Implementing GAAS 2018–19

Implementing GAAS 2018–19

A Practical Guide
to Auditing and Reporting

Ian Connon
BDO LLP

✳ **Croner-i**
HR · Tax · H&S · Audit & Accounting

CONTENTS

About the author   **xxxiii**

Preface   **xxxv**

1   The nature of auditing standards   **1**
1.1   Introduction   1
1.2   Limitations of standards   1
1.3   Authoritative bodies   2
1.4   International Auditing and Assurance Standards Board   2
        1.4.1   Background   2
        1.4.2   Structure and processes   3
        1.4.3   IAASB pronouncements   3
1.5   The Financial Reporting Council   4
        1.5.1   Role and structure   4
        1.5.2   Pronouncements   4
        1.5.3   Predecessor body – Auditing Practices Board   5
1.6   Development of International Standards on Auditing (UK)   5
        1.6.1   Original ISAs (UK and Ireland)   5
        1.6.2   IAASB's clarity project   6
        1.6.3   UK adoption of clarified ISAs   6
        1.6.4   EU audit directive and regulation   6
        1.6.5   Other changes to ISAs   7
        1.6.6   Application of ISAs (UK)   8
1.7   Other FRC guidance   9
        1.7.1   Practice Notes   9
        1.7.2   Bulletins   9
        1.7.3   Client Asset Reporting Standard   9
        1.7.4   Statements of Recommended Practice (SORPs)   9
        1.7.5   Standards for Reporting Accountants   9
1.8   Other guidance   10
1.9   Conventions   10
1.10   Accounting framework   10

2   Audit regulation and ethics   **11**
2.1   Introduction   11
        2.1.1   Ethical standards for auditors   12
        2.1.2   Audit regulations   12

Contents

2.2	Qualification	13
2.3	Control of audit firms	13
2.4	Fit and proper person	13
2.5	ICAEW code of ethics	13
	2.5.1 Background	13
	2.5.2 The fundamental principles	14
	2.5.3 Threats and safeguards	15
	2.5.4 Conflict resolution	16
	2.5.5 Conflicts of interest and confidentiality	16
	2.5.6 Control of confidentiality and independence	18
	2.5.7 Receipt of information in confidence by auditors	18
2.6	The FRC's Revised Ethical Standard 2016	18
	2.6.1 Scope	19
	2.6.2 Contents of the Revised Ethical Standard	21
	2.6.3 Ethical Standard – Introduction and Section 1 – Integrity, Objectivity and Independence	23
	2.6.4 Ethical Standard – Section 2: Financial, Business, Employment and Personal Relationships	28
	2.6.5 Ethical Standard – Section 3: Long Association with the Audit Engagement	32
	2.6.6 Ethical Standard Section 4: Fees, Remuneration and Evaluation Policies, Litigation, Gifts and Hospitality	34
	2.6.7 Ethical Standard Section 5 – Non-Audit Services Provided to Audited Entities	35
2.7	Section 6 – Provisions available for small entities	37
	2.7.1 Background	37
	2.7.2 Non-audit services	38
	2.7.3 Economic dependence	39
	2.7.4 Partners and other persons joining an audit client	39
	2.7.5 Audit report wording	40
2.8	Technical standards	41
	2.8.1 Acceptance of appointment and reappointment	41
	2.8.2 Quality control	41
2.9	Maintaining competence	42
2.10	Meeting of claims	42
2.11	Other areas	42
2.12	Oversight of the profession	43
2.13	Audit quality monitoring	43
2.14	Audit firm monitoring	44
2.15	Reports by registered auditors	45
2.16	Other international developments	45
3	**Quality control for audit work**	**47**
3.1	Introduction	47
3.2	ISQC (UK) 1 (Revised June 2016)	48
	3.2.1 Basic requirement	48
	3.2.2 Elements of a system of quality control	49

	3.2.3	Leadership	50
	3.2.4	Ethical requirements	50
	3.2.5	Client acceptance and continuance	51
	3.2.6	Human resources	54
	3.2.7	Engagement performance	55
	3.2.8	Engagement documentation	59
	3.2.9	Monitoring	60
	3.2.10	Complaints	63
	3.2.11	Documentation of quality control system	63
3.3	ISA (UK) 220 (Revised June 2016) Quality Control for an Audit of Financial Statements		64
	3.3.1	General requirement	64
	3.3.2	Leadership responsibilities for quality	65
	3.3.3	Ethical requirements	65
	3.3.4	Acceptance and continuance	65
	3.3.5	Assignment of the team	66
	3.3.6	Engagement performance	66
	3.3.7	Monitoring	67
	3.3.8	Documentation	67
3.4	FRC audit quality framework		68
	3.4.1	Background	68
	3.4.2	Promoting audit quality	69
	3.4.3	Factors outside the auditor's control	71
3.5	International developments		71
4	**The auditor's report**		**75**
4.1	Introduction		75
4.2	Standards and guidance		75
	4.2.1	Other guidance	76
4.3	Contents of this section		77
4.4	Forming an opinion		77
4.5	Contents of an audit report		78
	4.5.1	Entities that report on application of the code	79
	4.5.2	Public interest entities	80
4.6	Title		80
4.7	Addressee		80
4.8	Auditor's opinions		80
4.9	Basis for opinion		82
4.10	Going concern		82
4.11	Key audit matters		83
	4.11.1	Determining key audit matters	84
	4.11.2	Communicating key audit matters	84
	4.11.3	Circumstances in which a key audit matter is not communicated	85
	4.11.4	Interaction between key audit matters and going concern matters included in the auditor's report	85

Contents

	4.11.5	No matters to report	86
	4.11.6	Communicating other planning and scoping matters	86
	4.11.7	Communication with those charged with governance	87
	4.11.8	Documentation	87
4.12	Other information		88
4.13	Opinion on other matters		88
4.14	Reporting by exception		89
4.15	Responsibilities for the financial statements		90
4.16	Responsibilities of the auditor		90
4.17	Entities that report on application of the code		92
4.18	Public interest entities		93
4.19	Name of engagement partner		93
4.20	Signature		94
	4.20.1	Audit regulation	94
	4.20.2	Senior statutory auditor	94
	4.20.3	Signing	95
	4.20.4	Joint auditors	95
4.21	Auditor's location		96
4.22	Date		96
4.23	Unmodified auditor's reports examples		97
4.24	Directors' responsibility statements		107
4.25	Small companies		109
	4.25.1	Smaller entities and FRS 105	109
	4.25.2	The small companies regime	113
	4.25.3	Micro-entities	114
4.26	Reporting on the directors' remuneration report		115
	4.26.1	Introduction	115
	4.26.2	Companies affected by the rules	115
	4.26.3	The 'auditable part' of the directors' remuneration report	116
	4.26.4	Reporting on the directors' remuneration report	116
4.27	Electronic publication of audit reports		116
	4.27.1	Background	116
	4.27.2	Electronic publication of audit reports	116
4.28	The Bannerman case		117
	4.28.1	Introduction	117
	4.28.2	ICAEW Guidance	118
	4.28.3	Recommended wording and position in report	118
	4.28.4	Engagement letters	119
	4.28.5	Further developments	119
5	**Modified auditor's reports**		**121**
5.1	Introduction		121
5.2	Modifications		121
5.3	Modification to the auditor's opinion on the financial statements		122

	5.3.1	Financial statements not free from material misstatement	122
	5.3.2	Inability to obtain sufficient appropriate audit evidence	123
	5.3.3	Imposed limitation of scope	123
5.4	Types of modified opinion		124
	5.4.1	Adverse opinions or disclaimers of opinion	125
5.5	Form and content of the audit report when opinion is modified		126
	5.5.1	Opinion paragraph	126
	5.5.2	Qualified opinion	126
	5.5.3	Adverse opinion	126
	5.5.4	Disclaimer of opinion	126
	5.5.5	Basis for modification paragraph	127
	5.5.6	Description of auditor's responsibilities when the auditor disclaims an opinion	128
	5.5.7	Other considerations when the auditor disclaims an opinion	128
	5.5.8	Other implications of modified opinions	129
	5.5.9	ICAEW guidance	129
5.6	Examples		129
	5.6.1	Modifications to opinions on other matters	134
5.7	Emphasis of matter		136
5.8	Other matter paragraphs		137
5.9	Placement		138
5.10	Communication with those charged with governance		139
5.11	Communication with regulators and others		139
6	**Other reports on financial information**		**141**
6.1	Introduction		141
6.2	Revised financial statements and reports		142
	6.2.1	Legal background	142
	6.2.2	Guidance	142
	6.2.3	Types of revision	142
	6.2.4	Procedures	148
6.3	Preliminary announcements		149
	6.3.1	Background	149
	6.3.2	Guidance	150
	6.3.3	Terms of engagement	150
	6.3.4	Procedures	153
	6.3.5	Alternative performance measures	154
	6.3.6	Management commentary	154
	6.3.7	Directors' approval	155
	6.3.8	Modification of the auditor's report on the financial statements	155
	6.3.9	Reporting	155
	6.3.10	Announcements not agreed	157

Contents

6.4   New small companies regime   158
        6.4.1   Legal background   158
        6.4.2   Auditor's report   159
        6.4.3   Guidance   160
6.5   Summary financial statements   160

7   Other statutory reports by auditors   161
7.1   Introduction   161
7.2   Distributions   161
        7.2.1   Legal background   161
        7.2.2   Distributions made by reference to annual accounts 162
        7.2.3   Distributions made by reference to 'interim' accounts 165
        7.2.4   Distributions made by reference to 'initial' accounts 165
7.3   Purchase and redemption of own shares   167
        7.3.1   Legal background   167
        7.3.2   Guidance   167
7.4   Re-registration of companies   168
        7.4.1   Legal background   168
        7.4.2   Guidance   169
7.5   Allotment of shares otherwise than for cash   173
        7.5.1   Legal background   173
        7.5.2   Guidance   174
7.6   Transfer of non-cash assets to a public company by
        one of its members   176
        7.6.1   Legal background   176
        7.6.2   Guidance   176

**8   Compilation reports on accounts
         prepared by accountants   179**
8.1   Introduction   179
8.2   Guidance   179
        8.2.1   Professional ethics   179
8.3   Incorporated entities   180
        8.3.1   Terms of engagement   180
        8.3.2   Directors' responsibilities   182
        8.3.3   Accountants' procedures   183
        8.3.4   Misleading financial statements   183
        8.3.5   Approving financial statements   184
        8.3.6   Accountants' reports   184
8.4   Unincorporated entities   186
        8.4.1   Scope of guidance   186
        8.4.2   Accounting basis   186
        8.4.3   Terms of engagement   187
        8.4.4   Client's responsibilities   188
        8.4.5   Planning   189

	8.4.6	Procedures	189
	8.4.7	Misleading financial information	189
	8.4.8	Approval of financial information	189
	8.4.9	Accountants' reports	190
8.5		Companies claiming audit exemption	191
	8.5.1	Ineligible companies	191
	8.5.2	Requirements when a company becomes exempt	191
	8.5.3	Engagement letters	191
	8.5.4	Resignation procedures	191
9		**Reports to financial regulators**	**193**
9.1		Legal background	193
	9.1.1	Introduction	193
	9.1.2	Entities in the financial sector	193
	9.1.3	Public interest entities	194
9.2		Auditing and reporting standards and guidance	194
9.3		Types of report	195
9.4		Entities in the financial sector – auditor's responsibilities	195
9.5		Client assets	195
	9.5.1	Background	196
	9.5.2	Types of client assets report	196
	9.5.3	Scope of permissions	197
	9.5.4	The CASS rules	197
	9.5.5	Scope of the assurance standard	200
	9.5.6	Accepting the engagement	200
	9.5.7	Assurance procedures	201
	9.5.8	Planning the engagement	202
	9.5.9	Statutory and non-statutory trusts	203
	9.5.10	Reconciliations	204
	9.5.11	Custody arrangements	205
	9.5.12	Insurance intermediaries	205
	9.5.13	Debt management firms	206
	9.5.14	Mandates	206
	9.5.15	Using the work of the internal audit function	207
	9.5.16	Using the work of an expert	207
	9.5.17	Reporting	207
9.6		Special ad hoc reports	216
	9.6.1	Auditing standards and guidance	216
	9.6.2	Right and duty to report	217
	9.6.3	'Material significance'	218
	9.6.4	Procedures	220
	9.6.5	Reporting	222
	9.6.6	Form of report	223
	9.6.7	Communication by the regulator	224
	9.6.8	Relationship with other reporting responsibilities	225
9.7		Public interest entities	226

10	**Communicating with management and those charged with governance**	**227**
10.1	Introduction	227
10.2	Determining those charged with governance	228
10.3	Aims of reports to those charged with governance	228
10.4	The communication process	230
	10.4.1 Establishing expectations	230
	10.4.2 Form of communication and documentation	230
	10.4.3 Addressees	232
	10.4.4 Form of reports	232
10.5	Adequacy of communications	233
10.6	Matters to be communicated	234
	10.6.1 Overview	234
	10.6.2 Auditor's responsibilities	236
	10.6.3 Planned scope and timing	236
	10.6.4 Significant findings from the audit	237
	10.6.5 Integrity, independence and objectivity	240
10.7	Communication with audit committees	241
	10.7.1 Companies applying the UK Corporate Governance Code	241
	10.7.2 Public interest entities	241
10.8	Groups	243
10.9	Third parties	243
10.10	Communicating deficiencies in internal control	244
	10.10.1 Identifying and reporting deficiencies	244
	10.10.2 Significant deficiency	244
	10.10.3 Reporting of significant deficiencies	245
	10.10.4 Reporting of other deficiencies	246
11	**Going concern**	**247**
11.1	Introduction	247
11.2	Auditing standards and other guidance	248
11.3	General requirement	249
11.4	The entity's responsibilities	249
11.5	The auditor's responsibilities	251
11.6	Risk assessment procedures and related activities	251
	11.6.1 Significant doubt about the entity's ability to continue as a going concern	251
11.7	Evaluating the entity's assessment of going concern	253
	11.7.1 Possible audit procedures	254
	11.7.2 Borrowing facilities	255
11.8	Events after the period considered by those charged with governance	256
11.9	Additional procedures when events or conditions are identified	257
11.10	Auditor conclusions	257
	11.10.1 Entities applying the UK Corporate Governance Code	258

11.11	Adequacy of disclosures	259
	11.11.1 Adequacy of disclosures when events or conditions have been identified and a material uncertainty exists	259
	11.11.2 Adequacy of disclosures when events or conditions have been identified but no material uncertainty exists	260
11.12	Implications for the auditor's report	260
	11.12.1 Auditor's conclusions	260
	11.12.2 Going concern basis of accounting inappropriate	260
	11.12.3 Going concern basis of accounting is appropriate and no material uncertainty has been identified	261
	11.12.4 Use of going concern basis of accounting is appropriate but a material uncertainty exists	261
	11.12.5 Other considerations	262
	11.12.6 Small and micro-entities	262
	11.12.7 Entities applying the UK Corporate Governance Code	263
	11.12.8 Key audit matters	263
	11.12.9 Other information	263
11.13	Entity unwilling to make or extend its assessment	263
11.14	Communication with those charged with governance	264
	11.14.1 Public interest entities	264
11.15	Significant delay in the approval of financial statements	264
11.16	Example report extracts	264
11.17	Regulated entities	269
11.18	Groups	269
11.19	Preliminary announcements	269
11.20	Bulletin 2008/10	269
	11.20.1 The need for guidance	269
	11.20.2 General principles	270
	11.20.3 Detailed considerations	270
	11.20.4 Availability of finance	271
12	**Documentation**	**273**
12.1	Introduction	273
12.2	Purpose of documentation	273
12.3	Form and content	274
	12.3.1 Factors affecting form and content of working papers	275
	12.3.2 Documenting characteristics of items tested	276
	12.3.3 Judgment areas	277
	12.3.4 Documentation of departures from ISAs (UK)	278
	12.3.5 Identification of the preparer and reviewer of documentation	278
	12.3.6 Specific documentation requirements	278
12.4	Assembly of the final audit file	279
12.5	Changes to audit documentation	280
12.6	Other documentation requirements	280

12.7	Confidentiality, custody and ownership of working papers	282
12.8	Retention of working papers	283
12.9	Access to working papers	284
	12.9.1 Working paper ownership and access	284
	12.9.2 Further explanations	293
	12.9.3 Access for other parties	294
	12.9.4 Investigating accountants from the same firm as the auditor	296
	12.9.5 Change of auditor	296
13	**Planning**	**297**
13.1	Introduction	297
13.2	Planning the work	297
13.3	Preliminary engagement activities	298
13.4	The overall audit strategy	298
13.5	Audit plan	301
	13.5.1 Disclosures	302
13.6	Documentation	303
13.7	Initial audit engagements	303
13.8	Changes to planning decisions during the course of the audit	304
13.9	Direction, supervision and review	304
13.10	Communications with those charged with governance	304
14	**Engagement letters**	**305**
14.1	Introduction	305
14.2	Purpose	306
14.3	Preconditions for an audit	307
14.4	Contents	308
	14.4.1 Recurring audits	316
	14.4.2 Groups of companies	316
	14.4.3 Changes in terms	317
	14.4.4 Disengagement	317
14.5	Liability limitation	318
	14.5.1 Background	318
	14.5.2 FRC guidance	318
	14.5.3 Liability limitation agreements	318
	14.5.4 Liability limitation – other services	319
14.6	Small companies and micro-entities	319
15	**Materiality and the audit**	**321**
15.1	Introduction	321
15.2	Materiality	321
15.3	Materiality in the audit	322

15.4	Setting materiality	323
	15.4.1 Overall financial statement materiality	323
	15.4.2 Performance materiality	324
15.5	Revision to materiality assessments	325
15.6	Evaluation of uncorrected misstatements	325
	15.6.1 During the audit	326
	15.6.2 At the completion phase	327
	15.6.3 Disclosures	328
15.7	Documentation	329
15.8	Communication of misstatements	329
15.9	Written representations	329
15.10	FRC thematic reviews	329

16	**Fraud and error**	**331**
16.1	Introduction	331
16.2	Definitions	332
	16.2.1 Fraud	332
	16.2.2 Error	333
16.3	Responsibilities of those charged with governance	333
16.4	Responsibilities of the auditor	334
	16.4.1 Professional scepticism	335
	16.4.2 Engagement team discussion	335
	16.4.3 Risk assessment	336
	16.4.4 Identification and assessment of fraud risk	338
	16.4.5 Responses to fraud risk	339
16.5	Evaluating audit evidence	343
16.6	Auditor unable to continue the engagement	344
16.7	Management representations	344
16.8	Communication with management and those charged with governance	345
	16.8.1 Public interest entities	345
16.9	Communication with the authorities	346
	16.9.1 Public interest entities	346
16.10	Documentation	346

17	**Consideration of laws and regulations**	**347**
17.1	Introduction	347
17.2	Legal and regulatory framework	347
17.3	Management responsibility	348
17.4	Responsibility of the auditor	349
17.5	Consideration of compliance	350
	17.5.1 Laws with a direct effect on the financial statements	350
	17.5.2 Other laws and regulations	351
	17.5.3 Other procedures and written representations	351

17.6	Money laundering and tipping off	351
17.7	Non-compliance	352
17.8	Reporting	353
	17.8.1 Reporting to management and those charged with governance	353
	17.8.2 Reporting in the auditor's report	353
	17.8.3 Reporting to third parties	354
	17.8.4 Public interest entities	355
17.9	Resignation	355

18	**Money laundering and terrorist financing**	**357**
18.1	Introduction	357
18.2	Relevant legislation	357
18.3	Guidance for auditors and accountants	358
18.4	Money laundering and terrorist financing	359
18.5	Principal requirements	360
	18.5.1 Roles and responsibilities	360
	18.5.2 Policies and procedures	360
	18.5.3 Training	361
18.6	Risk based approach	361
18.7	Customer due diligence (CDD)	362
	18.7.1 Simplified CDD	363
	18.7.2 Enhanced CDD	363
	18.7.3 Politically exposed person (PEP)	365
18.8	Reporting suspicious activity	366
	18.8.1 Tipping off	366
	18.8.2 Reporting to regulators	367
	18.8.3 Privileged circumstances	368
18.9	The auditor's report on the financial statements	368
18.10	Resignation and communication with successor auditors	369

19	**Initial engagements, opening balances and comparatives**	**371**
19.1	Introduction	371
19.2	Initial engagements	371
19.3	Opening balances	372
	19.3.1 Modifications to the predecessor auditor's report	375
	19.3.2 Public interest entities	375
19.4	Comparatives	377
	19.4.1 Qualified reports	378
	19.4.2 Prior period financial statements issued by a predecessor auditor	382
	19.4.3 Prior period financial statements not audited	382

20	**Related parties**	**385**
20.1	Introduction	385
20.2	Auditing standards	386
20.3	General requirement	386
20.4	Materiality	387
20.5	Risk assessment	387
	20.5.1 Enquiries	388
	20.5.2 Understanding of controls	388
	20.5.3 Team discussion	388
	20.5.4 Remaining alert	389
	20.5.5 Assessment of risk	390
20.6	Response to risk	390
	20.6.1 Arm's length transactions	391
20.7	Control disclosures	392
20.8	Representations from those charged with governance	392
20.9	Communication with those charged with governance	393
20.10	Documentation	393
20.11	Reporting	393
20.12	The audit of related parties in practice	394
	20.12.1 Introduction	394
	20.12.2 The five-point action plan	394
21	**Audit risk assessment and the auditor's response**	**399**
21.1	Introduction	399
21.2	General overview	400
21.3	Identifying and assessing risks	400
	21.3.1 Requirements	400
	21.3.2 Risk assessment procedures and related activities	401
	21.3.3 Engagement team discussion	402
	21.3.4 Understanding the entity and its environment, including the entity's internal control	403
	21.3.5 Internal control	410
	21.3.6 Identifying and assessing the risks of material misstatement	417
	21.3.7 Communicating with those charged with governance	421
	21.3.8 Documentation	421
21.4	Responses to assessed risks	422
	21.4.1 Overall responses	422
	21.4.2 Responses at the assertion level	423
	21.4.3 Presentation of the financial statements	428
	21.4.4 Evaluating audit evidence	428
	21.4.5 Documentation	429
22	**Service organisations**	**431**
22.1	Introduction	431

22.2 Understanding the services provided by a service
organisation, including internal control 432
22.2.1 Using a type 1 or type 2 report 435
22.2.2 Accounting records 436
22.3 Responding to the assessed risks of material misstatement 437
22.4 Subservice organisations 438
22.5 Fraud, non-compliance with laws and regulations and
uncorrected misstatements 438
22.6 Reporting 438

23 Audit evidence **441**
23.1 Introduction 441
23.2 The nature of audit evidence 442
23.2.1 Concept of audit evidence 442
23.2.2 Sufficient appropriate evidence 442
23.2.3 Sources of evidence 444
23.2.4 Using assertions to gather audit evidence 444
23.2.5 Audit procedures 444
23.2.6 Selection and sampling of items for testing 446
23.2.7 Dealing with inconsistent or potentially
unreliable evidence 447
23.3 Management's experts 447
23.3.1 Using the work of a management's expert 447
23.3.2 Evaluating the expert's competence, capabilities and
objectivity 448
23.3.3 Obtaining an understanding of the expert's work 448
23.3.4 Evaluating the appropriateness of the expert's work 449
23.4 Specific considerations 449
23.5 Attendance at stocktaking 449
23.5.1 Introduction 449
23.5.2 Audit evidence 449
23.5.3 Planning 450
23.5.4 Evaluation of management's instructions
and procedures 450
23.5.5 Observation, inspection and test counts 451
23.5.6 Auditor unable to attend physical count 451
23.5.7 Inventory held by third parties 452
23.6 Enquiries about litigation and claims 452
23.6.1 Audit procedures 453
23.6.2 Written representations 456
23.7 Segment information 456
23.8 External confirmations 457
23.8.1 Use of external confirmations 457
23.8.2 Debtors' confirmations 459
23.9 Auditor scepticism 461
23.9.1 Background 461
23.9.2 A sceptical mind 462

23.9.3 Throughout the audit 463
23.9.4 The growing importance of scepticism 464
23.9.5 Difficulties for audit firms 465
23.9.6 Improving auditor scepticism 465

24 Bank confirmations 469
24.1 Introduction 469
24.2 Audit considerations 469
24.3 Request letters 469
24.4 Authority 470
24.5 Electronic confirmation 470

25 Analytical procedures 471
25.1 Introduction 471
25.2 What is meant by analytical procedures? 471
25.3 Problems in practice 473
25.4 Use of analytical procedures in risk assessment 474
25.5 Analytical procedures as a substantive procedure 474
25.5.1 Suitability of analytical procedures 475
25.5.2 Reliability of data 475
25.5.3 Precision of expected results 476
25.5.4 Acceptable differences 476
25.6 Analytical procedures near the end of the audit 476
25.7 Investigating variances 477

26 Audit sampling 479
26.1 Introduction 479
26.2 Use of sampling 479
26.3 Risk assessment 480
26.3.1 Sampling risk 480
26.3.2 Non-sampling risk 481
26.4 Design of the sample 481
26.4.1 Deciding whether to sample 481
26.4.2 Designing the sample 482
26.5 Sample size 483
26.6 Selecting the sample 485
26.7 Performing audit procedures 486
26.8 Deviations and misstatements 486
26.8.1 Tolerable misstatement/deviation 486
26.8.2 Expected error 487
26.8.3 Projecting errors 487
26.9 Evaluating results 488
26.10 Statistical and non-statistical sampling 489

27 Audit of accounting estimates 491

27.1 Introduction 491
27.2 Obtaining an understanding 492
27.3 Risk relating to the use of accounting estimates 492
27.4 Audit procedures 493
    27.4.1 Significant risks 494
    27.4.2 Testing management's methods 494
27.5 Evaluation of results 495
27.6 Disclosure 496
27.7 Indicators of possible management bias 496
27.8 Written representations 497
27.9 Documentation 497
27.10 International developments 497

28 Auditing financial instruments 499

28.1 Introduction 499
28.2 Guidance 499
28.3 Background information 500
28.4 Audit considerations 501
28.5 Using the work of an expert 502

29 The audit of retirement benefits 503

29.1 Introduction 503
29.2 Guidance for auditors 503

30 Audits of group financial statements 505

30.1 Introduction 505
30.2 Auditing standards and guidance 505
30.3 Definitions 506
30.4 Responsibilities 507
30.5 Acceptance and continuance 507
30.6 Overall audit strategy and audit plan 508
30.7 Understanding the group, its components and their environments 508
30.8 Understanding the component auditor 509
30.9 Materiality 511
30.10 Responding to assessed risks 511
    30.10.1 Involvement in the work performed by component auditors 514
30.11 The consolidation process 514
30.12 Subsequent events 515
30.13 Communication with the component auditor 516
30.14 Evaluating the sufficiency and appropriateness of audit evidence 517
30.15 Communication with those charged with governance of the group 518
    30.15.1 Public interest entities 520

30.16	Documentation	520
	30.16.1 External monitoring	521
	30.16.2 Examples	521
30.17	ICAEW practical guidance	523
30.18	International developments	524

31	**Reliance on others**	**527**
31.1	Introduction	527
31.2	Internal audit function	527
	31.2.1 Auditing Standards	527
	31.2.2 Understanding the internal audit function	528
	31.2.3 Use of the work of the internal audit function	529
	31.2.4 Using the work of the internal audit function	531
	31.2.5 Direct assistance	533
	31.2.6 Documentation	533
31.3	Auditors' experts	534
	31.3.1 Auditing standards	534
	31.3.2 Definition of an auditor's expert	535
	31.3.3 Determining the need for an auditor's expert	535
	31.3.4 The nature, timing and extent of audit procedures	535
	31.3.5 Competence, capabilities and objectivity of the expert	536
	31.3.6 Understanding the expert's field of expertise	537
	31.3.7 Agreement with the auditor's expert	537
	31.3.8 Evaluating the adequacy of the expert's work	537
	31.3.9 Reference to the expert in the auditor's report	538
	31.3.10 Documentation	538

32	**Management representations**	**539**
32.1	Introduction	539
32.2	Requirement to obtain written representations	539
32.3	Acknowledgement of directors' responsibilities	540
32.4	Other written representations required by ISAs	541
32.5	Additional written representations	542
32.6	Representations by management as audit evidence	543
32.7	Reliability of representations	544
32.8	Refusal to provide written confirmation	544
32.9	Example representation letter	544
32.10	Technical release 04/02 AAF	548
	32.10.1 The case	549
	32.10.2 Directors' ability to make representations	549

33	**Subsequent events**	**551**
33.1	Introduction	551
33.2	Subsequent events	551

Contents

33.3	Events occurring before the date of the auditor's report	552
33.4	Before the financial statements are issued	553
	33.4.1 Directors make the required amendments	554
	33.4.2 Failure to amend financial statements	554
33.5	Revising or withdrawing financial statements	555

34 The auditor's responsibilities in relation to other information — **557**

34.1	Introduction	557
34.2	Auditing standards	558
34.3	The auditor's consideration of other information	558
	34.3.1 Other information and statutory other information	558
	34.3.2 The auditor's responsibility	559
	34.3.3 Obtaining an understanding	560
	34.3.4 Obtaining the other information	560
	34.3.5 Reading and considering the other information	560
34.4	Responding to inconsistencies and misstatements	561
	34.4.1 Responding when a material misstatement of the other information exists	561
	34.4.2 Responding when a material misstatement in the financial statements exists or the auditor's understanding needs to be updated	562
34.5	Timing	563
34.6	Reporting	563
	34.6.1 All entities	563
	34.6.2 Directors' report and strategic report	564
	34.6.3 Separate corporate governance statement	564
34.7	UK Corporate Governance Code reporting	565
	34.7.1 Statement on the directors' assessment of the principal risks that would threaten the solvency or liquidity of the entity	566
34.8	Modified audit reports	567
34.9	Documentation	567
34.10	Electronic publication	567

35 Data analytics — **569**

35.1	Introduction	569
35.2	Guidance	569
35.3	Use of data analytics in external audits	570
	35.3.1 Audit quality	571
	35.3.2 Common data analytic routines	572
	35.3.3 ICAEW papers	572
	35.3.4 Audit quality thematic review	573
35.4	Future developments	574

36   The audit of small businesses   **575**
36.1   Introduction   575
36.2   Guidance   576
36.3   Characteristics of small businesses   576
36.4   The relationship between small businesses and their auditors   577
36.5   Responsibilities   578
        36.5.1   The auditor's responsibilities relating to fraud   578
        36.5.2   Consideration of laws and regulations   579
        36.5.3   Going concern   579
        36.5.4   Agreeing the terms of the engagement   580
        36.5.5   Subsequent events   580
36.6   Planning, controlling and recording   580
        36.6.1   Planning an audit of financial statements   580
        36.6.2   Identifying and assessing risks of material
                  misstatement   581
        36.6.3   Materiality   581
36.7   Accounting systems and internal control   582
        36.7.1   Identifying and assessing risks and the auditor's
                  responses to them   582
        36.7.2   Service organisations   583
36.8   Evidence   583
        36.8.1   Audit evidence and external confirmations   583
        36.8.2   Analytical procedures   584
        36.8.3   Audit sampling   585
        36.8.4   Written representations   585
        36.8.5   Initial audit engagements and comparative information   586
        36.8.6   Estimates and fair values   586
        36.8.7   Related parties   586
36.9   Reporting   587
        36.9.1   The independent auditor's report on
                  financial statements   587
        36.9.2   Communication with those charged with governance   587
36.10   Practice Note 26 and documentation   588
        36.10.1   Background   588
        36.10.2   The purpose of audit documentation   588
        36.10.3   Special considerations for smaller entities   589
        36.10.4   Audit documentation requirements in the ISAs   591
36.11   International guidance   591

37   Other operational issues   **593**
37.1   Introduction   593
37.2   The auditing implications of FRS 102   593
        37.2.1   Guidance for auditors   593
        37.2.2   Ethical considerations   594
        37.2.3   Potential problem areas   595
37.3   Implications of IFRS transition   596

37.4	XBRL tagging of information in financial statements		597
	37.4.1	Background	597
	37.4.2	Auditor's involvement	597
	37.4.3	Technical Release AAF 04/10	598
37.5	Paid cheques		600
	37.5.1	Existing guidance	600
	37.5.2	Audit evidence	600
	37.5.3	Cheques Act 1992	601
	37.5.4	Obtaining paid cheques	601
37.6	Auditing when financial market conditions are difficult		601
37.7	Auditing implications of Brexit		602

38	**Change of auditor**		**603**
38.1	Introduction		603
38.2	Procedures on cessation of office as auditor		604
	38.2.1	The Companies Act 2006 requirements	604
	38.2.2	All companies	605
	38.2.3	Non-public interest companies	605
	38.2.4	Section 519 statement	606
	38.2.5	Notifications – non-public interest companies	607
	38.2.6	Public interest companies	608
	38.2.7	Legal advice	610
38.3	Access to information by a successor auditor		617
	38.3.1	Requirements of the Act	617
	38.3.2	Technical Release AAF 01/08	618

39	**Review of interim financial information**		**627**
39.1	Introduction		627
39.2	Guidance for the auditor		628
39.3	General principles		628
39.4	Assurance provided		628
39.5	Engagement letters		629
39.6	Planning		631
39.7	Procedures and evidence		633
39.8	Documentation		634
39.9	Subsequent events		635
39.10	Going concern		635
39.11	Comparative periods		635
39.12	Management representations		636
39.13	Other information		638
39.14	Evaluating misstatements		638
39.15	Communication		638
39.16	Reporting		639
	39.16.1	Modification of the review report	640
	39.16.2	Prior period modifications	642
	39.16.3	Date of review report	642

39.17	Complete set of interim financial information	643
39.18	Requests to discontinue an interim review engagement	643

40	**Reports for special purposes and to third parties**	**645**
40.1	Introduction	645
40.2	Development of guidance	646
40.3	General guidance	647
	40.3.1 Accepting an engagement	647
	40.3.2 Managing professional liability	648
	40.3.3 Agreeing the terms of the engagement	648
40.4	Duties to lenders	649
	40.4.1 Case law	649
	40.4.2 Duties of care for the statutory audit report	649
	40.4.3 Draft accounts	650
	40.4.4 Disclaimer of responsibility	650
	40.4.5 The Contracts (Rights of Third Parties) Act 1999	651
	40.4.6 Separate engagements to provide specific assurances to lenders	651
40.5	Covenants in agreement for loans and other facilities	652
	40.5.1 Common financial and non-financial covenants	652
	40.5.2 The lender's requirement for evidence of covenant compliance	653
	40.5.3 The firm's duty of care	655
	40.5.4 The firm's consideration of acceptance of the engagement	657
40.6	Engagements to report on covenant compliance	658
	40.6.1 Scope of work performed	658
	40.6.2 The report	659
40.7	Reports on internal controls of service organisations	661
	40.7.1 Background	661
	40.7.2 Responsibilities of the service organisation	662
	40.7.3 Accepting the engagement	663
	40.7.4 Reporting accountant's procedures	667
	40.7.5 Reporting	667
40.8	Reports to other third parties	670
	40.8.1 Introduction	670
	40.8.2 TECH 10/12AAF: Reporting to third parties	670
	40.8.3 Requests for references on clients' financial status	678
40.9	Audit liability: Claims by third parties	680
	40.9.1 Potential investors	681
	40.9.2 Creditors and lenders	682
	40.9.3 Regulators and trade bodies	682
	40.9.4 Affiliates or associates of the audit client	682

Contents

41	**Other engagements**	**685**
41.1	Introduction	685
41.2	Review engagements	687
	41.2.1 Guidance	687
	41.2.2 Features of a review engagement	687
	41.2.3 Accepting the engagement	688
	41.2.4 Reliance by third parties	691
	41.2.5 Performing the engagement	691
	41.2.6 Written representations	692
	41.2.7 Reporting	692
41.3	Agreed upon procedures	693
41.4	Auditor's reports on special purpose financial statements	694
	41.4.1 Special purpose frameworks	695
	41.4.2 Reports on a single financial statement or a specific element	699
41.5	Assurance on non-financial information	702
	41.5.1 Non-financial information	702
	41.5.2 Current practices and guidance	702
	41.5.3 Considerations for practitioners	703

42	**Corporate governance**	**707**
42.1	Background	707
	42.1.1 Corporate governance framework	707
	42.1.2 Directors' remuneration	708
	42.1.3 Disclosure and transparency rules	708
42.2	Guidance	709
	42.2.1 FRC – companies and investors	709
	42.2.2 FRC – auditors	709
42.3	Terms of engagement	711
42.4	Auditor's responsibilities for the 'comply or explain' statement	711
42.5	Provisions of the UK Corporate Governance Code	712
42.6	Procedures	714
	42.6.1 Statement of compliance	714
	42.6.2 Specific procedures – the verifiable code provisions	715
	42.6.3 Non-compliance with the code	720
	42.6.4 Going concern	720
42.7	Other disclosures and reporting requirements	722
	42.7.1 Disclosures under the 'Disclosure Rules and Transparency Rules'	722
	42.7.2 Standard listed companies	725
42.8	Audit committees and the external auditor	725
	42.8.1 Role and responsibilities of the audit committee	725
	42.8.2 FRC guidance on audit committees	726
	42.8.3 Communication between the auditor and the audit committee	729

42.9   Monitoring   731
42.10 Other Codes   731
    42.10.1   Investment companies   731
    42.10.2   Smaller quoted companies   731
42.11 Future plans   732

43   **Charites**   **733**

43.1   Legal background   733
    43.1.1   General   734
    43.1.2   Independent examination   736
    43.1.3   Whistle-blowing duties for auditors and examiners   736
43.2   Audit guidance   737
43.3   Agreeing the terms of audit engagements   737
43.4   Quality control for an audit of financial statements   738
43.5   The auditor's responsibilities relating to fraud   739
43.6   Consideration of laws and regulations   740
    43.6.1   Laws and regulations relating directly to the
        preparation of financial statements   740
    43.6.2   Laws and regulations where non-compliance may
        have a material effect on the financial statements   740
43.7   The auditor's right and duty to report to regulators   741
43.8   Communication with those charged with governance   743
43.9   Communicating deficiencies in internal control   743
43.10 Planning an audit of financial statements   744
43.11 Identifying and assessing risks of material misstatement   745
    43.11.1   Control environment   745
    43.11.2   Accounting policies   746
    43.11.3   Risk of misstatement   746
43.12 Materiality in planning and performing an audit   747
43.13 The auditor's responses to assessed risks   748
    43.13.1   Completeness of income   748
    43.13.2   Overseas operations   749
    43.13.3   Restricted funds   750
    43.13.4   Heritage assets   750
    43.13.5   Grants payable   751
43.14 Audit considerations relating to an entity using a
    service organisation   751
43.15 Initial audit engagements – opening balances   751
43.16 Auditing accounting estimates, including fair value
    accounting estimates, and related disclosures   752
43.17 Related parties   752
43.18 Subsequent events   753
43.19 Going concern   753
43.20 Written representations   754
43.21 Audits of group financial statements   755

43.22	The auditor's report on financial statements	755
43.23	Other information	756
43.24	Summarised financial statements	757

44	**Pension schemes**	**759**
44.1	Introduction	759
44.2	Legal background	760
44.3	Accounting guidance	763
44.4	Schemes exempt from audit	764
44.5	Appointment and resignation	764
44.6	Considerations of fraud	765
44.7	Use of service organisations	767
44.8	Communication with trustees	768
44.9	Going concern	770
44.10	Other information	771
44.11	Reporting	772
44.11.1	Key audit matters	776
44.12	Contributions	776
44.13	Schemes in the process of winding up	780
44.14	Other reporting situations	781
44.15	Whistle-blowing responsibilities	781
44.16	Non-statutory audits	782
44.16.1	Appointment and removal	782
44.16.2	Engagement letter	782
44.16.3	Reporting to the Pensions Regulator (TPR)	782
44.16.4	Auditor's statement about contributions	783
44.16.5	Termination of appointment	783
44.16.6	Trustees' responsibilities statement	783
44.16.7	Auditor's report	783

45	**Solicitors' Accounts Rules**	**785**
45.1	Background	785
45.1.1	Summary of recent changes	785
45.1.2	Compliance with the rules	786
45.1.3	Objective	787
45.2	Engagement letter	788
45.2.1	'Whistle-blowing'	790
45.2.2	Termination of appointment	791
45.2.3	Independence	791
45.3	Procedures	792
45.3.1	The role of the reporting accountant	794
45.4	Common breaches	795
45.4.1	Debit balances	795
45.4.2	Client confidentiality	796
45.4.3	'Without delay'	796

	45.4.4 Receipt and transfer of costs – the '14 day rule'	796
	45.4.5 Reconciliations	796
	45.4.6 Prompt return of client money and residual balances	796
	45.4.7 Providing bank facilities	797
45.5	Reporting	797
45.6	Future developments	798

46 Investment businesses — **801**

46.1	PN 21 withdrawn	801

47 Registered Providers of Social Housing — **803**

47.1	Existing audit guidance	806
	47.1.1 Practice Note 14	806
47.2	Background	807
	47.2.1 The nature of Registered Providers	807
	47.2.2 Responsibilities of the board	809
	47.2.3 Responsibilities of audit committees	810
	47.2.4 Financial reporting requirements	810
	47.2.5 Responsibilities of the auditor	811
	47.2.6 Features of social housing audits	812
	47.2.7 The auditor's relationship with the Regulators	816
47.3	Audit engagement letters	816
47.4	Quality control	823
47.5	Responsibilities relating to fraud	823
47.6	Laws and regulations	824
	47.6.1 ISA (UK) 250 Section A (Revised December 2017) – Consideration of Laws and Regulations in an Audit of Financial Statements	824
	47.6.2 ISA (UK) 250 Section B (Revised June 2016)	826
47.7	Communication with those charged with governance	827
47.8	Identifying and assessing risks of material misstatement	828
47.9	Materiality	829
47.10	Responses to assessed risks	829
47.11	Using a service organisation	830
47.12	Audit evidence	830
47.13	External confirmations	831
47.14	Analytical procedures	831
47.15	Auditing accounting estimates	832
47.16	Related parties	833
47.17	Subsequent events	834
47.18	Going concern	834
47.19	Written representations	835
47.20	Using the work of internal auditors	835
47.21	Using the work of an auditor's expert	836
47.22	The auditor's report on financial statements	836
	47.22.1 UK Corporate Governance Code and enhanced audit reporting	840

47.23   Other information   841
47.24   Miscellaneous reports   842
47.25   Service charge audits   842

48   Public sector audits   845
48.1   Introduction   845
48.2   The role of the public sector auditor   845
48.3   Quality control   846
48.4   Overall objectives of the auditor and the conduct of an audit   847
48.5   Agreeing the terms of audit engagements   847
48.6   Quality control   848
48.7   The auditor's responsibilities relating to fraud   848
48.8   Consideration of laws and regulations   849
       48.8.1   Consideration of legislation on corruption   850
       48.8.2   Reporting non-compliance   850
48.9   Communication with those charged with governance   850
48.10 Identifying, assessing and responding to risks   851
48.11 Materiality in planning and performing an audit   853
48.12 Using a service organisation   853
48.13 Evaluation of misstatements   853
48.14 Opening balances   854
48.15 Accounting estimates   855
48.16 Related parties   856
48.17 Subsequent events   856
48.18 Going concern   856
       48.18.1   The auditor's other responsibilities relating to
                  going concern   857
       48.18.2   Circumstances affecting going concern   857
       48.18.3   Consideration of the foreseeable future   857
       48.18.4   The auditor's responsibilities in considering
                  going concern   857
       48.18.5   Entities that prepare their financial statements
                  on a cash basis   858
       48.18.6   Auditors' responsibilities for reviewing and
                  reporting on an entity's arrangements for
                  securing value for money   858
48.19 Written representations   859
48.20 Audits of group financial statements   859
48.21 Using the work of internal auditors   859
48.22 Using the work of an auditor's expert   859
48.23 Forming an opinion and reporting on financial statements   860
48.24 The auditor's responsibilities relating to other information
       in documents containing audited financial statements   861
48.25 Regularity   861
48.26 Grant claims   862

49   Regulated entities   865
49.1   Introduction   865
49.2   Duty of care and engagement contracts   866
        49.2.1   Tri-partite engagement contracts   866
        49.2.2   Bi-partite engagement contracts   866
49.3   Reporting   867
49.4   Materiality   867
49.5   Working with independent experts   868

Appendix 1   869
Existing guidance at 30 April 2018   869

Appendix 2   875
Specific ISA requirements relating to statutory audits of
public interest entities   875

Appendix 3   877
Glossary   877

Index   879

About the author

Ian Connon MA FCA

Ian Connon is Director of Audit and Assurance Advisory within the Technical Department at BDO LLP. He has many years of practical and technical experience in audit with BDO and previously with PKF, including the development of audit methodologies, writing audit manuals, development of automated audit tools and liaison with audit regulators. He is a long standing member of the ICAEW's Technical and Practical Auditing Committee and ISA Panel and contributes regularly to Audit and Assurance Faculty publications and helpsheets.

Preface

The past year has been a relatively quiet one in terms of changes to auditing standards, giving auditors time to ensure that the 2016 revisions to ISAs (UK) and the FRC's Ethical Standard are fully incorporated into their procedures.

New standards issued during the period were revisions to ISAs (UK) 250 Section A *Consideration of Laws and Regulations in an Audit of Financial Statements* (July 2017 and again in December 2017) and ISA (UK) 330 *The Auditor's Responses to Assessed Risks* (July 2017). The first revision of ISA (UK) 250 Section A followed limited changes to the international standard to align it with changes to the IESBA Code of Ethics resulting from IESBA's 'NOCLAR' (non-compliance with laws and regulations) project. The second revision incorporated a new Appendix providing guidance for auditors on money laundering following the introduction in June 2017 of new UK anti-money laundering and terrorist financing regulations. The revision to ISA (UK) 330 was a minor addition to application material prompted by the FRC's decision to withdraw Practice Note 16 *Bank reports for audit purposes in the United Kingdom.* Minor consequential and conforming amendments were made to a number of other standards as a result of these revisions. These amended standards were labelled by the FRC as being 'updated' in July 2017.

Other changes to FRC guidance include the withdrawal of Practice Notes – PN 12 Money laundering (replaced by the new Appendix to ISA (UK) 250 Section A), PN 21 *The audit of investment businesses* (dated material and largely superseded by FRC's Client Assets standard), PN 22 *The auditor's consideration of FRS 17* (also out of date) and PN 25 *Attendance at stocktaking* (disappeared from FRC's website).

Revised Practice Notes were issued for charities (PN 11) and pension schemes (PN 15). These PNs have been updated for ISAs (UK) as well as other developments relevant to the sector. They are not intended as standalone guides on how to perform an audit but provide additional guidance on application of ISAs in areas where specific sector related consideration apply.

Whilst the FRC's *Compendium of illustrative audit reports* provides guidance and examples of how to construct an audit report in accordance with ISAs (UK) 700 and 701, it is fairly limited in its scope and does not provide examples of how to construct reports containing modified or disclaimed opinions, or how to apply ISAs (UK) to audit reports for entities such as pension schemes, charities, LLPs and other types of entity. Some guidance is given in the relevant sections of this publication and in other Croner-i online publications but the ICAEW has also now produced a number of useful Audit and Assurance helpsheets in this area, providing detailed guidance and examples covering a variety of situations. Although produced by the Audit and Assurance Faculty these helpsheets are available to all ICAEW members via the website. More are on the way.

The other major development in the arena of audit reporting is an update to the Technical Release recommending the inclusion of a 'Bannerman' paragraph in auditors' reports. Following the issue of ISAs (UK), the ICAEW obtained updated legal advice regarding the wording and positioning of such paragraphs. The outcome, as set out in **Section 4** and elsewhere in this publication was that the recommended wording remained appropriate but the paragraph should be positioned at the end of the report, in a section of its own immediately before the signature.

As Brexit looms nearer and some of the implications become clearer, the auditor should not lose sight of the impact on his clients. Even in relatively stable businesses, forecasts, assumptions and judgments should be reconsidered with appropriate scepticism, especially where the business involves trading overseas or is dependent on other businesses that may be adversely affected by Brexit. Auditors also need to ensure that appropriate disclosures are made not only within the financial statements but also, where appropriate, in the 'front end' of the annual report.

With the collapse of Carillion, the role of the auditor is once again in the spotlight and 'auditor-bashing' a popular pastime. The case highlights the importance of issues such as independence, objectivity and professional scepticism and whilst the criticism, so far, has focussed on large firms engaged in the audits of public interest entities, the publicity, and consequent changes in the regulatory environment, are likely to have an impact for all auditors.

Of course, it is not all the fault of the auditor. Corporate governance plays its part and in December 2017, the FRC issued a public consultation on a revised UK Corporate Governance Code taking into account the FRC's work on corporate culture and the issues raised in a recent Government Green Paper and the report by the Business, Energy and Industrial Strategy (BEIS) Select Committee Inquiry. In addition, recognising that corporate governance is not just for public companies, in January 2018, the Government set up an industry group tasked with developing corporate governance principles for large privately-owned companies.

Meanwhile, the FRC awaits the outcome of an enquiry into whether it remains 'fit for purpose' as the UK's audit regulator.

On the standard setting front the IAASB remains busy. Its major project to revise ISA 540 *Auditing Accounting Estimates* is nearing completion with a revised draft due to be considered at the June meeting of the Board. A new standard is likely to have a significant impact on the way in which auditors approach the audit of accounting estimates and related disclosures.

Other IAASB projects include:

- a revision of ISA 315 *Identifying and Assessing the Risks of Material Misstatement*, which aims to establish more robust requirements and appropriately detailed guidance to drive auditors to perform appropriate risk assessment procedures in a manner commensurate with the size and nature of the entity, and consider how ISA 315 may be modified to promote a more effective risk assessment;
- revision of ISQC 1 and ISA 220 on quality control, including a greater emphasis on quality management procedures as well as after the event controls and creation of a new ISQC 2 standard dealing with the engagement quality control review (EQCR) procedures for listed and public interest entities;
- update to ISA 600 in respect of group audits; and
- consideration of the auditing implications of new data analytic techniques.

Scepticism remains high on the agenda and any new standards emerging from these projects will undoubtedly be infused with requirements for a healthy dose of professional scepticism.

As always, I am grateful to the many people who have contributed over the years to the material in this book. In particular, I should like to acknowledge the contributions of Don Bawtree, Ros Brickman, Simon Buss, Nick Carter-Pegg, Liz Kulczycki, Peter Lewis, Nigel Read and Paula Willock whose help in updating the book this year has been invaluable.

Any suggestions as to how this publication could be further improved would be welcome. Please e-mail your views to content.queries@croneri.co.uk.

Ian Connon

1 The nature of auditing standards

1.1 Introduction

For the purposes of this guide, Generally Accepted Auditing Standards (GAAS) are the rules which are acknowledged as those by which auditors can measure their performance and by which others can measure them. In the widest sense, these standards are set by a variety of groups:

- government, in the form of legislation;
- officially designated or generally recognised standard setting bodies, in the form of pronouncements of varying authority;
- professional bodies, in the form of guidance for members;
- courts in judgments on cases involving auditors; and
- regulators, whose interpretation of standards effectively determines what is or is not generally accepted.

1.2 Limitations of standards

Because of the nature of auditing, the development of a framework of auditing standards which will provide answers to all the questions and problems faced by auditors is not feasible. There will always be judgments over questions – such as how much evidence is enough in a given case? – to which auditing standards will not provide a solution. This is aggravated by the relationship between auditing and accounting. Auditors form opinions on financial statements, the preparation of which involves, amongst other things, appraisals of the likely outcome of uncertain future events. Auditing standards are also constrained by this uncertainty. As business practices and financial reporting practices evolve and adapt to changing circumstances, the auditor must also be able to adapt his approach. Whilst auditing standards aim to establish a principles-based set of requirements to which auditors must adhere, this can only be a framework to assist the auditor in making judgments and forming opinions, not a rigid system of rules.

1.3   Authoritative bodies

In the main, GAAS emanates from the pronouncements of authoritative bodies which have been granted the legal status to issue standards or which are accepted by audit practitioners and the bodies which regulate them as having the authority to issue guidance. From the point of view of this book, GAAS encompasses not only the standards issued by those bodies but also any guidance on their application.

What constitutes GAAS, in practice, is subject to evolution and change. Auditors in the UK must have regard to a large number of pronouncements issued by various bodies in order to ascertain what actually constitutes GAAS. The main bodies which either issue, or have issued, audit requirements, standards or related guidance are:

- the European Union, which issues Directives regarding the statutory audit of companies that must be incorporated into national law by Member States, and Regulations that have direct application for specific groups of entities;

- the UK Government which issues legislation governing the audit of companies and other legally constituted entities within the framework and context of EU legislation;

- International Federation of Accountants (IFAC) and its standard setting boards the International Auditing and Assurance Standards Board (IAASB) and the International Ethics Standards Board for Accountants (IESBA);

- the Financial Reporting Council (FRC), the UK's regulator and standard setter for auditors and accountants;

- professional accountancy bodies, for example, the Institute of Chartered Accountants in England and Wales (ICAEW) which issues guidance through its Audit and Assurance Faculty and other committees.

1.4   International Auditing and Assurance Standards Board

1.4.1   Background

The International Auditing and Assurance Standards Board (IAASB) is an independent standard-setting board within the International Federation of Accountants (IFAC). It was formed as the International Auditing Practices Committee in 1978, and develops auditing and assurance standards, guidance and other pronouncements used by professional accountants worldwide.

Over the years, the IAASB has established itself as an internationally accepted standard setter. Its stated objective is to serve the public interest by setting high-quality international standards for auditing, quality control, review, other assurance, and related services, and by facilitating the convergence of international and national standards. In doing so, the IAASB aims to enhance the quality and uniformity of practice throughout the world and strengthen public confidence in the global auditing and assurance profession. According to its website, over 113 jurisdictions worldwide, including the UK, have committed to using the IAASB's clarified auditing standards (see **1.6**).

1.4.2   Structure and processes

The Public Interest Oversight Board (PIOB) oversees the public interest activities of the whole of IFAC including the IAASB. The PIOB's objective is to increase confidence of investors and others by ensuring that the processes of IFAC are responsive to the public interest. This includes the setting of standards by the IAASB.

When setting standards and guidance, the IAASB gains input from its own Consultative Advisory Group, national auditing standard setters, IFAC member bodies and their members, and the general public. The Consultative Advisory Group (CAG) is comprised of representatives of regulators, business and international organisations, and users and preparers of financial statements who are interested in the development and maintenance of high quality international standards on auditing.

1.4.3   IAASB pronouncements

As well as the ISAs, the IAASB issues other guidance which is of relevance to UK auditors. IAASB pronouncements comprise:

- International Standards on Auditing (ISAs);
- International Standards on Assurance Engagements (ISAEs);
- International Standards on Review Engagements (ISREs);
- International Standards on Related Services (ISRSs);
- International Standards on Quality Control (ISQCs); and
- International Auditing Practice Statements (IAPSs).

In addition, the IAASB staff occasionally issue guidance notes such as practice alerts and bulletins. These are for information purposes only and have no authoritative status.

IAASB pronouncements have no direct authority in the UK, although the UK is committed to supporting IFAC and the FRC has largely adopted the auditing and quality control standards as the basis for its own standards. Through their membership of IFAC, professional accountancy bodies in the UK are also committed to using their best endeavours to promote IFAC standards.

1.5 The Financial Reporting Council

1.5.1 Role and structure

The Financial Reporting Council (FRC) is the UK's independent regulator, responsible for promoting high quality corporate governance and reporting to foster investment. The FRC sets the UK Corporate Governance and Stewardship Codes and UK standards for accounting work; monitors and takes action to promote the quality of corporate reporting; and operates independent enforcement arrangements for accountants. As the Competent Authority for audit in the UK, the FRC sets auditing and ethical standards and monitors and enforces audit quality.

The FRC Board is supported by the Codes and Standards Committee and the Conduct Committee.

The Codes and Standards Committee advises the FRC Board on matters relating to codes, standard-setting and policy questions, through its Corporate Reporting, Actuarial and Audit and Assurance Councils.

The Conduct Committee advises the Board on matters relating to conduct activities to promote high-quality corporate reporting, including monitoring, oversight, investigative and disciplinary functions through its Corporate Reporting Review, Audit Quality Review, and Case Management Committees.

1.5.2 Pronouncements

The FRC's *Scope and Authority of Audit and Assurance Pronouncements* issued in June 2016 sets out:

- an overview of the types of document issued by the FRC;
- the level of authority associated with each type of document; and
- the regulatory regime supporting FRC pronouncements derived from legislation and the rules of the accountancy bodies.

In order to act as auditors of UK companies, or of other entities that require auditors to be eligible for appointment as auditors under *Companies Act* 2006, s. 1212, auditors must be registered with, and eligible for appointment under the rules of a Recognised Supervisory Body (RSB) which is required under the Companies Act to have rules regarding the technical standards to be applied in audit work and the manner in which those standards are to be applied. Those rules must require statutory auditors to comply with standards determined by the FRC as the competent authority. Each RSB is also required to have arrangements in place for the effective monitoring and enforcement of compliance with those standards.

As members of The Consultative Committee of Accounting Bodies (CCAB), the five main accountancy bodies in the UK have undertaken to adopt the ethical and engagement standards and guidance issued by the FRC where the application of those standards is not required by law.

Failures by auditors to comply with applicable ethical or engagement standards may be investigated by the FRC or the relevant accountancy body. Auditors who do not comply with the applicable standards may be liable to regulatory action which may include the withdrawal of registration. All relevant FRC pronouncements are likely to be taken into account when the adequacy of the work of auditors is considered in a court of law or in other contested situations.

1.5.3   Predecessor body – Auditing Practices Board

As standard setter for the auditing profession, the FRC took over from the Auditing Practices Board (APB). At the time, all extant APB standards, Practice Notes and Bulletins were adopted by the FRC but most of these have subsequently been reissued as FRC pronouncements or withdrawn. A few APB Bulletins, however, remain extant.

1.6   Development of International Standards on Auditing (UK)

International Standards on Auditing (ISAs) are issued by the IAASB.

1.6.1   Original ISAs (UK and Ireland)

In May 2004, the APB announced its intention to adopt the ISAs issued by the IAASB for use in the UK and Ireland, first reviewing all of the existing Statements of Auditing Standards (SASs) to identify instances where they contained higher standards than those contained in the equivalent ISAs, and supplementing the ISAs accordingly. The resultant International Standards of Auditing (UK and Ireland) (ISAs (UK and Ireland)) were effective for the audit of financial statements for periods commencing on or after 15 December 2004.

1.6.2 IAASB's clarity project

At the same time, the IAASB began a comprehensive project to improve the clarity of its ISAs. The IAASB also took the opportunity to update and improve a number of the ISAs and the project was completed in March 2009 when 36 newly updated and clarified ISAs were issued. They were effective internationally for the audits of financial statements for periods commencing on or after 15 December 2009.

1.6.3 UK adoption of clarified ISAs

In the UK, the APB revised ISAs (UK and Ireland) on the basis of the new IAASB standards. Improvements to the ISAs meant that much of the original supplementary material was no longer required but the 'clarified' ISAs (UK and Ireland) nevertheless contained some additional paragraphs of supplementary material (grey-shaded paragraphs) which:

- addressed specific UK and Irish legal and regulatory requirements; and

- maintained a small number of other existing FRC/APB requirements and guidance considered necessary to prevent changes in audit practice to the detriment of audit quality.

These 'clarified' ISAs (UK and Ireland) were effective for audits of financial statements for periods ending on or after 15 December 2010.

One exception was ISA 700 *Forming an Opinion and Reporting on Financial Statements* which was not adopted by the APB. The APB instead issued ISA (UK and Ireland) 700 *The independent auditor's report on financial statements* which addressed the requirements of company law and also provided for a more concise auditor's report, addressing issues raised in the consultation process.

1.6.4 EU audit directive and regulation

In April 2014, the European Parliament and the Council of the European Union issued Regulation EU/537/2014 covering specific requirements regarding the statutory audit of public interest entities[1] (PIEs) (referred to as the Audit Regulation), and Directive 2014/56/EU which amended Directive 2006/43/EC covering the statutory audit of annual accounts and consolidated accounts (the Audit Directive). Both applied with effect from 17 June 2016. The Audit Regulation has the direct effect of law and EU member states are required to adopt appropriate provisions to ensure its effective application. The Audit Directive does not have a direct effect

---

[1] See glossary.

in law and EU member states are required to adopt and publish the measures necessary to comply with it.

The Audit Regulation and Audit Directive together required revisions to both the Ethical and Auditing Standards as well as changes to the UK Corporate Governance Code and amendments to UK law.

In the UK, the Government and the FRC decided to incorporate many of the detailed provisions of the Regulation and Directive directly into Auditing Standards, rather than as new requirements of the Companies Act and revised standards incorporating these amendments were published in June 2016. The revised standards are applicable for the audit of financial statements for periods commencing on or after 17 June 2016. This approach has the advantage of keeping detailed requirements for statutory audit in one place as well as providing greater flexibility for maintenance in the future given the difficulty involved in changing primary legislation. The downside is that the standards themselves contain much more UK specific material than previously, much more material that is applicable only to PIEs and some that is apparently duplicated where EU requirements and IAASB standards overlap. Requirements deriving from the Regulation and Directive are distinguished in the revised ISAs by being grey shaded material and by inclusion of 'R' or 'D' respectively in the paragraph number.

When the FRC issued the revisions to the ISAs in June 2016, it re-issued the full suite of ISAs as ISAs (UK), not just those that contained revisions to the requirements. This means that some ISAs have an implementation date (for example, periods ending on or after 15 December 2010) which apparently predates the issue date of June 2016. Some of the ISAs which were re-issued but were not revised did, however, have minor amendments or conforming changes made to the application material.

A number of the amendments made in June 2016 relate only to PIEs. These are reflected in the appropriate sections and also listed in a new **Appendix 2** for ease of reference.

1.6.5 Other changes to ISAs

As well as incorporating changes resulting from the Audit Directive and the Regulation, the revised standards issued in 2016 also included a number of changes to the IAASB's standards resulting from recent projects relating to the audit of other information and disclosures in the financial statements and to auditor reporting. These changes were widely spread throughout the suite of ISAs (UK).

A number of ISAs (UK) have also been updated or revised subsequently. Details are given in **Appendix 1**.

Reporting standards

In the June 2016 revisions, the FRC also took the opportunity to adopt (with some modifications) the IAASB's revised suite of reporting standards. Over recent years, the FRC has worked closely with the IAASB to develop the ISAs and incorporate reporting styles already introduced in the UK.

The resulting changes are reflected in the reporting sections of this book.

1.6.6 Application of ISAs (UK)

ISA (UK) 200 (Revised June 2016) *Objective and General Principles Governing an Audit of Financial Statements* sets out a number of basic principles and assumptions on which all other standards are based.

Each ISA (UK) sets out an objective for the auditor and specifies a number of requirements with which the auditor must comply, where relevant, in order to meet his objective. In order to meet the objective, it may be necessary for the auditor to carry out further procedures in addition to those required by ISAs (UK). In exceptional circumstances, it may be necessary for the auditor to depart from a relevant requirement in which case he will need to perform other procedures in order to achieve his objective. An example of such a situation may be where the ISA requires the auditor to carry out a specific procedure which, in the specific circumstances, would not be effective in achieving its aim. The ISAs (UK) also contain application and other explanatory material which is intended to assist auditors in interpreting and applying the standards but which is not prescriptive. The auditor is, however, required to have an understanding of the full text of an ISA, including the application and other explanatory material, in order to apply its requirements properly.

ISA (UK) 200 (Revised June 2016) requires auditors to conduct their audits in accordance with ISAs (UK) and with an attitude of professional scepticism throughout. Auditors are to recognise the possibility of a material misstatement due to facts or behaviour indicating irregularities, including fraud or error, notwithstanding the auditor's past experience of the honesty and integrity of the entity's management and of those charged with governance. This means that the audit should be approached with a questioning mind, with auditors making critical assessments of the evidence obtained, remaining alert for contradictions or evidence which makes them question the reliability of documents or management representations.

Auditors should also comply with the Revised Ethical Standard 2016 (see **Section 2**) and other ethical pronouncements issued by their professional body.

ISA (UK) 200 (Revised June 2016) requires auditors to plan and perform their work in order to reduce audit risk to an acceptably low level, having regard to the requirements of the ISAs (UK), their professional body, legislation and the terms of the engagement. Auditors must make an assessment of the audit risk, but are not responsible for the detection of misstatements that are not material to the financial statements taken as a whole.

1.7 Other FRC guidance

1.7.1 Practice Notes

The FRC also issues Practice Notes to assist auditors in applying auditing standards to particular circumstances in specific industries. Practice Notes are persuasive rather than prescriptive although they are indicative of good practice.

1.7.2 Bulletins

Bulletins have the same status as Practice Notes and are issued to provide auditors with timely guidance on new or emerging issues.

1.7.3 Client Asset Reporting Standard

The FRC has also issued one new assurance standard, *Providing assurance on client assets to the Financial Conduct Authority*, which applies to work carried out by auditors under Client Asset (CASS) Rules of the Financial Conduct Authority.

1.7.4 Statements of Recommended Practice (SORPs)

In particular industries or sectors, guidance for auditors may also be issued as SORPs which clarify how engagement standards may need to be applied in order to be relevant and provide useful information to users of audit reports or other information issued by the auditor. SORPs are persuasive rather than prescriptive and are indicative of good practice. Auditors should be aware of and consider SORPs applicable to the engagement. SORPs are issued by bodies recognised for this purpose by the FRC and are developed in accordance with the FRC's *Policy on Developing Statements of Recommended Practice (March 2016)*.

1.7.5 Standards for Reporting Accountants

The FRC also issues standards and guidance for accountants on assurance engagements closely related to audit. This includes the International Standards on Reporting Engagements ((ISRE) (UK and Ireland) 2410

Review of interim financial information performed by the independent auditor of the entity.

1.8 Other guidance

Since its formation in 1995, guidance on auditing matters has been issued by the Audit and Assurance Faculty of the ICAEW in the form of Technical Releases, many of which are referred to throughout this publication. Technical Releases are listed in **Appendix 1**.

1.9 Conventions

The reader should note that throughout this book, the male pronoun is used to cover references to both the male and female.

1.10 Accounting framework

Where this publication refers to the financial reporting framework, this should be taken to refer to the current relevant financial reporting standards applicable to the engagement. The applicable financial reporting framework also includes the requirements of applicable law.

In respect of the statutory accounts of a UK corporate entity, the relevant framework will be either:

- applicable law and UK Accounting Standards including [Financial Reporting Standard 102 *The Financial Reporting Standard applicable in the UK and the Republic of Ireland*]/[Financial Reporting Standard 101 *Reduced disclosure framework*]/[Financial Reporting Standard 105 *The Financial Reporting Standard applicable to the micro-entities regime*] (United Kingdom Generally Accepted Accounting Practice); or

- applicable law and International Financial Reporting Standards (IFRSs) as adopted by the European Union.

Other frameworks may apply in other situations.

2 Audit regulation and ethics

2.1 Introduction

Only registered auditors may accept appointment as company auditors in the UK. This has been the case since the relevant provisions of the *Companies Act* 1989 became effective on 1 October 1991 and this requirement is retained in the *Companies Act* 2006. In addition, where audits of other entities are required by law or regulations (e.g. certain charities and pension schemes), the auditor is required to be a registered auditor. Audit firms and individual audit engagement partners must be registered with a Recognised Supervisory Body (RSB). In order to qualify as an RSB, an organisation must have rules to ensure that its members, who are therefore qualified to accept appointments as company auditors, are properly regulated and monitored. To date the Institute of Chartered Accountants in England and Wales (ICAEW), the Institute of Chartered Accountants of Scotland (ICAS), the Institute of Chartered Accountants in Ireland (ICAI) (now operating as Chartered Accountants Ireland) and the Association of Chartered Certified Accountants (ACCA) have become RSBs for this purpose. In order to maintain registered auditor status, auditors registered with ICAEW, ICAS or ICAI must comply with Audit Regulations issued jointly by these bodies.

The definition of 'audit' includes audits of financial statements where required by law and any other function in respect of any of these entities that is required by law to be discharged by a registered auditor (for example, the report on the transfer of non-cash assets to a public company).

This publication is written with the presumption that the reader's audit firm is registered with the ICAEW as its RSB. Where this is not the case, and the firm is registered with an alternative RSB, this should be taken into account when reading example letters, for example those in **Section 38** which are addressed to the ICAEW.

The RSB's regulations must cover the following areas:

* qualification of auditors;
* control of audit firms by qualified individuals;
* fit and proper persons;
* professional integrity and independence;

- technical standards (see **2.8**);
- procedures to maintain competence (see **2.9**); and
- meeting claims (see **2.10**).

The rules must also provide for monitoring and enforcement, membership eligibility, investigation of complaints and discipline.

2.1.1 Ethical standards for auditors

Each RSB has its own Code of Ethics but in 2003, the responsibility for setting standards for independence, objectivity and integrity in respect of audit activities was transferred to the Auditing Practices Board (APB) who published a series of Ethical Standards for auditors including the *Ethical Standard – Provisions Available for Small Entities* (ES-PASE).

Responsibility for the issue of ethical standards for auditors was subsequently transferred to the Financial Reporting Council (FRC) who took over the functions of the APB and is now designated as the competent authority for the regulation of the auditing profession.

In June 2016, the FRC issued a single Revised Ethical Standard 2016 which is effective for audit and assurance engagements relating to periods commencing on or after 17 June 2016. This Revised Ethical Standard 2016 replaced the previous Ethical Standards for auditors and the ES-PASE.

This 2016 revision incorporated new requirements of the EU Audit Directive and EU Audit Regulation and largely affected auditors of public interest entities (PIEs). The revision resulted in one Ethical Standard divided into sections. The scope of the standard was also widened to cover 'all public assurance engagements' and as a result, the new standard applies to all audit and assurance engagements performed under the FRCs standards, including Standards for Investment Reporting (SIRs) and the standard for CASS reporting (see **Section 9**), although not all requirements apply equally to all types of engagement.

Further details of the FRC's Ethical Standard are given in **2.6** and **2.7**.

Further details of the ICAEW Code of Ethics are given in **2.5**.

2.1.2 Audit regulations

Audit Regulations are issued by the RSBs to govern the conduct of registered auditors. First issued in 1991, they have been subject to many changes and updates. Audit Regulations were revised in June 2016 to give effect to changes arising from the implementation of the EU Audit Directive and Regulation and were revised with effect from 1 April 2017 to take account of changes to Irish company law.

Amongst other things, the Regulations stipulate how audit reports must be signed (see **2.15**).

2.2 Qualification

The Companies Act states that for a qualification to be recognised, it must, among other things, involve:

- a course of theoretical instruction;

- examinations; and

- three years' practical training.

2.3 Control of audit firms

A firm may not be recognised as a registered auditor unless it is controlled by qualified persons. In simple terms, this means that a majority of the members of the firm are qualified persons although certain of the RSBs have in fact imposed more stringent requirements than this.

2.4 Fit and proper person

An RSB must have adequate rules and practices designed to ensure that persons eligible under its rules are fit and proper persons to be so appointed. This will normally involve ensuring that there is a suitable procedure for notification, both to the firm by partners and employees and to the RSB by the firms, of matters relating to partners and employees in respect of:

- financial integrity and reliability;

- convictions or civil liabilities; and

- good reputation or character – including previous disciplinary procedures with professional bodies or other regulatory organisations.

2.5 ICAEW code of ethics

2.5.1 Background

In July 2006, the ICAEW issued its own *Code of Ethics* ('the Code') to assist its members in meeting the highest standards of professional conduct and replacing the previous *Guide to Professional Ethics*. It has subsequently been updated and the current version was effective from 1 January 2011. The Code applies to all ICAEW members (including students), affiliates, employees of member firms and member firms themselves (together 'professional accountants'). It is applicable to all professional and business activities, whether remunerated or voluntary.

The Code was derived from the International Ethics Standards Board of Accountants' (IESBA) Code of Ethics issued in July 2009 by the International Federation of Accountants (IFAC), supplemented with additional requirements and guidance where this was considered appropriate by the ICAEW. It adopts a principles-based approach, with threats to the fundamental principles and related safeguards illustrated by a series of case studies. The IESBA Code of Ethics does not apply directly to ICAEW members or members of other UK accountancy bodies but the main accountancy bodies throughout the world, including ICAEW and the other CCAB bodies are required to comply with the principles included in the IESBA Code of Ethics.

2.5.2 *The fundamental principles*

The Code sets out five fundamental principles that must be complied with at all times. These are set out in **Table 1**.

TABLE 1: Five fundamental principles in the ICAEW Code of Ethics

Integrity

A professional accountant should be straightforward and honest in all professional and business relationships.

Objectivity

A professional accountant should not allow bias, conflict of interest or undue influence of others to override professional or business judgments.

Professional Competence and Due Care

A professional accountant should maintain professional knowledge and skill at the level required to ensure that a client or employer receives competent professional services based on current developments in practice, legislation and techniques and should act diligently and in accordance with applicable technical and professional standards.

Confidentiality

A professional accountant should respect the confidentiality of information acquired as a result of professional and business relationships and, therefore, should not disclose any such information to third parties without proper and specific authority, unless there is a legal or professional right or duty to disclose, nor use the information for the personal advantage of the professional accountant or third parties.

Professional Behaviour

A professional accountant should comply with relevant laws and regulations and should avoid any action that discredits the profession.

The environment in which professional accountants operate may lead to specific threats to these fundamental principles. As it is impossible to envisage every possible threat that may occur, the Code sets out a conceptual framework which requires professional accountants to identify, evaluate and address these threats individually rather than just comply with a predetermined set of rules. Where professional accountants identify significant threats they should apply suitable safeguards to eliminate them or reduce them to an acceptable level.

When considering whether a threat is significant, professional accountants should consider both quantitative and qualitative factors. Where suitable safeguards cannot be applied, the professional accountant should not accept, or should resign, from the engagement.

2.5.3 *Threats and safeguards*

The Code sets out the following types of threats to the fundamental principles:

- self-interest threats, as a result of the financial or other interests of a professional accountant or of an immediate or close family member;
- self-review threats, when a previous judgment needs to be re-evaluated by the professional accountant responsible for that judgment;
- advocacy threats, when a professional accountant promotes a position or opinion to the point that subsequent objectivity may be compromised;
- familiarity threats, when, because of a close relationship, a professional accountant becomes too sympathetic to the interests of others; and
- intimidation threats, when a professional accountant may be deterred from acting objectively by actual or perceived threats.

Each type of threat may arise in relation to the professional accountant themselves or in relation to a connected person such as a close family member, a fellow partner or other professional associate.

There are two main types of safeguard set out in the Code:

- safeguards created by the profession, legislation or regulation; and
- safeguards in the work environment.

The first category includes, but is not restricted to:

- educational, training and experience requirements for entry into the profession;
- continuing professional development requirements;

- corporate governance regulations;
- professional standards;
- professional or regulatory monitoring and disciplinary procedures; and
- external review by a legally empowered third party of the reports, returns, communications or information produced by a professional accountant.

The actual safeguards used will depend on the circumstances. In assessing whether the safeguards are reasonable, professional accountants should consider what a reasonable and informed third party would consider to be acceptable.

2.5.4 Conflict resolution

When applying the fundamental principles, conflicts may arise. The Code states that it is preferable for such conflicts to be resolved within the organisation before obtaining advice from the Institute or legal advisors. Where necessary, professional accountants should consult with other appropriate persons within the organisation.

When conflicts occur, professional accountants should consider:

- relevant facts;
- relevant parties;
- ethical issues involved;
- fundamental principles related to the matter in question;
- established internal procedures; and
- alternative courses of action.

If, having exhausted all possibilities, the conflict remains unresolved, the professional accountant should refuse to remain associated with the matter creating the conflict. This may involve a firm resignation from an engagement or an individual withdrawing from an engagement team or resigning from a firm.

2.5.5 Conflicts of interest and confidentiality

In January 2000, the ICAEW's Business Law Committee issued TECH 4/00 *Conflicts of interest and confidentiality* to provide guidance for accountants on the implications of the decision in the case of *Prince Jefri Bolkiah v KPMG*. The guidance was intended to be read in conjunction with the ICAEW's Guide to professional Ethics (now the Code of Ethics).

The judgment stresses that where an accountant is acting as a fiduciary, he cannot act for clients with conflicting interests without their informed consent. Since the law is unclear about when accountants act as fiduciaries, consent should be obtained whenever there is potential conflict. Such conflicts of interest could be wide ranging and could extend to audit clients who are competitors with one another in a particular market. This requirement does not apply to former clients, although duties of confidentiality will continue.

The guidance suggests additional paragraphs to be included in the engagement letter to deal with these issues. The paragraphs are set out in **Table 2**.

TABLE 2: Paragraphs to be included in an engagement letter where potential conflict of interest exists

Conflict and Confidentiality

You agree that we may reserve the right to act during this engagement for other clients whose interests are or may be adverse to yours, subject to the confidentiality requirements detailed here.

We confirm that where you give us confidential information, we shall at all times keep it confidential, except as required by law or as provided for in regulatory, ethical or other professional pronouncements applicable to our engagement.

You agree that it will be sufficient compliance with our duty of confidence for us to take such steps as we in good faith think fit to preserve confidential information both during and after termination of this engagement.

Although these paragraphs leave accountants potentially liable for any actual breach of confidence, this is only where they do not take appropriate steps to keep confidential information secure. This means that the erection of 'Chinese Walls' may be avoided.

Chinese Walls

Where an accountant is not able to obtain consent from his client in line with the paragraphs in **Table 2**, it is possible for a Chinese Wall to be effective within a firm. The *Prince Jefri* ruling states that the Chinese Wall must have the characteristics noted in **Table 3** to be effective.

TABLE 3: Characteristics of an effective Chinese Wall

- The physical separation of the various departments in order to insulate them from each other (this may include details such as separate dining arrangements).

- Training to emphasise the importance of not divulging confidential information.

> - Strict and defined procedures for when it is felt that the wall should be crossed and the maintaining of proper records where this occurs.
>
> - Monitoring of the effectiveness of the wall by compliance officers.
>
> - Disciplinary sanctions where there has been a breach of the wall.

In addition, an effective Chinese Wall needs to be an established part of an organisation, not created on an ad hoc basis. Physical segregation would not create an effective barrier within a single department.

2.5.6 Control of confidentiality and independence

A firm must have procedures to ensure that staff are aware of confidentiality and independence issues. Confidentiality applies to the information obtained during the course of professional work and the obligation not to disclose or use it. Firms need to be able to demonstrate that they have procedures to ensure that such issues have been brought to the attention of staff. This can be demonstrated by having staff certify their awareness of the procedures. Additionally, as regards independence, the firm should circulate details of listed companies of which it is the auditor to both partners and employees to enable them to identify any potential conflicts.

2.5.7 Receipt of information in confidence by auditors

In addition to the professional guidance found in the Code on the ethics of the disclosure and use of confidential information, guidance can also be found in the ICAEW's Technical Release TECH 10/14AAF *Receipt of information in confidence by auditors*. TECH 10/14AAF provides additional assistance in the resolution of ethical problems that may arise where auditors receive information from a source other than their client, with a request or the implication that the information or its source should be kept confidential. Such circumstances may arise in relation to information received from regulators, from employees or from third parties such as trading partners. In these circumstances, auditors should always act with integrity; take into account their legal obligations including potential duties to report to regulators or to report suspicions of money laundering; use best endeavours to protect the identity of informants; and consider the significance of any such matters raised in relation to the audit.

2.6 The FRC's Revised Ethical Standard 2016

The Revised Ethical Standard 2016 was issued in June 2016 and is effective for periods commencing on or after 17 June 2016. This replaced the APB's Ethical Standards 1–5 and the *Ethical Standard – Provisions Available for Small Entities* (ES-PASE). Many of the requirements are detailed and specific and the following information and guidance is intended only as a guide and is not a substitute for referring to the Revised Ethical Standard 2016 (the 'Ethical Standard').

2.6.1   Scope

The Ethical Standard applies to audit engagements and other public interest assurance engagements[1,2]. A fundamental objective of any such engagement is that the intended users trust and have confidence that the audit or assurance opinion is professionally sound and objective. This in turn should enhance the credibility for users of the information the opinion covers.

Although auditors and assurance practitioners are reporting to users, they are generally engaged to do so by the entity whose information they are reporting on. Accordingly, their contractual 'client' (the entity) is different to their beneficial 'client' (the users). These principal-agent relationships (where the users are the principals and the directors and auditors of the entity their agents) give rise to the potential for conflicts of interests that need to be addressed if the user is to have trust and confidence in the audit/assurance process, the subject matter information and the directors of the entity itself.

Users do not have all the information necessary for judging whether the firm, its partners and staff and any other covered persons are, in fact, acting with integrity and objectivity. Although the firm may be satisfied that the integrity, objectivity and independence of the firm or such persons will not in fact be compromised by a particular condition or relationship, an objective, reasonable and informed third party may reach a different conclusion. For example, if such a third party were aware that the firm, its partners or staff and/or other persons had certain financial, employment, business or personal relationships with an entity relevant to the engagement, that third party might reasonably conclude that the firm and such persons could be subject to undue influence from the directors of the entity or would not be impartial or unbiased. Public confidence in the integrity, objectivity and independence of the firm or such persons could

---

[1] Audits of financial statements undertaken in compliance with ISAs (UK) and other engagements undertaken in compliance with performance standards issued by the FRC which, as of 17 June 2016, comprise:

   (a) Reporting accountants acting in connection with an investment circular (the Standards for Investment Reporting – 'SIRs');

   (b) Review of interim financial information by the independent auditor of the entity (International Standard on Review Engagements (UK and Ireland) 2410); and

   (c) Engagements to provide assurance on client assets to the Financial Conduct Authority (the CASS Standard).

[2] In the public sector, the statutory scope of an audit can extend beyond the entity's financial statements to include reporting on an entity's arrangements for the proper conduct of its financial affairs, management of its performance or use of its resources.

therefore suffer as a result of this perception, irrespective of whether there is any actual impairment.

Ethical guidance on other matters, together with statements of fundamental ethical principles governing the work of all professional accountants, are issued by professional accountancy bodies. These also provide a basis for enhancing the trust and confidence of intended users that the engagement is professionally sound. Auditors and other accountants are required to comply with the relevant Ethical Codes of the professional accountancy bodies. The Ethical Standard imposes additional ethical considerations for auditors and those performing other public interest assurance engagements.

Part A of the Ethical Standard sets out the overarching principles of integrity, objectivity and independence, together with supporting ethical provisions. Together, these establish a framework, of ethical outcomes that are required to be met by the auditor or assurance practitioner, to provide a basis for user trust and confidence in the integrity and objectivity of the practitioner in performing the engagement.

Part B sets out specific requirements relevant to certain circumstances that may arise in audit and other public interest assurance engagements. These specific requirements are designed to assist in meeting the ethical outcomes required by the overarching principles and supporting ethical provisions. However, circumstances relating to engagements vary widely and meeting the ethical outcomes required by the overarching principles and supporting ethical provisions is paramount. Compliance with the specific requirements may not always be sufficient to achieve this as Part B does not, nor is it practicable for it to, address all possible circumstances that may exist. Accordingly practitioners need to be alert for, and respond appropriately to, other circumstances that create threats to meeting the ethical outcomes required by the overarching principles and supporting ethical provisions. Whether the ethical outcomes required by the overarching principles and supporting ethical provisions are achieved is always paramount and is a matter to be determined exercising professional judgment.

Importantly, consideration of whether the ethical outcomes required by the overarching principles and supporting ethical provisions have been met should be evaluated by reference to the perspective of an objective, reasonable and informed third party.

European Directive and Regulation

In April 2014, the European Commission published a Directive amending the Statutory Audit Directive and a new Audit Regulation. The Audit Directive establishes specific requirements concerning the statutory audit of annual and consolidated financial statements. The Audit Regulation establishes further specific requirements regarding the statutory audit of 'public interest entities'. Articles in both the Audit Directive and Audit Regulation establish provisions that relate to matters that are the subject of the Ethical Standard, and have been reflected in the Standard. In relation to a number of these provisions there are member state options that have been implemented in the Ethical Standard.

Compliance with IESBA Code

The Ethical Standard was developed with the intent that it should adhere to the principles of the Code of Ethics for Professional Accountants issued by the International Ethics Standards Board for Accountants (the IESBA Code) although it is more restrictive in some areas than the IESBA Code.

2.6.2 Contents of the Revised Ethical Standard

The Revised Ethical Standard 2016 consists of two parts:

- Part A – Overarching principles and supporting ethical provisions; and
- Part B which contains:
    - Section 1 – General requirements and guidance
    - Section 2 – Financial, business, employment and personal relationships;
    - Section 3 – Long association with engagements and with entities relevant to engagements;
    - Section 4 – Fees, remuneration and evaluation policies, gifts and hospitality, litigation;
    - Section 5 – Non-audit/additional services; and
    - Section 6 – Provisions available for small entities.

The main changes in the 2016 standard, other than the presentation and formatting changes, are set out in the following paragraphs.

General requirements

An audit firm is required to establish appropriate and effective operational and administrative arrangements to identify, manage and record incidents that may affect the integrity, objectivity and independence of its audit activities and be able to demonstrate to the competent authority (FRC) that the arrangements are appropriate given the complexity and size of the firm.

Where a firm is a member of a network, management of the UK firm will have a responsibility to make arrangements for ensuring that appropriate ethical policies are applied across the network and that policies, procedures and quality control systems are implemented and operating effectively.

A firm's policy on resolving differences of opinion should include differences of opinion between the Ethics Partner and those consulting him. The Ethics Partner also should not take on any role that would conflict with the role of Ethics Partner.

New provisions relate to identification of threats to independence where an audit client merges with or is acquired by another entity.

For public interest entities and other listed entities, specific requirements have been introduced to assess and document in the engagement working papers various matters including all significant threats to integrity or objectivity, and safeguards to mitigate them, compliance with the Ethical Standard, competence and adequacy of resources.

Terminology

Covered persons

'Covered person' is a new term and replaces the previous 'person in a position to influence the conduct and outcome of the audit' definition. It includes the following individuals:

- members of the audit engagement team;

- experts and specialists used as part of the audit engagement;

- any person in the audit firm with supervisory, management or other oversight responsibility over the audit engagement or the audit engagement partner or other key partners involved in the engagement. This also includes those individuals who are in a position to prepare, review or otherwise influence the performance appraisal and/or remuneration of most individuals whom are deemed a covered person; and

- other persons in a position to influence the audit engagement. This does not include any independent non-executive individuals on a supervisory or equivalent board. It is, however, intended to cover senior people in the firm or network firm who may be, for example, acting in a mentoring role, either for a newly appointed partner, or others in the team who that mentor might be able to influence.

Persons closely associated

A 'person closely associated' is a new term which replaces the previous 'immediate family' definition. It includes the following (but is not limited to):

- a spouse or a partner considered to be equivalent to a spouse in accordance with national law;

- a dependent child; and

- a relative who has lived in the same household as the person with whom they are associated for at least one year.

Partners

A 'partner' includes any individual with the authority to bind the firm with respect to the performance of a professional services engagement. This may therefore include certain staff members who have the ability to bind the firm by virtue of their roles and responsibilities.

The FRC's publication *Glossary of Terms (audit and accounting)* contains a comprehensive definition of 'covered person' and 'person closely associated'.

SME listed entity

An SME listed entity will have the following attributes:

- an average market capitalisation of less than €200m on the basis of year end quotes for the previous three calendar years; or

- an entity that issues exclusively non-equity financial instruments if:

  - the total nominal amount of the non-equity financial instruments issued and outstanding does not exceed €200m; or

  - according to the last annual or consolidated accounts, meets at least two of the following criteria:

    (a) an average number of employees during the financial year of less than 250;

    (b) a total balance sheet not exceeding €43m;

    (c) an annual net turnover not exceeding €50m.

2.6.3   Ethical Standard – Introduction and Section 1 – Integrity, Objectivity and Independence

The Ethical Standard defines the terms integrity, objectivity and independence as follows:

- integrity – being trustworthy, straightforward, honest, fair and candid; complying with the spirit as well as the letter of applicable ethical principles, laws and regulations; behaving so as to maintain the public's trust in the auditing profession; and respecting confidentiality except where disclosure is in the public interest or is required to adhere to legal and professional responsibilities;

- objectivity – acting and making decisions and judgments impartially, fairly and on merit (having regard to all considerations relevant to the task in hand but no other), without discrimination, bias, or compromise because of commercial or personal self-interest, conflicts of interest or the undue influence of others, and having given due consideration to the best available evidence; and

- independence is freedom from situations and relationships which, in the context of an engagement, would compromise the integrity or objectivity of the firm or covered persons.

The Standard requires firms to establish formal and written policies and procedures to ensure that those in a position to influence the conduct and outcome of an audit act with integrity, objectivity and independence. This should involve the leadership of the firm engendering an environment where ethics are considered more important than commercial considerations, and designating an 'ethics partner' to have overall responsibility for the firm's policies and procedures.

The Standard also requires that the firm and each covered person is not involved in the decision-making of an entity relevant to the engagement. Whilst it is not possible to specify all types of decision that are the responsibility of management, they typically involve leading and directing the entity, including making significant judgments and taking decisions regarding the acquisition, deployment and control of human, financial, physical and intangible resources.

The policies and procedures in place should include those set out in **Table 4**.

TABLE 4: Ethical policies and procedures

- Requirements for partners and staff to report where applicable:
  - family and other personal relationships involving an audit client of the firm;
  - financial interests in an audit client of the firm; and
  - decisions to join an audit client.

- Monitoring of compliance with the firm's policies and procedures relating to integrity, objectivity and independence. Such monitoring procedures include, on a test basis, periodic review of the audit engagement partners' documentation of their consideration of the auditors' objectivity and independence, addressing, for example:
  - financial interests in audit clients;
  - economic dependency on audit clients;

> – the performance of non-audit services; and
>
> – audit partner rotation.
>
> - Identification of the entities which partners and staff, and where applicable, persons closely associated with them, need to be independent from;
>
> - Prompt communication of identified breaches of the firm's policies and procedures to the relevant audit engagement partners.
>
> - Evaluation by audit engagement partners of the implications of any identified breaches of the firm's policies and procedures that are reported to them.
>
> - Reporting by audit engagement partners of particular circumstances or relationships as required by the Revised Ethical Standard 2016.
>
> - Operation of a disciplinary mechanism to promote compliance with policies and procedures.
>
> - Empowerment of staff to communicate to senior levels within the firm any issue of objectivity and independence that concerns them; this includes establishing clear communication channels open to staff, encouraging staff to use these channels and ensuring that staff who use these channels are not subject to disciplinary proceedings as a result.

All firms of more than three partners who are responsible individuals should designate a partner in the firm as 'ethics partner'. The ethics partner will have responsibility for:

- the adequacy of the firm's policies and procedures relating to integrity, objectivity and independence, their compliance with the Ethical Standards, and the effectiveness of their communications to partners and staff within the firm; and

- providing related guidance to individual partners to ensure a consistent approach to the application of the Ethical Standards.

The ethics partner should be suitably experienced and hold sufficient authority within a firm.

Firms with three or less partners where it is not practicable to designate an ethics partner should ensure that the relevant issues are regularly discussed by all partners. Sole practitioners should discuss with the ethics helpline of their professional body any matters where a difficult or objective judgment must be made.

The auditor should identify and assess threats to his objectivity and apply safeguards that will either eliminate or reduce the threat to an acceptable level. The principal types of threat are set out in **Table 5**.

A firm's policy on resolving differences of opinion should include differences of opinion between the Ethics Partner and those consulting him. The Ethics Partner also should not take on any role that would conflict with the role of Ethics Partner.

TABLE 5: Types of threat to objectivity

- Self-interest threat – the auditor has financial or other interest that would affect his decision making.

- Self-review threat – if auditing his own non-audit work.

- Management threat – the firm has made judgments or taken decisions that are the responsibility of management.

- Advocacy threat – the auditor has acted as an advocate and has supported a position taken by management in an adversarial context.

- Familiarity (or trust) threat – the auditor has a close personal relationship with the client.

- Intimidation threat – the auditor is influenced by fear or threats.

The significance of threats should be considered throughout the audit both individually and on a cumulative basis, but at least when:

- considering whether to accept or retain an audit engagement;

- planning the audit;

- forming an opinion on the financial statements;

- considering whether to accept or retain an engagement to provide non-audit services to an audit client; and

- potential threats are reported to the audit engagement partner.

This assessment of threats should be documented, together with details of actions taken as a result of identified threats. The firm should have procedures in place to ensure that any possible threats are reported to the audit engagement partner or the ethics partner. The audit engagement partner should not accept or continue an audit engagement if it is concluded that a threat to objectivity and independence cannot be reduced to an acceptable level.

A threat to independence may also arise from providing non-audit services to a third party who is connected to an audited entity and the outcome of that service has a material impact on the financial statements of the audited entity. Such arrangements should also be considered when assessing objectivity. Examples include providing actuarial advice to the pension scheme of an audited entity.

At the end of the audit process, but prior to issuing the audit report, the audit engagement partner should reach an overall conclusion on whether any threats to objectivity and independence have been properly addressed. If they are unable to conclude that this is the case, the audit report should not be issued, and the firm should resign.

In the case of listed companies and other public interest entities, the assessment and documentation of the assessment, should be reviewed by an independent partner and those charged with governance should be informed of any significant facts and matters that bear on the auditor's objectivity and independence on a timely basis.

For all clients, the key elements of the audit engagement partner's consideration of objectivity and independence should be communicated to those charged with governance. These may include:

- the principal threats, if any, to objectivity and independence identified by the auditor, including consideration of all relationships between the audit client, its affiliates and directors and the audit firm;

- any safeguards adopted and the reasons why they are considered to be effective;

- any independent partner review;

- the overall assessment of threats and safeguards; and

- information about the general policies and processes within the audit firm for maintaining objectivity and independence.

The minimum requirements for listed companies are set out in **Table 6**.

TABLE 6: Minimum contents of communications with those charged with governance for listed clients

- A written disclosure of relationships that bear on the auditor's objectivity and independence, any safeguards that are in place and details of non-audit services provided to the audited entity and the fees charged in relation thereto.

- Written confirmation that the auditor is independent.

- Details of any inconsistencies between Ethical Standards and the company's policy for the supply of non-audit services by the audit firm and any apparent breach of that policy.

- An opportunity to discuss auditor independence issues.

The Ethical Standard sets out in an appendix an illustrative template for disclosure of audit and non-audit services and fees for listed clients.

2.6.4 Ethical Standard – Section 2: Financial, Business, Employment and Personal Relationships

Section 2 sets out a number of requirements and prohibitions relating to auditor and client relationships.

Financial relationships

The Standard states that the audit firm, its partners and any covered persons, should not hold:

- any direct financial interest in an audit client or affiliate of an audit client;

- any indirect financial interest in an audit client or an affiliate of an audit client, where the investment is material to the audit firm or the individual or the intermediary (e.g. an open-ended investment company or a pension scheme); or

- any indirect financial interest in an audit client or an affiliate of an audit client, where the person holding it has both:

  - the ability to influence the investment decisions of the intermediary; and

  - actual knowledge of the existence of the underlying investment in the audit client.

There are no safeguards that can mitigate such threats and the individual involved should either dispose of the whole financial interest, dispose of part of the interest so that the remaining part is not material, or the firm or individual concerned should withdraw from the audit. The Ethical Standard gives further details of the remedies required.

This requirement also extends to any person closely associated with the partner or with the covered person.

Section 2 states that when a new partner or member of staff joins an audit firm, if they hold a prohibited financial interest, or if the financial interest is held by a person closely associated with them, the disposal of the financial interest should happen prior to them joining the firm. If disposal is not practicable prior to the individual joining the firm, that individual should not:

- be in a position to influence the conduct and outcome of the audit of that client;

- work in the same part of the firm as the audit engagement partner; and

- be involved in the provision of a non-audit service to that audit client.

The financial interest must be disposed of as soon as possible and records of such interests must be maintained by the Ethics Partner.

Financial interests held by audit firm pension schemes

There are no safeguards that can eliminate or reduce the self-interest threat to an acceptable level where the pension scheme of an audit firm has a financial interest in an audit client and the firm has any influence over the trustees' investment decisions. In such a situation, the audit firm would be required to resign from the audit. Where the pension scheme invests in a client through an intermediary such as a collective investment scheme, and the firm cannot influence the investment decisions, the ethics partner must consider whether the position is acceptable, having particular regard to the materiality of the investment to the pension scheme.

Loans and guarantees

There are similar restrictions as those for financial relationships where firms, covered persons and persons closely associated with them make loans to, or guarantee the borrowings of, an audit client or an affiliate of an audit client.

This also extends to accepting a loan from, or having borrowings guaranteed by, an audit client or an affiliate of an audit client.

The only exemptions for these restrictions are:

* the audit client is a bank or similar institution;

* the loan or guarantee is made in the ordinary course of business on normal business terms; and

* where the client makes the loan or guarantee to the audit firm, it is neither material to the audit firm or the client.

Business relationships

Audit firms and any covered persons[3] should not have a business or other relationship with audit clients that would compromise their independence.

Audit firms, covered persons and persons closely associated with them should not enter into business relationships with audit clients, its management or its affiliates except for the purchase of goods or services in the normal course of business where the transaction is not material to either party.

Examples of business relationships that may create self-interest, advocacy or intimidation threats include:

---

[3] See definition in **2.6.1**.

- joint ventures with the audit client or with a director, officer or other senior management;

- arrangements to combine services or products and market them with reference to both parties;

- acting as a distributor or marketer of any of the audit client's products or services; or

- other commercial transactions such as the audit firm leasing office space from the audit client.

Employment relationships

All partners and any covered persons should not:

- be employed by both audit firm and audit client;

- be loaned by the firm to the audit client, except if it is for a short period of time and does not involve staff or partners performing non-audit services which would not have been permitted under Section 5. Also, the audit client must agree that the member of staff will not hold a management position and will not have responsibility for management decisions or preparing or recording accounting entries; or

- be involved in auditing any work they performed whilst on loan with the client.

If a former partner of the firm joins an audit client, the firm must ensure that all connections with the partner are severed before any further audit work is performed for that client. This includes settling outstanding financial interests and ensuring that the partner does not participate or appear to participate in the firm's business or professional activities.

Firms should have procedures to ensure that partners or senior audit team members are required to notify the firm as soon as there is a potential for them to become employed by an audit client. Other members of the team should notify the firm as soon as their employment by an audit client becomes probable. Any such person must be removed from the audit team immediately and the work they performed on the current and most recent audit should be reviewed, ideally by someone of the same experience or by someone more senior.

When a partner (or former employee of the firm who was approved as a statutory auditor), having previously been a covered person, becomes a director, including a non-executive director, a member of the audit committee (or equivalent) or enters a key management position with an audit client within two years of acting as a covered person in the case of a partner and within one year of acting as a covered person in the case of any non-partner, the firm must resign as auditor. Reappointment cannot take place until a two-year 'cooling off' period has elapsed in the case of a partner and until a one year 'cooling off' period has elapsed in the case of any non-partner.

If a former partner of the firm (or former employee of the firm who was approved as a statutory auditor), has joined an entity as a director (including as a non-executive director), a member of the audit committee or body performing equivalent functions, or in a key management position, there is a similar 'cooling off' period prior to the firm accepting an engagement for the entity.

Similarly, the firm, a partner or an employee of an audit firm should not accept a governance role with an audit client. A prohibited governance role would be appointment to the board of directors or any subcommittee of that board or to any position in any entity which holds directly or indirectly, more than 20% of the voting rights of the audit client. Where a governance role is accepted by an immediate or close family member, or another partner or employee in the office, safeguards can usually be put in place to mitigate any threats.

When a director or a person able to exercise significant influence over the preparation of the financial statements transfers from audit client to audit firm, he should not be involved in the audit of that client for a period of at least two years from leaving the audit client, although a longer exclusion period may be appropriate depending on the auditor's assessment of threats and safeguards.

Family and other personal relationships

The Standard sets out that a relationship with a covered person does not generally affect the consideration of integrity and objectivity and the evaluation of whether independence is compromised.

However, this may not be the case where it is a relationship with a family member and that family member also has a financial, business or employment relationship with the audit client. The significance of any threat will depend on:

- the relevant person's involvement in the audit;

- the nature of the relationship between the relevant person and his or her family member; and

- the family member's relationship with the audit client.

Therefore partners and professional staff should report any 'persons closely associated' (i.e. spouse or equivalent and dependents), close family (i.e. parents, non-dependent children and siblings) and other personal relationships involving an audit client, to their firm where they consider it might create a threat to independence or objectivity. Such information should be passed to the engagement partner who will be able to assess the threat to independence and objectivity and apply appropriate safeguards.

The audit engagement partner should also consider whether any external consultant involved in the audit will be objective, and document the rationale for their conclusion.

2.6.5 Ethical Standard – Section 3: Long Association with the Audit Engagement

The Standard states that firms should monitor the length of time and extent of involvement that partners and staff in senior positions serve as members of the engagement team for each audit.

The Standard suggests rotating the audit partners and senior members of the audit team after a period of time. For listed and public interest entities, the maximum period is determined as five years. A suggested maximum of ten years is given for non-listed clients, although this is not mandatory and alternative safeguards could be applied. Where the individual is not rotated from the audit after ten years, the reasons for this should be documented and these facts communicated to those charged with governance.

For listed and public interest entities, the Standard states that partner rotation is the only permissible safeguard. **Table 7** sets out the time limits for rotation.

TABLE 7: Time limits for partner rotation for listed and public interest entities

In the case of listed companies and public interest entities, the audit firm should establish policies and procedures to ensure that:

- no one should act as audit engagement partner or key audit partner for a continuous period longer than five years;[4,5]

- no one should act as engagement quality control reviewer or a key partner involved in the engagement for a continuous period longer than seven years;

---

[4] This may be extended to seven years in exceptional circumstances where the audit committee (or equivalent) of the entity decide that such an extension is necessary to safeguard the quality of the audit and this is agreed by the audit firm involved. This may be where substantial change has recently been made or will be made to the nature or structure of the entity's business or there are unexpected changes in the senior management of the audited entity. In such circumstances, alternative safeguards should be put in place to reduce any threats to an acceptable level. Disclosure of the extension must be made to the shareholders as soon as possible and again in each of the subsequent years.

[5] Where an audit client becomes listed or a public interest entity the period before the listing etc. will be taken into account when calculating the five years elapsed. However, if on listing the partner has served four years or more, he can serve up to two further years.

- where an engagement quality control reviewer or key partner involved in the engagement becomes the audit engagement partner, the combined period of service in these positions should not exceed seven years;

- anyone who has previously acted as the audit engagement partner or key audit partner shall not subsequently participate in the audit until a further period of at least five years has elapsed;

- anyone who has previously acted as the audit engagement quality reviewer either continuously or in aggregate for seven years, shall not subsequently participate in the audit until a further period of at least five years has elapsed; and

- anyone who has previously acted as the key partner involved in the engagement either continuously or in aggregate for seven years, shall not subsequently participate in the audit until a further period of at least two years has elapsed.

A seven-year limit is imposed for rotation of 'key partners involved in the engagement'. A key partner involved in the engagement is a partner, or other person performing the function of a partner, of the engagement team (other than the audit engagement partner) who is involved at the group level and is responsible for key decisions or judgments on significant matters, such as on significant subsidiaries or divisions, or on significant risk factors that relate to the audit of that client. Additionally, the seven-year limit applies when the key partner involved in the audit becomes the engagement partner. The 'cooling off' period before the key partner involved in the engagement can assume any responsibility in relation to this client is two years.

The same seven-year limit is relevant to other partners and staff in senior positions after which time a review of the threats and safeguards relevant to objectivity and independence must be made. Where there are threats identified a suitable safeguard may be to remove the member of staff from the audit team.

A 'key audit partner' is a new role which is applicable to public interest entities only and is defined in the glossary.

A five-year limit is imposed for rotation of key audit partners with a cooling off period of five years before that partner can assume any responsibility in relation to that client.

For an audit of a public interest entity, the audit firm should establish an appropriate gradual rotation mechanism with regard to the most senior personnel involved in the audit. This is to ensure that rotation occurs on a timely basis to avoid senior members of the engagement team rotating off the client during the same period.

Mandatory firm rotation

For audits of public interest entities, there is a mandatory requirement for the audit firm to rotate after 20 years in office, with a mandatory tender at least after ten years. Transitional arrangements are in place for where the audit firm was appointed before this requirement came into effect.

2.6.6 Ethical Standard Section 4: Fees, Remuneration and Evaluation Policies, Litigation, Gifts and Hospitality

Fees

The Standard sets out the following requirements in relation to fees:

- sufficient partners and staff with appropriate skills must be used on an audit, irrespective of fees charged;

- an audit should not be undertaken on a contingent fee basis;

- a firm should not undertake an engagement to provide non-audit services in respect of an audited entity on a contingent fee basis where the:

  - contingent fee is material to the audit firm, or that part of the firm by reference to which the audit engagement partner's profit share is calculated;

  - non-audit service is a tax service where the outcome of the service (and, therefore, the amount of the fee) is based on uncertain or unestablished tax law, and may be material to present or future financial statements;

  - non-audit service is a tax service and the client is listed with a market cap of more than €200m; or

  - the outcome of those non-audit services (and, therefore, the amount of the fee) is dependent on a future or contemporary audit judgment relating to a material matter in the financial statements of the audited entity;

- for listed companies, the audit engagement partner should disclose to the audit committee in writing any contingent fee arrangements for non-audit services;

- fees and payment arrangements should be agreed with the client prior to the audit firm being appointed for the following period; and

- where overdue fees arise, the audit engagement partner, together with the ethics partner, should consider whether it is necessary to resign.

For audits of public interest entities, a cap (based on a 70% of the average audit fee over three years) will be imposed for the provision of certain non-audit services. This cap applies on a group wide basis and includes consideration of non-audit services provided by other firms in the auditor's network – whether or not those firms are involved in the audit of the group accounts

Remuneration and evaluation policies

The Standard states that the audit team should not include in its objectives the selling of non-audit services to the audit client, and team members should not be evaluated or remunerated based on their success in selling non-audit services.

When evaluating an individual's performance and considering promotions, a primary criterion will need to be the individual's contribution to the quality of the engagement.

Gifts and hospitality

The Standard states that the audit firm, its partners and any covered persons (and persons closely associated with them) should not accept gifts or favours, including hospitality, from an audit client unless an objective, reasonable and informed third party would consider the value as trivial or inconsequential. This is a change of emphasis and a simplification from previous rules.

The audit firm should establish policies on the nature and value of gifts and hospitality that may be accepted from and offered to audit clients, their directors, officers and employees.

Litigation

Unless insignificant, the audit firm should not continue or accept an audit engagement where litigation is in progress or is probable.

2.6.7   Ethical Standard Section 5 – Non-Audit Services Provided to Audited Entities

Section 5 states that a firm must consider whether acceptance of a non-audit service engagement may give rise to threats to objectivity. The test stated in the Standard is whether an objective, reasonable and informed third party would regard the objectives of the proposed engagement as being inconsistent with the objectives of the audit of the financial statements. If this is the case, they must either not accept the non-audit service engagement or provide the non-audit service having resigned their position as auditor. Procedures should be in place to ensure that the possible provision of non-audit services is notified to the audit engagement partner prior to accepting the work.

The audit engagement partner should ensure that those charged with governance of the audit client are informed of all significant facts relating to non-audit services that may have a bearing on the auditor's objectivity and independence. For listed clients, they should also be informed where their policy on obtaining non-audit services from their auditor is inconsistent with the requirements of the Ethical Standard, and if their own policy has been breached.

The Standard then details risks to objectivity that may arise from the provision of the following services:

- internal audit;
- information technology;
- valuation;
- actuarial valuation;
- litigation support;
- taxation;
- legal;
- recruitment and remuneration;
- corporate finance;
- transaction-related services; and
- accounting.

It also suggests safeguards which could be put in place, if any, to allow the auditor to continue his work in an independent and objective manner.

Threats to the independence and objectivity of the auditor arising from the provision of non-audit services has been one of the key themes of the EU audit reform project which culminated in changes to the Audit Directive and the Audit Regulation. As a result, the Revised Ethical Standard 2016 now includes an extensive list of prohibited non-audit services that may not be provided by auditors of public interest entities – although many of these were effectively prohibited under previous ethical standards.

In addition, the revised standard introduces a complex capping formula restricting, for such entities, the total value of non-audit services (where permitted) in comparison with audit fees, averaged over a three-year period. This cap applies on a group wide basis and includes consideration of non-audit services provided by other firms in the auditor's network – whether or not those firms are involved in the audit of the group accounts.

Although the most restrictive requirements derive from the EU Audit Regulation and therefore apply only to the audits of public interest entities, the FRC have decided to retain many of its existing restrictions in relation to listed companies that are not PIEs (for example companies traded on the AIM market). However, some of these restrictions have been relaxed so as not to apply to smaller listed non-PIE entities. Such 'SME listed' entities will, in general, be companies with equity shares with a market capitalisation of less than €200m or listed debt with a value of less than €200m, traded on a market that is not an EU regulated market.

The new rules are complex and auditors of public interest entities and other listed entities should give careful consideration to the requirements of the Ethical Standard which applies to audits of financial reporting periods commencing on or after 17 June 2016.

2.7   Section 6 – Provisions available for small entities

2.7.1   *Background*

The FRC is aware that a limited number of the requirements in the Sections 1 to 5 of the Ethical Standard are difficult for certain audit firms to comply with, particularly when auditing a small entity. Whilst the FRC is clear that the Sections 1 to 5 are appropriate in the interests of establishing the integrity, objectivity and independence of auditors, it accepts that certain dispensations are appropriate to facilitate the cost effective audit of the financial statements of small entities which are not public interest entities.

Section 6 of the *Ethical Standard – Provisions Available for Audits of Small Entities* sets out these dispensations. This section of the ES is not significantly different from the previous ES-PASE.

For purposes of the ES, a Small Entity client is defined in **Table 8**.

TABLE 8: Definition of a Small Entity client

For the purposes of the ES, in the UK a 'Small Entity' is:

- not a listed company, or an affiliate thereof;

- any company that qualifies as a small company under the *Companies Act* 2006 (or, where group accounts are prepared, any group that qualifies as a small group);

- any charity with an income of less than the turnover threshold applicable to small companies as defined in the *Companies Act* 2006 (currently £6.5m);

- any pension fund with less than 100 members including active, deferred and pensioner members (but excluding schemes in wind up that formerly had more than 100 members);

- any firm, bank and building society, regulated by the FSA, or its successors (including any mortgage firm or insurance broker), which is not required to appoint an auditor by the relevant regulator;

- any credit union which is a mutually owned financial cooperative established under the *Credit Unions Act* 1979 and the *Industrial and Provident Societies Act* 1965 (or equivalent legislation);

- any entity registered under the *Industrial and Provident Societies Act* 1965, incorporated under the *Friendly Societies Act* 1992 or registered under the *Friendly Societies Act* 1974 (or equivalent legislation), which meets the *Companies Act* 2006 definition of a small company, set out above;

- any registered social landlord with less than 250 units; and

- any other entity, such as a club, which would be a Small Entity if it were a company.

Where an entity falls into more than one of the above categories, it will only be a Small Entity if it meets the criteria for all relevant categories.

2.7.2 Non-audit services

When undertaking non-audit services for a Small Entity client, Section 6 states that the audit firm is not required to apply safeguards to address a self-review threat provided that the audited entity has 'informed management' and that the audit firm extends the cyclical inspection of completed audit engagements that is performed for quality control purposes to include a random selection of engagements where non-audit services have been provided.

When undertaking non-audit services for a Small Entity, the audit firm is not required to adhere to the same prohibitions in Section 5 relating to providing non-audit services that involve the audit firm undertaking part of the role of management, provided that:

- it discusses objectivity and independence issues related to the provision of non-audit services with those charged with governance, confirming that management accept responsibility for any decisions taken; and

- it discloses the fact that it has applied the *Ethical Standard – Provisions Available for Audits of Small Entities* (see **2.7.5**).

In addition, the auditor of a Small Entity will have exemption from the requirements of paragraphs 5.97 and 5.140(b) of Section 5 which prevent the audit firm from undertaking an engagement to provide tax services or restructuring services to an audit client provided that it discloses the fact that it has applied the *Ethical Standard – Provisions Available for Audits of Small Entities*.

See **2.7.5** for implications for the audit report and financial statements disclosures where advantage is taken of any of these exemptions.

2.7.3   Economic dependence

Where total audit and non-audit fees for a small entity client will regularly exceed 10% of the fee income of the firm (or the part of the firm by reference to which the audit partner's profit share is calculated) but will not regularly exceed 15%, Section 6 of the ES provides an exemption from the requirement in Section 4 that an external independent quality control review be performed. The exemption is available as long as the expectation that fees will amount to between 10 and 15% is disclosed to the ethics partner and to those charged with governance of the client.

2.7.4   Partners and other persons joining an audit client

The auditor of a Small Entity is not required to comply with paragraphs 2.53 and 2.57 of Section 2 regarding a cooling off period prior to joining an audit client or accepting a new engagement provided that the firm takes appropriate steps to ensure that there have been no significant threats to the audit team's integrity, objectivity and independence and discloses the fact that it has applied the *Ethical Standard – Provisions Available for Audits of Small Entities* in its audit report. Example steps for a Small Audit Firm to take are set out in **Table 9**.

Where this exemption is used, the fact must be disclosed in the auditor's report and further disclosures in line with the example in **Table 11** should be made in the financial statements or the auditor's report.

TABLE 9: Possible steps for a firm to take to guard against threats to independence relating to paragraph 2.53 and 2.57

- Assess significance of the self-interest, familiarity or intimidation threats having regard to:

  - the position the individual has taken at the audit client;

  - the nature and amount of any involvement the individual will have with the audit team or the audit process;

  - the length of time that has passed since the individual was a member of the audit team or firm; and

  - the former position of the individual within the audit team or firm.

- If that threat is anything other than clearly insignificant, apply alternative procedures such as:

  - considering the appropriateness or necessity of modifying the audit plan for the audit engagement;

> – assigning an audit team to the subsequent audit engagement that is of sufficient experience in relation to the individual who has joined the audit client;
>
> – involving an audit partner or senior staff member with appropriate expertise, who, where the firm already audits the entity, was not a member of the audit team, to review the work done or otherwise advise as necessary; or
>
> – perform an engagement quality control review of the audit engagement.

2.7.5 Audit report wording

Where advantage has been taken of one or more of the exemptions in the *Ethical Standard – Provisions Available for Audits of Small Entities* relating to provision of non-audit services or a former partner or other person approved as a statutory auditor joining the client, the auditor's report must disclose this fact and either the financial statements or the auditor's report must give details.

Examples are given in **Tables 10** and **11**.

TABLE 10: Example audit report wording where advantage taken of provisions available for small entities

Basis for opinion

We conducted our audit in accordance with International Standards on Auditing (UK) (ISAs (UK)) and applicable law. Our responsibilities under those standards are further described in the Auditor's responsibilities for the audit of the financial statements section of our report. We are independent of the company in accordance with the ethical requirements that are relevant to our audit of the financial statements in the UK, *including the FRC's Ethical Standard and the provisions available for small entities, in the circumstances set out in Note [...] to the financial statements*, and we have fulfilled our other ethical responsibilities in accordance with these requirements. We believe that the audit evidence we have obtained is sufficient and appropriate to provide a basis for our opinion.

Examples of the disclosures in the financial statements referred to in the example in **Table 10** are given in **Table 11**.

TABLE 11: Example disclosures in the financial statements where provisions available for small entities are used

Management threat/self-review threat in relation to non-audit services

Note [x]: In common with many other businesses of our size and nature, we use our auditor to prepare and submit returns to the tax authorities and assist with the preparation of the financial statements.

> *Advocacy threat – tax services*
>
> Note [x]: In common with many other businesses of our size and nature, we use our auditor to provide tax advice and to represent us, as necessary, at tax tribunals.
>
> *Partners joining an audit client*
>
> Note [x]: XYZ, a former partner of [audit firm] joined [audit client] as [a director] on [date].

2.8   Technical standards

The body must have rules and practices as to the technical standards to be applied in company audit work and the manner in which they are to be applied. In practice, the UK bodies have adopted the ISAs (UK) and registered auditors must be able to demonstrate compliance with these.

In practice, to comply with audit regulations, firms are required to have procedures covering, in addition to the areas mentioned above:

- acceptance of appointment and reappointments; and

- quality control and ISQC (UK) 1 (Revised June 2016) *Quality control for firms that perform audits and reviews of financial statements, and other assurance and related services engagements.*

2.8.1   *Acceptance of appointment and reappointment*

A firm will normally be expected to have procedures which ensure that before accepting an appointment, and also in considering whether to accept reappointment as auditor of a company, issues of the firm's independence and those of its competence to act are addressed. In addressing competence to act, the firm must assess whether or not the partners and employees have the necessary skills and training for the particular type of appointment.

2.8.2   *Quality control*

There must be an adequate system of quality control (see **Section 3**). This will involve not only ensuring adequate review procedures but also some measure of quality assurance procedures, for example, 'hot' review of work by independent partners before the opinion is signed off and also 'cold' review procedures to ensure that work has been properly carried out in accordance with the firm's procedures. Quality control will also ensure that the various procedures necessary to ensure compliance with the regulations of the RSB have been carried out.

2.9   Maintaining competence

There must be adequate arrangements to ensure that persons eligible for appointment as a company auditor continue to maintain an appropriate level of competence in the conduct of company audits. This is done by ensuring that there are satisfactory arrangements for training and continuing professional education (CPE) for members of bodies – the levels of desired CPE are normally set out in the rules of the various RSBs.

Although an audit firm's ability to audit rests with its partners and staff, these may change over time. As a result, to demonstrate its competence a firm must use audit manuals, audit programmes, checklists and standard procedures.

The amount of formal documentation and procedures will depend on the size of the firm and its clients. Even the smallest firm is likely to need some documentation such as audit programmes, but as it grows in size, or as its clients become more complex in their nature, procedures may need to be developed further to assist staff to carry out audit work in accordance with audit regulations.

2.10   Meeting of claims

There must be adequate rules to ensure that any registered auditor has adequate professional indemnity insurance (PII) cover to secure them against claims arising out of company audit work. In order to become a registered auditor, a firm must demonstrate that there is sufficient PII cover in place.

2.11   Other areas

In addition to the above, each RSB must have rules relating to eligibility for membership, disciplinary arrangements, investigation of complaints and keeping a published register of members. It must also take into account the costs of any rules it makes in terms of the benefit to be obtained and be involved in the promotion and maintenance of auditing standards.

In particular, audit regulations:

- explicitly state that a firm or member of an Institute must be registered by a RSB before accepting an audit appointment;

- require firms to formally apply before appointing a new Responsible Individual (RI), rather than just informing the registering Institute of the new RI; and

- clarify that the Regulations apply to all charities, not just those registered under the Charities Acts in England and Wales.

2.12   Oversight of the profession

Responsibility for oversight of the auditing profession was transferred from the Professional Oversight Board for Accountancy (POBA) to the FRC in 2012.

The FRC's Conduct Committee is now responsible for overseeing the Conduct Division in its work promoting high quality corporate reporting. Its responsibilities include overseeing:

- monitoring of recognised supervisory and recognised qualifying bodies;

- audit quality reviews;

- corporate reporting reviews;

- professional discipline; and

- oversight of the regulation of accountants and actuaries.

The FRC's Enforcement Division conducts investigations and will bring prosecutions, if appropriate, against auditors, accountants, accountancy firms, and actuaries where there appears to be misconduct or a breach of the relevant professional standards.

2.13   Audit quality monitoring

As the Competent Authority for audit regulation in the UK, the FRC is responsible for monitoring the quality of work done by statutory auditors. The FRC's Audit Quality Review (AQR) team monitors the quality of the audit work of statutory auditors and audit firms in the UK that audit Public Interest Entities (PIEs) and certain other entities within the scope retained by the FRC (these are currently large AIM companies/Lloyd's Syndicates/ and non-EEA entities with transferable securities (equity/debt) admitted to trading on a regulated market in the EEA and audited by a UK Registered Auditor.

Monitoring of all other statutory audits is delegated by the FRC to Recognised Supervisory Bodies including the ICAEW.

All UK audit firms that undertake PIE and large AIM/Lloyd's Syndicate/ Listed Non-EEA audits are subject to AQR inspections in respect of this audit work. The frequency of AQR inspections varies with larger firms inspected annually while other firms are generally inspected once every three years.

AQR activity comprises inspections of a sample of audits and related procedures supporting audit quality (firm-wide procedures) at individual audit firms. In addition, it undertakes thematic inspections which focus on particular aspects of audit across a sample of audits and firms.

The FRC publishes annually details of the scope of the AQR team's work and also the results of its reviews of individual firms as well as finding for its thematic inspections.

Each RSB must have in place arrangements for monitoring the quality of audits carried out by its members, other than those that fall within the remit of the AQR team's review. The ICAEW does this through its Quality Assurance Directorate (QAD), which is responsible for monitoring all other statutory audits conducted by ICAEW registered firms.

Adverse findings from a monitoring review may render the firm and the individuals responsible subject to disciplinary action.

2.14   Audit firm monitoring

As a Competent Authority, the FRC now has responsibility for the regular monitoring and mitigation of risks in the audit market. These include the risks of systematic deficiencies within an audit firm network, which could lead to the demise of any audit firm, disruption in the provision of statutory audit services whether in a specific sector or across sectors, and the impact on the overall stability of the financial sector. The largest audit firms are systemically important institutions; issues in one part of the firm's global network can affect the UK firm's reputation.

The FRC plans to develop and implement a new approach to the monitoring of the largest audit firms – the Big Six firms – which are core to the integrity and transparency of the UK's capital markets. This monitoring approach will inform the FRC's supervision of the firms. The FRC will set out expectations of each firm and seek evidence in relation to:

- leadership and governance;

- values and behaviours;

- business models and financial soundness;

- risk management and control; and

- evidence on audit quality, including from our programme of audit quality reviews conducted by the AQR team.

2.15 Reports by registered auditors

The Audit Regulations apply to audits of companies, LLPs, building societies, credit unions, registered charities, friendly and industrial and provident societies, and persons authorised under the *Financial Services and Markets Act* 2000. They also apply to audits of pension schemes, certain partnerships, OEICs and unit trusts.

Where the auditor issues a report in respect of an audit of financial statements, or any other function to which the regulations apply, the report must be signed in the name of the firm, together with the phrase 'Statutory auditor(s)'.

2.16 Other international developments

In April 2018, the IESBA released a completely rewritten Code of Ethics for Professional Accountants that is intended to be easier to navigate, use and enforce. Beyond the new structure, the Code brings together key ethics advances over the past four years, and is clearer about how accountants should deal with ethics and independence issues.

While the fundamental principles of ethics have not changed, major revisions have been made to the unifying conceptual framework – the approach used by all professional accountants to identify, evaluate and address threats to compliance with the fundamental principles and, where applicable, independence. The new Code includes:

- revised 'safeguards' provisions better aligned to threats to compliance with the fundamental principles;

- stronger independence provisions regarding long association of personnel with audit clients;

- new and revised sections dedicated to professional accountants in business (PAIBs) relating to:

    — preparing and presenting information; and

    — pressure to breach the fundamental principles;

- clear guidance for accountants in public practice that relevant PAIB provisions are applicable to them;

- new guidance to emphasise the importance of understanding facts and circumstances when exercising professional judgment; and

- new guidance to explain how compliance with the fundamental principles supports the exercise of professional scepticism in an audit or other assurance engagements.

Renamed the *International Code of Ethics for Professional Accountants (including International Independence Standards)*, the new Code becomes effective in June 2019.

As noted in **2.5.1**, these changes are likely to result in changes to the FRC's Ethical Standard and the ICAEW's Code of Ethics affecting UK auditors and accountants in due course.

3 Quality control for audit work

3.1 Introduction

This section examines the area of quality control relating both to audit firms and to individual audits.

Under audit regulation, each Recognised Supervisory Body (RSB) must ensure that its members have an adequate system of quality control (see **Section 2**).

Guidance on quality control is given by International Standard on Quality Control (ISQC) (UK) 1 (Revised June 2016) *Quality control for firms that perform audits and reviews of historical financial information, and other assurance and related services engagements* and ISA (UK) 220 (Revised June 2016) *Quality control for an audit of financial statements* both of which are effective for periods commencing on or after 17 June 2016. Both standards were updated in July 2017 to reflect conforming amendments following a revision to ISA (UK) 250 Section A *Consideration of laws and regulations in an audit of financial statements*.

ISQC (UK) 1 (Revised June 2016) sets out requirements and provides guidance for professional accountants on systems of quality control for audits and review work on historical financial information and ISA (UK) 220 (Revised June 2016) provides guidance on quality control procedures specifically applicable to audits.

The 2016 revisions incorporate amendments relating to the EU Audit Directive and Audit Regulation which are required to be implemented by all EU countries. The revisions mainly affect audits of public interest entities, in particular, surrounding independence requirements and engagement quality control reviews, and are covered in this section.

Audit quality continues to be an important theme for the FRC and for standard setters and regulators internationally as well as for companies themselves.

In November 2006, a discussion paper was issued by the Financial Reporting Council (FRC) entitled *Promoting Audit Quality*. This led to the publication in February 2008 of *The Audit Quality Framework* which was designed to support effective communication between auditors, audit committees, preparers, investors and other stakeholders on audit quality. Details of these papers are given in **3.4**.

In February 2014, the IAASB issued a paper entitled *A Framework for Audit Quality: Key Elements that create an Environment for Audit Quality*. The IAASB expects that the Framework will generate discussion, and positive actions to achieve a continuous improvement to audit quality (see **3.5**).

In March 2015, the FRC issued an Audit Quality Practice Aid for audit committees to assist them in evaluating audit quality in their assessment of the effectiveness of the external audit process. The FRC was responding to requests for guidance in this area, in light of the UK Corporate Governance Code provision that the audit committee report should include an explanation as to how it has assessed the effectiveness of the external audit process.

In addition, it is a key theme of the IAASB's consultation issued in December 2015. The Invitation to Comment, *Enhancing Audit Quality in the Public Interest: A Focus on Professional Scepticism, Quality Control and Group Audits* (the ITC) highlights the board's discussions on the topics of professional scepticism, quality control and group audits – and flags potential standard-setting activities the IAASB may undertake to enhance audit quality (see **3.5**).

3.2 ISQC (UK) 1 (Revised June 2016)

3.2.1 Basic requirement

ISQC (UK) 1 (Revised June 2016) requires firms to establish and maintain a system of quality control which is designed to provide reasonable assurance that the firm and its personnel comply with professional standards and regulatory and legal requirements, including relevant ethical requirements, and that reports issued by the firm or engagement partners are appropriate in the circumstances. The requirements set out in the ISQC (UK) are designed such that following these requirements should provide a sufficient basis to enable the firm to achieve this objective. However, because circumstances vary widely, the firm should also consider whether there are particular matters or circumstances that require the firm to establish policies and procedures in addition to those specifically required by the ISQC (UK) in order to meet that objective.

Firms need to take into consideration the scale and complexity of the firm's activities and be able to demonstrate to the competent authority that the policies and procedures designed to achieve compliance with the requirements of ISQC (UK) 1 (Revised June 2016) are appropriate given the scale and complexity of activities of the firm.

Personnel within the firm who are responsible for establishing and maintaining the firm's system of quality control are required to have an understanding of the entire text of ISQC (UK) 1 (Revised June 2016) in order to understand the objectives and to apply the requirements properly. The firm needs to comply with each requirement, unless the requirement is not relevant given the circumstances of the firm. For example, for a sole practitioner with no staff, requirements such as those for policies and procedures for the assignment of appropriate personnel to the engagement team or for the annual communication of the results of monitoring to engagement partners within the firm are not relevant.

ISQC (UK) 1 (Revised June 2016) has been written to apply to statutory audits of financial statements and other public interest assurance engagements (which means any other assurance engagement carried out in accordance with performance standards issued by the FRC). Not all requirements apply equally to all types of engagement. To avoid confusion, this section considers the requirements that apply to statutory audits.

3.2.2 Elements of a system of quality control

ISQC (UK) 1 (Revised June 2016) sets out six areas which should be addressed by a firm's quality control policies and procedures, documented and communicated to the firm's personnel:

- leadership responsibilities for quality within the firm (**3.2.3**);

- ethical requirements (**3.2.4**);

- acceptance and continuance of client relationships and specific engagements (**3.2.5**);

- human resources (**3.2.6**);

- engagement performance (**3.2.7**); and

- monitoring (**3.2.9**).

These are discussed in greater detail in subsequent paragraphs.

The policies and procedures are not restricted to professional staff, but the firm is required to ensure that its owners or shareholders, as well as the members of the administrative, management and supervisory bodies of the firm, do not intervene in the carrying out of an audit in any way which jeopardises the independence and objectivity of the engagement team. The firm is required to have:

- sound administrative and accounting procedures;

- internal quality control mechanisms that are designed to secure compliance with decisions and procedures at all levels of the firm;

- effective procedures for risk assessment; and

- effective control and safeguard arrangements for the firm's information processing systems.

3.2.3 Leadership

From the very top of the organisation, the firm should establish policies which promote a culture of quality. ISQC (UK) 1 (Revised June 2016) states that this should be demonstrated practically, with actions and messages from all levels of the firm's management emphasising their commitment to quality. This should also be demonstrated in the firm's overall business strategy, which should promote the need for quality.

The firm's managing board of partners, or equivalent, will maintain ultimate responsibility for the firm's system of quality control, but operational responsibility may be delegated to someone with sufficient and appropriate experience, ability and authority.

In order to promote an appropriate culture, firms should recognise that the overall business strategy is subject to an overriding requirement to achieve quality in its work and take care to ensure that:

- commercial considerations never override the quality of performance;

- audit partners and staff are always sufficiently independent and approach audits with a mindset of professional scepticism;

- performance evaluation, compensation and promotion demonstrate the firm's commitment to quality; and

- sufficient appropriate resources are devoted to the development, documentation and support of the firm's quality control policies and procedures.

3.2.4 Ethical requirements

The firm should have procedures in place to provide it with assurance that its personnel comply with relevant ethical requirements. The Audit Directive also requires the firm to establish appropriate and effective organisational and administrative arrangements for dealing with and recording incidents which have, or may have, serious consequences for the integrity of the firm's activities.

The application material in ISQC (UK) 1 (Revised June 2016) explains that 'relevant ethical requirements' ordinarily comprises Parts A and B of the International Ethics Standards Board for Accountants' *Code of Ethics for Professional Accountants* (the IESBA Code) and national requirements that are more restrictive. It also makes clear that in the UK, the firm and its personnel are subject to the Revised Ethical Standard 2016 (the

Ethical Standard) and ethical requirements imposed by the auditor's, or assurance practitioner's, own professional body (see **Sections 1** and **2**).

All audit partners and staff should have appropriate training on ethical matters including on the contents of the Ethical Standard (see **Section 2**), and specific guidance available within the firm. They should also be made aware of who or what to consult if they are uncertain on an ethical matter.

In relation to independence, the firm should ensure that it:

- is able to communicate its independence requirements to personnel and any others bound by them; and

- has established appropriate and effective organisational and administrative arrangements to prevent, identify, eliminate or manage and disclose any threats to the firm's independence.

To adhere to these requirements, sufficient information must be held about the engagements undertaken by the firm, including the scope of the services provided to each client. Changes to the information should be notified to the person responsible for maintaining it on a timely basis, personnel must notify the firm of any circumstances or relationships which create a threat to independence, and the firm or personnel must take appropriate action as required.

Firms should also ensure that they have policies and procedures for informing the relevant individual when breaches of independence take place. The engagement partner and others who need to take action should be informed of the breach promptly.

In addition, the firm should obtain annual declarations of independence from all personnel who are required to be independent by the Ethical Standard. This requirement can be most easily met by using a standard form.

Firms should set policies and procedures to be applied to mitigate the familiarity threat that may arise where the same senior personnel are used on an audit for a long period of time. These may include rotation of partners or other audit personnel. In the case of listed companies, rotation periods should be set in accordance with the requirements of the Ethical Standard.

3.2.5 Client acceptance and continuance

The firm's policies and procedures should ensure that, prior to accepting or continuing with client relationships, it:

- considers the integrity of each client;

- is competent and has the resources to provide the service; and

- can comply with ethical requirements.

These policies require the firm to gather or review information at the commencement of the relationship with the client, when accepting recurring work in second or subsequent years or when accepting a new engagement from an existing client. Example matters to be considered are set out in **Table 1**.

Where issues are discovered that cause concern, but the engagement continues, the issues, and their resolution should be fully documented.

If the firm later discovers something that would have led it to declining the engagement, it should take legal advice and consider resigning.

The firm also needs to have policies and procedures addressing the circumstances where the firm obtains information that would have caused it to decline the engagement had that information been available earlier. This will include considering:

(a) the professional and legal responsibilities that apply to the circumstances; and

(b) the possibility of withdrawing from the engagement or from both the engagement and the client relationship.

Where the auditor ceases to hold office as auditor, he provides the successor auditor with access to all relevant information concerning the entity, including information concerning the most recent audit (see **Section 38**).

Before accepting or continuing an audit engagement, the firm assesses:

(a) whether the firm complies with relevant independence and objectivity requirements in the Ethical Standard;

(b) whether there are threats to the firm's independence, and the safeguards applied to mitigate those threats;

(c) whether the firm has the competent personnel, time and resources needed in order to carry out the audit in an appropriate manner; and

(d) whether the key audit partner is eligible for appointment as a statutory auditor.

Public interest entities

In addition to points (a)–(d) in the previous paragraph, for a public interest entity, the firm assesses:

(a) whether the firm complies with the audit fees and the prohibition of the provision of non-audit services requirements in the Ethical Standard;

(b)   whether the conditions for the duration of the audit engagement in accordance with the Audit Regulation are complied with; and

(c)   without prejudice to UK anti-money laundering requirements, the integrity of the members of the supervisory, administrative and management bodies of the public interest entity.

TABLE 1: Examples of ' matters to consider when accepting or reaccepting a client

Client integrity

Consider:

- the identity and business reputation of the client's principal owners, key management, related parties and those charged with governance;

- the nature of the client's operations, including its business practices;

- information concerning the attitude of the client's principal owners, key management and those charged with governance towards such matters as aggressive interpretation of accounting standards and the internal control environment;

- whether the client is aggressively concerned with keeping the firm's fees as low as possible;

- indication of an inappropriate limitation in the scope of work;

- indications that the client might be involved in money laundering or other criminal activities;

- the identity and business reputation of related parties; and

- the reasons for the proposed appointment of the firm and non-reappointment of the previous firm (if relevant).

Firm resources and capabilities

Consider:

- whether firm personnel have knowledge of relevant industries or subject matters;

- if firm personnel have experience with relevant regulatory or reporting requirements or the ability to gain the necessary skills and knowledge effectively;

- whether the firm has sufficient personnel with the necessary capabilities and competence;

- the availability of experts, if needed;

- whether individuals meeting the criteria and eligibility requirements to perform engagement quality control reviews are available, where applicable; and

- whether the firm can complete the engagement within the reporting deadline.

3.2.6 Human resources

Firms should have policies and procedures to ensure that they have sufficient capable, competent and committed staff. These should, for example, cover:

- recruitment;
- performance evaluation;
- capabilities;
- competence;
- career development;
- promotion;
- compensation; and
- the number of staff needed.

Firms should allocate appropriately experienced and qualified staff to each engagement, together with an engagement partner who has the competence, capabilities and authority to perform the role and whose responsibilities are clearly defined and understood. The identity and role of the engagement partner should be communicated to key members of the client's management team and those charged with governance.

For audits, the firm must designate at least one key audit partner (including the engagement partner), who must be selected using the criteria of securing audit quality, independence and competence. The firm must assign to that key audit partner sufficient resources and personnel that have the necessary competence and capabilities to carry out the firm's duties appropriately.

Firms should also:

(a) establish appropriate policies and procedures to ensure that the firm's personnel and any other people under the firm's control who are directly involved in the audit activities, have appropriate knowledge and experience for the duties assigned; and

(b) have in place adequate remuneration policies, including profit sharing policies, providing sufficient performance incentives to secure audit quality. In particular, the revenue from providing non-audit services to the audited entity must not form part of the performance evaluation and remuneration of any person involved in, or able to influence, the audit.

The firm is also required to establish appropriate policies and procedures to ensure that outsourcing of important audit functions is not undertaken in such a way as to impair the quality of the firm's internal quality control and the ability of the competent authorities to supervise the firm's compliance with professional standards and applicable legal and regulatory requirements.

3.2.7 Engagement performance

ISQC (UK) 1 (Revised June 2016) requires firms to implement policies and procedures to provide it with assurance that its engagements are performed in accordance with professional and legal standards. The aim is to ensure consistently high quality engagements, and this can be accomplished through the use of manuals, software tools and standardised documentation as applicable.

The engagement team should be sufficiently briefed prior to commencing their work, adequately supervised throughout the engagement and their work reviewed by a more experienced team member.

Policies and procedures regarding the review of work are determined on the basis that work of less experienced team members is reviewed by more experienced engagement team members.

Firms also need to:

- establish an internal quality control system to ensure the quality of the audit which at least covers the policies and procedures for carrying out audits, coaching, supervising and reviewing employees' activities and organising the structure of the audit file;

- ensure that responsibility for the internal quality control system lies with a person who is eligible for appointment as a statutory auditor;

- establish appropriate policies and procedures for carrying out audits, coaching, supervising and reviewing the activities of the firm's personnel and organising the structure of the audit file; and

- use appropriate systems, resources and procedures to ensure continuity and regularity in the carrying out of the firm's audit activities.

Consultation

Firms need to establish policies and procedures for consultation and ensure that sufficient resources are available so that:

- appropriate consultation takes place on difficult or contentious issues;

- sufficient resources are available to enable the consultation to occur;

- the details of the consultation are documented and agreed with the consultee; and

- conclusions are implemented.

Small firms may need to make arrangements with others outside their firm in order to implement such policies. Arrangements for consultations with fellow professionals should be made as soon as it becomes clear that an issue exists and the person being consulted should be provided with full information on which to base his opinion. This includes the situation where the engagement team needs to consult with an individual, or organisation, with expertise in a specialised area of accounting or auditing, for example, a member of a financial reporting technical team, whether internal or external.

Engagement quality control review

For certain engagements, the firm should implement engagement quality control reviews to ensure that significant judgments made by the engagement team undergo an objective evaluation. The policies for such reviews should:

- require reviews for audits of listed companies; and
- set out criteria against which all other work should be assessed to see if it requires a review.

When setting these criteria, firms would consider the nature of the engagement, including the extent to which it involves a matter of public interest, any unusual circumstances or risks surrounding the work and whether a review is required by law.

The review should be completed before any report is issued.

Policies should also be developed to set out:

- the nature, extent and timing of the engagement quality control review;
- eligibility criteria for reviewers; and
- documentation requirements.

Nature, timing and extent of review

An engagement quality control review will usually involve discussions with the engagement partner, a review of the financial statements, consideration of the audit report and review of selected working papers. The engagement quality control review must be completed before the auditor's report is signed, however, documentation of that review may occur after the signing of the auditor's report providing that any matters raised by the reviewer were resolved before the audit report was signed.

In all engagement quality control reviews carried out in accordance with the firm's policy, the reviewer should consider the firm's compliance with the Ethical Standard in relation to the engagement, form an independent opinion as to the adequacy of any safeguards applied and consider the adequacy of the documentation of the engagement partner's consideration of the objectivity and independence of the firm and its personnel.

ISA (UK) 220 (Revised June 2016) requires the engagement quality control reviewer to perform an objective evaluation of the significant judgments made by the engagement team, and the conclusions reached. This includes:

- a discussion of significant matters with the engagement partner;
- a review of the financial statements and the proposed audit report;
- a review of selected audit documentation relating to the significant judgments made; and
- an evaluation of the conclusions reached in formulating the auditor's report and consideration of whether the proposed auditor's report is appropriate.

Engagement quality control reviews of audits of listed clients include considering:

- the engagement team's evaluation of the firm's independence in relation to the specific engagement;
- significant risks identified during the engagement and the responses to those risks;
- judgments made, particularly with respect to materiality and significant risks;
- whether appropriate consultation has taken place on matters involving differences of opinion or other difficult or contentious matters, and the conclusions arising from those consultations;
- the significance of corrected and uncorrected misstatements identified during the engagement and the actions taken in relation to them;
- the matters to be communicated to those charged with governance and other parties such as regulatory bodies;
- whether working papers selected for review reflect the work performed in relation to the significant judgments and support the conclusions reached; and
- the appropriateness of the report to be issued.

Where the review is for an engagement other than the audit of a listed company, some or all of these considerations will be relevant.

Public interest entities

For audits of public interest entities, the firm requires that:

Quality control for audit work

(a) before the audit report and the additional report to the audit committee are issued, an engagement quality control review is done to assess whether the key audit partner could reasonably have come to the opinion and conclusions expressed in the draft of these reports; and

(b) the review is to be performed by an engagement quality control reviewer who is eligible for appointment as a statutory auditor and not involved in the performance of the audit to which the EQCR relates.

Where the audit is carried out by a firm and all the statutory auditors of that firm were involved in the carrying-out of the audit, the firm needs to arrange for another firm to perform an engagement quality control review. Documents or information disclosed to the engagement quality control reviewer for this purpose shall be subject to professional secrecy.

Eligibility of reviewers

The firm's policies should set out the technical qualifications, experience and authority required of quality control reviewers together with the extent to which the quality control reviewer can be consulted by the engagement partner during the audit without compromising the reviewer's objectivity. Procedures should be in place to allow replacement of the quality control reviewer where his ability to perform an objective review is impaired.

What constitutes an appropriate degree of qualifications, experience and authority will depend on the circumstances of the engagement but for the audit of the financial statements of listed companies, for example, the application material to the standard suggests that the reviewer is likely to be someone who is sufficiently experienced to act as an engagement partner on listed company audits.

Care should be taken to ensure that the objectivity of the engagement quality control reviewer is not impaired and:

- where practicable, he is not appointed by the engagement partner;

- he takes no part in the audit (other than in connection with his review) and does not make decisions for the team;

- he is not used routinely for consultation by the engagement partner or team on significant matters of judgment; and

- he is not subject to other considerations that would threaten his objectivity.

For sole practitioners or small firms, suitably qualified external persons may be contracted to perform quality control reviews.

Review documentation

There should be documentation on file that the review has been performed in accordance with the firm's policies, that it was completed before the report was issued and that the reviewer is not aware of any unresolved matters that suggest that the conclusions of the engagement team were not appropriate.

Differences of opinion

There should be firm policies about resolution and documentation of differences of opinion within the engagement team, with those consulted and when applicable between the engagement partner and the engagement quality control reviewer. The firm's report should never be issued until any such differences have been resolved and the conclusions reached should be fully documented and implemented.

For public interest entities, the firm establishes procedures for determining the manner in which any disagreement between the key audit partner and the engagement quality control reviewer are to be resolved.

3.2.8 Engagement documentation

There should be policies and procedures for engagement teams to complete the assembly of final engagement files on a timely basis after the engagement reports have been finalised. For audits, this is 'ordinarily not more than 60 days after the date of the auditor's report'.

Policies and procedures should also be established that are designed to maintain the confidentiality, safe custody, integrity, accessibility and retrievability of engagement documentation.

ISQC (UK) 1 (Revised June 2016) states that firms may implement controls to avoid alteration or loss of engagement documentation, whether on paper, electronic or using other media, including those that:

- ensure that details of who created, changed or reviewed the working papers, and when that occurred, can be clearly seen;

- protect the integrity of the information, particularly if it is transmitted or shared with other members of the engagement team via the internet;

- prevent unauthorised changes to documentation; and

- allow access to the working papers to those that are authorised to have it.

Confidentiality, safe custody, integrity, accessibility and retrievability of engagement documentation may be improved by implementing further controls such as:

- the use of passwords to restrict access to electronic documentation to authorised users;

- appropriate back-up routines throughout the engagement;

- procedures for distributing documentation to audit team members, retrieving it and collating it at the end of the engagement; and

- procedures for restricting access to, and ensuring proper distribution and storage of, hardcopy engagement documentation.

Where hardcopy documentation is scanned for storage and retention purposes, the following controls may be relevant:

- ensuring scanned copies reflect the entire content of the original paper documentation, including manual signature, cross references and annotation;

- integrating scanned copies into the engagement file, including indexing them and signing them off as necessary; and

- enabling the scanned copies to be retrieved and printed as necessary.

ISQC (UK) 1 (Revised June 2016) also states that policies and procedures should be implemented to ensure that firms retain engagement documentation for the period required by law or regulation. Requirements for audit working papers are set out in **12.6**.

3.2.9 Monitoring

Monitoring the firm's quality control policies and procedures

Each firm should have procedures to monitor their quality control policies and to ensure that they are complied with in practice. Evaluation of the system of quality control will include:

- analysis of:

  - changes in professional standards and regulatory and legal requirements;

  - written confirmation by staff of compliance with policies and procedures on independence;

  - continuing professional development and training; and

  - decisions related to acceptance and continuance of engagements;

- suggestions for corrective actions and improvements to the system;

- communication of weaknesses in the system to those in authority; and

- follow-up procedures to ensure that modifications are made as suggested.

Monitoring should also include a periodic review of completed engagements on a cyclical basis, typically with at least one engagement for each engagement partner in an inspection cycle (which should be no longer than three years). The monitoring inspector will be separate from the engagement partner or the quality control reviewer and may select engagements without prior notification. For small firms or sole practitioners, an external person may be engaged, or arrangements established with another small firm to provide personnel on a reciprocal basis.

ISQC (UK) 1 (Revised June 2016) also requires firms to:

(a) monitor and evaluate the adequacy and effectiveness of the firm's systems, internal quality control mechanisms and arrangements established in accordance with ISQC (UK) 1 (Revised June 2016) and take appropriate measures to address any deficiencies;

(b) carry out an annual evaluation of the internal quality control system, referred to in **3.2.7**; and

(c) keep records of the findings of the evaluation required by paragraph (a) and any proposed measure to modify the internal quality control system.

The reviewer should consider whether any deficiencies found are:

- systemic, repetitive or significant which require prompt corrective action; or

- not indicative of failings in the firm's quality control system,

and an appropriate report should be given at the end of the work.

Where deficiencies are found, they should be communicated to the engagement partner and recommendations made for remedial action. Recommendations may include one or more of the following:

- taking action in relation to an individual engagement or member of personnel;

- informing those in charge of training and professional development;

- changing quality control policies and procedures; and

- disciplinary action against offenders.

Where an incorrect report is found to have been issued, firms should seek legal advice.

At least annually, a summary of the findings of the quality control review process should be provided to the engagement partners as well as the managing board of partners, or equivalent. This should include details of the monitoring procedures undertaken, conclusions drawn and information about any systemic failures and should be sufficient to enable the firm and the individuals to take prompt and appropriate action.

Where the firm is part of a network of firms, and some of the monitoring procedures to comply with ISQC (UK) 1 (Revised June 2016) are implemented on a network basis, then the network should communicate the overall scope, extent and results of the monitoring process to appropriate individuals within the network firms at least annually. It should also ensure it communicates promptly any identified deficiencies in the system of quality control so that the necessary action can be taken by the relevant individuals in the network firms.

External monitoring of group audits

Where the firm is subject to a quality assurance review or an investigation concerning a group audit, the firm is responsible for complying with, and ensuring the group engagement team also comply with, any request by the authority:

(a) for relevant audit documentation retained by the group engagement team;

(b) to deliver any additional documentation of the work performed by any component auditor from a non-EEA member state, including that component auditor's working papers relevant to the group audit, where the authority is unable to obtain audit documentation of the work carried out by that component auditor.

As such the firm needs to establish policies and procedures, which require that, in order to comply with any request under point (b) above, the group engagement team either:

(a) retain copies of the documentation of the work carried out by the relevant component auditor for the purpose of the group audit (including the component auditor's working papers relevant to the group audit);

(b) obtain the agreement of the relevant component auditor that the group engagement team shall have unrestricted access to such documentation on request;

(c) retain documentation to show that the group engagement team has undertaken the appropriate procedures in order to gain access to the audit documentation, together with evidence supporting the existence of any impediments to such access; or

(d) take any other appropriate action.

3.2.10 Complaints

ISQC (UK) 1 (Revised June 2016) also requires firms to have procedures for handling complaints or allegations that work performed does not comply with professional standards, or with the firm's own system of quality control, whether these arise from inside or outside the firm.

The firm is also required to keep records of any complaints made in writing about the performance of the audits carried out, as well as to establish policies and procedures requiring the documentation of complaints and allegations and the responses to them.

If, during the investigations into complaints and allegations, deficiencies in the design or operation of the firm's quality control policies and procedures or any non-compliance with them are identified, then the firm should take appropriate actions.

3.2.11 Documentation of quality control system

Firms are required to have sufficient documentation to provide evidence that their quality control system is operating effectively. ISQC (UK) 1 (Revised June 2016) does not set a standard form for this documentation, but points out that the content of documentation will vary depending on the size of the firm, the number of offices, and the nature and complexity of the firm's practice and organisation.

A frequently used method is to create an ISQC (UK) 1 (Revised June 2016) file documenting both the firm's policies and procedures. The level and length of the documentation required will depend on the size of the firm and need not be onerous. It is likely that documentation of a number of the areas is already covered by the firm's standard audit documentation, and cross references to other documentation may suffice in a number of areas. Alternatively, procedures may already be in place, but not formally documented. The documentation should be easily accessible by staff and partners involved in audit work and they should be required to read and understand it and be made aware of any updates or changes as they are made.

Firms also need to keep any engagement documentation that is of importance for monitoring compliance with this ISQC (UK) and other applicable legal requirements. This includes documenting whether:

(a) the firm complies with the independence and objectivity requirements in the Ethical Standard;

(b) there are threats to the firm's independence, and the safeguards applied to mitigate those threats;

(c) the firm has the competent personnel, time and resources needed in order to carry out the audit in an appropriate manner; and

(d) the key audit partner is eligible to be appointed as a statutory auditor.

Firms are required to keep the documents and information required by ISQC (UK) 1 (Revised June 2016) and the documentation requirements of other applicable ISAs (UK) for at least six years from the date of the auditor's report. This period may be longer if necessary to satisfy the requirements of any applicable laws or regulation relating to data protection and to meet the requirements for any applicable administrative and judicial proceedings.

The firm also needs to:

(a) keep records of any breaches (other than breaches which the firm reasonably considers to be minor breaches) of professional standards and applicable legal and regulatory requirements;

(b) keep records of any consequences of any breach recorded in (a), the measures taken to address such a breach and to modify the firm's internal quality control system; and

(c) prepare an annual report containing an overview of any measures taken under (b) and communicate that report internally.

ISQC (UK) 1 (Revised June 2016) also requires the firm to maintain a client account record detailing the following for each audit client:

(a) client's name, address and place of business;

(b) name of the key audit partner; and

(c) fees charged for the audit and fees charged for other services in any financial year.

3.3 ISA (UK) 220 (Revised June 2016) Quality Control for an Audit of Financial Statements

3.3.1 General requirement

ISA (UK) 220 (Revised June 2016) requires the auditor to implement quality control procedures for the individual audit engagement. ISQC (UK) 1 (Revised June 2016) (see **3.2**) sets out the detailed requirements for quality control systems for audits and reviews of historical financial information and ISA (UK) 220 (Revised June 2016) sets out the details of how those systems should be applied to audit engagements. The ISA deals largely with engagement partner responsibilities as set out in the following paragraphs.

3.3.2 Leadership responsibilities for quality

The engagement partner is responsible for the overall quality on each of his audit engagements. His actions and appropriate messages to the other members of the engagement team should emphasise:

- the importance to audit quality of:
  - performing work that complies with professional standards and applicable legal and regulatory requirements;
  - complying with the firm's quality control policies and procedures;
  - issuing audit reports that are appropriate to the circumstances; and
  - the team's ability to raise concerns without fear of reprisal; and
- the fact that quality is essential in performing audits.

3.3.3 Ethical requirements

Throughout the audit, the engagement partner is required to remain alert for any evidence of non-compliance by his team with relevant ethical requirements. If any such matters come to his attention, it is his responsibility, in consultation with others to determine the appropriate action.

He also forms a conclusion on compliance with independence requirements applicable to the audit engagement. In doing this, the ISA (UK) requires the engagement partner to obtain relevant information from the firm and, where applicable, network firms, to identify and evaluate any threats to independence and then to take appropriate action to eliminate such threats or reduce them to an acceptable level by applying safeguards. It is the engagement partner's responsibility to promptly report to his firm any inability to resolve a matter in order for appropriate action to be taken.

3.3.4 Acceptance and continuance

The engagement partner needs to be satisfied that appropriate procedures regarding the acceptance and continuance of client relationships and audit engagements have been followed and ensures conclusions reached are appropriate. If he obtains information that would have caused the firm to decline the engagement, had the information been available sooner, then he communicates that to the firm promptly so that the firm and engagement partner can take the necessary action.

3.3.5 Assignment of the team

The engagement partner is responsible for ensuring that the team, and any auditor's experts who are not part of the team, collectively have the appropriate competence and capabilities to perform the engagement in accordance with the relevant standards and enable an appropriate audit report to be issued.

3.3.6 Engagement performance

The engagement partner takes responsibility for:

- the direction, supervision and performance of the engagement in accordance with professional standards;

- his audit report being appropriate to the circumstances;

- reviews being performed in accordance with the firm's review policies and procedures;

- being satisfied that sufficient appropriate audit evidence has been obtained to support the conclusions reached and for the audit report to be issued;

- ensuring that members of the engagement team undertake appropriate consultation on difficult or contentious matters, that the resulting conclusions are agreed with the party consulted and that they are implemented;

- ensuring that an engagement quality control review is appropriately carried out, where required by the firm's policies, and that significant matters arising are discussed and resolved (further details of this are in the *Engagement quality control review* section in **3.2.7**); and

- ensuring that any differences of opinion, whether between the engagement team, those consulted, the engagement partner or the engagement quality control reviewer are dealt with and resolved in accordance with the firm's policies.

The key audit partner is also required to be actively involved in carrying-out the audit.

Public interest entities

For public interest entities, the engagement quality control reviewer, also considers the following:

(a) the independence of the firm from the entity;

(b) the significant risks relevant to the audit and which the key audit partner has identified during the audit and the measures that he has taken to adequately manage those risks;

(c)   the reasoning of the key audit partner, in particular with regard to the level of materiality and the significant risks referred to in (b);

(d)   any request for advice to external experts and the implementation of such advice;

(e)   the nature and scope of the corrected and uncorrected misstatements that were identified during the audit;

(f)   the subjects discussed with the audit committee and the management and/or supervisory bodies of the entity;

(g)   the subjects discussed with competent authorities and, where applicable, with other third parties; and

(h)   whether the documents and information selected from the file by the engagement quality control reviewer support the opinion of the key audit partner as expressed in the draft audit report and the additional report to the audit committee.

The engagement quality control reviewer discusses his assessment of these points and the results of his review with the key audit partner.

3.3.7   Monitoring

ISQC (UK) 1 (Revised June 2016) requires the firm to have a monitoring process in place (see **3.2.9**), designed to provide the firm with reasonable assurance that its policies and procedures relating to quality control are relevant, adequate and operating effectively. The engagement partner is responsible for considering the results of the firm's monitoring process and considering whether any deficiencies noted may affect the audit engagement.

3.3.8   Documentation

The engagement partner is responsible for ensuring that the audit is appropriately documented, including documentation of the following:

- issues identified regarding compliance with ethical requirements and how they were resolved;

- conclusions on compliance with applicable independence requirements;

- conclusions regarding the acceptance and continuance of client relationships and audit engagements;

- the nature and scope of, and conclusions from, consultations undertaken during the audit;

- all significant threats to the firm's independence as well as the safeguards applied to mitigate those threats; and

- those matters it is required to assess before accepting or continuing a statutory audit engagement in accordance with ISQC (UK) 1 (Revised June 2016).

The engagement quality control reviewer is responsible for documenting that:

- the procedures required by the firm's policies on EQCR have been performed;

- the EQCR has been completed on or before the date of the audit report; and

- he is not aware of any unresolved matters that would cause him to believe that the significant judgments the team made and the conclusions it reached were not appropriate.

Public interest entities

For public interest entities, the engagement quality control reviewer is required to:

(a) keep a record of the results of the review, together with the considerations underlying those results; and

(b) record at least the following:

   (i) the oral and written information provided by the key audit partner to support the significant judgments as well as the main findings of the audit procedures carried out and the conclusions drawn from those findings, whether or not at the request of the engagement quality control reviewer; and

   (ii) the opinions of the key audit partner, as expressed in the draft of his audit report and his report to the audit committee.

For public interest entities, the auditor is required to keep a record of the results of the EQCR, together with the considerations underlying those results in the audit documentation.

3.4 FRC audit quality framework

3.4.1 Background

In the early part of the 21st century, as a result of a number of high profile corporate collapses including Enron and WorldCom, and the subsequent break up of Arthur Andersen, a major international accounting firm, the quality of financial reporting and the effectiveness of the external audit process came under increasing scrutiny and criticism. Various reforms were introduced and legislators, including the UK government and the EU implemented measures aimed at improving corporate governance and financial reporting and increasing regulation of the auditing profession.

Against this background, in November 2006, the FRC issued a discussion paper, *Promoting Audit Quality*, addressing the FRC's objective of 'promoting and maintaining confidence in the audit process and the resulting audit report as a key component of the corporate reporting and governance regime and the effective operation of capital markets'. In order for this objective to be met, users of the financial statements must be able to rely on the audit report.

The paper notes that there is no single agreed definition of audit quality and that an auditor's opinion as to whether financial statements give a 'true and fair' view is subjective. Different views may be held as to the nature and extent of evidence needed to support such an opinion.

The approach taken in the paper is therefore to identify the 'drivers' that are central to achieving a high quality audit and consider the threats to them.

Following responses to the discussion paper in February 2008, the FRC issued its *Audit Quality Framework*. The Framework was intended to complement existing guidance and regulations and promote the previously identified key drivers of audit quality.

3.4.2 Promoting audit quality

Despite changes aimed at improving audit quality, the discussion paper identified the following concerns about audit quality which were still felt by commentators:

- changing business environment and increasing complexity of financial reporting, particularly in relation to the increasing requirement for estimates and valuations;
- audits possibly not detecting management fraud;
- relationships between executive management and the auditor;
- lack of transparency in auditor's work and judgments; and
- an increasingly prescriptive approach to audit.

The FRC identified four main drivers of audit quality. These were the:

- culture within the audit firm;
- skills and personal qualities of the audit partners and staff;
- quality of the audit process; and
- reliability and usefulness of audit reporting.

Audit firm culture

The discussion paper states that audit quality 'can be driven by audit firms creating an environment where achieving high quality is valued, invested in and rewarded'. It identifies a number of indicators that enhance audit quality, including respect for underlying auditing and ethical standards, partner and staff development systems and the promotion of consultation on difficult issues. Threats to quality oriented cultures include over-emphasis on winning and retaining audits or on non-audit services and excessive cost cutting in times of economic downturn.

Skills of partners and staff

The key drivers of audit quality in this area are subdivided into the skills required of partners and staff, the training provided to them and the appraisal process they undergo. Threats that may undermine quality in this area include failure to retain experienced staff, insufficient or ineffective training and lack of effective mentoring to develop the necessary personal characteristics.

Audit process

The discussion paper sets out the following characteristics of an effective audit process:

- an audit team appropriately structured for the engagement with relevant experience and knowledge;

- availability of high quality technical support;

- a well-structured audit methodology which provides a good framework to obtain sufficient appropriate audit evidence, ensures compliance with auditing standards, requires appropriate documentation and ensures effective review;

- objectives under ethical standards being achieved; and

- effective quality control procedures.

The paper identifies possible threats, including the increased use of computerised audit methodologies which may be over-prescriptive and reduce the importance of auditor judgment and a focus on producing documentation to the detriment of performing procedures properly.

Reliability of audit reporting

The discussion paper recognises that the structure of the audit report is specified by law and auditing standards and as such acts as 'a signal rather than a source of new information'. This means that confidence in the report is inextricably linked to the presumed quality of the audit process. This quality is best clarified through clear communication between the auditor and audit committee, as it is in this forum that the auditor can provide further information about the process followed, key risks identified and issues found.

The FRC are aware that confidence in the audit report may be undermined by the concerns of some users and commentators. These concerns include whether auditors are fulfilling their responsibilities in relation to the adequacy of a company's accounting records and whether audit reports should contain more information about key issues.

3.4.3 Factors outside the auditor's control

In addition, the discussion paper warns that some factors which affect audit quality will remain outside the control of the auditor. It lists these as:

- the approach taken by management;
- contributions made by audit committees;
- the role of shareholders and commentators;
- litigation as a driver of audit quality;
- the approach of regulators; and
- pressures caused by tight reporting deadlines.

3.5 International developments

In February 2014, the IAASB issued a paper entitled *A Framework for Audit Quality: Key Elements that create an Environment for Audit Quality.* The objectives of the Framework include:

- raising awareness of the key elements of audit quality;
- encouraging key stakeholders to explore ways to improve audit quality; and
- facilitating greater dialogue between key stakeholders on the topic.

The IAASB issued the Framework in order to generate discussion, and positive actions to achieve a continuous improvement to audit quality. It is not a substitute for auditing standards, standards of quality control or other regulatory requirements with which the auditor must comply, and does not itself create new standards or impose requirements on the auditor.

The framework identifies the following key elements that create an environment in which quality audits can be performed:

- inputs;
- processes;

- outputs;
- interactions with other in the supply chain; and
- contextual factors.

The Framework explains that quality audits involve the auditor exhibiting appropriate values, ethics and attitudes as well as being sufficiently knowledgeable, skilled and experienced, and having sufficient time to devote to the work. The auditor must also apply a rigorous audit process and quality control procedures.

Quality audits result in outputs that are useful and timely and involve the auditor interacting appropriately with other stakeholders including management, those charged with governance, users of financial statements and regulators.

Quality audits also require the auditor to respond appropriately to external factors including business practices and law, financial reporting and corporate governance frameworks and broader cultural factors.

In July 2015, the Public Company Accounting Oversight Board (PCAOB) in the US issued paper 2015-05 seeking public comment on the content and possible uses of a group of potential 'audit quality indicators'.

The indicators are a series of quantitative measures that may provide new insights about how to evaluate the quality of audits and how high quality audits are achieved. Taken together with qualitative context, the indicators may inform discussions among those concerned with the financial reporting and auditing process, for example, among audit committees and audit firms. Enhanced discussions, in turn, may strengthen audit planning, execution, and communication. Use of the indicators may also stimulate competition among audit firms focused on the quality of the firms' work and, thereby, increase audit quality overall.

Building on its 2014 Framework for Audit Quality, in December 2015, the IAASB released an Invitation to Comment, *Enhancing Audit Quality in the Public Interest: A Focus on Professional Scepticism, Quality Control and Group Audits* (the ITC). Specific issues it has identified that need to be addressed in revising its existing standards included:

- at the firm level:
  - monitoring (internal and external) and remediation activities;
  - quality control policies and procedures when operating as part of a network; and
  - transparency reports;

- and at an engagement level:
  - engagement partner responsibilities; and
  - engagement quality control reviews and reviewers.

Following this, the IAASB has been developing revisions to ISQC 1 and ISA 220 to address these and other issues with ISQC 1 focusing on the firms' responsibilities to design, implement and operate a system of quality management (rather than quality control) for audits of financial statements or other assurance or related services engagements and ISA 220 dealing with quality management at an engagement level for an audit of financial statements. It is intended that these revised standards will be supplemented by a proposed ISQC 2 dealing with requirements for engagement quality control (EQC) review including:

- criteria for determining which engagements should be subject to EQC review;
- establishing the objective of an EQC review;
- clarifying the nature timing and extent of the review; and
- eligibility of individuals who perform the review.

4 The auditor's report

4.1 Introduction

The form and content of the auditor's report are dictated by the nature of the engagement, the type of entity concerned and ISAs (UK). Where an entity is required by law to have an audit, the applicable law generally sets out the matters on which the auditor is required to report. In other cases, these may be determined by the auditor's engagement letter with the client. In all cases where the audit is carried out in accordance with ISAs (UK), the overall form of the report must comply with the ISAs, which also specify additional information to be included and how and when the auditor's opinion on the financial statements should be modified. The manner in which the audit report should be signed is set out in the *Companies Act* 2006 and Audit Regulations. This section examines the auditor's report on the annual financial statements of a company reporting in accordance with the *Companies Act* 2006. Modifications to the auditor's report are discussed in **Section 5**.

Other reports by auditors on financial information are considered in **Section 6**, while other reports under the Companies Act are considered in **Section 7**. Reports by the auditor to regulators of public interest entities and regulators of other entities in the financial sector are considered in **Section 9**. Compilation reports on accounts prepared by accountants are considered in **Section 8**. Reports by auditors on special purpose financial statements are considered in **Section 41**.

4.2 Standards and guidance

The current version of ISA (UK) 700 (Revised June 2016) *Forming an Opinion and Reporting on Financial Statements* was issued in June 2016. It is effective for periods commencing on or after 17 June 2016 and provides standards and guidance on the form and content of the auditor's report.

For guidance on the form and content of the auditor's report for periods commencing prior to this date, a previous version of this publication should be consulted.

Other ISAs relevant to audit reporting include:

- ISA (UK) 701 *Communicating Key Audit Matters in the Independent Auditor's Report* (see **4.11**);

- ISA (UK) 705 (Revised June 2016) *Modifications to the Opinion in the Independent Auditor's Report* (see **Section 5**);

- ISA (UK) 706 (Revised June 2016) *Emphasis of Matter paragraphs and Other Matter paragraphs in the independent auditor's report* (see **Section 5**);

- ISA (UK) 720 (Revised June 2016) *The Auditor's Responsibilities Relating to Other Information* (see **Section 34**); and

- ISA (UK) 570 (Revised June 2016) *Going Concern* (see **Section 12**).

The ISAs issued in June 2016 incorporate changes to align ISAs (UK) more closely with ISAs issued by the IAASB, as well as changes arising from the EU Audit Regulation and Directive.

The revisions to ISA (UK) 700 (Revised 2016) and related standards had a significant impact on the content, wording and format of the auditor's report which now starts with the opinion on the financial statements. Other wording changes include much more detailed explanation of the auditor's and directors' responsibilities, including responsibilities in relation to going concern, although much of this may be relegated to a website such as the one currently maintained by the FRC. There are also specific requirements for audit reports on public interest entities (see **4.18**).

4.2.1 Other guidance

The FRC has from time to time issued further guidance, including example reports, in the form of Bulletins. The most recent version is the Bulletin dated October 2016: *Compendium of illustrative auditor's reports on United Kingdom private sector financial statements for periods commencing on or after 17 June 2016*. This Bulletin superseded Bulletin 2010/2 *Compendium of Illustrative Auditor's Reports on United Kingdom Private Sector Financial Statements for periods ended on or after 15 December 2010 (Revised)* and Bulletin 4: *Recent Developments in Company Law, The Listing Rules and Auditing Standards that affect United Kingdom Auditor's Reports*.

The Audit and Assurance Faculty of the ICAEW has also issued a number of helpsheets providing guidance on how the examples in the FRC's Bulletin may be modified to cater for entities other than companies, and how the reporting principles of the standards may be adapted in other situations.

Further example reports can be found in *Preparing Audit Reports*, available online from Croner-i Tax and Accounting.

In January 2003, the Audit and Assurance Faculty of the ICAEW issued Technical Release Audit 1/03, *The Audit Report and Auditors' Duty of Care to Third Parties* following an earlier judgment in the Scottish courts, *Royal Bank of Scotland v Bannerman Johnstone Maclay* ('Bannerman'). The aim of Audit 1/03 is to assist the auditor in managing the risk of inadvertently assuming a duty of care to third parties in relation to his audit reports. A revised version of the Technical Release (01/03 AAF) was issued in May 2018. Further details are discussed in **4.28**.

APB Bulletin 2008/6 *The Senior Statutory Auditor under the United Kingdom Companies Act 2006* provides guidance on interpretation of the requirements of the Companies Act in respect of the role of the senior statutory auditor and the signature of the auditor's report.

4.3 Contents of this section

The objective of the audit report is covered in **4.4** with the contents of the main headings in the audit report covered by **4.5–4.22**.

Example unmodified audit reports are provided in **4.23**. Directors' responsibility statements are in **4.24**; considerations for small and micro entities in **4.25**; reporting on the directors' remuneration report in **4.26**; electronic publication in **4.27** and Bannerman clauses in **4.28**.

4.4 Forming an opinion

When reporting on a set of financial statements, the auditor's objective is to form an opinion on the financial statements, based on an evaluation of the conclusions drawn from the audit evidence obtained, and to express that opinion clearly in a written report.

ISA (UK) 700 (Revised June 2016) requires that the auditor forms an opinion on whether the financial statements are prepared, in all material respects, in accordance with the applicable financial reporting framework. In forming his opinion, he concludes as to whether he has obtained reasonable assurance that the financial statements are free from material misstatement whether due to fraud or error. This conclusion takes into account whether:

- sufficient appropriate audit evidence has been obtained;

- uncorrected misstatements are material, individually or in aggregate;

- the financial statements have been prepared in all material respects in accordance with the applicable financial framework (including consideration of the qualitative aspects of the entity's accounting practices and indicators of possible bias in management's judgments);

- in respect of a fair presentation framework, the financial statements achieve fair presentation (including consideration of the overall presentation, structure and content of the financial statements; and whether the financial statements represent the underlying transactions and events in a manner that achieves fair presentation); and

- the financial statements adequately refer to or describe the applicable financial reporting framework;

and, in particular, whether:

- the financial statements appropriately disclose the significant accounting policies selected and applied (including consideration of the relevance of the accounting policies and whether they are presented in an understandable manner);

- the accounting policies selected and applied are consistent with the applicable financial reporting framework, and are appropriate in the circumstances;

- accounting estimates are reasonable;

- the information presented in the financial statements is relevant, reliable, comparable and understandable (including considering whether the information that should have been included has been included, and whether it is appropriately classified, aggregated or disaggregated, and characterised; and whether the overall presentation of the financial statements has been undermined by including information that is not relevant or that obscures a proper understanding of the matters disclosed);

- the financial statements provide adequate disclosures to enable the intended users to understand the effect of material transactions and events on the information conveyed in the financial statements; and

- the terminology used in the financial statements, including the title of each financial statement, is appropriate.

4.5 Contents of an audit report

The ISA (UK) requires that an audit report is in writing, in clear and unambiguous language, and should contain:

- a title (see **4.6**);

- details of the addressee(s) of the report (see **4.7**);

- the auditor's opinion(s) on the financial statements (see **4.8**);

- basis for the opinion (see **4.9**);

- a going concern paragraph (see **4.10**);

- (where applicable) key audit matters together with the other matters required to be reported under ISA (UK) 701 (see **4.11**);

- the auditor's report on 'other information' in accordance with ISA (UK) 720 (see **4.12**);

- other matters on which the auditor is required to give an opinion (see **4.13**);

- details of the auditor's responsibilities to report by exception on certain matters (see **4.14**);

- the responsibilities of those charged with governance (see **4.15**);

- the responsibilities of the auditor (see **4.16**);

- (entities reporting on compliance with the UK Corporate Governance Code) matters the auditor is required to report on in relation to the Code and, where applicable, the Listing Rules (see **4.17**);

- (PIEs only) additional matters the auditor is required to address (see **4.18**);

- the name and signature of the auditor (see **4.19** and **4.20**);

- the location of the office where the auditor is based (see **4.21**); and

- the date of the auditor's report (see **4.22**).

The standard recommends that using a standard format with appropriate headings will help the user to understand the report. However, it also points out that the report should reflect the particular engagement.

In practice, most reports on unlisted companies follow a standard format based on that used by the FRC in its illustrative examples of audit reports.

4.5.1   Entities that report on application of the code

ISA (UK) 701 contains specific requirements for audit reports relating to entities that are required, or choose voluntarily, to report on how they have applied the Code. These include:

- a description of significant risks, description of how the auditor has applied the concept of materiality and an overview of the scope of the audit including how the auditor has responded to the significant risks;

- a report, by exception, where the auditor has identified 'other information' in the annual report that is materially incorrect or inconsistent with the knowledge he has gained in the course of the audit; and

- a statement regarding whether the auditor has anything to add to the directors' statements required by the Code in relation to risk assessment, going concern and liquidity.

Further details of these requirements are given in **4.17**.

4.5.2 Public interest entities

For public interest entities, the auditor is also required by ISA (UK) 700 to report on certain additional matters – see **4.18**.

4.6 Title

The report must have a title that clearly indicates that it is issued by an independent auditor, in order to distinguish the report from reports that might be issued by others.

4.7 Addressee

The report must identify to whom it is addressed. Where the auditor is reporting on the financial statements of a UK company, the *Companies Act* 2006 requires that he reports to the members of the company, as the audit is undertaken on their behalf. Audit reports for such companies are therefore usually addressed to 'the members' or 'the shareholders'.

For other types of reporting entity, the addressee of the report will depend on the terms of the engagement and/or applicable legislation. For example, in the case of an occupational pension scheme, the auditor is required to report to the trustees of the scheme. Where the addressee of the report is not specified in applicable legislation the auditor's terms of engagement should make clear to whom the auditor's report will be addressed.

Ensuring that the auditor's report is appropriately addressed not only helps users and others identify the intended recipients of the report but also helps the auditor in clarifying his responsibilities from a risk management point of view.

4.8 Auditor's opinions

ISA (UK) 700 (Revised June 2016) requires that the first section of the auditor's report should contain the auditor's opinion on the financial statements and have the heading 'Opinion'.

The opinion may be unmodified or modified. Modified opinions are considered in detail in **Section 5**.

The opinion required from the auditor will be dictated by the applicable reporting framework, including applicable legislation, and will be intended to provide the addressee of the report with reasonable assurance that the financial statements are free from material misstatement.

The Opinion section of the auditor's report also:

(a) identifies the entity whose financial statements have been audited;

(b) states that the financial statements have been audited;

(c) identifies the title of each statement comprising the financial statements;

(d) refers to the notes, including the summary of significant accounting policies; and

(e) specifies the date of, or period covered by, each financial statement comprising the financial statements.

For UK companies, the *Companies Act* 2006, s. 495(3) requires the auditor to express an opinion as to whether the financial statements:

- give a true and fair view of the entity's financial position at the end of the reporting period and of its profit/loss for that period;

- have been properly prepared in accordance with the applicable reporting framework; and

- have been prepared in accordance with the requirements of the *Companies Act* 2006.

The auditor's opinion should indicate the financial reporting framework upon which the financial statements are based. For UK companies, this will normally be stated as:

- applicable law and UK Accounting Standards (UK Generally Accepted Accounting Practice);

- applicable law and International Financial Reporting Standards (IFRSs) as adopted by the European Union; or

- (for consolidated financial statements of fully listed companies) applicable law and International Financial Reporting Standards (IFRSs) as adopted by the European Union and, as regards the consolidated financial statements, Article 4 of the IAS Regulation.[1]

---

[1] Article 4 of the IAS Regulation (1606/2002/EC) applies to companies with securities that are admitted to trading on a regulated market in an EU member state and requires such companies to apply EU adopted IFRS in their consolidated accounts. This requirement therefore applies to fully listed companies in the UK, but not to those traded on AIM, which is not a regulated market for this purpose.

Where UK Accounting Standards have been applied it is usual, in the interests of clarity, for the report to identify the applicable standard, e.g. 'the accounting framework that has been applied in their preparation is applicable law and United Kingdom Accounting Standards, including [Financial Reporting Standard 102 *The Financial Reporting Standard applicable in the UK and Republic of Ireland*]/[Financial Reporting Standard 101 *Reduced Disclosure Framework*] (United Kingdom Generally Accepted Accounting Practice)'.

Auditors may also be asked to report on compliance with a second financial reporting framework, such as International Financial Reporting Standards (IFRSs) as issued by the IAASB. In this situation, the second opinion must be clearly separated in the opinion section by the use of a subheading.

4.9   Basis for opinion

ISA (UK) 700 (Revised June 2016) requires that the auditor's report includes a section directly following the Opinion section, with the heading 'Basis for Opinion', that:

(a)   states that the audit was conducted in accordance with ISAs (UK) and applicable law;

(b)   refers to the section of the auditor's report that describes the auditor's responsibilities under the ISAs (UK);

(c)   includes a statement that the auditor is independent of the entity in accordance with the relevant ethical requirements relating to the audit, and has fulfilled the auditor's other ethical responsibilities in accordance with these requirements. In the UK, this will refer to the Revised Ethical Standard 2016, applied as required for the types of entity determined to be appropriate in the circumstances.

(d)   states whether the auditor believes that the audit evidence he has obtained is sufficient and appropriate to provide a basis for the auditor's opinion.

4.10   Going concern

ISA (UK) 700 (Revised June 2016) requires the auditor to report in accordance with ISA (UK) 570 (Revised June 2016) *Going Concern*.

For most reports, this will require a section in the report entitled 'Conclusions relating to going concern' or other appropriate heading in which the auditor reports by exception regarding the assessment of the appropriateness of management's use of the going concern basis of accounting and whether there are material uncertainties in relation to going concern that should be disclosed in the financial statements. Where a material uncertainty exists and is adequately disclosed in the financial statements this section of the report will instead be headed 'Material uncertainty in relation to going concern' and will draw attention to the disclosures in the financial statements relating to the uncertainty. This replaces the previous requirement to draw attention to disclosures by way of an emphasis of matter paragraph.

For entities reporting on compliance with the UK Code of Corporate Governance and for premium listed companies, there are additional matters that should be referred to in this section of the report.

This section of the report is considered in more detail in **11.12**.

4.11 Key audit matters

For audits of complete sets of general purpose financial statements of listed entities, public interest entities and other entities that are required, and those that choose voluntarily, to report on how they have applied the UK Corporate Governance Code, the auditor is required to communicate in his report in accordance with ISA (UK) 701 *Communicating Key Audit Matters in the Independent Auditor's Report*. The term 'listed entities' for this purpose includes all entities whose securities are publicly traded, so includes AIM companies and other entities whose securities are publicly traded on markets that are not EU regulated markets.

ISA (UK) 701 also applies if the auditor is required by law or regulation, or decides voluntarily, to communicate key audit matters in the audit report.

ISA (UK) 701 is a new standard based on ISA 701 issued by the IAASB in January 2015, with certain UK add-ons. The requirements are very similar to those applicable previously to entities reporting on compliance with the UK Corporate Governance Code, although ISA (UK) 701 now applies to a much wider range of entities.

Where ISA (UK) 701 applies, the auditor is required to determine key audit matters and, having formed an opinion on the financial statements, communicate those matters by describing them in his audit report.

Key audit matters are those matters that, in the auditor's professional judgment, were of most significance in the audit of the financial statements of the current period and include the most significant assessed risks of material misstatement identified by the auditor, including those which had the greatest effect on: the overall audit strategy; the allocation of resources in the audit; and directing the efforts of the engagement team. Key audit matters are selected from matters communicated with those charged with governance.

4.11.1 Determining key audit matters

The auditor decides, from the matters he has already communicated with those charged with governance, which were those matters that required significant auditor attention in performing the audit. In making this determination, he takes into account the following:

- areas of higher assessed risk of material misstatement, or significant risks identified in accordance with ISA (UK) 315 (Revised June 2016) (see **Section 21**);

- significant auditor judgments relating to areas in the financial statements that involve significant management judgment, including accounting estimates that have been identified as having high estimation uncertainty; and

- the effect on the audit of significant events or transactions that occurred during the period.

From the matters determined in this way, he determines which were of most significance in the audit of the current period financial statements and are therefore key audit matters.

4.11.2 Communicating key audit matters

The auditor describes each key audit matter, using an appropriate subheading, in a separate section of the auditor's report under the heading 'Key Audit Matters', unless the circumstances in **4.11.3** apply. The introductory language in this section of the audit report states that:

(a) key audit matters are those matters that, in the auditor's professional judgment, were of most significance in the audit of the financial statements and include the most significant assessed risks of material misstatement (whether due to fraud or error), including those which had the greatest effect on: the overall audit strategy; the allocation of resources in the audit; and directing the efforts of the engagement team; and

(b) these matters were addressed in the context of the audit of the financial statements as a whole, and in forming his opinion thereon, the auditor does not provide a separate opinion on these matters.

Key audit matters are not a substitute for expressing a modified opinion and the auditor should not communicate a matter in the key audit matters section of his report when he would be required, as a result of the matter, to modify his opinion in accordance with ISA (UK) 705 (Revised June 2016).

Descriptions of key audit matters

The description of each key audit matter in the audit report includes a reference to the related disclosure(s), if any, and addresses why the matter was considered to be one of the most significant in the audit and therefore a key audit matter, and how the matter was addressed in the audit.

In describing each of the key audit matters, the auditor's report is required to provide, in support of the audit opinion:

(a) a description of the most significant assessed risks of material misstatement, whether or not due to fraud;

(b) a summary of the auditor's response to those risks; and

(c) where relevant, key observations arising with respect to those risks.

In describing key audit matters, the auditor must make clear which matters are included because they were the most significant assessed risks of material misstatement (whether or not due to fraud) identified by the auditor.

4.11.3 *Circumstances in which a key audit matter is not communicated*

The auditor is required to describe each key audit matter in his report unless law or regulation prevents public disclosure about the matter; or, in extremely rare circumstances, the auditor determines that the matter should not be communicated in his report because the adverse consequences of doing so would reasonably be expected to outweigh the public interest benefits of such communication. This cannot be the case if the entity has already publicly disclosed information about the matter.

4.11.4 *Interaction between key audit matters and going concern matters included in the auditor's report*

Where matters related to going concern give rise to a modified opinion, or a material uncertainty related to events or conditions that may cast significant doubt on the entity's ability to continue as a going concern, these will, by their nature, be key audit matters. However, in such circumstances, these matters are not described in the Key Audit Matters section of the auditor's report. Instead, the auditor reports on these matters by modifying his opinion in accordance with ISA (UK) 705 (Revised June 2016) (see **Section 5**) and ISA (UK) 570 (Revised June 2016) (see **Section 11**) and includes a reference to the Basis for Qualified (Adverse) Opinion or the Material Uncertainty Related to Going Concern section(s) in the Key Audit Matters section.

4.11.5   No matters to report

If the auditor determines that there are no key audit matters to communicate or that the only key audit matters to communicate are those matters addressed in **4.11.4**, the auditor includes a statement to this effect in a separate section of his report under the heading Key Audit Matters.

4.11.6   *Communicating other planning and scoping matters*

The audit report is also required to include:

(a)   an explanation of how the auditor applied the concept of materiality in planning and performing the audit. This includes specifying the threshold used by the auditor as being materiality for the financial statements as a whole;

(b)   an overview of the scope of the audit, including an explanation of how such scope addressed each key audit matter and was influenced by the auditor's application of materiality.

In order to be useful to users of the financial statements, the explanations of the matters set out in the auditor's report need to be described:

(a)   so as to enable a user to understand their significance in the context of the audit of the financial statements as a whole and not as discrete opinions on separate elements of the financial statements;

(b)   in a way that enables them to be related directly to the specific circumstances of the entity and are not, therefore, generic or abstract matters expressed in standardised language; and

(c)   in the case of entities that are required, and those that choose voluntarily, to report on how they have applied the UK Corporate Governance Code, or to explain why they have not, in a manner that complements the description of significant issues relating to the financial statements, required to be set out in the separate section of the annual report describing the work of the audit committee in discharging its responsibilities. The auditor tries to coordinate descriptions of overlapping topics addressed in these communications, to avoid duplication of reporting about them, whilst having appropriate regard to the separate responsibilities of the auditor and the board for communicating information.

The explanation, of how the auditor applied the concept of materiality in planning and performing the audit, is tailored to the particular circumstances and complexity of the audit and, in addition to specifying the threshold used by the auditor as being materiality for the financial statements as a whole, might include, for example:

- materiality level or levels for those classes of transactions, account balances or disclosures where such materiality levels are lower than materiality for the financial statements as a whole;

- performance materiality;

- any significant revisions of materiality thresholds that were made as the audit progressed;

- the threshold used for reporting unadjusted differences to the audit committee; and

- significant qualitative considerations relating to the auditor's evaluation of materiality.

The content of the overview of the scope of the audit is tailored to the particular circumstances of the audit and how the scope was influenced by the auditor's application of materiality and addressed the key audit matters described in the auditor's report. Such a summary might also include, for example:

- the coverage of revenue, total assets and profit before tax achieved;

- the coverage of revenue, total assets and profit before tax of reportable segments achieved;

- the number of locations visited by the auditor as a proportion of the total number of locations, and the rationale underlying any program of visits;

- the effect of the group structure on the scope. The audit approach to a group consisting of autonomous subsidiary companies may differ from that applied to one which consists of a number of non-autonomous divisions;

- the nature and extent of the group auditor's involvement in the work of component auditors.

4.11.7 Communication with those charged with governance

The auditor communicates with those charged with governance those matters he determines to be the key audit matters or, if applicable, the fact that there are no key audit matters for the audit report.

4.11.8 Documentation

Audit documentation needs to include:

- the matters that required significant auditor attention and the rationale for the auditor's determination as to whether or not each of these matters is a key audit matter;

- where applicable, the rationale for the auditor's determination that there are no key audit matters to communicate in his report or that the only key audit matters to communicate are those matters addressed by a modified opinion or a material uncertainty related to going concern; and

- where applicable, the rationale for the auditor's determination not to communicate in his report a matter determined to be a key audit matter.

4.12   Other information

ISA (UK) 700 (Revised June 2016) also requires the auditor to report, where applicable, in accordance with ISA (UK) 720 (Revised June 2016) *The Auditor's Responsibilities Relating to Other Information*. This is covered in **Section 34**.

4.13   Opinion on other matters

When the auditor gives an opinion arising from other responsibilities, that opinion should be set out in a separate section of the auditor's report, with a heading titled 'Report on other legal and regulatory requirements' or otherwise appropriate to the content. If the topics addressed are the same as those required by ISAs (UK) then the matters may be presented in the same section of the audit report as the related report elements required by the ISAs (UK).

Other reporting requirements may be set out in legislation or by the terms of engagement agreed with the entity. Where this is the case, these opinions should be clearly distinguished from the opinion on the financial statements.

For UK companies, the *Companies Act* 2006 requires that the auditor expresses opinion(s), where applicable, on:

- strategic report and directors' report; and

- separate corporate governance statement (listed companies where required corporate governance disclosures not included in directors' report).

Further detail regarding these opinions is given in **Section 34**.

For quoted companies only the *Companies Act* 2006 also requires the auditor to report on the auditable part of the directors' remuneration report (see **4.26**).

Other reporting frameworks may require other additional opinions.

4.14   Reporting by exception

If the auditor is required to report by exception, he should describe his responsibilities under the heading 'Matters on which we are required to report by exception' and include a suitable conclusion(s) in respect of such matters.

All UK companies

For UK companies, the auditor is required by the *Companies Act* 2006 to consider, and report by exception if:

- in the light of the knowledge and understanding of the company and its environment obtained in the course of the audit the auditor has identified material misstatements in the strategic report or the directors' report; or

if in his opinion:

- adequate accounting records have not been kept by the company or returns adequate for the purposes of the audit have not been received from branches not visited by the auditor;

- the financial statements are not in agreement with the accounting records and returns;

- certain disclosures of directors' remuneration have not been made (that is the information required under the *Small Companies and Groups (Accounts and Directors' Report) Regulations* 2008 or the *Large and Medium-sized Companies and Groups (Accounts and Reports) Regulations* 2008, as applicable); or

- he has not received all the information and explanations he requires for his audit.

Small companies

Where a small company has prepared its accounts in accordance with the small companies regime or has taken advantage of either of the small companies' exemptions relating to the directors' report or the preparation of a strategic report, the auditor is required to report by exception if, in his opinion, the directors were not entitled to do so.

Other entities

Legislation and reporting frameworks applicable to other entities may require similar or additional exception reporting.

4.15   Responsibilities for the financial statements

Those charged with governance are responsible for the preparation of financial statements that give a true and fair view.

The auditor's report is required to include a section with a heading 'Responsibilities of Those Charged with Governance for the Financial Statements' or something similar. In the case of companies, the heading may instead refer to 'directors'.

This section needs to describe the responsibility of those charged with governance for preparing the financial statements in accordance with the applicable financial reporting framework, and for such internal control as they determine is necessary to enable the preparation of financial statements that are free from material misstatement, whether due to fraud or error; and for assessing the entity's ability to continue as a going concern and whether the use of the going concern basis of accounting is appropriate as well as disclosing, if applicable, matters relating to going concern. The explanation of the responsibility of those charged with governance for this assessment should include a description of when the use of the going concern basis of accounting is appropriate.

The statement also needs to include that those charged with governance are responsible for the preparation of financial statements that give a true and fair view.

This section of the report may also refer to a detailed director's responsibilities statement containing further detail. This statement is considered in **4.24**.

4.16   Responsibilities of the auditor

The auditor's report includes a section with the heading 'Auditor's Responsibilities for the Audit of the Financial Statements'.

This section of the auditor's report is required to state that:

(a) the objectives of the auditor are to:

  (i)   obtain reasonable assurance about whether the financial statements as a whole are free from material misstatement, whether due to fraud or error; and

  (ii) issue an auditor's report that includes the auditor's opinion;

(b) reasonable assurance is a high level of assurance, but is not a guarantee that an audit conducted in accordance with ISAs (UK) will always detect a material misstatement when it exists; and

(c) that misstatements can arise from fraud or error, and either:

    (i)   describe that they are considered material if, individually or in the aggregate, they could reasonably be expected to influence the economic decisions of users taken on the basis of these financial statements; or

    (ii) provide a definition or description of materiality in accordance with the applicable financial reporting framework.

The auditor's responsibilities section is also required to:

(a) state that, as part of an audit in accordance with ISAs (UK), the auditor exercises professional judgment and maintains professional scepticism throughout the audit; and

(b) describe an audit by stating that the auditor's responsibilities are:

    (i)   to identify and assess the risks of material misstatement of the financial statements, whether due to fraud or error; to design and perform audit procedures responsive to those risks; and to obtain audit evidence that is sufficient and appropriate to provide a basis for the auditor's opinion;

    (ii) to obtain an understanding of internal control relevant to the audit in order to design audit procedures that are appropriate in the circumstances, but not for the purpose of expressing an opinion on the effectiveness of the entity's internal control;

    (iii) to evaluate the appropriateness of accounting policies used and the reasonableness of accounting estimates and related disclosures made by management;

    (iv) to conclude on the appropriateness of management's use of the going concern basis of accounting and, based on the audit evidence obtained, whether a material uncertainty exists related to events or conditions that may cast significant doubt on the entity's ability to continue as a going concern. If the auditor concludes that a material uncertainty exists, he is required to draw attention in the auditor's report to the related disclosures in the financial statements or, if such disclosures are inadequate, to modify the opinion;

    (v) when the financial statements are prepared in accordance with a fair presentation framework, to evaluate the overall presentation, structure and content of the financial statements, including the disclosures, and whether the financial statements represent the underlying transactions and events in a manner that achieves fair presentation;

(c) when ISA (UK) 600 (Revised June 2016) applies, to further describe the auditor's responsibilities in a group audit engagement.

In addition, the auditor's responsibilities section also:

(a) states that the auditor communicates with those charged with governance regarding, among other matters, the planned scope and timing of the audit and significant audit findings, including any significant deficiencies in internal control that the auditor identifies during the audit;

(b) for audits of financial statements of listed entities, states that the auditor provides those charged with governance with a statement that the auditor has complied with relevant ethical requirements regarding independence and communicate with them all relationships and other matters that may reasonably be thought to bear on the auditor's independence, and where applicable, related safeguards; and

(c) for audits of financial statements of listed entities and any other entities for which key audit matters are communicated in accordance with ISA (UK) 701, state that, from the matters communicated with those charged with governance, the auditor determines those matters that were of most significance in the audit of the financial statements of the current period and are therefore the key audit matters. He describes these matters in the auditor's report unless, extremely rarely, he is prevented from doing so by either regulation or adverse consequences.

This description of the auditor's responsibilities for the audit of the financial statements can be provided either:

(a) within the body of the auditor's report;

(b) within an appendix to the auditor's report, in which case a reference to the appendix must be given from within the audit report; or

(c) by cross referring to 'Description of the Auditor's Responsibilities for the Audit of the Financial Statements' that is maintained on the FRCs website (www.frc.org.uk/auditorsresponsibilities).

Given the required content of this section, option (c) is likely to prove popular in practice in order to limit the length and complexity of the audit report and this is the approach taken in the examples in this section. Examples following the approaches in (a) and (b) are contained in the FRC's 2016 *Compendium*.

4.17 Entities that report on application of the code

For entities reporting on application of the UK Corporate Governance Code there are additional specific reporting requirements in relation to other information. For such entities, in addition to the normal wording describing the auditor's responsibilities in relation to other information the Other Information section of the report includes a statement covering:

- the statement by the directors that they consider the annual report as a whole to be fair, balanced and understandable;

- whether the section of the annual report describing the work of the audit committee appropriately addresses matters communicated by the auditor; and

- (for premium listed entities only) whether the parts of the directors' statement required by the Listing Rules relating to the company's compliance with those provisions of the Code specified for review by the auditor do not properly disclose a departure from a relevant provision of the Code.

Example wording is included in the audit report example in **Table 2**.

4.18 Public interest entities

For audits of financial statements of public interest entities, the auditor's report is also required to:

(a) state by whom or which body the auditor(s) was appointed;

(b) indicate the date of the appointment and the period of total uninterrupted engagement including previous renewals and reappointments of the firm;

(c) explain to what extent the audit was considered capable of detecting irregularities, including fraud;

(d) confirm that the audit opinion is consistent with the additional report to the audit committee (see **10.7.2**). Other than this reference, the auditor's report shall not contain any cross-references to the additional report to the audit committee;

(e) declare that the non-audit services prohibited by the Revised Ethical Standard 2016 were not provided and that the firm remained independent of the entity in conducting the audit; and

(f) indicate any services, in addition to the audit, which were provided by the firm to the entity and its controlled undertaking(s), and which have not been disclosed in the annual report or financial statements.

4.19 Name of engagement partner

The ISA (UK) specifically requires that the name of the engagement partner be included in the auditor's report on financial statements of listed entities unless, in rare circumstances, such disclosure is reasonably expected to lead to a significant personal security threat. In the rare circumstances that this applies, the auditor discusses his intention not to include the engagement partner's name with those charged with governance.

Where a listed entity is a UK company, it will in any case be covered by the senior statutory auditor rules (see **4.20.2**).

4.20   Signature

4.20.1   Audit regulation

Audit regulations require that an audit report in respect of the audit of UK entities must:

- state the name of the firm as it appears in the Register;

- include the words 'Statutory Auditor' or 'Statutory Auditors' after the name of the firm;

- and if required by law, state the name of the responsible individual who was in charge of the audit, be signed by this person in his own name and include the words 'Senior Statutory Auditor' after the name of the responsible individual.

An audit report has to include the description 'Statutory Auditor' but there is nothing to prevent a firm adding any other appropriate description, such as 'chartered accountants'.

4.20.2   Senior statutory auditor

Where the auditor is a firm, the *Companies Act* 2006 sets out the requirement for the senior statutory auditor to sign the auditor's report in his own name for and on behalf of the audit firm. Guidance with respect to the term *senior statutory auditor* was published by the APB in April 2008 as Bulletin 2008/6, *The 'senior statutory auditor' under the United Kingdom Companies Act 2006.*

The senior statutory auditor is required to sign in his own name for reports:

- prepared in accordance with the *Companies Act* 2006, s. 495, 496 and 497, that is audit reports which provide a true and fair opinion; and

- on voluntary revisions of annual accounts and reports (see **6.2**).

This requirement has applied since 6 April 2008.

In signing an auditor's report in his own name as the senior statutory auditor, the individual does not take on any additional legal responsibility for the audit or the report than he would previously have had prior to the *Companies Act* 2006.

If more than one partner is involved in an audit, it is important to determine which individual is acting as the engagement partner (as defined in ISAs (UK)) and therefore, assumes the role of senior statutory auditor.

The Bulletin suggests that it would be pragmatic for the audit firm to have a contingency plan as to who would succeed as senior statutory auditor in the event that the audit is at an advanced stage but the senior auditor is unable to sign the auditor's report.

4.20.3   Signing

The requirements of the *Companies Act* 2006 for the senior statutory auditor to physically sign the auditor's report in his own name, extends only to the copy of the auditor's report to be provided to the client upon completion of the audit. In all but this 'signing copy', the name of the senior statutory auditor needs to be stated, but the signature does not need to be reproduced. The copy of the auditor's report sent to the Registrar of Companies requires the name of the senior statutory auditor to be stated, together with the name of the statutory auditor, but does not require an actual signature.

Under s. 503(3) of the 2006 Act, only the senior statutory auditor can sign the 'signing copy' of the auditor's report. If he is absent at the time of signing, the signature can be obtained by electronic means, such as e-mail or fax. If, for example, due to illness or other absence, another partner needs to sign the audit report, he cannot do so on behalf of the senior statutory auditor but would need to take full responsibility for that role himself. This would involve familiarising himself with the audit and audit judgments made to the extent necessary for him to assume the role of senior statutory auditor.

4.20.4   Joint auditors

Where a company has appointed joint auditors, each audit firm will designate its own senior statutory auditor. When the auditor's report is signed, each firm's senior statutory auditor must sign the report in his own name for and on behalf of his firm.

4.21   Auditor's location

The report should also state the location of the auditor's office, typically, the city or town in which the auditor (or senior statutory auditor) responsible for the opinion is based.

4.22   Date

ISA (UK) 700 (Revised June 2016) requires that:

- before the auditor can give an opinion on the financial statements, they must have been approved by the directors and the auditor must have considered all of the available evidence; and

- the auditor's report has to be dated as at the date the opinion is expressed.

The significance of the date of the auditor's report is that he is informing the reader that he is aware of events up to that date and has considered the effect of these on the financial statements.

Before the auditor signs the audit report, the following must have occurred:

- receipt of the approved financial statements, together with any accompanying information, from the directors;

- review of all the documents which the auditor is required to consider in addition to the financial statements, for example, the strategic report (if any) and the directors' report; and

- completion of all the procedures thought necessary by the auditor to be able to form an opinion, including a post balance sheet events review.

The senior statutory auditor must sign and date the report expressing an opinion on the financial statements for distribution with the financial statements. Firms must therefore have procedures to ensure reports are not signed before the above events have occurred.

Although the date of the auditor's report has to be after the directors have approved the financial statements, it does not mean that the auditor cannot commence his work until the directors have approved the financial statements. Rather, he cannot conclude it until this has happened. In many cases, the preparation of the financial statements will take place at the same time as the auditor is gathering evidence.

Although he will normally be in a position to give his opinion at the same date as the financial statements are approved, it does not have to be on the same day. Unless the auditor has gathered all his evidence and completed his work at that time (including a post balance sheet event review), he is unable to sign his report despite the directors approving the financial statements.

Where the date the opinion is expressed is before the final printing of the financial statements, the auditor will have to ensure the drafts on which he forms his opinion are sufficiently clear for him to assess the overall presentation. One area to be especially aware of is where the directors have approved the profit and loss account and the balance sheet, but the notes have yet to be finally completed. In such cases, the auditor will have to delay giving his opinion until they are finished.

Where the date the auditor signs his report is later than the date of approval, he may need to obtain additional assurances from the directors that there have been no events in the intervening period that would affect the financial statements. He will also need to have his own procedures for reviewing subsequent events and assessing their impact on the financial statements.

4.23   Unmodified auditor's reports examples

ISA (UK) 700 (Revised June 2016) refers to example auditor's reports in the most recent version of the FRC's *Compendium of illustrative auditor's reports*. The current version is the Bulletin dated October 2016: *Compendium of illustrative auditor's reports on United Kingdom private sector financial statements for periods commencing on or after 17 June 2016*.

A simple auditor's report for an unlisted non-PIE company preparing group accounts is provided in **Table 1**. The example in **Table 2** is for a premium listed company. An example for a small company preparing single entity accounts is given in **Table 5**. Further variations are set out in the *Compendium of illustrative auditor's reports on United Kingdom private sector financial statements for periods commencing on or after 17 June 2016* but may need to be adapted to the entity's circumstances.

Further example reports can be found in *Preparing Audit Reports*, available online from Croner-i Tax and Accounting.

TABLE 1: Example simple auditor's report

- *Financial statements are prepared in accordance with FRS 102.*
- *Section 408 exemption taken for parent company's own profit and loss account.*
- *Company is not a listed or public interest entity.*
- *Company prepares group financial statements.*
- *Description of the auditor's responsibilities for the audit of the financial statements is included by reference to the FRCs website.*
- *Auditor is not required, and has otherwise not decided, to communicate key audit matters in accordance with ISA (UK) 701.*

Independent auditor's report to the members of XYZ Limited

Opinion

We have audited the financial statements of [XYZ Limited] (the 'parent company') and its subsidiaries (the 'group') for the year ended [date] which comprise [specify the titles of the primary statements]¹ and notes to the financial statements, including a summary of significant accounting policies. The financial reporting framework that has been applied in their preparation is applicable law and United Kingdom Accounting Standards, including Financial Reporting Standard 102 *The Financial Reporting Standard applicable in the UK and Republic of Ireland* (United Kingdom Generally Accepted Accounting Practice).

In our opinion, the financial statements:

- give a true and fair view of the state of the group's and of the parent company's affairs as at [date] and of the group's [profit/loss] for the year then ended;
- have been properly prepared in accordance with United Kingdom Generally Accepted Accounting Practice;
- have been prepared in accordance with the requirements of the *Companies Act* 2006.

Basis for opinion

We conducted our audit in accordance with International Standards on Auditing (UK) (ISAs (UK)) and applicable law. Our responsibilities under those standards are further described in the Auditor's responsibilities for the audit of the financial statements section of our report. We are independent of the group in accordance with the ethical requirements that are relevant to our audit of the financial statements in the UK, including the FRC's Ethical Standard, and we have fulfilled our other ethical responsibilities in accordance with these requirements. We believe that the audit evidence we have obtained is sufficient and appropriate to provide a basis for our opinion.

Conclusions relating to going concern

We have nothing to report in respect of the following matters in relation to which the ISAs (UK) require us to report to you where:

- the directors' use of the going concern basis of accounting in the preparation of the financial statements is not appropriate; or
- the directors have not disclosed in the financial statements any identified material uncertainties that may cast significant doubt about the group's or the parent company's ability to continue to adopt the going concern basis of accounting for a period of at least 12 months from the date when the financial statements are authorised for issue.

Other information

The directors are responsible for the other information. The other information comprises the information included in the annual report[2], other than the financial statements and our auditor's report thereon. Our opinion on the financial statements does not cover the other information and, except to the extent otherwise explicitly stated in our report, we do not express any form of assurance conclusion thereon.

In connection with our audit of the financial statements, our responsibility is to read the other information and, in doing so, consider whether the other information is materially inconsistent with the financial statements or our knowledge obtained in the audit or otherwise appears to be materially misstated. If we identify such material inconsistencies or apparent material misstatements, we are required to determine whether there is a material misstatement in the financial statements or a material misstatement of the other information. If, based on the work we have performed, we conclude that there is a material misstatement of this other information, we are required to report that fact.

We have nothing to report in this regard.

Opinions on other matters prescribed by the Companies Act 2006

In our opinion, based on the work undertaken in the course of the audit:

- the information given in the [Strategic Report and the] Directors' Report for the financial year for which the financial statements are prepared is consistent with the financial statements; and
- [the Strategic Report and] the Directors' Report [have/has] been prepared in accordance with applicable legal requirements.

Matters on which we are required to report by exception

In the light of the knowledge and understanding of the group and the parent company and its environment obtained in the course of the audit, we have identified no material misstatements in the Strategic Report or the Directors' Report.

We have nothing to report in respect of the following matters where the *Companies Act* 2006 requires us to report to you if, in our opinion:

- adequate accounting records have not been kept by the parent company, or returns adequate for our audit have not been received from branches not visited by us; or

- the parent company's financial statements are not in agreement with the accounting records and returns; or

- certain disclosures of directors' remuneration specified by law are not made; or

- we have not received all the information and explanations we required for our audit.

Responsibilities of directors

As explained more fully in the Directors' Responsibilities Statement [set out [on pages …]], the directors are responsible for the preparation of the financial statements and for being satisfied that they give a true and fair view, and for such internal control as the directors determine is necessary to enable the preparation of financial statements that are free from material misstatement, whether due to fraud or error.

In preparing the financial statements, the directors are responsible for assessing the group's and the parent company's ability to continue as a going concern, disclosing, as applicable, matters related to going concern and using the going concern basis of accounting unless the directors either intend to liquidate the group or the parent company or to cease operations, or have no realistic alternative but to do so.

Auditor's responsibilities for the audit of the financial statements

Our objectives are to obtain reasonable assurance about whether the financial statements as a whole are free from material misstatement, whether due to fraud or error, and to issue an auditor's report that includes our opinion. Reasonable assurance is a high level of assurance, but is not a guarantee that an audit conducted in accordance with ISAs (UK) will always detect a material misstatement when it exists.

Misstatements can arise from fraud or error and are considered material if, individually or in the aggregate, they could reasonably be expected to influence the economic decisions of users taken on the basis of these financial statements.

A further description of our responsibilities for the audit of the financial statements is located on the Financial Reporting Council's website at www.frc.org.uk/auditorsresponsibilities. This description forms part of our auditor's report.

Use of our report

This report is made solely to the company's members, as a body, in accordance with the *Companies Act* 2006, Pt 16, Ch. 3. Our audit work has been undertaken so that we might state to the company's members those matters we are required to state to them in an auditor's report and for no other purpose. To the fullest extent permitted by law, we do not accept or assume responsibility to anyone other than the company and the company's members as a body, for our audit work, for this report, or for the opinions we have formed.[3]

[Signature]

John Smith (Senior statutory auditor)

For and on behalf of ABC LLP, Statutory Auditor

Address

Date

[1] The terms used to describe the primary financial statements should be the same as those used by the directors.

[2] The term used to describe the annual report should be the same as that used by the directors.

[3] Optional 'Bannerman' paragraph (see **4.28**).

TABLE 2: Example auditor's report for a premium listed company using IFRSs

- *Company is a premium listed company, a quoted company and a public interest entity.*

- *Group and parent company financial statements not presented separately.*

- *IFRSs as adopted by the European Union used for both group and parent company financial statements.*

- *Company meets the Companies Act definition of a quoted company and has a premium listing in the UK.*

- *Corporate governance statement NOT incorporated into the directors' report, either directly or by incorporation by cross-reference.*

- *Section 408 exemption relating to parent company's own income statement taken.*

- *No separate opinion on compliance with IFRS as issued by IASB.*

- *Description of the auditor's responsibilities for the audit of the financial statements is included by reference to the FRC'S website.*

Independent auditor's report to the members of XYZ Limited

Opinion

We have audited the financial statements of [entity name] (the 'parent company') and its subsidiaries (the 'group') for the year ended [date] which comprise [specify the financial statements[4] such as the Group and Parent

Company Statements of Comprehensive Income, Statements of Changes in Equity, Balance Sheets and Statements of Cash Flow] and notes to the financial statements, including a summary of significant accounting policies. The financial reporting framework that has been applied in their preparation is applicable law and International Financial Reporting Standards (IFRSs) as adopted by the European Union and, as regards the parent company financial statements, as applied in accordance with the provisions of the *Companies Act* 2006.

In our opinion, the financial statements:

- give a true and fair view of the state of the group's and of the parent company's affairs as at ... and of the group's and the parent company's profit [loss] for the year then ended;

- the group financial statements have been properly prepared in accordance with IFRSs as adopted by the European Union;

- the parent company financial statements have been properly prepared in accordance with IFRSs as adopted by the European Union and as applied in accordance with the provisions of the *Companies Act* 2006; and

- the financial statements have been prepared in accordance with the requirements of the *Companies Act* 2006 and, as regards the group financial statements, Art. 4 of the IAS Regulation.

Basis for opinion

We conducted our audit in accordance with International Standards on Auditing (UK) (ISAs (UK)) and applicable law. Our responsibilities under those standards are further described in the Auditor's responsibilities for the audit of the financial statements section of our report. We are independent of the group in accordance with the ethical requirements that are relevant to our audit of the financial statements in the UK, including the FRC's Ethical Standard as applied to listed public interest entities, and we have fulfilled our other ethical responsibilities in accordance with these requirements. We believe that the audit evidence we have obtained is sufficient and appropriate to provide a basis for our opinion.

Conclusions relating to principal risks, going concern and viability statement

We have nothing to report in respect of the following information in the annual report, in relation to which the ISAs (UK) require us to report to you whether we have anything material to add or to draw attention to:

- the disclosures in the annual report[5] [set out on page...] that describe the principal risks and explain how they are being managed or mitigated;

- the directors' confirmation [set out on page...] in the annual report that they have carried out a robust assessment of the principal risks facing the group, including those that would threaten its business model, future performance, solvency or liquidity;

- the directors' statement [set out on page...] in the financial statements about whether they considered it appropriate to adopt the going concern basis of accounting in preparing the financial statements and the directors' identification of any material uncertainties to the group and the parent company's ability to continue to do so over a period of at least 12 months from the date of approval of the financial statements;

- whether the directors' statement relating to going concern required under the Listing Rules in accordance with Listing Rule 9.8.6R(3) is materially inconsistent with our knowledge obtained in the audit; or

- the directors' explanation [set out on page…] in the annual report as to how they have assessed the prospects of the group, over what period they have done so and why they consider that period to be appropriate, and their statement as to whether they have a reasonable expectation that the group will be able to continue in operation and meet its liabilities as they fall due over the period of their assessment, including any related disclosures drawing attention to any necessary qualifications or assumptions.

Key audit matters

Key audit matters are those matters that, in our professional judgment, were of most significance in our audit of the financial statements of the current period and include the most significant assessed risks of material misstatement (whether or not due to fraud) that we identified. These matters included those which had the greatest effect on: the overall audit strategy, the allocation of resources in the audit; and directing the efforts of the engagement team. These matters were addressed in the context of our audit of the financial statements as a whole, and in forming our opinion thereon, and we do not provide a separate opinion on these matters.

[Description of each key audit matter in accordance with ISA (UK) 701.]

Our application of materiality

[Insert an explanation of how the auditor applied the concept of materiality in planning and performing the audit. Such explanation shall specify the threshold used by the auditor as being materiality for the group and parent company financial statements as a whole but may include other relevant disclosures.][6]

An overview of the scope of our audit

[Insert an overview of the scope of the group and parent company audit, including an explanation of how the scope addressed each key audit matter and was influenced by the auditor's application of materiality.]

Other information

The other information comprises the information included in the annual report [set out on pages …][,including [*specify the titles of the other information*] [set out on pages …]], other than the financial statements and our auditor's report thereon. The directors are responsible for the other information. Our opinion on the financial statements does not cover the other information and, except to the extent otherwise explicitly stated in our report, we do not express any form of assurance conclusion thereon. In connection with our audit of the financial statements, our responsibility is to read the other information and, in doing so, consider whether the other information is materially inconsistent with the financial statements or our knowledge obtained in the audit or otherwise appears to be materially misstated. If we identify such material inconsistencies or apparent material misstatements, we are required to determine whether there is a material misstatement in the financial statements or a material misstatement of the other information. If, based on the work we have performed, we conclude that there is a material misstatement of the other information, we are required to report that fact.

We have nothing to report in this regard.

In this context, we also have nothing to report in regard to our responsibility to specifically address the following items in the other information and to report as uncorrected material misstatements of the other information where we conclude that those items meet the following conditions:

- **Fair, balanced and understandable [set out on page ...]** – [the statement given / the explanation as to why the annual report does not include a statement] by the directors that they consider the annual report and financial statements taken as a whole is fair, balanced and understandable and provides the information necessary for shareholders to assess the group's performance, business model and strategy, is materially inconsistent with our knowledge obtained in the audit; or

- **Audit committee reporting [set out on page ...]** – [the section describing the work of the audit committee does not appropriately address matters communicated by us to the audit committee / the explanation as to why the annual report does not include a section describing the work of the audit committee is materially inconsistent with our knowledge obtained in the audit]; or

- **Directors' statement of compliance with the UK Corporate Governance Code [set out on page ...]** – the parts of the directors' statement required under the Listing Rules relating to the company's compliance with the UK Corporate Governance Code containing provisions specified for review by the auditor in accordance with Listing Rule 9.8.10R(2) do not properly disclose a departure from a relevant provision of the UK Corporate Governance Code.

Opinions on other matters prescribed by the Companies Act 2006

In our opinion, the part of the Directors' Remuneration Report to be audited has been properly prepared in accordance with the *Companies Act* 2006.

In our opinion, based on the work undertaken in the course of the audit:

- the information given in the Strategic Report and the Directors' Report for the financial year for which the financial statements are prepared is consistent with the financial statements [and the reports have been prepared in accordance with applicable legal requirements;

- the information about internal control and risk management systems in relation to financial reporting processes and about share capital structures, given in compliance with rules 7.2.5 and 7.2.6 in the Disclosure Rules and Transparency Rules sourcebook made by the Financial Conduct Authority (the FCA Rules), is consistent with the financial statements and has been prepared in accordance with applicable legal requirements[7]; and
- information about the company's corporate governance code and practices and about its administrative, management and supervisory bodies and their committees complies with rules 7.2.2, 7.2.3 and 7.2.7 of the FCA Rules[8].

Matters on which we are required to report by exception

In the light of the knowledge and understanding of the group and the parent company and its environment obtained in the course of the audit, we have not identified material misstatements in:

- the Strategic Report or the Directors' Report; or
- the information about internal control and risk management systems in relation to financial reporting processes and about share capital structures, given in compliance with rules 7.2.5 and 7.2.6 of the FCA Rules[9].

We have nothing to report in respect of the following matters in relation to which the *Companies Act* 2006 requires us to report to you if, in our opinion:

- adequate accounting records have not been kept by the parent company, or returns adequate for our audit have not been received from branches not visited by us;
- the parent company financial statements and the part of the Directors' Remuneration Report to be audited are not in agreement with the accounting records and returns;
- certain disclosures of directors' remuneration specified by law are not made;
- we have not received all the information and explanations we required for our audit; or
- a corporate governance statement has not been prepared by the parent company[10].

Responsibilities of directors

As explained more fully in the Directors' Responsibilities Statement [set out [on page …]], the directors are responsible for the preparation of the financial statements and for being satisfied that they give a true and fair view and for such internal control as the directors determine is necessary to enable the preparation of financial statements that are free from material misstatement, whether due to fraud or error.

In preparing the financial statements, the directors are responsible for assessing the group's and the parent company's ability to continue as a going concern, disclosing, as applicable, matters related to going concern and using the going concern basis of accounting unless the directors either intend to liquidate the group or the parent company or to cease operations, or have no realistic alternative but to do so.

Auditor's responsibilities for the audit of the financial statements

Our objectives are to obtain reasonable assurance about whether the financial statements as a whole are free from material misstatement, whether due to fraud or error, and to issue an auditor's report that includes our opinion. Reasonable assurance is a high level of assurance, but is not a guarantee that an audit conducted in accordance with ISAs (UK) will always detect a material misstatement when it exists. Misstatements can arise from fraud or error and are considered material if, individually or in the aggregate, they could reasonably be expected to influence the economic decisions of users taken on the basis of these financial statements.

[*Explanation as to what extent the audit was considered capable of detecting irregularities, including fraud.*]

A further description of our responsibilities for the audit of the financial statements is located on the Financial Reporting Council's website at www.frc.org.uk/auditorsresponsibilities. This description forms part of our auditor's report.

Other matters which we are required to address

Following the recommendation of the audit committee, we were appointed by [*state by whom or which body the auditor was appointed*] on [*date*] to audit the financial statements for the year ending [*date*] and subsequent financial periods. The period of total uninterrupted engagement is [X] years, covering the years ending [*date*] to [*date*].

The non-audit services prohibited by the FRC's Ethical Standard were not provided to the group or the parent company and we remain independent of the group and the parent company in conducting our audit.

[*Indicate any services, in addition to the audit, which were provided by the firm to the group that have not been disclosed in the financial statements or elsewhere in the annual report.*]

Our audit opinion is consistent with the additional report to the audit committee.

Use of our report

This report is made solely to the company's members, as a body, in accordance with the *Companies Act 2006,* Pt. 16, Ch. 3. Our audit work has been undertaken so that we might state to the company's members those matters we are required to state to them in an auditor's report and for no other purpose.

To the fullest extent permitted by law, we do not accept or assume responsibility to anyone other than the company and the company's members as a body, for our audit work, for this report, or for the opinions we have formed.[11]

[Signature]

John Smith (Senior statutory auditor)

For and on behalf of ABC LLP, Statutory Auditor

Address

Date

[4] The terms used to describe the primary financial statements should be the same as those used by the directors.

[5] The term used to describe the annual report should be the same as that used by the directors.

[6] ISA (UK) 701, paragraph A59-1 includes other disclosures relevant to an explanation of how the auditor applied the context of materiality in planning and performing the audit – e.g.

- Materiality level or levels for those classes of transactions, account balances or disclosures where such materiality levels are lower than materiality for the financial statements as a whole (as described in paragraph 10 of ISA (UK) 320 (Revised June 2016)).

- Performance materiality (as described in paragraph 11 of ISA (UK) 320 (Revised June 2016)).

- Any significant revisions of materiality thresholds that were made as the audit progressed.

- The threshold used for reporting unadjusted differences to the audit committee.

- Significant qualitative considerations relating to the auditor's evaluation of materiality.

[7] Not required where relevant corporate governance information is included in the directors report.

[8] Not required where relevant corporate governance information is included in the directors report.

[9] Not required where relevant corporate governance information is included in the directors report.

[10] Not required where relevant corporate governance information is included in the directors report.

[11] Optional 'Bannerman' paragraph (see **4.28**).

4.24   Directors' responsibility statements

ISA (UK) 700 requires that the auditor's report should refer to the responsibilities of those charged with governance in relation to the financial statements. In the UK this is usually achieved through a combination of standard wording in the audit report and a cross reference to a separate statement of directors' responsibilities (which may be included in the directors' report or appear as a separate statement within the annual report).

Example wording for a description of the directors' responsibilities is given in **Table 3**. Auditors and directors may wish to amend or add to these responsibilities to reflect the particular circumstances of the entity and the legal and regulatory framework within which it prepares its financial statements.

Example wording of a paragraph for inclusion at the foot of the directors' responsibilities statement in situations where financial statements are to be published on a website is given in **Table 4**.

TABLE 3: Example wording of a description of the directors' responsibilities for inclusion in a non-publicly traded company's financial statements, reporting under UK GAAP

The directors are responsible for preparing the annual report and the financial statements in accordance with applicable law and regulations.

Company law requires the directors to prepare financial statements for each financial year. Under that law, the directors have elected to prepare the financial statements in accordance with United Kingdom Generally Accepted Accounting Practice (United Kingdom Accounting Standards and applicable law). Under company law, the directors must not approve the financial statements unless they are satisfied that they give a true and fair view of the state of affairs of the company and of the profit or loss of the company for that period.

In preparing these financial statements, the directors are required to:

* select suitable accounting policies and then apply them consistently;
* make judgments and accounting estimates that are reasonable and prudent;
* [except for small or medium-sized companies] state whether applicable UK Accounting Standards have been followed, subject to any material departures disclosed and explained in the financial statements;
* prepare the financial statements on the going concern basis unless it is inappropriate to presume that the company will continue in business.

The directors are responsible for keeping adequate accounting records that are sufficient to show and explain the company's transactions and disclose with reasonable accuracy at any time the financial position of the company and enable them to ensure that the financial statements comply with the *Companies Act* 2006. They are also responsible for safeguarding the assets of the company and hence for taking reasonable steps for the prevention and detection of fraud and other irregularities.

> **TABLE 4: Example paragraph for inclusion at the foot of the statement of directors' responsibilities where financial statements are to be published on a website**
>
> The directors are responsible for the maintenance and integrity of the corporate and financial information included on the company's website. Legislation in the United Kingdom governing the preparation and dissemination of the financial statements and other information included in annual reports may differ from legislation in other jurisdictions.

4.25   Small companies

4.25.1 Smaller entities and FRS 105

For accounting periods commencing from 1 January 2016, small companies preparing financial statements under UK GAAP will need to apply either FRS 102 *The Financial Reporting Standard applicable in the UK and Republic of Ireland* or where applicable, FRS 105 *The Financial Reporting Standard applicable to the Micro-entities Regime* or FRS 101 *Reduced Disclosure Framework*.

Example wording for an unmodified audit report for a small company preparing financial statements under FRS 102 is given in **Table 5**.

> **TABLE 5: Example unmodified auditor's report for a small company preparing financial statements under UK GAAP**
>
> - *Company qualifies as a small company.*
> - *Company does not prepare group financial statements.*
> - *Company does not prepare a strategic report.*
> - *Financial statements are prepared in accordance with FRS 102 (UK GAAP).*
> - *Description of the auditor's responsibilities for the audit of the financial statements is included by reference to the FRC's website.*
> - *Auditor is not required, and has otherwise not decided, to communicate key audit matters in accordance with ISA (UK) 701.*
>
> **Independent auditor's report to the members of XYZ Limited**
>
> *Opinion*
>
> We have audited the financial statements of [entity name] for the year ended [date] which comprise [state the primary financial statements such as the Profit and Loss Account, the Balance Sheet, the Cash Flow Statement, the Statement of Total Recognised Gains and Losses, the Reconciliation of Movements in Shareholders' Funds[12]] and notes to the financial statements,

including a summary of significant accounting policies. The financial reporting framework that has been applied in their preparation is applicable law and United Kingdom Accounting Standards, including Financial Reporting Standard 102 *The Financial Reporting Standard applicable in the UK and Republic of Ireland* (United Kingdom Generally Accepted Accounting Practice).

In our opinion, the financial statements:

- give a true and fair view of the state of the company's affairs as at … and of its profit [loss] for the year then ended;

- have been properly prepared in accordance with United Kingdom Generally Accepted Accounting Practice; and

- have been prepared in accordance with the requirements of the *Companies Act* 2006.

Basis for opinion

We conducted our audit in accordance with International Standards on Auditing (UK) (ISAs (UK)) and applicable law. Our responsibilities under those standards are further described in the Auditor's responsibilities for the audit of the financial statements section of our report. We are independent of the group in accordance with the ethical requirements that are relevant to our audit of the financial statements in the UK, including the FRC's Ethical Standard [, and the provisions available for small entities, in the circumstances set out in note [x] to the financial statements][13], and we have fulfilled our other ethical responsibilities in accordance with these requirements. We believe that the audit evidence we have obtained is sufficient and appropriate to provide a basis for our opinion.

Conclusions relating to going concern

We have nothing to report in respect of the following matters in relation to which the ISAs (UK) require us to report to you where:

- the directors' use of the going concern basis of accounting in the preparation of the financial statements is not appropriate; or

- the directors have not disclosed in the financial statements any identified material uncertainties that may cast significant doubt about the company's ability to continue to adopt the going concern basis of accounting for a period of at least 12 months from the date when the financial statements are authorised for issue.

Other information

The directors are responsible for the other information. The other information comprises the information included in the annual report[14], other than the financial statements and our auditor's report thereon. Our opinion on the financial statements does not cover the other information and, except to the extent otherwise explicitly stated in our report, we do not express any form of assurance conclusion thereon.

In connection with our audit of the financial statements, our responsibility is to read the other information and, in doing so, consider whether the other information is materially inconsistent with the financial statements or our knowledge obtained in the audit or otherwise appears to be materially misstated. If we identify such material inconsistencies or apparent material misstatements, we are required to determine whether there is a material misstatement in the financial statements or a material misstatement of the other information. If, based on the work we have performed, we conclude that there is a material misstatement of this other information, we are required to report that fact.

We have nothing to report in this regard.

Opinion on other matters prescribed by the Companies Act 2006

In our opinion, based on the work undertaken in the course of the audit:

- the information given in the directors' report for the financial year for which the financial statements are prepared is consistent with the financial statements; and

- the directors' report has been prepared in accordance with applicable legal requirements.

Matters on which we are required to report by exception

In the light of the knowledge and understanding of the company and its environment obtained in the course of the audit, we have not identified material misstatements in the directors' report.

We have nothing to report in respect of the following matters in relation to which the *Companies Act* 2006 requires us to report to you if, in our opinion:

- adequate accounting records have not been kept by the company, or returns adequate for our audit have not been received from branches not visited by us; or

- the company financial statements are not in agreement with the accounting records and returns; or

- certain disclosures of directors' remuneration specified by law are not made; or

- we have not received all the information and explanations we required for our audit; or

- the directors were not entitled to prepare the financial statements in accordance with the small companies regime and take advantage of the exemption in preparing the directors report and from the requirement to prepare a strategic report.

Responsibilities of directors

As explained more fully in the directors' responsibilities statement [set out [on pages …]], the directors are responsible for the preparation of the financial statements and for being satisfied that they give a true and fair view, and for such internal control as the directors determine is necessary to enable the preparation of financial statements that are free from material misstatement, whether due to fraud or error.

In preparing the financial statements, the directors are responsible for assessing the company's ability to continue as a going concern, disclosing, as applicable, matters related to going concern and using the going concern basis of accounting unless the directors either intend to liquidate the company or to cease operations, or have no realistic alternative but to do so.

Auditor's responsibilities for the audit of the financial statements

Our objectives are to obtain reasonable assurance about whether the financial statements as a whole are free from material misstatement, whether due to fraud or error, and to issue an auditor's report that includes our opinion. Reasonable assurance is a high level of assurance, but is not a guarantee that an audit conducted in accordance with ISAs (UK) will always detect a material misstatement when it exists.

Misstatements can arise from fraud or error and are considered material if, individually or in the aggregate, they could reasonably be expected to influence the economic decisions of users taken on the basis of these financial statements.

A further description of our responsibilities for the audit of the financial statements is located on the Financial Reporting Council's website at www. frc.org.uk/auditorsresponsibilities. This description forms part of our auditor's report.

Use of our report

This report is made solely to the company's members, as a body, in accordance with the *Companies Act 2006,* Ch. 3, Pt 16. Our audit work has been undertaken so that we might state to the company's members those matters we are required to state to them in an auditor's report and for no other purpose. To the fullest extent permitted by law, we do not accept or assume responsibility to anyone other than the company and the company's members as a body, for our audit work, for this report, or for the opinions we have formed.[15]

[Signature]

John Smith (Senior statutory auditor)

For and on behalf of ABC LLP, Statutory Auditor

> Address
>
> Date
>
> [12] The terms used to describe the primary financial statements should be the same as those used by the directors.
>
> [13] Include where advantage taken of special provisions available for audits of small entities in the Revised Ethical Standard 2016.
>
> [14] The term used to describe the annual report should be the same as that used by the directors.
>
> [15] Optional 'Bannerman' paragraph (see **4.28**).

4.25.2   The small companies regime

Small companies and groups, to which the small companies regime set out in the *Companies Act* 2006 applies, are subject to reduced accounting and reporting requirements in comparison with large and medium sized companies, and other companies not eligible to apply the small companies regime. The small company limits are set out in **Section 36**. These requirements and the conditions attached to their applicability are set out in the Act itself and in the *Small Companies and Groups (Accounts and Directors' Report Regulations)* 2008 (SI 2008/409) (as amended). These requirements are incorporated into Section A of FRS 102 so any small company entity applying Section A is automatically applying the small companies regime. Where a company prepares its accounts in accordance with the provisions applicable to small companies subject to the small companies regime, the balance sheet must contain a statement to that effect in a prominent position above the signature.

Companies subject to the small companies regime are entitled to take advantage of certain exemptions ('the small companies exemption') relating to the information required to be shown in the directors' report. Where they take advantage of this, the directors' report must include a statement to this effect.

Companies subject to the small companies regime are exempt from the requirement to prepare a strategic report but do not need to make a statement to that effect.

Where the directors of a company:

- have prepared accounts in accordance with the small companies regime; or

- take advantage of the small companies' exemption from the requirement to prepare a strategic report; or

- take advantage of the small companies' exemption in preparing the directors' report and, in the opinion of the auditor, were not entitled to do so, then the auditor must state that fact in his report.

See **Table 5** for example wording.

Changes to the small companies' regime were made by the *Companies, Partnerships and Groups (Accounts and Reports) Regulations* 2015 (SI 2015/980) including the introduction of 'abridged' accounts and changes to filing requirements including the abolition of abbreviated accounts. These changes apply for periods commencing on or after 1 January 2016 but may be applied early by some small companies for periods commencing on or after 1 January 2015. Further details including implications for the auditor's report are given in **Section 6**.

4.25.3 Micro-entities

A new category of small company, the 'micro-entity', was created by amendments to the *Companies Act* 2006 introduced by the *Small Companies (Micro-Entities Accounts) Regulations* 2013 (SI 2013/3008).

Subject to certain exceptions and conditions, a micro-entity is an entity falling within the small companies regime which meets two out of three of the following conditions in each of two consecutive years:

* turnover not more than £632,000;

* total assets not more than £316,000;

* number of employees not more than ten.

Micro-entities are subject to considerably simplified requirements relating to the preparation and filing of accounts. These are set out in the *Small Companies and Groups (Accounts and Directors' Report) Regulations* 2008 as amended by the *Small Companies (Micro-Entities' Accounts) Regulations* 2013. Where a company takes advantage of these provisions, the balance sheet must contain, in a prominent position above the signature, a statement to that effect.

The accounts of a micro-entity are still required to give a true and fair view but the *Companies Act* 2006 has been amended to clarify that, in their consideration of whether the accounts give a true and fair view, the directors must disregard:

* where the accounts contain only micro-entity minimum accounting items, any provisions of accounting standards that would require disclosure of information additional to those items; and

* in relation to a micro-entity minimum accounting item contained in the accounts, any provisions of accounting standards that would require the accounts to contain further information in relation to that item;

but where the accounts contain an item of information additional to the micro-entity minimum accounting items, they must have regard to any provision of an accounting standard which relates to that item.

Audit implications

Most companies entitled to the micro-entity provisions will also claim exemption from audit. However, in situations where an audit is required, in his consideration of whether the accounts give a true and fair view, the auditor must also disregard or have regard to the provisions of accounting standards as set out above.

In his report, the auditor should refer to the micro-entity provisions when describing the applicable reporting framework and in his opinion on the financial statements.

4.26 Reporting on the directors' remuneration report

4.26.1 Introduction

The *Companies Act* 2006 requires quoted companies to prepare a Directors' Remuneration Report for each financial year. Detailed requirements are set out in the *Large and Medium-sized Companies and Groups (Accounts and Reports) Regulations* 2008 (SI 2008/410), Sch. 8 (as amended).

The *Companies Act* 2006, s. 497 requires the auditor of quoted companies to include within his report on the annual accounts his opinion as to whether the 'auditable part' of the Directors' Remuneration Report has been properly prepared in accordance with the Companies Act.

4.26.2 Companies affected by the rules

The regulations apply to 'quoted' companies. A quoted company is defined as a company incorporated under the *Companies Act* 2006:

- whose equity share capital has been included in the official list; or

- is officially listed in an European Economic Area (EEA) state; or

- is admitted to dealing on either the New York Stock Exchange of the exchange known as Nasdaq.

The definition does not include companies traded on the Alternative Investment Market (AIM) or entities with listed debt or non-equity shares only.

4.26.3 The 'auditable part' of the directors' remuneration report

The auditor is required to report on the disclosures in the 'auditable part' of the Directors' Remuneration Report. The 'auditable part' is the part which contains the information required by the *Large and Medium-sized Companies and Groups (Accounts and Reports) Regulations* 2008 (SI 2008/410), Sch. 8, para. 4–17 as amended by the *Large and Medium-sized Companies and Groups (Accounts and Reports) (Amendment) Regulations* 2013 (SI 2013/1981).

4.26.4 Reporting on the directors' remuneration report

The auditor reports on the Directors' Remuneration Report as part of his report on the financial statements. As he is not required to audit all of the information in the Directors' Remuneration Report, he must clearly identify the elements that have been audited. If this cannot be done by cross-reference, the auditor should set out the particulars that have been audited within the auditor's report. It is not satisfactory, for example, for the auditor to describe what he has audited as 'the disclosures required by Pt. 3 of Sch. 8 to the *Large and Medium-sized Companies and Groups (Accounts and Reports) Regulations* 2008 (SI 2008/410)'.

An example of the auditor's report in relation to the Directors' Remuneration Report is included in **Table 2**, although it should be noted that the requirement is not restricted to reports on premium listed companies.

4.27 Electronic publication of audit reports

4.27.1 Background

APB Bulletin 2001/1 *The Electronic Publication of Auditors' Reports* was published in response to changes in company law enabling companies to meet their statutory reporting obligations to shareholders by distributing financial statements and certain other reports electronically, or by posting them on a website. This Bulletin was withdrawn in March 2012 as references contained in it were outdated and an updated version of much of the principal guidance is included in the Appendix to ISA (UK) 720 (Revised June 2016).

The *Companies Act* 2006 set out additional requirements to facilitate electronic communication with shareholders. It is discussed in **4.27.2**.

4.27.2 Electronic publication of audit reports

Companies and other entities now routinely publish annual financial statements on websites as well as in hard copy. In these circumstances, publication of information on the website and the maintenance of the website including checking the accuracy and completeness of information provided is the responsibility of the entity, not the auditor. In addition, as information published on websites may be available in many countries with different legal requirements, it is the responsibility of the entity to establish and ensure it complies with relevant legislation governing the preparation and dissemination of financial statements.

It is important to note that the auditor's duty of care is not extended solely as a result of his report being published in electronic rather than hard-copy form.

Additional work to provide assurance on the integrity of an entity's website would not normally be considered to be part of an audit engagement and is not covered here.

Directors' responsibilities

The fact that financial statements are reproduced or published electronically does not change the responsibilities of the directors concerning preparation, dissemination and signing of financial statements. Auditors may ask directors to include a statement in the annual report, usually as part of the directors' responsibilities statement, explaining the directors' responsibilities in respect of financial statements published on a website. Example wording is given in **Table 4**.

4.28 The Bannerman case

4.28.1 Introduction

As a result of the legal judgment in the Scottish Court of Session in the *Bannerman* case, auditors have considered whether they should include additional wording in their audit reports to protect against exposure to third party claims.

In the *Bannerman* case, the judge held that, although there was no direct contact between Bannerman (the auditor) and the third party, knowledge gained by Bannerman through the course of his normal audit work was sufficient, in the absence of any disclaimer, to create a duty of care towards the third party. The absence of a disclaimer was an important circumstance supporting the finding of a duty of care by the judge.

4.28.2 ICAEW Guidance

Having obtained advice from Leading Counsel the ICAEW issued Technical Release Audit 1/03 *The Audit Report and Auditors' Duty of Care to Third Parties* in January 2003. The Technical Release was clear that the responsibilities of the auditor were not changed as a result either of the *Bannerman* case or the release of Audit 1/03 and stated that 'the best risk management policy is for firms to take the steps that are necessary to carry out quality audits'. It did, however, provide a recommended form of words for inclusion in statutory audit reports to minimise the auditor's risk of unintentional exposure to liability. This form of wording has been almost universally adopted since then by UK auditors.

Following the issue of ISA (UK) 700 and the consequent changes in the format of the audit report the ICAEW, again following consultation with Leading Counsel, issued an update to Audit 1/03 in May 2018.

4.28.3 Recommended wording and position in report

It is clear that the auditor automatically assumes responsibility for the audit report to the shareholders as a body. The *Bannerman* case indicates that the absence of a disclaimer may, depending on the facts of the case, make the auditor liable to third parties.

Advice obtained by the ICAEW suggests that the disclaimer is likely to be most effective if it appears prominently within the report and if auditors adopt a consistent approach. The ICAEW therefore suggests the following wording be included in a separate section of the audit report entitled 'Use of [our/my] report', as the last section of the report immediately above the signature.

'*Use of our report*

This report is made solely to the company's members, as a body, in accordance with Chapter 3 of Part 16 of the *Companies Act* 2006. Our audit work has been undertaken so that we might state to the company's members those matters we are required to state to them in an auditor's report and for no other purpose. To the fullest extent permitted by law, we do not accept or assume responsibility to anyone other than the company and the company's members as a body, for our audit work, for this report, or for the opinions we have formed.'

The wording, or a variation of it, may also be suitable for inclusion in other reports issued by auditors, (except in the case of ISA (UK) 800 reports where a similar disclaimer is already incorporated into the example report wording provided in the standard).

It is important to note that the inclusion of this paragraph in audit reports does not mean that the auditor can never agree to take on responsibilities to third parties, or that they may inadvertently assume a duty of care through subsequent comments or actions inconsistent with the wording of this paragraph. Where the auditor is aware of circumstances which may give rise to a duty of care, he should disclaim this responsibility by writing a letter to the third party in line with guidance in Technical Release Audit 4/00 (see **Section 40**).

4.28.4   Engagement letters

The Technical Release also contains suggested wording for inclusion in an engagement letter, to inform clients about the clarification paragraph in the audit report. This is not mandatory, and is set out in **Section 14**.

4.28.5   Further developments

In February 2015, the High Court found in favour of Grant Thornton (GT) in relation to a negligence claim brought against it by Barclays Bank. The dispute arose after Barclays relied on two non-statutory audits carried out for the Von Essen Hotels Group (VEH) in 2006 and 2007 in continuing to fund VEH under a loan facility. The bank alleged GT had been negligent in producing the reports because it failed to uncover fraudulent overstatements of VEH's financial position, causing Barclays financial loss when VEH became insolvent and could not repay the loan.

Each of the reports produced by GT included a *Bannerman* style disclaimer which stated that the report was made solely to VEH's director and that the auditor did not accept responsibility to anyone other than VEH and its director for its audit work. Barclays argued that this disclaimer was 'unreasonable'. The judge, however, considered the disclaimer was 'clear on its face', 'could not have been misunderstood' and 'would have been read and understood by anyone at Barclays who had read the two page reports'. He noted that 'Grant Thornton made it clear that it was not prepared to assume responsibility to Barclays in respect of these reports. There was nothing unreasonable in that stance, as between two sophisticated commercial parties, where the approach of auditors limiting their responsibilities is well known'.

This is the first case in which the lawfulness of a *Bannerman* clause in an auditor's report had been considered. Although it related to non-statutory rather than statutory financial statements, it illustrates the potential value of a *Bannerman* clause, clearly identifying the addressee of the report and limiting or excluding liability to others by way of a prominent and clearly expressed disclaimer.

5 Modified auditor's reports

5.1 Introduction

In **Section 4**, the content and format of unmodified auditor's reports was considered. Where the auditor is unable to issue an unmodified report, his report may follow a number of formats, which are discussed in this section.

Standards relating to modified auditor's reports are provided by ISA (UK) 705 (Revised June 2016) *Modifications to the Opinion in the Independent Auditor's Report* and ISA (UK) 706 (Revised June 2016) *Emphasis of Matter Paragraphs and Other Matter Paragraphs in the Independent Auditor's Report*. Example wording in respect of modified opinions regarding statutory other information is also contained in the FRC's Bulletin issued in October 2016 *Compendium of illustrative auditor's reports on United Kingdom private sector financial statements for periods commencing on or after 17 June 2016*. Further example reports can be found in *Preparing Audit Reports*, available online from Croner-i Tax and Accounting. ICAEW Audit and Assurance Faculty helpsheets also provide guidance and example wording.

The current versions of ISA (UK) 705 (Revised June 2016) and ISA (UK) 706 (Revised June 2016) are effective for the audit of financial statements for periods commencing on or after 17 June 2016.

Whilst the revisions to the standards in 2016 did not significantly change the basic form of modified audit opinions (as set out in **5.4**), they did result in significant changes to the presentation of information in the auditor's report. One significant change was in relation to material uncertainties in respect of going concern, which are now dealt with under this heading in a separate section of the report (see **Section 11**) rather than as an 'Emphasis of Matter' in accordance with ISA (UK) 706.

5.2 Modifications

An auditor's report may be considered to be modified in the following situations:

- matters that affect the auditor's opinion on the financial statements (see **5.4**):

- disclaimer of opinion;
- adverse opinion;
- qualified opinion;

- matters that affect the auditor's opinion on other information (such as consistency of the strategic report and directors' report and their compliance with legal requirements, the directors' remuneration report, or separate corporate governance statement);

- matters that do not affect the auditor's opinions:

  - emphasis of matter;
  - other matter; and

- matters that the auditor is required to report by exception.

5.3 Modification to the auditor's opinion on the financial statements

Modified opinions on financial statements are issued where either:

- the auditor concludes that, based on the evidence obtained, the financial statements as a whole are not free from material misstatement; or

- the auditor is unable to obtain sufficient appropriate audit evidence to conclude that the financial statements are free from material misstatement.

5.3.1 Financial statements not free from material misstatement

A material misstatement of the financial statements may arise in relation to:

(a) the appropriateness of the selected accounting policies (for example, when the selected accounting policies are not consistent with the applicable financial reporting framework);

(b) the application of the selected accounting policies (for example, when management has not applied the selected accounting policies consistently with the financial reporting framework, including when management has not applied the selected accounting policies consistently between periods or to similar transactions and events); or

(c) the appropriateness or adequacy of disclosures in the financial statements (for example, when the financial statements do not include all of the disclosures required by the applicable financial reporting framework).

5.3.2   Inability to obtain sufficient appropriate audit evidence

The auditor's inability to obtain sufficient appropriate audit evidence (also called a limitation on the scope of the audit) may arise due to:

- circumstances beyond the control of the entity (e.g. the entity's accounting records have been destroyed);

- circumstances relating to the nature or timing of the auditor's work (e.g. the timing of the auditor's appointment is such that he is unable to observe the counting of the physical inventories); or

- limitations imposed by management (e.g. management prevents the auditor from observing the counting of the physical inventories).

An inability to perform a specific procedure does not limit the scope of the audit if the auditor is able to obtain sufficient appropriate audit evidence by performing alternative procedures. Where limitations are imposed by management, the auditor also needs to consider further implications, such as the auditor's assessment of fraud risks and consideration of engagement continuance.

5.3.3   Imposed limitation of scope

ISA (UK) 705 (Revised June 2016) refers to cases where directors or management restrict access to information such that an effective audit cannot be carried out. This may occur where there is a statutory requirement for an audit but the owners are indifferent to the requirement, for example:

- an owner-managed business; or

- an overseas controlled entity which requires an on-shore report.

In these cases, the owners or directors may be prepared to accept a disclaimed opinion for a nominal fee so long as they have a set of accounts that may be filed at Companies House.

If the auditor is aware, before accepting an audit engagement that the directors of the entity, or those who appoint its auditor, will impose a limitation on the scope of his work, which he considers is likely to result in the need to issue a qualified opinion or disclaimer of opinion on the financial statements, ISA (UK) 210 (Revised June 2016) *Agreeing the Terms of Audit Engagements* requires that he should not accept that engagement.

Where the auditor becomes aware after accepting an engagement of such a restriction, ISA (UK) 705 (Revised June 2016) requires that he should request management to remove the limitation. If management refuses to remove the limitation, he communicates the matter to those charged with governance and determines whether it is possible to perform alternative procedures to obtain sufficient appropriate audit evidence. If he cannot obtain sufficient appropriate evidence:

(a) if he concludes that the possible effects of undetected misstatements, if any, could be material but not pervasive, he qualifies his opinion; or

(b) if he concludes that the possible effects of undetected misstatements, if any, could be both material and pervasive so that a qualified opinion would not be enough to convey the seriousness of the situation, he withdraws from the audit. If withdrawal before issuing an opinion is not possible, he disclaims an opinion on the financial statements.

Factors he would take into account in deciding on the most appropriate course of action are the extent to which any work is complete and what is in the public interest.

Where the auditor does withdraw from the engagement as a result of the imposition of such a limitation, this may be a matter for the auditor to consider including in any statement of circumstances made in connection with his ceasing to hold office as auditor, or in response to professional enquiries made by the possible successor auditor.

In addition, before withdrawing, the auditor needs to communicate to those charged with governance any matters regarding misstatements identified during the audit that would have given rise to a modification of the opinion (see **5.10**). **Section 38** gives guidance on statements to be made on cessation as auditor.

5.4 Types of modified opinion

There are three possible outcomes, as illustrated in **Table 1**:

- *'qualified' opinion*, where the auditor concludes that the effects of the misstatements, individually or in aggregate, are material but not pervasive to the financial statements; or where the auditor is unable to obtain sufficient appropriate audit evidence on which to base his opinion, but he concludes that the possible effects of undetected misstatements, if any, could be material but not pervasive;

- *'adverse' opinion*, where the auditor concludes that the effects of misstatements, either individually or in aggregate, are both material and pervasive to the financial statements. Pervasive effects are those that in the auditor's judgment are not confined to specific elements or items of the financial statements, or if so confined represent a substantial proportion of the financial statements, or in relation to disclosures, are fundamental to users' understanding of the financial statements; and

- *'disclaimer' of opinion*, where the auditor is unable to obtain sufficient audit evidence on which to base an opinion on the financial statements and the possible effects of undetected misstatements could be both material and pervasive; or (rarely) where, despite having obtained sufficient audit evidence about each individual uncertainty, it is not possible to form an opinion on the financial statements due to the potential interaction of multiple uncertainties and their possible cumulative effect on the financial statements.

The effects of misstatements are considered to be pervasive when they are not limited to specific elements or items in the financial statements or, if they are so limited, the affected items represent a substantial proportion of the financial statements. In addition, misstatements in respect of disclosures will be pervasive if they are considered to be fundamental to a user's understanding of the financial statements.

TABLE 1: Types of modified opinion

Effect	Inability to obtain sufficient appropriate audit evidence	Financial statements are materially misstated
Material but not pervasive	Qualified opinion	
Material and pervasive	Disclaimer	Adverse

5.4.1 Adverse opinions or disclaimers of opinion

Where the auditor has expressed an adverse opinion or disclaimed an opinion on the financial statements as a whole, the auditor cannot issue an unmodified opinion on a part of the financial statements under the same financial reporting framework. To include an unmodified opinion in the same report in these circumstances would contradict the auditor's adverse opinion or disclaimer of opinion on the financial statements as a whole.

This does not, however, prevent the auditor from issuing a disclaimer of an opinion regarding the results of operations and cash flows, and an unmodified opinion on the balance sheet position. This is not a contradiction since the auditor has not expressed a disclaimer of opinion on the financial statements as a whole.

5.5 Form and content of the audit report when opinion is modified

5.5.1 Opinion paragraph

When the auditor modifies the audit opinion, the auditor shall use the heading *Qualified Opinion*, *Adverse Opinion*, or *Disclaimer of Opinion*, as appropriate, for the opinion paragraph.

5.5.2 Qualified opinion

When the auditor expresses a qualified opinion due to a material misstatement in the financial statements, he states that, in his opinion, except for the effects of the matter(s) described in the Basis for Qualified Opinion paragraph:

(a) the financial statements present fairly, in all material respects (or give a true and fair view of), when reporting in accordance with a fair presentation framework; or

(b) the financial statements have been prepared, in all material respects, in accordance with the applicable financial reporting framework, when reporting in accordance with a compliance framework.

When the modification arises from an inability to obtain sufficient appropriate audit evidence, the auditor uses the corresponding phrase 'except for the possible effects of the matter(s) ...' for the modified opinion.

5.5.3 Adverse opinion

When the auditor expresses an adverse opinion, he states that, in the auditor's opinion, because of the significance of the matter(s) described in the Basis for Adverse Opinion paragraph:

(a) the financial statements do not present fairly (or give a true and fair view of) when reporting in accordance with a fair presentation framework; or

(b) the financial statements have not been prepared, in all material respects, in accordance with the applicable financial reporting framework when reporting in accordance with a compliance framework.

5.5.4 Disclaimer of opinion

When the auditor disclaims an opinion due to an inability to obtain sufficient appropriate audit evidence, he is required to state that:

(a) because of the significance of the matter(s) described in the Basis for Disclaimer of Opinion paragraph, the auditor has not been able to obtain sufficient appropriate audit evidence to provide a basis for an audit opinion on the financial statements; and accordingly

(b) he does not express an opinion on the accompanying financial statements.

He also amends the introductory statement of his report to state that he was engaged to audit the financial statements, rather than that he has audited the financial statements.

5.5.5 Basis for modification paragraph

Where the auditor modifies his opinion, the auditor's report should include a paragraph, immediately after the opinion paragraph, describing the matter giving rise to the modification. This replaces the *Basis for Opinion* paragraph that would be in an unmodified report and should be headed *Basis for Qualified Opinion/Adverse Opinion/Disclaimer of Opinion*, as appropriate.

If there is a material misstatement of the financial statements that relates to specific amounts in the financial statements (including quantitative disclosures), the basis for modification paragraph should include a description and quantification of the financial effects of the misstatement, unless impracticable. For example, the auditor may be able to quantify the effects on income tax, income before taxes, net income and equity if inventory is overstated.

If it is not practicable to quantify the financial effects, this should be stated in this paragraph.

If there is a material misstatement that relates to narrative disclosures, the basis for modification paragraph should include an explanation of how the disclosures are misstated.

If there is a material misstatement of the financial statements that relates to the non-disclosure of information required to be disclosed, the auditor shall:

(a) discuss the non-disclosure with those charged with governance (see **5.10**);

(b) describe in the basis for modification paragraph the nature of the omitted information; and

(c) unless prohibited by law or regulation, include the omitted disclosures, provided it is practicable to do so and the auditor has obtained sufficient appropriate audit evidence about the omitted information.

If the modification results from an inability to obtain sufficient appropriate audit evidence, the auditor includes in the basis for modification paragraph the reasons for that inability.

When the auditor expresses a qualified or adverse opinion, the statement about whether the audit evidence obtained is sufficient and appropriate to provide a basis for the auditor's opinion should be amended to include the word 'qualified' or 'adverse', as appropriate.

When the auditor disclaims an opinion on the financial statements, the auditor's report should not include a reference to the section of the auditor's report where the auditor's responsibilities are described; nor a statement about whether the audit evidence obtained is sufficient and appropriate to provide a basis for the auditor's opinion.

Even if the auditor has expressed an adverse opinion or disclaimed an opinion on the financial statements, he should still describe in the basis for modification paragraph the reasons for any other matters of which the auditor is aware that would have required a modification to the opinion, and the effects thereof.

5.5.6 Description of auditor's responsibilities when the auditor disclaims an opinion

When the auditor disclaims an opinion due to an inability to obtain sufficient appropriate audit evidence, he amends the description of the auditor's responsibilities to include only:

(a) a statement that the auditor's responsibility is to conduct an audit of the entity's financial statements in accordance with ISAs (UK) and to issue an auditor's report;

(b) a statement that, however, because of the matter(s) described in the Basis for Disclaimer of Opinion section, he was not able to obtain sufficient appropriate audit evidence to provide a basis for an audit opinion on the financial statements; and

(c) the statement about auditor independence and other ethical responsibilities by ISA (UK) 700 (Revised June 2016).

5.5.7 Other considerations when the auditor disclaims an opinion

When the auditor disclaims an opinion on the financial statements, the auditor's report does not include a Key Audit Matters section (see **4.11**) or an Other Information section (see **Section 34**), except in the following circumstances, where he is still required to do so:

- for audits of financial statements of public interest entities, the auditor is required to communicate certain key audit matters in accordance with ISA (UK) 701 *Communicating key audit matters in the independent auditor's report*;

- for entities incorporated under the Companies Acts, the auditor is required to report in an Other Information section on the strategic report, the directors' report and, where one is prepared, the separate corporate governance statement in accordance with ISA (UK) 720 (Revised June 2016) *The Auditor's Responsibilities Relating to Other Information*; and

- for entities that are required, and those that choose voluntarily, to report on how they have applied the UK Corporate Governance Code, the auditor is required to report in an Other Information section on certain aspects of the entity's compliance with the UK Corporate Governance Code and the Listing Rules in accordance with ISA (UK) 720 (Revised June 2016).

5.5.8   Other implications of modified opinions

Where a matter gives rise to a qualified or adverse opinion or disclaimer of opinion on the financial statements, the auditor will need to consider the implications for his opinions on the strategic report and directors' report and, in particular, whether he is able to form an opinion as to whether the strategic report complies with legal requirements. Modifications may also need to be made to these opinions.

The auditor will also need to consider the implications for his reporting responsibilities in relation to other information and other matters on which he is required to report by exception. For example, a limitation in scope may well reflect inadequacies in a company's accounting records and will always result in the auditor concluding that he has not received all the information and explanations he requires.

5.5.9   ICAEW guidance

The Audit and Assurance Faculty of the ICAEW has issued a series of helpsheets covering the preparation of audit reports in a variety of situations. Each helpsheet explains how a 'standard' audit report, as illustrated in the FRC's Bulletin *Compendium of illustrative audit reports*, would be adapted in the relevant circumstances. Included in this series is a helpsheet *Preparing an audit report with a disclaimer of opinion*.

5.6   Examples

In the example in **Table 2**, the auditor was unable to obtain sufficient appropriate audit evidence, since the entity restricted his access to information. The restriction is considered by the auditor to be both material and pervasive such that he is unable to form an opinion on the financial statements and issues a report disclaiming an opinion on the financial statements. In this example the auditor's opinions in respect of the strategic report and directors' report are unmodified (see **5.5.8**).

The example in **Table 3** is qualified 'except for' any adjustments that might have been found to be necessary, had it been possible to obtain sufficient evidence concerning stock. The limitation on the scope of his work was determined by the auditor to be material but not pervasive to the financial statements.

The example in **Table 4** is an adverse opinion where the auditor has identified a misstatement, the possible effect of which is both material and pervasive to the financial statements. In this example, the auditor's opinions in respect of the strategic report and directors' report are unmodified (see **5.5.8**).

Table 5 is an example of a qualified opinion, indicating that the opinion is expressed except for the effects of the matter giving rise to the material misstatement.

TABLE 2: Extract from report with disclaimer of opinion: auditor unable to obtain sufficient appropriate audit evidence

Disclaimer of opinion

We were engaged to audit the financial statements of ...

We do not express an opinion on the financial statements of the company. Because of the significance of the matter described in the Basis for disclaimer of opinion section of our report, we have not been able to obtain sufficient appropriate audit evidence to provide a basis for an audit opinion on these financial statements.

Basis for disclaimer of opinion

The group's investment in its joint venture ABC Co is carried at £x in the group's consolidated statement of financial position which represents over 90% of the group's net assets at 31 December 20... We were not allowed access to ABC Co's management, accounting records or auditors and as a result we were unable to determine whether any adjustments were necessary in respect of the group's proportional share of ABC Co's assets that it controls jointly, its proportional share of liabilities for which it is jointly responsible or its proportionate share of ABC Co's income and expenses for the financial year.

Opinion on other matter prescribed by the Companies Act 2006

Notwithstanding our disclaimer of an opinion on the financial statements, in our opinion, based on the work undertaken in the course of the audit:

- the information given in the [strategic report and the] directors' report for the financial year for which the financial statements are prepared is consistent with the financial statements; and

- [the strategic report and] the directors' report have been prepared in accordance with applicable legal requirements.

Matters on which we are required to report by exception

In the light of the knowledge and understanding of the company and its environment obtained in the course of the audit, we have not identified material misstatements in [the strategic report or] the directors' report.

Arising from the limitation of our work referred to above, we have not obtained all the information and explanations that we considered necessary for the purpose of our audit.

We have nothing to report in respect of the following matters where the *Companies Act* 2006 requires us to report to you if, in our opinion:

- adequate accounting records have not been kept or returns adequate for our audit have not been received from branches not visited by us; or

- the financial statements are not in agreement with the accounting records and returns; or

- certain disclosures of directors' remuneration specified by law are not made.

TABLE 3: Extract from report with qualified opinion – auditor unable to obtain sufficient appropriate evidence

Qualified opinion

We have audited the financial statements of ...

In our opinion, except for the possible effects of the matters described in the Basis for qualified opinion section of our report, the financial statements:

- give a true and fair view of the state of the company's affairs as at [date] and of its profit [loss] for the year then ended;

- have been properly prepared in accordance with United Kingdom Generally Accepted Accounting Practice; and

- have been prepared in accordance with the requirements of the *Companies Act* 2006.

Basis for qualified opinion

With respect to stock having a carrying amount of £X the audit evidence available to us was limited because we did not observe the counting of the physical stock as at 31 December 20X1, since that date was prior to our appointment as auditor of the company. Owing to the nature of the company's records, we were unable to obtain sufficient appropriate audit evidence regarding the stock quantities by using other audit procedures.

We conducted our audit in accordance with International Standards on Auditing (UK) (ISAs (UK)) and applicable law. Our responsibilities under those standards are further described in the Auditor's responsibilities for the audit of the financial statements section of our report. We are independent of the company in accordance with the ethical requirements that are relevant to our audit of the financial statements in the UK, including the FRC's Ethical

Standard, and we have fulfilled our other ethical responsibilities in accordance with these requirements. We believe that the audit evidence we have obtained is sufficient and appropriate to provide a basis for our qualified opinion.

Opinion on other matter prescribed by the Companies Act 2006

In our opinion, based on the work undertaken in the course of the audit:

- the information given in the [strategic report and the] directors' report for the financial year for which the financial statements are prepared is consistent with the financial statements; and

- [the strategic report and] the directors' report have been prepared in accordance with applicable legal requirements.

Matters on which we are required to report by exception

In the light of the knowledge and understanding of the company and its environment obtained in the course of the audit, we have not identified material misstatements in [the strategic report or] the directors' report.

In respect solely of the limitation on our work relating to stock, described above:

- we have not obtained all the information and explanations that we considered necessary for the purpose of our audit; and

- we were unable to determine whether adequate accounting records had been kept.

We have nothing to report in respect of the following matters where the *Companies Act* 2006 requires us to report to you if, in our opinion:

- returns adequate for our audit have not been received from branches not visited by us; or

- the financial statements are not in agreement with the accounting records and returns; or

- certain disclosures of directors' remuneration specified by law are not made.

TABLE 4: Extract from report with adverse opinion: misstatements material and pervasive

Adverse opinion

We have audited the financial statements of . . .

In our opinion, because of the significance of the matter described in the Basis for adverse opinion section of our report, the financial statements:

- do not give a true and fair view of the state of the company's affairs as at 31 December 20 ... and of its profit for the year then ended;

- have not been properly prepared in accordance with United Kingdom Generally Accepted Accounting Practice; and

- have not been prepared in accordance with the requirements of the *Companies Act* 2006.

Basis for adverse opinion

As more fully explained in note X to the financial statements, no provision has been made for losses expected to arise on certain long-term contracts currently in progress, as the directors consider that such losses should be off-set against amounts recoverable on other long-term contracts. In our opinion, provision should be made for foreseeable losses on individual contracts as required by [*specify accounting standard*]. If losses had been so recognised the effect would have been to reduce the carrying amount of contract work in progress by £X, the deferred tax liability by £Y and the profit for the year and retained earnings at 31 December 20X1 by £Z.

We conducted our audit in accordance with International Standards on Auditing (UK) (ISAs (UK)) and applicable law. Our responsibilities under those standards are further described in the Auditor's responsibilities for the audit of the financial statements section of our report. We are independent of the company in accordance with the ethical requirements that are relevant to our audit of the financial statements in the UK, including the FRC's Ethical Standard, and we have fulfilled our other ethical responsibilities in accordance with these requirements. We believe that the audit evidence we have obtained is sufficient and appropriate to provide a basis for our adverse opinion.

Opinion on other matter prescribed by the Companies Act 2006

Notwithstanding our adverse opinion on the financial statements, in our opinion, based on the work undertaken in the course of the audit:

- the information given in the [strategic report and the] directors' report for the financial year for which the financial statements are prepared is consistent with the financial statements; and

- [the strategic report and] the directors' report have been prepared in accordance with applicable legal requirements.

Matters on which we are required to report by exception

In the light of the knowledge and understanding of the company and its environment obtained in the course of the audit, we have not identified material misstatements in [the strategic report or] the directors' report.

We have nothing to report in respect of the following matters where the *Companies Act* 2006 requires us to report to you if, in our opinion:

- adequate accounting records have not been kept or returns adequate for our audit have not been received from branches not visited by us; or

- the financial statements are not in agreement with the accounting records and returns; or

- certain disclosures of directors' remuneration specified by law are not made; or

- we have not received all the information and explanations we required for our audit.

TABLE 5: Extract from report with qualified opinion: misstatements material but not pervasive

Qualified opinion

We have audited the financial statements ...

In our opinion, except for the effects of the matter described in the Basis for Qualified Opinion section of our report, the financial statements:

- give a true and fair view of the state of the company's affairs as at 31 December 20 ... and of its profit for the year then ended;

- have been properly prepared in accordance with United Kingdom Generally Accepted Accounting Practice; and

- have been prepared in accordance with the requirements of the *Companies Act* 2006.

Basis for qualified opinion

Included in the debtors shown on the balance sheet is an amount of £ ... due from a company which has ceased trading. XYZ plc has no security for this debt. In our opinion, the company is unlikely to receive any payment and full provision of £ ... should have been made. Accordingly, debtors should be reduced by £Y, the deferred tax liability should be reduced by £X and profit for the year and retained earnings should be reduced by £Z.

We conducted our audit in accordance with International Standards on Auditing (UK) (ISAs (UK)) and applicable law. Our responsibilities under those standards are further described in the Auditor's responsibilities for the audit of the financial statements section of our report. We are independent of the company in accordance with the ethical requirements that are relevant to our audit of the financial statements in the UK, including the FRC's Ethical Standard, and we have fulfilled our other ethical responsibilities in accordance with these requirements. We believe that the audit evidence we have obtained is sufficient and appropriate to provide a basis for our qualified opinion.

5.6.1 Modifications to opinions on other matters

Where the auditor is unable to give an unqualified opinion regarding the consistency of the information given in the strategic report (where applicable) and the directors' report with the financial statements or where the strategic report (where applicable) or director's report do not comply with legal requirements, he should explain the reason for this and modify his opinion in the auditor's report accordingly. Where the opinion is modified, the Other information section, which describes the auditor's responsibilities in relation to other information, should conclude with a reference to the fact that the auditor has identified a material misstatement in the other information. The opinion required under the Companies Act should be qualified with a description of the matter giving rise to the qualification in a separate Basis for qualified opinion section immediately below the opinion. The Matters on which we are required to report by exception section will also need to contain a qualification regarding the identification of a material misstatement. See example wording in **Table 6**.

TABLE 6: Example qualified opinion on consistency of strategic report or directors' report:

Other information

...

As described in the Basis for qualified opinion on other matters prescribed by the *Companies Act* 2006 section of our report we have concluded that a material misstatement of the other information exists.

Qualified opinion on other matters prescribed by the Companies Act 2006

Except for the matter described in the Basis for qualified opinion on other matters prescribed by the *Companies Act* 2006 section of our report, in our opinion, based on the work undertaken in the course of the audit:

• the information given in the strategic report and the directors' report for the financial year for which the financial statements are prepared is consistent with the financial statements; and

• the strategic report and the directors' report have been prepared in accordance with applicable legal requirements.

Basis for qualified opinion on other matters prescribed by the Companies Act 2006

Based on the work undertaken in the course of the audit, the information given in the [*describe location*] of the [strategic/directors'] report is not consistent with the financial statements.

[*Description of material misstatement of statutory other information*]

Matters on which we are required to report by exception

Except for the material misstatement described in the Basis for qualified opinion on other matters prescribed by the *Companies Act* 2006 section of our report, in the light of the knowledge and understanding of the company and its environment obtained in the course of the audit, we have not identified material misstatements in the strategic report or the directors' report.

In the case of a quoted company, where the auditor is unable to provide an opinion as to whether the part of the Directors' Remuneration Report to be audited has been properly prepared in accordance with the *Companies Act* 2006, he should explain the reason for this and modify his opinion in the auditor's report accordingly. The auditor must also include in his report, so far as he is reasonably able to do so, a statement giving the required particulars.

5.7 Emphasis of matter

In some circumstances, the auditor may consider it necessary to draw the user's attention to a matter that is already presented or disclosed in the financial statements but which is, in the auditor's judgment, of such importance that it is fundamental to the user's understanding of the financial statements. The auditor does this by adding an Emphasis of Matter paragraph to his audit report to highlight the matter. Typical examples are:

- an uncertainty relating to the future outcome of major litigation;

- a subsequent event occurring between the date of the financial statements and the date of the auditor's report;

- early (permitted) application of a new accounting standard that has a pervasive effect on the financial statements in advance of its effective date; and

- a major catastrophe that has had a significant effect on the entity's financial position.

An Emphasis of Matter paragraph should not be used where the matter has been determined as a key audit matter for communication in the audit report (see **Section 4**). (In other words, where a matter is a key matter and key matters are reported separately in the audit report then the auditor cannot use Emphasis of Matter as an alternative presentation.) However, the application material notes that in the UK, law or regulation may require an Emphasis of Matter paragraph relating to something that is also disclosed as a key matter – in which case, the auditor is not precluded from doing so.

Where the auditor decides to include an Emphasis of Matter paragraph in his report, he:

- uses a separate section with an appropriate heading, such as *Emphasis of Matter*;

- includes a clear reference to the matter being emphasised and to where the relevant disclosures can be found in the financial statements; and

- indicates that the auditor's opinion is not modified in respect of the matter.

An Emphasis of Matter paragraph should only refer to information presented or disclosed in the financial statements and should not provide additional information, explanation or interpretation.

In order to provide further context, the heading for the paragraph may include an indication of the nature of the matter to which it relates e.g. 'Emphasis of matter – subsequent event'.

Table 7 gives an example of an Emphasis of Matter paragraph.

Unlike the previous version of the ISA, ISA (UK) 570 (Revised June 2016) *Going Concern* does not require the use of an Emphasis of Matter paragraph where there is a material uncertainty related to going concern that is adequately described in the financial statements. Instead this will be dealt with in the auditor's report by inclusion of a separate section in the report headed 'Material Uncertainty in Relation to Going Concern' (see **11.12.4**).

Where the use of the going concern basis is inappropriate and the entity is required, or elects, to prepare its financial statements on a basis other than that of going concern, the auditor may consider it appropriate or necessary to include an Emphasis of Matter paragraph in his report to draw the user's attention to the basis in which the financial statements have been prepared and the reasons for its use.

An Emphasis of Matter paragraph is not a substitute for expressing a qualified or adverse opinion, or for disclaiming an opinion, where the circumstances of the engagement require it.

TABLE 7: Example Emphasis of Matter paragraph:

Emphasis of Matter

We draw attention to note [..] to the financial statements which describes [*brief summary of the matter*]. Our opinion is not modified in this respect.

5.8 Other matter paragraphs

Where the auditor considers that a matter other than those presented or disclosed in the financial statements is relevant to the user's understanding of the audit, and that it is necessary to communicate it then ISA (UK) 706 (Revised June 2016) requires that this be done by the inclusion of a paragraph in the auditor's report setting out details of the matter. The information should be included in a separate section under the heading *Other Matter* or another appropriate heading.

An Other Matter paragraph may not be used where ISA (UK) 701 applies and the auditor has determined that the matter is a key matter to be communicated in the audit report.

Other Matter paragraphs may be used:

- when the matter has not been determined to be a key audit matter to be communicated in the auditor's report;

- where the entity has prepared another set of financial statements (e.g. consolidated financial statements prepared under IFRS and entity financial statements prepared in accordance with UK GAAP). In this case, the auditor may use an Other Matter paragraph referring to the fact that the entity has prepared another set of financial statements on which the auditor has reported separately; and

- where general purpose financial statements have been prepared for a specific purpose. In this situation, the auditor may include an Other Matter paragraph stating that the report is prepared solely for the intended users and may not be distributed to or used by third parties.

Where comparative information in the financial statements is derived from prior period financial statements that were not audited, ISA (UK) 710 *Comparative Information – Corresponding Figures and Comparative Financial Statements* requires that the auditor's report includes an Other Matter paragraph stating that comparative figures are unaudited.

ISA (UK) 560 *Subsequent Events* requires the use of an Emphasis of Matter paragraph or an Other Matter paragraph in circumstances where:

(a) a new or amended audit report is issued following amendment to the financial statements to reflect facts that became known after the date of the original audit report but before issue of the financial statements and where the auditor's procedures on subsequent events are restricted to the amendment of the financial statements as described in the relevant note therein; or

(b) management prepare new or amended financial statements to reflect facts that became known after the financial statements were originally issued and the auditor issues a new or amended audit report on those financial statements.

ISA (UK) 720 (Revised June 2016) requires an Other Matter paragraph to be included in the auditor's report where, on reading the other information, the auditor identifies a material inconsistency with the financial statements requiring revision of the other information and management refuses to make the revision.

5.9 Placement

Subject to rules in ISA (UK) 700 (Revised June 2016) regarding positioning of the Opinion and Basis for opinion sections of the report, the placement of an Emphasis of Matter paragraph or Other Matter paragraph in the auditor's report depends on the nature of the information to be communicated, and the auditor's judgment as to the relative significance of the information to intended users compared to other elements of the report.

For example, where an Emphasis of Matter paragraph relates to the applicable financial reporting framework, it may be appropriate to include it immediately below the Basis for opinion section of the report.

Where the report includes a Key Audit Matters section, an Emphasis of Matter paragraph may be presented either before or after this section depending on the auditor's judgment regarding the relative significance of the information included in the Emphasis of Matter paragraph.

5.10   Communication with those charged with governance

When the auditor expects to modify the opinion in his report, he should communicate with those charged with governance the circumstances that led to the expected modification and the proposed wording of the modification.

Similarly, if the auditor expects to include an Emphasis of Matter or an Other Matter paragraph in his report, he should communicate with those charged with governance regarding the proposed wording of this paragraph.

Doing this not only allows the auditor to give notice to those charged with governance of the intended modification and the reasons for the modification, but gives him the opportunity to seek the concurrence of those charged with governance regarding the facts of the matter; and gives those charged with governance an opportunity, where appropriate, to provide the auditor with further information and explanations in respect of the matter giving rise to the expected modification.

5.11   Communication with regulators and others

Where the auditor issues, or expects to issue, a modified audit report he may be required to notify regulators of this fact. In addition, in the case of a publicly traded company, it may be required or expected that any preliminary announcement of results would include an indication of any modification to the auditor's report.

In particular:

- in respect of a public interest entity, ISA (UK) 250 Section B (Revised June 2016) requires the auditor to report to the relevant regulator when he becomes aware of a matter which may bring about a material threat or doubt concerning the continuous function of the entity or the issue of an adverse or qualified opinion (see **Section 9**);

Modified auditor's reports

- for entities in the financial services sector regulated by the Financial Conduct Authority or the Prudential Regulation Authority, the auditor has a statutory duty to report matters of material significance to the regulator. This may include matters that would give rise to a modified auditor's report on the financial statements (see **Section 9**);

- where a premium listed company issues a preliminary statement of results, the statement must give details of the nature of any likely modification or emphasis of matter that may be contained in the auditor's report required to be included with the annual financial report (see **6.3.8**); and

- in the case of a registered charity in England or Scotland, the auditor or independent examiner has a duty to report matters of material significance to the regulator. Such matters include situations in which:

  - an auditor intends to offer a modified audit opinion, an audit opinion with an emphasis of matter or material uncertainty regarding going concern; or

  - a qualified independent examination report which identifies one or more concerns about the charity's accounts (see **Section 43**).

6 Other reports on financial information

6.1 Introduction

This section considers other reports that auditors may be required to make on a company's financial information. It covers reports on:

- revised financial statements and reports (**6.2**);
- preliminary announcements (**6.3**);
- reporting implications when a small company takes advantage of filing exemptions under the small companies regime (**6.4**); and
- summary financial statements (**6.5**).

This section does not cover engagements to review historical financial statements. Such engagements are covered in **Section 41**.

Engagements to report on special purpose financial statements are covered in **41.4**.

Rules regarding the preparation of abbreviated accounts for filing purposes and auditors' reports thereon have been repealed and abbreviated accounts are not permitted for filing purposes for accounting periods commencing on or after 1 January 2016. APB Bulletin 2008/4 *The special auditor's report on abbreviated accounts in the United Kingdom* has been withdrawn by the FRC. A new filing regime for small companies replaces the abbreviated accounts requirements and is described in **6.4**.

Rules regarding revision of financial statements or reports are contained in the *Companies (Revision of Defective Accounts and Reports) Regulations* 2008 (SI 2008/373). Guidance for auditors is found in Bulletin 2008/5 *Auditor's reports on revised accounts and reports, in the United Kingdom* for periods after 6 April 2008.

For preliminary announcements, guidance comes from FRC Bulletin *The auditors' association with preliminary announcements made in accordance with the requirements of UK listing rules* which was issued in December 2017 and replaces APB Bulletin 2008/2. The Listing Rules of the Financial Conduct Authority also contain rules regarding the issue of preliminary statements of results by listed companies.

6.2 Revised financial statements and reports

6.2.1 Legal background

The *Companies Act* 2006 allows directors to withdraw financial statements, strategic reports or directors' reports which have been found to be defective after they have been filed with the Registrar of Companies. In addition, the court, on application from the Secretary of State, has powers to make directors revise defective accounts or reports.

Detailed rules regarding revision of financial statements or reports are set out in the *Companies (Revision of Defective Accounts and Reports) Regulations* 2008 (SI 2008/373).

6.2.2 Guidance

Guidance for the auditor in these situations is contained in *Bulletin 2008/5 Auditor's reports on revised accounts and reports in the United Kingdom*. It should be noted that the Bulletin does not reflect revisions to the regulations arising from the *Companies (Revision of Defective Accounts and Reports) (Amendment) Regulations* 2013 (SI 2013/1971) relating to strategic reports, or revisions to ISA (UK) 700 (Revised June 2016) *Forming an opinion and reporting on financial statements*.

6.2.3 Types of revision

Revision may be by:

- issue of replacement financial statements and/or strategic or directors' reports, as applicable; or

- supplementary note, to be appended to the existing financial statements, strategic report or directors' report.

In each case, the auditor has to report on the revision and the directors' statement of the reason why the original financial statements, or report(s), are now considered incorrect. They must consider if the statement by the directors of the reason for the revision is sufficient for the reader to obtain a clear picture of the relevant facts. It is also necessary to consider if the method of revision is appropriate and whether any further adjustments are necessary.

Where the only revision is to the strategic report or directors' report, the auditor has to make a positive statement that it is consistent with the information in the financial statements.

Bulletin 2008/5 sets out individual example reports under the *Companies Act* 2006 for:

- revision by replacement; and
- revision by supplementary note

and both are reproduced in **Tables 1** and **2**.

Where either the full revision or supplementary note option is chosen, there should be a statement of directors' responsibilities under the Regulations. As with the annual financial statements, this may be either in the auditor's report or elsewhere in the financial statements or accompanying information. In addition to the normal responsibility statement that would accompany annual financial statements, the responsibilities that should be noted are shown in **Table 3**.

Where it is necessary to qualify such a report, the considerations are the same as for reports on other financial statements. For example, if the auditor considers that the reasons for the revision given by the directors are inadequate he should qualify and give further details in his report.

Where the auditor is a firm, the auditor's report must be signed by the senior statutory auditor in his own name for and on behalf of the auditor in the same way as for the audit report on the full financial statements.

TABLE 1: Annual financial statements revised by replacement under CA 2006

Independent auditor's report to the members of [XYZ Limited]

Opinion

We have audited the revised financial statements of [XYZ Limited] (the 'company') for the year ended [date] which comprise [specify the titles of the primary statements] and notes to the financial statements, including a summary of significant accounting policies. The financial reporting framework that has been applied in their preparation is applicable law and United Kingdom Accounting Standards, including Financial Reporting Standard 102 'The Financial Reporting Standard applicable in the UK and Republic of Ireland' (United Kingdom Generally Accepted Accounting Practice). These revised financial statements replace the original financial statements approved by the directors on […].

The revised financial statements have been prepared under the *Companies (Revision of Defective Accounts and Reports) Regulations* 2008 and accordingly do not take account of events which have taken place after the date on which the original financial statements were approved.

In our opinion, the revised financial statements:

- give a true and fair view, seen as at the date the original financial statements were approved, of the state of the company's affairs as at [date] and of its [profit/loss] for the year then ended;

- have been properly prepared in accordance with United Kingdom Generally Accepted Accounting Practice seen as at the date the original financial statements were approved;

- have been prepared in accordance with the requirements of the *Companies Act* 2006 as they have effect under the *Companies (Revision of Defective Accounts and Reports) Regulations* 2008; and

- the original financial statements for the year ended [...] failed to comply with the requirements of the *Companies Act* 2006 in the respects identified by the directors in the statement contained in note [...] to these revised financial statements.

Basis for opinion

We conducted our audit in accordance with International Standards on Auditing (UK) (ISAs (UK)) and applicable law. Our responsibilities under those standards are further described in the Auditor's responsibilities for the audit of the revised financial statements section of our report. We are independent of the company in accordance with the ethical requirements that are relevant to our audit of the revised financial statements in the UK, including the Revised Ethical Standard 2016, and we have fulfilled our other ethical responsibilities in accordance with these requirements. We believe that the audit evidence we have obtained is sufficient and appropriate to provide a basis for our opinion.

Conclusions relating to going concern

We have nothing to report in respect of the following matters in relation to which the ISAs (UK) require us to report to you where:

- the directors' use of the going concern basis of accounting in the preparation of the revised financial statements is not appropriate; or

- the directors have not disclosed in the revised financial statements any identified material uncertainties that may cast significant doubt about the company's ability to continue to adopt the going concern basis of accounting for a period of at least 12 months from the date when the original financial statements were authorised for issue.

Emphasis of matter – revision of [...]

In forming our opinion on the revised financial statements, which is not modified, we have considered the adequacy of the disclosures made in note [...] to these revised financial statements concerning the need to revise the [...]. The original financial statements were approved on [...] and our previous report was signed on [that date]. We have not performed a subsequent events review of the period from the date of our previous report to the date of this report.

Other information

The other information comprises the information included in the annual report, other than the revised financial statements and our auditor's report thereon. The directors are responsible for the other information. Our opinion on the revised financial statements does not cover the other information and, except to the extent otherwise explicitly stated in our report, we do not express any form of assurance conclusion thereon.

In connection with our audit of the revised financial statements, our responsibility is to read the other information and, in doing so, consider whether the other information is materially inconsistent with the revised financial statements or our knowledge obtained in the audit or otherwise appears to be materially misstated. If we identify such material inconsistencies or apparent material misstatements, we are required to determine whether there is a material misstatement in the revised financial statements or a material misstatement of the other information. If, based on the work we have performed, we conclude that there is a material misstatement of this other information, we are required to report that fact.

We have nothing to report in this regard.

Opinions on other matters prescribed by the Companies Act 2006

In our opinion, based on the work undertaken in the course of the audit:

- the information given in the [[revised] strategic report and the] [revised] directors' report for the financial year for which the revised financial statements are prepared is consistent with the revised financial statements; and

- the [[revised] strategic report and the] [revised] directors' report [has/ have] been prepared in accordance with applicable legal requirements.

Matters on which we are required to report by exception

In the light of the knowledge and understanding of the company and its environment obtained in the course of the audit, we have not identified material misstatements in the [[revised] strategic report and the] [revised] directors' report.

We have nothing to report in respect of the following matters in relation to which the *Companies Act* 2006 requires us to report to you if, in our opinion:

- adequate accounting records have not been kept, or returns adequate for our audit have not been received from branches not visited by us; or

- the revised financial statements are not in agreement with the accounting records and returns; or

- certain disclosures of directors' remuneration specified by law are not made; or

- we have not received all the information and explanations we require for our audit; [or

- the directors were not entitled to prepare the revised financial statements in accordance with the small companies regime and take advantage of the small companies' exemptions in preparing the directors' report and from the requirement to prepare a strategic report.]

Responsibilities of directors

As explained more fully in the directors' responsibilities statement [set out on page ...], the directors are responsible for the preparation of the revised financial statements and for being satisfied that they give a true and fair view, and for such internal control as the directors determine is necessary to enable the preparation of financial statements that are free from material misstatement, whether due to fraud or error.

In preparing the revised financial statements, the directors are responsible for assessing the company's ability to continue as a going concern, disclosing, as applicable, matters related to going concern and using the going concern basis of accounting unless the directors either intend to liquidate the company or to cease operations, or have no realistic alternative but to do so.

Auditor's responsibilities for the audit of the revised financial statements

Our objectives are to obtain reasonable assurance about whether the revised financial statements as a whole are free from material misstatement, whether due to fraud or error, and to issue an auditor's report that includes our opinion. Reasonable assurance is a high level of assurance, but is not a guarantee that an audit conducted in accordance with ISAs (UK) will always detect a material misstatement when it exists.

Misstatements can arise from fraud or error and are considered material if, individually or in the aggregate, they could reasonably be expected to influence the economic decisions of users taken on the basis of these revised financial statements.

The audit of revised financial statements includes the performance of additional procedures to assess whether the revisions made by the directors are appropriate and have been properly made.

A further description of our responsibilities for the audit of the revised financial statements is located on the Financial Reporting Council's website at www.frc. org.uk/auditorsresponsibilities. This description forms part of our auditor's report.

Use of our report

This report is made solely to the company's members, as a body, in accordance with the *Companies Act* 2006, Ch. 3, Pt. 16. Our audit work has been undertaken so that we might state to the company's members those matters we are required to state to them in an auditor's report and for no other purpose. To the fullest extent permitted by law, we do not accept or assume responsibility to anyone other than the company and the company's members as a body, for our audit work, for this report, or for the opinions we have formed.[1]

[Signature] John Smith (senior statutory auditor)

For and on behalf of ABC LLP, Statutory auditor

Address

Date

[1] Optional Bannerman paragraph.

TABLE 2: Annual financial statements revised by supplementary note under CA 2006

For financial statements revised by supplementary note the auditor's report is similar to that shown in **Table 1** with the following amendments:

(a) replace the introductory paragraph with:

'We have audited the revised financial statements of [XYZ Limited] (the "company") for the year ended [date] which comprise [specify the titles of the primary statements] and notes to the financial statements, including a summary of significant accounting policies. The financial reporting framework that has been applied in their preparation is applicable law and United Kingdom Accounting Standards, including Financial Reporting Standard 102 "The Financial Reporting Standard applicable in the UK and Republic of Ireland" (United Kingdom Generally Accepted Accounting Practice). These revised financial statements replace the original financial statements approved by the directors on [...] and consist of the attached supplementary note together with the original financial statements which were circulated to members on [...].'

(b) In the last bullet in the opinion paragraph and in the emphasis of matter paragraph refer to the supplementary note rather than note [...].

TABLE 3: Directors' responsibilities with regard to revised financial statements under CA 2006

Under the *Companies Act* 2006, s. 454, the directors have the authority to revise financial statements or a directors' report if they do not comply with the Act. The revised financial statements must be amended in accordance with the *Companies (Revision of Defective Account and Report) Regulations* 2008 and in accordance therewith do not take account of events which have taken place after the date on which the original financial statements were approved. The Regulations require that revised financial statements show a true and fair view as if they were prepared and approved by the directors, as at the date of the original financial statements.

There is no specific guidance on what the auditor should do if he does not agree that there are grounds for revision but the directors decide to go ahead with the revision. However, as the auditor must give an opinion on whether the revision is in accordance with the Regulations and these only permit revision in certain circumstances, where he disagrees with it, he will have to give an adverse opinion. This is because the revised financial statements have not been prepared in accordance with the Regulations and may also be on the grounds that in his opinion the original financial statements did comply with the requirements of the Companies Act.

The auditor will need to assess whether the discovery that leads to the revision indicates that adequate accounting records have not been kept and the effect this has on his report.

There is no duty on the auditor to search for further evidence after he has signed his report, but if he does become aware of anything that he should have known at the original date of signing he should inform the directors immediately and consider whether revision is necessary.

When deciding on the best course of action once an error is discovered, various factors should be taken into consideration, including the proximity to the next set of financial statements. It may be better to make a prior year adjustment rather than carry out a revision, if the error is discovered during the course of the next year's audit due to the costs and value of the information that will result from a revision. This is not precluded by the Regulations and will often be the best course of action if a significant amount of time has elapsed since the incorrect financial statements were produced.

6.2.4 Procedures

In determining the extent of audit procedures necessary, the auditor should analyse the matter giving rise to the revision and consider:

- whether the nature of the matter suggests that errors in the financial statements may be pervasive, for example the discovery of fraud;
- whether the facts discovered since the approval of the financial statements affect past assumptions in areas of judgment, for example provisions;
- the extent of any consequential changes to the form of financial statements which arise from the matter. For example, group financial statements may be required for the first time; and
- any steps taken by the directors to investigate and correct the defect.

Where the auditor has changed since the date of the original financial statements which have subsequently been found to be defective, the new auditor should make the required reports, unless the previous auditor has been specifically engaged by management and he is still eligible to report as 'registered auditor'.

Where the auditor reporting on the original and revised financial statements is the same, it is unlikely that a re-performance of the original audit will be required. However, in determining the extent of his examination, the auditor should assess the risk of other misstatements in the original accounts. Where different auditors are reviewing the revised accounts, the amount of work that is necessary will depend on the reason for the revision and their assessment of risk.

Based on their assessment of this, they should determine appropriate review procedures to identify any significant events in the period since the approval of the original financial statements. Such a review must be sufficient to:

- ensure that the factors which have led the directors to determine that the original financial statements were defective have been properly reflected in the proposed adjustments; and

- identify any further adjustments which should be made to the revised accounts.

The auditor would therefore normally undertake the following specific procedures:

- review of the original audit plans (and programmes) in the light of the analysis of the matter leading to revision and the extent to which additional audit evidence is required should be considered;

- reassessment of the various matters of judgment involved in the preparation of the original financial statements;

- obtaining evidence specific to the adjustments made to the original financial statements;

- review of the period after the date on which the original financial statements were approved;

- review of the revised financial statements to the extent that, in conjunction with the conclusions drawn from the other audit evidence obtained, there is a reasonable basis for the opinion on the financial statements; and

- consideration of any legal and regulatory consequences of the revision.

Each of these steps may in turn indicate a need for further procedures.

Engagements to report on revised directors' reports should be conducted following the principles outlined above.

6.3 Preliminary announcements

6.3.1 Background

Under the Listing Rules of the United Kingdom Listing Authority, a listed company may choose to publish a preliminary announcement, but is not required to do so. However, when a company does issue a preliminary announcement it is required by the Listing Rules to have agreed the announcement with the company's auditor prior to publication, although the Listing Rules do not set out what form the agreement with the auditor should take. Neither do they set out the extent of work expected of the auditor.

6.3.2 Guidance

The main guidance for auditors on this issue is in FRC Bulletin *The Auditors' Association with Preliminary Announcements Made in Accordance with the Requirements of UK Listing Rules*. The Bulletin replaces APB Bulletin 2008/2 and reflects:

- changes in the Listing Rules since 2008;

- changes to International Standards on Auditing (UK);

- guidance from the European Securities and Markets Authority (ESMA) about alternative performance measures; and

- changes to the UK Corporate Governance Code and the principle that the board should present a fair, balanced and understandable assessment of the company's position and prospects.

The Bulletin and the remainder of this section are based on the assumption that the company making the preliminary announcement is subject to the relevant requirements of the Listing Rules. However, this is obviously not the case for AIM companies or companies listed on other markets. AIM rules in particular do not require the auditor to agree to any preliminary announcement although it is likely that auditors of AIM companies would want to do so. The guidance in this section may be applied equally to such companies with omission of references to the Listing Rules, as appropriate.

6.3.3 Terms of engagement

It is in the interests of both the company and the auditor that the role of the auditor and the process of 'agreeing' to the release of the preliminary announcement be set out in an engagement letter.

Example paragraphs for inclusion in an engagement letter where a preliminary announcement is being made are shown in **Table 4** (audit complete) and **Table 5** (audit not yet complete). These may either be included in a separate engagement letter or incorporated within the audit engagement letter.

Where the auditor agrees to issue a report for publication with the preliminary announcement, it may be appropriate to refer also to this in the engagement letter.

TABLE 4: Example paragraphs for an engagement letter where audit will be complete

Review of preliminary announcement

The Listing Rules state that 'a preliminary statement of annual results ... must be agreed with the company's auditor prior to publication'. As directors of the company, you have accepted responsibility for preparing and issuing any preliminary announcement and ensuring that we agree to its release.

We undertake to review the preliminary announcement having regard to the Financial Reporting Council's Bulletin *The Auditors' Association with Preliminary Announcements Made in Accordance with the Requirements of UK Listing Rules*. Accordingly, our review will be limited to checking the accuracy of extraction of the financial information in the preliminary announcement from the audited financial statements of the company for that year, considering whether any 'alternative performance measures' and associated narrative explanations may be misleading and reading the management commentary, including any comments on, or separate presentation of, the final interim period figures, and considering whether it is in conflict with the information that we obtained in the course of our audit.

You will provide us with such information and explanations as we consider necessary for the purposes of our work. We shall request sight of the preliminary announcement in sufficient time to enable us to complete our work. The Board/Committee of the Board will formally approve the preliminary announcement before we agree to it.

The Listing Rules require that the preliminary announcement must include a statement including details of the nature of any likely modification or emphasis of matter paragraph that may be contained in the auditor's report required to be included with the annual financial report. We will also review the appropriateness of the wording of any such statement.

In the event that we disagree with the release of the preliminary announcement, we will write to you setting out the reasons why.

TABLE 5: Example paragraphs for an engagement letter where audit will not be complete

Review of preliminary announcement

The Listing Rules state that 'a preliminary statement of annual results ... must be agreed with the company's auditor prior to publication'. As directors of the company, you are responsible for preparing and issuing the preliminary announcement and ensuring that we agree to its release.

We undertake to review the preliminary announcement having regard to The Financial Reporting Council's Bulletin *The Auditors' Association with Preliminary Announcements Made in Accordance with the Requirements of UK Listing Rules* issued by the Auditing Practices Board. Accordingly, our review will be limited to checking the accuracy of extraction of the financial information in the preliminary announcement from the audited financial statements of the company for that year, considering whether any 'alternative performance measures' and associated narrative explanations may be misleading and reading the management commentary, including any comments on, or separate presentation of, the final interim period figures, and considering whether it is in conflict with the information that we have obtained in the course of our audit.

The Listing Rules require that the preliminary announcement must include a statement including details of the nature of any likely modification or emphasis of matter paragraph that may be contained in the auditor's report required to be included with the annual financial report. We will also review the appropriateness of the wording of any such statement.

You will provide us with such information and explanations as we consider necessary for the purposes of our work. We shall request sight of the preliminary announcement in sufficient time to enable us to complete our work. The Board/Committee of the Board will formally approve the preliminary announcement before we agree to it. You will also make available to us the proposed text of the company's annual report.

We will not agree to the release of the preliminary announcement until the audit is complete subject only to the following:

- clearing outstanding audit matters which we are satisfied are unlikely to have a material impact on the financial statements or disclosures insofar as they affect the preliminary announcement;

- completing audit procedures on the detail of note disclosures to the financial statements that will not have a material impact on the primary financial statements and completing our reading of the other information in the annual report in accordance with ISA (UK) 720 (Revised June 2016) *The auditor's responsibilities relating to other information*;

- updating the subsequent events review to cover the period between the date of the preliminary announcement and the date of our auditor's report on the financial statements; and

- obtaining final signed written representations from management and establishing that the financial statements have been reviewed and approved by the directors.

The scope of our work will be necessarily limited in that we will only be able to check the consistency of the preliminary announcement with draft financial statements on which our audit is incomplete. Accordingly, we shall not, at that stage, know whether further adjustments may be required to those draft financial statements. Consequently, there is an unavoidable risk that the company may wish to revise its preliminary announcement in the light of audit findings or other developments occurring between the preliminary announcement being notified to a regulatory information service and the completion of the audit.

In the event that we disagree with the release of the preliminary announcement, we will write to you setting out the reasons why.

6.3.4   Procedures

A preliminary announcement may be based on financial statements where the audit report has been finalised, or on financial statements whose audit is at an advanced stage. Whilst there is the expectation that the figures in the preliminary announcement will be consistent with those in the final audited financial statements, this cannot be guaranteed where the full financial statements are yet to be approved. Currently, the majority of companies making preliminary announcements do so based on audited financial information.

The Bulletin defines an 'advanced stage' as being where the audit has been completed, including engagement quality control review, subject only to the following:

- clearing outstanding audit matters which the auditor is satisfied are unlikely to have a material impact on the financial statements or disclosures in the preliminary announcement;

- completing audit procedures on the detail of note disclosures to the financial statements that will not have a material impact on the primary financial statements and completing their reading of the other information in the annual report in accordance with ISA (UK) 720 (Revised June 2016) *The auditor's responsibilities relating to other information*;

- updating the subsequent events review to cover the period between the issue of the preliminary announcement and the date of the auditor's report on the financial statements; and

- obtaining final signed written representations, where relevant, from management and establishing that the financial statements have been reviewed and approved by the directors.

Regardless of whether the preliminary announcement is based on draft financial statements or extracted from audited financial statements, the auditor's procedures will normally include:

- checking that the figures in the preliminary announcement covering the full year have been accurately extracted from the audited or draft financial statements and reflect the presentation to be adopted in the audited financial statements. For example, any summarisation should not change the order in which items are presented where this is specified by law or accounting standards;

- considering whether the information (including the management commentary) is consistent with other expected contents of the annual report of which the auditor is aware; and

- considering whether the financial information in the preliminary announcement is misstated. A misstatement exists when the information is stated incorrectly or presented in a misleading manner. A misstatement may arise, for example, as a result of an omission of a significant change of accounting policy disclosed or due to be disclosed in the audited financial statements.

The auditor should also consider whether the preliminary announcement includes the directors' statements in connection with the publication of non-statutory accounts required by the *Companies Act* 2006, s. 435.

6.3.5 Alternative performance measures

As well as reporting in accordance with the applicable financial reporting framework, companies often choose to report non-GAAP performance measures or other measures of performance, position or cash flows, other than financial measures defined in the framework. Whilst such 'alternative performance measures' (APMs) are often helpful to shareholders, they have the potential to be misleading or deceptive. In the context of the preliminary announcement, the auditor should therefore consider whether:

- appropriate prominence is given to statutory financial information;
- the use, relevance and reliability of APMs is explained;
- APMs are clearly defined and have been given meaningful labels; and
- APMs have been reconciled to the most nearly reconcilable line item in the financial statements and comparatives are included and any change in basis over time is explained.

6.3.6 Management commentary

The auditor should read any management commentary in the preliminary statement, together with any other narrative disclosures and any final interim period figures (together referred to as 'other information'), and consider whether:

- management commentary is fair balanced and understandable;
- there is any material inconsistency between the other information and the financial statements; and
- there is any material inconsistency between the other information and the auditor's knowledge obtained in the audit.

The principles to be applied here are similar to those set out in ISA (UK) 720 (Revised June 2016) regarding other information accompanying a full set of audited financial statements.

6.3.7   Directors' approval

The preliminary statement should state the date on which it was approved by the directors. The auditor does not agree the preliminary announcement until the Board has formally approved its entire content.

6.3.8   Modification of the auditor's report on the financial statements

The Listing Rules require that where an auditor is likely to issue a modified report (that is a qualified or adverse opinion, disclaimer of opinion or emphasis of matter), any preliminary announcement should make reference to this. The directors should give adequate prominence to this information in the announcement and the auditor should consider whether this is the case.

When giving details of the likely modification, care should be taken to comply with the *Companies Act* 2006, s. 435 which states that an auditor's report on the statutory accounts cannot be published with non-statutory accounts.

6.3.9   Reporting

The auditor is not required to prepare an audit report on the preliminary announcement. However, the Bulletin recommends that, to avoid possible misunderstanding and to make explicit his agreement to the preliminary announcement, he should issue a letter to the company to signify his agreement. An example of this letter is shown in **Table 6**. This letter should not be published with the announcement.

TABLE 6: Example letter to the directors agreeing preliminary announcement

Dear Sirs

In accordance with the terms of our engagement letter dated [ ], we have reviewed the attached proposed preliminary announcement of XYZ plc for the year ended [ ]. Our work was conducted having regard to The Financial Reporting Council's Bulletin *The Auditor's Association with Preliminary Announcements Made in Accordance with the Requirements of UK Listing Rules*. As directors, you are responsible for preparing and issuing the preliminary announcement.

Our responsibility is solely to give our agreement to the preliminary announcement having carried out the procedures specified in the Bulletin as providing a basis for such agreement. In this regard, we agree to the preliminary announcement being notified to [a Regulatory Information Service].

> [*Insert paragraph* below only where the preliminary announcement is made before the audit is complete.*]
>
> Yours faithfully
>
> * As you are aware we are not in a position to sign our auditor's report on the annual financial statements as they have not yet been approved by the directors and we have not yet [*insert significant procedures that are yet to be completed, for example completing the subsequent events review and obtaining final representations from directors*]. Consequently, there can be no absolute certainty that we will be in a position to issue an unmodified audit opinion on financial statements consistent with the results and financial position reported in the preliminary announcement. However, at the present time, we are not aware of any matters that may give rise to a modification to our report. In the event that such matters do come to our attention, we will inform you immediately.

The auditor may also agree to inclusion within the preliminary announcement of a voluntary report by the auditor setting out the responsibilities of the directors and the auditor, the procedures performed in relation to the preliminary announcement and the status of the audit of the financial statements. Where the audit is complete, this may also refer to key audit matters and other matters addressed in the audit report in accordance with ISA (UK) 701. An example of such a report (without key audit matters) is given in **Table 6A**.

> **TABLE 6A: Independent auditor's report to the shareholders of [...] on the preliminary statement of annual results**
>
> As the independent auditor of [...] we are required by UK Listing Rule LR 9.7A.1 (2) R to agree to the publication of the company's preliminary statement of annual results for the period ended [...].
>
> The preliminary statement of annual results includes [description of the content of the preliminary announcement which the auditor has agreed to be published, including disclosures required by the Listing rules and any additional content such as highlights/overview, Chairman's Statement, narrative disclosures, management commentary, press release etc.]. We are not required to agree to the publication of [description of additional information published alongside the preliminary statement of annual results, which may include presentations to analysts, trading statement, interim management statement or half-yearly financial report].
>
> The Directors of [...] are responsible for the preparation, presentation and publication of the preliminary statement of annual results in accordance with the UK Listing Rules.
>
> We are responsible for agreeing to the publication of the preliminary statement of annual results, having regard to the Financial Reporting Council's Bulletin *The Auditor's Association with Preliminary Announcements made in accordance with the requirements of UK Listing Rules*.

Status of our audit of the financial statements

[Our audit of the annual financial statements of XYZ PLC is complete and we signed our auditor's report on [Date]. Our auditor's report [is not modified and contains no emphasis of matter paragraph]/[description of modification/ emphasis of matter].]

[We are not in a position to sign our auditor's report on the annual financial statements [of XYZ PLC] as they have not yet been approved by the Directors. In accordance with the FRC's Bulletin *The Auditor's Association with Preliminary Announcements made in accordance with the requirements of UK Listing Rules* our audit is complete to an advanced stage, except for [insert significant procedures that are yet to be completed, for example completing the subsequent events review and obtaining final signed written representations from Directors ...]. Consequently, there can be no absolute certainty that we will be in a position to issue an unmodified audit report on financial statements consistent with the results and financial position reported in the preliminary announcement. However, at the present time, we are not aware of any matters that may give rise to a modification to our report and/or and emphasis of matter paragraph.]

Procedures performed to agree to the preliminary announcement of annual results

In order to agree to the publication of the preliminary announcement of annual results of [...] we carried out the following procedures:

[Insert description of procedures carried out]

[Signature]

John Smith (Senior Statutory Auditor)

For and on behalf of ABC LLP, Statutory Auditor

[Address]

[Date]

6.3.10 Announcements not agreed

Where the auditor is not in agreement with the content of the preliminary announcement, he should communicate this to the directors in a letter setting out the reasons for this disagreement and advising the directors not to release the announcement to a Regulatory Information Service.

Where he becomes aware that the company has released the announcement, without first obtaining his consent, he should first ascertain the reasons for this. If the announcement was released inadvertently, the Bulletin advises the auditor to remind the directors of their obligations under the Listing Rules to obtain the auditor's agreement. However, where an announcement with which the auditor disagrees has been released, the Bulletin advises taking legal advice with a view to notifying the Listing Authority of the fact that the announcement had not been agreed.

6.4 New small companies regime

6.4.1 Legal background

The *Companies, Partnerships and Groups (Accounts and Reports) Regulations* 2015 (SI 2015/980) made various amendments to the *Companies Act* 2006 and the *Small Companies and Groups (Accounts and Directors' Report) Regulations* 2008 (SI 2008/409) and introduced significant changes to the small companies regime. Companies are entitled to adopt the new provisions of the Act and Regulations for periods commencing on or after 1 January 2015 and are required to apply them for periods commencing on or after 1 January 2016.

Under the new regime, small companies may prepare their accounts for members using the full small company formats set out in the regulations or may alternatively prepare simplified accounts (referred to as 'abridged accounts') in which certain of the prescribed format items are combined. For example, an abridged format 1 profit and loss account will start at the gross profit/loss line rather than turnover and in an abridged format 2 profit and loss account, the first five lines in the format are combined into one heading of 'gross profit or loss'. In an abridged balance sheet, items need only be analysed to the levels indicated by letters and roman numerals in the formats. For example, within fixed assets, tangible assets would need to be disclosed, but would not need to be further analysed into land and buildings and plant and machinery. Companies preparing abridged accounts should note, however, that such accounts must still give a true and fair view and FRS 102 notes that in order to achieve this, small entities may need to provide additional disclosure that is necessary in the notes to the financial statements, for example in relation to disaggregating the information in the income statement or balance sheet.

If a company wishes to prepare abridged accounts, it must obtain unanimous agreement of all shareholders. This means that if one shareholder does not agree to the abridgement, then the company must instead prepare a full set of financial statements for the period in question. It is worth noting that shareholders' agreement to prepare abridged accounts for the preceding financial year does not cover all subsequent accounting periods and such a decision must be taken on an annual basis.

Abbreviated accounts are not permitted under the new regime and instead the accounts filed with the registrar must be the same accounts as those prepared for members. There are, however, a number of filing exemptions and a small company need not file its directors' report or its profit and loss account (or notes thereto). This applies whether the accounts prepared for members were full accounts or abridged accounts. Where advantage is taken of either of these exemptions, there must be a statement on the balance sheet to the effect that the annual accounts and reports have been delivered to the registrar in accordance with the provisions of the small companies regime.

Where a company has prepared abridged accounts, the Companies Act also requires a statement from the directors to the registrar that all shareholders have consented to the abridgement.

6.4.2 Auditor's report

Where the accounts are audited, the auditor's report is essentially the same regardless of whether the accounts are full accounts or abridged accounts although, where applicable, the auditor may choose to make reference to the fact that the accounts have been prepared as abridged accounts. Unlike abbreviated accounts, there is no requirement for a 'special' auditor's report.

As noted in **6.4.1**, the accounts prepared for members, whether abridged or not, need to be filed at Companies House, although the profit and loss account may be removed before filing. Where the accounts have been audited but no profit and loss account is filed the auditor's report should also not be filed. Instead the notes to the filed accounts should include a note summarising the auditor's report on the full financial statements. An example is given in **Table 7**. The note must:

(a) state whether the auditor's report was qualified or unqualified;

(b) where that report was qualified, disclose the basis of the qualification (reproducing any statement under s. 498(2)(a) or (b) (accounting records) or s. 498(3) (information and explanations not obtained), if applicable);

(c) where that report was unqualified, include a reference to any matters to which the auditor drew attention by way of emphasis; and

(d) state:

   (i)   the name of the auditor and (where the auditor is a firm) the name of the person who signed the auditor's report as senior statutory auditor; or

   (ii) if the conditions in s. 506 (circumstances in which names may be omitted) are met, that a resolution has been passed and notified to the Secretary of State in accordance with that section.

> **TABLE 7: Example auditor's report**
>
> *Note X – Auditor's report on the financial statements*
>
> The financial statements of the company for the financial year ended 31 December 20XX prepared for members, from which these financial statements have been extracted, were audited by the company's auditors, ABC LLP.
>
> The auditor's report on those financial statements was [unqualified/qualified] (explain basis of qualification/unqualified but contain an emphasis of matter paragraph as follows (…)]. The report was signed by [name] as senior statutory auditor for and on behalf of ABC LLP, statutory auditor on [date].

6.4.3   Guidance

The ICAEW issued a helpsheet, *Abridged accounts for small companies* in December 2015. The helpsheet provides example formats for financial statements under the new rules.

6.5   Summary financial statements

Under the *Companies Act* 2006, s. 426(1) and the *Companies (Summary Financial Statement) Regulations* 2008, companies in the United Kingdom used to be able to send summary financial statements (SFSs) to their shareholders instead of the full report and accounts.

These summary financial statements used to be accompanied by a statement from the company's auditor that the summary statement was consistent with the full accounts and that it complied with s. 426(1) and the Regulations.

This concept of summary financial statements, however, was removed from the *Companies Act* 2006, s. 426 by the *Strategic Report and Directors' Report Regulations* 2013. With effect from 1 October 2013, companies are now able to send to shareholders, with their agreement, a copy of the strategic report instead of the full annual financial statements. There is no requirement to include the auditor's report.

Other entities, for example, non-corporate registered charities may still choose to produce summary financial statements and companies may produce summary financial statements for other purposes. Whilst the FRC has withdrawn APB Bulletin 2008/3 *The Auditor's Statement on the Summary Financial Statement in the United Kingdom* which related to the statutory requirement, many auditors still refer to this for guidance on procedures to be applied and the form of their report. Alternatively, reference may be made to the IAASB's ISA 810 (Revised) *Engagements to Report on Summary Financial Statements*, the latest version of which was issued in March 2016.

Further guidance on charities is given in **Section 43**.

7 Other statutory reports by auditors

7.1 Introduction

This section considers the other types of reports that auditors may be required to make under the *Companies Act* 2006. It covers the reports on:

- distributions;
- purchase and redemption of own shares;
- re-registration of companies;
- allotment of shares otherwise than for cash; and
- transfer of non-cash assets.

The guidance on the form of these is contained in Bulletin 2008/9 *Miscellaneous reports by auditors required by the United Kingdom Companies Act 2006*. For some reports, there is additional guidance on the procedures necessary to support such reports and the source of this has been noted.

7.2 Distributions

7.2.1 Legal background

A company may only make a distribution out of distributable reserves and must justify any distribution by reference to profits, losses, assets, liabilities, provisions, share capital and reserves shown in the 'relevant accounts'. Generally, the relevant accounts will be the company's last annual accounts except where:

- a distribution would be found to contravene the requirements of the *Companies Act* by reference to the last annual accounts – in which case special 'interim' accounts may be used instead (**7.2.3**); or
- a distribution is proposed to be declared in the company's first accounting reference period, before any annual accounts have been prepared – in which case special 'initial' accounts may be prepared for the purpose of justifying the distribution (**7.2.4**).

Where interim or initial accounts are prepared, these accounts should be sufficient to enable a reasonable judgment to be made as to profits, losses, assets, liabilities, provisions, share capital and reserves of the company and hence, as to the availability of distributable profits. However, in the case of a public company, the accounts must be 'properly prepared' or have been so prepared except for matters not material for the purposes of determining distributable profits. 'Properly prepared' in this context means prepared under the accounting provisions of the Companies Act for individual company accounts, applying such modifications as are necessary to reflect the fact that the accounts are not the annual accounts of the company.

In the case of a parent company, group accounts are not required.

7.2.2 *Distributions made by reference to annual accounts*

The *Companies Act* 2006, s. 837(4) requires that where the auditor's report on a company's annual financial statements contains a qualification, before those statements may be used to justify a distribution, it is necessary for the company's auditor to make a further statement as to whether the qualification is material for the purposes of determining the company's distributable profits. This statement must, in the case of a private company, be circulated to members of the company or, in the case of a public company, be laid before the members in general meeting.

The auditor's statement may be issued as a separate report to the members and sent to the company for distribution to members, or as an additional paragraph in the normal auditor's report on the financial statements. This will depend upon the individual circumstances.

The required statement is restricted to the consideration of the effect of the last qualification on the company's distributable profits. The auditor is required to state whether the subject matter of the qualification is material for determining whether the proposed distributions, and any which have not yet been proposed, are permitted. Some qualifications will not be material because of their nature, for example, if the qualification related to the misclassification of creditors due within one year, there would be no effect on distributable profits.

Other qualifications will by their nature be potentially material. For example, a qualification for failure to make a provision in respect of the carrying value of properties could have an adverse effect on the distributable reserves of the company. Here the auditor would have to assess the maximum potential write down, if known, before he could say whether the proposed distribution was permitted.

It should be noted that an emphasis of matter paragraph which states that the auditor's opinion on the financial statements is not qualified does not count as a qualification of the auditor's report for this purpose and as a consequence will not result in the need for a report under s. 837(4).

If the auditor is unable to quantify the effect of the qualification, its effect would have to be assessed as material for the purposes of determining the distributable reserves, unless he can conclude that the qualification either does not impact distributable profits or that its possible impact could only be favourable. In this case, the auditor would have to state either that the qualification is material or that he is unable to form an opinion whether it is material.

A disclaimer of opinion on the financial statements as a whole would be material as the auditor would be unable to form an opinion on the amount at which the company's distributable profits are stated.

Whatever opinion is given, legally the company could pay a dividend so long as a statement, irrespective of its conclusion, is laid before the members. It is only when the auditor does not provide such a statement that the distribution is illegal. However, where the auditor has concluded that the effect of a qualification is or could be material, the directors would be unwise to make a distribution without first establishing that the company did in fact have sufficient distributable reserves.

The following tables provide suitable wordings for these reports. **Table 1** is where a separate report is given and the amount of the proposed distribution is known. If the proposed dividend is as yet unquantified, the wording in **Table 2** should be used or if a statement is to be made about 'any distribution' **Table 3** should be used. If a separate report is not required, the additional paragraph should be based on **Table 4**.

If a separate statement is made, the date used should be that on which the statement is completed and will need to be by the date of the distribution.

TABLE 1: Report required on company's ability to make a distribution

Statement of the Independent Auditor to the [members/shareholders] of XYZ Limited pursuant to the Companies Act 2006, s. 837(4)

We have audited the financial statements of XYZ Limited for the year ended … in accordance with International Standards on Auditing (United Kingdom) and have expressed a qualified opinion thereon in our report dated …

Respective responsibilities of directors and auditor

[*Summarisation of directors' responsibilities with respect to the financial statements referred to in the introductory paragraph.*] They are also responsible for considering whether the company, subsequent to the balance sheet date, has sufficient distributable profits to make a distribution at the time the distribution is made.

Other statutory reports by auditors

Our responsibility is to report whether, in our opinion the subject matter of our qualification of our auditors' report on the financial statements for the year ended … is material for determining, by reference to those financial statements, whether the distribution proposed by the company is permitted under the *Companies Act* 2006, s. 830 [s. 831/832[1]]. We are not required to form an opinion on whether the company has sufficient distributable reserves to make the distribution proposed at the time it is made.

Opinion

In our opinion, the subject matter of that qualification is not material for determining, by reference to those financial statements, whether [the distribution of £ … /the interim/final dividend for the year ended … of £ …] proposed by the company is permitted under the *Companies Act* 2006, s. 830 (*s. 831/832*).[2]

Statutory Auditor

Address

Date

Notes

[1] Section 831 should be used for public companies and s. 831 and 832 if the company is also an investment company.

[2] The auditor may include a 'Bannerman Statement' as part of the final section of his report (see **4.28**).

TABLE 2: Alternative opinion paragraph where amount of distribution not known

In our opinion, the subject matter of that qualification is not material for determining, by reference to those financial statements, whether a distribution of not more than £ … by the company is permitted under the *Companies Act* 2006, s. 830 (*s. 831/832*).

TABLE 3: Alternative opinion paragraph concerning ability to make 'any distribution'

In our opinion, the subject matter of that qualification is not material for determining, by reference to those financial statements, whether any distribution proposed by the company is permitted under the *Companies Act* 2006, s. 830 (*s. 831/832*).

TABLE 4: Additional paragraphs concerning ability to make a distribution for audit report on annual accounts

Statement pursuant to Companies Act 2006, [s. 837(4)/839(6[1])].

Respective responsibilities of directors and auditor

In addition to their responsibilities described above, the directors are also responsible for considering whether the company, subsequent to the balance sheet date, has sufficient distributable profits to make a distribution at the time the distribution is made.

Our responsibility is to report whether, in our opinion the subject matter of our qualification of our auditors' report on the financial statements for the year ended ... is material for determining, by reference to those financial statements, whether the distribution proposed by the company is permitted under the *Companies Act* 2006, s. 830 [s. 831/832[2]]. We are not required to form an opinion on whether the company has sufficient distributable reserves to make the distribution proposed at the time it is made.

Opinion on other matter required by the Companies Act

In our opinion, the subject matter of the above qualification is not material for determining whether [the distribution of £ ... /the interim/final dividend for the year ended ... of £ ...] proposed by the company is permitted under the *Companies Act* 2006, s. 830 (*s. 831/832*).

Notes

[1] Section 837(4) applies where the last annual accounts are used. Section 839(6) applies where initial accounts are used and are qualified.

[2] Section 831 should be used for public companies and s. 831 and 832 if the company is also an investment company.

7.2.3   Distributions made by reference to 'interim' accounts

Where interim accounts are prepared to justify a distribution, no auditor's report is required, although, in the case of a public company, the interim accounts must be filed with the Registrar of Companies.

7.2.4   Distributions made by reference to 'initial' accounts

Where a company wishes to make a distribution during its first accounting period, or after its end but before the accounts for that period have been circulated to members or laid before the members in general meeting, initial accounts have to be prepared in accordance with the *Companies Act* 2006, s. 839, as set out in **7.2.1**. In the case of a private company, there is no requirement for a report by the auditor, but in the case of a public company, the auditor must report in accordance with the *Companies Act* 2006, s. 839(5) whether, in his opinion, the initial accounts have been properly prepared.

The auditor's report may be addressed to the directors and should identify the period covered by the initial accounts.

The auditor is required to express an opinion on whether the accounts have been properly prepared in accordance with the *Companies Act* 2006, s. 395–397 with any modifications necessary to reflect the fact that the accounts are not prepared in respect of a financial year of the company.

This means, in effect, that the accounts give a true and fair view and are prepared in accordance with the accounting provisions of the Act.

Although the opinion provided by the auditor is not an audit opinion, the work done by the auditor in order to determine whether the accounts are properly prepared will not be dissimilar to that required to support an audit opinion on annual financial statements.

An example unqualified report is shown in **Table 5**.

If the auditor's opinion on the initial accounts is qualified, then the auditor must make a statement as to whether, in his opinion, the subject matter of the qualification is material for the purposes of determining whether the company has sufficient distributable reserves. See **Table 4** for example paragraphs for inclusion in the report.

In the case of a distribution by a public company based on initial accounts, the initial accounts, the auditor's report thereon, and any statement made by the auditor in respect of a qualified opinion on the initial accounts, must be filed with the Registrar of Companies.

TABLE 5: Report on initial accounts of a public company wishing to make a distribution

Report of the Independent Auditor to the directors of XYZ Plc under the Companies Act 2006, s. 839(5)

We have examined the initial accounts of XYZ plc for the period from ... to ... which comprise [state the primary financial statements such as the Profit and Loss Account, the Balance Sheet, the Cash Flow Statement, the Statement of Total Recognised Gains and Losses] and the related notes. The initial accounts have been prepared under the accounting policies set out therein.

Respective responsibilities of directors and auditor

As described ... the directors are responsible for the preparation of the initial accounts in accordance with applicable law and United Kingdom Accounting Standards (United Kingdom Generally Accepted Accounting Practice).

Our responsibility is to report to you our opinion as to whether the initial accounts have been properly prepared within the meaning of the *Companies Act* 2006, s. 839(4).

Opinion

In our opinion, the initial accounts for the period from ... to ... have been properly prepared within the meaning of the *Companies Act* 2006, s. 839(4).[1]

[Signature]

John Smith (senior statutory auditor)

for and on behalf of ABC LLP, Statutory Auditor

Address

Date

Note

[1] The auditor may include a 'Bannerman Statement' as part of the final section of his report (see **4.28**).

7.3 Purchase and redemption of own shares

7.3.1 Legal background

Where a private company decides to redeem or purchase its own shares wholly or partly out of capital, this has to be approved by a special resolution of the company. A directors' declaration is required concerning the amount by which the purchase price exceeds any available profits (the permissible capital payment) and the solvency of the company. This statement has to be accompanied by an auditor's report.

The auditor's report should be addressed to the directors and states that the amount specified as the permissible capital payment has been properly determined and that the solvency statement is reasonable. The report should be made and dated in the week prior to the meeting which passes the special resolution.

7.3.2 Guidance

The auditor's report:

- should not be dated earlier than the declaration;
- cannot be qualified and should not be issued unless unqualified.

An example of the report is shown in **Table 6**.

There is no published guidance on the procedures that are necessary to support such a report. In general, before giving the report the auditor must:

- be satisfied that the directors' assumptions are realistic and consistently applied;
- review the cash flow forecasts;
- review asset and liability values, including provisions and future commitments;
- confirm that any support being received from lenders or group companies will be continued; and

167

- ensure that the permissible capital payment calculation is correct, taking into account any movements since the relevant accounts were prepared. These relevant accounts need not be audited but must be sufficient to enable a reasonable judgment to be made as to the financial position of the company.

TABLE 6: Report for private company redeeming or purchasing shares out of capital

Report of the Independent Auditor to the Directors of XYZ Limited pursuant to the Companies Act 2006, s. 714(6)

We report on the attached statement of the directors dated ..., prepared pursuant to the *Companies Act* 2006, in connection with the company's proposed [purchase]/[redemption] of ... (*number*) [ordinary]/[preferred] shares by a payment out of capital.

Basis of opinion

We have inquired into the state of the company's state of affairs in order to review the bases for the directors' statement.

Opinion

In our opinion, the amount of £ ... specified in the directors' statement as the permissible capital payment for the shares to be [purchased]/[redeemed] is properly determined in accordance with the *Companies Act* 2006, s. 710–712.

We are not aware of anything to indicate that the opinion expressed by the directors in their statement as to any of the matters mentioned in the *Companies Act* 2006, s. 714(3) is unreasonable in all the circumstances.[1]

Statutory Auditor

Address

Date

Note

[1] The auditor may include a 'Bannerman Statement' as part of the final section of his report (see **4.28**).

7.4 Re-registration of companies

7.4.1 Legal background

When a private company wishes to re-register as a public company, it has to deliver certain documents to the Registrar of Companies before it will be issued with a new certificate of incorporation. These include a copy of the company's balance sheet, at a date not more than seven months before the application, together with an auditor's report on that balance sheet which is either:

- unqualified; or

- qualified and the auditor expresses an opinion that the qualification is not material for determining the net assets of the company,

and a further written statement from the auditor. If the last financial statements are at a date more than seven months before, an up-to-date balance sheet will need to be prepared and audited.

The auditor's statement should confirm that the company's net assets are not less than the total of its share capital and non-distributable reserves.

7.4.2   Guidance

The procedures to support such a report may be restricted to a simple examination of the amounts in the relevant financial statements. The report should indicate that the work is limited to such an examination.

If the balance sheet is qualified, the auditor will have to state that this is not material for the purposes of determining whether at the balance sheet date the net assets of the company were not less than the aggregate of its called-up share capital and non-distributable reserves. The considerations required for this are similar to those for the effect of qualifications on distributions. Where this is the case, an extra paragraph will need to be inserted in the auditor's statement as illustrated in **Table 7**.

The auditor's report should not be dated earlier than the date of the audit report on the relevant balance sheet.

If there has been a change of auditor, the new auditor can accept the balance sheet audited by his predecessor unless the audit report contains a material qualification. The new auditor should refer in his report to the firm that has carried out the audit of the relevant balance sheet.

The following examples should be used:

- a balance sheet from the previous annual financial statements is reported on without qualification (**Table 7**);

- a balance sheet from the previous annual financial statements is reported on with a qualification in respect of proper preparation in accordance with the *Companies Act* 2006, but the qualification is not material (**Table 8**);

- a specially prepared balance sheet is reported on without qualification (**Table 9**); and

- a specially prepared balance sheet is reported on with a qualification in respect of proper preparation in accordance with the *Companies Act* 2006, but the qualification is not material (**Table 10**).

TABLE 7: Statement required when a private company wishes to re-register as a public company – previous balance sheet with no qualification

Statement of the Independent Auditor to the directors of XYZ Limited for the purpose of the Companies Act 2006, s. 92(1)(b) and (c)

We have examined the balance sheet and related notes of XYZ Limited as at … which formed part of the financial statements for the year then ended which were audited by [us]/[name of firm].

Respective responsibilities of directors and auditor

The company's directors are responsible for the preparation of the balance sheet and related notes.

It is our responsibility to:

- report on whether the balance sheet has been properly prepared in accordance with the requirements of the *Companies Act* 2006; and

- form an independent opinion, based on our examination, concerning the relationship between the company's net assets and its called up share capital and undistributable reserves at the balance sheet date.

Opinion concerning proper preparation of balance sheet

In our opinion, the audited balance sheet as at … has been properly prepared in accordance with the requirements of the *Companies Act* 2006.

Statement on net assets

In our opinion, at … the amount of the company's net assets (within the meaning given to that expression by the *Companies Act* 2006, s. 831(2)) was not less than the aggregate of its called-up share capital and undistributable reserves.[1]

Statutory Auditor

Address

Date

Note

[1] The auditor may include a 'Bannerman Statement' as part of the final section of his report (see **4.28**).

TABLE 8: Statement required when a private company wishes to re-register as a public company – previous balance sheet with non-material qualification

Statement of the Independent Auditor to the directors of XYZ Limited for the purpose of the Companies Act 2006, s. 92(1)(b) and (c)

We have examined the balance sheet and related notes of XYZ Limited as at … which formed part of the financial statements for the year then ended which were audited by [us]/[name of firm].

Respective responsibilities of directors and auditor

The company's directors are responsible for the preparation of the balance sheet and related notes.

It is our responsibility to:

- report on whether the balance sheet has been properly prepared in accordance with the requirements of the *Companies Act* 2006; and

- form an independent opinion, based on our examination, concerning the relationship between the company's net assets and its called up share capital and undistributable reserves at the balance sheet date.

Qualified opinion concerning proper preparation of balance sheet

[We]/[Name of firm] audited the financial statements for the year ended ... and expressed a qualified opinion regarding the proper preparation of the balance sheet in accordance with the requirements of the *Companies Act* 2006.

The matter giving rise to [our]/[the] qualification is not material for determining by reference to the balance sheet at ... whether, at that date, the amount of the company's net assets (within the meaning given to that expression by the *Companies Act* 2006, s. 831(2)) was not less than the aggregate of its called-up share capital and undistributable reserves.

Statement on net assets

In our opinion, at ... the amount of the company's net assets (within the meaning given to that expression by the *Companies Act* 2006, s. 831(2)) was not less than the aggregate of its called-up share capital and undistributable reserves.[1]

Statutory Auditor

Address

Date

Note

[1] The auditor may include a 'Bannerman Statement' as part of the final section of his report (see **4.28**).

TABLE 9: Report for re-registration where new balance sheet prepared and is unqualified

Report of the Independent Auditor to the directors of XYZ Limited for the purpose of the Companies Act 2006, s. 92(1)(b) and (c)

We have audited the balance sheet and related notes of XYZ Limited as at ... set out on pages ... to ... which have been prepared under the accounting policies set out therein.

Respective responsibilities of directors and auditor

The company's directors are responsible for the preparation of the balance sheet and related notes.

It is our responsibility to:

- report on whether the balance sheet has been properly prepared in accordance with the requirements of the *Companies Act* 2006 that would have applied if it had been prepared for a financial year of the company with such modifications as are necessary by reason of that fact; and

- form an independent opinion concerning the relationship between the company's net assets and its called up share capital and undistributable reserves at the balance sheet date.

Opinion concerning proper preparation of balance sheet

In our opinion, the audited balance sheet as at … has been properly prepared in accordance with the requirements of the *Companies Act* 2006, which would have applied had the balance sheet been prepared for a financial year of the company.

Statement on net assets

In our opinion, at … the amount of the company's net assets (within the meaning given to that expression by the *Companies Act* 2006, s. 831(2)) was not less than the aggregate of its called-up share capital and undistributable reserves.[1]

Statutory Auditor

Address

Date

Note

[1] The auditor may include a 'Bannerman Statement' as part of the final section of his report (see **4.28**).

TABLE 10: Report for re-registration where new balance sheet prepared and has a non-material qualification

Report of the Independent Auditor to the directors of XYZ Limited for the purpose of the Companies Act 2006, s. 92(1)(b) and (c)

We have audited the balance sheet and related notes of XYZ Limited as at … set out on pages … to … which have been prepared under the accounting policies set out therein.

Respective responsibilities of directors and auditor

The company's directors are responsible for the preparation of the balance sheet and related notes.

It is our responsibility to:

- report on whether the balance sheet has been properly prepared in accordance with the requirements of the *Companies Act* 2006 that would have applied if it had been prepared for a financial year of the company with such modifications as are necessary by reason of that fact; and

- form an independent opinion concerning the relationship between the company's net assets and its called up share capital and undistributable reserves at the balance sheet date.

Qualified opinion concerning proper preparation of balance sheet

[Except for [*describe area of non-compliance with CA 2006*] in our opinion the balance sheet and related notes as at ... have been properly prepared in accordance with the provisions of the *Companies Act* 2006, which would have applied had the balance sheet been prepared for a financial year of the company.][1]

[Because [*describe area of non-compliance with CA 2006*] in our opinion the balance sheet and related notes as at ... have not been properly prepared in accordance with the provisions of the *Companies Act* 2006, which would have applied had the balance sheet been prepared for a financial year of the company.][2]

However, in our opinion, this matter is not material for determining by reference to the balance sheet at ... whether, at that date, the amount of the company's net assets (within the meaning given to that expression by the *Companies Act* 2006, s. 831(2)) was not less than the aggregate of its called-up share capital and undistributable reserves.

Statement on net assets

In our opinion, at ... the amount of the company's net assets (within the meaning given to that expression by the *Companies Act* 2006, s. 831(2)) was not less than the aggregate of its called-up share capital and undistributable reserves.[3]

Statutory Auditor

Address

Date

Notes

[1] Use this wording if the auditor has expressed a qualified opinion concerning the proper preparation of the balance sheet.

[2] Use this wording if the auditor has expressed an adverse opinion concerning the proper preparation of the balance sheet.

[3] The auditor may include a 'Bannerman Statement' as part of the final section of his report (see **4.28**).

7.5 Allotment of shares otherwise than for cash

7.5.1 Legal background

All companies may allot shares and receive payment for them in something other than cash. However, where the company concerned is a public company, during the six months prior to the allotment, it is necessary to obtain a report on the value of the asset to be received instead of cash.

This report should be prepared by independent accountants. This is either the company's auditor, or a firm suitably qualified to be the company's auditor, i.e. a registered auditor. The accountants are entitled to rely on an expert, who is not connected with the company, to make a valuation of part or all of the asset.

If the company's own statutory auditor is requested to undertake a valuation in accordance with the *Companies Act* 2006, s. 599, the standards and guidance in Revised Ethical Standard 2016 are applied (see **Section 2**).

The report should be addressed to the company and sent to the company secretary for distribution to the allottees. It should include the following information:

- the nominal value of the shares in question;
- any premium payable on them;
- a description of the consideration;
- a description of the part of the consideration valued by the independent accountants, the method used and the date of the valuation; and
- the extent to which the nominal value of the shares and any premium are to be treated as paid up by the consideration and in cash.

If the valuation was carried out by someone else, the independent accountants should give their opinion on whether that valuation is reasonable and provide details on the expert's qualifications, the method used, and the amount and the date of the valuation. The expert must be independent of the company.

Where the allotment of shares represents only part of the consideration for the asset, the report should apply to as much of the value as is attributable to the shares. It must state what valuations have been made to determine the proportion of the consideration and the reasons for and methods of that valuation.

7.5.2 *Guidance*

The accountants' work will consist of:

- either valuing the consideration themselves or assessing whether it is reasonable to accept an external valuation;
- confirming that the value of the consideration is not less than the total amount to be treated as being paid up on the shares, together with any premium; and

- considering whether there has been any change in the value of the asset since the valuation and confirming that it has not diminished. Where they have used an expert to provide the valuation it may be necessary to obtain written confirmation that there has been no diminution since the original valuation exercise.

The report, which must not be qualified, is shown in **Table 11**. If it were qualified the company registrars would be unable to issue the share certificates.

TABLE 11: Report where shares allotted other than for cash

Report of the Independent [Valuer] [Auditor] to XYZ Plc for the purposes of the Companies Act 2006, s. 593(1)

We report on the value of the consideration for the allotment to … [*name of allottee*] of … shares, having a nominal value of […] each, to be issued at a premium of … pence per share. The shares and share premium are to be treated as fully paid up.

The consideration for the allotment to … [*name of allottee*] is [the freehold building situated at … [*address*]] and … [*number*] shares, having a nominal value of […] each in Blue Chip plc.

Basis of valuation

The freehold building was valued on the basis of open market value by [*name of expert*], a Fellow of the Royal Institution of Chartered Surveyors.

The shares in Blue Chip plc were valued by us on … on the basis of the price shown in The Stock Exchange Daily Official List at …

Opinion

In our opinion:

- it is reasonable to accept the valuation made by [name of expert];

- the methods of valuation of the freehold building and of the shares in Blue Chip plc were reasonable in all the circumstances; and

- there appears to have been no material change in the value of either part of the consideration since the date(s) at which the valuations were made.

On the basis of the valuations, in our opinion, the value of the total consideration is not less than the aggregate of the nominal value and share premium to be treated as paid up by the consideration.[1]

Qualified independent person

Address

Date

Note

[1] The auditor may include a 'Bannerman Statement' as part of the final section of his report (see **4.28**).

7.6 Transfer of non-cash assets to a public company by one of its members

7.6.1 Legal background

A similar report to that described in **7.5** is required when a public company, in the first two years following its registration, purchases a non-cash asset from one of its members for a consideration of at least one-tenth of the nominal value of its issued share capital. The Act does not allow such a purchase without approval by an ordinary resolution of the company and the submission of a report by independent accountants.

7.6.2 Guidance

This report must be prepared by independent accountants and must be made to the company in the six months preceding the allotment of shares.

As with the report made in **7.5**, if the company's own statutory auditor is requested to undertake a valuation in accordance with the *Companies Act* 2006, s. 599, the standards and guidance in the Revised Ethical Standard 2016 are applied (see **Section 2**).

Instead of being sent to the allottees, it will be addressed to the company and sent to the members and will detail the asset to be purchased by the company, together with details of the valuation. Again, this report must not be qualified.

An example report is set out in **Table 12**.

TABLE 12: Report where non-cash assets are transferred to a public company by certain of its members

Report of the Independent [Valuer] [Auditor] to XYZ Plc for the purposes of the Companies Act 2006, s. 599

We report on the transfer of non-cash assets to XYZ plc ('the Company') by subscribers to the Company's memorandum of association.

The consideration to be received by the Company is [a freehold building situated at … [*address*]] ('the consideration to be received').

The consideration to be given by the Company is [number] shares, having a nominal value of […] each in LMN plc ('the consideration to be given').

Basis of valuation

The freehold building was valued on the basis of open market value by [name of expert], a Fellow of the Royal Institution of Chartered Surveyors.

The shares in LMN Plc were valued by us on … on the basis of the price shown in The Stock Exchange Daily Official List at …

Opinion

In our opinion:

- it is reasonable to accept the valuation made by [name of expert];

- the methods of valuation of the freehold building and of the shares in LMN Plc were reasonable in all the circumstances; and

- there appears to have been no material change in the value of either part of the consideration since the date(s) at which the valuations were made.

On the basis of the valuations, in our opinion, the value of the total consideration to be received by the Company is not less than the value of the consideration to be given by the Company.[1]

Qualified independent person

Address

Date

Note

[1] The auditor may include a 'Bannerman Statement' as part of the final section of his report (see **4.28**).

8 Compilation reports on accounts prepared by accountants

8.1 Introduction

As audit exemption thresholds have crept steadily upwards over recent years, accountants have found themselves increasingly preparing financial statements for companies and charities where no audit is required. Statutory financial statements will, however, still be required to give a true and fair view and will be used by clients for the same purposes as audited financial statements. Although not required to do so, accountants will often wish to attach a report to financial statements they have prepared or compiled to indicate their involvement in the process and to make clear the extent of their responsibilities.

Some of the considerations arising when companies become exempt from the audit requirement are detailed in **8.5**.

8.2 Guidance

The Audit and Assurance Faculty of the ICAEW has issued guidance on the form and content of reports issued by accountants who prepare accounts on behalf of clients. The most recent versions are:

- TECH 07/16 AAF *Chartered accountants' reports on the compilation of financial statements of incorporated entities* (Revised March 2016), which replaced AAF 02/10; and

- TECH 08/16 AAF *Chartered accountants' reports on the compilation of historical financial information of unincorporated entities* (Revised March 2016), which replaced AAF 03/10.

The guidance in TECH 07/16 AAF for incorporated entities is also applicable to the compilation of financial statements of Limited Liability Partnerships (LLPs).

8.2.1 Professional ethics

TECH 07/16 AAF and TECH 08/16 AAF remind accountants that the five fundamental ethical principles of integrity, objectivity, competence, confidentiality and professional behaviour apply to compilation engagements as they do to audits. It also reminds them that no tests are required on the assertions underlying the information they are presented with and therefore reporting accountants can express no assurance on the financial statements.

When compiling historical financial information, accountants are bound by all ethical and other guidance laid down by the ICAEW. They should not, therefore compile, or allow their names to be associated with, financial information which they consider to:

- contain a materially false or misleading statement;

- contain statements or information furnished recklessly; or

- omit or obscure information required to be included where such omission or obscurity would be misleading.

If the accountant has been associated with such information, he should take steps to disassociate himself.

8.3 Incorporated entities

8.3.1 Terms of engagement

TECH 07/16 AAF states that there must be clear understanding between the client and the accountants regarding the terms of the engagement. An example engagement letter extract is given in **Table 1**.

In addition, accountants should consider whether it is appropriate to include a section on the limitation of the accountants' liability.

TABLE 1: Engagement letter extracts for the compilation of unaudited financial statements

Your responsibilities as directors

As directors of the company, you are responsible for maintaining adequate accounting records and for preparing financial statements which give a true and fair view and which have been prepared in accordance with the *Companies Act* 2006 ('the Act'). As directors, you must not approve the financial statements unless you are satisfied that they give a true and fair view of the assets, liabilities, financial position and profit or loss of the company.

In preparing financial statements, you are required to:

(1) select suitable accounting policies and then apply them consistently;

(2) make judgments and estimates that are reasonable and prudent; and

(3) prepare financial statements on a going concern basis unless it is inappropriate to presume that the company will continue in business.

You are also responsible for such internal control as you determine is necessary to enable the preparation of financial statements that are free from material misstatement whether due to fraud or error.

You are also responsible for safeguarding the assets of the company and hence for taking reasonable steps to prevent and detect fraud and other irregularities.

You have undertaken to make available to us, as and when required, all the company's accounting records and related financial information, including minutes of management and shareholders' meetings, necessary to carry out our work. You will make full disclosure to us of all relevant information.

Scope of the accountants' work

You have asked us to assist you in the preparation of the financial statements. We will compile the annual financial statements for your approval based on the accounting records maintained by you and the Information and explanations given to us by you. We shall plan our work on the basis that no report is required by statute or regulation for the year, unless you inform us in writing to the contrary. In carrying out our engagement, we will make enquiries of management and undertake any procedures that we judge appropriate but are under no obligation to perform procedures that may be required for assurance engagements such as audits or reviews.

You have advised us that the company is exempt from an audit of the financial statements. We will not carry out any work to determine whether or not the company is entitled to audit exemption. However, should our work indicate that the company is not entitled to the exemption, we will inform you of this.

Our work will not be an audit of the financial statements in accordance with International Standards on Auditing (UK). Consequently, our work will not provide any assurance that the accounting records or the financial statements are free from material misstatement, whether caused by fraud, other irregularities or error and cannot be relied on to identify weaknesses in internal controls.

Since we have not carried out an audit, nor confirmed in any way the accuracy or reasonableness of the accounting records maintained by the company, we are unable to provide any assurance as to whether the financial statements that we prepare from those records present a true and fair view.

We have a professional duty to compile financial statements that conform with generally accepted accounting principles from the accounting records and information and explanations given to us. Furthermore, as directors, you have a duty to prepare financial statements that comply with the Act and applicable accounting standards. Where we identify that the financial statements do not conform to accepted accounting principles or if the accounting policies adopted are not immediately apparent this will need to be disclosed in the financial statements.

We have a professional responsibility not to allow our name to be associated with financial statements which may be misleading. Therefore, although we are not required to search for such matters, should we become aware, for any reason, that the financial statements may be misleading, we will discuss the matter with you with a view to agreeing appropriate adjustments and/ or disclosures in the financial statements. In such circumstances where adjustments and/or disclosures that we consider appropriate are not made or where we are not provided with appropriate information, and as a result, we consider that the financial statements are misleading, we will withdraw from the engagement.

As part of our normal procedures, we may request you to provide written confirmation of any information or explanations given by you orally during the course of our work.

Form of the accountants' report

We shall report to the Board of Directors, with any modifications that we consider may be necessary, that in accordance with this engagement letter and in order to assist you to fulfil your responsibilities, we have compiled, without carrying out an audit, the financial statements from the accounting records of the company and from the information and explanation supplied to us.

Liability provisions

We will perform the engagement with reasonable skill and care. The total aggregate liability to the Company and the Board of Directors, as a body, of whatever nature, whether in contract, tort or otherwise, of [name of accountants] for any losses whatsoever and howsoever caused arising from or in any way connected with this engagement shall not exceed [amount].

8.3.2 Directors' responsibilities

Although they have asked their accountants to compile the financial statements, directors are ultimately responsible for ensuring that the company maintains adequate accounting records and for preparing financial statements which give a true and fair view. The accounts of micro-entities, where the exemptions available are taken advantage of and the legal disclosure requirements are met, are presumed to give a true and fair view. Other company accounts must have been prepared in accordance with the *Companies Act* 2006 and the applicable financial reporting framework.

In addition, directors are required to:

- select suitable accounting policies and then apply them consistently;

- make judgments and estimates that are reasonable and prudent;

- state whether applicable UK accounting standards have been followed, subject to any material departures disclosed and explained in the financial statements; and

- prepare financial statements on a going concern basis unless it is inappropriate to presume that the company will continue in business.

They are also responsible for safeguarding the assets of the company and for taking steps for the prevention and detection of fraud and other irregularities.

8.3.3   Accountants' procedures

Accountants will plan their work, and this includes obtaining a general understanding of the business and operations of the company and the accounting principles and practices of the industry in which the company operates.

Accountants also consider whether the financial statements are consistent with their understanding of the company, but are under no obligation to perform procedures that may be required for an audit or other type of assurance engagement.

There is no mandatory requirement to document the work that has been carried out; however, adequate documentation will demonstrate that the work performed is of the requisite quality and has been performed in accordance with the terms of engagement. Accountants may use a disclosure checklist or software package to check that all relevant disclosures have been made.

Accountants will also consider obtaining written confirmation of oral representations made by management.

8.3.4   Misleading financial statements

Although accountants are not reviewing or auditing the financial statements, they may become aware that the financial statements are misleading. For example, they may be aware that there are significant misclassifications or disclosure omissions within the financial statements, or instances of non-compliance with applicable requirements of the Companies Act or accounting standards. If this is the case, the matter should be discussed with management with a view to making adjustments or giving additional disclosures. If such amendments are not made, accountants should withdraw from the engagement.

It should be noted that where accounts have been prepared using the micro-entity option, there is no requirement for the disclosure of a going concern note or a note of accounting policies. If the accounts have been properly prepared to include the minimum requirements under this regime, they will be presumed to give a true and fair view. However, should the micro-entity choose to include items in addition to the minimum requirements, the accountant must consider the relevant accounting standard in relation to that item and whether proper disclosure has been made.

Accountants also need to remember that they are bound by the Code of Ethics not to be knowingly associated with misleading information, including instances where the information may be misleading because of omissions. This may be relevant where the accounts of micro-entities are presumed to be true and fair but, on rare occasions, may be considered misleading perhaps due to the absence of key information.

If the accountant considers the financial statements to be misleading, he should discuss the matter with the client and hope to make relevant adjustments or disclosures. If management refuse to take any action, the accountant will consider withdrawing from the engagement.

In rare circumstances, accountants may conclude that they do not need to withdraw from the engagement despite apparent departures from accounting standards or incomplete information, for example due to inadequacies in the accounting records. In these situations, where appropriate disclosure has been made in the financial statements, the accountants may wish to highlight the matter by inclusion of an explanatory paragraph in their compilation report.

There may be rare occasions when professional accountants consider that the information disclosed in accordance with the micro-entity regime is misleading and they need to take appropriate action.

8.3.5 Approving financial statements

The financial statements should be approved and signed by the directors before the accountants' report is signed.

The directors are statutorily responsible for their company's accounts. They are required to approve the accounts and the balance sheet should state the name of the directors signing the accounts on behalf of the board.

Under the *Companies Act* 2006, s. 475, a company is not entitled to audit exemption unless its balance sheet contains a statement by the directors to that effect. In addition, the directors must, on the face of the balance sheet, state that the members of the company have not required the company to obtain an audit of its accounts and acknowledge their responsibilities for complying with the requirements of the Companies Act with respect to keeping accounting records and the preparation of accounts.

8.3.6 Accountants' reports

The aim of the accountants' report is for readers to draw comfort from the fact that the accounts have been compiled by a chartered accountant who is subject to the ethical and other guidance issued by the ICAEW. The report will normally be addressed to the directors of the company.

The report should not be signed as 'registered auditor' or 'statutory auditor'.

An example report is given in **Table 2**.

The financial statements should contain a reference to the fact that they are unaudited, either on the front cover or on each page of the financial statements.

TABLE 2: Example accountants' report

Chartered Accountants'/Accountant's Report to the Board of Directors on the preparation of the Unaudited Statutory Accounts of XYZ Ltd for the year ended xxx

In order to assist you to fulfil your duties under the *Companies Act* 2006, we have prepared for your approval the accounts of XYZ Limited for the year ended xxx [as set out on pages x-x which comprise [*insert name of statements*] and the related notes from the company's accounting records and from information and explanations you have given us.

As a practising member/member firm of the Institute of the Chartered Accountants in England and Wales (ICAEW), we are subject to its ethical and other professional requirements which are detailed at www.icaew.com/en/members/regulations-standards-and-guidance/.

[It is your duty to ensure that XYZ Limited has kept adequate accounting records and to prepare statutory accounts that give a true and fair view of the assets, liabilities, financial position and profit [/loss] of XYZ Limited. You consider that XYZ Limited is exempt from the statutory audit requirement for the year.]

[We have not been instructed to carry out an audit or a review of the accounts of XYZ Limited. For this reason, we have not verified the accuracy or completeness of the accounting records or information and explanations you have given to us and we do not, therefore, express any opinion on the statutory accounts.]

[We draw your attention to note x in the financial statements which discloses and explains ...]

[This report is made to the Board of Directors of XYZ Limited, as a body, in accordance with the terms of our engagement letter dated xxx. Our work has been undertaken [solely to prepare for your approval the accounts of XYZ Limited and state those matters that we have agreed to state to the Board of Directors of XYZ Limited, as a body, in this report] in accordance with ICAEW

Technical Release 07/16 AAF. To the fullest extent permitted by law, we do not accept or assume responsibility to anyone other than XYZ Limited and its Board of Directors, as a body, for our work or for this report.]

Signature

Typed name of professional accountant

Chartered Accountants

Address

Date

8.4 Unincorporated entities

8.4.1 Scope of guidance

TECH 08/16 AAF is intended to give general guidance to accountants when they compile historical financial information for their clients, and covers situations where the request is by unincorporated entities for a specific purpose, such as for tax purposes, partnership accounts or for grant claims.

However, where a set of financial statements which comply fully with the provisions of UK GAAP are requested for an unincorporated entity, the guidance in TECH 07/16 AAF should be followed (see **8.3**).

TECH 08/16 AAF may also be of use when accountants compile historical financial information, other than financial statements, for incorporated entities.

8.4.2 Accounting basis

Accountants are not required to test assertions underlying the information which they are compiling and therefore are not able to express any assurance on the financial information being compiled.

There is no statutory requirement for the financial information of most unincorporated entities to give a true and fair view and it is acceptable to compile the information on an accounting basis other than full UK GAAP. The appropriate accounting basis should be discussed with the clients and clearly defined so that the accountants can compile the information.

The accounting basis, purpose and limitations of the information presented should be fully disclosed in a note to the financial information and referred to in the accountants' report.

8.4.3   Terms of engagement

As with compilations performed under TECH 07/16 AAF, there must be clear understanding between the client and the accountants regarding the terms of the engagement. An example engagement letter extract for the compilation of historical financial information under TECH 08/16 AAF is provided in **Table 3**.

In addition, accountants should consider whether it is appropriate to include a section on the limitation of the accountants' liability.

TABLE 3: Engagement letter extracts for the compilation of historical financial information for unincorporated entities

Client's responsibilities

You will be responsible for the reliability, accuracy and completeness of the accounting records.

You have undertaken to make available to us, as and when required, all your accounting records and related financial information, including minutes of management meetings, necessary to carry out our work. You will provide us with all the information and explanations relevant to the purpose and compilation of the financial information.

Scope of the accountants' work

You have asked us to assist you in the preparation of [insert type of information required] for [insert purpose]. We will compile the financial information for your approval based on the accounting records maintained by you and the information and explanations given to us by you.

We shall plan our work on the basis that no report is required by statute or regulation, unless you inform us in writing to the contrary. In carrying out our engagement, we will make enquiries of [management] and undertake any procedures that we judge appropriate but are under no obligation to perform procedures that may be required for assurance engagements such as audits or reviews.

Our work will not be an audit of the financial information in accordance with Auditing Standards. Consequently, our work will not provide any assurance that the accounting records or the financial information are free from material misstatement, whether caused by fraud, other irregularities or error and cannot be relied on to identify weaknesses in internal controls.

Since we have not carried out an audit, nor confirmed in any way the accuracy or reasonableness of the accounting records maintained by the company, we are unable to provide any assurance as to whether the financial information that we prepare from those records presents a true and fair view.

We have a professional duty to compile financial information that conforms with generally accepted accounting principles selected by management as being appropriate for the purpose for which the information is prepared. The accounting basis on which the information has been compiled, its purpose

---

and limitations will be disclosed in an accounting policy note to the financial information and will be referred to in our accountants' report.

We also have a professional responsibility not to allow our name to be associated with financial information which we believe may be misleading. Therefore, although we are not required to search for such matters, should we become aware, for any reason, that the financial information may be misleading, we will discuss the matter with you with a view to agreeing appropriate adjustments and/or disclosures in the financial information. In circumstances where adjustments and/or disclosures that we consider appropriate are not made or where we are not provided with appropriate information, and as a result we consider that the financial information is misleading, we will withdraw from the engagement.

As part of our normal procedures, we may request you to provide written confirmation of any information or explanations given by you orally during the course of our work.

You will approve and sign the financial information thereby acknowledging responsibility for it, including the appropriateness of the accounting basis on which it has been compiled, and for providing us with all information and explanations necessary for its compilation.

Form of the accountants' report

We shall report to you that in accordance with this engagement letter we have compiled, without carrying out an audit, the financial information from the accounting records of the entity and from the information and explanation supplied to us. The report should not be used for any purpose other than as set out in this engagement letter.

Liability provisions

We will perform the engagement with reasonable skill and care. The total aggregate liability to you, of whatever nature, whether in contract, tort or otherwise, of [name of accountants] for any losses whatsoever and howsoever caused arising from or in any way connected with this engagement shall not exceed [amount].

8.4.4 Client's responsibilities

The client is responsible for the reliability, accuracy and completeness of the accounting records of the entity and for disclosing all relevant information to the accountant.

The client is also responsible for safeguarding the assets of the entity and for taking steps for the prevention and detection of fraud and other irregularities.

Where required by the applicable financial reporting framework, e.g. UK GAAP, the client needs to satisfy himself that it is appropriate for the financial statements to be prepared on a going concern basis.

8.4.5   Planning

Having agreed a basis and format for the financial information, the accountant will plan the engagement. The level of planning will vary depending on the complexity and completeness of the client's accounting records and the reporting accountant's experience of the business.

8.4.6   Procedures

As in **8.3.3**, reporting accountants will obtain a general understanding of the operations of the entity, consider whether the financial information is consistent with their understanding of the business and check whether relevant disclosures have been made. In addition, they will obtain written representations from management, particularly in relation to estimates and the reliability, accuracy and completeness of information provided to them.

The accountants are under no obligation to perform procedures that would be necessary to enable them to give assurance on the financial information.

There is no mandatory requirement to document the work carried out, although full documentation will assist with performing a good quality engagement.

8.4.7   Misleading financial information

Accountants compiling financial information for unincorporated entities have the same responsibilities towards misleading financial information as accountants working for incorporated entities (see **8.3.4**).

8.4.8   Approval of financial information

Although there is no statutory duty for the financial information of unincorporated entities to be signed or approved by the client, it is recommended that the client does sign the information to acknowledge their responsibility for it. An example wording is given in **Table 4**.

TABLE 4: Example wording for approval of financial information

In accordance with the engagement letter dated [...], I/we approve the financial information which comprises [state the financial information compiled]. I/we acknowledge my/our responsibility for the financial information, including the appropriateness of the applicable financial reporting framework as set out in note [x], and for providing [the accountants] with all information and explanations necessary for its compilation.

8.4.9 Accountants' reports

As stated in **8.3.6**, the aim of the accountants' report is to help users derive comfort from the fact that the financial information has been compiled by an accountant who is subject to the ethical and other guidance issued by the ICAEW. It also clarifies that an audit has not taken place. An example report wording for the compilation of financial information for unincorporated entities is given in **Table 5**.

TABLE 5: Example accountants' report for the compilation of financial information for unincorporated entities

Chartered Accountants'/Accountant's Report to [Entity] on Unaudited Financial Information of XYZ

In accordance with the engagement letter dated [date], we have prepared for your approval the financial information of [the entity] for the year [/period] which comprises [insert names of statements] and the related notes from the entity's accounting records and from information and explanations you have given to us.

As a practising member [/member firm] of the Institute of Chartered Accountants in England and Wales (ICAEW), we are subject to its ethical and other professional requirements which are detailed at www.icaew.com/en/members/regulations-standards-and-guidance/.

[You have approved the [financial information] [for the year/period] and have acknowledged your responsibility for it, for the appropriateness of the financial reporting framework adopted and for providing all information and explanations necessary for its compilation.

We have not verified the accuracy or completeness of the accounting records or information and explanations you have given to us and we do not, therefore, express any opinion on the financial information.]

[This report is made solely to you in accordance with the terms of our engagement letter dated [date].] Our work has been undertaken [solely to prepare for your approval the financial information of [entity] and state those matters that we have agreed to state to you in this report] in accordance with ICAEW Technical release TECH 08/16AAF. [To the fullest extent permitted by law, we do not accept or assume responsibility to anyone other than [addressee of this report] for our work or for this report.]

Signature

Typed name of professional accountant

Chartered Accountants

Address

Date

8.5   Companies claiming audit exemption

8.5.1   Ineligible companies

Many companies that fulfil the size criteria for audit exemption (profit and loss, balance sheet or number of employees) are still required to have an audit. This may be because they are 'ineligible' under the legislation, such as public, banking and insurance companies, trade unions, employers' associations, certain companies that are members of groups and companies regulated under *Financial Services and Markets Act* 2000. An audit may also be required where the company's constitution requires it or where it is requested by the provider of finance.

8.5.2   Requirements when a company becomes exempt

Where a client company becomes audit exempt, either as a result of changing exemption limits, or due to changes in its size, the auditor should not continue to perform an audit without telling the client about the options available. Discussing these options will allow the auditor to point out the advantages of continuing with the annual audit process.

8.5.3   Engagement letters

Where there is a significant change in the nature of the services provided, a new engagement letter will be required. Therefore, when a client becomes audit exempt and takes advantage of that exemption a new engagement letter will be required, assuming the practitioner continues to act in some other capacity for that client. Where the client becomes entitled to take advantage of audit exemption but chooses not to do so it may nevertheless be desirable to issue a new engagement letter setting out the situation clearly.

8.5.4   Resignation procedures

Where a client becomes audit exempt and an audit is no longer requested for other reasons, the auditor does not, in theory, have to resign from office.

However, in order to avoid unnecessary risk relating to his position as auditor and risk arising should the exemption status of the company change in future, the auditor may wish to resign from office when an audit is no longer required. Normal procedures should be followed regarding statements to be made by the auditor on cessation of office (see **Section 38**).

The former Department of Trade and Industry (now Department for Business, Energy and Industrial Strategy) has advised that audit exemption is not, in itself, an issue that should be brought to the attention of members or creditors on the resignation of an auditor.

9 Reports to financial regulators

9.1 Legal background

9.1.1 Introduction

The auditor of an entity subject to statutory regulation (a 'regulated entity') may be required to report direct to a regulator certain information which comes to the auditor's attention in the course of the work undertaken in his capacity as auditor of the regulated entity. This may include work undertaken to express an opinion on the entity's financial statements, other financial information or on other matters specified by legislation or by a regulator.

9.1.2 Entities in the financial sector

The auditor of certain regulated entities in the financial sector has special reporting responsibilities in addition to his responsibility to report on the financial statements of the entity. These may include:

- requirements to report to regulators on certain specific matters, such as the entity's procedures with regard to client assets;

- a more general statutory duty to report to regulators where matters come to the attention of the auditor in the course of his audit that may be of significance to the regulator in the performance of its functions; and

- a right to report to the regulator matters that fall outside the statutory duty to report, where the auditor considers it appropriate to do so in the public interest.

Regulators for this purpose are primarily the Financial Conduct Authority (FCA) and the Prudential Regulation Authority (PRA) but may include other bodies if empowered to act in this capacity by future legislation.

Details regarding the auditor's responsibilities are set out in applicable legislation, for example, the *Financial Services and Markets Act* 2000, the *Financial Services Act* 2012 and the EU Audit Regulation (Regulation EU 537/2014 of the European Parliament and of the Council) and the rules of the relevant regulator. Auditors of regulated entities should ensure that they are aware of their responsibilities in this respect.

Whilst this is a familiar area to auditors in the financial services sector, the widening scope of businesses now authorised and regulated by the FCA has broadened the auditor's responsibilities in this area which now covers insurance intermediaries, consumer credit and debt management activities as well as businesses more usually thought of as falling under a financial services umbrella.

9.1.3   Public interest entities

In addition, as a result of the EU Audit Regulation which applies from 17 June 2016, public interest entities are now all also included in the definition of regulated entities, and auditors of public interest entities, regardless of sector, have a statutory duty to report to a regulator should certain matters come to their attention (see **9.7**).

9.2   Auditing and reporting standards and guidance

The following standards and guidance are relevant:

- ISA (UK) 250 Section B (Revised June 2016) – *The Auditor's Statutory Right and Duty to Report to Regulators of Public Interest Entities and Regulators of Other Entities in the Financial Sector*; and

- FRC Assurance Standard *Providing Assurance on Client Assets to the Financial Conduct Authority*, issued November 2015 (the Client Asset Assurance Standard).

The current version of ISA (UK) 250 Section B (Revised June 2016) is effective for periods commencing on or after 17 June 2016.

The Client Asset Reporting Standard, which was issued in November 2015 and effective for periods commencing 1 January 2016 superseded not only the client asset material in Practice Note 21 but also APB Bulletin 2011/2 and FRC Bulletin 3 (March 2013). It applies to auditors reporting to the Financial Conduct Authority (FCA) in accordance with its SUP (Supervision Manual) Rules in respect of engagements to report on regulated firms' compliance with the FCA's rules relevant to the holding of client assets.

Practice Note 19 (Revised) *The audit of banks and building societies in the United Kingdom* and Practice Note 20 (Revised) *The audit of insurers in the United Kingdom* also contain guidance relating to the provision of special reports on a routine basis on other matters specified by regulators of these regulated businesses.

Practice Note 21 (Revised) *The audit of investment businesses in the United Kingdom* was issued in December 2007 but was withdrawn by the

FRC in November 2017 as much of the material had been superseded by the Client Asset Reporting Standard and the remaining material was considered to be dated.

This section considers only the reports of auditors to regulators.

9.3   Types of report

Three types of report made by the auditor to the regulator are covered in this section:

- opinions on client money and custody assets (**9.4** and **9.5**);
- special ad hoc reports on regulatory matters of material significance (**9.6**); and
- reports to the regulator in respect of public interest entities (**9.7**).

Opinions on interim profits are not covered here. Guidance in this area was formerly contained in Practice Note 21 which has now been withdrawn. Guidance is however given in Practice Note 19 (Revised) *The audit of banks and building societies in the United Kingdom.*

9.4   Entities in the financial sector – auditor's responsibilities

Details of the reporting Rules applicable to auditors are contained within the FCA and PRA Handbooks.

The auditor should always be aware of any changes to the regulator's Rules during the period and the impact this will have on his report.

The auditor must notify the FCA or PRA, as applicable, if he is removed from office, resigns before the end of his term of office or is not reappointed. Any matters relevant to the removal, resignation or non-reappointment should be included in this communication. If there are no such matters, this must also be stated.

9.5   Client assets

The main purpose of the CASS (Client Asset) Rules, which are contained in the Business Standards section of the FCA's Handbook, is to ensure that the regulated business safeguards client assets, both in its day-to-day business and in the event of its insolvency. Chapter 6 of the CASS Rules contains the rules which a regulated business must comply with when it holds and/or safeguards and administers custody assets, whilst Chapter 7 sets out rules relating to when such a firm holds client money. Chapter 5 deals with client money arising in relation to insurance mediation (for example, broking) activities. Chapter 11 deals with client money arising in connection with debt management activities. Auditors have to report on this compliance under section 3.10 of the Supervision (SUP) section of the Handbook.

9.5.1 Background

Most firms that carry on investment business fall within the ambit of FCA rule SUP 3.10 regarding client assets. Such firms must appoint an auditor (a 'CASS auditor') to prepare and submit a Client Assets Report to the FCA. This may be the statutory auditor or another auditor engaged for this purpose. Similar rules apply to insurance intermediaries although not all insurance intermediaries are required to appoint a CASS auditor (see **9.5.12**). The CASS auditor's report must be made annually (or for a period of not more than 53 weeks) and provide an opinion on whether the firm:

- has maintained systems adequate to enable it to comply with the FCA's client money and custody rules (and if relevant, collateral and mandate rules) throughout the year; and

- was in compliance with those rules at the period end date.

The CASS auditor is also required to provide a schedule of breaches of CASS rules.

Where no CASS auditor has been appointed, the statutory auditor should be alert for circumstances that indicate that a CASS audit is required. If the statutory auditor becomes aware of such circumstances, a report should be made to the firm and the FCA.

9.5.2 Types of client assets report

A client assets report will take one of two forms:

- reasonable assurance report – a report providing a high but not absolute level of assurance which is obtained when the CASS auditor has obtained sufficient appropriate assurance evidence to reduce assurance engagement risk to an acceptably low level in the circumstances of the engagement, as the basis for a positive form of expression of the CASS auditor's conclusion;

- limited assurance report – a report providing a level of assurance where the engagement risk is reduced to a level that is acceptable in the circumstances of the engagement but which is obtained when that risk is greater than the level of assurance that would be provided in a reasonable assurance client assets report, as the basis for a negative form of expression of the CASS auditor's conclusion.

The form of report will depend on the entity, the scope of its permissions and its circumstances.

Examples of reasonable assurance reports are given in **Tables 3, 4** and **5**. Examples of limited assurance reports are given in **Tables 6, 7** and **8**.

9.5.3   Scope of permissions

Firms must not hold client money or assets unless they have the correct authority from the FCA to do so. CASS auditors are required to determine whether the firm is acting within its scope of permissions. In order to determine whether this is the case, the CASS auditor will discuss the matter with those charged with governance and view the firm's Scope of Part IV Permissions notice.

If the auditor determines that the firm is acting outside its permission in relation to holding client money, custody assets or both client money and custody assets, a report should be made to the FCA.

9.5.4   The CASS rules

The main role of the CASS rules is to ensure that client assets are protected in the event of an insolvency of the firm. The provisions within CASS include the following suffixes:

- 'R' – Rule;
- 'E' – Evidential Provision, a rule which is not binding in its own right, but will be linked to a binding rule; and
- 'G' – Guidance.

A rule is a binding obligation on firms that the FCA regulates and if contravened, a firm commits a 'breach' which renders it subject to potential enforcement action and in some circumstances an action for damages.

A reportable breach will occur whenever a rule is contravened. Where a firm has not followed a guidance provision, the CASS auditor should consider whether the linked rule has been breached.

Key principles underlying the CASS rules

Table 1 sets out the key principles underlying the CASS rules, which the CASS auditor should consider:

TABLE 1: Principles underlying the CASS rules

Principle	CASS 3 Collateral	CASS 5 Insurance Intermediaries	CASS 6 Custody Assets	CASS 7 Client Money	CASS 8 Mandates	CASS 11 Debt Management Firms
Identification: The firm should identify all sources of client assets and mandates in its business	X	X	X	X	X	X
Protecting client assets: The firm should make adequate arrangements to safeguard client ownership rights on the insolvency of the firm	X	X	X	X		X
Organisational arrangements: The firm's organisational arrangements should be adequate such that they comply with the CASS Rules	X	X	X	X	X	X
• Arrangements in respect of registration and recording of legal titles			X			
• Segregation of client money		X		X		X
• Safe custody assets used only as permitted by the CASS Rules	X		X			
Accurate records and accounts: The firm should have records and accounts that are maintained with sufficient accuracy (and on a timely basis) to enable the firm to comply with the CASS Rules	X	X	X	X	X	X

Principle	CASS 3 Collateral	CASS 5 Insurance Intermediaries	CASS 6 Custody Assets	CASS 7 Client Money	CASS 8 Mandates	CASS 11 Debt Management Firms
Reconciliations: The firm should perform internal and external reconciliations in accordance with the CASS Rules at the requisite frequency in order to rectify discrepancies		X	X	X		X
Rectify discrepancies in reconciliations: The firm should ensure that discrepancies arising from reconciliations are rectified appropriately		X	X	X		X
Trust: The firm should notify and obtain acknowledgement of trust status over client money		X		X		X
Non-statutory trust: The firm should ensure that the conditions for establishing a non-statutory trust are met		X				
Custody agreements: The firm should have appropriate custody agreements setting out the status of client custody accounts and prohibiting inappropriate liens			X			
Client money distributions: The firm should ensure that client money distributions are carried out in accordance with the CASS Rules		X		X		X

9.5.5 Scope of the assurance standard

The Client Asset Assurance Standard covers the following CASS Rules:

- **Collateral** (CASS 3) – these rules address arrangements whereby a firm is given the right to use a client's asset, and is allowed to treat the asset as if the firm has legal title and associated rights to it, subject to the requirement to return equivalent assets to the client upon satisfaction of the client's obligation to the firm;

- **Client Money** (CASS 5, 7 and 11) – money of any currency that a firm holds for or on behalf of a client in connection with investment business or insurance mediation activity or debt management activities;

- **Client Money Distributions** (CASS 5.6 and 7A) – these rules aim to facilitate the timely return of client money to a client if the firm or a third party holding the client money fails;

- **Custody Assets** (CASS 6) – in relation to a non-MiFID ('Markets in Financial Instruments Directive' which allows firms incorporated and authorised in an EEA member state to provide those authorised services in another EEA member state) business, custody assets include:

  - a designated investment held for or on behalf of a client (otherwise known as a safe custody investment); and

  - any other asset, which is or may be held with a designated investment, held for, or on behalf of, a client.

  For MiFID businesses, custody assets are financial instruments that the firm holds which belong to a client; and

- **Mandates** (CASS 8) – these rules apply to a firm in respect of any authority from the client under which engagements where the firm controls rather than holds client assets or can enter arrangements that create liabilities on behalf of a client.

9.5.6 Accepting the engagement

In accordance with ISQC (UK) 1 *Quality Control for Firms that Perform Audits and Reviews of Historical Financial Information and Other Assurance and Related Services Engagements*, see **Section 3**, an engagement partner and the audit staff must have appropriate experience and competence to act for a client. Therefore, members of the CASS engagement team must have a knowledge and understanding of the CASS and other FCA Rules sufficient to perform the engagement. This may mean that the statutory audit team are not best placed to perform the CASS audit for complex firms and a specialist team may be used instead.

Where the statutory audit team and the CASS audit team are from the same firm, the terms of engagement for the CASS audit may be included in a separate section of the main engagement letter. Typically, the CASS auditor will refer in the engagement letter to the:

- responsibility of the directors or senior management to comply with applicable legislation and the FCA Handbook rules and guidance including the need to keep the FCA informed about the affairs of the firm;

- statutory right and duty of the CASS auditor to report directly to the FCA in certain circumstances; and

- requirement to cooperate with the CASS auditor, including allowing access to records information and explanations.

The FCA do not approve the appointment of the CASS auditor and so is not usually an addressee of the engagement letter. However, CASS auditors are required to cooperate with the FCA and notify them when they cease to hold office.

9.5.7 Assurance procedures

The FRC's Client Asset Assurance Standard sets out the requirements with which a CASS auditor is required to comply in performing a CASS audit for both reasonable assurance and limited assurance engagements. The process for forming the auditor's opinions in a reasonable assurance engagement is set out, in diagram form, in **Table 2**.

Actual or potential breaches of the rules may be identified at any stage of the process.

The Standard also sets out examples of specific procedures for limited assurance engagements.

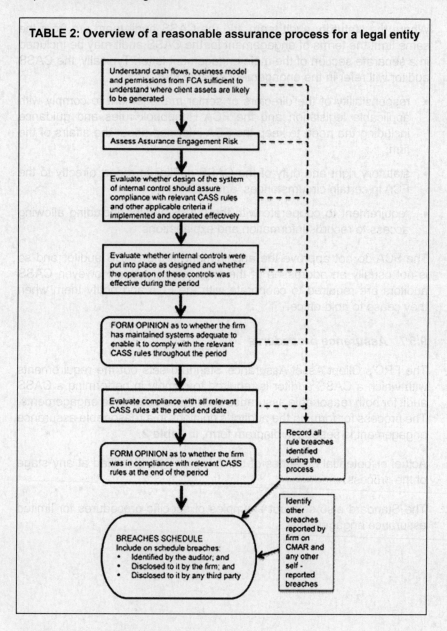

TABLE 2: Overview of a reasonable assurance process for a legal entity

Understand cash flows, business model and permissions from FCA sufficient to understand where client assets are likely to be generated

Assess Assurance Engagement Risk

Evaluate whether design of the system of internal control should assure compliance with relevant CASS rules and other applicable criteria if implemented and operated effectively

Evaluate whether internal controls were put into place as designed and whether the operation of these controls was effective during the period

FORM OPINION as to whether the firm has maintained systems adequate to enable it to comply with the relevant CASS rules throughout the period

Evaluate compliance with all relevant CASS rules at the period end date

FORM OPINION as to whether the firm was in compliance with relevant CASS rules at the end of the period

Record all rule breaches identified during the process

Identify other breaches reported by firm on CMAR and any other self-reported breaches

BREACHES SCHEDULE
Include on schedule breaches:
- Identified by the auditor; and
- Disclosed to it by the firm; and
- Disclosed to it by any third party

9.5.8 Planning the engagement

The objective of the CASS Rules is to ensure that client assets are safeguarded if the firm becomes insolvent. For this reason, the FRC's Assurance Standard requires that CASS auditors develop an 'insolvency mind-set', meaning that they should conduct their procedures against a level of stress which presumes that the firm may become insolvent.

Also in contrast to a typical financial statements audit, the CASS auditor will not apply the concept of materiality when identifying and reporting breaches of CASS Rules to the FCA. All breaches, of whatever monetary value, must be reported.

The extent of the CASS auditor's work will depend on the assessment of assurance engagement risk. This is the risk that the auditor incorrectly expresses an unmodified opinion when reporting to the FCA that the firm has maintained adequate systems during the period or that it was in compliance with the relevant rules at the period end when in fact it was not.

In making the initial assessment of engagement risk, the CASS auditor will meet with senior management, the CASS compliance officer and the CF10a (individual approved for the CASS oversight function) for CASS medium and CASS large firms. The auditor would also consider:

- operations manuals;
- the firm's documentation of systems and controls (control framework) mapped to individual CASS rules;
- the firm's CASS risk assessment;
- compliance monitoring programmes and results;
- records maintained by the firm of any rule breaches and notifications to the FCA that may have occurred during the period;
- the results of recent inspection visits made by the FCA;
- the register of client complaints; and
- any section 166 Skilled Persons Reports that may have been performed.

CASS auditors must ensure that they consider all systems used by the entity in relation to client assets. This is particularly relevant where client assets are held on deposit overnight, and are, therefore subject to different arrangements at different times of the day.

9.5.9   *Statutory and non-statutory trusts*

The CASS rules require that client bank accounts, client transaction accounts held with a clearing house or broker and money held in respect of mediation activity are named to show that they are client money and that the bank or other institution holding them acknowledges in writing the status of the money held in the account and the limitation of right of set off or counterclaim with other entity accounts.

The CASS auditor should consider whether the:

- client bank accounts and client transaction accounts include in their titles an appropriate description to distinguish them as client money;

- relevant acknowledgement letters relating to the trust status have been sent to and received from the bank/institution at which accounts have been opened;

- acknowledgement from the bank/institution has been received in the prescribed period set out by the CASS rules;

- body of the notification letters complies with the specific requirements set out in CASS 7;

- acknowledgment letters sufficiently distinguish the account to which they refer; and

- letters can be dated and attributed to the responsible party (i.e. the letterhead and signatory identifies their position within the firm).

9.5.10 Reconciliations

The CASS auditor is required to review client asset reconciliations as part of his work. These can often be complex in nature and a suitably senior member of the CASS audit team should be involved in performing this review to evaluate whether the justifications given for reconciling items are reasonable.

The CASS auditor should be particularly cautious in relation to:

- infrequent or sporadic reconciliations;

- poorly implemented system changes which lead to reconciling items;

- an excessive number of manual corrections or corrections caused by poor systems;

- the inclusion of non-client bank accounts in the reconciliation;

- client staff appearing to lack understanding of the CASS rules;

- a failure to escalate reconciling items to the appropriate level of management by client staff;

- poor documentation; and

- the reconciliation being performed by a person involved in the recording or movement of assets, resulting in a lack of segregation of duties.

9.5.11   Custody arrangements

The CASS auditor is required to ensure that the firm has complied with the rules in CASS 6.3 where custody assets held on behalf of a client are placed in an account with a third party.

The auditor should:

- obtain and document an understanding of the contractual terms between the firm and the third party;
- understand how the firm monitors the systems and controls in place at the third party;
- consider relevant reports from the third party's statutory auditor, internal auditor or other regulatory agencies; and
- consider whether they have access to all the information they require from the third party.

Failure to obtain sufficient information from the third party will result in a limitation in scope, which will affect the opinion in the client assets report.

9.5.12   Insurance intermediaries

CASS 5 governs firms undertaking insurance mediation activity and holding client money. Many of the requirements are similar to those governing client money held by investment businesses, however there are some significant differences of which CASS auditors must be aware and these are set out in the rules themselves.

In addition:

- insurance intermediaries holding no more than £30,000 client money in a statutory trust are not required to appoint a CASS auditor; and
- insurance intermediaries are not required to appoint a CASS auditor to give a limited assurance report when they claim not to hold client money.

Insurance intermediaries may use non-statutory trusts in accordance with rule CASS 5.4. This allows them to make advances of credit from the client money account to the firm's clients. The conditions and requirements surrounding use of non-statutory trusts are many and varied, including ensuring that the firm obtains, and keeps current, written confirmation from its CASS auditor that the firm has in place systems and controls which are adequate to ensure that the firm is able to monitor and manage its client money transactions and any credit risk arising from the operation of non-statutory trusts.

9.5.13 Debt management firms

Debt management firms fall within the scope of FCA regulation. CASS 11 extends CASS Rules and reporting requirements to such firms which are defined as firms which:

(a) carry on the activities of debt counselling or debt adjusting, alone or together, with a view to an individual entering into a particular debt solution;

(b) carry on the activity of debt counselling where an associate carries on debt adjusting with that aim (or vice versa); or

(c) are not a not-for-profit debt advice body.

During a transitional period, some debt management firms are operating under interim permissions from the FCA and may not be required to comply in full with the FCA rules. Auditors of such firms should check the firm's authorisation status and the rules that apply in the particular circumstances.

9.5.14 Mandates

Where a firm holds a mandate in respect of investment business or insurance mediation activity (except where it relates to a reinsurance contract) which allows the firm to control a client's assets or liabilities, that firm must establish and maintain adequate systems and internal controls which include:

- an up-to-date list of the authorities and any conditions placed by the client or the firm's management on their use;

- a record of all transactions entered into using the authority and internal controls to ensure that they are within the scope of the authority of the person and the firm entering into the transaction;

- the details of the procedures and authorities for giving and receiving of instructions under the authority;

- where the firm holds a passbook or similar document belonging to the client, internal controls for the safeguarding (including against loss, unauthorised destruction, theft, fraud or misuse) of any passbook or similar document belonging to the client and held by the firm.

The CASS auditor is required to perform procedures in relation to mandates to provide reasonable assurance that the firm maintained systems adequate to enable it to comply with the mandate rules and that the firm was in compliance with the mandate rules at the period end date.

9.5.15   Using the work of the internal audit function

Where the client entity has an internal audit function, the scope of which covers control over client assets, the CASS auditor should consider the extent to which the work of the internal audit function is relevant for his purposes. The CASS auditor will, at least, wish to familiarise himself with the findings of the internal audit function and consider the implications thereof for his own work and reporting responsibilities.

Further guidance on matters to be considered when using the work of the internal audit function are set out in the FRC's Client Asset Assurance Standard and in **Section 31**.

The findings of internal audit in relation to breaches of CASS rules are of particular importance to the CASS auditor because the CASS auditor must report all CASS breaches in his CASS report and this includes any CASS breaches identified by the internal audit function. However, the responsibility for the client asset report remains entirely with the CASS auditor.

9.5.16   Using the work of an expert

Although CASS auditors are expected to have a good knowledge of the CASS rules, there can sometimes be complex arrangements in place which may mean that CASS Rules are not applicable to an individual client money or asset balance or to the overall holdings of a particular client.

In these situations, it is important that the CASS auditor understands the underlying terms of client agreements to ascertain whether exemption provisions are correctly applied. The involvement of a legal specialist is likely to be required in such situations, and the guidance in **31.3** will apply.

9.5.17   Reporting

A report on a client asset engagement is quite different to a report on financial statements as the engagement is specifically undertaken to address the needs of the FCA who are the users of the report.

If there has been any breach of a CASS rule during the year, a qualified or adverse opinion must be given as the concept of materiality does not apply as in the audit of financial statements. However, if all breaches identified in the period have been rectified by the period end, the CASS auditor may give a modified opinion on the period and a clean opinion on the period end compliance with CASS rules (see **Table 3**).

An adverse opinion is likely to be given where the breaches identified are indicative of a 'systemic or pervasive failure to comply with the principle of protecting client assets'. Considerations include:

- the extent to which clients might lose their assets if the firm had gone into administration while the breach persisted;

- whether there has been a breach of the requirement to keep proper records of client assets; and

- whether the firm has failed to carry out, or incorrectly carried out to a significant extent, the reconciliations or client money calculations required by the CASS Rules.

The client asset report contains two parts:

- the CASS auditor's opinion; and

- the breaches schedule.

Every breach within the period identified by the CASS auditor, the firm or notified by another party including the FCA itself, must be listed in the breaches schedule and if no breaches were found, a nil return must be made. Information about the severity, duration and frequency of each breach must also be given, together with details of the circumstances that gave rise to each breach and any remedial action undertaken.

The CASS auditor must deliver a draft of its client asset report to the firm prior to submitting it to the FCA so that the firm has an adequate period of time to consider the findings and provide the CASS auditor with comments explaining the circumstance that gave rise to the breaches included in the breaches schedule and to provide details of remedial action.

CASS auditors are required to submit their report to the FCA within four months of the end of the period covered with a copy of the final report also provided to the firm. For insurance intermediaries, the report must be delivered to the firm, rather than the FCA, within the same time period.

Examples of qualified, adverse, and unmodified reasonable assurance reports are set out in **Tables 3–8**.

TABLE 3: Example qualified reasonable assurance report

Reasonable assurance report on client assets by the independent auditor to the Financial Conduct Authority in respect of [name of firm], FCA reference number [number]

Part 1: Auditor's Opinion on Client Assets

We report in respect of [Firm name] ('the firm') on the matters set out below for the period started [dd/mm/yyyy] and ended [dd/mm/yyyy] ('the period').

Our report has been prepared as required by SUP 3.10.4R and is addressed to the Financial Conduct Authority (FCA) in its capacity as regulator of financial services firms under the *Financial Services and Markets Act* 2000.

Basis of opinions

We have carried out such procedures as we considered necessary for the purposes of this report in accordance with the Client Asset Assurance Standard issued by the Financial Reporting Council.

The opinions relate only to the period, or as at the date, specified. The opinions do not provide assurance in relation to any future period or date as changes to systems or controls subsequent to the date of this report may alter the validity of our opinions.

Qualified opinion on adequacy of systems during the period

In our opinion, except for the failure of the firm to perform a reconciliation of ... in March 20xx, as described in item 1 of the attached breaches schedule, the firm has maintained systems adequate to enable it to comply with the custody rules, collateral rules, mandate rules and client money rules throughout the period since the last date at which a report was made.

Unmodified opinion on compliance at period end date

In our opinion, the firm was in compliance with the custody rules, collateral rules, the mandate rules and the client money rules as at the period end date.

Other matters

This report should be read in conjunction with the Breaches Schedule that we have prepared and which is appended.

[Signature]

Address

John Smith for and on behalf of [Name of audit firm]

Date

Breaches Schedule

Part 2: Identified CASS Breaches that have occurred during the period

[Firm name], FCA reference number [number], for the period started [dd/mm/yyyy] and ended [dd/mm/yyyy]

In accordance with SUP 3.10.9AR, Columns A to D have been completed by and are the responsibility of the auditor. In accordance with SUP 3.11.1G, Column E has been completed by the firm. The auditor has no responsibility for the content of Column E.

Column A	Column B	Column C	Column D	Column E
Item No	Rule Reference(s)	Identifying Party	Breach Identified	Firm's Comment
1. (Illustrative details to be inserted)				

TABLE 4: Example adverse reasonable assurance report

Assurance report on client assets by the independent auditor to the Financial Conduct Authority in respect of [name of firm], FCA reference number [number]

Part 1: Auditor's Opinion on Client Assets

We report in respect of [Firm name] ('the firm') on the matters set out below for the period started [dd/mm/yyyy] and ended [dd/mm/yyyy] ('the period').

Our report has been prepared as required by SUP 3.10.4R and is addressed to the Financial Conduct Authority (FCA) in its capacity as regulator of financial services firms under the *Financial Services and Markets Act* 2000.

Basis of opinions

We have carried out such procedures as we considered necessary for the purposes of this report in accordance with the Client Asset Assurance Standard issued by the Financial Reporting Council.

The opinions relate only to the period, or as at the date, specified. The opinions do not provide assurance in relation to any future period or date as changes to systems or controls subsequent to the date of this report may alter the validity of our opinions.

Adverse opinion on adequacy of systems during the period

In our opinion, because of the systemic failure of the firm to carry out reconciliations of ... as described in lines 1–5 of the attached breaches schedule the firm did not maintain systems adequate to enable it to comply with the client money rules throughout the period since the last date at which a report was made.

Adverse opinion on compliance at period end date

In our opinion, because of the failure to perform the reconciliations described in lines 1–5 of the attached breaches schedule the firm was not in compliance with the client money rules as at the period end date.

Claim not to hold custody assets

The scope of the firm's permissions did not allow it to hold custody assets.

The directors of the firm have stated that the firm did not hold custody assets during the period. Based on review procedures performed, nothing has come to our attention that causes us to believe that the firm held custody assets during the period.

Other matters

This report should be read in conjunction with the Breaches Schedule that we have prepared and which is appended.

[Signature]

Address

John Smith for and on behalf of [Name of audit firm]

Date

Breaches schedule

Part 2: Identified CASS Breaches that have occurred during the period

[Firm name], FCA reference number [number], for the period started [dd/mm/yyyy] and ended [dd/mm/yyyy].

In accordance with SUP 3.10.9AR, Columns A to D have been completed by and are the responsibility of the auditor. In accordance with SUP 3.11.1G, Column E has been completed by the firm. The auditor has no responsibility for the content of Column E.

Column A	Column B	Column C	Column D	Column E
Item No	Rule Reference(s)	Identifying Party	Breach Identified	Firm's Comment
1. (Illustrative details to be inserted)				

TABLE 5: Example unmodified reasonable assurance report

Reasonable assurance report on client assets by the independent auditor to the Financial Conduct Authority in respect of [name of firm], FCA reference number [number]

Part 1: Auditor's Opinion on Client Assets

We report in respect of [Firm name] ('the firm') on the matters set out below for the period started [dd/mm/yyyy] and ended [dd/mm/yyyy] ('the period').

Our report has been prepared as required by SUP 3.10.4R and is addressed to the Financial Conduct Authority (FCA) in its capacity as regulator of financial services firms under the *Financial Services and Markets Act* 2000.

Basis of opinions

We have carried out such procedures as we considered necessary for the purposes of this report in accordance with the Client Asset Assurance Standard issued by the Financial Reporting Council.

The opinions relate only to the period, or as at the date, specified. The opinions do not provide assurance in relation to any future period or date as changes to systems or controls subsequent to the date of this report may alter the validity of our opinions.

Unmodified opinions on adequacy of systems during the period

In our opinion, the firm has maintained systems adequate to enable it to comply with the custody rules, collateral rules, mandate rules and client money rules throughout the period since the last date at which a report was made.

In our opinion [name of nominee companies], subsidiaries of the firm which are nominee companies during the period in whose name custody assets are registered, those nominee companies have maintained throughout the period systems for the custody, identification and control of custody assets which:

(a) were adequate; and

(b) included reconciliations at appropriate intervals between the records maintained (whether by the firm or the nominee company) and statements or confirmations from custodians or from the person who maintained the record of legal entitlement.

Unmodified opinion on compliance at period end date

In our opinion, the firm was in compliance with the [custody rules,] [collateral rules,] [the mandate rules] [and] [the client money rules] as at the period end date.

Unmodified opinion on secondary pooling event

In our opinion, in relation to the secondary pooling event during the period, the firm has complied with the rules in [CASS 5.6] [and] [CASS 7A] in relation to that pooling event.

Other matters

Our opinion expressed above does not extend to the appended Breaches Schedule.

[Signature]

Address

John Smith for and on behalf of [Name of audit firm]

Date

Breaches schedule

Part 2: Identified CASS Breaches that have occurred during the period

[Firm name], FCA reference number [number], for the period started [dd/mm/yyyy] and ended [dd/mm/yyyy].

In accordance with SUP 3.10.9AR, Columns A to D have been completed by and are the responsibility of the auditor. In accordance with SUP 3.11.1G, Column E has been completed by the firm. The auditor has no responsibility for the content of Column E.

Column A	Column B	Column C	Column D	Column E
Item No	Rule Reference(s)	Identifying Party	Breach Identified	Firm's Comment
			No breaches were identified	

TABLE 6: Example unmodified opinion limited assurance report where firm has permission to hold both client money and client assets and claims to hold neither

Limited assurance report on client assets by the independent auditor to the Financial Conduct Authority in respect of [name of firm], FCA reference number [number]

We report in respect of [Firm name] ('the firm') on the matters set out below for the period started [dd/mm/yyyy] and ended [dd/mm/yyyy] ('the period').

Our report has been prepared as required by SUP 3.10.4R and is addressed to the Financial Conduct Authority (FCA) in its capacity as regulator of financial services firms under the *Financial Services and Markets Act* 2000.

Basis of opinion

We have carried out such procedures as we considered necessary for the purposes of this report in accordance with the Client Asset Assurance Standard issued by the Financial Reporting Council.

The opinions relate only to the period, or as at the date, specified. The opinions do not provide assurance in relation to any future period or date.

Unmodified opinion

The directors of the firm have stated that the firm did not hold client money or custody assets during the period. Based on review procedures performed, nothing has come to our attention that causes us to believe that the firm held client money or custody assets during the period.

[Signature]

Address

John Smith for and on behalf of [Name of audit firm]

Date

TABLE 7: Example unmodified opinion limited assurance report where firm does not have permissions to hold client money or custody assets and claims to hold neither

Limited assurance report on client assets by the independent auditor to the Financial Conduct Authority in respect of [name of firm], FCA reference number [number]

We report in respect of [Firm name] ('the firm') on the matters set out below for the period started [dd/mm/yyyy] and ended [dd/mm/yyyy] ('the period').

Our report has been prepared as required by SUP 3.10.4R and is addressed to the Financial Conduct Authority (FCA) in its capacity as regulator of financial services firms under the *Financial Services and Markets Act* 2000.

Basis of opinion

We have carried out such procedures as we considered necessary for the purposes of this report in accordance with the Client Asset Assurance Standard issued by the Financial Reporting Council.

The opinions relate only to the period, or as at the date, specified. The opinions do not provide assurance in relation to any future period or date.

Unmodified opinion

The scope of the firm's permissions did not allow it to hold client money or custody assets.

The directors of the firm have stated that the firm did not hold client money or custody assets during the period. Based on review procedures performed, nothing has come to our attention that causes us to believe that the firm held client money or custody assets during the period.

[Signature]

Address

John Smith for and on behalf of [Name of audit firm]

Date

TABLE 8: Example modified limited assurance report on client assets where a firm holds client money but does not have permission to do so

Limited assurance report on client assets by the independent auditor to the Financial Conduct Authority in respect of [name of firm], FCA reference number [number]

We report in respect of [Firm name] ('the firm') on the matters set out below for the period started [dd/mm/yyyy] and ended [dd/mm/yyyy] ('the period').

Our report has been prepared as required by SUP 3.10.4R and is addressed to the Financial Conduct Authority (FCA) in its capacity as regulator of financial services firms under the *Financial Services and Markets Act* 2000.

Basis of opinion

We have carried out such procedures as we considered necessary for the purposes of this report in accordance with the Client Asset Assurance Standard issued by the Financial Reporting Council.

The opinions relate only to the period, or as at the date, specified. The opinions do not provide assurance in relation to any future period or date.

Modified opinion on client money

The scope of the firm's permissions allowed it to hold custody assets but not to hold client money.

The directors (or equivalent corporate officers) of the firm have stated that the firm did not hold client money or custody assets during the period. Arising from the findings of our review procedures, it came to our attention that, contrary to its permissions, the firm held client money [include information about how much client money is involved and the circumstances leading to the firm holding such client money] during [specify period during which client money was held].

Unmodified opinion on custody assets

Based on review procedures performed, nothing has come to our attention that causes us to believe that the firm held custody assets during the period.

[Signature]

Address

John Smith for and on behalf of [Name of audit firm]

Date

9.6 Special ad hoc reports

The *Financial Services and Markets Act* 2000, the *Financial Services Act* 2012 and regulations made under them (including the *FSMA 2000 (Communications by Auditors) Regulations* 2001 (SI 2001/2587)) impose a statutory duty on the auditors of an authorised firm, or the auditor of an entity closely linked to an authorised firm, to communicate certain matters to the regulator relevant to the regulator's functions, which has come to his attention 'in the capacity of auditor' during his audit work. The FRC's Assurance Standard on Client Assets notes that the FCA has confirmed that this duty applies also to a CASS auditor who is not appointed as statutory auditor of the entity.

Other regulations clarify the matters to be reported and extend the application of the statutory duty to information to which auditors of a financial institution become aware in their capacity as auditors of other entities with close links to the financial institution.

The EU Audit Regulation which applies for audits of accounting periods commencing on or after 17 June 2016 also imposes a new duty to report to regulators on auditors of public interest entities. This is reflected in the requirements of ISA (UK) 250 Section B (Revised June 2016) and is considered in **9.7**.

9.6.1 Auditing standards and guidance

Standards and guidance on the implications of and the procedures necessary under these regulations are contained in ISA (UK) 250 Section B (Revised June 2016). This includes:

- the right and duty to report to regulators;
- material significance;
- procedures;
- reporting;
- communication with the regulator; and
- relationship with other reporting responsibilities.

Practice Notes have also been developed for different types of entity – for example, Practice Note 19 covers Banks and Building Societies and Practice Note 20 covers Insurers. Where entities are governed by more than one regulator, the auditor should ensure that they follow the guidance in each relevant Practice Note.

9.6.2 Right and duty to report

The auditor of a regulated entity is required to bring to the attention of the regulator information of which he becomes aware in the course of the work required to fulfil his audit responsibilities, which in his opinion is:

- relevant to the regulator's functions (such as breaches of regulator's Rules or concerns about the fit and proper status of management); and
- of material significance to the regulator.

For this purpose, ISA (UK) 250 Section B (Revised June 2016) defines a regulated entity as being an individual, company or other type of entity which is:

(i) authorised to carry on business in the financial sector which is subject to statutory regulation; or

(ii) a public interest entity (defined in the glossary in **Appendix 3**).

The auditor has a statutory duty to report certain other information, typically breaches of regulations which may come to his attention during his work. The auditor is not required to perform any additional procedures to search out these matters. This statutory duty applies only to information which comes to the auditor in his capacity as auditor. Guidance on what constitutes information gained in his capacity as auditor is given in the ISA (UK).

If the information is discovered by someone not involved in the audit, but it is of relevance to the audit, and the work that it related to, it should be taken into account as if it were audit evidence. If the work is not relevant to the audit, then it is unlikely that it will give rise to a duty to report.

Where information is discovered in the course of work performed for another client, the auditor has no right to breach his duty of confidentiality in respect of it. However, he may choose to make enquiries during the audit of the regulated entity to establish whether the information can be substantiated from that source.

The guidance stresses that firms should ensure that they have suitable lines of communication so that any information which may give rise to a duty to report is brought to the attention of the partner responsible for the audit, usually by enquiries of other members of the firm as part of the audit planning and completion.

The statutory right to report to the regulator is not affected if the auditor ceases to hold office. Hence, if he is aware of information, this may be reported either before or after ceasing to hold office.

The auditor may have a right to report certain matters direct to the regulator in addition to those which he has a duty to report. This right will usually be exercised where the auditor considers that doing so is necessary to protect the interests of those for whose benefit the regulator is required to act.

9.6.3 *'Material significance'*

'Material significance' is defined in ISA (UK) 250 Section B (Revised June 2016) as being where the regulator is likely to investigate a matter because of its nature or potential financial impact. Material significance does not mean the same as materiality in the context of the audit of financial statements. Whilst an event may be trivial in its financial impact, it may be of a nature or type likely to change the perception of the regulator. Further guidance concerning particular types of regulated entity is contained in the Practice Notes.

Under the *Financial Services and Markets Act* 2000, statutory definitions are provided for matters giving rise to a duty to report. They are generally matters which the auditor has a reasonable cause to believe will, or may be, of material significance in determining whether:

- a person is a fit and proper person to carry on investment or other regulated business; or

- disciplinary action or powers of intervention should be used to stop investors suffering loss.

Although the particular nature of the various sectors are considered in the legislation, in general the definitions incorporate the following terms:

- circumstances indicating that the regulated entity's authorisation could be revoked;

- there is, has been, or may have been, either:

  - a failure to fulfil specified requirements; or

  - a contravention of other provisions of the Rules which is likely to be of material significance to the regulator concerned for the exercise of its functions;

- there is a doubt as to the entity's status as a going concern; and

- the auditor concludes that his report on the entity's financial statements should include a qualified opinion.

Status of regulated entities, directors and senior management as fit and proper persons

When planning the audit, the auditor must familiarise himself with any guidance issued by the regulator on the information that it takes into consideration when deciding whether the fit and proper requirement has been met.

Generally, the regulator assesses entities against three broad measures:

- honesty;
- competence; and
- solvency.

Although the auditor cannot be expected to make judgments on competence, soundness of judgment and diligence, there may be persuasive evidence which calls the appropriateness of some of the entity's actions into question. Therefore, the auditor should be alert for any indication of shortfalls in any of the following areas:

- probity, honesty, skill, care and integrity;
- attention to establishing satisfactory compliance arrangements;
- attention to compliance with notification requirements;
- observing appropriate standards of market practice; and
- openness with the regulator.

Any report on the fitness and propriety of the entity, or any of its directors or management, should be made to the regulator without prior reference to the directors of the entity.

Risk of loss – client assets

The auditor should report any identified deficiency in client assets which cannot be explained or accounted for, as well as any suspicions that misappropriation of assets may occur. Immediate action is required to ensure that the regulator can take appropriate action to protect client assets from future loss.

Risk of loss – financial position

Areas of material significance to the regulator will be those that indicate:

- the occurrence or possibility of a material loss to the regulated entity; or
- the breach, or likelihood of breach, by the entity of the requirements concerning the adequacy of its financial resource or solvency requirements.

A material loss to the business will include an event leading to a loss which is material in meeting the entity's solvency or capital adequacy requirements, or the requirement of a subsidiary, related or nominee company. This may include litigation against the entity, which may give rise to contingent liabilities and costs in defending the action.

An entity may be required to notify the regulator if its financial resources fall below a multiple of the financial requirement (e.g. 110%). Failure to make this notification will also be regarded by the regulator as having material significance.

Compliance with requirements for the management of its affairs

Areas that the auditor is likely to be aware of as a result of his work include:

- significant concerns over the internal control environment;
- disagreements or lack of evidence about amounts in the financial statements which cannot be resolved;
- material breaches of client asset rules and the rules requiring suitable systems in relation to client assets;
- evidence of business being conducted outside the entity's authorised scope; and
- significant matters affecting the regulated businesses' appointed representatives.

Doubt as to the entity's status as a going concern

Any doubt as to the entity's ability to continue to undertake investment business should be reported to the regulator.

9.6.4   Procedures

ISA (UK) 250 Section B (Revised June 2016) stresses that neither the legislation nor the ISA require the auditor to perform any extra work to discover information that may give rise to a duty to report. The duty relates only to work performed to fulfil other reporting responsibilities where the auditor must be alert to instances which would give rise to a duty to report.

Planning

When obtaining an understanding of the entity, the auditor of a regulated entity should ensure that he has an appropriate understanding of its current activities, the scope of its authorisation an effectiveness of the control environment, including the attitude of management to compliance with the relevant regulator's rules.

This understanding will inform the auditor's risk assessment which should consider the risk of failure by the entity to comply with regulatory or other requirements and possible consequences of such failure including fines, regulatory action or other implications for the financial statements.

Supervision and control

ISA (UK) 250 Section B also requires that all staff involved in the audit of a regulated business have an understanding of the provisions of relevant legislation, the regulator's rules and guidance and any specific requirements applicable to the entity appropriate to their role in the audit and sufficient to enable them to identify situations that may give rise to a need to report to the regulator.

Audit firms should establish procedures to ensure that any relevant matters that are discovered in the course of an audit are brought to the attention of the engagement partner.

Identifying matters requiring a report

When the auditor becomes aware of matters that he suspects may give rise to a report to a regulator, he should:

- obtain evidence to assess the implications for reporting;
- determine whether the matter is of material significance to the regulator; and
- consider whether the breach is criminal conduct that gives rise to criminal property, and therefore should be reported to the relevant authority.

The specific matters to report derive from the relevant legislation but generally relate to:

- the financial position of the regulated entity;
- compliance with rules or regulatory requirements for the conduct of its business; or
- the status or conduct of those charged with governance.

Further guidance is given in the Practice Notes relating to regulated businesses and in rules and guidance issued by regulators.

Not all breaches of regulatory requirements will be immediately reportable and the question of whether they reflect matters of material significance may only become apparent after further investigation. Minor breaches which have been rectified and (where appropriate) reported by the entity itself may not normally need to be reported by the auditor. On the other hand, minor breaches may be reportable if they indicate a general lack of compliance which calls into question the fit and proper status.

It is not necessary to collect sufficient evidence to determine the full implications of the matter before deciding to report. It is only necessary that there are reasonable grounds. What constitutes reasonable grounds is a matter for professional judgment. Such a judgment will be based on:

- discussions with management and staff; and

- a review of correspondence and documents relating to the matter.

Certain matters, such as a loss of client money, may be so serious as to necessitate an immediate report to the regulator to prevent further losses being sustained.

The evidence obtained by the auditor should be documented so that his decision whether to proceed with a report can be clearly demonstrated should the need arise in the future.

Cumulative minor breaches

Minor breaches would not normally be of material significance to the regulator and give rise to an ad hoc report. However, the auditor of a regulated entity is required to review whether the cumulative effect of a number of minor breaches is such as to give rise to a duty to report to the regulator. The auditor may wish to seek legal advice on whether such a report would be necessary.

The facts and circumstances of his decision to report or not should be clearly documented in the audit working papers.

Use of other auditors

In group audit situations, the group auditor is not necessarily expected to have all the knowledge of components of the group that component auditors may have acquired in the course of their audits. However, the auditor of a regulated entity (including a public interest entity) should establish arrangements such that other auditors bring to their attention any matters that may give rise to a duty to report to a regulator.

9.6.5 Reporting

Auditor's statutory duty to report to a regulator

Where the auditor concludes that there is a matter that gives rise to a statutory duty to report to a regulator, ISA (UK) 250 Section B (Revised June 2016) requires that the auditor should bring the matter to the attention of the regulator as soon as practicable in a form and manner which will facilitate appropriate action. Where a statutory duty to report arises, the auditor must report the matter, even if it has already been reported by another party, including the entity or those charged with governance.

The report should be made without delay and may be made orally, so long as the auditor makes a contemporaneous written record of the oral report and the report. Except where the matter reported casts doubt on the integrity or competence of those charged with governance, or would constitute 'tipping off', the auditor sends a copy of the report to those charged with governance of the entity.

In normal circumstances, the auditor would wish to communicate with the regulator with the knowledge and agreement of those charged with governance. This should not, however, be used as a reason for delaying or failing to report a matter to the regulator.

Where the matter in question casts doubt on the integrity of those charged with governance or their competence to conduct the business of the regulated entity, then the auditor should report as soon as practicable to the regulator without informing those charged with governance. Application material in the ISA notes that in such extreme cases speed is of the essence and that the auditor may wish to take legal advice.

Where the matter involves evidence or suspicion of fraud or criminal activity that would fall within the scope of money laundering regulations, auditors need also to consider their responsibilities under these regulations (see **Section 18**) and be careful to avoid any activity that would amount to 'tipping off'.

Auditor's right to report directly to regulators

Under FSMA 2000, auditors are not held to breach any duty by communicating in good faith to the regulator, information or an opinion on a matter that they reasonably believe is relevant to any functions of the regulator. This only applies to information obtained as auditors. Auditors should ensure compliance with legislation relating to 'tipping off' (see **Section 18**).

In addition to the statutory duty to report directly, the auditor has a right to do so where he believes the matter to be relevant to the regulator's function and the entity has not informed the regulator itself. On discovery of such a matter, the auditor should inform those charged with governance in writing that, in his opinion, it should be reported, and if he does not obtain evidence within a reasonable period that they have done so, he should report to the regulator himself.

The auditor may wish to take legal advice before deciding on what, and in what form, to report. However, it is important to balance this against the need for prompt reporting to protect the interests of investors.

9.6.6 *Form of report*

ISA (UK) 250 Section B (Revised June 2016) states that a report to a regulator should include:

- the name of the regulated entity;

- the statutory power under which the report was made;

- a statement that it has been prepared in accordance with ISA (UK) 250 Section B (Revised June 2016);

- a description of the context in which the report is given;

- a description of matters giving rise to the report;

- a request that the regulator confirms receipt of the report; and

- the name of the auditor making the report, the date of the written report and, if appropriate, the date of the oral report and the name of the person to whom it was made.

The description of the matter should give an indication of the extent of any discussions with the directors on the matter.

The context of the report will depend on several matters such as:

- the nature of the appointment from which the report derives;

- the interpretation of the relevant legislation;

- the extent to which the auditor has investigated the matter;

- whether the matter has been discussed with the directors; and

- whether steps have been taken to rectify the matter.

9.6.7 Communication by the regulator

The regulator may pass on to the auditor any information which it considers relevant to his function. Auditors are bound by the confidentiality provisions set out in the *Financial Services and Markets Act* 2000, Pt. XXIII (Public record, disclosures of information and cooperation). Communications of this nature must be treated as confidential by the auditor and must not be disclosed to his client or any other party without the express permission of the regulator or the other party. The regulator will indicate if anyone at the client has been informed of the matter.

The regulator has confirmed that it will take the initiative in communicating with auditors. The most likely matters are those which may affect the opinion that the auditor gives on the financial statements. However, the auditor should not assume that no communication from the regulator means that there is nothing that may be materially significant.

Where information has been brought to his attention, the auditor may need to amend his approach, but there is no requirement to change the scope of his work or actively investigate the matter further, unless specifically requested to do so by the regulator.

9.6.8 Relationship with other reporting responsibilities

Where matters have been reported directly to regulators, the auditor should consider the implications for his report on the financial statements. Such matters may give rise to contingencies or other uncertainties which should be disclosed in the financial statements.

Table 9 provides a flowchart showing actions to be taken when a breach is suspected.

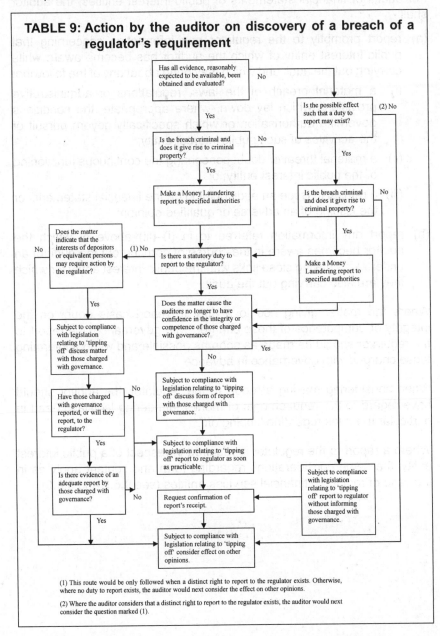

TABLE 9: Action by the auditor on discovery of a breach of a regulator's requirement

(1) This route would be only followed when a distinct right to report to the regulator exists. Otherwise, where no duty to report exists, the auditor would next consider the effect on other opinions.

(2) Where the auditor considers that a distinct right to report to the regulator exists, the auditor would next consider the question marked (1).

9.7   Public interest entities

A new requirement was introduced into ISA (UK) 250 Section B (Revised June 2016) by virtue of the EU Audit Regulation imposing a duty on auditors of public interest entities to report to the appropriate regulator where certain matters come to their attention, in a manner similar to that applied to auditors of regulated entities in the financial sector.

For audits of financial statements of public interest entities, the auditor shall:

(a) report promptly to the regulator any information concerning that public interest entity of which the auditor has become aware while carrying out the audit and which may bring about any of the following:

(i)   a material breach of the laws, regulations or administrative provisions which lay down, where appropriate, the conditions governing authorisation or which specifically govern pursuit of the activities of such public interest entity;

(ii) a material threat or doubt concerning the continuous functioning of the public interest entity; or

(iii) a refusal to issue an audit opinion on the financial statements or the issuing of an adverse or qualified opinion;

(b) report any information referred to in (i)–(iii) above of which the auditor becomes aware in the course of carrying out the audit of an undertaking having close links with the public interest entity for which they are also carrying out the audit.

Where the matter giving rise to a duty to report casts doubt on the integrity or competence of those charged with governance, the report to the regulator should be made as soon as possible and without informing those charged with governance in advance.

When considering making a report to the regulator, the auditor should have regard to the requirements of money laundering legislation and in particular the rules regarding 'tipping off'.

Where a report to the regulator is required in respect of a public interest entity, the same considerations regarding form and content apply as in the case of regulated financial services entities (see **9.6.5** and **9.6.6**).

10 Communicating with management and those charged with governance

10.1 Introduction

Auditors are required by ISAs (UK) to communicate with management and/or those charged with governance on a number of matters relating to the audit.

In addition, auditors may be requested to provide other reports to management and those charged with governance in connection with their audit work – for example, on the adequacy of the company's system of internal control, on significant findings and on possible improvements to the financial and accounting efficiency of the business. The timing, form and content of such reports should be covered in the engagement letter between the auditor and his client.

This section considers the principal requirements of the ISAs, particularly in the context of ISA (UK) 260 (Revised June 2016) *Communication with those Charged with Governance* and ISA (UK) 265 *Communicating Deficiencies in Internal Control to those Charged with Governance and Management*.

ISA (UK) 260 (Revised June 2016) is effective for the audit of financial statements for periods commencing on or after 17 June 2016 but was updated in July 2017 for conforming amendments following a revision of ISA (UK) 250 Section A.

Changes made in the 2016 revision to ISA (UK) 260 include changes affecting public interest entities due to the Audit Regulation and Directive; these are detailed in the section and include the requirement to communicate certain matters in an additional report to the audit committee (see **10.7.2**). In addition, the communication surrounding planned scope and timing of audit work has been clarified and this is covered in **10.6.3**.

ISA (UK) 260 (Revised June 2016) sets standards and provides guidance on:

- determining the appropriate person(s) within the governance structure for communications;

- matters to be communicated;
- the communication process; and
- documentation of that communication.

ISA (UK) 265 considers the specific case of reporting significant deficiencies in internal control. The current version of ISA (UK) 265 was issued in October 2009 and is effective for the audit of financial statements for periods ending on or after 15 December 2010. ISA (UK) 265 is discussed in **10.10**. It was not revised by the FRC but was reissued as ISA (UK) 265 in June 2016 with some amended application material in respect of public interest entities.

10.2 Determining those charged with governance

ISA (UK) 260 (Revised June 2016) defines those charged with governance as including 'the directors (executive and non-executive) of a company or other body, the members of an audit committee where one exists, the partners, proprietors, committee of management or trustees of other forms of entity, or equivalent persons responsible for directing the entity's affairs and preparing its financial statements'.

Depending on the nature and circumstances of the entity, management, i.e. those persons who perform senior management functions, may include some or all of those charged with governance, for example the executive directors of a company. Non-executive directors are not usually part of management.

The auditor needs to determine the appropriate person or people within the governance structure with whom to communicate. Where the auditor communicates with a sub-group of those charged with governance, for example, an audit committee, he should consider whether it is appropriate also to communicate with the governing body as a whole.

For audits of public interest entities, ISAs require certain matters to be communicated to an audit committee, and ISA (UK) 260 (Revised June 2016) requires the auditor to include these matters in an additional report to the audit committee (see **10.7.2**). If the entity does not have an audit committee, the additional report to the audit committee is to be submitted to the body performing equivalent functions within the entity.

10.3 Aims of reports to those charged with governance

The auditor should aim to develop a constructive working relationship with those charged with governance, whilst retaining his independence and objectivity, and under ISA (UK) 260 (Revised June 2016), one of his objectives is to promote effective two-way communication with those charged with governance.

The main purposes of such communication are:

- to assist the auditor and those charged with governance in understanding matters related to the audit. This includes communicating clearly the responsibilities of the auditor in relation to the audit and an overview of the planned timing and scope of the work;

- to assist the auditor in obtaining information from those charged with governance that is relevant to the audit. This includes the auditor making enquiries of those charged with governance regarding their knowledge of actual or suspected fraud, non-compliance with laws and regulations and their reasons for not adjusting misstatements in the financial statements detected by the auditor; and

- to assist those charged with governance in fulfilling their responsibilities in relation to the financial reporting process, thereby reducing the risks of material misstatement in the financial statements. This includes communication by the auditor of audit findings and other matters of governance interest.

All reports to the client should be relevant to the particular client, and the auditor should consider the extent, form and frequency of reports in relation to the size and nature of the client. The attitude of those charged with governance and the importance of the issues to be raised may also affect the format and timing of reports. For example, reports of relatively minor matters to a small client may be best handled orally via a meeting or telephone conversation rather than by a formal written report. These considerations are discussed further in **10.4**.

All reports should be made on a timely basis to allow those charged with governance to take appropriate action. Timely communication throughout the audit contributes to the achievement of robust two-way dialogue between those charged with governance and the auditor. The speed with which the auditor reports will depend on the nature of the issue arising, but matters relating to the qualitative aspects of the entity's accounting and financial reporting will usually be communicated prior to the approval of the financial statements. When ISA (UK) 701 *Communicating key audit matters in the independent auditor's report* applies (see **Section 4**), the auditor may communicate preliminary views about key audit matters when discussing the planned scope and timing of the audit, and he also may have more frequent communications to further discuss such matters when communicating about significant audit findings.

ISA (UK) 260 acknowledges that law or regulation may restrict or specifically prohibit the auditor's communication of certain matters with those charged with governance, for example where this might prejudice an investigation by an appropriate authority into an actual, or suspected, illegal act, including alerting the entity when the auditor is required to report identified or suspected non-compliance with laws and regulations pursuant to anti-money laundering legislation. In these circumstances, the issues considered by the auditor may be complex and the auditor may consider it appropriate to obtain legal advice.

10.4 The communication process

10.4.1 Establishing expectations

At an early stage in their relationship, the auditor should agree the level of detail and timing of communication between himself and those charged with governance. This will vary depending on the circumstances of the client. The auditor should also clarify that he will only report matters which he considers relevant to those charged with governance as a result of his normal audit procedures, and will not perform additional procedures specifically to determine other matters to report.

Such communication is often made in the engagement letter (see **Section 14**). The auditor is also required to set out his responsibilities, as in **10.6.2**.

10.4.2 Form of communication and documentation

Certain communications need to be made in writing. These are:

- agreement to the terms of the engagement (engagement letter);
- in the case of a listed[1] entity:
    - the communications regarding auditor independence specified in **10.6.5**; and
    - any contingent fee arrangements for non-audit services provided by the auditor or members of the same network;
- in the case of a public interest entity[2]:
    - the communications regarding independence set out in **10.6.5**;
    - the additional report to the audit committee must be in writing. This report is to be signed and dated by the engagement partner, and submitted to the audit committee no later than the date of submission of the audit report; and

---

[1] See glossary for definition.
[2] See glossary for definition.

   – upon request by either the auditor or the audit committee, the auditor shall discuss key matters arising from the audit, referred to in the additional report to the audit committee (see **10.7.2**), and in particular any deficiencies communicated;

- significant deficiencies in internal control (see **10.10**); and

- matters on which the auditor is required to obtain written representations (representation letter – see **32.4**).

In addition, the auditor should communicate in writing with those charged with governance regarding significant findings from the audit if, in his professional judgment, oral communication would not be adequate.

Due to the nature and sensitivity of fraud involving senior management, or fraud that results in a material misstatement in the financial statements, the auditor may also consider it necessary to report such matters in writing.

Other communications may be made orally. However, the auditor may judge that for effective communication a written communication is issued even if its content is limited to explaining that there is nothing he wishes to draw to the attention of those charged with governance. To avoid doubt, where there are no matters the auditor wishes to communicate in writing, he may issue a written communication to that effect.

Where communication has been made in writing, the auditor should retain a copy as part of the audit documentation.

ISA (UK) 260 (Revised June 2016) requires that where matters are communicated orally, a record should be retained in the audit documentation showing what was communicated, to whom and when. In many cases, this will be a copy of the minutes of a meeting at which the issue was discussed.

Additionally, for audits of public interest entities, the auditor is required to retain any other data and documents that are important in supporting the additional report to the audit committee (see **10.7.2**) as part of the audit documentation.

Typically, the auditor will discuss his findings with management or those with direct responsibility for an area, where appropriate to do so, before reporting them to those charged with governance. This should ensure that all facts are clarified as well as providing management with an opportunity to provide further explanations. Where it will aid the understanding of those charged with governance, the auditor may include details of comments made by management in his final communication.

10.4.3 Addressees

The auditor should use judgment to determine to whom he communicates certain matters. This may be contrary to the arrangement agreed at the start of the audit if the matter is sufficiently important to require reporting directly to the board or governing body.

For listed companies and other entities where they have been constituted, reports will often be made to the audit committee. However, auditors and boards should understand that a report to the audit committee will only form part of the auditor's overall obligation to report to those charged with governance and additional reports to other parts of the client's organisation may also be required, such as reports direct to the remuneration committee or to individual departments. In any case, it is important that the report is seen by those who have the authority to implement the recommendations included therein. If the report is presented in sections of varying importance, it may be appropriate for the more detailed matters to be referred directly to the division or branch to which they relate.

10.4.4 Form of reports

Where a written report is made, the form of report will depend on the type of organisation concerned and the matters to be communicated. A report covering findings from the audit may typically be formed of a covering letter (see **Table 1**) and a schedule of points raised.

TABLE 1: Reports to those charged with governance covering letter

Private & Confidential

The Directors

XYZ Plc

1 High Street

London W1

24 June 20XX

Dear Sirs

XYZ Plc

Following our recent audit of your company, we are writing to advise you of various matters which came to our attention.

We set out on the attached schedule the major areas of weakness which we noted, together with our recommendations. These recommendations have already been discussed with … and their comments have been included.

As the purpose of the audit is to form an opinion on the company's financial statements, you will appreciate that our examination cannot necessarily be

---

expected to disclose all shortcomings of the system and for this reason, the matters raised may not be the only ones which exist.

We should appreciate your comments as to how you propose to deal with the matters raised in this letter. If you require any further information or advice, please contact us.

We have prepared this letter for your use only. It should not be disclosed to a third party and we can assume no responsibility to any person to whom it is disclosed without our written consent.

We would like to take this opportunity to thank you and your staff for your help and co-operation during the course of our audit.

Yours faithfully

ABC & Co

10.5   Adequacy of communications

The responsiveness of those charged with governance to communications from the auditor may be considered when assessing the effectiveness of the entity's control environment. This may also affect the auditor's assessment of the risks of material misstatements. The auditor may consider:

- the appropriateness and timeliness of actions taken by those charged with governance following the auditor's recommendations;

- how open those charged with governance appear to be when communicating with the auditor;

- the willingness of those charged with governance to meet with the auditor; and

- the ability of those charged with governance to comprehend the recommendations made by the auditor.

ISA (UK) 260 (Revised June 2016) also requires the auditor to evaluate, as part of the audit process, whether the two-way communication between him and those charged with governance has been adequate for the purposes of his audit. In other words, have those charged with governance provided all the information expected of them in response to the auditor's enquiries and have they understood and responded appropriately to matters communicated to them by the auditor. If not, the auditor should consider the effects on his risk assessment and his ability to obtain sufficient appropriate audit evidence and take further action as necessary.

10.6 Matters to be communicated

10.6.1 Overview

There are a number of matters that the auditor is required to communicate to those charged with governance which are covered in this section:

- his responsibilities in relation to the audit of the financial statements (**10.6.2**);

- the form, timing and expected general content of communications (**10.4**);

- an overview of the planned scope and timing of the audit (**10.6.3**);

- significant findings from the audit (**10.6.4**);

- significant deficiencies in internal control (**10.10**); and

- certain matters regarding independence and objectivity (**10.6.5**); and

- (for audits of public interest entities) matters to be contained in an additional report to the audit committee (**10.7.2**).

In addition to ISAs (UK) 260 and 265, a number of other ISAs (UK) also contain specific requirements relating to matters to be communicated to those charged with governance in specific circumstances. Where appropriate, these requirements are referred to in other sections and a summary of these is provided here:

- ISQC (UK) 1 (Revised June 2016), identity and role of the engagement partner (see **3.2.6**);

- ISA (UK) 240 (Revised June 2016), requires the auditor to make enquiries of those charged with governance to determine whether they have knowledge of any actual, suspected or alleged fraud affecting the entity (see **16.4.3**); where applicable to discuss reasons for withdrawal from the engagement (see **16.6**); and when applicable to inform the entity of any suspected irregularities, including fraud and ask them to take action (see **16.8.1**);

- ISA (UK) 250 Section A (Revised December 2017), requires the auditor to make enquiries as to whether the entity is in compliance with laws and regulations (see **17.5.1**); and to inform those charged with governance of any suspected non-compliance (see **17.8.1** and **17.8.4**);

- ISA (UK) 450 (Revised June 2016), requires uncorrected misstatements and their effects to be communicated (see **15.9**);

- ISA (UK) 505, requires communication if management refuse to allow the auditor to send a confirmation request and it is considered unreasonable (see **23.8.1**);

- ISA (UK) 510 (Revised June 2016), requires communication if any errors in opening balances result in material misstatements in the current period's financial statements (see **19.3**);

- ISA (UK) 550, requires communication of any significant matters arising during the audit in connection with the entity's related parties (see **20.8**);

- ISA (UK) 560, requires the auditor to:

  - enquire of management and those charged with governance as to whether any subsequent events have occurred (see **33.3**);

  - discuss with management any facts which become known to the auditor after the date of his report but before the date the financial statements are issued (see **33.3**);

  - in certain situations, to ask those charged with governance not to issue the financial statements (see **33.4**);

  - discuss facts that become known after the financial statements have been issued (see **33.5**); and

  - communicate circumstances in which the auditor believes the financial statements need to be amended (see **33.5**);

- ISA (UK) 570 (Revised June 2016), requires communication of events or conditions identified that may cast significant doubt on the entity's ability to continue as a going concern (see **11.14**);

- ISA (UK) 600 (Revised June 2016), requires communication of certain matters in a group situation (see **30.15**);

- ISA (UK) 610 (Revised June 2013), requires communication about the use of the work of the internal audit function (see **31.2.3**);

- ISA (UK) 700 (Revised June 2016), communication where the auditor does not intend to disclose the name of the engagement partner in the audit report (see **4.19**);

- ISA (UK) 701, requires communication of key audit matters (see **4.11**);

- ISA (UK) 705 (Revised June 2016), requires certain communications where there is an imposed limitation of scope or an inability to obtain sufficient appropriate audit evidence (see **5.3.3**), material misstatements due to the non-disclosure of information (see **5.5.5**) and expected modifications to the opinion (see **5.10**);

- ISA (UK) 706 (Revised June 2016), communication of an expected Emphasis of Matter or Other Matter paragraph (see **5.10**);

- ISA (UK) 710, where the auditor concludes that a material misstatement exists in prior period financial statements on which a predecessor auditor had reported without modification of his opinion (see **19.3**); and

- ISA (UK) 720 (Revised June 2016), requires certain communications where misstatements are identified in other information (see **34.4.1**).

The auditor communicates 'audit matters of governance interest' to those charged with governance. These are matters arising from the audit of financial statements and which, in the opinion of the auditor, are both important and relevant to those charged with governance in their role of overseeing the financial statements and disclosure process. Only matters which have come to the auditor's attention as a result of the audit will be reportable, and the auditor is not required to perform additional procedures to identify matters of governance interest.

10.6.2   Auditor's responsibilities

The auditor needs to communicate his responsibilities to those charged with governance, including that:

- he is responsible for forming and expressing an opinion on the financial statements that have been prepared by management with oversight from those charged with governance; and

- the audit does not relieve management or those charged with governance of their responsibilities.

This is usually covered by the engagement letter (see **Section 14**). In all cases, the auditor should ensure that those charged with governance are provided with a copy of the engagement letter.

10.6.3   Planned scope and timing

The ISA states that auditors of all entities should inform those charged with governance of the planned scope and timing of the work they plan to perform, including any limitations thereon. This includes communicating about the significant risks identified by the auditor. Also where the auditor is required or decides to communicate key audit matters (see **Section 4**), the overview of the planned scope and timing of the audit should include communication about the most significant assessed risks of material misstatement (whether or not due to fraud) the auditor identified, including those that had the greatest effect on the overall audit strategy; the allocation of resources; and directing the efforts of the engagement team. Matters that might be communicated in outline include:

- how the auditor plans to address the significant risks of material misstatement, whether due to fraud or error;

- how the auditor plans to address areas of higher assessed risks of material misstatement;

- the concept of materiality and its application to the audit;

- the approach the auditor will use in relation to assessing and relying on internal controls;

- the nature and extent of specialised skill or knowledge needed to perform the planned audit procedures or evaluate the audit results, including the use of an auditor's expert;

- the extent, if any, that reliance can be placed on the internal audit function;

- where relevant, the work to be performed by other auditors and how the auditor intends to ensure the adequacy of the work of those other auditors;

- when ISA (UK) 701 applies (see **Section 4**), the auditor's preliminary views about matters that may be areas of significant auditor attention in the audit and therefore may be key audit matters; and

- the auditor's planned approach to addressing the implications on the individual statements and the disclosures of any significant changes within the applicable financial reporting framework or in the entity's environment, financial condition or activities.

The nature and detail of the planning information communicated will depend on the size and nature of the entity and precisely how those charged with governance operate. The auditor needs to take care when communicating with those charged with governance about the planned scope and timing of the audit to ensure that he does not compromise the effectiveness of the audit, particularly where some or all of those charged with governance are involved in managing the entity. For example, communicating the nature and timing of detailed audit procedures may reduce the effectiveness of those procedures by making them too predictable.

Where the audit team considers that there has been no change in this information from one year to the next, there is no requirement to reproduce it. Instead, the auditor need only make those charged with governance aware that no change has taken place.

10.6.4   Significant findings from the audit

The following areas are those that the auditor should communicate to those charged with governance:

- the auditor's views on the qualitative aspects of the entity's accounting practices and financial report – this will include the auditor's opinions on the accounting policies used, the appropriateness of accounting estimates, the potential impact of uncertainties and apparent misstatements in other material issued with the financial statements;

- any significant difficulties encountered during the audit, such as:
  - significant delays by management, the unavailability of entity personnel or an unwillingness by management to provide information necessary for the auditor to perform his procedures;
  - an unreasonably brief time within which to complete the audit;
  - extensive unexpected effort required to obtain sufficient appropriate audit evidence;
  - the unavailability of expected information;
  - restriction imposed on the auditor by management; and
  - management's unwillingness to make or extend its assessment of the entity's ability to continue as a going concern when required;
- significant matters discussed with management, unless all of those charged with governance are involved in managing the entity, such as:
  - significant events or transactions that occurred during the year;
  - business conditions affecting the entity, and business plans and strategies that may affect the risks of material misstatement;
  - concerns about management's consultations with other accountants on accounting or auditing matters;
  - discussions or correspondence in connection with the initial or recurring appointment of the auditor regarding accounting practices, the application of auditing standards, or fees for audit or other services; and
  - significant matters on which there was disagreement with management, except for initial differences of opinion because of incomplete facts or preliminary information that are later resolved by the auditor obtaining additional relevant facts or information.
- written representations the auditor is requesting, unless all of those charged with governance are involved in managing the entity;
- any other significant matters which the auditor considers relevant to the oversight of the financial reporting process, this may include modifications to the overall audit strategy and audit plan, material misstatements of the other information that have been corrected, and other matters considered by the engagement quality control reviewer;
- uncorrected misstatements (see following paragraph);
- the final draft of the management letter for signature;
- any circumstances which affect the form and content of the auditor's report, such as expected modifications to his report – to ensure that those charged with governance are aware of the proposed

modification, that there are no disputed facts and that those charged with governance have an opportunity to provide further information so that a modification is no longer required;

- significant deficiencies in internal control identified during the audit;

- matters specifically required by other ISAs (UK) to be communicated to those charged with governance; and

- any other matters of governance interest.

ISA (UK) 260 (Revised June 2016) also requires the auditor to explain, where relevant, why significant accounting policies, which are acceptable under the applicable financial reporting framework are not considered appropriate in the particular circumstances of the entity. Examples may include the effect of accounting policies in controversial or emerging areas where there may be a lack of guidance, areas where estimates are significant, or the effect of the timing of a transaction in relation to the period in which they are recorded.

Unadjusted misstatements

Where the auditor finds uncorrected misstatements, he should report them to the entity's management and request that they be corrected. These misstatements should be clearly distinguished as either errors of fact or matters of judgment. There is no requirement to report those misstatements which are 'clearly trivial' or inconsequential whether taken individually or in aggregate.

Where any of these misstatements are not corrected by management they are reported to those charged with governance. If those charged with governance refuse to make any of the adjustments, the auditor should discuss the matter with them and consider the implications for his report. The auditor should also obtain written representations from those charged with governance that explain why they have not been corrected.

Even where management has corrected the misstatements, the auditor may consider that including the details of the misstatement in his communications may assist those charged with governance with their role, including considering the effectiveness of the system of internal control.

Where matters previously reported have not been rectified by those charged with governance, the auditor considers repeating the point. Failing to do so may lead to the auditor giving the impression that he is satisfied that the matter has been addressed.

Guidance on unadjusted misstatements is detailed in ISA (UK) 450 (Revised June 2016) *Evaluation of Misstatements Identified During the Audit* (see **Section 15**).

10.6.5 *Integrity, independence and objectivity*

For all companies, listed and unlisted, the Revised Ethical Standard 2016 requires that those charged with governance should be told of any significant facts and matters which may impact the auditor's objectivity and independence.

The communication should include the key issues considered by the engagement partner such as:

- the principal threats, if any, to objectivity and independence identified by the auditor;

- any safeguards implemented with an explanation of why they were thought to be effective;

- any independent partner review;

- the overall assessment of threats and safeguards; and

- information about the general policies and processes employed by the audit firm to maintain independence and objectivity.

Listed entities

ISA (UK) 260 (Revised June 2016) states that for listed companies, the auditor should, at least annually:

- disclose in writing and discuss as appropriate:

  - all relationships between the audit firm and its related entities and the client entity and its related entities that may reasonably be thought to bear on the firm's independence and the objectivity of the audit engagement partner and audit staff; and

  - the related safeguards that are in place to eliminate identified threats to independence or reduce them to an acceptable level; and

- where it is the case, confirm in writing to the audit committee that, in his professional judgment, the firm is independent within the meaning of regulatory and professional requirements and the objectivity of the audit engagement partner and audit staff is not impaired.

In addition, for listed entities, the engagement partner should provide the audit committee with details of all non-audit services provided to the entity and the fees charged in relation thereto as well as details of any inconsistencies between the Revised Ethical Standard 2016 and the company policy for the supply of non-audit services and any apparent breach of that policy.

Public interest entities

ISA (UK) 260 (Revised June 2016) requires that for all public interest entities, the auditor shall:

- confirm annually in writing to the audit committee that the statutory auditor, the audit firm and partners, senior managers and managers, conducting the statutory audit are independent from the audited entity; and

- discuss with the audit committee the threats to the auditor's independence and the safeguards applied to mitigate those threats.

This includes identifying the ethical requirements relevant to the group audit that are applicable to component auditors.

10.7 Communication with audit committees

10.7.1 Companies applying the UK Corporate Governance Code

In the case of entities that are required, and those that choose voluntarily, to report on how they have applied the UK Corporate Governance Code, or to explain why they have not, the auditor shall communicate to the audit committee the information that the auditor believes will be relevant to:

- the board (in the context of fulfilling its responsibilities under Code provisions C.1.1, C.1.3, C.2.1, C.2.2 and C.2.3) and, where applicable, the audit committee (in the context of fulfilling its responsibilities under Code provision C.3.4) – see **42.5**; and

- the audit committee (in the context of fulfilling its responsibilities under Code provision C.3.2) to enable them to understand the rationale and the supporting evidence the auditor has relied on when making significant professional judgments in the course of the audit and in reaching an opinion on the financial statements.

This will include information about the auditor's views on business risks, significant accounting policies, valuations of assets and liabilities and disclosure thereof, the effectiveness of internal control, the robustness of the directors' risk assessment process and the directors' explanation in the annual report as to how they have assessed the prospects of the entity. ISA (UK) 260 (Revised June 2016) gives further details of these matters.

10.7.2 Public interest entities

In addition to this, for public interest entities, the auditor is required to submit an additional written report to the audit committee of the entity not later than the date of the auditor's report explaining the results of the audit. This report should cover a number of matters set out in ISA (UK) 260 (Revised June 2016), including at least, where applicable:

(a) the declaration of independence referred to in **10.6.5**;

(b) the identity of key audit partner(s);[3]

(c) where any of the auditor's activities are carried out by another firm that is not a member of the same network or by an external expert, that fact together with confirmation of the independence of external experts or other firms used (see **31.3.5**);

(d) a description of the nature, frequency and extent of communication with the audit committee;

(e) a description of the scope and timing of the audit;

(f) where more than one auditor has been appointed, a description of the distribution of tasks;

(g) a description of the methodology used, including an explanation of any substantial differences to the previous year, even if the previous year's audit was carried out by another firm. This includes being able to describe the methodology used, including which categories of the balance sheet have been directly verified and which categories have been verified based on system and compliance testing, including an explanation of any substantial variation in the weighting of system and compliance testing when compared to the previous year (see **19.3.2**);

(h) the quantitative level(s) of materiality applied and the qualitative factors considered when setting the levels;

(i) a report and explanation of judgments about events or conditions identified that may cast significant doubt on the entity's ability to continue as a going concern and provide a summary of all support measures that have been taken into account when making a going concern assessment;

(j) a report on any significant deficiencies in the internal financial control system and/or in the accounting system and whether or not they have been resolved by management;

(k) any significant matters involving actual or suspected non-compliance with laws and regulations identified in the course of the audit;

(l) valuation methods applied including any impact of changes of such methods (see **21.4.2**);

---

[3] See glossary for definition.

(m) the scope of consolidation and the exclusion criteria applied by the entity to the non-consolidated entities, if any;

(n) identify any audit work performed in relation to consolidated financial statements other than by members of the same network to which the group auditor belongs;

(o) whether all requested explanations and documents were provided by the entity;

(p) a report of any significant difficulties encountered in the course of the audit, any significant matters arising from the audit, and any other matters arising from the audit that in the auditor's professional judgment, are significant to the oversight of the financial reporting process.

10.8   Groups

Where a parent undertaking is preparing group financial statements, the auditor brings to the attention of those charged with governance any matters arising through the audit of components which he judges to be of significance in the context of the group.

There is a statutory requirement for the auditor of corporate subsidiaries in the UK to supply information, on request, to the parent company auditor. Where no statutory obligation exists (for example, for non-corporate or overseas components), the group auditor may need to seek permission to communicate with the component auditor.

Further detail on communicating with those charged with governance in group situations is given in **30.15**.

10.9   Third parties

Reports issued by the auditor to those charged with governance on the matters referred to in this section will usually be solely for the use of the addressees. If the auditor wishes to disclose its contents to a third party, he should obtain permission from the client before releasing it. In practical terms, once the report has been sent, the auditor has little control over it and it may be given to third parties without the knowledge of the auditor. The auditor should therefore ensure that his report contains an appropriate disclaimer, as shown in **Table 1**, so that any third parties who see the report understand it was not prepared for their benefit.

In the public or regulated sectors, the auditor may have a duty to submit a copy of his report to the relevant regulatory or funding bodies and therefore the disclaimer will not be appropriate. However, any communication with those charged with governance is confidential and the auditor will require prior consent from those charged with governance before sending a copy to the regulator or funding body.

Where reports are required by such third parties, the auditor should show due consideration for the requirements of those bodies when compiling his reports.

10.10   Communicating deficiencies in internal control

10.10.1   Identifying and reporting deficiencies

The auditor is required to obtain an understanding of internal control sufficient to allow him to identify and assess risks of material misstatement and to plan audit procedures which address those risks. The auditor is not required to identify deficiencies with the sole purpose of reporting them to those charged with governance or management.

Where the auditor has identified deficiencies in internal control, ISA (UK) 265 sets out the requirements that apply in determining the manner in which they are communicated to management or those charged with governance, as appropriate. This does not preclude the auditor from reporting any other deficiencies in internal control identified during the course of his work.

10.10.2   Significant deficiency

A deficiency in internal control exists when:

- a control is designed, implemented or operated in such a way that it is unable to prevent, or detect and correct, misstatements in the financial statements on a timely basis; or

- a control necessary to prevent, or detect and correct, misstatements in the financial statements on a timely basis is missing.

A deficiency is a 'significant deficiency' when, either in isolation or in combination with other deficiencies, it is of sufficient importance to merit the attention of those charged with governance. This will depend not only on whether a material misstatement has actually occurred, but also on the likelihood that a misstatement could occur, and the potential magnitude of the misstatement. Therefore, significant deficiencies can exist without a misstatement having been identified.

When determining whether a deficiency or combination of deficiencies in internal control constitutes a significant deficiency, the auditor may consider:

- likelihood of the deficiencies leading to material misstatements in the financial statements in the future;
- susceptibility to loss or fraud of the related asset or liability;
- subjectivity and complexity of determining estimated amounts, such as fair value accounting estimates;
- financial statements amounts exposed to the deficiencies;
- volume of activity that has occurred or could occur in the account balance or class of transactions exposed to the deficiency or deficiencies;
- importance of the controls to the financial reporting process; for example:
    - general monitoring controls (such as oversight of management);
    - controls over the prevention and detection of fraud;
    - controls over the selection and application of significant accounting policies;
    - controls over significant transactions with related parties;
    - controls over significant transactions outside the entity's normal course of business;
    - controls over the period-end financial reporting process (such as controls over non-recurring journal entries);
- cause and frequency of the exceptions detected as a result of the deficiencies in the controls; and
- interaction of the deficiency with other deficiencies in internal control.

10.10.3   *Reporting of significant deficiencies*

All significant deficiencies should be reported on a timely basis and in writing to those charged with governance. In addition, management should also be notified in writing of any significant deficiencies reported to those charged with governance.

When reporting significant deficiencies to those charged with governance, the auditor should include in his written communication:

- a description of the deficiencies and an explanation of their potential effects; and
- sufficient information to allow those charged with governance and management to understand the context of the communication. In particular, the auditor should explain that the:

- purpose of the audit was for the auditor to express an opinion on the financial statements;

- audit included consideration of internal control relevant to the preparation of the financial statements in order to design audit procedures that are appropriate in the circumstances but not for the purpose of expressing an opinion on the effectiveness of internal control; and

- matters being reported are limited to those deficiencies that the auditor has identified during the audit and that the auditor has concluded are of sufficient importance to merit being reported to those charged with governance.

The auditor may include suggestions for remedial actions and management's own responses as well as details of any steps taken to verify whether management's responses have been implemented.

The auditor may also include in his reports:

- an indication that if he had performed more extensive procedures on internal control more reportable deficiencies may have been discovered, or it may have been concluded that some of the reported deficiencies may not have needed to be reported; and

- an indication that the report has been provided for the purposes of those charged with governance only, and that it may not be suitable for other purposes.

Public interest entities

For audits of public interest entities, ISA (UK) 260 (Revised June 2016) requires the auditor to communicate in the additional report (see **10.7.2**) to the audit committee any significant deficiencies in the entity's internal financial control system or in the accounting system, and whether or not the deficiencies reported have been resolved by management.

10.10.4 *Reporting of other deficiencies*

Other deficiencies not considered to be significant deficiencies need not be reported in writing but should be communicated to management at an appropriate level of responsibility on a timely basis. Obviously, such deficiencies may be included in the written report to those charged with governance if the auditor and client consider it appropriate to do so.

11 Going concern

11.1 Introduction

The auditor's consideration of the appropriateness of the use of the going concern basis of accounting and of the adequacy of disclosures relating to the future solvency or liquidity of the entity is an area that continues to attract much attention.

Changes to auditing standards in 2016 now require the auditor to report specifically on the directors' use of the going concern basis and whether management has failed to disclose material uncertainties that may cast significant doubt on the entity's ability to continue as a going concern for a period of at least 12 months from the date of approval of the financial statements.

The UK Corporate Governance Code ('the Code') and accompanying guidance for directors, Listing Rules and ISAs (UK) on going concern and auditor reporting have also made changes in this area for companies that explain their compliance with the Code.

Directors have a responsibility to prepare financial statements using the going concern basis of accounting unless it is inappropriate to do so. This involves an assessment of, and judgments about, the future. If they decide the basis is inappropriate, assets may need to be written down to recoverable amounts or reclassified, and liabilities restated to reflect changes in amount or date of maturity. Directors must also consider whether there are material uncertainties regarding the entity's ability to continue as a going concern (or to continue to adopt the going concern basis of accounting) and ensure that these are disclosed in the financial statements where appropriate. The auditor must assess whether directors have carried out this assessment on a realistic basis and whether the consequences, where relevant, and any disclosures regarding uncertainties are adequately reflected in the financial statements.

Recent changes to auditing standards and related guidance make a distinction between the use of the going concern basis of accounting, which is prescribed except in specific limited circumstances, and adequacy of disclosures regarding the directors' consideration of the company's viability, including risks and uncertainties relating to the company's future solvency or liquidity that may impact on its ability to continue in business as a going concern.

11.2 Auditing standards and other guidance

ISA (UK) 570 (Revised June 2016) *Going Concern* is effective for the audit of financial statements for periods commencing on or after 17 June 2016.

Changes in the 2016 version of the ISA were numerous and result from the EU Directive, IAASB updates and UK specific amendments.

Key changes include:

- use of the term 'going concern basis of accounting' rather than 'going concern assumption';

- an EU Directive requirement for the auditor to maintain professional scepticism when reviewing future cash flow relevant to the entity's ability to continue as a going concern;

- requirement for a specific auditor conclusion regarding management's use of the going concern basis of accounting;

- greater emphasis on consideration of adequacy of disclosures including a requirement for the auditor to consider adequacy of disclosures where there are matters that may cast significant doubt on the entity's ability to continue as a going concern but no material uncertainty exists; and

- consideration of whether going concern is a key audit matter for the purposes of ISA (UK) 701 *Communicating key audit matters in the independent auditor's report* even where no material uncertainty has been identified.

Guidance for directors of companies applying the UK Corporate Governance Code is available in *Guidance on Risk Management, Internal Control and Related Financial and Business Reporting* issued by the FRC in September 2014.

For those entities which do not apply the Code, guidance was issued in April 2016, titled *Guidance on the Going Concern Basis of Accounting and Reporting on Solvency and Liquidity Risks*.

Older, but still potentially relevant, guidance is also contained in the APB's Bulletin 2008/10 *Going concern issues during the current economic conditions* published in December 2008 to supplement Bulletin 2008/1 *Audit issues when financial market conditions are difficult and credit facilities may be restricted*, which provided more general guidance and is covered in **Section 37**. Bulletin 2008/10 is discussed in **11.20**.

11.3   General requirement

In preparing financial statements, it is the responsibility of those charged with governance to determine whether it is appropriate to apply the going concern basis of accounting and whether any assumptions and uncertainties are adequately disclosed.

The auditor's objectives are to:

- obtain sufficient appropriate audit evidence regarding, and conclude on, the appropriateness of those charged with governance's use of the going concern basis of accounting in the preparation of the financial statements;

- conclude, based on the audit evidence obtained, whether a material uncertainty exists related to events or conditions that may cast significant doubt on the entity's ability to continue as a going concern; and

- report in accordance with ISA (UK) 570 (Revised June 2016).

The ISA focuses on the auditor's responsibility to assess how the directors have satisfied themselves that the financial statements have been prepared on an appropriate basis and whether the financial statements contain adequate disclosures relating to going concern, including the existence of any material uncertainties in relation to the entity's ability to continue as a going concern.

11.4   The entity's responsibilities

Under the going concern basis of accounting, an entity will be assumed to continue in business for the foreseeable future without the intention or need to liquidate, cease trading or seek protection from its creditors. Assets and liabilities will, therefore, be recorded assuming that they will be traded or settled in the normal course of business.

Those charged with governance may prepare financial statements under either IFRS or UK accounting standards. The requirements relating to going concern are similar under the two frameworks and entities should prepare their accounts on a going concern basis unless the entity has ceased trading or is being liquidated, or the directors either intend or have no realistic alternative but to cease trading or liquidate the entity. Most financial statements will therefore be prepared on a going concern basis even where there is uncertainty regarding the entity's ability to remain a going concern.

Going concern

Under UK accounting standards, in assessing whether the going concern basis of accounting is appropriate, those charged with governance take into account all available information about the future, which is at least, but is not limited to, 12 months from the date when the financial statements are authorised for issue.

When those charged with governance are aware, in making their assessment, of material uncertainties related to events or conditions that cast significant doubt upon the entity's ability to continue as a going concern, the entity must disclose those uncertainties. When an entity does not prepare financial statements on a going concern basis, it shall disclose that fact, together with the basis on which it prepared the financial statements and the reason why the entity is not regarded as a going concern.

IAS 1 contains almost identical requirements to UK accounting standards but requires that the directors' assessment covers a period of at least 12 months from the balance sheet date. In practice, however, for UK entities, those charged with governance are usually expected to consider a period of 12 months from the date of approval, and where this is not the case, the auditor is required to request management to extend its assessment period.

Non-compliance with an accounting standard will usually lead to a qualification of the auditor's opinion. Where the assessment period is less than 12 months from the date of approval of the financial statements, under either framework, the auditor may need to refer to this in the audit report.

When making their assessment, those charged with governance should be aware that:

- the outcome of an event is less certain the further it is likely to occur from the date the assessment is made;

- judgments can only be made on the basis of information available at the time. Subsequent events can contradict a decision which was reasonable at the time it was made; and

- any judgment will be affected by the size and complexity of the entity, its type of business and how susceptible its activities are to outside influences.

The auditor should also consider these factors when forming an opinion on the assessment made by those charged with governance.

11.5   The auditor's responsibilities

The auditor's responsibilities are to evaluate the assessment made by those charged with governance of the use of the going concern basis of accounting, conclude on the existence of material uncertainties, consider the disclosures made in the financial statements and in other information (see **Section 34**) and to report appropriately.

11.6   Risk assessment procedures and related activities

When carrying out his risk assessment procedures (see **Section 21**), the auditor should consider whether events or conditions exist that may cast significant doubt over the entity's ability to continue as a going concern. He should determine whether those charged with governance have already performed a preliminary assessment of their ability to continue as a going concern, and:

- if such an assessment has been performed, he should discuss it with those charged with governance to determine whether they have identified events or conditions that, individually or collectively, may cast significant doubt on the entity's ability to continue as a going concern, and, if so, their plans to address them; or

- if such an assessment has not yet been performed, the auditor discusses with those charged with governance the basis for the intended use of the going concern basis of accounting, and inquires of them whether events or conditions exist that, individually or collectively, may cast significant doubt on the entity's ability to continue as a going concern.

The auditor should also remain alert throughout the audit for evidence of events or conditions that may cast significant doubt on the entity's ability to continue as a going concern.

If such events or risks are identified, the auditor may need to revise his risk assessment and may need to reconsider the nature and timing of his procedures in response to the assessed risks of material misstatement (see **Section 21**).

11.6.1   *Significant doubt about the entity's ability to continue as a going concern*

Examples of events or circumstances which may cause doubt about the entity's ability to continue as a going concern are given in **Table 1**.

TABLE 1: Events or circumstances which may cause doubt about the entity's ability to continue as a going concern

Financial

- net liability or net current liability position;

- necessary borrowing facilities have not been agreed;

- fixed-term borrowing approaching maturity without realistic prospects of renewal or repayments; or excessive reliance on short-term borrowings to finance long-term assets;

- major debt repayment falling due where refinancing is necessary to the entity's continued existence;

- major restructuring of debt;

- indications of withdrawal of financial support by debtors and other creditors;

- negative operating cash flows indicated by historical or prospective financial statements;

- adverse key financial ratios;

- substantial operating losses or significant deterioration in the value of assets used to generate cash flows;

- major losses or cash flow problems which have arisen since the balance sheet date;

- arrears or discontinuance of dividends;

- inability to pay creditors on due dates;

- inability to comply with the terms of loan agreements;

- reduction in normal terms of trade credit;

- change from credit to cash-on-delivery transactions with suppliers;

- inability to obtain financing for essential new product development or other essential investments;

- substantial sales of fixed assets not intended to be replaced.

Operating

- loss of key management without replacement;

- loss of key staff without replacement;

- loss of a major market, franchise, licence or principal supplier;

- labour difficulties or shortages of important suppliers;

- fundamental changes in the market or technology to which the entity is unable to adapt adequately;

- excessive dependence on a few product lines where the market is depressed;

- technical developments which render a key product obsolete.

Other

- non-compliance with capital or other statutory requirements;

- pending legal or regulatory proceedings against the entity that may, if successful, result in claims that are unlikely to be satisfied;

- changes in legislation or government policy expected to adversely affect the entity;

- issues which involve a range of possible outcomes so wide that an unfavourable result could affect the appropriateness of the going concern basis.

11.7   Evaluating the entity's assessment of going concern

ISA (UK) 570 (Revised June 2016) requires that the auditor evaluates the assessment made by those charged with governance of the entity's ability to continue as a going concern. It also requires that the auditor maintains professional scepticism throughout the audit and in particular when reviewing future cash flow relevant to the entity's ability to continue as a going concern.

In his evaluation, the auditor should consider the same period as used by those charged with governance. If this covers a period of less than 12 months from the date of approval of the financial statements, the auditor should request those charged with governance to extend the period of their assessment. If they fail to do so, this may have implications for the auditor's report.

In making his evaluation, the auditor considers whether those charged with governance's assessment has included all relevant information of which the auditor is aware as a result of the audit.

The auditor's procedures may involve:

- holding discussions with those charged with governance;

- examining appropriate supporting documentation; and

- planning and performing procedures designed to identify any material matters which could impact on the entity's ability to continue as a going concern, including considering the process followed to make the assessment, the assumptions on which the assessment is based, and plans for the future.

The issues the auditor should consider may include the:

- period assessed by those charged with governance;
- system for identifying future risks;
- existence/quality of budgets or forecasts;
- appropriateness of assumptions;
- sensitivity of budgets;
- adequacy of borrowing facilities; and
- the entity's plans for resolving going concern problems.

The extent of the procedures carried out will depend on the headroom between financial requirements and the facilities available. The more demonstrably healthy the company, the less extensive the procedures may need to be.

11.7.1 *Possible audit procedures*

Some possible procedures that the auditor may consider are shown in **Table 2**.

TABLE 2: Possible audit procedures

Forecasts and budgets

Review cash flow forecasts and budgets, where available, from the expected date of approval of the financial statements. Perform sensitivity analysis on the key components of forecasts and budgets.

Consider the assumptions used in preparing the forecasts, for example:

- anticipated levels of sales;
- projected winning of new customers;
- expected cash collection performance;
- capital expenditure programme;
- timing of anticipated payments to HMRC;
- basis of payment terms to existing suppliers;
- ensure forecasts represent the timing of cash flows, not profits;
- where forecasts assume an increase in sales, ensure that associated costs (advertising, sales/admin staff, distribution, increased stock levels etc), are also factored in; and
- ensure the entity has the capacity to deliver at the increased sales level forecast.

Assess reliability of directors' previous forecasting.

Borrowing facilities

Confirm the existence and terms of facilities, for example:

- establish the date for renewal of facilities.
- assess the future intentions of lenders via discussion or correspondence.
- assess possible breaches of any borrowing covenants imposed by lenders.
- check for any arrears of interest on current borrowings.
- review the value of any assets granted as security for borrowings.
- review correspondence between directors and lenders.

Contingent liabilities

Consider possible exposure to contingent liabilities arising, for example, from:

- legal proceedings;
- guarantees or warranties; and
- retentions.

Assess potential intra-group guarantees (e.g. unlimited multilateral guarantees).

Review possible breaches of grant conditions leading to repayment of grants.

Financial risk

Review directors' assumptions about projected foreign currency exchange rates.

Consider exposure to major fixed-price contracts.

Financial adaptability

Assess entity's ability to adapt to unexpected events, for example:

- disposal of fixed assets;
- leasing;
- debt restructuring;
- share capital issue;
- financial support from group companies; and
- new sources of finance.

11.7.2   Borrowing facilities

When considering adequacy of borrowing facilities, the auditor may need to make an assessment of the intentions of the company's bankers or other providers of finance, where:

- there is a low margin of financial resources available;
- the company's facilities are shortly due for renewal;
- he is aware of previous difficulties in agreeing facilities and the bankers have imposed further conditions for continued lending;
- the directors have projected a significant deterioration in the cash position; or
- the company has recently breached or is likely to breach its borrowing covenants.

Such an assessment may include:

- reviewing correspondence between directors and their bankers; and
- meeting with the directors and bankers to clarify the latter's intentions.

The auditor may, despite the above, decide it is necessary to obtain confirmation from bankers of the existence and terms of facilities.

If he is neither able to satisfy himself about the existence and terms of facilities or about the bankers' future intentions, the auditor needs to consider whether this represents a material uncertainty that should be disclosed in the financial statements and may have implications for his report (see **11.11**).

11.8 Events after the period considered by those charged with governance

The 12-month period is not intended to be a hard cut-off point and the auditor should also make enquiries regarding management's knowledge of events or conditions beyond the period of their assessment that may cast significant doubt on the entity's ability to continue as a going concern.

Events this far in the future are unlikely to be certain, but the auditor should consider the possible significance of any such event which is made known to him up until the date of his audit report. For example, it may be that the company's cash flow forecasts show a significant dependence on the availability of a loan facility. Where those charged with governance know, or suspect, that the company's situation will make renewal of the facility difficult they should take this into account in their assessment, even where the renewal date is later than 12 months after the date of approval of the financial statements.

However, the auditor has no responsibility to design audit procedures, other than enquiry, to discover such events or conditions.

11.9 Additional procedures when events or conditions are identified

If events or conditions have been identified that may cast significant doubt on the entity's ability to continue as a going concern, the auditor shall obtain sufficient appropriate audit evidence to determine whether or not a material uncertainty exits related to events or conditions that may cast significant doubt on the entity's ability to continue as a going concern. This is done through performing additional audit procedures, including consideration of mitigating factors. These procedures shall include:

- where those charged with governance have not yet performed an assessment of the entity's ability to continue as a going concern, requesting them to make their assessment;

- evaluating those charged with governance's plans for future actions in relation to their going concern assessment, whether the outcome of these plans is likely to improve the situation and whether their plans are feasible in the circumstances;

- where the entity has prepared a cash flow forecast, and analysis of the forecast is a significant factor in considering the future outcome of events or conditions in the evaluation of those charged with governance's plans for future action:

  - evaluating the reliability of the underlying data generated to prepare the forecast; and

  - determining whether there is adequate support for the assumptions underlying the forecast.

- considering whether any additional facts or information have become available since the date on which those charged with governance made their assessment; and

- requesting written representations from those charged with governance regarding their plans for future action and the feasibility of these plans.

11.10 Auditor conclusions

The auditor evaluates whether sufficient appropriate audit evidence has been obtained and concludes on the appropriateness of management's use of the going concern basis of accounting.

Based on the audit evidence obtained, the auditor concludes whether, in his judgment, a material uncertainty exists related to events or conditions that, individually or collectively, may cast significant doubt on the entity's ability to continue as a going concern. A material uncertainty exists when the magnitude of its potential impact and the likelihood of occurrence is

257

such that, in the auditor's judgment, appropriate disclosure of the nature and implications of the uncertainty is necessary for the fair presentation of the financial statements.

11.10.1 Entities applying the UK Corporate Governance Code

For those entities required, or who voluntarily choose to report on how they have applied the UK Corporate Governance Code, the auditor shall read the following and consider them in the light of the auditor's knowledge obtained in the audit:

- the directors' confirmation in the annual report that they have carried out a robust assessment of the principal risks facing the entity, including those that would threaten its business model, future performance, solvency or liquidity (Code Provision C2.1);

- the disclosures in the annual report that describe those risks and explain how they are being managed or mitigated (Code Provision C2.1);

- the directors' statement in the financial statements about whether they considered it appropriate to adopt the going concern basis of accounting in preparing them, and their identification of any material uncertainties to the entity's ability to continue to do so over a period of at least 12 months from the date of approval of the financial statements (Code Provision C1.3); and

- the directors' explanation in the annual report as to how they have assessed the prospects of the entity, over what period they have done so and why they consider that period to be appropriate, and their statement as to whether they have a reasonable expectation that the entity will be able to continue in operation and meet its liabilities as they fall due over the period of their assessment, including any related disclosures drawing attention to any necessary qualifications or assumptions (Code Provision C2.2).

The auditor determines whether he has anything material to add or to draw attention to in his audit report in relation to these disclosures and reports.

Matters the auditor considers when determining whether there is anything to add or to emphasise in his audit report, include:

- whether he is aware of information that would indicate that the annual report and accounts taken as a whole are not fair, balanced and understandable in relation to the principal risks facing the entity including those that would threaten its business model, future performance, solvency or liquidity; and

- matters relating to the robustness of the directors' assessment of the principal risks facing the entity and its outcome, including the related disclosures in the annual report and accounts, that the auditor communicated to the audit committee and that are not appropriately addressed in the section of the annual report that describes the work of the audit committee.

11.11 Adequacy of disclosures

The auditor has a responsibility to consider the requirements of the applicable financial reporting framework and the adequacy of disclosures, whether or not he considers a material uncertainty to exist.

A material uncertainty exists when the potential impact of the events or conditions and the likelihood of them occurring is such that appropriate disclosure is necessary to achieve fair presentation. The auditor needs to conclude on whether such a material uncertainty exists regardless of whether or how the applicable financial reporting framework defines a material uncertainty.

Even when no material uncertainty exists, the auditor is required to evaluate whether the financial statements provide adequate disclosure about events or conditions that may cast significant doubt on the entity's ability to continue as a going concern.

See **11.11.1** which considers the situation where events or conditions have been identified and a material uncertainty does exist and **11.11.2** where no material uncertainty exists.

11.11.1 Adequacy of disclosures when events or conditions have been identified and a material uncertainty exists

If the auditor concludes that the use of the going concern basis of accounting is appropriate but that there remains a material uncertainty, he should determine whether the financial statements:

- disclose adequately the principal events or conditions that may cast significant doubt on the entity's ability to continue as a going concern and those charged with governance's plans to deal with these events or conditions; and

- disclose clearly that the material uncertainty exists and that it may cast significant doubt on the entity's ability to continue as a going concern and, therefore, that it may be unable to realise its assets and discharge its liabilities in the normal course of business.

11.11.2 Adequacy of disclosures when events or conditions have been identified but no material uncertainty exists

If events or conditions have been identified that may cast significant doubt on the entity's ability to continue as a going concern but, based on the audit evidence obtained the auditor concludes that no material uncertainty exists, the auditor evaluates whether, in view of the requirements of the applicable financial reporting framework, the financial statements provide adequate disclosures about these events or conditions.

11.12 Implications for the auditor's report

11.12.1 Auditor's conclusions

The auditor may conclude that:

- use of the going concern basis of accounting is not appropriate in the circumstances;

- use of the going concern basis is appropriate and no material uncertainty exists; or

- use of the going concern basis is appropriate but one or more material uncertainties exist.

11.12.2 Going concern basis of accounting inappropriate

Where the financial statements have been prepared using the going concern basis of accounting, but in the auditor's judgment, the use of the going concern assumption is inappropriate, the auditor would give an adverse opinion in his report, as shown in **Table 3**. This applies regardless of whether the financial statements include disclosure of the inappropriateness of those charged with governance's use of the going concern basis of accounting.

Where the use of the going concern basis of accounting is inappropriate and those charged with governance have elected to prepare the financial statements on an alternative basis (such as a liquidation basis), which the auditor considers to be acceptable, and have made appropriate disclosures in the financial statements regarding the basis of preparation and the reasons for it then the auditor may be able to give an unqualified opinion on the financial statements. In these circumstances he may consider it appropriate or necessary to include an Emphasis of Matter paragraph (see **Section 5**) drawing attention to the basis of preparation and the relevant disclosures in the financial statements.

11.12.3 Going concern basis of accounting is appropriate and no material uncertainty has been identified

Where the auditor concludes that management's use of the going concern basis of accounting is appropriate in the circumstances and no material uncertainty has been identified, the auditor reports by exception in a separate section in the auditor's report with the heading 'Conclusions Relating to Going Concern', or other appropriate heading, as to whether:

(i) management's use of the going concern basis of accounting in the preparation of the entity's financial statements is not appropriate; or

(ii) management has not disclosed in the entity's financial statements any identified material uncertainties that may cast significant doubt about the entity's ability to continue to adopt the going concern basis of accounting for a period of at least 12 months from when the financial statements are authorised for issue.

An example is shown in **Table 4** in **11.16** and in the simple audit report example **Table 1** in **4.23**.

For entities explaining compliance with the Code, the reporting requirement is slightly different and the auditor reports whether he has anything material to add or draw attention to in relation to the directors' statement in the financial statements about whether the directors considered it appropriate to adopt the going concern basis of accounting in preparing the financial statements, and the directors' identification of any material uncertainties to the entity's ability to continue to do so over a period of at least 12 months from the date of approval of the financial statements.

An example for a premium listed company is shown in **Table 2** in **4.23**.

If the auditor is required or has decided to communicate key audit matters (see **Section 4**), where he concludes that the use of the going concern basis of accounting is appropriate and no material uncertainty has been identified, he nevertheless needs to consider whether a key audit matter relating to going concern exists. If so, he communicates it in his report in accordance with ISA (UK) 701, see **4.11**.

11.12.4 Use of going concern basis of accounting is appropriate but a material uncertainty exists

Adequate disclosure of a material uncertainty is made in the financial statements

If adequate disclosure is made, the audit opinion would be unmodified, but the auditor's report would contain a separate section under the heading 'Material Uncertainty Related to Going Concern' to bring readers' attention to the note(s) disclosing the matter(s) in the financial statements. The section should also state that these events or conditions indicate that a material uncertainty exists that may cast significant doubt on the entity's ability to continue as a going concern and that the auditor's opinion is not modified in respect of the matter. This paragraph replaces what used to be an Emphasis of matter paragraph under previous ISAs (UK and Ireland).

Where the auditor is also reporting key audit matters in accordance with ISA (UK) 701, **Table 5** sets out example report paragraphs.

Adequate disclosure of a material uncertainty is not made in the financial statements

Where the relevant disclosures about the material uncertainty are not made or are inadequate, the auditor expresses a qualified or adverse opinion, as appropriate. In the 'Basis for Qualified (Adverse) Opinion' section of the auditor's report, he states that a material uncertainty exists that may cast significant doubt on the entity's ability to continue as a going concern and that the financial statements do not adequately disclose this matter. See examples in **Tables 6** and **7**.

11.12.5 Other considerations

Where those charged with governance have not extended their assessment when required to do so, the auditor needs to consider whether they have complied with the relevant accounting framework and needs to consider the implications for his report.

Where financial statements have been prepared on a basis other than that of going concern and the auditor considers that adequate disclosure of this has not been made, then he may need to qualify his opinion or express an adverse opinion.

In extreme circumstances, where there are multiple significant uncertainties, a disclaimer of opinion may be suitable.

11.12.6 Small and micro-entities

In the case of small and micro-entities in the UK, the applicable accounting framework may not contain the same requirements in relation to disclosure of material uncertainties as are imposed on other entities. The auditor is nevertheless required to consider management's assessment of the applicability of the going concern basis and the adequacy of disclosures in relation to any material uncertainties that exist and should consider the implications for his report where he considers that disclosure of such uncertainties is not adequate for the purposes of a true and fair view (see **8.3.4**).

11.12.7 Entities applying the UK Corporate Governance Code

Having considered the various disclosures and reports referred to in **11.10.1**, the auditor determines whether he has anything material to add or to draw attention to in his audit report in relation to these disclosures and reports, and he reports in accordance with ISA (UK) 720 (Revised June 2016) *The Auditor's Responsibilities Relating to Other Information.* Where he has nothing to add or to draw attention to, he reports that fact. See **4.17** and **34.7**.

11.12.8 Key audit matters

Whilst the existence of a material uncertainty in relation to going concern may well be a key audit matter, it nevertheless warrants separate reference in a 'material uncertainties' or basis for opinion paragraph even where key audit matters are disclosed in the audit report. In this situation, the introductory paragraph to the key audit matters section is modified to indicate that the matters referred to therein are in addition to the matter(s) disclosed in the material uncertainty paragraph or basis for qualified/ adverse opinion as appropriate. See **Table 8** for example wording.

11.12.9 Other information

A qualified or adverse opinion or the existence of a material uncertainty may have an impact on the auditor's opinions on statutory and non-statutory other information if the relevant matter is not referred to appropriately in other information such as the strategic report or if the other information is not consistent with the information in the financial statements.

11.13 Entity unwilling to make or extend its assessment

If the auditor believes it is necessary to request those charged with governance to make or extend their assessment, and they are unwilling to do so, the auditor considers the implications for his audit report. In such circumstances, a qualified opinion or a disclaimer of opinion may be appropriate, because it may not be possible for the auditor to obtain sufficient appropriate audit evidence regarding the use of the going concern basis of accounting, for example, such as evidence regarding the existence of plans that those charged with governance have put in place or the existence of other mitigating factors.

11.14 Communication with those charged with governance

Unless all those charged with governance are involved in managing the entity, the auditor communicates with those charged with governance, those events or conditions identified that may cast significant doubt on the entity's ability to continue as a going concern. This includes whether the events or conditions constitute a material uncertainty, whether the use of the going concern basis of accounting for the preparation of the financial statements is appropriate, the adequacy of related disclosures in the financial statements, and, where applicable, the implications for the audit report.

11.14.1 Public interest entities

For audits of public interest entities, ISA (UK) 260 (Revised June 2016) *Communication with those charged with governance* requires the auditor in the additional report to the audit committee to:

- explain the judgments about events or conditions identified in the course of the audit that may cast significant doubt on the entity's ability to continue as a going concern and whether they constitute a material uncertainty; and

- provide a summary of all guarantees, comfort letters, undertakings of public intervention and other support measures that have been taken into account when making a going concern assessment.

11.15 Significant delay in the approval of financial statements

If there is a significant delay in the approval of the financial statements by those charged with governance, the auditor inquires as to the reasons. If the auditor believes the delay may be related to events or conditions relating to the going concern assessment, he performs additional audit procedures as necessary as well as considering the effect on his conclusion regarding the existence of a material uncertainty.

11.16 Example report extracts

The extracts of example audit reports in **Tables 3** to **8** illustrate the following situations:

Table 3 – an example adverse opinion, where the auditor considers that the directors' use of the going concern basis is inappropriate.

Table 4 – an example of conclusions relating to going concern where use of the going concern basis is appropriate and no material uncertainties exist.

Table 5 – an example of material uncertainty paragraph conclusions relating to going concern where use of the going concern basis is appropriate but a material uncertainty exists that is adequately disclosed in the financial statements.

Table 6 – an example of a qualified opinion where use of the going concern basis is appropriate but a material uncertainty exists that is not adequately disclosed in the financial statements.

Table 7 – an example of an adverse opinion where use of the going concern basis is appropriate but a material uncertainty exists that is not adequately disclosed in the financial statements.

Table 8 – illustration of how the introduction to the Key Audit Matters section is modified where a material uncertainty exists.

These examples do not apply to public interest entities or other entities choosing to report on how they applied the provisions of the UK Corporate Governance Code as in these cases there are additional considerations that would need to be addressed in the auditor's report.

TABLE 3: Example adverse opinion – use of the going concern basis is inappropriate

Adverse opinion

We have audited the financial statements of XYZ Limited (the company), which comprise …

In our opinion, because of inappropriate use of the going concern basis for the preparation of the financial statements referred to in the Basis for adverse opinion section of our report, the financial statements:

- do not give a true and fair view of, the state of the company's affairs as at …, and of its profit or loss for the year then ended;

- have not been properly prepared in accordance with UK Generally Accepted Accounting Practice; and

- have not been prepared in accordance with the requirements of the *Companies Act* 2006.

Basis for adverse opinion

[As described in note x to the financial statements] the company's financing arrangements have expired and an amount of £x is overdue for payment. The company is currently unable to pay this debt and has been unable to obtain replacement financing. In our opinion, in these circumstances the directors have no realistic alternative but to cease trading and as a result, the use of the going concern basis for the preparation of the financial statements is

---

inappropriate. The financial statements do not contain the adjustments that may be necessary to reflect that fact that the company is not a going concern.

We conducted our audit in accordance with International Standards on Auditing (UK) (ISAs (UK)). Our responsibilities under those standards are further described in the Auditor's responsibilities for the audit of the financial statements section of our report. We are independent of the company in accordance with the ethical requirements that are relevant to our audit of the financial statements in the UK, including the FRC's Ethical Standard, and we have fulfilled our ethical responsibilities in accordance with these requirements. We believe that the audit evidence we have obtained is sufficient and appropriate to provide a basis for our adverse opinion.

TABLE 4: Example conclusions relating to going concern where use of the going concern basis is appropriate and no material uncertainty exists

Opinion

...

Basis for opinion

...

Conclusions relating to going concern

We have nothing to report in respect of the following matters in relation to which the ISAs (UK) require us to report to you where:

- the directors' use of the going concern basis of accounting in the preparation of the financial statements is not appropriate; or

- the directors have not disclosed in the financial statements any identified material uncertainties that may cast significant doubt about the group's or the parent company's ability to continue to adopt the going concern basis of accounting for a period of at least 12 months from the date when the financial statements are authorised for issue.

TABLE 5: Example material uncertainty paragraph – use of the going concern basis appropriate but a material uncertainty exists and is adequately disclosed

Opinion

...

Basis for opinion

...

Material uncertainty related to going concern

We draw attention to note x to the financial statements, which indicates that the company incurred a net loss of £A during the year ended 31 December 20X1 and, as at that date, the company's current liabilities exceeded its total assets by £B. As stated in note x, these events or conditions, along with other matters as set out in note X, indicate that a material uncertainty exists that may cast significant doubt on the company's ability to continue as a going concern. Our opinion is not modified in respect of this matter.

TABLE 6: Example qualified opinion – use of the going concern basis appropriate but a material uncertainty exists and is not adequately disclosed

Qualified opinion

We have audited the financial statements of XYZ Limited (the company), which comprise ....

In our opinion, except for the incomplete disclosure of the information referred to in the Basis for qualified opinion section of our report, the accompanying financial statements:

- give a true and fair view of, the state of the company's affairs as at ..., and of its profit or loss for the year then ended;

- have been properly prepared in accordance with UK Generally Accepted Accounting Practice; and

- have been prepared in accordance with the requirements of the *Companies Act* 2006.

Basis for qualified opinion

As explained in note x, the company's financing arrangements expire and amounts outstanding are payable on 19 March 20X2. The company has been unable to conclude renegotiations or obtain replacement financing. This situation indicates that a material uncertainty exists that may cast significant doubt on the company's ability to continue as a going concern. The financial statements do not adequately disclose this matter.

We conducted our audit in accordance with International Standards on Auditing (UK) (ISAs (UK)). Our responsibilities under those standards are further described in the Auditor's responsibilities for the audit of the financial statements section of our report. We are independent of the company in accordance with the ethical requirements that are relevant to our audit of the financial statements in the UK, including the FRC's Ethical Standard, and we have fulfilled our ethical responsibilities in accordance with these requirements. We believe that the audit evidence we have obtained is sufficient and appropriate to provide a basis for our qualified opinion.

TABLE 7: Example adverse opinion – use of the going concern basis appropriate but a material uncertainty exists and is not adequately disclosed

Adverse opinion

We have audited the financial statements of XYZ Limited (the company), which comprise ...

In our opinion, because of the omission of the information mentioned in the Basis for adverse opinion section of our report, the financial statements:

- do not give a true and fair view of, the state of the company's affairs as at ..., and of its profit or loss for the year then ended;

- have not been properly prepared in accordance with UK Generally Accepted Accounting Practice; and

- have not been prepared in accordance with the requirements of the *Companies Act* 2006.

Basis for adverse opinion

The company's financing arrangements expired and the amount outstanding was payable on .... The company has been unable to conclude re-negotiations or obtain replacement financing and as a result the company may be unable to continue trading. This situation indicates that a material uncertainty exists that may cast significant doubt on the company's ability to continue as a going concern. The financial statements do not adequately disclose this fact.

We conducted our audit in accordance with International Standards on Auditing (UK) (ISAs (UK)). Our responsibilities under those standards are further described in the Auditor's responsibilities for the audit of the financial statements section of our report. We are independent of the company in accordance with the ethical requirements that are relevant to our audit of the financial statements in the UK, including the FRC's Ethical Standard, and we have fulfilled our ethical responsibilities in accordance with these requirements. We believe that the audit evidence we have obtained is sufficient and appropriate to provide a basis for our adverse opinion.

TABLE 8: Key audit matters – introductory paragraph where material uncertainty exists or the auditor expresses a qualified or adverse opinion

Key audit matters are those matters that, in our professional judgment, were of most significance in our audit of the financial statements of the current period. These matters were addressed in the context of our audit of the financial statements as a whole, and in forming our opinion thereon, and we do not provide a separate opinion on these matters. In addition to the matter described in the Material uncertainty related to going concern section[1], we have determined the matters described below to be the key audit matters to be communicated in our report.

[1] Refer here to where the matter is described elsewhere in the report e.g a Material uncertainty paragraph as illustrated here or a Basis for qualified opinion paragraph, as appropriate. Note that whilst the ISA acknowledges that a material uncertainty is, by its nature a 'key audit matter' it is not reported under this heading in the audit report but in a separate paragraph.

11.17   Regulated entities

Where the entity is regulated, it may be necessary to inform the regulator at an early stage of the intention to use an explanatory paragraph or qualify the audit report. This may lead to corrective action being requested by the regulator, which may serve to reduce the concerns that led to the proposal to include the explanatory paragraph or qualify the audit report.

11.18   Groups

The provisions of ISA (UK) 570 (Revised June 2016) apply to group financial statements as well as individual company ones. However, the going concern basis may be appropriate for the preparation of group financial statements, even though it may not be for one or more of the individual entities within the group. Where this is the case, the auditor should ensure that he documents his considerations, and those of the directors, fully.

11.19   Preliminary announcements

Where a company prepares a preliminary announcement, the Listing Rules of the UK Listing Authority require that the preliminary announcement of full year results include a reference to any likely modification or emphasis of matter paragraph that may be contained in the auditor's report to be issued with the annual financial report. The announcement should also be agreed with the auditor. Although there is no reference in these requirements to going concern, best practice suggests that the auditor would not agree a preliminary statement that made no reference to significant concerns where these existed.

11.20   Bulletin 2008/10

11.20.1   The need for guidance

As referred to in **11.2**, Bulletin 2008/10 *Going Concern issues during the current economic conditions* was issued in response to the severe economic conditions described as the 'credit crunch' affecting the UK and Irish economies in the latter half of 2007 and subsequently. Economic conditions had deteriorated and the APB considered it appropriate to issue further guidance regarding the auditor's evaluation of the directors' assessment of going concern, and the implications for the auditor's report.

11.20.2 General principles

An important principle underlying the Bulletin is that economic recession in itself would not give rise to a material uncertainty that causes significant doubt and causes the auditor to issue a report containing an emphasis of matter paragraph. It is only where there are matters which are specific to the entity that such an uncertainty would arise.

It is still therefore necessary for the process set out in ISA (UK) 570 (Revised June 2016) to be followed whereby those charged with governance assess the applicability of the going concern basis of accounting and make disclosures regarding any material uncertainty around it, whilst the auditor assesses and evaluates what those charged with governance have done and reports accordingly where there is a material uncertainty that may cast significant doubt on the entity's ability to continue as a going concern.

11.20.3 Detailed considerations

The Bulletin goes into more detail about how economic recession may affect the various stages of this process and amongst other things makes the following points:

- the process directors go through to make the disclosures around risk referred to above will provide useful audit evidence;

- the need for the assessment by both the directors and the auditor to start early. As this process will often result in board papers or possibly in remediation plans so the earlier the issues are addressed the better;

- because the risks in relation to the entity not being a going concern are so pervasive, they must be borne in mind throughout the audit;

- because the future outcome of implementing plans may be an important part of the assessment of going concern, then specific representations relating to these matters may be needed;

- the understandability of disclosures is an important feature given that the disclosures may be made in numerous places in the financial statements;

- the extent of disclosure is not an indicator that there is a material uncertainty that causes significant doubt. A lengthy disclosure may be as a result of explaining why this is not the case; and

- the issue of facility renewal is likely to be problematic but need not result in significant doubt (see **11.20.4**).

11.20.4   Availability of finance

One impact of difficult economic conditions may be the limited availability of finance from both suppliers and customers as well as banks and other lenders. Companies often find themselves needing to renew facilities before the end of the period over which going concern is being assessed. In these cases, bankers may be reluctant to confirm that facilities will continue to be available. This in itself is not a reason to doubt the ability of the entity to continue as a going concern.

The Bulletin refers to a number of reasons why a bank may be reluctant to confirm that a facility will be available in the future, including:

- the bank responding that in the current economic environment, as a matter of policy, it is not providing such confirmations to its customers and their auditors;

- the entity and its bankers are engaged in negotiations about the terms of a facility (e.g. the interest rate), so there is no evidence that the bank is reluctant to lend to the company; or

- the bank renewed a rolling facility immediately prior to the date of the issuance of the annual report and accounts and is reluctant to go through the administrative burden to confirm that the facility will be renewed on expiry.

The absence of a confirmation on its own does not constitute a significant doubt. The Bulletin makes the point that there needs to be other reasons specific to the entity which lead to the belief that the bankers are refusing to confirm ongoing facilities.

Even in this event, directors and auditors should consider whether alternative strategies or sources of finance are available. The auditor should assess the directors' plans for future action, including plans to liquidate assets, borrow money or restructure debt, reduce or delay expenditure or increase capital. Where alternative strategies are in place, the auditor should consider whether these:

- are realistic;

- have a reasonable expectation of resolving the problem; and

- are likely to be put into place effectively by the directors.

If this is the case, the auditor may decide it is unnecessary to include an emphasis of matter paragraph in his report.

12 Documentation

12.1 Introduction

ISA (UK) 230 (Revised June 2016) *Audit Documentation* is effective for the audit of financial statements for periods commencing on or after 17 June 2016. The ISA provides standards on documentation covering:

- form of working papers;

- content of working papers;

- changes to audit documentation after the date of the auditor's report;

- assembly of the final audit file; and

- confidentiality, safe custody and retention of audit documentation.

Changes made in the 2016 revision to ISA (UK) 230 include Audit Directive requirements for statutory audits regarding retention of documents and closure of the audit file (see **12.3**, **12.4** and **12.7**).

Other ISAs contain documentation requirements and application material relating to specific aspects of the audit. These are covered in the sections of this book dealing with the relevant topics and are summarised in **12.6**.

ISQC (UK) 1 and Audit Regulations also contain requirements regarding ownership, custody and confidentiality of working papers (see **12.7**).

Whilst audit documentation remains the property of the auditor, Audit Regulation 3.09 and the Companies Act require certain information to be made available to successor auditors (see **Section 38**).

Auditors may also be asked in other situations to grant access to their files to third parties, usually acting on behalf of a prospective purchaser of, or provider of finance to, the entity. Guidance on steps that may be taken by the auditor to mitigate risk in these situations is provided in ICAEW Technical Release Audit 04/03 *Access to Working Papers by Investigating Accountants* (see **12.9**).

12.2 Purpose of documentation

ISA (UK) 230 (Revised June 2016) requires that the auditor should document matters which are important in providing audit evidence to support his opinion and evidence that the audit was carried out in accordance with ISAs (UK).

Working papers are any material the auditor obtains, prepares or retains in the course of his audit. This may be in paper form but may also include, for example, film, scanned documents, computer discs or electronic files, including e-mail.

Working papers provide a record of supervision and review, the planning and performance of the audit by the staff and the evidence to support the audit opinion. They provide the individuals responsible for approving the audit report with the means to satisfy themselves that the work delegated has been properly performed. Other advantages of working papers are that they are seen as providing a source of reference that may be used in subsequent years and that they encourage a methodical approach.

12.3　Form and content

Working papers should be sufficiently complete and detailed so as to provide an overall understanding of the audit. They should contain information on planning the audit, the nature, timing and extent of the audit procedures performed and the results and conclusions from the procedures.

Working papers should be sufficient to allow an 'experienced auditor, having no previous connection with the audit' to be able to understand:

- the nature, timing and extent of the audit procedures performed to comply with the ISAs (UK) and applicable legal and regulatory requirements;

- the results of the audit procedures performed, and the audit evidence obtained; and

- significant matters arising during the audit, the conclusions reached thereon, and significant professional judgments made in reaching those conclusions.

For statutory audits of financial statements, the ISA requires the auditor to retain any other data and documents in the audit documentation that are of importance in support of his report.

An experienced auditor is an individual (whether internal or external to the firm) who has practical audit experience, and a reasonable understanding of:

- audit processes;

- ISAs and applicable legal and regulatory requirements;

- the business environment in which the entity operates; and

- auditing and financial reporting issues relevant to the entity's industry.

The ISA states that it may be necessary for that experienced auditor to hold discussions with the auditor to obtain a detailed understanding.

Because of a wide variety of circumstances in which working papers have to be prepared and the many types of business transactions to which they relate, it is not practicable to lay down a standard form for their preparation suitable for each and every situation. How the relevant information can best be shown, what audit procedures need to be applied and how their results can best be summarised is a matter for the particular circumstances. They should, however, be set out in such a fashion that the salient facts are readily apparent.

12.3.1 Factors affecting form and content of working papers

Working papers should be designed for each assignment and the factors set out in **Table 1** will determine their extent.

TABLE 1: Factors affecting form and content and extent of working papers

- the nature of the engagement;

- the identified risks of material misstatement;

- the extent of judgment required in performing the work and evaluating the results;

- the significance of the audit evidence obtained;

- the nature and extent of exceptions identified;

- the need to document a conclusion or the basis for a conclusion not readily determinable from the documentation of the work performed or audit evidence obtained; and

- the specific methodology and technology the auditor uses.

The use of standardised working papers, such as checklists, specimen letters and a standard index may aid efficiency and control, but the auditor should be aware of the dangers of following a standard approach mechanically. Professional judgment should be exercised when such aids are used.

If schedules have been drawn up by the client, the auditor requires evidence that they have been properly prepared before relying on them.

The term 'working papers' refers to the record of all of the evidence that the auditor considers it necessary to collect in order to support an opinion.

This may relate to the current year or be of a permanent nature, i.e. of continuing importance and as a result, be filed separately. The specific nature will depend on the assignment. Examples of the content of working papers are shown in **Table 2**.

TABLE 2: Contents of working papers

- information on the legal nature of the client, including copies of important documents;

- information concerning the industry and the economic and legislative environments within which the entity operates;

- evidence of the planning process, including any changes;

- notes on the accounting and internal control systems including extracts from the entity's internal control manual;

- assessment of inherent and control risks at the financial statements and assertion level;

- consideration of and conclusions on the work of internal audit;

- analyses of transactions and balances, including significant ratios and trends;

- audit programmes showing the nature, timing and extent of the audit procedures performed in response to risks at the assertion level, and the conclusions thereon;

- evidence that the work performed by assistants was supervised and reviewed;

- an indication as to who performed the audit procedures and when they were performed;

- correspondence with other auditors, experts and third parties;

- details of audit procedures applied where components of the financial statements are audited by another auditor;

- correspondence with the entity, including reports to management and notes of discussions with management concerning audit matters;

- letters of representation from management;

- a summary of the significant aspects of the audit, the conclusions reached and how matters have been resolved and the views of those charged with governance; and

- copies of the approved financial statements and auditor's reports.

12.3.2 Documenting characteristics of items tested

The ISA requires the auditor to include in his documentation details of the identifying characteristics of the items or matters tested. The characteristics recorded will vary depending on the items being tested, but may specifically identify the actual items tested, e.g. for a detailed test of entity-generated purchase orders, the auditor may identify the actual documents tested by providing their purchase order number, or alternatively, indicate the population as a whole, e.g. for a review of credit notes over a certain amount, the auditor may document the scope of the procedure and the threshold value above which items were reviewed.

Recording the items tested at this level of detail allows the subsequent investigation of exceptions or inconsistencies as well as enabling the audit team to be accountable for its work.

Typically, however, copies of the entity's records will only be required when they are necessary for an experienced auditor to understand the work performed and the conclusions reached.

12.3.3   Judgment areas

ISA (UK) 230 requires that working papers should include the auditor's reasoning on all significant matters which require the exercise of judgment, together with the auditor's conclusions thereon.

The ISA provides examples of items which would be deemed to be 'significant matters':

- matters that give rise to significant risks;
- results of audit procedures which indicate either that financial information could be materially misstated or that there is a need to revise the auditor's previous assessment of the risks of material misstatement;
- circumstances where the auditor has significant difficulty in performing his procedures;
- the entity's ability to continue as a going concern; and
- findings that could result in a modification to the auditor's report.

The working papers should note the relevant facts at the time the judgment was reached. This is particularly important where it concerns a difficult area which may be questioned later with the benefit of hindsight. The ISA suggests that use of a summary of significant matters cross-referenced to detailed working papers may aid consideration of these matters together with assisting with review of the work performed and conclusions reached. This may form part of a 'completion memorandum'.

The ISA also requires the auditor to document any discussion held with management and others, including those charged with governance, about significant matters.

Where the auditor has found information that contradicts his final conclusion on a significant matter, the inconsistency should be documented on file, together with an explanation of how the final conclusion was reached. This does not mean, however, that incorrect or superseded documentation should be retained on file.

12.3.4 Documentation of departures from ISAs (UK)

Where it is necessary to depart from the requirements of the basic or essential procedures in an ISA, the auditor is required to document the alternative procedures followed and the reasons for the departure. This does not apply to procedures that are not relevant to the engagement, e.g. in the second and subsequent years of an audit the auditor need not apply the standards in ISA (UK) 510 (Revised June 2016) regarding initial engagements.

12.3.5 Identification of the preparer and reviewer of documentation

The performer of audit work should be clearly identified on each piece of documentation, including the date on which his work was performed. There is no requirement to provide on each piece of documentation evidence of who reviewed the audit work. The documentation should indicate, however, who reviewed each element of the audit work and when. This may be on a control sheet rather than by, for example, initialling and dating each sheet of documentation itself.

12.3.6 Specific documentation requirements

In addition to documentation requirements specified elsewhere in ISAs, ISQC (UK) 1 (Revised June 2016) requires that for statutory audits, the engagement documentation must include any other data and documents that are of importance for monitoring compliance with the ISQC and other applicable legal requirements.

This includes documenting whether:

(a) the firm complies with the independence and objectivity requirements in the Revised Ethical Standard 2016;

(b) there are threats to the firm's independence, and the safeguards applied to mitigate those threats;

(c) the firm has the competent employees, time and resources needed in order to carry out the audit in an appropriate manner; and

(d) the key audit partner is eligible to be appointed as a statutory auditor.

Firms are required to keep the documents and information required by ISQC (UK) 1 and the documentation requirements of other applicable ISAs (UK) for at least six years from the date of the auditor's report. This period may be longer if necessary to satisfy the requirements of any applicable laws or regulation relating to data protection and to meet the requirements for any applicable administrative and judicial proceedings.

ISA (UK) 220 (Revised June 2016) specifies certain documentation requirements where engagement quality control reviews are carried out.

ISQC (UK) 1 (Revised June 2016) also specifies certain matters that need to be documented at the firm level regarding the firm's systems, procedures and controls. These matters are further considered in **Section 3**.

12.4   Assembly of the final audit file

ISA (UK) 230 (Revised June 2016) requires the final audit file to be assembled on a timely basis. The requirements of ISQC (UK) 1 (Revised June 2016) suggest this should be within 60 days of the date of the auditor's report (see **3.2.8**) and for statutory audits, ISA (UK) 230 (Revised June 2016) requires the file to be closed within this 60-day period.

For statutory audits of financial statements, the auditor is required to keep any other data and documents that are of importance for monitoring compliance with ISAs (UK) and other applicable legal requirements.

The final assembly of the audit file is an administrative process and should not involve any further audit work or the drawing of new conclusions. Only administrative changes can be made to the audit documentation, such as:

- deleting or discarding superseded documentation;

- sorting, collating or cross-referencing working papers;

- signing off completion checklists relating to the file assembly process; or

- documenting audit evidence that the auditor has obtained, discussed and agreed with the relevant members of the audit team before the date of his report.

Other audit documentation must not be deleted or discarded before the end of the retention period.

12.5 Changes to audit documentation

ISA (UK) 230 (Revised June 2016) states that exceptional circumstances may arise which require the auditor to perform new procedures after the date of the audit report or modify existing documentation, such as in response to comments received during monitoring inspections performed by internal or external parties. The ISA requires the auditor to record who made the changes and when, the consequential changes to documentation, the reasons for the changes and the effect on his previous conclusions.

12.6 Other documentation requirements

In addition to the requirements of ISA (UK) 230 (Revised June 2016), a number of other ISAs specify requirements relating to audit documentation. These include:

- ISA (UK) 210 (Revised June 2016) (Updated July 2017) – the engagement letter;

- ISA (UK) 220 (Revised June 2016) (Updated July 2017) – matters required to be considered before acceptance/continuance of an audit engagement; nature and scope of consultations undertaken in the course of the audit; and issues with respect to ethical matters and conclusions on independence requirements, including details of threats to independence and safeguards (new);

- ISA (UK) 240 (Revised June 2016) (Updated July 2017) – matters relating to fraud including conclusions from the team discussion, communications with management and those charged with governance, fraud risk and the audit response thereto; the results of procedures designed to address the risk of management override and the reasons (if any) for rebutting the presumed risk of fraud in relation to revenue recognition;

- ISA (UK) 250 Section A (Revised December 2017) – identified or suspected non-compliance with laws or regulations and the results of discussions with management, those charged with governance and others, as applicable;

- ISA (UK) 260 (Revised June 2016) (Updated July 2017) – where matters required to be communicated with those charged with governance are communicated orally, details including when and to whom they communicated. For public interest entities, other data and documents important in supporting the additional report to the audit committee (new);

- ISA (UK) 300 (Revised June 2016) – the overall audit strategy and audit plan including any changes thereto and reason for such changes;

- ISA (UK) 315 (Revised June 2016) – the engagement team discussion; key elements of understanding of the entity and its environment, sources of information and risk assessment procedures performed; risks identified and controls related to significant risks;

- ISA (UK) 320 (Revised June 2016) – materiality levels including overall financial statement materiality, specific materiality, performance materiality and any changes to these levels as the audit progressed;

- ISA (UK) 330 (Revised July 2017) – overall responses to address assessed risks at the financial statement level and audit procedures performed; linkage with risks at the assertion level and the results of the audit procedures; (where applicable) the conclusion reached about relying on controls tested in previous periods. Documentation should also demonstrate that information in the financial statements agrees or reconciles with underlying accounting records, Including agreeing or reconciling disclosures derived from outside the general and subsidiary ledgers (new);

- ISA (UK) 450 (Revised June 2016) (Updated July 2017) – 'clearly trivial' level; accumulated misstatements and the auditor's conclusion as to whether misstatements are material;

- ISA (UK) 540 (Revised June 2016) – basis for conclusions about the reasonableness of accounting estimates and their disclosure that gave rise to significant risks and indicators of possible management bias (if any);

- ISA (UK) 550 (Revised June 2016) – names of identified related parties and nature of related party relationships;

- ISA (UK) 600 (Revised June 2016) – matters relating to group audits including:
  - analysis of components showing which are significant and the type of work performed on each component;
  - nature timing and extent of involvement in the work of component auditors;
  - written communications with component auditors;
  - nature timing and extent of work performed by component auditors including, where applicable, the group audit team's review of relevant parts of the component auditor's documentation (new);
  - sufficient appropriate documentation to enable the competent authority to review the work of the group auditor (new); and
  - the group audit team must make arrangements to ensure that the competent authority will be able to gain access to audit documentation of the work carried out by a component auditor, should they wish to inspect it in connection with a quality assurance review or investigation (new).

- ISA (UK) 610 (Revised June 2016) – evaluation of the internal audit function, where the auditor uses the work of internal audit;

- ISA (UK) 620 (Revised June 2016) – any request for advice from an auditor's expert together with the advice received (new);

- ISA (UK) 701 – where applicable, determination of key audit matters to include in the auditor's report;

- ISA (UK) 720 (Revised June 2016) – procedures performed on 'other information' accompanying the financial statements and a copy of the final version of such other information;

- ISCQ (UK) 1 (Revised June 2016) also imposes requirements regarding:

  - documentation of the engagement quality control review (EQCR) where applicable;

  - documentation to facilitate external monitoring of group audits by regulators;

  - records of any complaints made in writing about the performance of audit engagements; and

  - documentation of the system of quality control.

12.7 Confidentiality, custody and ownership of working papers

ISQC (UK) 1 (Revised June 2016) (see **3.2.8**) contains specific requirements that the auditor should adopt appropriate procedures for maintaining the confidentiality and safe custody of his working papers. It is the auditor's responsibility to ensure that the audit working papers are kept safely. He should bear in mind that his work is strictly confidential.

These include Audit Directive requirements regarding establishment of policies and procedures designed to apply adequate provision on confidentiality and professional secrecy in relation to all information and documents to which the firm has access and to ensure that the firm complies with legal and regulatory requirements regarding confidentiality of information received in the course of an audit.

The audit working papers are the property of the auditor. Papers relating to accountancy work will normally be the property of the client although this will depend on the particular circumstances. Certain papers may be made available to clients but care should be taken not to undermine the independence or validity of the audit process. Because of their confidential nature, they should not be divulged to third parties without the client's permission, although some third parties, for example HMRC, may have a right of access in certain circumstances. However, whatever the circumstances, they should not be seen as a substitute for the client's accounting records.

12.8   Retention of working papers

Audit Regulation 3.11 states that 'A Registered Auditor must keep all audit working papers which auditing standards require for an audit for a period of at least six years. The period starts with the end of the accounting period to which the papers relate'. The actual length of time they are kept for will be a matter of judgment based on the auditor's own needs, those of the client and any regulatory requirements. However, it suggests that prior to their destruction, a review is carried out to ensure that there is no need to refer to them again.

There is a difference in the start date of the working paper retention period, however, following the recently implemented EU Audit Directive, ISQC (UK) 1 (Revised June 2016) now requires that for statutory audits, engagement documentation must be retained for at least six years from the date of the audit report.

Where evidence is held electronically, audit firms should ensure that they retain at least one version of any, otherwise superseded, information technology applications required to access old audit documentation. This may include both proprietary word-processing or spreadsheet tools which may have been upgraded, or any internally developed audit tools which have become obsolete or have been replaced or revised. The ability to retrieve working papers and other documentation is also an issue if it was originally prepared on paper and has later been scanned for storage.

It is important that the auditor has procedures in place to ensure that the integrity of data is maintained when it is stored electronically such as introducing appropriate back-up routines and use of restricted passwords.

Where working papers are produced by sub-contractor auditors, Audit Regulation 3.12 requires that 'A Registered Auditor must make arrangements so that if any of its audit work is carried out by another firm, then:

(a)   all the audit working papers created by that firm are returned to the Registered Auditor; or

(b)   the other firm agrees to keep those papers as required by Regulation 3.11 and allows the Registered Auditor unrestricted access to the papers for whatever reason.'

Working papers of component auditors in group situations are considered in **Section 30**.

12.9   Access to working papers

When a company becomes a target for potential purchasers, the purchaser's investigating accountants will frequently want access to the audit working papers to assist in their investigations. The granting of access to working papers in these circumstances involves issues of confidentiality and also the possibility that the auditor may be alleged to have accepted an additional duty of care.

The Audit Faculty of the ICAEW issued Audit 4/03: *Access to Working Papers by Investigating Accountants*, to attempt to facilitate the agreement of access to working papers in these situations and update previous guidance. It recommends that access to papers is granted on the basis of client authorisation and 'release' letters. These seek to deal with confidentiality issues and limit as far as possible additional risks.

12.9.1   *Working paper ownership and access*

The working papers of the auditor are his legal property and he has the right to restrict or decline access to them, except where there is a change of auditor, as described in **Section 38**. The auditor would not normally provide access to his working papers or provide explanations in relation to those papers until he has received:

- an authorisation letter signed by the vendor and the target company permitting the auditor to give access (**Table 3**); and

- a release letter signed by the prospective purchaser and its investigating accountant in which they agree that the auditor does not assume any duties or liabilities as a result of granting access (**Table 4**).

The release letter also requires the purchaser to indemnify the auditor for any loss suffered in the event of the purchaser or investigating accountant failing to comply with his obligations in the release letter.

In addition, to assist in excluding any other duty of care which may arise, and to reinforce the importance and purpose of audit working papers, the guidance suggests:

- attaching a 'notice' to the working papers when access is provided which summarises the characteristics, and records the exclusion of liability (see Attachment 1 in the example letter in **Table 4**); and

- obtaining an undertaking from the purchaser and investigating accountants to include such a standard notice in the text of their due diligence report.

This assumes that the purchaser and investigating accountant will not allow the working papers to be viewed by another third party without written consent from the auditor. Whether this will be granted depends on the circumstances, and will usually be dependent on the signing of a formal release letter. In many cases, the auditor controls access to the files by requiring the investigating accountants to view them on the auditor's premises.

The auditor would normally give access to all working papers. If some are withdrawn, he should inform the investigating accountants and purchaser that this is the case.

The example letters in **Tables 3** and **4** should be tailored to the circumstances. In particular, references to tax papers should be omitted where access to such papers is not provided.

TABLE 3: Client authorisation letter

Private and Confidential

The Directors
[Vendor]
[Address]

The Directors
[The Company]
[Address]
[Date]

Dear Sirs

Proposed sale of [Company Limited ('the Company') by [XYZ plc] ('the Vendor') to [ABC plc] ('the Purchaser')

In relation to the proposed sale by the Vendor [of the ordinary shares of the Company] to the Purchaser ('the Proposed Transaction') in which you requested this firm to allow [the Purchaser and/or] the Purchaser's accountants [PQR & Co] ('the Investigating Accountants') access to this firm's working papers relating to the statutory audit[s] of the Company's [and its subsidiaries'] financial statements for the year ended 31 December 20XX ('the Audit Working Papers').]

[As you are aware, this firm has not yet completed this year's statutory audit[s] of the Company's [and its subsidiaries'] financial statements, and therefore, the Audit Working Papers for this year are incomplete. Further this firm is not able to give any opinion on those financial statements and has not done so. Nevertheless, I understand that the Purchaser and the Investigating Accountants still wish the Investigating Accountants to review such Audit Working Papers as are available to date.]

[In addition, you requested this firm to allow the Investigating Accountants to review the taxation returns and computations of the Company [and its subsidiaries], so far as in the possession of this firm, as submitted to and/or agreed with the UK HM Revenue & Customs for each of the last [insert number] years[, working papers relating to those returns and computations]

---

and copies of the correspondence and related documents passing between this firm and the UK HM Revenue & Customs in respect of those returns and computations (together, 'the Tax Papers').]

This firm's general policy is not to allow third parties to have access to the working papers in the possession of this firm. However, this firm is content to allow such access to the Audit Working Papers [and the Tax Papers] ([together] 'the Papers'), but only on the basis of the guidance contained in Technical Release 04/03 issued by the Institute of Chartered Accountants in England and Wales. In accordance with that guidance I am now writing to confirm your agreement to the terms set out in this letter and to secure the authorisation of the Company [and its subsidiaries] for that access.

As a condition of providing access to the Investigating Accountants and responding to any requests for information and explanations in relation to the Papers in the course of or in connection with their review of the Papers, this firm requires that the Purchaser and the Investigating Accountants agree to the terms of the letter enclosed.

As you will appreciate, the Audit Working Papers were created for the sole purpose of the statutory audit[s] of the Company's [and its subsidiaries'] financial statements [and the Tax Papers were prepared and/or obtained for the purpose of calculating and agreeing the Company's [and its subsidiaries'] UK tax liabilities]. The Papers were not created for the purpose of the Proposed Transaction. Consequently, the information in the Papers should not be treated as suitable for the purposes of the Proposed Transaction. Furthermore, it is not this firm's function or responsibility to provide to the Purchaser or the Investigating Accountants any Papers that may come into existence, or information that may come to this firm's attention, after [date].

Accordingly, this firm requires the Vendor and its directors and the Company [(and its subsidiaries)] and [its] [their] directors to agree to the following conditions:

(a) They each accept the risk, and do not and will not hold this firm responsible, if the Investigating Accountant's review of the Papers or any information or explanations that this firm gives to them in relation to the Papers or in connection with their review of the Papers:

    (i) results in or contributes to the termination or reduction of the interest of the Purchaser in, or to the alternation to the proposed terms of, the Proposed Transaction, or otherwise affects the Proposed Transaction or the prospects of its maturing into a binding transaction; or

    (ii) causes an action or proceeding to be brought at any time against the Vendor or its directors or the company [(or any of its subsidiaries)] or [its] [their] directors [respectively]; or

    (iii) results in the Purchaser, the Investigating Accountants or any other person or entity using or misusing any confidential information obtained from a review of the Papers or from any information or explanations given by this firm.

(b) They each accept that, to the fullest extent permitted by law, this firm owes them no duty of care or other obligation and has no liability to them, in relation to or in connection with the Proposed Transaction as a result of granting the Investigating Accountants access to the Papers or any information or explanations that this firm gives in relation to the Papers or in connection with the review by the Investigating Accountants of the Papers.

The audit of the financial statements of the [Company/Companies] was undertaken by and is the sole responsibility of this firm, that is [insert full, exact name of UK firm carrying out the audit]. In paragraph (a) and (b) above references to 'this firm', where appropriate in the context, shall have an extended meaning so that they include, in addition to [insert full, exact name of the UK firm carrying out the audit], [partners/directors/members], employees and agents of this firm [and any person or organisation associated with this firm through membership of the international association of professional service firms to which this firm belongs and their [partners/directors/members], employees and agents]. This letter is for the benefit of all those included within the reference to this firm and each of them may enforce in their own right all of the terms of this letter.

Please confirm that the Company [and its subsidiaries] authorise[s] this firm to allow access to the Papers and to give information or explanations on the terms described above by signing the enclosed copy of this letter on behalf of the Vendor and its directors and the Company and its directors [and its subsidiaries and their directors] and returning it to this firm marked for the attention of ....

Yours faithfully

....

ACKNOWLEDGEMENT

Acknowledged and agreed, for and on behalf of [Vendor] and the directors of [Vendor].

....

Director   Date

Acknowledged and agreed, for and on behalf of [the Company] and the directors of [the Company].

....

Director   Date

[Acknowledged and agreed, for and on behalf of [subsidiaries] and the directors of [subsidiaries].

....

Director   Date]

TABLE 4: Release letter to prospective purchaser and investigating accountants

(The Release Letter assumes a proposed purchase of a company and that both Audit Working Papers and Tax Papers are to be made available. It must be amended as appropriate for the circumstances of each transaction.)

Private and Confidential

[Purchaser]
[Address]

[Investigating Accountants]
[Address]
[Date]

Dear Sirs

Proposed Acquisition of [Company] Limited

(1) In connection with the proposed acquisition by [ABC plc] ('the Purchaser') of [Company] Limited ('the Company') ('the Proposed Transaction') the Company [(and the subsidiary undertakings identified in Attachment 2)] [(together 'the Companies')] [has/have] requested this firm to allow [the Purchaser and/or] [name of Firm of Accountants] (the 'Investigating Accountants') access to this firm's working papers relating to the statutory audit[s] [(including the audits currently in progress)] of the financial statements of the [Company/Companies] for the year[s] ended [date] ('the Audit Working Papers') [and the taxation returns and computation of the [Company/Companies], so far as in this firm's possession, as submitted to and/or agreed with the UK HM Revenue & Customs for each of the last [number] years[, working papers relating to those returns and computations] and copies of the correspondence and related documents passing between this firm and the UK HM Revenue & Customs in respect of those returns and computations (together 'the Tax Papers')]. [[The Company/Companies] [has/have] authorised this firm at this firm's discretion to give information or explanations in relation to the Audit Working Papers [and the Tax Papers]]. The Audit Working Papers [and the Tax Papers together] are also referred to below as 'the Papers'.

(2) The Purchaser and the Investigating Accountants should note that this firm has not reported on the [Company's/Companies'] financial statements for any period subsequent to [date] [nor have any tax liabilities of the [Company/Companies] been agreed for any subsequent period to [date]] and significant events may well have occurred since [that date/those dates]. It is not this firm's function or responsibility to provide to the Purchaser or the Investigating Accountants any Audit Working Papers [or Tax Papers] that may come into existence, or information that may come to this firm's attention, at any point after [date].

(3) This firm does not accept or assume responsibility to anyone other than the [Company/Companies] and the [Company's/Companies' respective] members as a body, for its audit work, for its audit report(s) or for the

---

opinions it has formed. The statutory audit is undertaken in order that this firm might report to the [Company's/Companies' respective] members, as a body, in accordance with the *Companies Act* 2006, Ch. 3, Pt. 16. The audit procedures and the Audit Working Papers were designed and created solely for the purpose of enabling this firm to form and state an opinion to the [Company's/Companies' respective] members as a body, in accordance with the statutory requirements for audit, on whether the financial statements of [the Company/the Companies], which are the responsibility of the directors of the [the Company/the Companies], give a true and fair view of the state of affairs of [the Company/the Companies] as at the end of the relevant financial year and of the profit and loss for the period then ended. This firm's auditing procedures were designed to enable this firm to express an opinion on [the Company's/the Companies' respective] financial statements as a whole or not, for example and save where otherwise expressly stated, on individual account balances, financial amounts, financial Information or the adequacy of financial, accounting or management systems. [The Tax Papers were prepared and/or obtained solely for the purpose of calculating and/or agreeing [the Company's/the Companies'] tax liabilities.]

(4)   This firm's audit(s) of the [Company's/Companies'] financial statements, and the Audit Working Papers prepared or obtained in connection therewith, [was/were] not planned or conducted in contemplation, or for the purpose, of the Proposed Transaction. [Nor were the Tax Papers.] Further, the scope of an audit is normally substantially narrower than an investigation on behalf of a potential purchaser. Moreover, there are a number of inherent limitations in audited financial statements [and the calculation or agreement of tax liabilities] as the Investigating Accountants will be able to advise.

(5)   Therefore, items of possible interest to the Purchaser may not have been specifically addressed for the purposes of the audit [or of calculating and agreeing [the Company's/the Companies'] tax liabilities]. The user of professional judgment and assessment of materiality for the purpose of this firm's audit [or of calculating and agreeing [the Company's/the Companies'] tax liabilities] means that matters may have existed that would have been assessed differently by the Purchaser or the Investigating Accountants for the purposes of the Proposed Transaction. This firm does not warrant or represent that the information in the Papers, or that information or explanations given by this firm in relation to the Papers or in connection with the review by the Investigating Accountants of the Papers, is appropriate for the purposes of the Purchaser or the Investigating Accountants. The Audit Working Papers were not created for, and should not be treated as suitable for, any purpose other than the Statutory Audit. [The Tax Papers were not created for, and should not be treated as suitable for, any purpose other than [calculating and agreeing [the Company's/the Companies'] tax liabilities.]

(6)   For the foregoing reasons, neither the Papers nor the information or explanations given by this firm in relation to the Papers or in connection with the review by the Investigating Accountants of the Papers can in any way serve as a substitute for other enquiries and procedures

that the Purchaser and Investigating Accountants would (or should) otherwise undertake and judgments they must make for the purpose of satisfying themselves regarding [the Company's/the Companies' respective] financial condition or for any other purpose in connection with the Proposed Transaction. No one should rely for any purpose whatsoever upon the Papers or any information or explanations that this firm may give in relation to them or in connection with the review by the Investigating Accountants of them.

(7) This firm is prepared to grant the [Purchaser and/or the] Investigating Accountants access to the papers and at this firm's discretion to give information and explanations in relation to the Papers or in connection with the review by the Investigating Accountants of the Papers, on condition that the Purchaser and the Investigating Accountants acknowledge and accept the foregoing paragraphs (including that the position in respect of this firm's audit reports on the [Company's/Companies'] financial statements will remain as stated in paragraph 3 above following the grant of access to the Papers and giving of information and explanations in relation to the Papers) and agree to the following conditions upon which access to the Papers is granted and the explanations and information referred to are given:

(1) The Purchaser and the Investigating Accountants accept, agree and acknowledge:

(a) for the purposes of this letter, the expression 'the information' shall mean the Papers and any information and explanations given by this firm in relation to the Papers or in connection with the review by the Investigating Accountants of the papers;

(b) where any information or explanation is given by this firm, the onus shall be upon the Purchaser and the Investigating Accountants to verify any such information or explanation direct with [the Company/the Companies] rather than seek to rely on this firm;

(c) to the fullest extent permitted by law, this firm owes no duty to them, whether in contract or in tort or under statute or otherwise (including in negligence) with respect to or in connection with the information or its provision or in relation to the audit reports on the [Company's/Companies'] financial statements;

(d) if, notwithstanding the terms of this letter, they do rely upon any of the information or the audit reports on the [Company's/Companies] financial statements for any purpose, they will do so entirely at their own risk;

(e) they will not bring any actions, proceedings, or claims against this firm where the action, proceeding or claim in any way relates to or concerns or is connected with the use of or reliance on the information or the audit reports on the [Company's/Companies'] financial statements;

(f)   to the fullest extent permitted by law, this firm has no liability to them for any loss or damage suffered or costs incurred by them, arising out of or in connection with the information or its use or the audit reports on the [Company's/Companies'] financial statements, however such loss or damage is caused;

(g)   they will not refer to the information nor allow access to it or any report derived therefrom to any person or entity without this firm's prior written consent. (However the Investigating Accountants will not need to obtain such consent in order to disclose and discuss the same (i) with [the Company/ the Companies] for the purpose of obtaining information or verification from [the Company/the Companies] in respect of any report to be prepared by the Investigating Accountants in connection with the Proposed Transaction; (ii) with the Purchaser's legal advisers but then only on the basis that the firm will have no duty or liability to them; or (iii) otherwise as required by a Court or by statute.) Where this firm is willing to give written consent, this firm will require as a condition of such consent that the other person or entity agrees in writing to be bound by and to observe the terms set out in this letter, as if references to the Purchaser were a reference to the other person or entity.

(2)   To the fullest extent permitted by law, the Purchaser agrees to indemnify and hold harmless this firm against all actions, proceedings and claims brought or threatened against this firm, and all loss, damage and expense (including legal expenses) relating thereto where such action, proceeding or claim has arisen out of or results from or is connected with the failure of the Purchaser, or any of its professional advisers or the Investigating Accountants to comply with the terms of this letter.

(3)   Without limiting the obligation in paragraph 7(1)(g) above, the Purchaser and the Investigating Accountants agree to ensure that the notice attached as Attachment 1 to this letter is attached to any document obtained as a result of the Investigating Accountants' access to the Papers and is included in any note or report or other document in which they make reference to the information.

(8)   The audit of the financial statements of the [Company/Companies] was undertaken by and is the sole responsibility of this firm, that is [insert full, exact name of UK firm carrying out the audit]. In paragraph 7(1)(c)–(g) and 7(2) of this letter all references to 'this firm' (except for the first and the last two references in the paragraph 7(1)(g) shall have an extended meaning so that they include, in addition to [insert full, exact name of the UK firm carrying out the audit], [partners/directors/members], employees and agents of this firm [and any person or organisation associated with this firm through membership of the international association of professional service firms to which this firm belongs and their [partners/ directors/members], employees and agents. This letter is for the benefit

of all of those referred to in the previous sentence and each of them may enforce in their own right all of the terms of this letter.

(9) This letter sets out the entire agreement as between the Purchaser and the Investigating Accountants and this firm in relation to the conditions upon which access to the Papers is given by this firm and upon which information and explanations in relation to the Papers or in connection with the review by the Investigating Accountants are given by this firm to the Purchaser and the Investigating Accountants. It replaces all prior agreements or understandings (if any) between or amongst the Purchaser, the Investigating Accountants and this firm in that regard.

(10) The terms of the agreement shall be governed solely by English law, and the Courts of England and Wales shall have exclusive jurisdiction in respect of any dispute arising out of it or in connection with it. [The Purchaser, the Investigating Accountants, and this firm irrevocably waive any right to object to proceedings being brought in those Courts, to claim that the proceedings have been brought in an inappropriate forum, or to claim that those Courts do not have jurisdiction.]

(11) Please confirm the agreement of the Purchaser and the Investigating Accountants to, and acceptance of, the provisions of this letter by signing, dating and returning to us a copy of this letter.

Yours faithfully

[Firm]

The Purchaser hereby acknowledges that it agrees to and accepts the provisions of this letter.

_____   [Date]

Director

The Investigating Accountants hereby acknowledge that they agree to and accept the provisions of this letter.

_____   [Date]

Director

Attachment 1 to Release Letter

Notice of the Auditor

(1) [Firm name] ('the Auditor'), the auditor of [Company name] ('the Company') [and the subsidiary undertakings identified in the attached List of Subsidiary Undertakings (together 'the Companies')], has, on certain conditions, allowed [name of Investigating Accountants] ('the Investigating Accountants') to have access to the Auditor's working papers relating to the statutory audit of the [Company's/Companies'] financial statements for the [year/period] ended [date] ('the Audit Working Papers') and certain matters in the Auditor's files relating to the Auditor's engagement as the [Company's/Companies'] tax agent and adviser ('the Tax Papers').

(2) The Auditor does not accept or assume responsibility to anyone other than [the Company/the Companies] and the [Company's/Companies' respective] members as a body, for its audit work, for its audit report[s] or for the opinions it has formed. To the fullest extent permitted by law, the Auditor does not accept or assume responsibility to anyone as a result of the access given to the Audit Working Papers and Tax Papers or for any information or explanation given to the Investigating Accountants in relation to the Audit Working Papers and Tax Papers or in connection with the review by the Investigating Accountants of the Audit Working Papers and Tax Papers.

(3) The Audit Working Papers were not created for, and should not be treated as suitable for, any purpose other than the statutory audit. The statutory audit is undertaken in order that the Auditor might report to the [Company's/Companies' respective] members, as a body, in accordance with *Companies Act* 2006, Pt. 16, Ch. 3. The audit work of the Auditor is undertaken so that the Auditor might state to the [Company's/Companies' respective] members those matters it is required to state to them in an auditor's report and for no other purpose. The Tax Papers were not created for, and should not be treated as suitable for, any purpose other than calculating and agreeing the [Company's/Companies'] tax liabilities.

Attachment 2 to Release Letter

List of companies referred to in paragraph 1 for which access to the Audit Working Papers [and the Tax Papers] is to be provided.

12.9.2 *Further explanations*

If an auditor provides further explanation which extends to matters beyond the content of his working papers, he increases the risk of assuming a duty of care. In particular, the auditor should take care not to give oral representations about matters arising after the date of the audit report.

If further explanations are sought, the auditor is advised to re-emphasise the matters in the Notice in Attachment 1 to the release letter, in **Table 4**, at the time, perhaps by reading this out, or circulating a copy of the Notice at the beginning of the meeting any meeting at which such matters are to be discussed.

If matters outside the auditor's working papers are to be discussed, the auditor considers whether this is appropriate. If the risks can be managed, he may wish to structure this as a separate engagement with appropriate liability protection in a separate engagement letter.

Auditors are recommended not to agree to any request by the investigating accountants to review or approve their due diligence report. Such requests do not give the auditor any added protection and may serve to confuse auditors' roles in transactions.

12.9.3   *Access for other parties*

The example release letter in **Table 4** assumes a simple investment transaction where an existing corporate entity purchases a subsidiary of the vendor. There are other situations where the release letter may require amendment.

Syndicated financings

In syndicated financings, the investigating accountants may be requested to provide copies of their investigation report, incorporating information derived from the audit working papers, to other parties who were not identified at the time the release letter was signed, and therefore could not be party to it. Providing this information without the auditor's consent would be in breach of paragraph 7(1)(g) of the release letter.

It might be appropriate for the lead bank or equity provider to sign a modified release letter containing the following paragraph:

> 'This letter is addressed to [Lead Bank/Lead Equity Provider] for itself and on behalf of all [Banks/Equity Providers] listed in the [Loan/Equity Agreement] (together "the [Banks/Equity Providers"). By signing and accepting the terms of this letter, [Lead Bank/Equity Provider] warrants and represents that it has authority to accept the same on its own behalf and as agent for the [Banks/Equity Providers].'

The lead bank or equity provider may seek to amend paragraph 7(2) of the letter to seek to provide an indemnity for its own breaches only. If this is agreed, the auditor should be aware of the risks of another bank or equity provider passing information on to another party.

Alternatively, each bank or equity provider should sign a release letter in its own right. This may be difficult where the draft investigating accountants' report is circulated to potential finance parties as a basis for their decision whether or not to go ahead with the finance. Technical Release Audit 4/03 contains detailed guidance on this situation.

Flotations

Where access is provided in connection with a flotation, the auditor is advised to obtain a release letter signed by the:

- firm acting as reporting accountants;

- new company incorporated for the purpose of the float; and

- sponsor.

The auditor should obtain legal advice about limiting liability where no new company has been incorporated.

Where the reporting accountants are preparing an accountants' report (a short form report), there is no need to attach or refer to the Notice. Paragraph 7(3) of the release letter should be amended accordingly.

Vendor due diligence

Where a vendor has instructed a firm of accountants to prepare a due diligence report that will eventually be addressed to a purchaser, the auditor will require the vendor and the target company to sign an authorisation letter. The wording of that letter will be extended to include an indemnity from the vendor, as it is the vendor, rather than the purchaser, who will control the distribution of the due diligence report.

The auditor will also require a release letter signed by the investigating accountants, based on **Table 4**, but without the indemnity paragraph 7(2). Risks to unknown potential purchasers will be managed in much the same way as for financing syndicates.

Alternatively, the auditor may be prepared to acknowledge that the investigating accountants will require permission to circulate his report to prospective purchasers, and replace paragraphs 7(1)(g) and 7(2) with **Table 5**.

TABLE 5: Alternative paragraph 7(1)(g) and 7(2) for use in vendor due diligence situations

(g) they will not refer to the Information nor allow access to it or any report derived therefrom to any person or entity without this firm's prior written consent. The Investigating Accountants may allow access to the Information or any part thereof, in the form of a report of Investigating Accountants incorporating or referring to any part of the Information, to any prospective purchaser of the Company ('Prospective Purchaser') provided that the Investigating Accountants obtain the express prior agreement and acknowledgement of each Prospective Purchaser, addressed to this firm, that (a) this firm has, to the fullest extent permitted by law, no duty or liability and assumes no responsibility to the Prospective Purchaser or its professional advisers, whether in contract or tort or under statue or otherwise (including in negligence), with respect to or in connection with the Information or any part thereof the report and that (b) Prospective Purchaser will not disclose (including by reference or by copy, in whole or in part) any Information, including without limitation the report, to any other person or entity. Prior to the Investigating Accountants addressing to any party acquiring interest in the Company ('Purchaser') any report incorporating or referring to any part of the Information, the Investigating Accountants shall procure that Purchaser binds itself to this firm and accepts all the provisions of a letter in the terms of this letter (but adjusted to refer to Purchaser), together with an obligation in the following terms:

---

(2) To the fullest extent permitted by law, Purchaser agrees to indemnify and hold harmless this firm against all actions, proceedings and claims brought or threatened against this firm and all loss, damage and expense (including legal expenses) relating thereto, where such action, proceedings or claim has arisen out of or results from or is connected with the failure of Purchaser, or any of its professional advisers or Investigating Accountants to comply with the terms of this letter.

Where the vendor due diligence report is prepared by the same firm as the auditor, the firm may manage its risk relating to the purchaser or prospective purchaser by:

- requiring the purchaser to agree the terms of the release letter before agreeing to address the vendor due diligence report to them; or

- placing an obligation on the vendor to ensure that the purchaser signs the release letter.

Business refinancing where there is no acquisition

Where a firm of accountants are instructed to report to funders in respect of a proposed refinancing of the entity, it is recommended that the auditor obtains a signed release letter from the funders and investigating accountants prior to releasing the audit working papers.

12.9.4 *Investigating accountants from the same firm as the auditor*

Where the auditor and investigating accountants are from the same firm, there still remains a risk from releasing audit working papers to a purchaser.

In this situation, some firms will wish to amend the release letter so that it is addressed only to the purchaser. The indemnity may also be restricted to breaches by the purchaser only.

12.9.5 *Change of auditor*

Where there is a change of auditor, guidance on access to working papers by the successor auditor is covered in **Section 38**.

13 Planning

13.1 Introduction

ISA (UK) 300 (Revised June 2016) *Planning an Audit of Financial Statements* is effective for the audit of financial statements for periods commencing on or after 17 June 2016. The ISA provides guidance on the planning process covering:

- the role and timing of planning;
- involvement of key engagement team members;
- preliminary engagement activities;
- planning activities;
- documentation; and
- considerations for initial audit engagements.

Changes made in the 2016 revision of the ISA include additional application material specifically relating to the audit of disclosures in the financial statements (see **13.5.1**). These derive from the IAASB's disclosures project (see **Section 1**) which identified a need to focus the auditor's attention on disclosures at an early stage in the audit process.

13.2 Planning the work

Planning is discussed in the context of recurring audits and is described as 'not a discrete phase of an audit, but rather a continual and iterative process that often begins shortly after (or in connection with) the completion of the previous audit and continues until the completion of the current audit engagement'. However, some planning activities will, by necessity, have to be completed at the beginning of the audit, such as understanding the legal and regulatory framework within which the entity operates and briefing the audit team.

The objectives of planning include:

- ensuring that appropriate attention is directed to important areas of the audit;
- ensuring that potential problems are identified;
- organising and managing the engagement properly;

- assisting with proper allocation of work to engagement team members;

- where appropriate, assisting with the coordination of work performed by other auditors or specialists;

- facilitating review; and

- enabling the audit to be performed in an effective and timely manner.

The guidance stresses that planning varies according to the size of the entity and complexity of the audit. In the case of a smaller audit where accountancy assistance is provided by the auditor, the audit plan should take account of any areas of audit risk identified, and evidence obtained, during that exercise.

13.3   Preliminary engagement activities

In order to ensure that the auditor has considered any events or circumstances which may affect his ability to plan to reduce the risk of material misstatement to an acceptable level, he should:

- perform client and audit engagement acceptance procedures in accordance with ISA (UK) 220 (Revised June 2016) *Quality Control for an Audit of Financial Statements* (see **Section 3**);

- evaluate compliance with ethical and independence requirements (see **Sections 2** and **3**); and

- establish the terms of the engagement, in accordance with ISA (UK) 210 (Revised June 2016) *Agreeing the Terms of Audit Engagements* (see **Section 14**).

The factors affecting client acceptance and ethical and independence issues should be continually re-evaluated during the audit as circumstances may change. However, the main element of this work should be performed before any other audit procedures are started and, for continuing engagements, this may be at the end of the prior year's audit.

13.4   The overall audit strategy

The auditor should set an overall strategy for the audit which sets the scope, timing and direction of the audit and assists with the development of the more detailed audit plan. This will involve:

- identifying the characteristics of the engagement that define its scope, i.e. what reporting requirements are there, what financial reporting framework is the client using, what group companies are covered;

- ascertaining the reporting objectives of the engagement to plan the timing of the audit and the nature of the communications required;

- considering the factors that, in the auditor's professional judgment, are significant in directing the engagement team's efforts;

- considering the results of preliminary engagement activities and, where applicable, whether knowledge gained on other engagements performed by the engagement partner for the entity is relevant; and

- ascertaining the nature, timing and extent of resources necessary to perform the engagement.

Developing this overall audit strategy helps the auditor to determine matters such as which members of the audit team should be used for specific audit areas and whether experts are needed for complex areas. For example, using appropriately experienced team members for high risk areas, how many team members to attend the inventory count, the extent of review of other auditor's work, the timing of such work and how these team members and resources are to be managed, directed and supervised.

Table 1 sets out a list of matters the auditor may consider when determining his overall audit strategy.

TABLE 1: Matters to consider when determining the overall audit strategy

Scope of the audit engagement

- the financial reporting framework on which the financial information to be audited has been prepared, including any need for reconciliations to another financial reporting framework;

- industry specific reporting requirements such as reports mandated by industry regulators;

- the expected audit coverage, including the number of locations of components to be included;

- the nature of the control relationships between a parent and its components that determine how the group is to be consolidated;

- the extent to which components are audited by other auditors;

- the nature of the business segments to be audited, including the need for specialised knowledge;

- the reporting currency to be used including any need for currency translation for the financial information audited;

- the need for a statutory audit of standalone financial statements in addition to an audit for consolidation purposes;

- whether the entity has an internal audit function and if so, whether, in which areas and to what extent, the work of the function can be used for the purposes of the audit;

- the entity's use of service organisations and how the auditor may obtain evidence concerning the design or operation of controls performed by them;

- the expected use of audit evidence obtained in prior audits, for example, audit evidence related to risk assessment procedures and tests of controls;

- the effect of information technology on the audit procedures, including the availability of data and the expected use of computer-assisted audit techniques;

- the coordination of the expected coverage and timing of the audit work with any reviews of interim financial information and the effect on the audit of the information obtained during such reviews; and

- the availability of client personnel and data.

Reporting objectives, timing of the audit and communications required

- the entity's timetable for reporting, such as at interim and final stages;

- the organisation of meetings with management and those charged with governance to discuss the nature, extent and timing of the audit work;

- the discussion with management and those charged with governance regarding the expected type and timing of reports to be issued and other communications, both written and oral, including the auditor's report, management letters and communications to those charged with governance;

- the discussion with management regarding the expected communications on the status of audit work throughout the engagement and the expected deliverables resulting from the audit procedures;

- communication with auditors of components regarding the expected types and timing of reports to be issued and other communications in connection with the audit of components;

- the expected nature and timing of communications among engagement team members, including the nature and timing of team meetings and timing of the review of work performed; and

- whether there are any other expected communications with third parties, including any statutory or contractual reporting responsibilities arising from the audit.

Significant factors and preliminary activities

- with respect to materiality:

  - setting materiality for planning purposes;

  - setting and communicating materiality for auditors of components;

  - reconsidering materiality as audit procedures are performed during the course of the audit;

  - identifying significant components (where applicable) and material classes of transactions, account balances and disclosures;

- identification of audit areas where there is a higher risk of material misstatement;
- the impact of the assessed risk of material misstatement at the overall financial statement level on direction, supervision and review;
- the manner in which the auditor emphasises to engagement team members the need to maintain a questioning mind and to exercise professional scepticism in gathering and evaluating audit evidence;
- results of previous audits that involved evaluating the operating effectiveness of internal control including the nature of identified weaknesses and action taken to address them;
- discussion of matters that may affect the audit with firm personnel responsible for providing other services to the entity;
- evidence of the commitment of those charged with governance to the design and operation of sound internal control including evidence of appropriate documentation of such internal control;
- changes within the applicable financial reporting framework, such as changes in accounting standards, which may involve significant new or revised disclosures, particularly relevant with the introduction of new UK GAAP;
- volume of transactions which may determine whether it is more efficient for the auditor to rely on internal control;
- importance attached to internal control throughout the entity to the successful operation of the business;
- processes management uses to identify and prepare the disclosures required by the applicable financial reporting framework, including disclosures containing information that is obtained from outside the general and subsidiary ledgers;
- significant business developments affecting the entity, including changes to information technology and business process, changes in key management and acquisitions, mergers and divestments;
- significant industry developments such as changes in industry regulations and new reporting requirements; and
- other significant relevant developments such as changes in the legal environment affecting the entity.

13.5   Audit plan

As well as setting an overall audit strategy, ISA (UK) 300 (Revised June 2016) requires the auditor to develop a detailed audit plan to address the various matters identified in the overall audit strategy in detail. The plan needs to include:

- a description of the nature, timing and extent of planned risk assessment procedures sufficient to assess the risks of material misstatement in accordance with ISA (UK) 315 (Revised June 2016)

Identifying and Assessing the Risks of Material Misstatement through Understanding of the Entity and its Environment (see **Section 21**);

- a description of the nature, timing and extent of planned further audit procedures at the assertion level for each material class of transactions, account balance and disclosure in accordance with ISA (UK) 330 (Revised July 2017) *The Auditor's Responses to Assessed Risks* (see **Section 21**); and

- details of other planned procedures that are required to be carried out so that the engagement complies with ISAs (UK).

The audit plan is more detailed than the overall audit strategy in that it includes the specific nature, timing and extent of audit procedures to be performed by engagement team members. Planning for these audit procedures takes place over the course of the audit as the audit plan for the engagement develops. For example, planning of the auditor's risk assessment procedures occurs early in the audit process. However, planning the nature, timing and extent of specific further audit procedures depends on the outcome of those risk assessment procedures. In addition, the auditor may begin the execution of further audit procedures for some classes of transactions, account balances and disclosures before planning all remaining further audit procedures.

Although audit firms may have a bank of standard tests which are used to form the basis of an audit plan, these must be tailored to the individual circumstances of each audit.

13.5.1 Disclosures

Determining the nature, timing and extent of planned risk assessment procedures, and further audit procedures, as they relate to disclosures is important in light of both the wide range of information and the level of detail that may be encompassed in those disclosures. Further, certain disclosures may contain information that is obtained from outside of the general and subsidiary ledgers, which may also affect the assessed risks and the nature, timing and extent of audit procedures to address them.

Rather than leaving disclosures until the end of the audit, consideration of disclosures early in the audit assists the auditor in giving appropriate attention to, and planning adequate time for, addressing disclosures in the same way as classes of transactions, events and account balances. Early consideration may also help the auditor to determine the effects on the audit of:

- significant new or revised disclosures required as a result of changes in the entity's environment, financial condition or activities (for example, a change in the required identification of segments and reporting of segment information arising from a significant business combination);

- significant new or revised disclosures arising from changes in the applicable financial reporting framework (for example, the introduction of new UK GAAP, changes to disclosures where a small company ceases to be eligible for the small companies regime or a change in framework from UK GAAP to IFRS);

- the need for the involvement of an auditor's expert to assist with audit procedures related to particular disclosures (for example, disclosures related to pension or other retirement benefit obligations); and

- matters relating to disclosures that the auditor may wish to discuss with those charged with governance.

13.6 Documentation

ISA (UK) 300 (Revised June 2016) requires that the auditor should document the overall audit strategy, the audit plan and any significant changes made during the audit engagement to the overall audit strategy or the audit plan, and the reasons for such changes.

This will act as a record of the key decisions considered necessary to properly plan the audit and communicate significant matters to the engagement team.

Documentation of the audit plan also acts as a record that the planning has been properly completed, which can be reviewed and approved before further work is undertaken.

13.7 Initial audit engagements

Much of the planning for ongoing or initial engagements will be identical, however, the first time auditor will not be able to draw on his knowledge of the client from earlier work. In addition to the procedures detailed elsewhere in this section, the first time an auditor acts for a client, as part of planning he should also:

- perform the client acceptance procedures set out by ISA (UK) 220 (Revised June 2016);

- follow up any matters discussed with management or those charged with governance as part of the process followed to select him as auditor;

- communicate with the predecessor auditor to arrange review of his working papers (see **Section 38**);

- consider the audit procedures necessary to obtain sufficient appropriate audit evidence regarding opening balances (see **Section 19**);

- assign appropriately experienced audit firm personnel; and

- perform the procedures required by the firm's quality control systems, such as appointment of a technical or concurring partner.

13.8 Changes to planning decisions during the course of the audit

The ISA explains that the planning decisions should be reviewed and revised as necessary during the course of the audit. The results of the audit tests or new information may lead to changes in the approach adopted or the assessment of risks and materiality and these should be formally documented.

13.9 Direction, supervision and review

As part of the audit planning, the auditor needs to plan time for the direction, supervision and review of others' work. The nature, timing and extent of the direction and supervision of audit team members and review of their work will depend on a number of factors including their experience and the complexity of the areas in which they are working. For areas of higher risk of material misstatement, the extent of direction and supervision may be increased.

Direction, supervision and review is not relevant where the audit work is carried out by the audit engagement partner who is a sole practitioner. However, that individual must be content that the audit has been performed in accordance with ISAs, and a sole practitioner may plan to consult with an outside source on particularly difficult or complex areas.

13.10 Communications with those charged with governance

ISAs require certain elements of planning to be discussed with those charged with governance to improve the efficiency and effectiveness of the audit – see **Section 10**. However, the overall audit strategy and the audit plan remain the auditor's responsibility.

14 Engagement letters

14.1 Introduction

ISAs require that prior to commencing an engagement, the auditor and the client should agree on the terms of that engagement and these terms should be recorded in writing. Guidance on this is contained in ISA (UK) 210 (Revised June 2016) *Agreeing the Terms of Audit Engagements*, which is effective for the audit of financial statements for periods commencing on or after 17 June 2016. The ISA provides guidance on engagement letters issued by the auditor covering:

- agreeing terms of engagement in writing;
- respective responsibilities of the auditor and those charged with governance;
- imposed limitations on audit scope;
- changes to the terms of the audit engagement;
- recurring audits; and
- changes in engagements.

In addition, ISA (UK) 210 (Revised June 2016) includes guidance on the preconditions for an audit (see **14.3**).

Changes made in the 2016 revision of ISA (UK) 210 (Revised June 2016) are confined to the application material and relate largely to additional information that the auditor may request from management for the audit along with example paragraphs for inclusion in an engagement letter. In addition, the application material considers the implications of the special financial reporting frameworks applicable to small companies and micro-entities (see **14.6**).

ISA (UK) 210 (Revised June 2016) was updated in July 2017. Following a revision of ISA (UK) 250 Section A, the application material now suggests it may be relevant to refer, in the engagement letter, to the auditor's responsibilities to report identified or suspected non-compliance with laws or regulations.

In June 2008, the Financial Reporting Council issued guidance on auditor liability limitation agreements. It is outlined in **14.5**.

Further guidance from Croner-i can be found in our Engagement Letter Toolkit, which includes a comprehensive online tool for creating engagement letters.

ICAEW guidance includes TECH 09/15BL *Managing the professional liability of accountants* and a helpsheet *Engagement Letters*, which provides example wording for engagement letters in a variety of scenarios. This helpsheet was last issued in July 2016 and reviewed in October 2017.

14.2 Purpose

ISA (UK) 210 (Revised June 2016) requires that the auditor and the client should agree on the terms of the engagement and these terms should be recorded in writing.

The purpose of an engagement letter is to:

- define clearly the extent of the auditor's responsibilities;

- minimise the possibility of any misunderstanding between the client and the auditor; and

- provide written confirmation of the auditor's acceptance of appointment, the scope of the audit and the form of the report.

There may be occasions when an engagement letter is not appropriate, but the terms should still be agreed in some other form of contract.

It is important that the letter takes account of the relevant legislative requirements and should be tailored for each assignment.

The ISA is primarily concerned with the audit of annual financial statements but the guidance to it notes that its principles can be applied to other audit related assignments, such as reporting on interim financial information or review of UK Corporate Governance Code compliance statements (see **Sections 39** and **42** for examples of appropriate engagement letters).

The guidance in the ISA does not encompass other services such as tax and accounting and separate letters may be required for each such service. Such services may be included in the audit engagement letter, but if so, the paragraphs must be clearly distinguished from those relating to the audit.

14.3   Preconditions for an audit

An auditor should only accept or continue with an audit when the basis upon which it is to be performed has been agreed. This will involve:

- establishing whether the preconditions for an audit are present; and
- confirming the understandings of the auditor and those charged with governance.

The preconditions for an audit are only present when the auditor can determine that the financial reporting framework to be applied by those charged with governance is acceptable and that those charged with governance understand and acknowledge their responsibility for:

- the preparation of the financial statements in accordance with that financial reporting framework;
- internal control systems that are adequate to ensure that financial statements can be prepared that are free from material misstatement; and
- providing the auditor with access to information relevant to the preparation of the financial statements, additional information requested by the auditor and individuals from whom the auditor may wish to gather audit evidence.

If those charged with governance impose a limitation on the scope of the auditor's work such that the auditor believes the limitation will result in him disclaiming an opinion on the financial statements, then the auditor should not accept such a limited engagement as an audit engagement, unless he is required by law or regulation to do so.

If the preconditions for an audit are not present, the auditor discusses the matter with those charged with governance. Unless required by law or regulation to do so, the auditor shall not accept the proposed audit engagement where he has determined that the financial reporting framework being applied is unacceptable, or where those charged with governance have not agreed to provide the auditor with additional information that he may request for purposes of the audit.

Additional information that the auditor may request from management for the purpose of the audit may include when applicable, matters related to other information in accordance with ISA (UK) 720 (Revised June 2016) *The Auditor's Responsibilities Relating to Other Information* – see **Section 34**.

14.4 Contents

An engagement letter should be sent to each new client as soon after the acceptance of the appointment as possible and certainly before the commencement of any audit work.

The contents of an audit engagement letter may vary for each client, but reference should be made to:

- the objective of the audit of the financial statements;

- the responsibilities of the auditor;

- those charged with governance's responsibility for the financial statements;

- the scope of the audit, including reference to applicable legislation, regulations or pronouncements of professional bodies to which the auditor adheres;

- identification of the applicable financial reporting framework for the preparation of the financial statements;

- the form of any reports or other communication of results of the engagement; and

- a statement that there may be circumstances in which a report may differ from its expected form and content.

Where these matters are prescribed by law or regulation they need not be included in the letter, except to set out that such law or regulation applies and obtain confirmation form those charged with governance that they acknowledge and understand their responsibilities as set out in **14.3**

The auditor may also include in the engagement letter:

- where applicable, the requirement for the auditor to communicate key audit matters in the auditor's report in accordance with ISA (UK) 701 *Communicating Key Audit Matters in the Independent Auditor's Report* (see **Section 4**);

- the fact that because of the test nature and other inherent limitations of an audit, together with the inherent limitations of internal control, there is an unavoidable risk that even some material misstatement may remain undiscovered;

- arrangements regarding the planning and performance of the audit;

- expectation of receiving written confirmation of oral representations made by management and those charged with governance;

- expectation that management will provide access to all information of which management is aware that is relevant to the preparation of the financial statements, including information relevant to disclosures;

- agreement of management to make draft financial statements available to the auditor on a timely basis including all information relevant to their preparation, whether obtained from within or outside of the general and subsidiary ledgers (including all information relevant to the preparation of disclosures), and any 'other information', as defined in ISA (UK) 720 (Revised June 2016) – see **Section 34**;

- expectation that management will inform the auditor of any facts that may affect the financial statements of which management may become aware during the period from the date of the auditor's report to the date the financial statements are issued;

- descriptions of any other letters or reports the auditor expects to issue to the client;

- any confidentiality of other letters and reports to be issued and, where appropriate, the conditions, if any, on which permission might be given to make those reports available to others;

- basis on which fees are computed and any billing arrangements;

- complaint procedures;

- arrangements concerning the involvement of other auditors, experts or internal audit;

- for an initial audit, arrangements to be made with the predecessor auditor;

- a description of the auditor's responsibilities under law, regulation or relevant ethical requirements that address reporting identified or suspected non-compliance with laws and regulations to an appropriate authority;

- a restriction of audit liability, where this is possible;

- a reference to any further agreements between auditor and client; and

- a request for the client to confirm acceptance of the terms of engagement.

When the auditor is not required to communicate key audit matters, it may be helpful for him to make reference in the terms of the audit engagement to the possibility of communicating key audit matters in the auditor's report.

Extracts from an example engagement letter for a company preparing financial statements under the *Companies Act* 2006 is shown in **Table 1**.

TABLE 1: Example terms for inclusion in an engagement letter for the audit of a non-listed company

Your responsibilities as directors

1.1 As directors of the company, you are responsible for ensuring that the company maintains adequate accounting records and an appropriate system of internal control for the company. You are also responsible for preparing and approving the annual report and financial statements which give a true and fair view and have been prepared in accordance with the applicable financial reporting framework, the *Companies Act* 2006 and any other applicable law and regulations. As directors, you must not approve the financial statements unless you are satisfied that they give a true and fair view of the assets, liabilities, financial position and profit or loss of the company.

1.2 The financial reporting framework you have chosen to apply is applicable law and [UK accounting standards (UK GAAP)/International Financial Reporting Standards as adopted by the European Union].

1.3 In preparing the financial statements, you are required to:

- select suitable accounting policies and then apply them consistently;

- make judgments and estimates that are reasonable and prudent;

- state whether applicable accounting standards have been followed, subject to any material departures disclosed and explained in the financial statements; and

- prepare the financial statements on the going concern basis unless it is inappropriate to presume that the company will continue in business.

1.4 You are responsible for keeping adequate accounting records that:

- show and explain the company's transactions;

- disclose with reasonable accuracy at any time the company's financial position; and

- enable you to ensure that the financial statements comply with the Act.

1.5 You are also responsible for safeguarding the assets of the company and hence for taking reasonable steps to prevent and detect fraud and other irregularities. You are also responsible for ensuring that the company complies with laws and regulations that apply to its activities, and for preventing non-compliance and detecting any that occurs.

1.6 You are responsible for making an assessment of the company's ability to continue as a going concern and the appropriateness of the going concern basis of accounting for the preparation of the financial statements. This assessment should cover a period of not less than 12 months from the date of approval of the financial statements.

1.7 You are also responsible for the preparation of a directors' report and, where applicable, a strategic report which complies with the requirements of the *Companies Act* 2006.

1.8 It is usual for a statement of your responsibilities to be included in the directors' report or elsewhere in the annual report.

1.9 You are responsible for filing the financial statements at Companies House and any other registration bodies within the requisite time limit. Failure to do so can result in action being taken against yourself and the company.

1.10 You are also responsible for making available to us, as and when required, all the company's accounting records and all other relevant records and related information, including minutes of all management and shareholders' meetings. We are entitled to require from the company's officers such other information and explanations as we think necessary for the performance of our duties as auditors.

1.11 The Act also requires that the directors, having made enquiries of fellow directors and the company's auditors, state in the directors' report that:

- so far as they are aware, there is no relevant audit information of which the company's auditors are unaware; and

- they have taken all reasonable steps they ought to have taken as directors in order to make themselves aware of any relevant audit information and to establish that the company's auditors are aware of that information.

1.12 If financial information, which includes a report by us or is otherwise connected to us, is to be published on the company's website or by other electronic means, you agree to inform us in advance of the electronic publication. You agree that any such information will only be published in an appropriate context and be presented in a manner that is not misleading. The maintenance and integrity of the company's website is the responsibility of the directors. The directors' responsibility also extends to the ongoing integrity of the financial statements contained therein.

Our responsibilities as auditor

2.1 We shall endeavour to plan our audit so that we have a reasonable expectation of detecting material misstatements in the financial statements or accounting records (including those resulting from fraud, error or non-compliance with law or regulations), but our examination should not be relied upon to disclose all such material misstatements or frauds, errors or instances of non-compliance as may exist.

We have a statutory responsibility to report to the members whether in our opinion the financial statements give a true and fair view and have been properly prepared in accordance with the relevant financial reporting framework and whether they have been prepared in accordance with the *Companies Act* 2006.

2.2 We are also required to report whether, based on the work undertaken in the course of the audit, in our opinion, the information given in the strategic report (if any) and the directors' report is consistent with those financial statements, and whether any such strategic report and the directors' report have been prepared in accordance with applicable legal requirements. We are required to state whether we have identified any material misstatements and, if so, give an indication of their nature.[1]

In forming our opinions, we are required to have regard to your duty as directors not to approve the financial statements unless you are satisfied that they give a true and fair view.

2.3 In arriving at our opinions, we are required to consider the following matters, and to report on any in respect of which we are not satisfied:

(a) whether, in the light of the knowledge and understanding of the company and its environment obtained in the course of the audit, we have identified material misstatements in the director's report and where applicable the strategic report;

(b) whether adequate accounting records have been kept by the company and proper returns adequate for our audit have been received from branches not visited by us;

(c) whether the company's financial statements are in agreement with the accounting records and returns; and

(d) whether we have obtained all the information and explanations which we consider necessary for the purposes of our audit.

In addition, there are certain other matters which, according to the circumstances, may need to be dealt with in our report. For example, where the financial statements do not give details of directors' remuneration or of their transactions with the company, the *Companies Act* 2006 requires us to disclose such matters in our report.

2.4 We have a professional responsibility to report if the financial statements do not comply in any material respect with applicable accounting standards, unless in our opinion the non-compliance is justified in the circumstances. In determining whether or not the departure is justified, we consider:

(a) whether the departure is required in order for the financial statements to give a true and fair view; and

(b) whether adequate disclosure has been made concerning the departure.

2.5 In connection with our audit of the financial statements, we have a responsibility to read the other information and, in doing so, consider whether the other information is materially inconsistent with the financial statements or our knowledge obtained in the audit or otherwise appears to be materially misstated. If we identify such material inconsistencies or apparent material misstatements, we are required to determine whether there is a material misstatement in the financial statements or a material misstatement of the other information. If, based on the work we have performed, we conclude that there is a material misstatement of this other information, we are required to report that fact.

2.6 We are required to consider your assessment of the use of the going concern basis in preparing the financial statements and the adequacy of any disclosures in the financial statements relating to going concern.

We will report by exception where, in our opinion:

- the directors use of the going concern basis of accounting in the preparation of the financial statements is not appropriate; or

- the directors have not disclosed in the financial statements any identified material uncertainties that may cast doubt about the group's and the company's ability to continue to adopt the going concern basis of accounting for a period of at least 12 months from the date when the financial statements are authorised for issue.

2.7 Our audit report will be made solely to the company's members, as a body, in accordance with *Companies Act* 2006, Pt. 16, Ch. 3. Our audit work will be undertaken so that we might state to the company's members those matters we are required to state to them in an auditor's report and for no other purpose. To the fullest extent permitted by law, we do not accept or assume responsibility to anyone other than the company and the company's members as a body, for our audit work, the audit report, or for the opinions we will form.

2.8 [Where appropriate] As the company is a subsidiary undertaking we may be requested to co-operate with auditors of the parent undertaking and to provide them with information and explanations as necessary for the purposes of their audit of the parent undertaking. You agree that we may communicate with group auditors and respond to any reasonable requests for information for this purpose.

2.9 In the event that we cease to act as statutory auditors for the company, we are required to make available, if requested, all relevant information concerning the audit to our successors (if any) as statutory auditors. You agree to cover any reasonable costs of making such information available that we may incur in fulfilling our statutory duty.

Scope of Audit

3.1 Our audit will be conducted in accordance with International Auditing Standards (UK). Those standards require us to comply with ethical requirements. In carrying out the audit, we will exercise professional judgment and maintain professional scepticism throughout the audit.

3.2 We shall:

- obtain an understanding of the accounting and internal control systems in order to assess their adequacy as a basis for the preparation of the financial statements and to establish whether adequate accounting records have been maintained by the company;

- identify and assess the risks of material misstatement of the financial statements, whether due to fraud or error and design and perform audit procedures responsive to those risks; and

- expect to obtain such appropriate evidence as we consider sufficient to enable us to form a reasonable basis for our conclusions.

3.3 Our procedures will include an assessment of:

- whether the accounting policies are appropriate to the company's circumstances and have been consistently applied and adequately disclosed;

- the reasonableness of significant accounting estimates made by the directors;

- the appropriateness of management's use of the going concern basis of accounting and, based on the audit evidence obtained, whether a material uncertainty exists related to events or conditions that may cast significant doubt on the Company's ability to continue as a going concern; and

- the overall presentation of the financial statements.

If we conclude that a material uncertainty exists in relation to the Company's ability to continue as a going concern, we are required to draw attention in our auditor's report to the related disclosures in the financial statements or, if such disclosures are inadequate, to modify our opinion.

In addition, we will read all the financial and non-financial information to be published with the financial statements to identify material inconsistencies with the audited financial statements and to identify any information that is apparently materially incorrect based on, or materially inconsistent with, the knowledge acquired by us in the course of performing the audit. If we become aware of any apparent material misstatements or inconsistencies, we will discuss them with you and consider the implications for our report.

3.4 The nature and extent of our procedures will vary according to our assessment of the company's accounting system and, where we wish to place reliance on it, the internal control system, and may cover any aspect of the business's operations that we consider appropriate. Our audit is not designed to identify all significant weaknesses in the company's systems but, if such weaknesses come to our notice during the course of our audit which we think should be brought to your attention, we shall report them to you. Any such report may not be provided to third parties without our prior written consent. Such consent will be granted only on the basis that such reports are not prepared with the interests of anyone other than the company in mind and that we accept no duty or responsibility to any other party as concerns the reports.

3.5 As part of our normal audit procedures, we may request you to provide written confirmation of certain oral representations which we have received from you during the course of the audit on matters having a material effect on the financial statements. In connection with representations and the supply of information to us generally, we draw your attention to the *Companies Act* 2006, s. 501, under which it is an offence for an officer of the company to mislead the auditors.

3.6 In order to assist us with the examination of your financial statements, we shall request sight of all documents or statements, including any chairman's statement, strategic review and the directors' report, which are due to be issued with the financial statements. We are also entitled to attend all general meetings of the company and to receive notice of all such meetings.

3.7 The responsibility for safeguarding the assets of the company and for the prevention and detection of fraud, error and non-compliance with law or regulations rests with yourselves. However, we shall endeavour to plan our audit so that we have a reasonable expectation of detecting material misstatements in the financial statements or accounting records (including those resulting from fraud, error and non-compliance with law or regulations), but our examination should not be relied upon to disclose all such material misstatements or frauds, errors or instances of non-compliance as may exist.

3.8 (**Where appropriate**) We shall not be treated as having notice, for the purposes of our audit responsibilities, of information provided to members of our firm other than those engaged on the audit (e.g. information provided in connection with accounting, taxation and other services).

3.9 In respect of the expected form and content of our report, we refer you to the most recent bulletin on auditors' reports published by the Financial Reporting Council. The form and content of our report may need to be amended in the light of our findings.

3.10 Once we have issued our report, we have no further direct responsibility in relation to the financial statements for that financial year. However, we expect that you will inform us of any material event occurring between the date of our report and that of the Annual General Meeting which may affect the financial statements.

3.11 To ensure that there is effective two-way communication between us and to comply with the requirements of International Standards on Auditing (UK) we will:

- contact you prior to the audit to discuss any relevant matters, the planned scope and timing of the audit and to agree any required action; and

- contact you after the audit to discuss any matters arising from the audit and to confirm any agreed action.

We will of course contact you more frequently and regularly about audit and other matters during the course of the audit.

> 3.12 The scope of the audit does not extend to providing assurance on the accuracy of iXBRL tagging in the financial statements. We therefore accept no responsibility for tagging inaccuracies detected by HMRC or others.
>
> [1] Applies for periods commencing on or after 1 January 2016 or where small company accounting regulations have been applied early.

14.4.1 Recurring audits

Once agreed, the letter will remain in force until it is replaced, but should be reviewed annually to ensure that it is appropriate to the client's circumstances. If a change has taken place, then a new letter may need to be sent.

A new engagement letter may be appropriate when there is:

- any indication that the client misunderstands the objective and scope of the audit;
- any revised or special terms of the audit engagement;
- a recent change of management;
- a significant change in ownership;
- a significant change in the client's business;
- a change in the financial reporting framework adopted for the preparation of the financial statements; or
- a change in legal or professional requirements.

Where a new letter is not considered necessary, it may nevertheless be appropriate to remind the client of the original letter.

14.4.2 Groups of companies

The ISA does not deal with group or joint audits. However, accepted practice suggests that where the same firm of auditors is appointed for several companies within a group, they should consider whether separate letters should be sent to each board. The decision will be influenced by:

- who appoints the auditor of the component;
- whether a separate audit report is to be issued on the component;
- whether the terms are the same for each component;
- legal requirements;
- the extent of any work performed by other auditors; and
- the degree of ownership by the parent.

Where a group letter is sent, it should clearly identify the companies concerned and confirmation should be obtained from each board.

Where joint auditors are appointed, the audit engagement should be described in similar terms by each firm and a joint letter be sent if there are no additional services provided by either party.

Further guidance on group audits is in **Section 30**.

14.4.3 Changes in terms

The ISA states that the auditor 'shall not agree to a change in the terms of the audit engagement where there is no reasonable justification for doing so'. If he considers the changes appropriate, the auditor obtains written agreement to them.

Such situations arise from:

- changes in circumstances affecting the need for the service;

- misunderstandings as to the nature of the audit originally requested; or

- restrictions of the scope of the engagement.

Where the auditor considers the changes inappropriate, normally because it may lead to the recipients of his report being misled in some way, he should consider his position and, if necessary, take legal advice. If he decides to withdraw from the engagement, he should consider whether the reasons for this have to be notified to any party. For example, under the *Companies Act* 2006, the outgoing auditor must send a notice of any circumstances which he considers should be brought to the attention of the members or creditors of the company. He may also need to provide a statement of reasons for his ceasing to hold office to the appropriate audit authority (see **Section 38**).

14.4.4 Disengagement

Where the auditor ceases to hold office in circumstances where no other auditor is appointed, it may be appropriate to write to the client to formally terminate the appointment. This situation may arise where an audit client becomes eligible for and claims exemption from audit or where an insolvency practitioner is appointed as administrator or liquidator. Further guidance is in **Section 38**.

14.5 Liability limitation

14.5.1 Background

The *Companies Act* 2006, s. 532 provides that any provision that exempts an auditor from any liability in connection with the audit shall be void, except in the case of liability limitation agreements as set out in **14.5.3**.

From 6 April 2008, when the *Companies Act* 2006, s. 532–538 came into force, auditors were permitted to limit their liability to their statutory audit clients as long as they obtain the agreement (under a liability limitation agreement) of the company and its shareholders.

Other legislation may permit or prohibit liability limitation arrangements in respect of statutory audit for other types of entities. Where legislation is silent on the subject, contractual limitation of liability may well be possible, provided that the contract terms do not fall foul of the *Unfair Contract Terms Act* 1977.

Provisions of the *Companies Act* 2006, s. 532–538 do not apply to statutory audit of limited liability partnerships (LLPs).

14.5.2 FRC guidance

Guidance on the use of auditor liability agreements was published by the Financial Reporting Council in June 2008. The guidance outlines the measures to improve auditor liability that are allowed under the *Companies Act* 2006, gives specimen clauses for use in agreements, and explains the process to be followed for obtaining shareholder approval.

However, there were issues with introducing this into practice, mainly caused by the US authorities' non-acceptance of these agreements and the unwillingness of major companies and auditors to implement them without acceptance by the US authorities. As a result, these agreements are rarely used in practice.

14.5.3 Liability limitation agreements

A liability limitation agreement will limit the liability owed by the auditor in relation to negligence, breach of duty or breach of trust occurring during the course of the audit. In order for the liability agreement to be valid, it must:

- cover only one financial year;
- be approved by a resolution of the company's shareholders, as follows:

- for public companies, at a general meeting;

- for private companies, by written resolution, if preferred;

- for group companies, by each company in the group, not just the holding company; and

● be 'fair and reasonable'.

The courts can ultimately decide whether a liability limitation agreement is 'fair and reasonable'.

The actual limit on liability can be set out a number of different ways:

● based on the auditor's proportionate share of the responsibility for any loss;

● purely by reference to the 'fair and reasonable' test;

● a cap of liability (either in monetary terms or the basis of an agreed formula); or

● a combination of some or all of the above.

The FRC guidance sets out specimen 'principal terms' for each method of limiting liability above, together with example clauses which can be added to the relevant principal terms to form a liability limitation agreement.

The liability limitation agreement can be entered into at any time before the accounts for the year are approved. The existence of any such agreement and its principal terms must be disclosed in a note to the company's annual accounts.

14.5.4   Liability limitation – other services

Where an engagement letter covers both an audit in respect of which limitation of liability is prohibited and non-audit services in respect of which the auditor wishes to limit his liability, the letter should make clear that any limitation of liability applying to the non-audit services does not apply to the audit.

14.6   Small companies and micro-entities

The application material in ISA (UK) 210 (Revised June 2016) notes that EU law imposes restrictions on the number of disclosures that can be prescribed by law or accounting standards for small companies and micro-entities even though the financial statements of those entities are required to give a true and fair view. This means that such companies, when preparing financial statements in compliance with prescribed requirements may not include all the disclosures considered necessary for the purposes of a true and fair view, particularly in relation to matters relating to the use of the going concern assumption.

In the case of a small company, it is not sufficient for the auditor to conclude that the financial statements give a true and fair view simply because they contain all the prescribed disclosures and the auditor in this case may wish to draw attention in the engagement letter to the fact that additional disclosures may be required if he is to give an unqualified opinion.

In the case of micro-entities, the situation is slightly more complicated, although it is expected that the vast majority of such companies will take advantage of audit exemption. For these companies, the law presumes that compliance with the prescribed requirements is sufficient to give a true and fair view. The auditor is thus precluded from insisting on additional disclosures. As this financial reporting framework does not acknowledge that to achieve fair presentation of the financial statements, it may be necessary for management to either provide additional disclosures or to depart from a requirement of the framework, it is not considered to be a fair presentation framework as defined in ISA (UK) 200 (Revised June 2016) *Overall objectives of the independent auditor and the conduct of an audit in accordance with International Standards on Auditing (UK)*. Accordingly, this financial reporting framework is considered to be a compliance framework. Under ISA 700 (UK) (Revised June 2016) *Forming an opinion and reporting on financial statements*, an auditor can only provide an unmodified opinion in respect of a fair presentation framework and would therefore be unable to do so for micro-entities as to do so may result in the auditor's report being misunderstood by users.

The guidance notes that it may be possible for the auditor to mitigate the potential misunderstanding through the prominent inclusion of an Other Matter paragraph, addressing this in the auditor's report in accordance with ISA (UK) 706 (Revised June 2016) *Emphasis of matter paragraphs and other matter paragraphs in the independent auditor's report*. In this situation, the engagement letter should also refer to the proposed form of report.

15 Materiality and the audit

15.1 Introduction

ISA (UK) 320 (Revised June 2016) *Materiality in Planning and Performing an Audit* and ISA (UK) 450 (Revised June 2016) *Evaluation of Misstatements Identified During the Audit* are both effective for the audit of financial statements for periods commencing on or after 17 June 2016. An updated version of ISA (UK) 450 was issued in July 2017.

Materiality considerations in the context of a group audit engagement are also considered in ISA (UK) 600 (Revised June 2016) *Special Considerations – Audits of Group Financial Statements* (see **Section 30**).

Changes made in the 2016 revisions to ISAs (UK) 320 and 450 derive from the IAASB's disclosure project (see **Section 1**) and emphasise that consideration of the nature of potential misstatements in disclosures is relevant to the design of audit procedures relating to those disclosures and that in evaluating the overall effect of all misstatements, the auditor should consider the nature of uncorrected misstatements as well as their size.

15.2 Materiality

The term 'materiality' is used in financial reporting frameworks in relation to the preparation and presentation of financial statements. Misstatements are considered to be material if they, individually or in aggregate, can be reasonably expected to influence the economic decisions of users of the financial statements. Materiality is determined both by the size and nature of an item, judged in relation to the surrounding circumstances.

The auditor's determination of materiality is a matter of professional judgment and will be affected by the auditor's perception of the financial information needs of users of the financial statements. There is no mathematical definition of materiality, as it has both qualitative and quantitative aspects.

In considering the needs of users the auditor may assume that users:

- have a reasonable knowledge of business and economic activities and accounting and a willingness to read the information in the financial statements carefully;

- understand that financial statements are prepared and audited to a certain level of materiality;

- recognise uncertainties inherent in the measurements of amounts based on estimates or where judgment is applied – given that financial statements are prepared at a point in time and that complete, accurate financial information may not be available or may be impractical to obtain.

Whilst the primary users of financial statements are presumed to be the shareholders (or equivalent), the auditor should bear in mind that other user groups may have a legitimate interest in the financial statements and may make economic decisions based on them. These may include employees, suppliers, customers, providers of finance, government agencies and regulators.

15.3 Materiality in the audit

The auditor plans and performs audits so as to obtain reasonable assurance that the financial statements are free from material misstatement.

The concept of materiality is applied by the auditor in both planning and performing the audit and when evaluating the effect of identified misstatements on the audit as it progresses. Materiality judgments are also used when considering the effect of any uncorrected misstatements on the financial statements.

In planning the audit, the auditor makes judgments about misstatements that will be considered material. These judgments provide a basis for:

(a) determining the nature, timing and extent of risk assessment procedures;

(b) identifying and assessing the risks of material misstatement; and

(c) determining the nature, timing and extent of further audit procedures.

As well as quantitative misstatements, the auditor also needs to be aware of qualitative misstatements. For example, an inadequate description of an accounting policy which would mislead users of financial statements is material to those users. The auditor should remain alert for possible bias in management judgments, particularly in relation to the entity's accounting practices. A misstatement may also arise due to the omission of a disclosure needed for the financial statements to achieve a fair presentation beyond those disclosures specifically required by the accounting framework; for an example in relation to disclosures for small companies and micro-entities, see **8.3.4**.

Other relevant factors may include:

- the circumstances of the entity for the period (for example, the entity may have undertaken a significant business combination during the period);

- the applicable financial reporting framework, including changes therein (for example, a new financial reporting standard may require new qualitative disclosures that are significant to the entity);

- qualitative disclosures that are important to users of the financial statements because of the nature of an entity (for example, liquidity risk disclosures may be important to users of the financial statements for a financial institution).

15.4 Setting materiality

15.4.1 Overall financial statement materiality

At the commencement of the audit, the auditor sets a materiality level for the financial statements as a whole.

If there are specific classes of transactions, account balances or disclosures, in which a misstatement of less than the materiality set for the financial statements as a whole could be expected to influence the decision making of users, then the auditor may set specific materiality levels, lower than materiality for the financial statements as a whole, for these classes of transactions, account balances or disclosures. This is often appropriate where the balance sheet contains significant items affected by fair value adjustments, such as property or investments.

Lower materiality levels may also be applied to sensitive areas of disclosure such as directors' emoluments or certain related party transactions.

In determining materiality the auditor may use a benchmark such as a percentage of turnover, net assets or profit before tax as a starting point. Factors that may affect the choice of benchmark include:

- the elements of the financial statements (asset, liabilities, equity, revenue, expenses) and their relative significance;

- whether there are items on which the attention of users of the financial statements tends to be focused (e.g. profit, turnover, asset values etc.). This will often depend on the nature of the entity and its business but may also depend on the users themselves (e.g. are they long-term investors);

- the nature of the entity, where it is in its lifecycle and the industry and economic environment in which it operates;

- the entity's ownership structure and the way it is financed; and
- relative volatility of the benchmark.

Having determined an appropriate benchmark, the auditor usually then applies a percentage to determine materiality. The choice of an appropriate percentage is a matter of judgment and may be influenced by the auditor's understanding of the users. For example, a lower materiality percentage may be applied for a company whose shares are publicly traded than for an owner managed business with no external providers of finance.

Materiality for the financial statements as a whole is set by reference to the needs of users and the level of misstatement that would influence their decisions. It is therefore not influenced by the auditor's assessment of risk. The procedures performed by the auditor are however influenced by his assessment of the risk that material misstatements may exist which in turn depends on his assessment of materiality. The assessment of materiality helps the auditor to determine the type and extent of testing required to reduce audit risk (the risk that material misstatements exist and are not detected by the audit) to an acceptably low level.

15.4.2 Performance materiality

'Performance materiality' is the amount or amounts set by the auditor at less than the materiality level for the financial statements as a whole, so that the probability of the aggregate of uncorrected and undetected misstatements exceeding materiality is reduced to an appropriately low level. Performance materiality may be set as a single figure for the financial statements as a whole or, separately for some or all individual classes of transactions, account balances or disclosures. The level of performance materiality is a matter of judgment. It will depend on the auditor's understanding of the entity and the nature and extent of misstatements identified in previous audits, which determine expectations relating to misstatements in the current period.

Although not a simple mechanical calculation, performance materiality is often set at between 50% and 75% of overall financial statement materiality or the specific level of materiality applied to the particular transactions, balances or disclosures in question.

Unlike materiality for the financial statements as a whole, performance materiality is directly affected by the auditor's assessment of risk. A high risk of misstatement means that the auditor has a greater expectation of finding errors and in this situation it is generally appropriate to use a performance materiality towards the lower end of the auditor's normal range. Conversely, where there is a low expectation of errors, a performance materiality towards the upper end of the range will still leave enough margin within the overall materiality level to allow for the possibility of aggregation risk.

In the case of first time audits, the auditor may set performance materiality lower than normal to allow for greater uncertainty regarding competence of management and the history of errors in prior periods.

15.5 Revision to materiality assessments

Materiality levels are often set initially based on incomplete or estimated figures which are adjusted during the course of the audit, either as part of the entity's normal procedures or as a result of identified misstatements.

ISA (UK) 320 (Revised June 2016) sets out additional guidance in relation to revisions to materiality assessments. If information comes to light during the course of the audit which would have influenced the auditor's assessment of materiality had it been known when materiality was determined, the materiality level (or levels for particular classes of transactions, account balances or disclosures) should be adjusted. The amendment and the reason for it should be clearly documented on the audit file.

In any case, the auditor is required to reassess materiality levels at the conclusion of the audit in the context of the final financial statements.

If materiality levels are lowered, the auditor should consider whether performance materiality should also be decreased. In addition, where misstatements are found during the audit which exceed the auditor's initial expectations, consideration should be given to the need to reduce performance materiality.

Where revisions are made to materiality, the auditor should consider the implications for his audit approach and, if necessary, modify the nature, timing and extent of planned audit procedures. If his revised assessment results in a lower level of materiality, the auditor may find it necessary to carry out more audit work.

15.6 Evaluation of uncorrected misstatements

In evaluating whether the financial statements give a true and fair view, the auditor is required to assess the materiality of the aggregate of uncorrected misstatements. Uncorrected misstatements may arise from:

(a) inaccuracies in gathering or processing data from which the financial statements are prepared;

(b) omissions of an amount or disclosure required by the accounting framework, including inadequate or incomplete disclosures;

(c) errors in accounting estimates arising from overlooking, or misinterpretation of, facts;

(d) judgments made by management that the auditor considers unreasonable or the selection and application of accounting policies that the auditor considers inappropriate;

(e) an inappropriate classification, aggregation or disaggregation, of information;

(f) inclusion of material that is not relevant or obscures a proper understanding of information in the financial statements; and

(g) for financial statements prepared in accordance with a fair presentation framework, the omission of a disclosure necessary for the financial statements to achieve fair presentation beyond disclosures specifically required by the framework.

Further examples of misstatements arising from fraud are given in ISA (UK) 240 (Revised June 2016) *Auditor's Responsibilities Relating to Fraud in an Audit of Financial Statements.*

15.6.1 During the audit

Misstatements found during the audit should be assessed individually and in aggregate as the audit progresses. If the auditor is of the opinion that these may be material, he will need to consider reducing audit risk by extending audit procedures or requesting management to adjust the financial statements.

Where a number of individually immaterial misstatements have been identified within the same account balance or class of transactions, this may lead the auditor to reconsider his assessment of the risk of material misstatement for that account balance or class of transactions.

Where the circumstances of individual misstatements indicate that other misstatements may exist, or where the aggregate of misstatements approaches materiality, the auditor should reassess his audit strategy and plan. This should include a reconsideration of performance materiality and the implications this may have for testing procedures and sample sizes.

Misstatements that are individually and in aggregate 'clearly trivial' can be omitted from this aggregation. If there is debate over whether an item is 'clearly trivial', the ISA states that by generating such a debate the item cannot be considered trivial.

Misstatements in disclosures that are not 'clearly trivial' also need to be accumulated to enable the auditor to evaluate their effect on the disclosures and financial statements as a whole. Such misstatements often cannot simply be added together as monetary amounts can be, but the auditor still needs to evaluate those misstatements individually and in aggregate to determine whether they are material.

If the aggregate of uncorrected errors approaches materiality, the auditor should consider whether undetected errors could make this total material. In other words, the aggregate of uncorrected misstatements reduces the 'headroom' or 'margin for error' in the remaining untested part of the population. In such a situation, he may perform additional procedures or request that the identified errors be adjusted, or both.

15.6.2   At the completion phase

Before evaluating the effect of uncorrected misstatements, ISA (UK) 320 (Revised June 2016) requires that the auditor should reassess his previously determined materiality levels in the context of the entity's actual financial results.

The auditor should then consider whether any uncorrected misstatements are material either individually or in aggregate.

Each individual misstatement should be evaluated, considering the size of the misstatement and the particular circumstances, to determine its effect on relevant account balances, transactions or disclosures. The auditor should also consider whether any materiality levels for each account balance, transaction or disclosure have been breached as well as considering the impact on the financial statements as a whole.

The auditor should include in this consideration the effect of uncorrected misstatements in prior periods that have an impact on the current period. For example, an uncorrected sales cut-off error in the prior period would have a compensating effect on reported turnover and profit in the current period which, when taken together with identified errors arising in the current period could be material.

In evaluating misstatements, it may be useful to distinguish:

- factual misstatements, or undisputed errors;

- judgmental misstatements – where the auditor disagrees with management on a matter of judgment. Where there are a number of judgmental misstatements with a similar effect on the view given by the financial statements, this may be an indication of management bias or fraud;

- projected misstatements – where identified misstatements in a sample are extrapolated to provide an estimate of the level of misstatements in the population as a whole.

The auditor should also be aware of areas where errors are likely to be material by their nature and without aggregation, for example the disclosure of directors' emoluments.

In addition to simply aggregating the monetary value of misstatements, the auditor also needs to consider the circumstances surrounding the misstatement as some may be considered to be material, even if they are lower than materiality levels. For example, where the misstatement has an effect on compliance with regulatory requirements or compliance with covenants, or where it affects a value on which management bonuses are calculated, such circumstances would be likely to affect the auditor's consideration of materiality.

15.6.3 *Disclosures*

When considering misstatements in disclosures at the completion stage, any misstatements that are not clearly trivial are also accumulated, to help the auditor to evaluate the effect of the misstatements on the relevant disclosures and the financial statements as a whole.

Determining whether a misstatement in a qualitative disclosure is material, and aggregating such misstatements, is a matter that involves the exercise of professional judgment. Some examples of where such misstatements may be material include:

- inaccurate or incomplete descriptions of information about the objectives, policies and processes for managing capital for entities with insurance and banking activities;

- the omission of information about the events or circumstances that have led to an impairment loss (e.g. a significant long-term decline in the demand for a metal or commodity) in an entity with mining operations;

- the inclusion of significant accounting policies that are incorrectly described, not relevant to the entity, or otherwise not presented in an understandable manner;

- the inadequate description of the sensitivity of an exchange rate in an entity that undertakes international trading activities;

- inappropriate or inadequate description of estimation uncertainty in relation to an impairment (or otherwise) of an intangible asset; and

- inclusion of material in the financial statements that is not relevant or that obscures an understanding of the matters disclosed.

15.7   Documentation

ISA (UK) 450 (Revised June 2016) sets out a number of documentation requirements in relation to misstatements identified during the audit. The requirements are to clearly document on file:

- the amount below which a misstatement would be regarded as clearly trivial;

- all misstatements accumulated during the audit and whether they have been corrected; and

- the auditor's conclusions as to whether uncorrected misstatements are material individually or in aggregate, and the basis for that conclusion.

15.8   Communication of misstatements

The auditor should provide details of all misstatements, other than those which are clearly trivial, to the appropriate level of management, with a request that they be corrected. Uncorrected misstatements will need to be brought to the attention of those charged with governance, and the auditor may consider it appropriate to bring corrected misstatements to their attention as well, in accordance with ISA (UK) 260 (Revised June 2016) (see **Section 10**).

15.9   Written representations

The auditor should obtain written representations from those charged with governance to confirm their opinion that uncorrected misstatements are immaterial both individually and in aggregate. The ISA requires that this representation, which would normally be contained in a management representation letter (see **Section 32**), be accompanied by a list of uncorrected misstatements.

Where misstatements that have been reported to those charged with governance remain uncorrected, the auditor should obtain a written representation from those charged with governance as to their reasons for not making the necessary corrections.

15.10   FRC thematic reviews

In December 2013, the FRC published the results of an Audit Quality Thematic Review on the subject of materiality. The review looked at the consideration and application of materiality by the six largest audit firms and the disclosures made in published audit reports and identified a number of key messages for firms including:

- promoting the use of judgment in setting materiality levels, including performance materiality;

- that auditors should demonstrate consideration of risk in setting performance materiality and not automatically default to the highest level allowed under the firm's guidance; and

- that auditors should ensure that materiality is appropriately addressed when planning analytical procedures. For example, analytical procedures where expected or permitted variances exceed performance materiality are unlikely to provide much in the way of useful audit evidence.

This was followed in 2017 with another thematic review, this time covering the largest eight firms, the results of which were published in December 2017. In its conclusions and key messages for audit firms the FRC noted:

- that it was pleased that the majority of the key messages for audit firms in its last report had been addressed by the firms. These included an increase in the emphasis within the firms' methodologies on the application of judgment when determining overall materiality and performance materiality; providing industry-specific guidance for many sectors and demonstrating the consideration of risk in setting performance materiality;

- three of the audit firms had introduced guidance to encourage audit teams to reduce performance materiality to reflect the increased risk of first year audits;

- audit teams should ensure that if adjusted profit is used as a benchmark, it is a true reflection of the needs of users of the financial statements. If adjusted profit is used, auditors should explain why they have made the adjustments and how the benchmark selected better responds to the need of users of the financial statements;

- audit firms should provide audit teams with guidance on setting component materiality including both how to address the relative sizes of components and the particular risks arising in certain components; and

- audit firms should consider how they can better explain the concept of performance materiality in their reports. As one of the influences on performance materiality is the auditor's view of the control environment at the entity, the difference between overall materiality and performance materiality can give investors some insight into this area.

16 Fraud and error

16.1 Introduction

This section covers the responsibilities of the auditor in relation to fraud. It does not cover non-compliance with law and regulations, which is covered in **Section 17**.

ISA (UK) 240 (Revised June 2016) *The Auditor's Responsibilities Relating to Fraud in an Audit of Financial Statements* is effective for the audit of financial statements for periods commencing on or after 17 June 2016. It was updated in July 2017, following revisions to ISA (UK) 250 Section A *Consideration of Laws and Regulations in an Audit of Financial Statements.* The ISA covers:

- the definition of fraud and error;

- the responsibilities of those charged with governance;

- auditor's responsibilities;

- assessment of the risks of material misstatement due to fraud;

- evaluating audit evidence;

- written representations;

- reports to management;

- communication with those charged with governance;

- communication with the authorities; and

- documentation.

Changes made in the 2016 revision related largely to Audit Regulation requirements for statutory audits of public interest entities regarding communication with the entity and reporting to relevant authorities where the auditor suspects that irregularities have occurred, or may do so (see **16.8** and **16.9**).

The 2017 update recognises that the auditor may have responsibilities in relation to fraud and error that are additional to those set out in the standard, particularly in relation to reporting matters to an appropriate authority, and that the auditor's actions and communication with those charged with governance may be constrained by law or regulations or by professional ethics where fraud is identified or suspected. Requirements in respect of communication with those charged with governance were modified to include an exception where such communication is prohibited by law or regulation. Application and other explanatory material was similarly updated.

16.2   Definitions

The auditor plans and performs audit procedures to reduce audit risk to an acceptably low level. As part of this process, the ISA requires him to consider the risk of material misstatement in the financial statements due to fraud.

Misstatements can arise from either fraud or error. The main difference between fraud and error is whether the action that resulted in the misstatement was intentional or unintentional.

16.2.1   Fraud

Fraud is an intentional act by one or more individuals among management, those charged with governance, employees, or third parties, involving the use of deception to obtain an unjust or illegal advantage.

Although fraud has a wide legal definition, for the purpose of the ISA, the auditor is only concerned with fraud that causes a material misstatement in the financial statements.

Fraudulent financial reporting involves intentional misstatements in financial statements to deceive the users of those financial statements. It may be a result of:

- falsification or alteration of records and documents;

- misappropriation of assets or theft;

- suppression or omission of the effects of transactions from records or documents;

- recording fictitious transactions;

- wilful misrepresentation of transactions or of an entity's state of affairs; or

- intentional misapplication of accounting policies.

Fraud often involves management override of controls using such techniques as intentionally:

- recording fictitious journal entries, particularly close to the end of the accounting period;

- adjusting assumptions and changing judgments used when performing accounting estimates;

- omitting, advancing or delaying recognition of items in the financial statements;

- omitting, obscuring or misstating disclosures required by the applicable financial reporting framework, or disclosures that are necessary to achieve fair presentation;

- concealing facts that could affect the amounts recorded in the financial statements;

- engaging in complex transactions which aim to misrepresent the financial position or performance of the entity; or

- altering records and terms related to significant and unusual transactions.

16.2.2 Error

Error is distinguished from fraud and is defined as unintentional mistakes in the financial statements. It may arise from:

- mathematical or clerical mistakes in the underlying records and accounting data;

- oversight or misinterpretation of facts; or

- unintentional misapplication of accounting policies.

As part of his assessment of an error, the auditor should decide its cause and whether it was intentional or unintentional.

16.3 Responsibilities of those charged with governance

As stewards of the company, both those charged with governance and management have a fiduciary duty towards the owners of the company. Those charged with governance also have a statutory duty to maintain adequate accounting records and prepare financial statements that give a 'true and fair view'. Those charged with governance are responsible for the prevention and detection of fraud and error. It is not possible to achieve absolute assurance against fraud and error, but the implementation and continued operation of adequate accounting and internal control systems may reduce the likelihood of such occurrences.

An additional responsibility is that, under the *Companies Act* 2006, s. 501, it is a criminal offence to give auditors information or explanations which are misleading, false or deceptive.

Those charged with governance should take steps to prevent and detect fraud, and these may include:

- creating a culture of honesty and ethical behaviour, including setting a proper tone;

- developing an appropriate control environment;

- hiring, training and promoting appropriate employees; and

- requiring periodic confirmation by employees of their responsibilities and taking appropriate action in response to actual, suspected or alleged fraud.

16.4   Responsibilities of the auditor

The position has not altered since the pronouncement of Lord Justice Lopes in *Re Kingston Cotton Mill Company* (1896) that an auditor 'is a watchdog … not a bloodhound'. The auditor's responsibilities are thus very much tied in with the duty to report on financial statements and are restricted by the concept of 'reasonable assurance'.

ISA (UK) 240 (Revised June 2016) expects the auditor to recognise that fraud or error may materially affect the financial statements when planning his work and when evaluating and reporting his findings.

Compliance with auditing standards will not guarantee that the financial statements are free from material misstatement. The risk of undetected misstatement will be higher with regard to those resulting from fraud or error due to:

- the inherent limitations of the accounting and internal control systems and the use of audit sampling to test them;

- the persuasive, rather than conclusive, nature of the evidence generally obtained by the auditor;

- frauds sometimes taking place over a number of years but only being discovered when they become material;

- audit procedures which are planned to detect error may not be appropriate to detect fraud which does not immediately affect the financial statements; and

- frauds often involving collusion or intentional misrepresentations to the auditor.

Often auditors are less likely to detect fraud perpetrated by management than fraud perpetrated by employees. This is because management are frequently in a position to directly or indirectly manipulate accounting records or override control procedures.

Because fraud or errors are subsequently discovered which were not detected by the audit, it does not mean that the audit was defective. The guidance stresses that although the auditor cannot prevent fraud and error, the very fact that an annual audit is carried out may act as a deterrent.

16.4.1   Professional scepticism

Auditors should maintain an attitude of professional scepticism throughout the audit. Professional scepticism requires an enquiring mind and a critical questioning of the audit evidence, and is particularly important when considering the risks of material misstatement due to fraud. Even when management and those charged with governance have been found previously to be honest and trustworthy, a sceptical view should be maintained. However, as auditors are not trained to be experts in the authentication of documents, they will accept records and documents as genuine as long as there is no evidence to the contrary.

16.4.2   Engagement team discussion

ISA (UK) 315 (Revised June 2016) *Identifying and Assessing the Risks of Material Misstatement through Understanding of the Entity and its Environment* requires the auditor to discuss any susceptibilities of the financial statements to material misstatement (see **21.3.3**), and ISA (UK) 240 (Revised June 2016) requires this discussion to include particular emphasis on those risks arising from fraud.

The discussion should include the engagement partner and key staff, and the engagement partner has a responsibility to ensure that those engagement team members not present at the discussion are informed of matters relevant to their work. Areas that the discussion would normally consider are set out in **Table 1**.

TABLE 1: Considerations for the engagement team discussion

- how and where they believe the financial statements (including disclosures) may be susceptible to material misstatement due to fraud, how management could perpetrate and conceal fraudulent financial reporting and how assets of the entity could be misappropriated;

- circumstances that might be indicative of earnings management and how earnings may be managed fraudulently;

- the risk that management may attempt to present disclosures in a manner that may obscure a proper understanding of the matters disclosed (for example, by including too much immaterial information or by using unclear or ambiguous language);

- the known external and internal factors affecting the entity that may create an incentive for management or others to commit fraud;

- management's involvement in overseeing employees with access to cash or other assets susceptible to misappropriation;

- any unusual or unexplained changes in behaviour or lifestyle of management or employees which have come to the attention of the engagement team;

- the importance of maintaining an air of professional scepticism;

- types of circumstances that might be indicative of fraud;

- how an element of unpredictability will be incorporated into the nature, timing and extent of the audit procedures to be performed;

- the audit procedures selected to respond to the risk of fraud and whether some types of procedures are more effective than others;

- any allegations of fraud that have come to the auditor's attention; and

- the risk of management override of controls.

After the initial discussion, it is important that the engagement team members continue to communicate and discuss their findings.

Where a small audit is being carried out entirely by the engagement partner, that partner must consider the susceptibility of the entity to fraud during the planning and execution of the work.

16.4.3 Risk assessment

ISA (UK) 240 (Revised June 2016) requires an assessment of the risk that fraud or error may lead to misstatement. It sets out the following areas for consideration.

Management and others within the entity

The auditor should enquire about the entity's:

- assessment of the risk that the financial statements may be materially misstated by fraud;

- process for identifying and responding to the risks of fraud in the entity including any specific risks of fraud that have been identified or account balances, classes of transactions or disclosures for which a risk of fraud is likely to exist;

- communication, if any, with those charged with governance regarding its fraud risk identification procedures; and

- communication, if any, to employees regarding its views on business practices and ethical behaviour.

The auditor should also ask those charged with governance, management and the internal audit function about any actual, suspected or alleged fraud affecting the entity. Where there is an internal audit function, the auditor should ask appropriate individuals within the function about the risk of fraud, whether the internal audit function has performed any procedures to detect fraud in the period and whether management and those charged with governance have responded satisfactorily to any findings resulting from those procedures.

Others to whom the auditor may direct enquiries about fraud include:

- operating personnel not directly involved in the financial reporting process;

- employees with different levels of authority;

- employees involved in initiating, processing or recording complex or unusual transactions and those who supervise or monitor such employees;

- in-house legal counsel;

- chief ethics officer or equivalent; and

- the person or persons who deal with allegations of fraud.

Those charged with governance

Those charged with governance have a duty to oversee the systems for monitoring risk, financial control and compliance with the law and this will include the entity's assessment of the risks of fraud and controls put in place to mitigate specific risks of fraud that have been identified. The auditor should understand how those charged with governance fulfil this responsibility, and this may give insight into the susceptibility of the entity to fraud, the adequacy of internal control and the competence and integrity of management.

Unusual or unexpected relationships

Any unusual results from analytical review work should make the auditor consider the possibility of fraudulent financial reporting.

Other information

Any other information that comes to the auditor's attention should be considered as a possible indicator of fraudulent financial reporting. The engagement team discussion (see **16.4.2**) may be particularly useful in this respect. In addition, work performed as part of acceptance or reacceptance procedures, and work done for the entity in other capacities may be of use.

Fraud risk factors

After his work on understanding the entity and its environment is complete, the auditor should consider whether it indicates that one or more fraud risk factor is present. Examples include the:

- need to meet expectations of third parties to obtain additional financing; or

- granting of significant bonuses if unrealistic profit targets are met.

Fraud risk factors may not necessarily indicate that a fraud has occurred or is likely to occur and the auditor uses his judgment to assess whether the existence of a fraud risk factor does actually affect the risk of material misstatement of the financial statements.

Fraud risk factors are generally classified as:

- an incentive or pressure to commit fraud, e.g. profitability being threatened by changes in the market;

- a perceived opportunity to commit fraud, e.g. the handling of large amounts of cash; and

- an ability to rationalise the fraudulent action, e.g. a known history of violations against laws and regulations.

Auditors are encouraged to increase their focus on identifying fraud risk factors when assessing the risks of the financial statements being materially misstated due to fraud and in particular, they should ensure their approach is tailored to the entity they are auditing.

16.4.4 Identification and assessment of fraud risk

As part of his work of identifying and assessing the risk of material misstatement at the financial statements and assertion level, the auditor should assess the risks of material misstatement due to fraud. Fraud risks will automatically be significant risks (see **21.3.6**) and therefore, the auditor should evaluate the design of the related controls and determine whether they have been implemented.

The assessment of fraud risk is a three-stage process. The auditor uses his professional judgment to:

- identify risks of fraud through risk assessment procedures;

- relate the risks of fraud to the assertions; and

- consider the likely size of the potential misstatement and the likelihood of the risk occurring.

Not all fraud risks will have related controls, as the entity's management and those charged with governance may believe that some risks are so remote that the implementation of controls to mitigate them is not necessary.

Revenue recognition

As material misstatement due to fraud often results in an understatement or overstatement of revenue, ISA (UK) 240 (Revised June 2016) states that the auditor ordinarily assumes that there are risks of fraud in revenue recognition. This means that these risks will be significant risks and the three-stage assessment noted above should be followed, together with consideration of associated controls.

The assumption that there are risks of fraud in revenue recognition may be rebutted, for example, where there is a single type of simple revenue transaction, such as leasehold revenue from a single unit rental property.

16.4.5   Responses to fraud risk

Responses to fraud risk

Where the risk of material misstatement in the financial statements due to fraud has been identified, the auditor will respond in ways that have an overall effect on how the audit is conducted. This means that professional scepticism will be increased in all areas, which may lead to an increased need to corroborate explanations and representations, and take greater care when examining documentation in relation to material matters.

In his overall response to the risk of material misstatement due to fraud, the auditor is required by ISA (UK) 240 (Revised June 2016) to pay particular attention to:

- the assignment and supervision of suitably experienced personnel and experts;

- the accounting policies used by the entity, particularly those related to subjective and complex areas; and

- the selection, nature and timing of audit procedures, including incorporating an element of unpredictability in his audit plan.

Responses at the assertion level

The auditor's responses to the risk of material misstatement from fraud at the assertion level may include changing the nature, extent and timing of tests planned. He will aim to obtain more relevant and reliable audit evidence and additional corroborative evidence. This may include a greater reliance on observation and inspection procedures or, where relevant, CAATs. The auditor may conclude that better quality evidence will be obtained by performing more, or all, of his procedures at the period end, rather than during an interim visit, unless the fraud risk has arisen from improper revenue recognition during an interim period, which may be best investigated earlier in the audit process. More extensive testing may also be suitable in response to the increased risk assessment.

Table 2 sets out possible audit procedures to address the assessed risks of material misstatement due to fraud.

TABLE 2: Example audit procedures to address the assessed risks of material misstatement due to fraud

- visiting locations or performing certain tests on a surprise or unannounced basis. For example, observing stock at locations where auditor attendance has not been previously announced or counting cash at a particular date on a surprise basis;

- requesting that stocks be counted at the end of the reporting period or on a date closer to period end to minimise the risk of manipulation of balances in the period between the date of completion of the count and the end of the reporting period;

- altering the audit approach in the current year. For example, contacting major customers and suppliers orally in addition to sending written confirmations, sending confirmation requests to a specific party within an organisation, or seeking more or different information;

- performing a detailed review of the entity's year end adjusting entries and investigating any that appear unusual as to nature or amount;

- for significant and unusual transactions, particularly those occurring at or near year end, investigating the possibility of related parties and the sources of financial resources supporting the transactions;

- performing substantive analytical procedures using disaggregated data. For example, comparing sales and costs of sales by location, line of business or month to expectations developed by the auditor;

- conducting interviews of personnel involved in areas where a risk of material misstatement due to fraud has been identified, to obtain their insights about the risk and whether, or how, controls address the risk;

- when other independent auditors are auditing the financial statements of one or more subsidiaries, division or branches, discussing with them the extent of work necessary to be performed to address the risk of material misstatement due to fraud resulting from transactions and activities among these components;

- if the work of an expert becomes particularly significant with respect to a financial statement item for which the risk of misstatement due to fraud is high, performing additional procedures relating to some or all of the expert's assumptions, methods or findings to determine that the findings are not unreasonable, or engaging another expert for that purpose;

- performing audit procedures to analyse selected opening balance sheet accounts of previously audited financial statements to assess how certain issues involving accounting estimates and judgments, for example, a provision for sales returns, were resolved with the benefit of hindsight;

- performing procedures on account or other reconciliations prepared by the entity, including considering reconciliations performed at interim periods;

- performing computer-assisted techniques to test for anomalies in a population;

- testing the integrity of computer-produced records and transactions;

- seeking additional audit evidence from sources outside of the entity being audited.

Responses to management override of controls

The extent of the risk that management may use their position to override controls to manipulate accounting records and prepare fraudulent financial statements will vary from entity to entity. However, there will be some risk in all entities, and the ISA deems this to be a significant risk (see **21.3.6**). Therefore, in accordance with ISA (UK) 315 (Revised June 2016), specific procedures should be planned and performed to address this risk. ISA (UK) 240 (Revised June 2016) requires the auditor to:

- test the appropriateness of journal entries recorded in the general ledger and other adjustments made in the preparation of financial statements;

- review accounting estimates for biases that could result in material misstatement due to fraud; and

- obtain an understanding of the business rationale of significant transactions that the auditor becomes aware of that are outside the normal course of business for the entity, or that otherwise appear to be unusual given the auditor's understanding of the entity and its environment.

The auditor's assessment of the risk of material misstatement due to fraud may lead him to perform additional procedures to those set out here.

Journal entries

The financial reporting process is often manipulated by the recording of inappropriate or unauthorised journal entries or other adjustments. When considering which journals or adjustments to test, the auditor considers:

- his assessment of the risks of material misstatement, which may indicate a type of class or adjustments for testing;

- whether there are effective controls over journal entries and adjustments;
- the nature of evidence that can be obtained, particularly when journal entries are made electronically;
- the typical characteristics of fraudulent journal entries, including entries:
  - made to unrelated, unusual or seldom-used accounts;
  - made by individuals who do not usually make journal entries;
  - recorded at the end of the period or as post-closing entries that have little or no explanation or description;
  - made either before or during the preparation of the financial statements; or
  - containing round numbers or consistent ending numbers;
- the nature and complexity of the accounts involved, as fraudulent entries may be made to accounts that:
  - contain transactions that are complex or unusual in nature;
  - contain significant estimates and period end adjustments;
  - have been prone to misstatements in the past;
  - have not been reconciled on a timely basis or contain unreconciled differences;
  - contain intercompany transactions; or
  - are otherwise associated with an identified risk of material misstatement due to fraud; and
- those journals processed outside the normal course of business.

Accounting estimates

Fraudulent financial reporting is often performed through intentional misstatement of accounting estimates. Therefore, the ISA suggests that, when the auditor is reviewing accounting estimates, he should consider whether the estimates indicate a bias on the part of the entity's management. The auditor may also perform a retrospective review of management judgments and assumptions in the prior year to see if any bias is indicated in the current period.

If a bias is indicated, the auditor should consider whether the circumstances represent a risk of material misstatement due to fraud.

Business rationale of transactions

The auditor aims to understand the rationale of unusual business transactions in order to consider whether the transactions have been entered into to conceal fraudulent financial reporting or misappropriation of assets. The auditor should consider whether:

- the transaction appears overly complex;

- management has discussed the nature of, and accounting for, the transaction with those charged with governance;

- management is placing emphasis on the need for a particular accounting treatment;

- transactions involving related parties have been properly reviewed and approved by those charged with governance; and

- the transaction involves previously unidentified related parties or parties that do not have the substance to support the transaction without the assistance of the entity being audited.

16.5 Evaluating audit evidence

In accordance with ISA (UK) 330 (Revised June 2016)*The auditor's responses to assessed risks*, once audit evidence has been obtained, the auditor should revisit his assessment of the risk of material misstatement and consider whether it remains valid or needs amendment. This includes the risk of material misstatement due to fraud. If the risk assessment requires amendment, further audit procedures may be required.

The auditor's overall analytical review procedures at the end of the audit should include consideration of whether there is an indication of material misstatement due to fraud. For example, uncharacteristically large amounts of income being reported in the last few weeks of the accounting period may indicate fraudulent activity.

Any misstatements discovered during the audit process should be considered as possible indicators of fraud. If fraud is indicated, the auditor should reconsider the reliability of management representations.

The auditor must consider the severity of the fraud and its impact on his report. Where a suspected fraud has caused a misstatement that is not material to the financial statements, the auditor considers its implications to the rest of his evidence. For example, a petty cash fraud perpetrated by a clerk is not likely to impact the auditor's opinions. However, if the same fraud was perpetrated by management, the auditor may consider that it is indicative of a more pervasive problem with the integrity of management.

16.6   Auditor unable to continue the engagement

ISA (UK) 240 (Revised June 2016) states that there may be situations where the auditor is required to question his ability to continue performing an audit. These may include:

- the entity does not take the appropriate action regarding fraud that the auditor considers necessary in the circumstances, even where the fraud is not material to the financial statements;

- auditor's consideration of the risk of material misstatement due to fraud and the results of audit tests indicate a significant risk of material and pervasive fraud; or

- the auditor has significant concerns about the competence or integrity of management or those charged with governance.

In such situations, the auditor should:

- consider whether it is appropriate to withdraw from the engagement;

- determine his professional and legal responsibilities, including responsibilities to report his inability to continue the engagement with the person or persons who made the audit appointment or any relevant regulatory authority.

16.7   Management representations

ISA (UK) 240 (Revised June 2016) requires the auditor to obtain written representations from management and those charged with governance that:

- it acknowledges its responsibility for the design, implementation and maintenance of internal controls to prevent and detect fraud;

- it has disclosed to the auditor the results of its assessment of the risk that the financial statements may be materially misstated as a result of fraud;

- it has disclosed to the auditor its knowledge of fraud or suspected fraud affecting the entity involving:

  - management;

  - employees who have significant roles in internal control; or

  - others where the fraud could have a material effect on the financial statements; and

- it has disclosed to the auditor its knowledge of any allegations of fraud, or suspected fraud, affecting the entity's financial statements, communicated by employees, former employees, analysts, regulators or others.

16.8   Communication with management and those charged with governance

Where the auditor has identified a fraud, or has obtained indications that a fraud may exist, this should be communicated, unless prohibited by law or regulation, to an appropriate level of management as soon as possible.

If fraud is identified involving:

- management;

- employees who have significant roles in internal control; or

- others where the fraud could have a material effect on the financial statements,

the auditor should communicate with those charged with governance as soon as practicable. Such communications with those charged with governance are required, unless the communication is prohibited by law or regulation.

Communication may be oral or in writing, but where fraud involves senior management or results in material misstatement of the financial statements, the nature and sensitivity of such matters may be such that the auditor considers it appropriate to report in writing.

If the integrity or honesty of management or those charged with governance is doubted, the auditor may consider seeking legal advice before deciding on an appropriate course of action.

In addition, the auditor should inform those charged with governance about any significant deficiencies in the design and implementation of internal controls to prevent and detect fraud, or other matters related to fraud which may have come to his attention.

16.8.1   Public interest entities

For public interest entities, when the auditor suspects that irregularities, including fraud with regard to the financial statements, may occur or have occurred, he informs the entity and asks it to investigate the matter and take appropriate measures to deal with the issue and to prevent any recurrence. Where the entity does not investigate these matters, the auditor informs the relevant authorities (see **16.9**).

If the entity investigates the matter but does not, in the auditor's judgment, take appropriate measures to deal with any fraud and prevent future occurrences, the auditor considers whether he needs to take further action.

16.9   Communication with the authorities

The auditor's duty of confidentiality will be overridden by the requirements of anti-money laundering legislation including the *Money Laundering, Terrorist Financing and Transfer of Funds (Information on the Payer) Regulations* 2017, the *Proceeds of Crime Act* 2002 and the *Terrorism Act* 2000 which impose a duty on the auditor to report knowledge or suspicions of criminal activity gained in the course of his work. Further details are given in **Section 18**.

16.9.1   Public interest entities

The disclosure in good faith to the relevant authorities, by the auditor, of any irregularities referred to in **16.8** does not constitute a breach of any contractual or legal restriction on disclosure of information in accordance with the Audit Regulation.

16.10   Documentation

As part of his understanding of the entity as required by ISA (UK) 315 (Revised June 2016), the auditor should document:

- the significant decisions reached during the engagement team discussion about the susceptibility of the entity's financial statements to material misstatement due to fraud (see **16.4.2**); and

- the identified and assessed risks of material misstatement due to fraud at the financial statements level and at the assertion level.

The auditor should also document:

- his planned responses to the assessed risk of material misstatement due to fraud at the financial statements level and the nature, timing and extent of audit procedures planned, with those procedures linked back to the assessed risks of material misstatement due to fraud at the assertion level;

- the results from the procedures planned;

- communications about fraud made to management and those charged with governance; and

- if he has assessed that there is no risk of material misstatement due to fraud related to revenue recognition, his reasons for this conclusion.

17 Consideration of laws and regulations

17.1 Introduction

This section covers the responsibility of the auditor to consider laws and regulations in the context of an audit. It does not cover fraud and error, which are covered in **Section 16** or money laundering, which is covered in **Section 18**.

ISA (UK) 250 Section A (Revised December 2017) *Consideration of Laws and Regulations in an Audit of Financial Statements* is based on the IAASB's ISA 250 with some additional UK specific material. It was revised in June 2016 and issued as part of the FRC's suite of ISAs (UK). The standard was subsequently revised in July 2017 to incorporate minor changes made by the IAASB to the international standard and revised again in December 2017 to incorporate updated guidance reflecting changes to the money laundering regime in the UK. This section is based on the December 2017 version although the changes made in July 2017 and December 2017 are stated as being effective for audits of financial periods commencing on or after 15 December 2017.

Further guidance on the auditor's responsibility to report to regulators of public interest entities and entities in the financial sector is contained in ISA (UK) 250 Section B (Revised June 2016) *The Auditor's Statutory Right and Duty to Report to Regulators of Public Interest Entities and Regulators of Other Entities in the Financial Sector*. This is covered in **Section 9**.

17.2 Legal and regulatory framework

An entity's legal and regulatory framework is the laws and regulations to which it is subjected. The legal and regulatory framework will vary from entity to entity. Some laws and regulations will have a direct effect on the financial statements as they determine the amounts to be reported and disclosures in the financial statements. Examples of such laws and regulations include those governing taxation and pension rights.

Other laws and regulations do not have a direct effect on the amounts in the financial statements, but compliance with them is fundamental to the ability of the business to operate. These include compliance with the terms of an operating licence, compliance with regulatory solvency requirements or compliance with environmental regulations. Non-compliance with these laws and regulations may result in fines, litigation, adverse publicity or regulatory action affecting the ability of the business to operate and may have a material effect on the financial statements.

The amount of law and regulation that an entity is governed by will depend on the industry it operates in and its constitution. For example, some sectors are heavily regulated, such as banks or pharmaceutical companies, whilst others are only subject to 'general' laws such as health and safety regulations.

17.3   Management responsibility

It is management's responsibility to ensure that the entity complies with laws and regulations and to establish procedures to prevent and detect non-compliance. Management would normally be expected to have procedures that enable them to:

- maintain a register of significant laws and regulations as they affect the entity;

- monitor relevant legal requirements and ensure operating procedures and conditions meet them;

- institute and operate an appropriate system of internal control;

- develop and publish within the entity relevant codes of conduct;

- ensure employees are properly trained and understand the relevant codes of conduct;

- monitor compliance with the code;

- engage legal advisers to assist in monitoring; and

- maintain a record of complaints.

In larger entities, particular responsibilities may be assigned to:

- an internal audit function;

- a compliance department; or

- an audit committee.

In certain industries, such as the financial sector, certain compliance procedures and functions may be mandated by regulations.

Non-compliance with laws and regulations may lead to financial penalties being imposed on an entity or a loss of its business. Therefore, the implications of any non-compliance, either suspected or actual, should be assessed under the applicable financial reporting framework with regard to the possible inclusion and/or disclosure in the financial statements of liabilities, provisions, contingent liabilities or other relevant information. In serious cases, this may also affect the directors' consideration of going concern.

17.4   Responsibility of the auditor

The auditor is responsible for obtaining reasonable assurance that the financial statements are free from material misstatement whether due to fraud or error. In carrying out the audit, he takes account of the legal and regulatory framework within which the entity operates but, with some limited exceptions, he has no direct responsibility for the detection of non-compliance with laws or regulations.

ISA 250 Section A distinguishes between laws and regulations that have a direct effect on the preparation of the financial statements and the determination or presentation of items within them, and those other laws and regulations which, whilst not directly related to the financial statements, are such that non-compliance could have a material impact on the financial statements. The ISA specifies different approaches to be taken by the auditor in respect of possible non-compliance in these two categories.

The objectives of the auditor are to obtain evidence regarding compliance with those laws and regulations that directly affect the financial statements, to carry out procedures to help identify instances of non-compliance with other laws or regulations where this could have material effect on the financial statements and, where non-compliance is identified or suspected, to respond appropriately including reporting to management, those charged with governance or external authorities.

As part of the planning process, the auditor should obtain a general understanding of the legal and regulatory framework applicable to the client and its industry. The auditor should also consider the procedures the entity follows to ensure that it complies with this framework. Procedures may include:

- using and updating existing knowledge of the entity's industry, regulatory and other external factors;

- enquiring of those charged with governance about the entity's policies and procedures for complying with laws and regulations;

- enquiring of those charged with governance as to the regulations that may be expected to have a fundamental effect on the operations of the entity;

- discussing the policies for identifying, evaluating and accounting for litigation claims with those charged with governance; and

- discussing the legal and regulatory framework with auditors of subsidiaries in other countries.

During the audit, the auditor may also become aware of non-compliance with laws or regulations which do not materially affect the financial statements. In these situations, the auditor is mindful of the 'Professional conduct in relation to defaults or unlawful acts guidance' attached to the ICAEW Code of Ethics and of his obligations to report potential money laundering offences and certain other activities to an appropriate authority (see **17.6**).

17.5 Consideration of compliance

17.5.1 *Laws with a direct effect on the financial statements*

Where laws and regulations are generally recognised to have a direct effect on material amounts and disclosures in the financial statements, the ISA requires that the auditor should obtain sufficient appropriate evidence of compliance. Examples of such laws are:

- those which determine the form and content of an entity's financial statements – for example, the *Large and Medium-sized Companies and Groups (Accounts and Reports) Regulations* 2008 (SI 2008/410) or the *Small Companies and Groups (Accounts and Directors' Report) Regulations* 2008 (SI 2008/409);

- those which determine when a company is prohibited from making a distribution – for example, the *Companies Act* 2006, s. 830;

- those which oblige the auditor to report in accordance with specific statutory requirements – for example, failure of a company to maintain adequate accounting records, or disclosure of directors' remuneration; and

- financial reporting requirements for specific industry sectors.

The auditor's responsibility to express an opinion on financial statements does not extend to determining whether the entity has complied with every aspect of applicable tax legislation. The auditor needs only to obtain sufficient appropriate evidence to give reasonable assurance that the amounts included in the financial statements and related disclosures are not materially misstated.

17.5.2   Other laws and regulations

Other laws and regulations may also have a material effect on the financial statements. Such laws and regulations include those that have a fundamental effect on the operations of the entity or its ability to continue as a going concern. For example, non-compliance with the terms of a licence or other entitlement to perform operations (such as a failure by a bank to comply with capital maintenance requirements) may not directly affect the financial statements but may give rise to penalties or withdrawal of the licence to operate.

To identify instances of non-compliance with other laws and regulations which have a material effect on the financial statements, the ISA requires the auditor to:

- review correspondence with relevant authorities; and
- make enquiries of management and those charged with governance as to whether the entity is in compliance with such laws and regulations.

17.5.3   Other procedures and written representations

The auditor should remain alert during the audit to the possibility that other audit procedures may indicate non-compliance with laws or regulations.

In all cases, the auditor should obtain written confirmation from those charged with governance that they have disclosed to the auditor all known or suspected instances of non-compliance where this may have an effect on the financial statements.

Unless the auditor becomes aware of, or suspects, non-compliance, he is not required to carry out procedures regarding the entity's compliance with laws or regulations other than those set out in this section.

17.6   Money laundering and tipping off

The auditor should be aware that instances of possible or actual non-compliance with laws and regulations discovered during the audit may result in obligations for partners and staff to report to the authorities.

When considering actual or suspected non-compliance with laws or regulations, the auditor needs to be mindful of the requirements of anti-money laundering legislation and other similar legal obligations to report suspicious activity to an appropriate authority. In particular, the auditor needs to be mindful of 'tipping off' rules under the *Proceeds of Crime Act* 2002 which may restrict the auditor's ability to discuss matters with management or those charged with governance or carry out further investigations. Further guidance is given in **Section 18**.

17.7 Non-compliance

Information that may alert the auditor to the possibility of non-compliance may include, for example:

- evidence of investigation by government departments;
- payment of fines or penalties;
- large payments for unspecified services or loans to consultants;
- excessive sales commissions;
- purchasing at prices significantly above or below market price;
- unusual payments in cash, cheques payable to bearer or transfers to numbered bank accounts;
- unusual transactions with companies registered in tax havens;
- payments for goods or services made to a country other than that where goods originated;
- existence of an accounting system or part of one which fails, whether by design or accident, to give an adequate audit trail;
- unauthorised or improperly recorded transactions; or
- media comment.

When the auditor becomes aware of or suspects non-compliance, he should obtain an understanding of the nature of the act and the circumstances in which it has occurred, and sufficient other information to evaluate the possible effect in the financial statements.

Evaluating the effect on the financial statements involves considering:

- the potential financial consequences of non-compliance including fines, compensation, penalties, damages, expropriation of assets, forced discontinuance of operations and litigation;
- whether the potential financial consequences require recognition of liabilities or disclosure in the financial statements;
- whether the going concern assumption remains appropriate; and
- whether potential consequences are so serious as to call into question the presentation of the financial statements or otherwise make them misleading.

If the auditor suspects non-compliance he should, unless prohibited by law or regulation (see **17.6**), discuss the matter with management and, where appropriate, those charged with governance. Where management does not provide sufficient information about the suspected non-compliance, the auditor should consider taking legal advice. If there is still insufficient information concerning the non-compliance, then the auditor should consider the implications for his audit opinion.

However, it is not just the effect on the audit report that should be considered. The auditor needs to assess the impact on other areas of the audit including his risk assessment, the reliability of management representations and the integrity of management and those charged with governance. This may be particularly important where the non-compliance includes:

- an apparent failure of specific control procedures;

- involvement of management; and

- any concealment of the act.

17.8 Reporting

17.8.1 *Reporting to management and those charged with governance*

The discovery of non-compliance should, unless prohibited by law or regulation, be reported to those charged with governance unless clearly inconsequential. Where the non-compliance is believed to be intentional and material this report should be made as soon as is practicable.

Where it is suspected that management or those charged with governance are involved in the non-compliance, the matter should be reported to the next higher level of management who are not suspected of being involved. Legal advice may be required if the auditor believes that no higher authority exists or that his report may not be acted on. If money laundering or some other reportable event is suspected, the auditor may be prevented by 'tipping off rules' from communicating with management and it may be appropriate to report suspicions directly to the relevant authority.

Specific requirements apply in the case of audits of public interest entities. See **17.8.4**.

17.8.2 *Reporting in the auditor's report*

Where a non-compliance has a material effect on the financial statements, and it has not been adequately reflected in those financial statements, the auditor should issue a qualified or adverse opinion on the financial statements.

If management or those charged with governance have failed to provide sufficient appropriate evidence for the auditor to form a conclusion as to whether non-compliance may be material to the financial statements, a limitation of scope opinion should be given. This will be either a disclaimer of opinion or a qualified opinion depending on the severity of the limitation.

If the auditor is unable to determine whether a non-compliance has occurred as a result of circumstances other than management intervention, a limitation of scope opinion will also be suitable.

In all these situations, and where there is the suspicion of money laundering, the auditor must consider whether issuing his audit report would be considered to be 'tipping off' (see **Section 18**). In such a situation, the auditor should obtain specialist legal advice.

The auditor should not refrain from qualifying his report or omitting an explanatory paragraph simply because the matter has since been corrected. He should base his assessment on the adequacy of the view given by the financial statements.

In considering the implications of non-compliance on the financial statements, the auditor should consider the requirements of the accounting framework, bearing in mind that although immediate financial consequences may not be material, there may be future material consequences arising from, e.g. fines, civil litigation, criminal proceedings or loss of business.

17.8.3 Reporting to third parties

Where the auditor becomes aware of an actual or suspected non-compliance which gives rise to a statutory duty or right to report, he should do so to the appropriate authority without delay.

ISA (UK) 250 Section B (Revised June 2016) covers reporting to regulators of public interest entities and other entities in the financial sector, and is covered in **Section 9**. ISA (UK) 250 Section B (Revised June 2016) may also be adapted for situations in which the auditor of other entities identifies an instance of non-compliance with law or regulations which he is under a statutory duty to report.

In addition to those circumstances in which the auditor has a statutory duty to report, the application material in ISA (UK) 250 Section A (Revised June 2016) requires the auditor who becomes aware of suspected or actual non-compliance to:

- consider if the matter should be reported to 'a proper authority in the public interest'; and where this is the case

- discuss the matter with the board and the audit committee, except in cases where he no longer has confidence in the integrity of the directors.

Once he has reached a decision, the auditor should then notify the directors in writing that he is of the opinion that the matter is reportable. If the directors do not report the matter themselves, or do not provide evidence that they have already reported the matter, the auditor should report directly. The auditor may take legal advice before making a decision on whether the matter needs to be reported.

Where the auditor has lost confidence in the integrity of the directors as a result of the suspected or actual non-compliance, he may report extreme cases directly to the proper authority in the public interest, without discussing the matter with the board.

Reporting to third parties may lead to some concerns regarding the apparent breach of confidentiality and what is meant by the public interest. The guidance in the ISA considers both in detail.

17.8.4   Public interest entities

For public interest entities, ISA (UK) 250 Section A requires that when the auditor suspects that irregularities, including fraud with regard to the financial statements, may occur or have occurred, he informs the entity and asks it to investigate the matter and take appropriate measures to deal with the issue and to prevent any recurrence. Where the entity does not investigate these matters, the auditor is required to inform the relevant authorities.

The disclosure in good faith to the relevant authorities, by the auditor, of any such irregularities does not constitute a breach of any contractual or legal restriction on disclosure of information in accordance with the Audit Regulation.

The auditor considers whether to take further action when the entity investigates the matter but where the measures taken by management or those charged with governance, in the auditor's judgment, were not appropriate to deal with the actual or potential risks of fraud identified or would fail to prevent future occurrences of fraud or other irregularities.

17.9   Resignation

The guidance suggests that as a last resort, where the auditor cannot obtain the necessary information, or where management or those charged with governance do not take the remedial action that the auditor considers appropriate in the circumstances, or the auditor wishes to inform the shareholders and creditors of his concerns but has no immediate opportunity to do so, or where management refuse to issue financial statements, he should consider withdrawing from the engagement.

18 Money laundering and terrorist financing

18.1 Introduction

Section 17 deals with laws and regulations and the need for the auditor to take them into account in the course of his audit. However, one area of particular concern to auditors and accountants is compliance with the UK's anti-money laundering (AML) and terrorist financing legislation. This is a complex area in which the auditor needs to be careful both to fulfil the obligations imposed on him and avoid 'tipping off' those who may be involved in criminal activity. Penalties and other consequences of non-compliance can be severe.

18.2 Relevant legislation

The law comprising the AML and terrorist financing (AMTF) regime is contained in:

- the *Money Laundering, Terrorist Financing and Transfer of Funds (Information on the Payer) Regulations* 2017 (the 2017 Regulations);

- the *Proceeds of Crime Act* 2002 (POCA 2002) as amended by the *Serious Organised Crime and Police Act* 2005 (SOCPA 2005);

- the *Terrorism Act* 2000 (TA 2000) (as amended by the *Anti-Terrorism Crime and Security Act* 2001 (ATCSA) and the *Terrorism Act* 2006 (TA 2006));

- the *Terrorist Asset-Freezing Act* 2010;

- the *Anti-terrorism, Crime and Security Act* 2001;

- the *Counter-terrorism Act* 2008, Sch. 7; and

- the *Criminal Finances Act* 2017.

The 2017 Regulations came into force on 26 June 2017 and replace the *Money Laundering Regulations* 2007 (SI 2007/2157) and the *Transfer of Funds (Information on the Payer) Regulations* 2007 (SI 2007/3298). The Regulations contain updated provisions that implement in part the EU's Fourth Money Laundering Directive and Funds Transfer Regulation.

The regime applies to all businesses which provide defined services. This includes anyone acting as:

- a trust or company service provider;
- an auditor;
- an external accountant;
- an insolvency practitioner; or
- a tax adviser.

An accountant or firm of accountants that is unclear as to whether particular services provided are 'defined services' is advised to seek professional or legal advice.

Principal changes in the 2017 Regulations were:

- more prescriptive risk assessments;
- requirements for policies and procedures to mitigate money laundering and terrorist financing risks;
- enhanced transparency over beneficial ownership;
- customer due diligence procedures;
- changes to the definition of politically exposed persons;
- requirement for a nominated person responsible for compliance at Board (or equivalent) level; and
- enhanced training requirements.

18.3 Guidance for auditors and accountants

In March 2018, the Consultative Committee of Accounting Bodies (CCAB) published new guidance to replace its guidance previously issued in 2008. *Anti-Money Laundering Guidance for the Accountancy Sector* has been updated for the 2017 Anti-Money Laundering Regulations and is approved by HM Treasury. It has also been adopted by the UK accountancy AML supervisory bodies.

In an audit context, further guidance is provided in an Appendix to ISA (UK) 250 Section A (Revised December 2017) *Consideration of Laws and Regulations in an Audit of Financial Statements*. The Appendix is entitled *Money Laundering, Terrorist Financing and Proceeds of Crime Legislation in the United Kingdom* and replaces Practice Note 12 *Money Laundering – Guidance for Auditors on UK Legislation (Revised)* which was issued in 2010 and has now been withdrawn.

This publication provides only a brief overview of the law in this area and is no substitute for reading the CCAB guidance and, where applicable, the Appendix in ISA (UK) 250 Section A. To obtain a full understanding of the requirements, reference should be made to relevant legislation and accountants and auditors may need to seek legal advice.

18.4   Money laundering and terrorist financing

For the purposes of the legislation, money laundering is widely defined and encompasses all forms of using or possessing criminal property, or facilitating its use or possession, regardless of how it was obtained.

Money laundering offences are largely set out in POCA 2002 as amended by SOCPA 2005 and an offence will be committed by anyone who:

- conceals, disguises, converts, transfers or removes criminal property from any part of the UK; or

- enters into or becomes involved in any arrangement which they know, or suspect, facilitates the acquisition, retention, use or control of criminal property by or on behalf of another person; or

- acquires, uses or possess criminal property for which adequate consideration was not given.

Money laundering may involve conduct overseas if this would have been an offence if carried out in the UK, regardless of whether any proceeds of criminal activity pass through the UK.

For accountants and others providing defined services, it is also an offence to fail to report suspicions of money laundering or to disclose that a suspicious activity report has been made or is contemplated, in a way likely to prejudice any subsequent investigation.

The *Terrorism Act* 2000 sets out similar offences in relation to terrorist financing. These relate in particular to:

- fundraising – with an intention that money or other property raised will be used for terrorism or a reasonable suspicion that it will;

- using or possessing terrorist funds;

- entering into funding arrangements – where money will be used for terrorism or there is a reasonable suspicion that it will;

- money laundering;

- disclosing information related to the commission of an offence; and

- failing to disclose information.

There are some exceptions but these are complex and likely to be limited in their application.

18.5   Principal requirements

18.5.1   Roles and responsibilities

Businesses to which the Regulations apply, including sole practitioners, must set up systems and controls to enable them to comply with the 2017 Regulations and must ensure that all staff are aware of these systems and controls and are properly trained. Businesses are responsible also for monitoring and managing their own continuing compliance with the regulations.

Businesses must nominate a member of senior management to be responsible for the business' compliance with the AML regime. They must also appoint a 'nominated officer' who will be responsible for receiving internal suspicious activity reports (SARs) and for making SARs to the appropriate authority in a timely manner. These roles may be combined. The money laundering supervisory authority for the business should be notified of the names of the individual(s) concerned. The 2017 Regulations do not refer to Money Laundering Reporting Officer (MLRO). Businesses with an existing MLRO should check that the role and responsibilities are defined in such a way as to comply with the 2017 Regulations.

18.5.2   Policies and procedures

Policies and procedures must cover matters such as:

- risk based approach, risk assessment and management;

- client due diligence;

- record keeping;

- internal control;

- ongoing monitoring;

- reporting procedures; and

- compliance management communication.

Policies and procedures should be proportionate to the size of the business and should be subject to regular review and update, with a written record kept.

18.5.3 Training

All relevant staff must be made aware of their legal responsibilities and be given regular training in how to recognise and deal with suspicious activity.

Customer (or client) due diligence (CDD)

Appropriate CDD must be carried out for all new clients and at other appropriate points during the lifetime of a relationship with the client. This is now done using a risk based approach (see **18.6** and **18.7**). Records must be kept.

Scope of audit

AML legislation does not extend the scope of the audit but does impose on the auditor a requirement to report known or suspected instances of money laundering or terrorist financing activity.

Reporting

Known instances of money laundering or terrorist financing activity, or any suspicion thereof gained by the auditor or accountant in the course of his work, must be reported to the appropriate authority.

This is normally one of the functions of the MLRO.

Anti-money laundering supervisory authority

The Regulations designate a number of bodies as anti-money laundering supervisory authorities, which are empowered to supervise the compliance of businesses with the regulations. For accountants and auditors, the relevant authority is likely to be the professional accountancy body with which they are registered.

18.6 Risk based approach

The risk based approach is fundamental to the money laundering or terrorist financing (MLTF) regime. It requires governments, supervisors and business to analyse MLTF risk and take proportionate responses. It allows business to tailor responses in proportion to perceptions of risk which means that CDD procedures will not necessarily be the same for all clients.

In designing and implementing systems, businesses should ensure that they document the reasons for considering a particular approach to be appropriate and that these should be supported by evidence. Systems should also be created to monitor effectiveness.

Businesses must be able to demonstrate to their anti-money laundering supervisory authority how they assess and seek to mitigate MLTF risks.

The CCAB document provides guidance on applying the risk based approach to particular AML procedures and controls.

18.7   Customer due diligence (CDD)

The purpose of CDD is to establish the client's identity and understand the nature of its business activities so that MLTF risks can be properly identified and managed.

CDD involves:

- identifying the client and then verifying their identity (i.e. establishing that they are who they say they are) using appropriate documentation and other information sources;

- identifying beneficial owners – where the client is an incorporated or unincorporated entity or other organisation, steps should be taken to understand the ownership and control structure and to identify the individuals who are owners or otherwise control the organisation. Further checks may need to be taken to verify the identities of one or more individuals as above;

- gathering information on the nature and intended purpose of the business relationship.

CDD must be carried out:

- on all clients at the start of a business relationship;

- at appropriate points during the lifetime of a relationship; and

- when an occasional transaction is to be undertaken – this is defined as a transaction that takes place outside of a business relationship and has a value of more than €15,000.

The CCAB guidance suggests that CDD can be broken down into three stages.

(1) Identification – who is the client, who owns/controls the client, what is the legal structure, what does the client do, what is the source of their funds, what is the service to be provided etc.

(2) Risk assessment – consideration of factors such as client risk, service risk, geographic risk, sector risk and delivery channel risk. Appendix E to the CCAB guidance provides a more extensive list of risk factors that may be considered.

(3) Verification – collection of documents or other evidence to demonstrate that what the service provided has been told is true and other information that may be needed to mitigate specific risks identified.

At each stage there is a feedback loop so that the risk assessment may highlight a need for more information at the identification stage and the verification process may highlight additional risks to consider.

18.7.1   Simplified CDD

The regulations and CCAB guidance allow for simplified CDD to be carried out where a client is considered to be low risk and there is no suspicion of MLTF. CDD measures are still required but extent and timing may be adjusted to reflect risk, for example in determining what constitutes reasonable verification.

18.7.2   Enhanced CDD

In high risk situations, 'enhanced' due diligence must be applied. This will include situations:

- where a high risk of MLTF is identified;

- in any business relationship or occasional transaction with a person established in a high risk country;

- if the client is a politically exposed person (PEP) or a family member or close associate of a PEP;

- where the client has provided false or stolen identification documents or other information; and

- where a transaction is complex, unusually large and there is no obvious economic or legal purpose.

The business' MLTF procedures should clearly set out the circumstances in which a client will qualify for CDD.

CDD procedures must include examining the background and purpose of the engagement and increasing the degree and nature of monitoring of the business relationship. They must also include one or more of:

- seeking additional independent sources to verify information including identity information;

- taking additional measures to better understand the background, ownership and financial situation of the client and other relevant parties;

- taking further steps to be satisfied that a transaction is consistent with the intended nature of the business relationship; and

- increasing monitoring of the relationship, including greater scrutiny of transactions.

The auditor must ensure that he has on file sufficient evidence to prove that the identity of the client has been verified and suitable evidence has been retained. The CCAB guidance provides suggested evidence for companies and individuals, and this is reproduced in **Tables 1** and **2**.

TABLE 1: Client identification and verification procedures suggested by the CCAB guidance

For private companies and LLPs

The following information must be obtained and verified:

- full name of company;

- registered number;

- registered office address and principal place of business;

- shareholders/members ultimately controlling more than 25% of shares or voting rights;

- identity of any agent or intermediary purporting to act on behalf of the entity and their authorisation to act;

- the law to which the entity is subject;

- its constitution; and

- full names of all directors or equivalent and other senior persons responsible for the operations of the company.

Note: company registers of beneficial ownership may be useful but not solely relied on.

Listed or regulated entity

The full name, address and membership or registration number should be obtained.

Identity may be verified by obtaining either (a) a printout from the relevant regulator's or exchange's website (which should be annotated); or (b) direct written confirmation from the regulator or exchange of the entity's regulatory status. A copy should be retained.

Government or similar bodies

The full name of the body, the main place of operation and the name of the government or supra-national agency which controls it should be obtained.

Identity may be verified by obtaining a printout from the relevant body's website (which should be annotated). Additionally for housing associations the printout must contain its registered number, registered company number and registered address. Copies should be retained.

TABLE 2: Client identification procedures suggested by the CCAB guidance for individuals

For individuals, the full name, date of birth and residential address should be obtained.

Normal risk individuals

Original or certified copy of one or more of:

● valid passport;

● valid photocard driving licence;

● national identity card (for non-UK nationals); or

● identity card issued by the Electoral Office for Northern Ireland.

A copy should be retained.

High risk individuals

In addition to the above, a second document should be seen. This may be:

● valid UK driving licence;

● recent evidence of entitlement to state or local authority funded benefits in the UK;

● instrument of a court appointment;

● current council tax demand or statement;

● HMRC issued tax notification (not P60);

● end of year tax deduction certificate;

● current bank account or credit/debit card statement; or

● current utility bill.

A copy should be retained.

18.7.3 Politically exposed person (PEP)

Under the 2017 Regulations, a politically exposed person is an individual who is entrusted with prominent public functions, other than as a middle-ranking or more junior official. Prominent public functions include head of state, head of government, minister and deputy or assistant ministers; members of parliament or of similar legislative bodies; members of the governing bodies of political parties; members of supreme courts, members of constitutional courts or of any judicial body the decisions of which are not subject to further appeal except in exceptional circumstances; members of courts of auditors or of boards of central banks; ambassadors, charges d'affaires and high ranking officers in the armed forces; members of the administrative, management or supervisory bodies of state-owned enterprises; directors, deputy directors and members of the board or equivalent function of an international organisation.

18.8 Reporting suspicious activity

A business to which the Regulations apply must have internal reporting procedures that require relevant employees and partners to report knowledge or suspicions of MLTF to a nominated person, who may be designated as the Money Laundering Reporting Officer (MLRO).

Suspicion involves:

- a state of mind more definite than speculation but falling short of evidence based knowledge;
- a positive feeling of apprehension or mistrust;
- a slight opinion, without sufficient evidence.

Suspicion is not idle wondering, a vague feeling of unease or simple speculation.

The MLRO will then determine whether or not an external suspicious activity report (SAR) needs to be made to the National Crime Agency (NCA).

Matters should be reported where:

- the auditor knows or suspects or has reasonable grounds to know or suspect that a person is engaged in money laundering or terrorist financing;
- the auditor can identify the other person or the whereabouts of any laundered property or it is reasonable to believe that the information the auditor has obtained will or may assist in identifying that person or the whereabouts of the laundered property; and
- the information has come to the auditor in the course of the auditor's business.

There is no de minimis provision – all suspicions should be reported.

It is a criminal offence for any relevant member of staff to fail to report suspicions of MLTF to the MLRO.

Partners and staff making internal SARs need to be mindful of the rules relating to 'tipping off'.

18.8.1 Tipping off

Auditors with knowledge or suspicion that a money laundering offence has occurred must be careful not to breach 'tipping off' requirements. An offence is committed where a relevant individual discloses that:

- a SAR has been made and this disclosure is likely to prejudice any subsequent investigation; or

- an investigation into allegations of MLTF is underway (or being contemplated) and this disclosure is likely to prejudice that investigation.

Considerable care must therefore be taken when communicating with clients or third parties to avoid tipping off.

There are some limited exemptions to the disclosure rule; for example no offence is committed if disclosure is made to a relevant employee in the same firm or to an anti-money laundering supervisory authority.

In the context of an audit, a SAR is likely to give rise to particular problems and auditors should:

- be careful, and consult with the MLRO before discussing matters or suspicions with management or those charged with governance that may be indicative of a money laundering issue;

- ensure that any further investigation consists only of steps that the auditor would have performed as part of his normal audit work;

- obtain clearance from their MLRO before any further investigation is performed;

- consider whether the wording of a qualified audit report will fall foul of the tipping off regulations, consulting with the law enforcement agency for agreement as necessary;

- avoid unnecessary delay in issuing an auditor's report as this may itself be construed as tipping off; and

- take advice on the precise wording and dating of any statement made in connection with ceasing to hold office if they decide to resign from the engagement.

18.8.2   *Reporting to regulators*

Reporting to the NCA does not relieve the auditor from other statutory duties. Examples include:

- reporting 'matters of material significance' to regulators of public interest entities and other entities in the financial sector;

- in certain public sector engagements, the auditor's duty to report on the regularity and propriety of financial transactions; or

- for auditors of certain other entities, the auditor's duty to report matters of material significance to a regulator (e.g. charities and pension schemes).

Knowledge or suspicion of involvement in money laundering by the entity's management or those charged with governance, or failure of a regulated business to comply with AML legislation, would normally be regarded as being of material interest to a regulator.

A report to a regulator in these circumstances would not constitute a tipping off offence where disclosure is not likely to prejudice an investigation.

18.8.3 Privileged circumstances

As is the case with lawyers, a 'relevant professional adviser' may be exempt from being required to make a SAR if information came to him in privileged circumstances. This only applies to an accountant, auditor or tax adviser who is a member of a relevant professional body which:

- tests the competence of those seeking admission; and

- imposes and maintains professional and ethical standards, as well as imposing sanctions for non-compliance with those standards.

Examples where relevant professional advisers may fall within privileged circumstances include:

- advice on tax law to assist a client in understanding their tax position;

- representing a client at a tax tribunal;

- advice on the legal aspects of a takeover bid;

- when instructed as an expert witness by a solicitor on behalf of a client;

- advice on duties of directors under the Companies Act;

- advice to directors on legal issues relating to the *Insolvency Act* 1986; and

- advice on employment law.

Audit work, book-keeping, preparation of accounts or tax compliance assignments are unlikely to take place in privileged circumstances.

18.9 The auditor's report on the financial statements

Where money laundering has occurred or is suspected the auditor considers the potential impact on the financial statements, including the potential outcome of any subsequent investigation by relevant authorities.

If it is known that money laundering has occurred and management or those charged with governance were involved, the auditor needs to consider whether his audit report should be modified or contain an emphasis of matter paragraph.

However, the auditor also needs to consider whether including information in the auditor's report would constitute 'tipping off'. Timing of issue of the report may also be critical as a delay in issuing the auditor's report pending the outcome of an investigation may be impractical and could itself constitute 'tipping off'. In these situations, the auditor should consult with his MLRO and if necessary, seek legal advice and consult with the NCA or other relevant authority regarding an appropriate course of action.

18.10   Resignation and communication with successor auditors

In some situations, the auditor may wish to resign from the engagement, particularly where he considers that a normal relationship of trust can no longer be maintained with the entity, those charged with governance or its employees.

Again, the auditor needs to be careful to avoid tipping off in such a situation and will need to carefully consider the wording of any s. 519 statement. It may be necessary to consult the NCA and seek legal advice.

Where a successor audit requests information regarding suspicious activity, the CCAB guidance recommends that such requests be declined – in order to avoid the risk of tipping off. The guidance in the Appendix to ISA (UK) 250 Section A notes however that under AML legislation, information provided to a successor auditor would not be regarded as tipping off if it was done to prevent the successor from committing a money laundering offence.

Where the audit files contain information regarding a money laundering offence, or suspicions thereof, the auditor needs to consider the extent to which this is relevant audit information that should be made available to the successor auditor on request. In general, where the files contain only details of matters that give rise to suspicions, then the auditor will not be committing an offence if the information is passed to a successor auditor. Where on the other hand the work papers indicate that suspected irregularities also constituted suspicions of money laundering the auditor should consult the MLRO and if appropriate consult the NCA and take legal advice.

19 Initial engagements, opening balances and comparatives

19.1 Introduction

When performing a first-time audit where the prior period financial statements were not audited or were audited by a predecessor auditor (initial engagements), the auditor must consider whether material errors in the opening balances might give rise to errors in the current financial period.

ISA (UK) 510 (Revised June 2016) *Initial Audit Engagements – Opening Balances* was issued in June 2016 and is effective for periods commencing on or after 17 June 2016. It deals with the auditor's responsibilities in relation to opening balances, including matters requiring disclosure such as contingent liabilities, in initial engagements. Changes made in the 2016 version of ISA (UK) 510 (Revised June 2016) relate to the audit of public interest entities (see **19.3.2**).

ISA (UK) 300 (Revised June 2016) *Planning an Audit of Financial Statements* also contains requirements and guidance applying to initial audits.

Whether or not the audit is an initial engagement, the auditor must consider whether comparative information is properly presented in the financial statements.

ISA (UK) 710 *Comparative Information – Corresponding Figures and Comparative Financial Statements* was issued in October 2009, although in June 2016 an additional paragraph was added to the application material relating to initial engagements for public interest entities. It was not revised by the FRC but was reissued as ISA (UK) 710 in June 2016.

19.2 Initial engagements

When planning an initial engagement, ISA (UK) 300 (Revised June 2016) requires the auditor to perform procedures required by ISA 220 (UK) (Revised June 2016) *Quality Control for an Audit of Financial Statements* regarding the acceptance of the client relationship (see **13.3**) and to communicate with the predecessor auditor, where there was one, in accordance with ethical requirements. An engagement letter will be required.

When planning an initial engagement the auditor may also consider any major issues regarding the application of accounting principles or auditing standards discussed with management in connection with the auditor selection process, and will need to consider how he plans to obtain sufficient appropriate audit evidence regarding opening balances.

The auditor may wish to make arrangements to review the predecessor auditor's working papers for the last financial period audited. This will often provide the auditor with useful information regarding the client's organisation, operations and accounting systems and potential risk areas as well as providing audit evidence regarding opening balances and comparative information. Where the entity is a UK company the auditor has a statutory right to obtain information from the predecessor auditor's working papers (see **38.3**).

In the case of a public interest entity, the auditor is required to obtain an understanding of the methodology used by the predecessor auditor sufficient to enable him to explain to those charged with governance any planned substantial variation in the weighting of system and compliance testing compare with the previous audit.

19.3   Opening balances

The auditor should obtain appropriate evidence about whether the opening balances contain material misstatements that could affect the current period's financial statements by checking that:

- the prior period's closing balances have been appropriately brought forward into the current period; and

- opening balances reflect the application of appropriate accounting policies.

In order to do this, he may:

- review the predecessor auditor's working papers;

- consider whether audit procedures performed in the prior period provide evidence regarding the opening balances;

- perform specific procedures in order to gain assurance over opening balances; or

- carry out a combination of the above.

If the auditor obtains evidence that the opening balances contain misstatements that may affect the current period, he should perform procedures to evaluate the potential misstatement. Where he establishes that a misstatement exists, he should consider its impact on the financial statements in the context of other misstatements detected in the course of the audit.

Where material misstatements in opening balances exist and are not corrected, the auditor should consider the implications for his report. Similarly, where he is unable to obtain sufficient evidence to establish that there is no material misstatement he may need to issue a qualified opinion or, in extreme cases, a disclaimer of opinion.

A commonly encountered situation is where there was no predecessor auditor and the auditor is appointed after the end of the financial year. As a consequence, the auditor was unable to observe a physical stock count or carry out normal year-end audit procedures regarding stock existence and condition, or cut-off testing in relation to stock movements. In these situations, it is often difficult, if not impossible, for the auditor retrospectively to obtain sufficient evidence to support the opening stock figure, with consequent implications for reported revenue and profit in the current period.

Cash balances, on the other hand, can usually be established relatively easily and debtor and creditor positions can often be largely reconstructed by examination of receipts and payments in the current period. It is unusual therefore for an auditor to be unable to obtain audit evidence in relation to all opening balances and a qualified audit report should not be seen as an alternative to carrying out appropriate audit procedures.

An example of a report with a qualified opinion is shown in **Table 1**.

TABLE 1: Unable to obtain evidence regarding opening balances

Extract from the independent auditor's report to the shareholders of XYZ Ltd

Qualified Opinion

We have audited the financial statements of [XYZ Limited] (the 'company') for the year ended [*date*] which comprise [*specify the titles of the primary statements*] and notes to the financial statements, including a summary of significant accounting policies. The financial reporting framework that has been applied in their preparation is applicable law and United Kingdom Accounting Standards, including Financial Reporting Standard 102 *The Financial Reporting Standard applicable in the UK and Republic of Ireland* (United Kingdom Generally Accepted Accounting Practice).

In our opinion, except for the possible effect of the matter described in the Basis for Qualified Opinion paragraph, the financial statements:

- give a true and fair view of the state of the company's affairs as at [*date*] and of its profit [loss] for the year then ended;

- have been properly prepared in accordance with United Kingdom Generally Accepted Accounting Practice; and

---

- have been prepared in accordance with the requirements of the *Companies Act* 2006.

Basis for Qualified Opinion

The evidence available to us was limited because we were not appointed as auditor of the company until [*date*] and in consequence it was not possible for us to perform the auditing procedures necessary to obtain sufficient appropriate audit evidence as regards [*specify and evaluate the balances involved*] included in the preceding years' financial statements at £ ... Any adjustment to [*these figures*] would have a consequential effect on the profit for the year ended 31 December 20 ...

We conducted our audit in accordance with International Standards on Auditing (UK) (ISAs (UK)) and applicable law. Our responsibilities under those standards are further described in the Auditor's responsibilities for the audit of the financial statements section of our report. We are independent of the company in accordance with the ethical requirements that are relevant to our audit of the financial statements in the UK, including the FRC's Ethical Standard, and we have fulfilled our other ethical responsibilities in accordance with these requirements. We believe that the audit evidence we have obtained is sufficient and appropriate to provide a basis for our qualified opinion.

Matters on which we are required to report by exception

In the light of the knowledge and understanding of the company and its environment obtained in the course of the audit, we have not identified material misstatements in the [strategic report or the] directors' report.

In respect solely of the limitation on our work relating to [*specify balances involved*]:

- we have not obtained all the information and explanations that we considered necessary for the purpose of our audit; and

- we were unable to determine whether adequate accounting records had been maintained.

We have nothing to report in respect of the following matters where the *Companies Act* 2006 requires us to report to you if, in our opinion:

- returns adequate for our audit have not been received from branches not visited by us; or

- the financial statements are not in agreement with the accounting records and returns; or

- certain disclosures of directors' remuneration specified by law are not made.

The auditor should also consider the accounting policies applied in the determination of the opening balances. Were they appropriate, in accordance with the relevant accounting framework and have they been consistently applied in the current period, or are changes to policies adequately disclosed.

Where the auditor concludes that accounting policies are not consistently applied or a change in policy is not appropriately reflected in the financial statements, he may need to issue a qualified or adverse audit opinion, as appropriate.

19.3.1 Modifications to the predecessor auditor's report

Where the predecessor auditor's report contained a modification to the opinion, the auditor should consider the implications for his assessment of the risk of material misstatements arising in the current period.

Where the predecessor auditor's report contained a modification to the opinion that remains relevant and material to the current period's financial statements, the auditor will consider the implications for his own report and modify his own opinion on the current period's financial statements in accordance with ISA (UK) 705 *Modifications to the Opinion in the Independent Auditor's Report* and ISA (UK) 710.

In cases where a matter giving rise to a modified opinion in the prior period has been resolved, this may nevertheless have resulted in income or expense being recognised in the wrong accounting period or uncertainty regarding the accuracy of comparative information and the auditor may need to issue a modified opinion as a result (see **19.4.1**).

19.3.2 Public interest entities

For public interest entities, an incoming auditor is also required to obtain an understanding of the predecessor auditor's methodology used to carry out the audit, sufficient to enable him to communicate with those charged with governance those matters required by ISA (UK) 260 (Revised June 2016) *Communication with those Charged with Governance* (see **10.7.2**). This includes being able to describe the methodology used, including which categories of the balance sheet have been directly verified and which categories have been verified based on system and compliance testing, including an explanation of any substantial variation in the weighting of system and compliance testing when compared to the previous year. This applies even where the previous year's audit was carried out by a predecessor auditor and may lead to the incoming auditor becoming aware of a possible misstatement in corresponding figures.

For public interest entities, the Audit Regulation also specifically requires the predecessor auditor to grant the successor auditor access to the additional report to the audit committee in respect of previous years.

TABLE 2: Previous year's figures are unaudited

Extract from the independent auditor's report to the shareholders of XYZ Limited

Qualified opinion

We have audited the financial statements of [XYZ Limited] (the 'company') for the year ended [*date*] which comprise [*specify the titles of the primary statements*] and notes to the financial statements, including a summary of significant accounting policies. The financial reporting framework that has been applied in their preparation is applicable law and United Kingdom Accounting Standards, including Financial Reporting Standard 102 *The Financial Reporting Standard applicable in the UK and Republic of Ireland* (United Kingdom Generally Accepted Accounting Practice).

In our opinion, except for the possible effects of the matter described in the Basis for Qualified Opinion paragraph, the financial statements:

- give a true and fair view of the state of the company's affairs as at [date] and of its profit [loss] for the year then ended;

- have been properly prepared in accordance with United Kingdom Generally Accepted Accounting Practice; and

- have been prepared in accordance with the requirements of the *Companies Act* 2006.

Basis for qualified opinion

The evidence available to us was limited because we were appointed as auditors during the year and we have been unable to carry out auditing procedures necessary to obtain adequate assurance regarding the opening balances and comparative figures because the financial statements for the year ended 31 December 20 … were unaudited. Any adjustments to the opening balances would have a consequential effect on the profit for the year. In addition, the amounts shown as corresponding amounts for the year ended 31 December 20 … may not be comparable with the figures for the current period.

We conducted our audit in accordance with International Standards on Auditing (UK) (ISAs (UK)) and applicable law. Our responsibilities under those standards are further described in the Auditor's responsibilities for the audit of the financial statements section of our report. We are independent of the company in accordance with the ethical requirements that are relevant to our audit of the financial statements in the UK, including the FRC's Ethical Standard, and we have fulfilled our other ethical responsibilities in accordance with these requirements. We believe that the audit evidence we have obtained is sufficient and appropriate to provide a basis for our qualified opinion.

Other matter

Comparative information in the financial statements is derived from the company's prior period financial statements which were not audited.

Matters on which we are required to report by exception

In the light of the knowledge and understanding of the company and its environment obtained in the course of the audit, we have not identified material misstatements in the [strategic report or the] directors' report.

In respect solely of the limitation on our work relating to opening balances:

- we have not obtained all the information and explanations that we considered necessary for the purpose of our audit; and

- we were unable to determine whether adequate accounting records had been maintained.

We have nothing to report in respect of the following matters where the *Companies Act* 2006 requires us to report to you if, in our opinion:

- returns adequate for our audit have not been received from branches not visited by us;

- the financial statements are not in agreement with the accounting records and returns; or

- certain disclosures of directors' remuneration specified by law are not made.

19.4　Comparatives

The auditor should determine whether the financial statements include the comparative information required by the applicable financial reporting framework and obtain evidence that such information is appropriately classified. ISA (UK) 710 requires that evidence is obtained to confirm that:

- accounting policies in the comparative information are consistent with those in the current period, or if there has been a change that this is properly accounted for and adequately presented and disclosed;

- the comparative information agrees with the amounts and other disclosures presented in the prior period or, where appropriate, have been restated.

Where the auditor is unable to obtain such evidence, he should consider the implications for his report.

For the continuing auditor, as long as he has no concerns about prior year items, procedures are normally restricted to ensuring that the comparatives have been correctly brought forward and disclosed.

The ISA requires the auditor to obtain a written representation for all periods referred to in his opinion and also a specific written representation regarding any restatement made to correct a material misstatement in prior period financial statements that affects the comparative information.

19.4.1 Qualified reports

The reasons for a qualified report in one period may have knock-on effects into the next. The effect of a qualification on a subsequent period depends on whether or not the matter has been resolved:

(a) when the matter is unresolved, and is material in the context of the current period's opening balances as well as comparatives, the auditor should qualify the current period audit report in respect of opening balances and comparatives;

(b) where the matter is unresolved and does not affect the opening balances, but is material to the comparatives shown in the current financial statements, the auditor should qualify his report in respect of the comparatives; and

(c) where the matter has been resolved, but is material to the current period, the auditor should include an emphasis of matter paragraph in his report on the current period explaining how it has been dealt with.

In (a), the qualified opinion would describe the matter and its effect on the current and preceding years' figures. An example of this would be where in a previous year the company had made a provision for the permanent diminution in value of a fixed asset which the auditor did not believe was necessary. In subsequent years, the auditor would qualify his report in respect of the consequential understatement of the depreciation charge and corresponding understatement of the asset and give an 'except for' opinion.

A further example would be a disagreement over the necessity for a provision against a debtor. **Table 3** shows the opinion paragraph that would be appropriate.

Where an auditor's report on the previous year contained a limitation of scope disclaimer covering all aspects of the report, it would be unlikely that the auditor could satisfy himself on the profit and loss account or the cash flow statement in the next year, even if he obtained sufficient evidence that the balance sheet for that year showed a true and fair view.

TABLE 3: Preceding period was qualified and the matter has not been resolved

Extract from independent auditor's report to the shareholders of XYZ Ltd

Qualified opinion

We have audited the financial statements of [XYZ Limited] (the 'company') for the year ended [date] which comprise [specify the titles of the primary statements] and notes to the financial statements, including a summary of significant accounting policies. The financial reporting framework that has

---

been applied in their preparation is applicable law and United Kingdom Accounting Standards, including Financial Reporting Standard 102 The Financial Reporting Standard applicable in the UK and Republic of Ireland (United Kingdom Generally Accepted Accounting Practice).

In our opinion, except for the possible effects of the matter described in the Basis for Qualified Opinion paragraph, the financial statements:

- give a true and fair view of the state of the company's affairs as at [date] and of its profit [loss] for the year then ended;

- have been properly prepared in accordance with United Kingdom Generally Accepted Accounting Practice; and

- have been prepared in accordance with the requirements of the *Companies Act* 2006.

Basis for qualified opinion

Included in the debtors shown on the balance sheet of 31 December 20 ... and 31 December 20 ... is an amount of £Y which is the subject of litigation and against which no provision has been made. In our opinion, full provision of £Y should have been made in the year ended 31 December 20 ... reducing profit before tax for the year ended 31 December 20 ... and net assets at 31 December 20 ... and 31 December 20 ... by that amount.

We conducted our audit in accordance with International Standards on Auditing (UK) (ISAs (UK)) and applicable law. Our responsibilities under those standards are further described in the Auditor's responsibilities for the audit of the financial statements section of our report. We are independent of the company in accordance with the ethical requirements that are relevant to our audit of the financial statements in the UK, including the FRC's Ethical Standard, and we have fulfilled our other ethical responsibilities in accordance with these requirements. We believe that the audit evidence we have obtained is sufficient and appropriate to provide a basis for our qualified opinion.

Matters on which we are required to report by exception

In the light of the knowledge and understanding of the company and its environment obtained in the course of the audit, we have not identified material misstatements in the [strategic report or the] directors' report.

We have nothing to report in respect of the following matters where the *Companies Act* 2006 requires us to report to you if, in our opinion:

- adequate accounting records have not been kept or returns adequate for our audit have not been received from branches not visited by us; or

- the financial statements are not in agreement with the accounting records and returns; or

- certain disclosures of directors' remuneration specified by law are not made; or

- we have not received all the information and explanations we required for our audit.

Initial engagements, opening balances and comparatives

Where this occurs, it normally affects areas such as stock and work in progress or debtors and creditors at the beginning of the period, uncertainty about which directly affects the profit and loss account and the cash flow statements. Where the effect is material, either a qualification or disclaimer on the grounds of limitation of scope is needed, depending on the effect of the limitation on the audit procedures and the significance of the amounts involved to the financial statements. An example of such a disclaimer is shown in **Table 3** of **Section 5**.

An example of (b) might be a limitation of scope in respect of the accounting records kept in the first six months of the year which had been destroyed by a fire but which had not led to a qualification in respect of the balance sheet. In the subsequent year, there would be an 'except for' opinion in respect of the corresponding profit and loss figures as the auditor would still not have sufficient evidence on them.

Similarly, if there was a change in auditor in the previous period and that previous report contained the limitation of scope shown in **Table 5** of **Section 5**, the subsequent report will refer to this, as shown in **Table 4**.

Situation (c) would result from a fundamental uncertainty which was not properly disclosed in the previous financial statements resulting in a disagreement which has now been resolved.

TABLE 4: Previous qualification not affecting opening balances

Extract from independent auditor's report to the shareholders of XYZ Ltd

Qualified opinion

We have audited the financial statements of [XYZ Limited] (the 'company') for the year ended [date] which comprise [specify the titles of the primary statements] and notes to the financial statements, including a summary of significant accounting policies. The financial reporting framework that has been applied in their preparation is applicable law and United Kingdom Accounting Standards, including Financial Reporting Standard 102 The Financial Reporting Standard applicable in the UK and Republic of Ireland (United Kingdom Generally Accepted Accounting Practice).

In our opinion, except for the possible effects of the matter described in the Basis for Qualified Opinion paragraph, the financial statements:

- give a true and fair view of the state of the company's affairs as at [date] and of its profit [loss] for the year then ended;

- have been properly prepared in accordance with United Kingdom Generally Accepted Accounting Practice; and

- have been prepared in accordance with the requirements of the *Companies Act* 2006.

Basis for qualified opinion

The evidence available to us was limited in relation to the comparatives in the current year's financial statements which are derived from the financial statements for the year ended 31 December 20 … In our report on those financial statements we stated that, because we were appointed as auditor on 30 June 20 … it was not possible for us to perform the auditing procedures necessary to obtain sufficient appropriate audit evidence concerning the quantities and condition of certain stock and work in progress included in the balance sheet at 31 December 20 … at £ … Any adjustment to this figure would have a consequential effect on the profit for the year ended 31 December 20 … and, consequently, our opinion on the financial statements for the year ended 31 December 20 … was qualified because of this limitation in audit scope. Accordingly the amounts shown as cost of sales and profit for the year ended 31 December 20 … may not be comparable with the figures for the current period.

We conducted our audit in accordance with International Standards on Auditing (UK) (ISAs (UK)) and applicable law. Our responsibilities under those standards are further described in the Auditor's responsibilities for the audit of the financial statements section of our report. We are independent of the company in accordance with the ethical requirements that are relevant to our audit of the financial statements in the UK, including the FRC's Ethical Standard, and we have fulfilled our other ethical responsibilities in accordance with these requirements. We believe that the audit evidence we have obtained is sufficient and appropriate to provide a basis for our qualified opinion.

Matters on which we are required to report by exception

In the light of the knowledge and understanding of the company and its environment obtained in the course of the audit, we have not identified material misstatements in the [strategic report or the] directors' report.

In respect solely of the limitation on our work relating to stock and work in progress:

- we have not obtained all the information and explanations that we considered necessary for the purpose of our audit; and

- we were unable to determine whether adequate accounting records had been maintained.

We have nothing to report in respect of the following matters where the *Companies Act* 2006 requires us to report to you if, in our opinion:

- returns adequate for our audit have not been received from branches not visited by us; or

- the financial statements are not in agreement with the accounting records and returns; or

- certain disclosures of directors' remuneration specified by law are not made.

In contrast, where the auditor issues a qualified report because of disagreement over an accounting policy, but this no longer exists following a change in accounting policy, which has been properly disclosed and adjustments made to the prior year, no qualification is necessary as the matter has been resolved and dealt with correctly.

Where an issue over which there was a disagreement has been resolved but not satisfactorily, for example, where the disagreement over the accounting policy was resolved by adjusting the current year's figures when the auditor considered a prior year adjustment was required, then both current period and comparatives would be qualified on the basis of disagreement.

For audits under the *Companies Act* 2006, there is no direct requirement to report on comparatives, apart from the fact that they are a 'disclosure requirement' under relevant UK law. Any qualification should therefore be in terms of this requirement. If corresponding amounts are presented solely as good practice, the audit report reference should be made as an explanatory paragraph.

The guidance to the ISA considers what the auditor should do when he becomes aware of a material misstatement which affects the previous financial statements, which had an unqualified audit opinion. If the previous financial statements have been revised (see **Section 6**) the auditor needs to ensure that the comparatives agree with the revised financial statements. Where the previous year's financial statements have not been reissued but the comparatives adjusted, no qualification is necessary as long as the matter is properly disclosed. Where no adjustment or disclosure has been made, the auditor needs to consider whether the misstatements in the opening balances will give rise to misstatements in this period's financial statements or whether the comparatives are materially misstated. Both of which, in the absence of adjustments, will lead to qualifications as discussed above.

19.4.2 Prior period financial statements issued by a predecessor auditor

Where the comparative figures have been audited by a predecessor auditor, the new auditor assumes responsibility for them as part of the financial statements as a whole. He should assess them in the light of his knowledge of the client and the previous financial statements.

19.4.3 Prior period financial statements not audited

If the comparative figures have not been audited, for example, where advantage had been taken of audit exemption, the auditor should ensure that the financial statements clearly disclose the fact that the comparatives are unaudited, but also needs to ensure that he is not aware of any possible material misstatement in those figures. In situations where the auditor is unable to satisfy himself that no material misstatement exists in the comparative figures, he will qualify his opinion on the financial statements on the basis that the comparative information may not be comparable.

If the auditor encountered significant difficulty in obtaining sufficient appropriate audit evidence that the opening balances do not contain misstatements that materially affect the current period's financial statements, he may determine this to be a key audit matter in accordance with ISA (UK) 701 *Communicating Key Audit Matters in the Independent Auditor's Report* – see **4.11**.

Regardless of any potential qualification of the auditor's opinion, in all situations where the previous financial statements were not audited, the auditor should include an 'Other Matter paragraph' (see **5.8**) in his report stating that comparative figures are unaudited. An example is shown in **Table 2**.

20 Related parties

20.1 Introduction

Accounting frameworks often require disclosures in financial statements to draw attention to the possibility that the financial position of the entity or its profit or loss may have been affected by the existence of related parties and by transactions and outstanding balances with such related parties.

Different frameworks may use different definitions of 'related party' but the term usually encompasses those with control or significant influence over the entity, key management personnel and close family members of such persons. It will also include other entities controlled by such persons or over which they have significant influence. In some situations, the list of potential related parties can be quite extensive.

Challenges for the auditor include identification of related parties, including controlling parties, identification of transactions and balances with related parties, completeness and accuracy of disclosures in the financial statements and considering the overall presentation of related party information in the financial statements. In evaluating the adequacy of disclosures, the auditor should bear in mind that materiality for related party transactions and balances is influenced not only by the size of the transaction or balance but also by its nature.

Related party transactions are also often used to conceal fraud and have featured in a number of high profile corporate scandals. The auditor therefore needs to consider fraud risk factors associated with related parties and be alert to the possibility of fraud.

Standards and guidance for the auditor are found in ISA (UK) 550 *Related Parties* which was issued in October 2009 and is effective for the audit of financial statements for periods ending on or after 15 December 2010. It was not revised by the FRC but was reissued as ISA (UK) 550 in June 2016.

Further guidance on the audit of related parties was issued by the Audit and Assurance Faculty of the ICAEW in 2010. Further details are provided in **20.12**.

20.2   Auditing standards

ISA (UK) 550 covers:

- responsibilities of the auditor;
- risk assessment procedures and related activities;
- responses to risk;
- evaluation of accounting and disclosure;
- management representations;
- communication with those charged with governance; and
- documentation.

20.3   General requirement

The auditor has a responsibility to perform audit procedures to identify, assess and respond to the risks of material misstatement arising from the entity's failure to appropriately account for, or disclose, related party relationships, transactions or balances in accordance with the requirements of the financial reporting framework. Even where the requirements of the accounting framework are minimal, the auditor needs to consider whether the financial statements, insofar as they are affected by related party relationships or transactions achieve a fair presentation and are not misleading.

In order to do this, the auditor firstly needs to understand, as part of his knowledge of the business, the relevant disclosure requirements in legislation and accounting standards.

Many related party transactions are in the normal course of business and may carry no higher risk of material misstatement of the financial statements than similar transactions with unrelated parties. However, related party transactions may be difficult to detect due to:

- reticence on the part of the directors to disclose sensitive transactions;
- accounting systems not being designed to identify these transactions;
- a lack of controls over such transactions; and
- the complexity of the definition of a related party in applicable accounting standards.

In certain instances, related party transactions may be concealed in whole, or in part, from the auditor for fraudulent purposes. ISA (UK) 240 (Revised June 2016) *The Auditor's Responsibilities Relating to Fraud in an Audit of Financial Statements* (see **Section 16**) provides guidance on the auditor's responsibility to consider fraud and error in financial statements and this includes fraudulent related party transactions. The auditor's understanding of related parties is relevant when considering whether one or more fraud risk factors is present.

The auditor's risk of not detecting related party transactions is compounded when transactions are:

- without charge;
- not self-evident to the auditor;
- with a party that the auditor could not reasonably know was a related party; or
- actively concealed by the directors.

Directors are responsible for the identification and disclosure of related party transactions. However, in addition to their responsibility to ensure that the disclosures are complete and accurate, the auditor should consider the effect they may have on other items within the financial statements, such as the tax liability. He must also be aware that the reliability of evidence may be reduced if it is obtained from related parties and also that transactions with them may be motivated by considerations other than ordinary business, such as window dressing.

20.4 Materiality

Where related parties are concerned, it is particularly important for the auditor to consider not just the monetary amount of any misstatements, but also their nature. A misstatement of a related party transaction may be significant to users of the financial statements (and hence material) even if its monetary value is low, depending on the nature of the relationship with the related party or the nature of the transaction.

20.5 Risk assessment

The auditor's risk assessment procedures will include:

- making enquiries of management;
- obtaining an understanding of the entities procedures and controls;
- consideration of fraud risk factors and the susceptibility of the financial statements to material misstatement as a result of fraud or error as part of the engagement team discussion;
- remaining alert throughout the audit for indications of undisclosed relationships or transactions; and
- making an assessment of risk of material misstatement associated with related parties.

Related parties

20.5.1 Enquiries

As part of his initial risk assessment procedures in accordance with ISA (UK) 315 (Revised June 2016) *Identifying and Assessing the Risks of Material Misstatement through Understanding of the Entity and its Environment*, the auditor is required to make enquiries of management regarding:

- the identity of related parties, including changes from prior periods;

- the nature of relationships with those related parties; and

- whether any transactions were entered into with those related parties during the period, and if so, the type and purpose of those transactions.

20.5.2 Understanding of controls

The ISA requires that the auditor also gains an understanding of controls in place over related party transactions by understanding controls over the:

- identification, accounting and disclosure of related party relationships and transactions;

- authorisation and approval of significant transactions and arrangements with related parties; and

- authorisation and approval of significant transactions and arrangements outside the normal course of business.

As transactions between related parties may not be at arm's length, there may be an actual or perceived conflict of interest. For this reason, many entities will require that such transactions are authorised by those charged with governance. This means that such transactions are often recorded in the minutes of meetings, for example, meetings of directors. This is less likely for owner-managed entities where procedures are often less formalised.

20.5.3 Team discussion

ISA (UK) 550 requires that the audit team discussion required by ISA (UK) 315 (Revised June 2016) (see **Section 21**), shall include specific consideration of fraud or error that may arise as a result of related party relationships and transactions.

Matters that may be addressed in this discussion include:

- nature and extent of the entity's relationships and transactions with related parties;

- any known changes to the auditor's list of related parties;

- an emphasis on maintaining professional scepticism throughout the audit regarding the potential for material misstatement in respect of related parties;

- circumstances or conditions that may indicate the existence of undisclosed related parties or transactions;

- records or documents that may indicate the existence of related parties or transactions;

- attitude of management and those charged with governance to the identification of and disclosure of related parties and related party transactions;

- existence of special purpose entities and how these may be used to facilitate fraud;

- how transactions with persons or entities connected with a key member of management could be used to facilitate fraud.

Relevant information about related parties should be shared with the whole audit team including those not present at the engagement team discussion.

20.5.4   Remaining alert

The auditor should remain alert to indicators of the existence of related parties and related party transactions when inspecting records and documents throughout the audit. ISA (UK) 550 requires the auditor to inspect the following documents for indications of unidentified related parties:

- bank and legal confirmations obtained as part of the auditor's procedures;

- minutes of meetings of shareholders and of those charged with governance; and

- such other records or documents considered necessary by the auditor.

Table 1 sets out other documents that the auditor is likely to view as part of his audit procedures which may indicate the existence of previously undisclosed related parties.

TABLE 1: Records or documents that may indicate undisclosed related parties

- third party confirmations obtained by the auditor (in additional to bank and legal confirmations);

- entity income tax returns;

- information supplied by the entity to regulatory authorities;

- shareholder registers to identify the entity's principal shareholders;

- statements of conflicts of interest from management and those charged with governance;

- records of the entity's investments and those of its pension plans;

- contracts and agreements with key management or those charged with governance;

- significant contracts and agreements not in the entity's ordinary course of business;

- specific invoices and correspondence from the entity's professional advisors;

- life insurance policies acquired by the entity;

- significant contracts re-negotiated by the entity during the period;

- reports of the internal audit function; and

- documents associated with the entity's filings with a securities regulator (such as prospectuses).

In addition, where the auditor identifies transactions outside the entity's normal course of business he should make further enquiries of management to establish the nature of the transactions and whether related parties could be involved.

20.5.5 Assessment of risk

Based on his knowledge and enquiries, the auditor makes an assessment of the risk of material misstatement in connection with the accounting for and disclosure of transactions, balances and relationships with related parties.

Where the auditor identifies a transaction with a related party that is outside the normal course of business, this is always treated as giving rise to a significant risk as defined in ISA (UK) 315 (Revised June 2016) (see **21.3.6**).

20.6 Response to risk

Depending on his assessment of risk, the auditor designs appropriate audit procedures to obtain sufficient appropriate audit evidence in respect of the assessed risks.

If previously unidentified related parties are discovered, they should be reported to all members of the audit team immediately, as this information could affect the results of work they are performing or have already performed, including the assessment of the risk of material misstatement, which may need revision. The auditor should request management to identify all transactions with the newly identified related party so that they can be evaluated and should make enquiries as to why the entity's own procedures and controls had failed to identify the relate party.

The auditor should then carry out substantive procedures as necessary regarding the newly identified related party and any transactions and balances with the related party.

If non-disclosure of the related party by management appears intentional, it may be indicative of a risk of material misstatement due to fraud, and the auditor should evaluate the implications for the audit and his report. It may also cast doubt over other representations made by management.

Where significant related party transactions appear to be outside the entity's normal course of business, they will have been assessed as giving rise to a significant risk. In this case, the auditor examines any underlying contracts or agreements to determine whether there are any indications of fraud, whether the terms of the agreements are consistent with management's expectations and whether the transactions have been properly accounted for and disclosed. The auditor will also seek evidence that the transactions were appropriately authorised.

Table 2 sets out a number of examples of transactions outside the entity's normal course of business.

TABLE 2: Transactions outside the normal course of business

- complex equity transactions such as restructurings or acquisitions;

- transactions with offshore entities in jurisdictions with weak corporate laws;

- leasing of premises or rendering of services by the entity at no charge;

- sales or other transactions with unusually large discounts or generous terms;

- transactions with circular arrangements;

- transactions under contracts whose terms are changed before expiry.

20.6.1 *Arm's length transactions*

If management asserts that a related party transaction has been conducted on terms equivalent to an arm's length transaction, ISA (UK) 550 requires that the auditor should obtain evidence to support that assertion.

In order to support its assertion, management may:

- compare the terms of the related party transaction with those of an identical or similar transaction with an unrelated party;

- engage an external expert to determine a market value and confirm market terms and conditions for the transaction; or

- compare the terms of the transaction with broadly similar transactions in the open market.

Evaluating the information provided by management may include:

- considering the appropriateness of the processes undertaken by management to support their assertion;

- verifying internal or external data used as evidence by management;

- evaluating whether assumptions used by management are reasonable.

20.7   Control disclosures

Accounting frameworks usually require disclosures relating to the control of the entity. Where this is the case, ISA (UK) 550 expects the auditor to obtain appropriate evidence in this respect, usually via enquiry of management or those charged with governance. It is suggested that these management representations may be confirmed with the controlling party if considered appropriate.

20.8   Representations from those charged with governance

ISA (UK) 550 requires the auditor to obtain written confirmation from those charged with governance that information concerning related parties and control provided to the auditor is complete, that transactions have been properly accounted for and that the disclosures in the financial statements regarding related party transactions are appropriate and in accordance with the relevant accounting framework (see **Section 32**).

Where an entity requires its management and those charged with governance to make individual declarations regarding related party relationships and transactions, the auditor should inspect these documents. In such cases, the guidance suggests that the confirmations may be jointly addressed to the company and the auditor. Alternatively, the auditor may seek direct confirmation from those concerned.

20.9 Communication with those charged with governance

Examples of items which the auditor may report in his communications with those charged with governance in respect of related party transactions include:

- intentional or unintentional non-disclosure of related parties or significant related party transactions, which may alert those charged with governance to relationships and transactions of which they had not previously been aware;

- significant related party transactions which have not been appropriately authorised and approved, which may give rise to suspected fraud;

- disagreements with management regarding the accounting for and disclosure of significant related party transactions;

- non-compliance with laws and regulations which prohibit or restrict certain types of related party transactions; and

- difficulties in identifying the party that ultimately controls the entity.

20.10 Documentation

ISA (UK) 550 includes a formal requirement for the names and nature of the relationship with all related parties be documented on the audit file.

20.11 Reporting

In forming his opinion, the auditor must evaluate whether the identified related party relationships and transactions are appropriately accounted for and disclosed and also whether the effects of these relationships and transactions prevent the financial statements from achieving fair presentation. Related party transactions and relationships should be presented in a way that is understandable, which may not be the case if the business rationale and effects of the transactions are unclear or if key terms or conditions necessary for an understanding of the transactions are not disclosed.

If the auditor is unable to obtain sufficient appropriate evidence on related party matters or the disclosures are not adequate, he should consider the implications for his report.

Where the auditor believes that there is more information which could have been obtained but he has been unable to do so, this is a limitation of scope which could lead to a qualified or disclaimed opinion as set out in **5.4**. For example, such a report would be appropriate where he suspects a related party transaction but has not been able to obtain all the evidence to which he is reasonably entitled to determine the matter.

In instances where the auditor has sufficient evidence to know that the disclosure is incorrect or he considers the disclosures inadequate because the directors are unwilling to disclose information, he should consider giving a qualified or adverse opinion on the basis of misstatement of the financial statements (see **5.4**). ISA (UK) 705 (Revised June 2016) *Modifications to the Opinion in the Independent Auditor's Report* requires that, where practicable and unless prohibited by law or regulation, the auditor should include in his report a description and quantification of any misstatement and details of any omitted disclosures. The *Companies Act* 2006 also requires the auditor to include details in his report of omitted or misstated disclosures where these relate to details of directors' remuneration, pensions, or compensation for loss of office required under the Act.

20.12   The audit of related parties in practice

20.12.1   Introduction

In February 2010, the Audit and Assurance Faculty of the ICAEW issued a paper entitled *The Audit of Related Parties in Practice* as it believed that revisions to ISA 550 required a significant shift in the focus of work carried out by the auditor in this area, with a stronger emphasis on procedures to identify, assess and respond to risks of material misstatement associated with related parties and a focus in particular on fraud risk factors linked to related party transactions.

The Audit and Assurance Faculty guidance highlights common pitfalls when auditing related parties and related party transactions, and provides suggestions to improve audit quality in this area. It emphasises the importance of proper planning in this area, involving the whole audit team.

20.12.2   The five-point action plan

The Audit and Assurance Faculty guidance contains a five-point plan highlighting specific areas where existing audit work on related parties and related party transactions could be enhanced to improve the quality of the audit. It is reproduced in **Table 3**.

TABLE 3: The five-point action plan

(1) Plan your work on the audit of related parties and related party transactions thoroughly.

   (a) Plan the audit of related parties and related party transactions by updating existing information, and where possible, obtain a list of related parties from clients or compile a list based on discussions with clients.

   (b) Ask management about changes from the prior period, the nature of the relationships, whether any transactions have been entered into and the type and purpose of the transactions.

   (c) Ensure that the client understands what related parties are and why the relevant disclosure requirements are necessary.

   (d) Speak to the right person 'in authority' at the client who can answer questions.

   (e) Plan for concerns raised by audit team members and others to be considered and reviewed by suitably experienced staff.

   (f) Brief all audit team members on related party relationships and transactions and the risks of material misstatement due to fraud or error that could arise from such transactions.

   (g) Ensure that all staff are informed about any changes to related party relationships throughout the engagement and are aware of the need to bring such changes to the attention of the rest of the team.

(2) Focus on the risk of material misstatement that might arise from related party transactions.

   (a) Understand the nature, size and complexity of the businesses and use family trees or document group structures to help identify related parties and relationships between the client and related parties.

   (b) Follow up indicators of the existence of undisclosed related parties or related party transactions.

   (c) Consider the impact of undisclosed related party relationships and transactions as a potential fraud risk.

   (d) Consider the qualitative aspects of materiality.

   (e) Emphasise the importance of the audit team remaining alert for related party relationships and transactions as the audit proceeds.

   (f) Discuss related party relationships with others within the firm who provide services to the client, such as tax, accounting or corporate finance departments.

(3) Understand the internal controls at the company to identify related parties and to record related party transactions.

   (a) Understand the controls, if any, that management has put in place to identify, account for and disclose related party transactions and to approve significant transactions with related parties, and significant transactions outside the normal course of business.

   (b) If few or no processes are in place for dealing with related party relationships and transactions, seek to obtain an understanding of those relationships and transactions by asking management.

(4) Design procedures to respond to risks identified.

   (a) Perform procedures to confirm identified related party relationships and transactions and identify others including:

- inspecting bank and legal confirmations obtained as part of other audit procedures;

- inspecting minutes of shareholder and management meetings and any other records or documents considered necessary, such as regulatory returns, tax returns and records of investments.

   (b) Where the existence of related party relationships or transactions that management has not previously identified or disclosed is indicated, communicate the information to team members promptly, and:

- request management to identify all such transactions;

- ask why controls failed to identify or disclose the related parties or transactions;

- perform appropriate substantive procedures;

- reconsider the risk that further unidentified or undisclosed relationships or transactions may exist and evaluate the implications for the audit.

   (c) Consider any fraud risk factors in the context of the requirements of ISA (UK) 240 (Revised June 2016).

   (d) Establish the nature of significant transactions outside the company's normal course of business and whether related parties could be involved, by inquiring of management.

   (e) Consider any arm's-length transactions and obtain supporting evidence from third parties.

   (f) Treat significant related party transactions outside the normal course of business as significant risks and inspect relevant documentation to evaluate the business rationale of the transactions, whether they have been appropriately authorised and approved, whether the terms are consistent with management's explanations and whether they have been appropriately accounted for.

(g) Document the identity of related parties and the nature of related party relationships.

(5) Perform completion procedures.

(a) Obtain a representation that management has disclosed the identity of related parties, relationships and transactions of which they are aware and that related parties and transactions have been appropriately accounted for and disclosed.

(b) Communicate significant related party matters arising during the audit to those charged with governance unless all of those charged with governance are involved in its management.

(c) Ensure that the accounting for and disclosures of related parties and related party transactions are appropriate.

(d) Consider the implications of the findings from work performed on related parties and related party transactions for the audit opinion.

21 Audit risk assessment and the auditor's response

21.1 Introduction

ISA (UK) 200 (Revised June 2016) *Overall Objectives of the Independent Auditor and the Conduct of an Audit in Accordance with International Standards on Auditing (UK)* explains that as the basis for his opinion, ISAs (UK) require the auditor to obtain reasonable assurance that the financial statements as a whole are free from material error whether due to fraud or error. Reasonable assurance is a high level of assurance, albeit not an absolute level of assurance.

In order to obtain this reasonable assurance, the auditor exercises professional judgment and maintains professional scepticism in carrying out his work and is required, among other things:

- to identify and assess the risks of material misstatement in the financial statements based on an understanding of the entity and its environment, including the entity's internal control; and

- to obtain sufficient appropriate audit evidence through designing and implementing appropriate responses to the assessed risks.

Three ISAs deal specifically with the process of obtaining an understanding of the entity, identifying and assessing risks and designing and implementing appropriate audit responses. These are:

- ISA (UK) 315 (Revised June 2016) *Identifying and Assessing the Risks of Material Misstatement through Understanding the Entity and its Environment*;

- ISA (UK) 330 (Revised July 2017) *The Auditor's Responses to Assessed Risks*; and

- ISA (UK) 240 (Revised June 2016) (Updated July 2017) *The Auditor's Responsibilities Relating to Fraud in an Audit of Financial Statements*, which is covered in **Section 16**.

These ISAs are largely effective for the audit of financial statements for periods commencing on or after 17 June 2016 although relatively minor updates in July 2017 are effective for audits commencing on or after 15 December 2017.

Changes made in the 2016 revision to ISA (UK) 315 relate to the audit of disclosures as a result of the IAASB's disclosure project (see **Section 1**). These changes are covered at various points throughout the section and include:

- a requirement that the auditor's understanding of relevant information systems should extend to systems relating to information that is disclosed in the financial statements but comes from outside the general and subsidiary ledgers;

- a requirement for the auditor to consider both quantitative and qualitative aspects of disclosures when identifying and assessing risks of misstatement; and

- application material suggesting that consideration should be given to disclosure requirements as part of the engagement team discussion to assist in early identification of risks relating to disclosures.

Changes in ISA (UK) 330 included Audit Regulation requirements for public interest entities (see **21.4.2**) and audit of disclosures (covered in **21.4.2**, **21.4.3** and **21.4.5**). A further minor change to ISA (UK) 330 was made in July 2017 to introduce additional application and other explanatory material regarding external confirmations (see **Section 24**) following withdrawal of Practice Note 16 *Bank reports for audit purposes in the UK* (PN 16).

The update to ISA (UK) 240 in July 2017 related to communication with those charged with governance and the auditor's legal responsibilities to report suspicions of fraud.

21.2   General overview

The auditor is required to perform risk assessment procedures to provide a basis for the identification and assessment of risks of material misstatement at the financial statements and assertion levels. Risk assessment procedures do not, of themselves, provide sufficient appropriate audit evidence on which to base the audit opinion but enable the auditor to determine the nature, timing and extent of further audit procedures necessary to obtain sufficient appropriate audit evidence.

21.3   Identifying and assessing risks

21.3.1   Requirements

ISA (UK) 315 (Revised June 2016) sets out requirements on understanding the entity, including its internal control, and using this understanding to assess the risks of material misstatement in the financial statements. The ISA covers:

- risk assessment procedures and related activities;

- the required understanding of the entity and its environment, including the entity's internal control;

- identifying and assessing the risks of material misstatement; and

- documentation.

21.3.2 Risk assessment procedures and related activities

Procedures

Although concentrated at the early stages of the audit, procedures to obtain an understanding of the entity, its environment and internal control, will be performed throughout the audit. Audit procedures designed and performed to obtain such an understanding are defined by the ISA as 'risk assessment procedures'. Such procedures may also provide evidence about transactions, balances, disclosures or the operation of controls, although they were not specifically designed to.

The ISA requires the auditor to perform the following risk assessment procedures to obtain an understanding of different aspects of the entity and its environment:

- enquiries of management, of appropriate individuals within the internal audit function (if the function exists) and others within the entity;

- analytical procedures; and

- observation and inspection.

Much information may come from management, but other directors or staff may be able to provide different perspectives which highlight the risk of material misstatement. Information may also be obtained through enquiries with the internal audit function, if the entity has such a function. For example, talking to sales personnel may uncover a change in sales trends or contractual arrangements with customers, or meeting with the internal audit function may highlight potential problems with the design or effectiveness of the internal control system.

Analytical procedures may identify unusual transactions or trends which may indicate material misstatements. At the risk assessment stage such analytical procedures tend to be at a high level and are therefore likely only to provide a broad initial indication of a misstatement which will require further investigation.

Observation and inspection may support management representations or may provide information directly. Procedures will normally include:

- observation of entity activities and operations;

- inspection of documents (such as business plans and strategies), records and internal control manuals;

- reading reports (such as quarterly management reports and minutes of directors' meetings);

- visits to the entity's premises; and

- tracing transactions through the information systems relating to financial reporting, i.e. walkthroughs.

Prior year information

For ongoing audits, information gained at the prior year's audit will be of use when performing risk assessment procedures in the current year. However, the ISA requires the auditor to determine whether changes have occurred since the previous audit that may affect the relevance of such information in the current audit. The continuing relevance of such information can be determined by performing system walkthroughs.

Information gathered during any interim review may also be relevant to the year end risk assessment procedures, but its ongoing accuracy should also be confirmed.

In addition, information gathered in previous audits may highlight particular types of transactions and other events or account balances (and related disclosures) where the auditor experienced difficulty in performing the necessary audit procedures, for example, due to their complexity.

21.3.3   Engagement team discussion

ISA (UK) 315 (Revised June 2016) introduced a requirement for the engagement partner and other key members of the engagement team to discuss the susceptibility of the entity's financial statements to material misstatement. This meeting is often combined with the fraud discussion outlined in **16.4.2**. The meeting should include all key members of the engagement team, but the exact participants, timing and extent of the meeting are matters of professional judgment. Typically, such a discussion would include the engagement partner, audit manager and senior and tax manager, where such services are provided. More junior members of the engagement team may be included to enable them to gain a better understanding of how the results of the work assigned to them affect other aspects of the audit. The presence of the engagement partner is not to be underestimated as he is key in setting the overall tone and direction of the audit and his knowledge and experience both of the client, its industry and auditing in general will provide essential inputs to the risk assessment process.

The engagement team must also consider whether experts assigned to the team, such as IT or valuation specialists, should participate in the meeting.

The discussion provides an opportunity for more experienced engagement team members to share their knowledge of the entity. It allows the engagement team members to exchange information about the business risks to which the entity is subject and about how and where the financial statements might be susceptible to material misstatement due to fraud or error. It is an opportunity for the engagement team members to gain a better understanding of the potential for material misstatement of the financial statements in the specific areas assigned to them, and to understand how the results of the audit procedures that they perform may affect other aspects of the audit including the decisions about the nature, timing, and extent of further audit procedures.

The discussion should emphasise the need for professional scepticism and, in accordance with the requirements of ISA (UK) 240 (Revised June 2016) particular importance should be given to the susceptibility of the entity's financial statements to material misstatement due to fraud.

As part of the discussion, there should be consideration of the disclosure requirements of the applicable financial reporting framework to assist in identifying early in the audit where there may be risks of material misstatement in relation to disclosures.

Further meetings may be held during the course of the engagement to allow team members to communicate and share information gained during the audit which may affect the assessment of risk or the audit procedures performed.

21.3.4 Understanding the entity and its environment, including the entity's internal control

Detailed areas

The following areas should be included in the auditor's understanding of the entity and its environment:

- industry, regulatory and other external factors, including the applicable financial reporting framework;

- nature of the entity, including:

  - its operations;

  - its ownership and governance structures;

  - the types of investment that the entity is making and plans to make, including investments in special-purpose entities; and

- – the way that the entity is structured and how it is financed to enable the auditor to understand the classes of transactions, account balances, and disclosures to be expected in the financial statements;
- the selection and application of accounting policies;
- objectives and strategies and the related business risks that may result in a material misstatement of the financial statements; and
- measurement and review of the entity's financial performance.

Table 1 sets out examples of items that the auditor may consider in relation to these areas. Internal control is considered in **21.3.5**.

Nature of the entity

A full understanding of the nature of the entity, its operations, governance and the way it is structured will help to ensure that any risks relating to group structures or the need for consolidation are identified. Such knowledge will also assist with identifying related party transactions.

The ISA also requires the auditor to consider whether the accounting policies selected and applied by the entity are suitable given the business and its industry. The auditor should consider new financial reporting standards that may be relevant to the entity and situations where the entity has changed its accounting policies, as well as ensuring adequate disclosure has been made of all relevant issues in the financial statements.

Objectives, strategies and related business risks

A business will define overall plans, or 'objectives' to respond to a variety of internal and external factors. To implement these objectives, practical 'strategies' are used. The risk that events or circumstances will mean that strategies cannot be implemented and objectives are not achieved is 'business risk'.

Business risk is a wider concept than the risk of material misstatement of the financial statements, but understanding business risk will increase the likelihood of identifying such risk. Whether a business risk will result in a risk of material misstatement will depend on the entity's circumstances. Examples of conditions that may indicate a risk of material misstatement are given in **Table 2**.

Smaller entities may not have formal, documented objectives and strategies. Therefore, to understand the business risk for such entities, the auditor must make enquiries and observations of management.

TABLE 1: Example items to consider when gaining an understanding of the entity and its environment

Industry, regulatory and other external factors

- Industry conditions:

    - the market and competition, including demand, capacity and price competition;

    - cyclical or seasonal activity;

    - product technology relating to the entity's products; and

    - energy supply and cost.

- Regulatory environment:

    - accounting principles and industry-specific practices;

    - regulatory framework for a regulated industry, including requirements for disclosures;

    - legislation and regulation that significantly affect the entity's operations, including direct supervisory activities;

    - taxation (corporation tax and other);

    - government policies currently affecting the conduct of the entity's business such as:

        – monetary, including foreign exchange controls:

        – fiscal;

        – financial incentives (e.g. grant programmes);

        – tariffs and trade restrictions; and

    - environmental requirements affecting the industry and the entity's business.

- Other external factors:

    - general level of economic activity (e.g. recession or growth);

    - interest rates and availability of financing; and

    - inflation, currency revaluation.

Nature of the entity

- Business operations:

    - nature of revenue sources (e.g. manufacture, wholesale, banking, insurance or other financial services, import/export trading, utilities, transportation and technology products and services);

    - products or services and markets (e.g. major customers and contracts, terms of payment, profit margins, market share, competitors, experts, pricing policies, reputation of products, warranties, order book, trends, marketing strategy and objectives, manufacturing processes);

- conduct of operations (e.g. stages and methods of production, business segments, delivery or products and services, details of declining or expanding operations);

- alliances, joint ventures and outsourcing activities;

- involvement in electronic commerce including internet sales and marketing activities;

- geographic dispersion and industry segmentation;

- location of production facilities, warehouses and offices;

- key customers;

- important suppliers of goods and services (e.g. long-term contracts, stability of supply, terms of payment, imports. methods of delivery such as 'just in time');

- employment (e.g. by location, supply, wage levels, union contracts, pension benefits, share option or incentive bonus arrangements and government regulation related to employment matters);

- research and development activities and expenditure; and

- transactions with related parties.

- Investments:

  - acquisitions, mergers or disposals of business activities (planned or recently executed);

  - investment and dispositions of securities and loans;

  - capital investment activities, including investments in plant and equipment and technology and any recent or planned changes; and

  - investments in non-consolidated entities, including partnerships, joint ventures and special-purpose entities.

- Financing:

  - group structure – major subsidiaries and associated entities, including consolidated and non-consolidated structures;

  - debt structure, including covenants, restrictions, guarantees and off-balance sheet financing arrangements;

  - leasing of property, plant or equipment for use in the business;

  - parent companies (local, foreign, business reputation and experience);

  - related parties; and

  - use of derivate financial instruments.

- Financial reporting practices:

  - accounting principles and industry specific practices;

  - revenue recognition;

  - accounting for fair values;

  - stock (e.g. locations and quantities);

  - foreign currency assets, liabilities and transactions;

  - industry specific significant classes of transactions, account balances and related disclosures in the financial statements (e.g. loans and investments for banks, trade debtors and stock for manufacturers, research and development for pharmaceuticals);

  - accounting for unusual or complex transactions including those in controversial or emerging areas; and

  - financial statements presentation and disclosure.

Objectives and strategies and related business risks

- Existence of objectives relating to:

  - industry developments (a potential business risk might be that the entity does not have the personnel or expertise to deal with the changes in the industry);

  - new products and services (a potential related business risk might be that there is increased product liability);

  - expansion of the business (a potential business risk might be that the demand has not been accurately estimated);

  - new accounting requirements (a potential business risk might be incomplete or improper implementation or increased costs);

  - regulatory requirements (a potential business risk might be increased legal exposure);

  - current and prospective financing requirements (a potential business risk might be the loss of financing due to the entity's inability to meet requirements); and

  - use of IT (a potential business risk might be that systems and processes are incompatible).

- Effects of implementing a strategy, particularly any effects that will lead to new accounting requirements (a potential business risk might be incomplete or improper implementation).

Measurement and review of the entity's financial performance

- Key ratios and operating statistics;

- key performance indicators;

- employee performance measures and incentive compensation policies;

- trends;

- use of forecasts, budgets and variance analyses;

- analyst reports and credit rating reports;

- competitor analyses;

- period-on-period financial performance (revenue growth, profitability, leverage).

TABLE 2: Examples of conditions that may indicate a risk of material misstatement, including risks relating to disclosures

- operations in regions that are economically unstable, e.g. countries with significant currency devaluation or highly inflationary economies;

- operations exposed to volatile markets, e.g. futures trading;

- high degree of complex regulation;

- going concern and liquidity issues including loss of significant customers;

- constraints on the availability of capital and credit;

- changes in the industry in which the entity operates;

- changes in the supply chain;

- developing or offering new products or services, or moving into new lines of business;

- expanding into new locations;

- changes in the entity such as large acquisitions or reorganisations or other unusual events;

- entities or business segments likely to be sold;

- complex alliances and joint ventures;

- use of off-balance sheet finance, special purpose entities and other complex financing arrangements;

- significant transactions with related parties;

- lack of personnel with appropriate accounting and financial reporting skills;

- changes in key personnel including departure of key executives;

- weaknesses in internal control, especially those not addressed by management;

- incentives for management and employees to engage in fraudulent financial reporting;

- inconsistencies between the entity's IT strategy and its business strategies;

- changes in the IT environment;

- installation of significant new IT systems related to financial statements;

- enquiries into the entities' operations or financial results by regulatory or government bodies;

- past misstatements, history of errors or a significant amount of adjustments at period end;

- significant amount of non-routine or non-systematic transactions including intercompany transactions and large revenue transactions at period end;

- transactions that are recorded based on management's intent, e.g. debt refinancing, assets to be sold and classification of marketable securities;

- application of new accounting pronouncements;

- accounting measurements that involve complex processes;

- events or transactions that involve significant measurement uncertainty, including accounting estimates, and related disclosures;

- omission, or obscuring, of significant information in disclosures;

- pending litigation and contingent liabilities, e.g. sales warranties, financial guarantees and environmental remediation.

Measurement and review of financial performance

By understanding which areas management are keen to monitor and review, the auditor can make assumptions about the areas which management perceive to be of relatively high risk. In turn, the existence of such performance measures may create a pressure on management, which may lead to motivation to misstate the financial statements.

Information used by management to monitor performance may include key performance indicators (both financial and non-financial), budgets, variance analysis, segment information and divisional, departmental or other level performance reports, and comparison of an entity's performance with that of competitors. Much of this information is likely to be internally generated and the auditor must consider whether it is likely to be accurate and precise enough to detect material misstatement.

Although smaller entities may not have formal performance review procedures, management are still likely to focus on a number of performance indicators. The auditor can observe these in the same way as for larger entities.

21.3.5 Internal control

Components of internal control

ISA (UK) 315 (Revised June 2016) requires the auditor to obtain an understanding of internal control relevant to the audit in order to identify types of misstatement and design audit procedures. Internal control is the process designed, implemented and maintained to provide reasonable assurance about the achievement of the entity's objectives with regard to reliability of financial reporting, effectiveness and efficiency of operations and compliance with applicable laws and regulations.

Internal control consists of five components:

- the control environment;
- the entity's risk assessment process;
- the information system, including the related business processes, relevant to financial reporting and communication;
- control activities; and
- monitoring of controls.

Each of these is considered in detail in the following paragraphs.

The design and implementation of internal control will vary from entity to entity and will differ depending on the entity's size and complexity. For smaller entities, the five components of internal control may be blurred with an owner-manager taking sole responsibility for elements of each of them. Although the components of internal control may not be clearly distinguished in a smaller entity, their purpose will still stand.

Ordinarily, the auditor will be concerned with those controls relevant to the preparation of financial statements. Controls over information not directly relevant to the financial statements may also be of concern to the auditor if that information is used in the design or performance of an audit procedure, for example production statistics or controls, or pertains to the detection of non-compliance with laws and regulations. Therefore in assessing whether a control is relevant to the audit, the auditor considers:

- materiality;
- the significance of the related risk;
- the size of the entity;
- the nature of the entity's business;
- the diversity and complexity of the entity's operations;
- applicable legal and regulatory requirements;

- the circumstances and the applicable component of internal control;

- the nature and complexity of the systems that are part of the entity's internal control; and

- whether, and how, a specific control, individually or in combination with others, prevents, or detects and corrects, material misstatement.

Once the auditor has determined which controls are relevant to the audit, he should evaluate the design of each control and determine whether it has been properly implemented. When evaluating the design of the control, the auditor considers whether it is capable of preventing, detecting or correcting material misstatements. If a control is poorly designed, it may lead to a weakness which should be reported to those charged with governance.

Obtaining an understanding of a control Is not the same as testing its operating effectiveness. In order to obtain assurance that a control is mitigating the risk of material misstatement, the control must be found to be operating effectively throughout the period.

Control environment

ISA (UK) 315 (Revised June 2016) states that the auditor should obtain an understanding of the control environment. This includes the governance and management functions and the attitudes, awareness, and actions of those charged with governance and management concerning the entity's internal control and its importance in the entity. The control environment sets the tone of an organisation, influencing the control consciousness of its people.

When evaluating the entity's control environment, the auditor considers how the following elements have been incorporated:

- communication and enforcement of integrity and ethical values;

- commitment to competence;

- participation of those charged with governance, including their independence from management;

- management's philosophy and operating style, their approach to taking risks and attitude to financial reporting and financial reporting staff;

- organisational structure and how activities are planned, executed, controlled and reviewed;

- assignment of authority and responsibility; and

- human resources policies and practices, such as recruitment, training and evaluating.

In understanding the control environment, the auditor must also consider whether the entity's policies have actually been implemented. This will involve enquiries and corroboration using observation techniques or review of documents. For some elements, documentary evidence may be limited. For example, a commitment to ethical values is often demonstrated rather than documented. In smaller entities, communication between management and other personnel may be particularly informal. In such situations, the auditor's observations will be important.

An entity's control environment has a pervasive effect on assessing the risk of material misstatement. Even the best documented and implemented internal control system will be rendered useless by a poor management attitude which allows control environment weaknesses and thinks little of overriding controls. However, the existence of a satisfactory control environment can be a positive factor when assessing the risk of material misstatement, and may allow the auditor to have more confidence in the reliability of internally generated audit evidence.

The risk assessment process

The entity's risk assessment process is the way in which they identify the business risks that are relevant to financial reporting and determine actions to address those risks. The auditor is required to obtain an understanding of this process. This will involve considering how management identifies business risks, estimates their significance, assesses the likelihood of them occurring and determines actions to manage them.

The entity's process can assist the auditor in identifying risks of material misstatement, however, if the auditor discovers material risks which were not identified by the entity's process he considers whether there is a weakness which should be reported to those charged with governance.

The information system

The auditor is required to obtain an understanding of the information system insofar as it relates to financial reporting objectives. This will include gaining an understanding of the accounting system. The ISA sets out the following areas that the auditor should consider:

- the classes of transactions which are significant to the financial statements;

- the procedures by which transactions are initiated, recorded, processed and reported in the financial statements (these may be IT based or manual);

- the records supporting the above processes, held either electronically or manually;

- how other events are captured, i.e. those that are not normal transactions for the entity;
- the process used to prepare the financial statements from the accounting records; and
- controls surrounding journal entries, including non-standard journal entries used to record non-recurring, unusual transactions or adjustments.

This understanding of the information system relevant to financial reporting needs to include relevant aspects of that system relating to information disclosed in the financial statements that is obtained from within or outside of the general and subsidiary ledgers.

Financial statements may contain information that is obtained from outside of the general and subsidiary ledgers, such as information:

- from lease agreements, such as renewal options or future lease payments;
- produced by an entity's risk management system;
- on fair values;
- from models, or from other calculations used to develop estimates, including information relating to the underlying data and assumptions used in those models;
- about sensitivity analyses derived from financial models that demonstrates that management has considered alternative assumptions;
- obtained from an entity's tax returns and records; and
- obtained from analyses prepared to support management's assessment of the entity's ability to continue as a going concern.

The auditor should also be aware of whether and how controls are overridden and how incorrect processing of transactions is dealt with once it has been discovered. In addition, the auditor should consider how information is transferred from the processing system to the general ledger or the financial reporting systems.

The auditor should also consider whether the entity's information system is suitable for its circumstances. This will involve gaining an understanding of the entity's business processes and how transactions originate during these processes.

As part of understanding the information system, the auditor should also consider how the roles and responsibilities within the system are communicated to the individuals involved in the day-to-day running of that system. A risk of material misstatement may be reduced by the entity ensuring that all roles are set out in suitably detailed policy or financial reporting manuals.

Control activities

The auditor's risk assessment procedures performed to date will have provided a good indication of the areas where a risk of material misstatement exists. When assessing an entity's control activities, the auditor will concentrate on those areas where material misstatements are more likely to occur.

Control activities are the policies and procedures that help ensure that management directives are carried out. In order to understand an entity's control activities, the auditor considers how a particular activity, individually or in conjunction with others, prevents, detects or corrects a material misstatement. Specific control activities may include:

- authorisation (e.g. of payments);
- performance reviews;
- information processing;
- physical controls (e.g. over assets); or
- segregation of duties.

Specifically, the ISA requires the auditor to consider how the entity has responded to risks arising from IT. The auditor should consider how control activities have responded to different risks posed by the advent of IT systems, and consider whether the integrity of the information and security of the data has been maintained. **Table 3** provides examples of areas where risks may differ when the system is automated rather than manual.

TABLE 3: Traits of an automated system

Examples of areas where risk may differ from that associated with a manual system include:

- lack of transaction trails;

- uniform processing of transactions – clerical error is less of a risk in an information systems (IS) environment but there is a risk of a programming error resulting in large numbers of similar transactions being incorrectly processed;

- lack of segregation of duties;

- potential to alter data without visible signs of this being done;

- lack of human involvement may mean that errors are not detected as quickly;

> - automatic transactions carried out by the IS;
> - potential for increased management supervision using analytical tools available via the IS; and
> - potential for using computer assisted audit techniques.

IT controls can be categorised as 'general IT controls' or 'application controls'. General IT controls are policies and procedures that relate to many applications and assist with ensuring that the information system operates properly. Examples are controls over access to IT systems or development of new systems. Application controls typically operate at a more detailed level, can be preventative or detective in nature and aim to ensure the integrity of the accounting records. Examples include numerical sequence checks or checks to ensure that items are suitably authorised.

Monitoring of controls

ISA (UK) 315 (Revised June 2016) requires the auditor to gain an understanding of what the entity does to monitor its own controls. This monitoring should encompass both the day-to-day operation of the controls and the overall design of the control system. Where the information used to monitor the controls is taken from the information system itself, the auditor considers how the entity ensures it is reliable.

Where the entity has an internal audit function, the auditor should obtain an understanding of the nature of the internal audit function's responsibilities, its organisational status and the activities performed, or to be performed. Further guidance can be found in **Section 31**.

Manual and automated elements of internal control

An entity's system of internal control is likely to include both manual and automated elements. For smaller companies, there is likely to be a greater emphasis on manual procedures, but even for some large entities, elements of their internal control system may still rely heavily on manual intervention. The benefits and risks of using automated controls are set out in **Table 4**.

> **TABLE 4: Benefits and risks of using automated controls**
>
> *Benefits – an entity is able to:*
>
> - consistently apply predefined business rules and perform complex calculations in processing large volumes of transactions or data;
> - enhance the timeliness, availability and accuracy of information;
> - facilitate the additional analysis of information;

- enhance the ability to monitor the performance of the entity's activities and its policies and procedures;

- reduce the risk that controls will be circumvented; and

- enhance the ability to achieve effective segregation of duties by implementing security controls in applications, databases and operating systems.

Risks

- reliance on systems or programmes that are inaccurately processing data, processing inaccurate data, or both;

- unauthorised access to data that may result in destruction of data or changes to data, including the recording of unauthorised or non-existent transactions or inaccurate recording of transactions. Particular risks occur where multiple users access a common database;

- the possibility of IT personnel gaining access privileges beyond those necessary to perform their assigned duties thereby breaking down segregation of duties;

- unauthorised changes to data in master files;

- unauthorised changes to systems or programmes;

- failure to make necessary changes to systems or programmes;

- inappropriate manual interventions; and

- potential loss of data or inability to access data as required.

Manual systems or elements of systems may be more suitable when judgment and discretion are required, such as for:

- large, unusual or non-recurring transactions;

- circumstances where errors are difficult to define, anticipate or predict;

- changing circumstances that require a control response outside the scope of an existing automated control; or

- monitoring the effectiveness of automated controls.

However, manual controls are generally less reliable than automated controls as they rely on people to perform them. Therefore, it cannot be assumed that a manual control has been applied consistently.

Limitations of internal control

Internal control, however well designed and implemented, can at best only provide reasonable assurance about achieving an entity's financial reporting objectives. Even automated controls are subject to some human involvement and, therefore, human error. There may have been errors at the programming stage, operatives may input data incorrectly and individuals receiving reports from the system may not understand the purpose of such reports.

In addition, all controls are subject to override by collusion of one or more individuals. In smaller entities formal segregation of duties may be impossible, and the potential for override of controls by an owner-manager may be great.

21.3.6   Identifying and assessing the risks of material misstatement

Relating risks to assertions

The auditor identifies risks in the financial statements by obtaining an understanding of the entity and its environment, including relevant controls that relate to risks and by considering the classes of transactions, account balances and disclosures (including both the qualitative and quantitative aspects of disclosures). He then relates the risks identified to the financial statements assertions. The assertions considered by the auditor are set out in **Table 5**, although the audit approaches of different firms may use different terminologies. This means that each risk is considered in terms of the financial statements balance or balances it may affect and what that effect might be. For example, a risk that goods may have been incorrectly invoiced to customers without being despatched may impact the existence and valuation of turnover and trade debtors.

The auditor then considers whether the risk is such that the effect on the financial statements would be material and then how likely it is that this will occur. Potential misstatements in individual statements and disclosures may be judged to be material due to size, nature or circumstances.

The auditor will next consider whether controls have been identified which are likely to prevent or detect and correct material misstatement arising from each risk. Often individual controls do not completely address a risk, but the controls within a particular process or system may together address an assertion. However, the less directly a control relates to an assertion, the less effective that control may be in preventing or detecting and correcting risks related to the assertion.

Once risks have been allocated to assertions and matched with controls, the auditor can plan tests of controls and substantive tests to gain his audit evidence.

TABLE 5: Audit assertions

Assertions about classes of transactions and events, and related disclosures, for the period under audit

- occurrence – transactions and events that have been recorded or disclosed have occurred, and such transactions and events pertain to the entity;

- completeness – all transactions and events that should have been recorded have been recorded, and all related disclosures that should have been included in the financial statements have been included;

- accuracy – amounts and other data relating to recorded transactions and events have been recorded appropriately, and related disclosures have been appropriately measured and described;

- cut-off – transactions and events have been recorded in the correct accounting period;

- classification – transactions and events have been recorded in the proper accounts;

- presentation – transactions and events are appropriately aggregated or disaggregated and clearly described, and related disclosures are relevant and understandable in the context of the requirements of the applicable financial reporting framework.

Assertions about account balances, and related disclosures, at the period end

- existence – assets, liabilities and equity interests exist;

- rights and obligations – the entity holds or controls the right to assets, and liabilities are the obligations of the entity;

- completeness – all assets, liabilities and equity interests that should have been recorded have been recorded, and all related disclosures that should have been included in the financial statements have been included;

- accuracy, valuation and allocation – assets, liabilities and equity interests have been included in the financial statements at appropriate amounts and any resulting valuation or allocation adjustments have been appropriately recorded, and related disclosures have been appropriately measured and described;

- classification – assets, liabilities, and equity interests have been recorded in the proper accounts;

- presentation – assets, liabilities, and equity interests are appropriately aggregated or disaggregated and clearly described, and related disclosures are relevant and understandable in the context of the requirements of the applicable financial reporting framework.

> *Assertions about other disclosures*
>
> The assertions described above, adapted as appropriate, may also be used by the auditor in considering the different types of potential misstatements that may occur in disclosures not directly related to recorded classes of transactions, events, or account balances. As an example of such a disclosure, the entity may be required to describe its exposure to risks arising from financial instruments, including how the risks arise; the objectives, policies and processes for managing the risks; and the methods used to measure the risks.

Pervasive risks

Although many risks can be related to specific assertions, some risks may affect the financial statements as a whole, typically as a result of a weak control environment. Examples would be concerns about the integrity of the entity's management or untrained or inexperienced staff in a key accounting role.

In severe situations, the weakness of internal control may raise doubts about the auditability of the financial statements, for example unscrupulous management may lead to a very high risk of management misrepresentation in the financial statements or very poor accounting records may mean that insufficient audit evidence is available to support an unqualified audit opinion. In such cases, the auditor may issue a qualification or disclaimer of opinion, but if the situation is severe, the only action available to the auditor is to resign.

Significant risks

As part of his risk assessment, the auditor may decide that certain risks are 'significant risks'. Significant risks require special audit consideration as a result of the nature of the risk or the magnitude or likelihood of the error which may result. Significant risks often arise from non-routine transactions or judgmental matters as a result of:

- greater management intervention to specify the accounting treatment;

- greater manual intervention during data collection and processing;

- complex calculations or accounting principles, which may also be unfamiliar; and

- the difficulty of planning and implementing effective controls over non-routine transactions.

In determining whether a risk is a significant risk, the ISA requires the auditor to consider:

- whether the risk is a risk of fraud;
- whether the risk is related to recent significant economic, accounting or other developments and, therefore, requires specific attention;
- the complexity of transactions;
- whether the risk involves significant transactions with related parties;
- the degree of subjectivity in the measurement of financial information related to the risk, especially those measurements involving a wide range of measurement uncertainty; and
- whether the risk involves significant transactions that are outside the normal course of business for the entity, or that otherwise appear to be unusual.

Having identified significant risks, the auditor considers the controls, if any, in place to mitigate those risks. As such risks are often as a result of non-routine transactions, there may not be controls specific to each risk, but rather general procedures for responding to such risks such as approval processes for any transaction falling outside of the standard accounting process.

If the auditor wishes to rely on the operating effectiveness of controls to mitigate a significant risk, he will plan and perform tests of controls. In addition, substantive procedures should be planned to address the significant risk. This is covered further in ISA (UK) 330 (Revised July 2017), which is discussed below in **21.4**.

Other ISAs identify certain matters that are presumed to give rise to significant risks and will therefore warrant special audit consideration:

- ISA (UK) 240 (Revised June 2016) states that:
  - where assessed risks of material misstatement are due to fraud, they must be treated as significant risks;
  - there is a presumed risk of fraud in relation to revenue recognition. This presumption may be rebutted, otherwise revenue recognition will be a significant risk; and
  - when making his assessment of risks due to fraud, in all entities the auditor should presume that there is a risk of fraud arising from management override of controls. This presumption may not be rebutted, and as a fraud risk, this will always give rise to a significant risk;
- ISA (UK) 550 *Related Parties* requires that the auditor should treat identified significant related party transactions that are outside the entity's normal course of business as giving rise to significant risks.

Risks that cannot be mitigated by substantive procedures alone

At the risk assessment stage, the auditor should be aware of any risks which may not be mitigated by planning and performing substantive tests alone. Such risks are likely to arise in an environment where much of the entity's information is initiated, recorded, processed or reported electronically with little or no manual intervention. In such an integrated system, audit evidence may only be available electronically and its sufficiency and appropriateness will depend on the effectiveness of the controls over its accuracy and completeness. If such controls are not operating properly, the potential for fictitious transactions to be created or existing transactions to be amended without detection may be large.

In such a situation, the auditor should plan and perform tests of controls to satisfy themselves that controls are working to eliminate any risk of material misstatement. Due to the nature of such systems, the use of CAATs will be required (see **Section 37**).

Revision of risk assessment

The auditor's assessment of the risks of material misstatement at the assertion level may change during the course of the audit as additional audit evidence is obtained. Where audit evidence is obtained from performing further audit procedures, or new information is obtained, either of which is inconsistent with the audit evidence on which the auditor originally based the assessment, the auditor should revise the assessment and modify the further planned audit procedures accordingly.

21.3.7   Communicating with those charged with governance

Where the auditor finds significant deficiencies in the design or implementation of internal control, or a risk of material misstatement which has not been addressed by one or more controls, he should inform those charged with governance as soon as practical.

21.3.8   Documentation

ISA (UK) 315 (Revised June 2016) requires the auditor to document:

- the engagement team's discussion about the likelihood of material misstatement arising from fraud or error and the significant decisions reached;

- his understanding of the entity and its environment, assessment of the component parts of internal control, risk assessment procedures and sources of his information;

- risks of material misstatement by financial statement area and assertion;

- significant risks; and
- risks that cannot be mitigated by substantive tests alone.

There are many techniques that may be used to document these areas:

- narrative descriptions;
- questionnaires;
- checklists; and
- flow charts.

These may be used in isolation or in combination. The extent and form of the documentation to support the assessment will depend on the complexity of the systems and the extent of the auditor's procedures required to assess them.

21.4   Responses to assessed risks

ISA (UK) 330 (Revised July 2017) covers:

- overall responses;
- audit procedures responsive to the assessed risks of material misstatement at the assertion level;
- adequacy of presentation and disclosure;
- evaluating the sufficiency and appropriateness of audit evidence; and
- documentation.

21.4.1   Overall responses

The first stage is for the auditor to respond to any risks of material misstatement at the overall financial statements level. Responses may include:

- emphasising the need for professional scepticism;
- assigning more experienced audit staff;
- using specialists or experts;
- providing additional supervision; and
- incorporating further elements of unpredictability in the selection of audit tests.

The auditor may also decide to perform all audit procedures at the period end date rather than during any interim visit. Only if the auditor has confidence in the effectiveness of the control environment may some audit procedures be performed at an interim date.

Where there are concerns about the control environment, the auditor is likely to use a substantive approach, rather than a combined approach which also relies on tests of controls.

21.4.2   Responses at the assertion level

Procedures planned by the auditor should link directly to his risk assessment. The auditor should consider:

- the significance of the risk;
- the likelihood that a material misstatement will occur;
- the characteristics of the class of transactions, account balance or disclosure involved;
- the nature of the specific controls used by the entity and in particular whether they are manual or automated; and
- whether the auditor expects to obtain audit evidence about related controls.

The auditor may plan to perform tests of controls alone, tests of controls combined with substantive procedures or follow a purely substantive testing route. The latter approach may be used where the risk assessment procedures have not identified any effective controls relevant to the assertion or because testing the operating effectiveness of controls would be inefficient. For smaller entities a fully substantive approach would probably be used as the number of control activities are likely to be limited.

Nature of procedures

The higher the auditor's assessment of risk, the more reliable and relevant the audit evidence must be. This will affect both the types of audit procedures performed and their mix. Where the auditor has considered related controls in his assessment of material misstatement, he should test the effective operation of those controls. Where the auditor uses information produced by the entity's information system in his testing, the accuracy and completeness of that information should be verified. For example, if analytical procedures include comparisons to budget data, the accuracy and completeness of the budget data should be considered.

Timing of procedures

The higher the assessed risk of material misstatement, the more likely the auditor is to consider that performing substantive procedures at period end rather than at an interim date would be most effective. A disadvantage of performing all procedures at the period end is that the auditor may lose the ability to identify and address significant matters at an early stage. Another strategy might be to perform procedures unannounced or at unpredictable times.

In considering when to perform his procedures, the auditor considers:

- the control environment;

- when information is available;

- the nature of the risk, for example risks relating to the state of work in progress would be performed at the period end;

- the period or date to which the audit evidence relates; and

- the timing of the preparation of the financial statements, particularly for those disclosures that provide further explanation about amounts recorded in the statement of financial position, the statement of comprehensive income, the statement of changes in equity or the statement of cash flows.

Extent of procedures

The extent of any audit procedure is a matter of judgment based on the materiality, the assessed risk and the degree of assurance the auditor plans to obtain. The use of CAATs may allow more extensive testing of electronic transactions and account files (see **Section 37**).

Tests of controls

The auditor should perform tests of controls when:

- substantive procedures alone do not provide sufficient evidence; or

- the auditor's risk assessment includes the expectation that controls are operating effectively.

Typically, an enquiry will form part of the auditor's testing of controls, but an enquiry will not be sufficient in itself and should be combined with other procedures such as observation, inspection or reperformance. The type of testing will be determined by the details of the control itself. For example, some controls are documented and review of this documentation may provide evidence about the effective operation of the control. Others may not be documented, such as control activities performed by a computer, where the use of CAATs may be required.

Controls are generally tested throughout the period. Testing at one point in time only may be effective for some areas such as for controls over the entity's physical stock count at the period end. When testing has only covered part of the period, alternative audit procedures should normally be used for the remainder.

Relying on prior periods' assessments

If the auditor plans to rely on evidence about the operating effectiveness of controls obtained in prior periods he should ensure, through observation or inspection, that the controls have not changed. If controls have changed, he must test the operating effectiveness of those controls in the current audit. Even if they have not changed, the ISA requires that the operating effectiveness should be retested at least once every third audit. When there are a number of controls which are not being retested each year, a proportion of them should be tested at each audit.

In considering whether it is acceptable to rely on the testing carried out in prior periods, the auditor considers:

- the effectiveness of other elements of internal control, including the control environment, the entity's monitoring of controls and risk assessment process;

- the characteristics of the control, including whether it is manual or automated;

- the effectiveness of general IT controls;

- the effectiveness of the control and its application by the entity, including the nature and extent of failures of the control in prior audits;

- whether the lack of change in a control is itself a risk, given changing circumstances elsewhere; and

- the risk of material misstatement and the extent of reliance placed on the control.

Where the operation of one or more controls is intended to mitigate a significant risk (see **21.3.6**), evidence about the operating effectiveness of the control must be made in the current period.

Extent of tests of controls

Matters that the auditor considers when deciding on the extent of tests of controls include:

- how frequently the control is performed during the period;

- the length of time during the audit period that the auditor is relying on the operating effectiveness of the control;

- the quality of the audit evidence likely to be obtained;

- the extent to which other controls related to the assertion will provide audit evidence;

- the extent to which the control is relevant to the assessment of risk; and

- expected deviations in the control (although if this is too high, no reliance may be placed on the control).

The more the auditor relies on the operating effectiveness of controls, the greater the extent of testing required.

Where controls are automated, the auditor will not gain additional assurance from increasing the extent of testing of the control. The control should function consistently throughout the period unless the application is changed. Once the auditor is content that the control is operating as intended, usually by testing it once only, testing should concentrate on ensuring that the application is not changed without appropriate change controls and testing.

Substantive procedures

The auditor should plan and perform substantive procedures for each material class of transactions, account balance and disclosure, regardless of their risk. In addition, the auditor is required by the ISA to:

- agree or reconcile information in the financial statements to the underlying accounting records, including agreeing or reconciling information in disclosures, whether such information is obtained from within or outside of the general and subsidiary ledgers; and

- examine material journal entries and other adjustments made during the course of preparing the financial statements.

Where the risk assessment process has identified a significant risk (see **21.3.6**), substantive procedures should be planned and performed in response to that risk. Substantive procedures may be analytical procedures or tests of detail. Substantive analytical procedures are generally more applicable to large volumes of transactions that tend to be predictable over time and suit gathering evidence about existence and valuation assertions. When designing substantive analytical procedures, the auditor should consider:

- the suitability of using substantive analytical procedures given the assertions;

- the reliability of the data, whether internal or external, used to generate ratios and comparisons;

- whether the expected results are sufficiently precise to identify a material misstatement and the desired level of assurance; and

- the amount of any difference in recorded amounts from expected values that is acceptable.

If substantive procedures are performed at an interim date, the auditor should perform further tests (either tests of controls, substantive tests or a combination of both) to cover the remaining time to the period end. The decision whether it is worthwhile performing substantive procedures at an interim date will depend on the:

- control environment and other relevant controls;
- availability of information at the date of the interim procedure;
- the objective of the test;
- the assessed risk of material misstatement;
- the nature of the class of transactions or account balance and related assertions being tested; and
- the ability of the auditor to perform additional tests to cover the period between the interim testing and the period end.

If testing has occurred at an interim date and has detected misstatements, the auditor would usually modify the assessment of risk and the nature, timing or extent of further audit procedures to be performed at the period end.

Relying on prior periods' work

Unlike for tests of controls, it is not sufficient to rely on substantive procedures performed in prior periods to obtain evidence to address a risk of material misstatement in the current period. If any assurance is to be taken from work performed in prior periods, the audit evidence and related subject matter must not change fundamentally. An example would be where legal opinion was obtained about the structure of a securitisation in the prior period, and that securitisation has not changed.

Extent and nature of substantive procedures

The greater the risk of material misstatement, the greater the extent of substantive procedures. Substantive procedures may also be extended if there are unsatisfactory results from the work performed on tests of controls.

For tests of detail, the extent of testing is often thought of in terms of the sample size. ISA (UK) 530 contains details on the use of sampling and other methods to select items for testing (see **Section 26**).

The auditor should also consider whether external confirmation procedures should be performed. External confirmations may be relevant in some situations and further details can be found in **Section 23**. Although external confirmations may provide relevant audit evidence relating to certain assertions, there are some assertions in respect of which they may be less relevant. For example, an external confirmation provides more evidence about the existence of a debtor balance than it does about its recoverability.

Confirmation procedures may also provide an opportunity to obtain evidence about other matters. Bank balance confirmation requests, for example, may be used to seek information about trade finance transactions, guarantees and securities. The decision whether to seek such confirmation will depend on the auditor's risk assessment.

Public interest entities

For public interest entities, the ISA includes an explicit requirement (derived from the Audit Regulation) that the auditor needs to assess the valuation methods applied to the various items in the financial statements including the impact of any changes. He is also required to communicate in his additional report to the audit committee, his assessment of the valuation methods used including the impact of any changes in such methods (see **10.7.2**). Such procedures may also be appropriate for other entities.

21.4.3 Presentation of the financial statements

The ISA requires the auditor to plan and perform procedures to determine that the overall presentation of the financial statements is in line with the requirements of the applicable accounting framework. In making this evaluation, the auditor considers whether the financial statements are presented in a manner that reflects the appropriate:

- classification and description of financial information and the underlying transactions, events and conditions; and

- presentation, structure and content of the financial statements.

21.4.4 Evaluating audit evidence

Throughout the audit, the auditor is required to evaluate whether his original assessment of the risk of material misstatement requires amending. For example, the auditor may be required to amend his assessment as a result of:

- a higher level of misstatements being discovered than planned during the performance of substantive procedures;

- failures of the entity's controls during the period; or

- discrepancies coming to light as a result of the overall analytical review of the financial statements at the completion stage of the audit.

Changes to the assessment may require changes to the nature, timing and extent of the audit procedures.

At the completion of the audit procedures, the auditor is required to conclude whether sufficient appropriate audit evidence has been obtained to reduce the risk of material misstatement in the financial statements to an acceptably low level. The factors influencing what constitutes sufficient appropriate audit evidence are set out at **23.2.2**. Where he concludes that the evidence obtained is not sufficient, the auditor should attempt to gather further information. Where this is not possible, he should issue a qualified or disclaimer of opinion audit report.

21.4.5   Documentation

The auditor should ensure that the following are fully documented:

- overall responses to address the assessed risks of material misstatement at the financial statements level;

- nature, timing and extent of further audit procedures;

- linkage of those procedures with assessed risks at the assertion level;

- results of audit procedures; and

- where using evidence about the operating effectiveness of controls obtained in prior audits, the justification for relying on that work.

The auditor's documentation should demonstrate that information in the financial statements agrees or reconciles with the underlying accounting records, including agreeing or reconciling disclosures.

22 Service organisations

22.1 Introduction

ISA (UK) 402 *Audit Considerations Relating to an Entity using a Service Organisation* was issued in October 2009 and is effective for the audit of financial statements for periods ending on or after 15 December 2010. It was not revised by the FRC but was reissued as ISA (UK) 402 in June 2016.

ISA (UK) 402 sets out requirements on the procedures necessary to assess the impact of a reporting entity's use of a service organisation, specifically:

- understanding the services provided by a service organisation, including internal control;

- responding to the assessed risks of material misstatement;

- subservice organisations;

- responding to the risks of material misstatement;

- fraud, non-compliance with laws and regulations and uncorrected misstatements; and

- reporting by the auditor of the user entity ('the user auditor').

A 'service organisation' is defined for this purpose as a third-party organisation (or segment of a third-party organisation) that provides services to user entities that are part of those entities' information systems relevant to financial reporting. Use of service organisations is often referred to as 'outsourcing'.

Guidance on issuing reports on service organisations is given in AAF 01/06 *Assurance reports on internal controls of service organisations made available to third parties* and ISAE 3402 *Assurance Reports on Controls at a Third Party Service Organisation*. These are covered in **Section 40**.

22.2 Understanding the services provided by a service organisation, including internal control

The auditor is required to identify whether the reporting entity uses service organisations and then to consider the impact of this on the client's internal control, the auditor's assessment of the risk of material misstatement and his procedures. The guidance notes that the outsourcing of an activity by an entity to a service organisation does not relieve its directors of their responsibilities nor does it alter those of the auditor. As not all outsourced activities have a significant effect on the reporting entity's financial statements, the auditor needs to assess initially whether those activities are relevant to financial reporting and hence whether the service provider is a service organisation as defined in **22.1**.

Service organisation services that are relevant to the audit include:

- information processing;

- maintenance of the user entity's accounting records;

- management or custody of assets; and

- initiation or execution of transactions on behalf of the entity.

Examples of ways in which different activities undertaken by service organisations can affect the risk of misstatement are given in **Table 1**.

TABLE 1: Characteristics of service organisation activities which may increase risk

Outsourced Accounting Functions

Degree of risk	Characteristics	Examples
High	• Complex transactions	• Maintenance of both accounting records and preparation of budgets and reports control
	• Those undertaking accounting work need extensive business or specialist knowledge	• Accounting records of retail business
	• Delegated authority to initiate and execute transactions	
	• Effective controls only possible on 'real time' basis	
	• Reversal of outsourcing costly/difficult	

Degree of risk	Characteristics	Examples
	• High cost of performance failure (e.g. misleading management reports leading to poor decision making)	
	• High proportion of finance functions outsourced	
Medium	• Some business knowledge needed but parameters for necessary judgments can be identified and agreed in advance	• Outsourcing of accounting records by a supplier of raw materials
	• Transactions can be initiated but execution requires approval from entity	• Credit control
	• Execution of transactions on instruction from entity	• Leasing arrangements
	• Analytical techniques insufficient for adequate degree of control	
	• Discrete functions outsourced	
Low	• Little requirement for judgment in processing transactions	• Processing salary payments
	• Non-complex transactions	• Preparation of invoices
	• Little business knowledge required	• Data entry
	• Analytical control techniques effective	
	• Effects of failure can be contained	
	• Easy to rearrange/ find alternative service organisations	
	• Low proportion of discrete functions outsourced	

Services provided by a service organisation will be relevant when those services, and the controls over them, effectively form part of the entity's information system relevant to financial reporting. Controls at the service organisation may be relevant to the audit, such as controls over the safeguarding of assets. A service organisation's services will be part of the entity's information system if those services affect any of the following:

- the classes of transactions that are significant to the user entity's financial statements;

- the procedures by which the user entity's transactions are initiated, recorded, processed, corrected as necessary, transferred to the general ledger and reported in the financial statements;

- the related accounting records, supporting information and specific accounts in the user entity's financial statements;

- how the user entity's information system captures events and conditions, other than transactions, that are significant to the financial statements;

- the financial reporting process used to prepare the financial statements; and

- controls surrounding recurring and non-recurring journal entries.

The auditor should obtain and document an understanding of the contract terms, whether agreed orally or in writing, and the way in which the reporting entity monitors the service organisation's activities so that it can meet its fiduciary and other legal responsibilities. This will assist the auditor in his consideration of the impact of the arrangement on his assessment of risk (see **22.3**).

When obtaining an understanding of internal control relevant to the audit, the user auditor evaluates the design and implementation of relevant controls at the user entity that relate to the services provided by the service organisation, including those that are applied to the transactions processed by the service organisation.

For example, if a user entity uses a service organisation to process payroll, the user entity may establish controls over the submission and receipt of payroll information that could prevent, or detect, material misstatements. These controls may include comparing the data submitted to the service organisation with reports received from the service organisation after the data has been processed and recomputing a sample of the payroll amounts for accuracy and reviewing the total payroll amount for reasonableness. In such a situation, the user auditor may perform tests of the user entity's controls over payroll processing that would provide a basis for him to conclude that the user entity's controls are operating effectively for the assertions related to payroll transactions.

The user auditor determines whether a sufficient understanding of the nature and significance of the services provided by the service organisation and their effect on the user entity's internal control relevant to the audit has been obtained to provide a basis for the identification and assessment of risks of material misstatement.

If the auditor is unable to ascertain sufficient information about the operation of controls at the service organisation from the user entity, ISA (UK) 402 requires that he performs one or more of the following procedures:

- obtain a type 1 report on the description and design of controls, or a type 2 report (see **22.2.1**) on the description and design of controls and their operating effectiveness, if available;
- contact the service entity, through the user entity, to obtain specific information;
- visit the service organisation and perform procedures that will provide the necessary information about controls; or
- use another auditor to perform those procedures for him.

22.2.1   *Using a type 1 or type 2 report*

Type 1 and type 2 reports are prepared under International Standards on Assurance Engagements (ISAE) 3402 *Assurance Reports on Controls at a Third Party Service Organisation* with guidance from AAF 01/06 (see **40.7**) and are used to support the auditor's understanding of the service organisation. Type 1 and type 2 reports provide differing levels of assurance to the user auditor and, as a result, have different impacts on the remaining work to be carried out.

A type 1 report is a report on the description and design of the controls at a service organisation and contains:

(i)   the service organisation's description of its system;

(ii)   a written assertion by the service organisation that, in all material respects, and based on suitable criteria, the description fairly presents the service organisation's system as designed and implemented as at the specified date and the controls related to the control objectives stated in the service organisation's description of its system were suitably designed as at the specified date; and

(iii)   a service auditor's assurance report that gives reasonable assurance on (ii) above.

A type 2 report is a report on the description and design and also operating effectiveness of the controls at a service organisation and contains:

(i)   the service organisation's description of its system;

(ii)   a written assertion by the service organisation that, in all material respects, and based on suitable criteria, the description fairly presents the service organisation's system as designed and implemented throughout the specified period, the controls related to the control objectives stated in the service organisation's description of its system were suitably designed throughout the specified period, and the controls operated effectively throughout the specified period; and

(iii) a service auditor's assurance report that gives reasonable assurance on (ii) above and also includes a description of the tests of controls and the results thereof.

In order to determine the sufficiency and appropriateness of the audit evidence provided by the type 1 or type 2 report, the auditor needs to be satisfied as to:

- the service auditor's professional competence and independence from the service organisation; and

- the adequacy of the standards under which the report was issued, particularly where the service auditor practices outside of the United Kingdom.

Where the auditor plans to use a type 1 or type 2 report as audit evidence to support his understanding about the design and implementation of controls at the service organisation, the ISA requires him to:

- evaluate whether the description and design of controls at the service organisation is at a date or for a period that is appropriate for the auditor's purposes;

- evaluate the sufficiency and appropriateness of the evidence provided by the report for the understanding of the user entity's internal control relevant to the audit; and

- determine whether complementary user entity controls identified by the service organisation are relevant to the user entity and, if so, obtain an understanding of whether the user entity has designed and implemented such controls.

22.2.2 Accounting records

Outsourcing all or part of their accounting records does not diminish the responsibilities of those charged with governance in relation to those records. Therefore, for each material element of the accounting records maintained by a service organisation, the auditor should obtain and document an understanding of the way the accounting records are maintained and how those charged with governance ensure the accounting records meet any relevant legal obligations. Under UK company law, those charged with governance must retain ownership of the accounting records and allow the auditor to access them at any time.

The ISA requires that the auditor should assess whether the arrangements for maintaining all or part of the entity's accounting records by a service organisation have any effect on his reporting responsibilities in relation to accounting records.

The guidance notes that the wording of UK company law is such that it requires companies to keep records rather than cause them to be kept, and thus the wording of the contract with the service organisation will need to be reviewed to determine whether the entity retains ownership of those records. It is suggested that the auditor may wish to seek legal advice where there is any doubt on this matter.

22.3   Responding to the assessed risks of material misstatement

The ISA requires the auditor to use his understanding of the arrangement to:

* assess whether he can obtain sufficient appropriate audit evidence on the relevant financial statement assertions from the records held at the reporting entity; and if not

* determine effective procedures to obtain audit evidence either by direct access to the records kept by the service organisation or through information obtained from the service organisation or its auditor.

Where the auditor requires evidence concerning balances representing assets held by or transactions undertaken by the service organisation, he may consider the efficiency and effectiveness of the following procedures:

* inspecting records and documents held by the reporting entity;

* establishing the effectiveness of controls;

* obtaining representations to confirm balances and transactions from the service organisation;

* performing analytical review procedures on the records maintained by the reporting entity or the returns from the service organisation;

* inspecting records and documents held by the service organisation;

* requesting the service organisation auditor or the reporting entity's internal audit function to perform specified procedures; and

* reviewing information from the service organisation and its auditor concerning the design and operation of its controls systems.

As noted in **22.2**, when the user auditor's risk assessment includes an expectation that controls at the service organisation are operating effectively, he obtains evidence about this from one or more of the following:

- obtaining a type 2 report;

- performing appropriate tests of control at the service organisation; or

- using another auditor to perform tests of control at the service organisation on his behalf.

22.4   Subservice organisations

If the service organisation itself outsources some of its activities to another service organisation, the auditor should consider whether those activities are relevant to the audit of the user entity's financial statements. If they are, the requirements of ISA (UK) 402 should be applied also to the operations of the other service organisations.

22.5   Fraud, non-compliance with laws and regulations and uncorrected misstatements

ISA (UK) 402 requires the auditor to enquire of management of the user entity whether the service organisation has reported to them any incidences of fraud, non-compliance with applicable laws and regulations and uncorrected misstatements affecting the financial statements of the user entity. Terms of the contract between the user entity and the service organisation may require that such disclosure is made.

If such incidents have been reported, the auditor should consider any impact they may have on the nature, timing and extent of his audit procedures.

22.6   Reporting

If the auditor is unable to obtain sufficient appropriate audit evidence regarding the services provided by the service organisation which are relevant to the audit of the financial statements, then the auditor should modify his opinion in accordance with ISA (UK) 705 (Revised June 2016) *Modifications to the Opinion in the Independent Auditor's Report* . Such a limitation on scope may arise where:

- the auditor is unable to obtain a sufficient understanding of the services provided by the service organisation and does not have a basis for the identification and assessment of the risks of material misstatement;

- the auditor's risk assessment includes an expectation that controls at the service organisation are operating effectively but he is unable to obtain sufficient appropriate audit evidence about the operating effectiveness of these controls; or

- sufficient appropriate audit evidence is only available from records held at the service organisation and the auditor is unable to obtain direct access to those records.

Whether the auditor expresses a qualified opinion or disclaims an opinion depends on the individual situation and circumstances.

Where the auditor's report is not modified, it should not refer to the work of a service auditor.

If reference to the work of the service auditor is relevant to an understanding of a modification in the auditor's report, the report should make clear that the reference does not diminish the auditor's responsibility for the audit opinion. The auditor may also need to seek the consent of the service auditor before making such a reference.

Examples of modifications in audit reports arising from limitations in scope are shown in **Tables 3** and **5** in **Section 5**.

23 Audit evidence

23.1 Introduction

There are three ISAs covering various elements of the subject of audit evidence. These are:

- ISA (UK) 500 *Audit Evidence*;
- ISA (UK) 501 *Audit Evidence – Specific Considerations for Selected Items*; and
- ISA (UK) 505 *External Confirmations.*

The current versions of these ISAs (UK) are effective for the audit of financial statements for periods ending on or after 15 December 2010. They were not revised by the FRC but were reissued as ISAs (UK) in June 2016. See **1.6.4** for further details. ISAs (UK) 500 and 505 were updated in July 2017 following revisions to ISAs (UK) 250 Section A and 330.

ISA (UK) 500, including the use of management's experts, is considered in **23.2** and **23.3**.

ISA (UK) 501 covers:

- attendance at stocktaking – see **23.5**;
- enquiries about litigation and claims – see **23.6**; and
- segment information – see **23.7**.

ISA (UK) 505 is considered in **23.8**.

In addition to the guidance on external confirmations given in this section, guidance on bank confirmations is contained in **Section 24**.

Professional scepticism is an essential feature of an audit and is necessary to the critical assessment of audit evidence. Following criticism from regulators and other commentators, the exercise of professional scepticism by auditors and the role of standards in influencing this, continue to be matters of debate and an area of focus for standard setters. This is considered in **23.9**.

23.2   The nature of audit evidence

23.2.1   Concept of audit evidence

ISA (UK) 500 *Audit Evidence* requires the auditor to obtain sufficient appropriate audit evidence to be able to draw reasonable conclusions on which to base his opinion. The *Auditor's Code* (see **1.5**) also requires the auditor to act with professional skill which demands an expertise in accumulating and assessing the evidence necessary to form an audit opinion.

Audit evidence is obtained from a combination of enquiry, inspection, observation, tests of controls and substantive procedures (including confirmation, recalculation, reperformance and analytical procedures).

It is defined as information used by the auditor in arriving at the conclusions on which his opinion is based and includes:

- information from source documents and accounting records underlying the financial statement assertions; and

- information from other sources such as previous audits and a firm's client acceptance procedures.

23.2.2   Sufficient appropriate evidence

The ISA contains a discussion on what 'sufficient appropriate evidence' means. Sufficiency is seen as a measure of the quantity of audit evidence, and appropriateness is a measure of its quality, including its relevance and its reliability.

The auditor is rarely able to rely on conclusive evidence, but uses persuasive evidence which is supported by information from different sources. He seeks reasonable, but not absolute, assurance that there are no material misstatements and may choose to rely on sample data, extracted either statistically or judgmentally, in order to form his opinion on a particular balance or class of transaction. Reasonable assurance will be obtained when the auditor has obtained sufficient appropriate audit evidence to reduce audit risk (i.e. the risk that the auditor expresses an inappropriate opinion when the financial statements are materially misstated) to an acceptably low level.

Audit evidence is cumulative in nature and the decision on whether there is sufficient appropriate evidence is a matter for the auditor's judgment and is influenced by:

- the assessment of the nature and degree of risk of material misstatement at both the financial statement level and at the account balance or transaction level;

- the nature of the accounting and internal control systems and the assessment of the control environment;

- the materiality of the item being examined;

- previous experience of the client and the auditor's knowledge of the business;

- the results of auditing procedures and work on preparing the financial statements; and

- the source and reliability of information available.

The reliability of audit evidence can be judged using the following general criteria:

- external evidence, for example, confirmation obtained from third parties, is generally more reliable than internal evidence;

- evidence from the entity's records and systems is generally more reliable when the related accounting and internal control system is satisfactory;

- evidence obtained directly by the auditor is generally more reliable than that obtained from the entity;

- evidence in the form of documents and written representations is generally more reliable than oral representations; and

- original documents are generally more reliable than photocopies or facsimiles.

Where the auditor performs procedures on information produced by the entity, he should first satisfy himself as to the accuracy and completeness of the information. For example, if the auditor is verifying provisions against debtors outstanding at the year end, using an aged debts list prepared by the entity, he should first satisfy himself that the listing is complete and correctly aged by checking invoices raised in the period for inclusion on the listing where appropriate and amounts on the listing back to dated invoices. He also needs to ensure that the information is sufficiently precise and detailed for his purposes, for example, performance measures used by management may not be precise enough to detect material misstatements where the same information is used by the auditor.

Consistency is obviously important in deciding the sufficiency and appropriateness of the evidence obtained – see **23.2.7**. The auditor also needs to consider the relationship between the cost of obtaining evidence and its usefulness bearing in mind that the difficulty and expense of obtaining evidence is not a valid reason for not obtaining it.

23.2.3   Sources of evidence

Some audit evidence is obtained by performing procedures to test the accounting records. For example, analysis and review, reperforming procedures followed in the financial reporting process, and reconciling information may help the auditor to determine that the accounting records are internally consistent and agree to the financial statements.

Where the auditor is able to corroborate evidence from different sources or items of a different nature, he will usually obtain more assurance than from those items considered individually. For example, corroborating information obtained from a source independent of the entity, may increase the assurance the auditor obtains from internally generated information, such as accounting records, minutes of meetings, etc.

23.2.4   Using assertions to gather audit evidence

ISA (UK) 315 (Revised June 2016) *Identifying and Assessing the Risks of Material Misstatement through Understanding the Entity and its Environment* requires that the auditor's consideration of the risk of material misstatement is made at assertion level (see **Section 21**). When seeking to obtain audit evidence from audit procedures, the auditor should consider the extent to which the evidence supports the relevant financial statement assertions.

The term 'assertions' refers to the individual representations made by management and which make up the financial statements. The assertions considered by the auditor are set out in **21.3.6**, although the audit approaches of different firms may use different terminologies.

23.2.5   Audit procedures

The auditor uses audit procedures to:

- obtain an understanding of the entity and its environment and determine audit risk;
- test the operating effectiveness of controls; and
- detect material misstatements at the assertion level.

The objective of testing the operating effectiveness of controls is to test the design of control systems by aiming to establish whether the system is capable of preventing and detecting material misstatement. When testing the operation of controls, the auditor seeks to establish whether the controls have operated for the whole of the period under review. Where controls are not effective, such testing may indicate the existence of audit risk.

Substantive procedures are planned and performed in order to determine audit risk and then in response to the risk of material misstatement assessed at the planning stage. The auditor uses one or more of the types of audit procedure listed in the following paragraphs.

The nature and timing of audit procedures will depend on the information available to the auditor. Where information is held in electronic form, the auditor may carry out Computer Assisted Audit Techniques (CAATs) (see **37.4**).

Inspection of records or documents

This consists of examining records or documents whether internal or external, in paper form, electronic form or other media. It provides evidence of different degrees of persuasiveness depending on the nature and source of the documentation. The criteria used in assessing the reliability of evidence in general are noted at **23.2.2**, and they should be applied to the type of evidence that can be obtained by inspection. For example, depending on the case, different degrees of reliability will apply to documentary evidence:

- created and provided by third parties;
- created by third parties and held by the entity; and
- created and held by the entity.

Some documentation will give direct evidence about existence, but may not provide evidence of ownership or value, for example share or bond certificates.

Inspection of tangible assets

This consists of physical examination of the assets. Again, the inspection of tangible assets provides evidence of their existence but alone is not sufficient to provide evidence of their ownership or value.

Observation

This consists of inspecting a particular process or procedure being performed by others. It is particularly useful where an internal control procedure does not leave an audit trail or for 'one off' procedures such as stocktakes. It is normally used in combination with other procedures.

Enquiry

This consists of seeking information from knowledgeable persons both inside and/or outside the entity. This may either be written or oral. Its reliability will vary depending on its source in a similar way to the evidence resulting from inspection.

An important part of the enquiry process is evaluation of the responses received, which may lead to amending the audit plan or performing additional audit procedures.

Enquiry alone is not sufficient to provide evidence of material misstatement or to confirm the effectiveness of controls. For example, in relation to management intentions, in addition to making enquiries, the auditor should consider management's past history of carrying out its stated intentions and obtain written representation of oral responses.

Confirmation

Confirmation is a type of enquiry and involves obtaining information directly from a third party. For example, a debtors' circularisation obtains confirmation of outstanding balances directly from the entity's debtors. Further information is provided in ISA (UK) 505 (see **23.8**).

Recalculation

Recalculation involves checking the mathematical accuracy of documents or records, and may be done through the use of CAATs (see **37.4**).

Reperformance

This describes the independent reperformance of calculations, for example, the calculations on a sales invoice or on a debtors' listing. Again, CAATs may be used to perform this task.

Analytical procedures

These involve the analysis of relationships between items of financial data both within the financial statements and between the financial statements and other internally and externally produced data. These are discussed in greater detail in **Section 25**.

23.2.6   Selection and sampling of items for testing

Where the auditor designs tests of controls or substantive procedures, he determines the best method of selecting the items for testing so as to be effective in meeting the purpose of the audit procedure. The methods available for selecting the items to test are:

- selecting all items (100% examination);
- selecting specific items; and
- audit sampling.

The auditor chooses which method, or combination of methods, is appropriate depending on the particular circumstances, including the risks related to the assertion being tested and the practicality and efficiency of the different means. Further details on these selection methods are given in **26.4**.

23.2.7   Dealing with inconsistent or potentially unreliable evidence

Where evidence is inconsistent, for example, one piece of evidence leads the auditor to believe a company owns an asset whilst another piece of evidence throws doubt on this, or where the auditor has doubts about the reliability of information to be used as evidence, he will need to consider what modifications or additional procedures are necessary to resolve the matter. He will also need to consider the effect of the matter on other areas of the audit and ultimately on his opinion.

23.3   Management's experts

23.3.1   Using the work of a management's expert

Where information to be used as audit evidence has been prepared using the work of a management's expert, such as actuarial calculations, valuations or engineering data, the auditor should ensure that, to the extent necessary, he:

(a) evaluates the competence, capabilities and objectivity of that expert;

(b) obtains an understanding of the work of that expert; and

(c) evaluates the appropriateness of that expert's work as audit evidence for the relevant assertion.

Where the auditor uses his own expert (as opposed to work of the management's expert), reference should be made to ISA (UK) 620 (Revised June 2016) *Using the Work of an Auditor's Expert* (see **Section 31**).

The nature, timing and extent of audit procedures in relation to work performed by management's experts will be affected by many factors such as:

- the nature and complexity of the matter;

- the risks of material misstatement;

- the availability of alternative sources of evidence;

- the nature, scope and objectives of the management's expert's work;

- whether the management's expert is employed by the entity, or is a party engaged by it to provide relevant services;

- the extent to which management can exercise control or influence over the work of the management's expert;

- whether the management's expert is subject to technical performance standards or other professional or industry requirements;

- the nature and extent of any controls over the management's expert's work;

- the auditor's knowledge and experience of the management's expert's field of expertise; and

- the auditor's previous experience of the work of that expert.

23.3.2 Evaluating the expert's competence, capabilities and objectivity

In order to evaluate the competence, capabilities and objectivity of management's expert, the auditor will need to evaluate evidence from a variety of sources, such as:

- personal experience with previous work of that particular expert;

- discussions with the expert and with others familiar with his work;

- knowledge of the expert's qualifications, membership of a professional body or industry association, licence to practice, etc.;

- published books or papers written by the expert;

- an auditor's expert, where used, who assists the auditor in obtaining sufficient appropriate audit evidence with respect to the information produced by the management's expert.

The auditor may also need to consider the relevance of the management's expert's competence for the matter in question. For example, a particular actuary used by management may specialise in property insurance but have limited expertise regarding pension calculations.

The auditor will also need to consider the objectivity of the management's expert, which may be threatened by a range of circumstances, such as self-interest, advocacy, familiarity, self-review and intimidation threats. Although safeguards may reduce such threats, they are unlikely to eliminate all threats to a management's expert's objectivity.

23.3.3 Obtaining an understanding of the expert's work

The auditor needs to obtain an understanding of the work of the management's expert including:

- whether the expert's work has any areas of speciality within it that are relevant to the audit;

- whether any professional standards or regulatory requirements apply;

- what assumptions and methods are used by the management's expert and whether they are generally accepted within that expert's field and appropriate for financial reporting purposes; and

- the nature of the internal and external data the expert uses.

23.3.4 Evaluating the appropriateness of the expert's work

In order to evaluate the appropriateness of the management's expert's work as audit evidence, the auditor needs to consider:

- the relevance and reasonableness of the expert's findings or conclusions, their consistency with other audit evidence, and whether they are appropriately reflected in the financial statements;

- the relevance and reasonableness of any significant assumptions and methods used by the expert; and

- the relevance, completeness and accuracy of any source data used by the expert.

23.4 Specific considerations

ISA (UK) 501 *Audit evidence – specific considerations for selected items* provides guidance on:

- attendance at stocktaking;

- enquiries about litigation and claims; and

- segment information.

These are discussed in **23.5**, **23.6** and **23.7**.

23.5 Attendance at stocktaking

23.5.1 Introduction

ISA (UK) 501 sets outs requirements and provides guidance for the auditor regarding audit evidence in relation to inventory where this is material to the financial statements. Practice Note 25 *Attendance at stocktaking* which used to provide additional guidance in this area was withdrawn by the FRC in 2017.

23.5.2 Audit evidence

Where inventory is material, ISA (UK) 501 requires the auditor to obtain appropriate evidence by:

(a) attending a stocktake, unless it is 'impracticable' to do so; and

(b) performing audit procedures over the entity's final inventory records to determine whether they accurately reflect actual inventory count results.

As part of his stocktake attendance procedures, the auditor should:

(a) evaluate management's instructions and procedures for recording and controlling the results of the entity's physical inventory counting;

(b) observe the performance of management's count procedures;

(c) inspect the inventory; and

(d) perform test counts.

23.5.3 Planning

Table 1 outlines a number of matters that may be relevant in planning attendance at a physical inventory counting (or in designing and performing audit procedures).

TABLE 1: Planning

Planning procedures may include, for example, consideration of:

- risks of material misstatement related to inventory;

- the nature of the internal control related to inventory;

- whether adequate procedures are expected to be established and proper instructions issued for physical inventory counting;

- the timing of physical inventory counting;

- whether the entity maintains a perpetual inventory system;

- the locations at which inventory is held, including the materiality of the inventory and the risks of material misstatement at different locations, in deciding at which locations attendance is appropriate. ISA (UK) 600 (Revised June 2016) may be relevant if other auditors are involved with regard to attendance at stocktakes at a remote location; and

- whether the assistance of an auditor's expert is needed. ISA (UK) 620 (Revised June 2016) deals with the use of an auditor's expert to assist the auditor to obtain sufficient appropriate audit evidence.

23.5.4 Evaluation of management's instructions and procedures

Matters relevant in evaluating management's instructions and procedures for recording and controlling the physical inventory counting include whether they address, for example:

- the application of appropriate control activities, for example, collection of used physical inventory count records, accounting for unused physical inventory count records, and count and recount procedures;
- the accurate identification of the stage of completion of work in progress, of slow-moving, obsolete or damaged items and of inventory owned by a third party, for example, on consignment;
- the procedures used to estimate physical quantities, where applicable, such as may be needed in estimating the physical quantity of a coal pile; and
- control over the movement of inventory between areas and the shipping and receipt of inventory before and after the cut-off date.

23.5.5 Observation, inspection and test counts

Observing the performance of management's count procedures, for example those relating to control over the movement of inventory before, during and after the count, assists the auditor in obtaining audit evidence that management's instructions and count procedures are adequately designed and implemented. In addition, the auditor may obtain copies of cutoff information, such as details of the movement of inventory, to assist the auditor in performing audit procedures over the accounting for such movements at a later date.

Inspecting inventory when attending physical inventory counting assists the auditor in ascertaining the existence of the inventory (though not necessarily its ownership), and in identifying, for example, obsolete, damaged or ageing inventory.

Performing test counts, for example by tracing items selected from management's count records to the physical inventory and tracing items selected from the physical inventory to management's count records, provides audit evidence about the completeness and the accuracy of those records. In addition to recording the auditor's test counts, obtaining copies of management's completed physical inventory count records assists the auditor in performing subsequent audit procedures to determine whether the entity's final inventory records accurately reflect actual inventory count results.

23.5.6 Auditor unable to attend physical count

If the auditor is unable to attend physical inventory counting due to unforeseen circumstances, he should make or observe some physical counts on an alternative date and perform audit procedures on intervening transactions.

If attendance at physical inventory counting is impracticable, for example where the nature or location of the inventory may pose physical threats to the safety of the auditor, the auditor will need to perform alternative audit procedures to obtain sufficient appropriate audit evidence regarding the existence and condition of inventory.

In some cases where attendance is impracticable, alternative audit procedures, for example inspection of documentation of the subsequent sale of specific inventory items acquired or purchased prior to the physical inventory counting, may provide sufficient appropriate audit evidence about the existence and condition of inventory.

Where it is not possible to obtain sufficient appropriate audit evidence regarding the existence and condition of inventory by performing alternative audit procedures, the auditor will need to modify his audit opinion as a result of the scope limitation.

23.5.7   *Inventory held by third parties*

If inventory under the custody and control of a third party is material, the auditor is required to perform one or both of the following:

- request confirmation from the third party as to the quantities and condition of inventory held on behalf of the entity; and

- perform inspection or other audit procedures appropriate in the circumstances.

Other procedures may include:

- attending, or arranging for another auditor to attend, the third party's physical counting of inventory, if practicable;

- obtaining another auditor's report, or a service auditor's report, on the adequacy of the third party's internal control for ensuring that inventory is properly counted and adequately safeguarded (see **Section 22**);

- inspecting documentation regarding inventory held by third parties, for example, warehouse receipts; and

- requesting confirmation from other parties when inventory has been pledged as collateral.

23.6   Enquiries about litigation and claims

Requirements and guidance for the auditor when dealing with pending litigation against the company on which he is reporting is given in ISA (UK) 501.

In addition, useful guidance can be found in the old, but still relevant, ICAEW statement AUDIT 2/95 – *The Ascertainment and Confirmation of Contingent Liabilities Arising from pending Legal Matters* which covers the auditor's problems concerning contingencies arising from pending litigation against the entity upon which he is reporting.

23.6.1 Audit procedures

The auditor should design and perform audit procedures to determine whether a risk of material misstatement may arise from any litigation or claims involving the entity. These must include:

- enquiries of management and, where applicable, others within the entity;

- reviewing minutes of meetings with those charged with governance and correspondence between the entity and its legal advisers; and

- reviewing legal expense accounts.

Procedures the auditor may use to verify the existence of claims, although they will not necessarily provide sufficient evidence of the likely amount that the company may be responsible for, include:

- reviewing the system of recording claims and the procedure for bringing these to the attention of management;

- discussing with management arrangements for instructing solicitors;

- examining board minutes and correspondence for potential claims;

- examining legal expense accounts, bills from solicitors or estimates of unbilled charges;

- obtaining a list of matters referred to solicitors with estimates of the possible ultimate liabilities;

- making enquiries of those charged with governance; and

- obtaining written representations that there are no further matters of which the directors are aware.

If the auditor assesses a risk of material misstatement regarding litigation or claims that have been identified, or where audit procedures indicate that other material litigation or claims might exist, the auditor must seek direct communication with the entity's external legal advisers. This should be done through a letter of enquiry prepared by management and sent by the auditor requesting that the legal advisers communicate directly with the auditor. If management refuses to give permission for this communication or the legal advisers refuse, or are prohibited from responding appropriately, and the auditor is unable to obtain sufficient appropriate evidence from alternative procedures, then he will modify his opinion (see **Section 5**).

The auditor may make a general enquiry to the legal advisor, asking the advisor to inform the auditor of any litigation and claims of which they are aware, together with an assessment of the outcomes and the financial implications. However, the Council of the Law Society has advised solicitors in the UK that they are not recommended to comply with such general requests for information. As such, the auditor may seek communication through a letter of specific enquiry which includes:

- a list of litigation and claims;

- where available, management's assessment of the outcome of each identified litigation and claim, along with management's estimate of the financial implications; and

- a request that the legal advisor confirms the reasonableness of management's assessments and provides further information if management's list is considered to be incomplete or incorrect.

Example extracts from a letter of enquiry to be sent to the client's legal advisor are included in **Tables 2** and **3**. They are to be typed on the client's headed notepaper and sent out by the auditor.

The example in **Table 2** is to be used in situations where management is not aware of litigation or claims that the auditor considers to be relevant to his audit and **Table 3** in situations where management is already aware of litigation or claims that the auditor considers to be relevant to his audit.

TABLE 2: Example of a 'negative' enquiry

Dear Sirs

[*Client name/List of companies*]

In connection with the preparation and audit of our accounts for the year ended [*date*], we as the directors of the company/ies stated above, have confirmed to our auditors that there are no litigation or claims on which you have been consulted greater than £[*amount*].

We should be grateful if you would write directly to our auditors on the following:

(1) Confirming that you are not aware of any litigation or claims on which you have been consulted greater than £[*amount*]. If this is not the case, providing detail of the litigation or claims including:

    (a) an assessment of the outcome of the litigation or claim;

    (b) an estimate of the financial implications; and

    (c) an estimate of the legal costs to complete.

---

(2)   Details of monies held by you on behalf of the company/ies; and

(3)   Giving an estimate of the amount of any unbilled fees and expenses due to you at [*date*].

Please send your response to:

For the attn of: [*Name*]

[*Name of Audit Firm*]

[*Audit Firm address*]

Your letter should include matters that existed at [*date*] and during the period from that date to the date of your letter.

Yours faithfully

_____

[*Client Signatory*]

TABLE 3: Example of a 'positive' enquiry

Dear Sirs

[*Client name/List of companies*]

In connection with the preparation and audit of our accounts for the year ended [*date*], we as the directors of the company/ies stated above, have given our auditors details of litigation and claims on which you have been consulted. These are as follows:

[*List of litigation and claims. Where available this to include management's assessment of the outcome of each identified litigation or claim and their estimate of the financial implications, including costs involved.*]

Claims where the outcome is likely to be less than £[*amount*] have been excluded.

We should be grateful if you would write directly to our auditors on the following:

(1)   Confirming whether in your opinion our assessments are reasonable;

(2)   Providing any additional information that you consider necessary including an explanation of those matters on which your view may differ from those stated;

(3)   Confirming that you are not aware of any items which should be included but which have been omitted;

(4)   Details of monies held by you on behalf of the company/ies; and

(5)   Giving an estimate of the amount of any unbilled fees and expenses due to you at [*date*].

> Please send your response to:
>
> For the attn of: [*Name*]
>
> [*Name of Audit Firm*]
>
> [*Audit Firm address*]
>
> Your letter should include matters that existed at [*date*] and during the period from that date to the date of your letter.
>
> Yours faithfully
>
> _____
>
> [*Client Signatory*]

There may also be situations where the auditor considers it necessary to meet with the entity's legal advisers to discuss the likely outcome of claims. This may be the case where the auditor determines the matter is a significant risk or is complex, or if there is disagreement between management and the entity's legal advisers. Where such meetings take place, they usually include a representative of management and they take place with management's permission.

Where there are matters which are being dealt with by solicitors but the auditor is unable to take photocopies of documents because of legal privilege, he should prepare file notes of the evidence he has reviewed.

There are occasions when solicitors do not reply directly to requests on the grounds that letters written concerning the merits of litigation involving a client would be discoverable by the other party to the litigation. In such situations, the auditor needs to consider the adequacy of the evidence available to him to support the treatment and disclosure of the issue in the financial statements.

23.6.2 *Written representations*

The auditor also needs to obtain written representations from management and those charged with governance that all known actual or possible litigation and claims that should be considered in relation to the financial statements have been disclosed to the auditor and accounted for and disclosed in accordance with the applicable financial reporting framework.

23.7 Segment information

When segmental information is material to the financial statements, the auditor should plan and perform procedures to obtain sufficient appropriate audit evidence about the presentation and disclosure of the segment information. This will usually be by:

- obtaining an understanding of the methods used by management to determine the segmental information and:

  - evaluating whether such methods are likely to result in disclosure in accordance with the financial reporting framework; and

  - where necessary, testing the application of those methods; and

- performing analytical or other procedures considered appropriate in the circumstances.

This is likely to involve discussion with those charged with governance about the techniques used to determine the segmental information and analytical techniques. Guidance is given in ISA (UK) 501.

23.8   External confirmations

23.8.1   Use of external confirmations

As stated in **23.2.2**, audit evidence is more reliable when it is obtained from independent sources outside the entity. ISA (UK) 505 provides guidance on using external confirmations to provide sufficient appropriate audit evidence at assertion level.

External confirmations are frequently used in connection with account balances and their components, such as debtors' circularisations, which are discussed in detail in **23.8.2**. However, they need not be limited to this and may be used to confirm the terms of agreements or transactions an entity has with third parties. Examples of where external confirmations may be used are:

- bank balances and other information with bankers (see **Section 24**);

- stocks held by third parties at bonded warehouses for processing or on consignment;

- property title deeds held by lawyers or financiers for safe custody or as security;

- investments purchased from stockbrokers but not delivered at the balance sheet date;

- loans from lenders; and

- accounts payable and receivable balances.

The assertions covered by external confirmations will vary. For example, in the case of goods held on consignment, evidence will be obtained about existence and rights and obligations assertions, but not about the value. Confirmation about the completeness assertion can be obtained by contacting certain parties. For example, evidence about completeness of accounts payable balances can be obtained by circularising suppliers with a nil balance at the year end to determine whether all liabilities to them have been recorded. This means that external confirmation requests must be tailored to the specific audit objective.

All confirmation requests are usually sent on the entity's headed paper and contain the management's authorisation to disclose the information requested. ISA (UK) 505 states that in order to have control over the process, the auditor must design the confirmation request, determine the parties to contact and the information to be requested, send the requests himself and make all follow up requests, where applicable. All responses should be sent directly to the auditor, not to the entity.

The auditor may use positive or negative confirmations, or a combination of both. Positive confirmations ask respondents to reply and either confirm information or provide data themselves. Negative confirmations ask for responses only in the event of a disagreement with the information provided in the request. There is an additional risk with negative confirmations that the auditor will assume that information was correct when the respondent simply chooses not to respond. The auditor should not use negative confirmation requests as the sole substantive audit procedure to address an assessed risk of material misstatement unless:

- the risk of material misstatement has been assessed as low and the related controls have been assessed as operating effectively;

- the population subject to negative confirmation comprises a large number of small, homogeneous account balances, transactions or conditions;

- a very low exception rate is expected; and

- the auditor is not aware of circumstances or conditions that would cause recipients of negative confirmation requests to disregard such requests.

With positive confirmations, the response rate tends to be lower the more information the auditor requests. However, by requesting information from respondents, the value of audit evidence is greater than where they are asked only to confirm a balance included in the request. In order to obtain good quality responses, the auditor should consider to whom the confirmation request is addressed.

If those charged with governance refuse to allow the auditor to obtain direct confirmations, the auditor should consider whether this is reasonable, whether alternative suitable audit evidence is available and whether a limitation of audit scope has arisen. Similarly, where no response is obtained from a positive confirmation or where the response has not provided sufficient reliable evidence, the auditor should perform alternative procedures. Where no response has been obtained he would normally first attempt to contact the recipient of the confirmation to elicit a response.

ISA (UK) 505 requires that where the auditor has doubts about the reliability of a response he should consider whether additional procedures are required. Doubts about the reliability of a response may arise because it was not received by the auditor directly or appeared not to come from the original intended confirming party. If a confirming party uses a third party to coordinate its response, the auditor should perform procedures to confirm that the respondent was indeed authorised to respond on behalf of the original contact.

Once any alternative procedures have been performed, the auditor evaluates whether the results in total have provided sufficient appropriate audit evidence, and where this is not the case, he considers the implications for his report.

23.8.2 Debtors' confirmations

As noted in **23.8.1**, the auditor may decide to carry out a circularisation of the company's trade debtors as part of his audit procedures.

The auditor cannot approach the debtors directly as only the client can authorise third parties to divulge information to the auditor but generally, if asked, the management will authorise the circularisation. Where the client refuses, the auditor needs to consider whether he is able to obtain sufficient alternative evidence and the implications for his report.

Where a circularisation is performed on a sample basis, it may not provide sufficient evidence on its own, but may influence the extent of any other tests carried out.

There are two methods that can be used when requesting information from the debtor. These are:

- *positive*: where the debtor is requested to confirm the accuracy of the balance shown or state in what respect he disagrees; or

- *negative*: where the debtor only replies if the amount stated is disputed.

In either case, the reply should be sent directly to the auditor. The choice of method will be a matter for the auditor's judgment, but there are certain factors which may influence this decision, including:

- the strength of the system of internal controls;

- whether there are any suspicions of irregularities;
- the number and size of accounts;
- whether there are amounts which are likely to be in dispute; and
- the number of bookkeeping errors.

Where there are doubts about the accuracy of the sales ledger or where there is a small number of large balances, more confidence will be gained from a positive circularisation. However, if errors are not expected or there is a large number of small balances then a negative one may be more appropriate.

In most cases, a sample of debtors' balances based on the complete population will be tested. However, the following should be considered when selecting the sample:

- old, unpaid accounts;
- accounts written off during the period;
- accounts with credit balances;
- accounts with nil balances; and
- accounts which have been paid by the date of the examination.

The request is usually accompanied by a statement of the account, either the normal monthly statement if the circularisation is carried out at the same time as these are sent out, or a specially printed one if the circularisation is at any other time. Where a positive response is required, a pre-paid reply envelope is normally included.

The request may be as a specially prepared letter or as an attachment to the statement. An example of a positive circularisation is shown in **Table 4**.

Where requests are returned as undelivered, they should be sent to the auditor, who will need to consider what action to take.

When the positive method is used and replies are not received, the auditor should make every effort to ensure that some response is obtained. It may be that a member of the client's staff can be used to do this, but the auditor will need to ensure that the clearance procedure is properly performed. It may be necessary to use other audit tests to provide evidence of the validity of the debtor where no reply is received in a positive circularisation, as every item selected must be concluded upon.

The responses may indicate inaccuracies in the part of the population that is not tested and further work may be necessary.

TABLE 4: Example of positive debtors' circularisation letter

[Client entity letter head]

[Trade Debtor Name and Address]

Dear Sir

As part of their normal audit procedures, we have been requested by our auditors, ABC & Co, to ask you to confirm direct to them the balance on your account at 31 December 20 ... This request is made for audit purposes only and remittances should be sent to us in the normal way.

According to our records, the balance at that date in our favour was as shown by the enclosed statement of your account. If the balance is in agreement with that shown by your records, please sign the confirmation below and return it in the enclosed reply-paid envelope to ABC & Co. Please do this even if the account has been settled.

If the balance is not in agreement with that shown by your records, will you please send the confirmation to our auditors showing, if possible, details of the items making up the difference.

Your co-operation in this matter is greatly appreciated.

Yours faithfully

[Client]

....

ABC & Co Auditors

1 High Street

London

Dear Sirs

We confirm that according to our records a balance of £ ... was owing by us to XYZ plc at 31 December 20 ...

Name of company or individual: _____

Signed: _____

Position held: _____

Items making up difference if any: _____

23.9 Auditor scepticism

23.9.1 Background

Professional scepticism is an essential feature of an audit, particularly in relation to the auditor's evaluation of the sufficiency and appropriateness of audit evidence. ISAs (UK) define professional scepticism as 'an attitude that includes a questioning mind, being alert to conditions which may indicate possible misstatement due to error or fraud, and a critical assessment of audit evidence'.

In recent years, a number of papers have been issued on the subject, including:

- in August 2010, the Auditing Practices Board's Discussion Paper *Auditor Scepticism: Raising the Bar* following challenges from regulators on whether sufficient auditor scepticism was shown by audit firms in relation to the banking crisis;

- in March 2012, a feedback paper based on the responses received, together with a further APB Paper *Professional Scepticism: Establishing a Common Understanding and Reaffirming its Central Role in Delivering Audit Quality*;

- in February 2012, the IAASB issued a question and answer paper on the issue; and

- in December 2015, the IAASB issued an *Invitation to Comment, Enhancing Audit Quality in the Public Interest: A Focus on Professional Skepticism, Quality Control and Group Audits.*

23.9.2 A sceptical mind

The papers all accept that a sceptical mind is a requirement of a rigorous audit performed with due professional care. The degree of scepticism required is less clear cut. Too little scepticism influences both the effectiveness and efficiency of the audit, too much risks an unnecessary increase in costs.

Prior to commencement of an audit, an auditor may have a neutral mindset (that is he does not assume either that the financial statements are misstated or correct or that management are honest or dishonest) or a more questioning approach, sometimes known as 'presumptive doubt'. Both ISA (UK) 200 (Revised June 2016) *Overall Objectives of the Independent Auditor and the Conduct of an Audit in Accordance with International Standards on Auditing (UK)* and ISA (UK) 240 (Revised June 2016) *The Auditor's Responsibilities Relating to Fraud in an Audit of Financial Statements* suggest that the auditor should lean towards holding a position of presumptive doubt at the start of the audit 'recognising the possibility that a material misstatement due to fraud could exist'. This initial mindset is largely a personal attribute, and audit firms need to consider a number of character traits which underlie auditor scepticism when recruiting auditors:

- curiosity and a questioning mind;
- deferral of judgment and not making premature conclusions;
- understanding management behaviour and motivations;
- self-confidence; and
- freedom of action.

Such a sceptical mindset can be acquired or learned through effective training and procedures and auditors are also likely to become more sceptical when they have been personally involved in an investigation of an audit failure.

Audit firm procedures are also of particular importance when responding to negative findings from audit testing. The nature and extent of additional work to be performed is likely to be a decision taken by the hierarchy of the audit team and will be strongly influenced by the firm's policies, procedures and methodologies.

23.9.3 *Throughout the audit*

An attitude of professional scepticism is necessary throughout all stages of the audit, it is not simply something to attempt to document at the end of the engagement.

At the acceptance stage, the engagement partner should be challenging the integrity of the client. This top down approach is essential and the partner should drive the audit approach from planning through to sign off and he should encourage staff to adopt a more questioning mentality. Its importance must be stressed at the audit team discussion in relation to fraud (see **16.4.2**) and the engagement partner should set expectations regarding the importance of professional scepticism through his direction and supervision of the engagement, particularly in his review of the work involved. Due to the characteristics of fraud, which may include sophisticated schemes, concealment and collusion, professional scepticism is particularly relevant when considering fraudulent activity. The engagement partner should also encourage members of the audit team to seek guidance on difficult or contentious matters.

Professional scepticism also includes being alert to audit evidence that contradicts other evidence obtained or causes the auditor to question the reliability of documents or responses by management. This requires the auditor to assess audit evidence critically, and exercise judgment in reaching conclusions. Professional scepticism is closely interrelated with professional judgment and both are key elements of audit quality.

Whilst scepticism is important at all stages of the audit, it is particularly relevant where there are areas which are more complex, significant or highly judgmental, such as:

- accounting estimates and related disclosures;

- going concern, particularly when evaluating management's plans for the future;

- related party relationships and transactions;

- consideration of laws and regulations; and

- the audit of significant unusual or highly complex transactions.

Audit scepticism should be clearly documented in working papers, particularly in relation to discussions with those charged with governance and where difficult or contentious issues have been discussed between members of the audit team or experts from others areas in the firm. Documentation needs to show, for example that where any doubts arose about an explanation provided, the audit team have questioned the entity appropriately and not just taken the client at their word.

Reviewers should also review with an open mind, not placing any reliance on, nor forming expectations based on the previous year's audit. Every review should be treated with the same sceptical attitude as if it were a new client.

23.9.4 *The growing importance of scepticism*

Changes in accounting requirements, particularly the increase in estimates involved in preparing financial statements in accordance with IFRS means that auditor scepticism is increasingly important in determining audit quality. Auditor scepticism should be directed at management, to challenge them about the appropriateness of accounting estimates, and also directed inward to the audit team to determine whether appropriate audit evidence has been obtained to support management's estimates.

The *Auditor Scepticism: Raising the Bar* paper suggested that findings from audit failures, as well as reports from audit regulators tended to show audit scepticism may have been lacking. The paper cites the following particular areas of concern:

- over reliance on management representations;

- failure to investigate conflicting explanations; and

- failure to obtain appropriate third party confirmations.

Judgments relating to the fair value of impairment of goodwill and other intangibles were noted as lacking, with audit firms tending to look for evidence to corroborate management's valuations rather than seeking to challenge them.

23.9.5   Difficulties for audit firms

The *Auditor Scepticism: Raising the Bar* paper notes the difficulties facing firms in today's markets where costs and profitability are increasingly under scrutiny and typically a sceptical approach may be more expensive in terms of both costs and time. This is of particular importance for listed clients who are likely to have set their reporting deadline prior to the commencement of the audit, and where delays caused by additional audit procedures may damage the client relationship. The paper does point out, however, that too little scepticism can lead to audit failures which can expose the firm to litigation and reputational damage in the long and medium term.

23.9.6   Improving auditor scepticism

Audit firms can improve audit scepticism by employing staff with the appropriate attitude (perhaps through the increased use of electronic screening of character traits) and by having effective training and development programmes.

However, classroom training can only be effective if it is reinforced through the culture of the firm. In part, this will be through the firm's mentoring and compensation system, by rewarding those who demonstrate the required skills.

Auditors also need to be aware of the dangers of 'detachment' associated with highly complex but standardised audit methodologies, and their effect on scepticism. As audit firms take advantage of electronic working papers, checklists and schedules there is the danger that the auditor becomes distanced from observing and inspecting the company's operations, spending increasingly large proportions of time away from discussions with clients or review of client records, and focusing instead on sitting in the audit room completing electronic schedules. A return to asking more open questions of clients may improve the levels of audit scepticism, as well as providing audit juniors with invaluable experience which will make them more effective reviewers of work at a later date.

Teams should also be warned against asking clients to prepare too many schedules and analyses prior to the audit commencing as academic research suggests that, whilst reducing audit costs, such client co-operation arrangements may make the auditor over-trusting.

A useful summary of conditions which would help the auditor demonstrate scepticism was included in the Feedback paper issued by the APB in

2012 following comments received on the *Auditor Scepticism: Raising the Bar* paper. These are set out in **Table 5**.

TABLE 5: Conditions necessary for professional scepticism

The individual auditor

- develop a good understanding of the entity and its business;

- have a questioning mind and be willing to challenge management assertions;

- assess critically the information and explanations obtained in the course of his work and corroborate them;

- seek to understand management motivations for possible misstatement of the financial statements;

- investigate the nature and cause of deviations or misstatements identified and avoid jumping to conclusions without appropriate audit evidence;

- be alert for evidence that is inconsistent with other evidence obtained or calls into question the reliability of documents and responses to enquiries; and

- have the confidence to challenge management and the persistence to follow things through to a conclusion – even if predisposed to agree with management's assertion, the auditor should actively consider the alternative views and challenge management to demonstrate that they are not more appropriate.

Engagement teams

- have good business knowledge and experience;

- actively consider in what circumstances management numbers may be misstated, whether due to fraud or error, and the possible sources of misstatement, notwithstanding existing knowledge and relationships;

- develop a good understanding of the entity and its business in order to provide a basis for identifying unusual events or transactions and share information on a regular basis;

- partners and managers are actively involved in assessing risk and planning the audit procedures to be performed – they think about the changes that are taking place in the entity and its environment and plan audit tests that are responsive to them;

- partners and managers actively lead and participate in audit team planning meetings to discuss the susceptibility of the entity's financial statements to material misstatement including through fraud and the misuse of related parties;

- partners and managers are accessible to other staff during the audit and encourage them to consult with them on a timely basis;

- engagement teams document their key audit judgments and conclusions, especially those reported to the audit committee, in a way that clearly demonstrates that they have exercised an appropriate degree of challenge to management and professional scepticism. In particular, the reasons why the audit team concurs with management's assertions are clearly articulated in a way that, where appropriate, discusses the appropriateness of reasonably credible alternative views and the reasons why they have not been adopted; and

- partners and managers bring additional scepticism to the audit through taking the steps necessary to carry out, face to face where appropriate, a diligent challenge and review of the audit work performed, and the adequacy of the documentation prepared, by other members of the engagement team.

Audit firms

- the culture within the firm emphasises the importance of:

    - understanding and pursuing the perspective of the shareholders (and other stakeholders) of the audited entity in making audit judgments;

    - coaching less experienced staff to foster appropriate scepticism;

    - sharing experiences about difficult audit judgments within the firm;

    - consultation with others about difficult audit judgments; and

    - supporting audit partners when they need to take and communicate difficult audit judgments;

- scepticism is embedded in the firm's training and competency frameworks used for evaluating and rewarding partner and staff performance;

- the firm requires rigorous engagement quality control reviews that challenge engagement teams' judgments and conclusions; and

- firm methodologies and review processes emphasise the importance of, and provide practical support for the auditor in:

    - developing a thorough understanding of the entity's business and its environment, sufficient to enable the auditor to carry out a robust risk assessment through his own fresh eyes;

    - identifying issues early in the planning cycle to allow adequate time for them to be investigated and resolved;

    - rigorously taking such steps as are appropriate to the scale and complexity of the financial reporting systems, to identify unusual transactions;

    - changing risk assessments, materiality and the audit plan in response to audit findings;

    - documenting audit judgments in a conclusive rather than a conclusionary manner and therefore setting out not only the conclusion but also the rationale for the conclusion, relating it to the nature of the challenges raised in the underlying work and reviews, the strength of the evidence obtained and the perspective of shareholders (and other stakeholders);

- raising matters with the audit committee (or those charged with governance) in relation to which the auditor believes the perspective of shareholders (and other stakeholders) about the treatment or disclosure of the matter in the financial statements or related narrative reports could well be different from that adopted by the entity; and

- ensuring that the disclosures relating to such matters are carefully assessed to ensure that those of relevance to shareholders (and other stakeholders) are sufficient and appropriate in the circumstances, having regard to the auditor's consideration of the true and fair view.

The role of audit committees and management

Both the audit committee and management will also have an important role in influencing the scepticism the auditor is able to exhibit. The audit committee should:

- promote a culture which ensures staff respond constructively to challenges from the auditor;

- challenge whether the auditor has a sufficiently deep understanding of the entity and its environment to perform the risk assessment;

- ensure that contentious issues which have been resolved between management and auditor are brought to the attention of the audit committee; and

- understand whether the challenge made by the auditor was rational, whether alternative conclusions were considered and why the final judgment was considered to be the most appropriate of the alternatives.

24 Bank confirmations

24.1 Introduction

Until recently, guidance on the form of request letters, as agreed between the auditing profession and the BBA (formerly British Bankers' Association), was included in Practice Note 16 *Bank Reports for Audit Purposes,* the latest version of which was issued in February 2011. However, in July 2017, the FRC issued ISA (UK) 330 (Revised July 2017) *The Auditor's Responses to Assessed Risks*, with conforming amendments to ISA (UK) 505 *External Confirmations*, effective for audits of financial statements for periods commencing on or after 15 December 2017. The revisions are intended to integrate the guidance relating to obtaining bank reports for audit purposes into the auditing standards and, consequently, the FRC has withdrawn Practice Note 16 from the date from which the revised standard is effective.

24.2 Audit considerations

ISA (UK) 330 requires that the auditor perform substantive procedures for each material class of transactions, account balance and disclosure. The auditor must also perform substantive procedures that are specifically responsive to any identified significant risk.

In determining the nature and extent of substantive procedures to apply, the auditor should consider whether external confirmations are to be performed and the extent to which they will provide relevant audit evidence. In this respect, it is noted that as well as providing evidence in relation to balances, a bank confirmation request may provide relevant evidence in relation to other matters such as guarantees, assets pledged as security, trade finance or other banking arrangements. Depending on his risk assessment, the auditor should take this into consideration when deciding whether to seek confirmation from the bank and the form such a request should take.

24.3 Request letters

The BBA is now formally part of UK Finance. It has, however, retained its old website and template request letters and guidance on their use remain available at www.bba.org.uk/policy/financial-and-risk-policy/financialreporting/audit/instructions-for-using-pn16-templates.

When using these templates, auditors need to provide the customer's main sort code and account number for each legal entity on their audit request and a facility account number for trade finance or derivative and commodity trading information (if required). This will enable the banks to find the right details for their customer and prevent them from searching for facilities that may not exist. For requests submitted by paper or email, there are three specially designed request templates to help auditors gather relevant information:

- standard (which includes the option to request additional information on trade finance and derivative and commodity trading);

- fast-track (only to be used in circumstances whereby the reporting deadline is a month or less after the year end/audit confirmation date); and

- incomplete information (use this form in exceptional circumstances; the auditor will be expected to acknowledge that the bank's response may take longer than usual to process).

24.4 Authority

Customers have to give explicit authority to their banks before any information can be released to their auditor. Where possible, this should take the form of an ongoing standing authority rather than as a separate authority each time information is requested.

Although auditors do not need to provide a new Authority to Disclose (ATD) for a client each time they submit an audit request, auditors should ensure that the ATD for each client is reviewed with that client and make sure all legal entities are covered and the authorisation signatures are appropriate.

Auditors should also note that a new authority will be needed in the case of a new audit entity and an updated authority will be needed in the case of entity changes (e.g. new group entities/auditor changes).

24.5 Electronic confirmation

Online confirmation is becoming increasingly popular as a faster, more efficient way to obtain bank confirmations. In 2014, the BBA also launched BBA Confirmations (bba.confirmation.com), to provide a secure online solution for performing audit confirmations.

25 Analytical procedures

25.1 Introduction

ISA (UK) 315 (Revised June 2016) *Identifying and Assessing the Risks of Material Misstatement through Understanding the Entity and its Environment* requires the auditor to use analytical procedures as part of his risk assessment procedures (see **21.3.2**) and ISA (UK) 330 (Revised July 2017) *The Auditor's Responses to Assessed Risks* contains standards and guidance relating to the use of substantive analytical procedures when responding to assessed risks (see **21.4**). ISA (UK) 520 *Analytical Procedures* sets out additional requirements and guidance when performing substantive analytical procedures and also requires the use of analytical procedures near the end of the audit when the auditor is forming an overall conclusion on the financial statements.

The current ISA (UK) 520 *Analytical Procedures* is effective for the audit of financial statements for periods ending on or after 15 December 2010. It was not revised by the FRC but was reissued as ISA (UK) 520 in June 2016. It provides a definition of analytical procedures and covers the use of analytical procedures:

- as substantive procedures to provide relevant and reliable audit evidence; and

- to assist the auditor in forming an overall conclusion as to whether the financial statements are consistent with his understanding of the entity.

25.2 What is meant by analytical procedures?

Analytical procedures may be applied at the planning, execution and overall review stages of an audit. Analytical procedures are the examination and comparison of the financial and non-financial information of a business with internal and external information, for both the current and different periods. This is usually achieved by calculating ratios and trends and investigating fluctuations and inconsistencies. It may be described as the process of reviewing the figures to see if they make sense. Methods used range from simple comparisons to complex analyses using advanced statistical techniques. Analytical procedures may be applied to consolidated financial statements, financial statements of components, such as subsidiaries or divisions, and individual elements of financial information.

As well as comparing the current year information with that of prior periods, analytical review also includes comparisons with:

- budgets;

- estimates prepared by the auditor, such as depreciation; and

- similar industry information.

It also includes the consideration of various relationships among elements of financial information that are expected to conform to a predictable pattern based on the entity's experience, such as gross profit margin percentages, and between financial information and relevant non-financial information, such as payroll costs to number of employees. An example of this is shown in **Table 1**.

TABLE 1: Variable relationships

A company had 50 employees last year with total wages of £420,000 and 50 employees this year with a wage bill of £525,000, an increase of 25%. It is known that the annual pay rise was 12% and the level of business has remained approximately constant.

At first sight, the figures do not appear to make sense because the increase is substantially greater than expected. There may, however, be satisfactory explanations. For example, there may have been a change in sales mix with previously bought-in goods being replaced by goods manufactured in-house, resulting in substantial authorised overtime. This could be verified by looking at the sales figures for different products as well as the payroll. Alternatively, there could have been a switch to more skilled, and hence more expensive, labour; this could be verified from payroll and production records.

If no such explanation is available, it is possible that the payroll has been inflated by, for example:

(a) misposting in the general ledger;

(b) 'dummy' employees on the payroll;

(c) unauthorised overtime being paid; or

(d) employees being paid at higher rates of pay than authorised.

The auditor may direct his substantive testing towards finding any errors of this nature.

Comparisons should also be made with other branches or divisions in the same line of business, which are part of the same company or group or with other companies within the same industry. It is often helpful to make comparisons on a monthly or quarterly basis where such figures are available. This can eliminate any distorting effects of seasonal trade and may enable the auditor to distinguish genuine seasonal fluctuations from window dressing around the year end.

25.3   Problems in practice

Although analytical procedures are a useful source of evidence, there are certain pitfalls in relying on conclusions drawn from such comparisons. In particular, care must be taken that:

- *they are computed on a consistent basis for each period or location under review.* Where there is a change in the basis of the calculation of a ratio or in the relationships which make up the ratio, comparability may be lost. The ratio for the prior year may be restated to obtain a meaningful comparison. For example, if stock turnover is calculated using average stocks for the previous period, there is little point trying to make a comparison with a ratio for this year using year end stocks. Major changes in pricing policy and product lines may also render past relationships inconsistent with current results;

- *there ought to be a meaningful relationship between the items being compared.* For example, there is little point in comparing head office overheads with sales since there is unlikely to be any connection between them. Similarly, there is little point in examining the relationship between sales and gross profit if stocks are valued by reference to a fixed gross profit ratio;

- *results and balance sheet values are not distorted by the effects of changing price levels.* For example, under historical cost accounting, assets acquired at different times are stated at different price levels. This means that any ratio involving fixed assets is affected by when the assets were purchased. Hence, ratios such as return on capital employed and fixed asset turnover can be distorted and comparisons between different companies made meaningless unless they are carried out on a current cost basis;

- *they are not distorted by unusual items.* Such items are often first detected by means of analytical review procedures and once detected, they should be investigated separately and their effects removed from any ratios and trends;

- *they are not distorted by changes in accounting policy or accounting estimates.* It is necessary to adjust the figures for the prior year in order that comparisons can be made. It may also be useful to calculate the figures or ratios using the old accounting policy or estimate; this is not always possible but, if it is, it may give some indication of the effect, if any, of the change.

25.4   Use of analytical procedures in risk assessment

Guidance relating to the use of analytical procedures as risk assessment procedures is set out in ISA (UK) 315 (Revised June 2016). That ISA requires that the auditor 'applies analytical procedures to assist in planning the nature, timing and extent of other audit procedures', including obtaining 'an understanding of the entity and its environment'.

The use of analytical procedures at the planning stage may also indicate aspects of the business of which the auditor is unaware but which he should take into account in planning his audit.

Analytical procedures at the planning stage are usually based on interim financial information, budgets and management accounts. For smaller entities such management information is often not extensive, and performance is monitored and controlled by less formal means. In such cases, it is suggested that the auditor extracts information from the existing accounting records, such as VAT returns and bank statements, as well as any draft financial statements and then discusses variations with management.

25.5   Analytical procedures as a substantive procedure

There is no requirement for analytical procedures to be used as substantive procedures, and the decision whether to use them, and the extent of such use is a matter for the auditor's professional judgment. Guidance on the nature, timing and extent of audit procedures in relation to assessed risks can be found in ISA (UK) 330 (Revised July 2017) (see **Section 21**).

The auditor should consider whether sufficient reliable information is available to apply analytical procedures and the results of any similar procedures already performed by the entity. In addition, when designing and performing substantive analytical procedures, the auditor should consider:

- the suitability of substantive analytical procedures for particular assertions;

- the reliability of the data, whether internal or external, from which the expectation of recorded amounts or ratios is developed;

- whether the expected results are precise enough to show when a material misstatement has occurred; and

- the difference between expected and actual results which would be acceptable to the auditor.

Each item is considered in more detail in **25.5.1 – 25.5.4**.

25.5.1   *Suitability of analytical procedures*

Substantive analytical procedures are generally most effective when directed at high volumes of transactions that tend to be predictable over time. Where a financial statements amount is a result of few transactions, year-on-year comparisons are less likely to be a useful source of evidence, as the components of the balance are likely to be different year on year.

In addition, if the auditor notes weak controls over an area, analytical procedures may be less conclusive than extensive detailed substantive tests. Similarly, an area with a historical problem of high error levels may be best tested using tests of detail as analytical procedures may show little or no trends for comparison purposes.

ISA (UK) 330 (Revised July 2017) requires that where the approach to a significant risk consists only of substantive procedures, those procedures must include tests of detail, i.e. substantive analytical procedures alone will not provide sufficient evidence in relation to that particular assertion.

25.5.2   *Reliability of data*

The reliability of data will depend on its nature, source and how it was obtained, i.e. direct from a third party or via the client. The auditor should consider:

- the source of the information available: information is normally more reliable when it is obtained from a source outside the entity;

- comparability of the information available: general industry data may need to be supplemented when the particular client deals only in a specialised area within the industry;

- nature and relevance of the information available: does the entity set attainable budgets, therefore making them a good benchmark for analytical procedures;

- controls over the preparation of the information: are budgets amended during the period to bring them closer in line to actual results? If so, this will lessen their use for comparative purposes;

- prior year knowledge and understanding: what data has been previously reliable and useful;

- whether the information has been produced internally: internal information will be less reliable than external information, but its reliability is enhanced if it is produced independently of the accounting system or there are adequate controls over its preparation; and

- whether controls over the preparation of the data are reliable.

25.5.3   Precision of expected results

The auditor must consider whether he can determine what the expected results of the analytical procedure will be with suitable precision before the test is performed. Precise expectations are required to allow the auditor to determine when results indicate that a material misstatement has occurred. The auditor should consider:

- the accuracy with which the expected result can be determined. Some results can be more easily predicted than others, such as gross margins compared to discretionary expense payments;

- the degree to which information can be disaggregated. Results may be more easily predicted for individual sections of an operation;

- the availability of information; and

- the frequency with which a relationship is observed.

25.5.4   Acceptable differences

The amount of difference from expectation that the auditor may accept without further investigation depends on the materiality of the item and the level of assurance he wishes to derive from the procedure.

25.6   Analytical procedures near the end of the audit

ISA (UK) 520 requires that the auditor should also apply analytical procedures at or near the end of the audit when forming an overall conclusion as to whether the financial statements as a whole are consistent with the auditor's understanding of the entity.

The results from this review should corroborate the results of the detailed audit testing, both in individual areas and in forming the final conclusion. They may also indicate areas where further work needs to be carried out.

The auditor should consider the following when carrying out such procedures:

- whether the financial statements adequately reflect the information and explanations previously obtained and conclusions previously reached during the course of the audit;

- whether the procedures reveal any new factors that may affect the presentation of, or disclosures in, the financial statements;

- whether analytical procedures applied when completing the audit, such as comparing the information in the financial statements with other pertinent data, produce results which support the overall conclusion that the financial statements as a whole are consistent with his knowledge of the entity's business;

- whether the presentation adopted in the financial statements may have been unduly influenced by the desire of those charged with governance to present matters in a favourable or unfavourable light; and

- the potential impact on the financial statements of the aggregate of uncorrected misstatements (including those arising from bias in making accounting estimates) identified during the course of the audit and the preceding period's audit, if any.

The results of analytical procedures may identify a previously unrecognised risk in which case the auditor should revise his assessment of risk and plan and perform additional audit procedures accordingly.

25.7   Investigating variances

ISA (UK) 520 requires that, when analytical procedures identify fluctuations or relationships that are inconsistent with other relevant information or that differ from expected values by a significant amount, the auditor should investigate and obtain adequate explanations and appropriate corroborative audit evidence.

Unexpected results may arise as a result of:

- actions of the client of which the auditor is unaware when he performs the review;

- external factors not controllable by the client of which the auditor is unaware when he carries out his review;

- other errors or omissions in the auditor's understanding resulting in inappropriate expectations being set; or

- errors or omissions in the recorded amounts subject to review.

The investigation of significant variances will usually involve discussion between the client and the auditor. The auditor will then corroborate management's explanations by:

- considering them in the light of the auditor's understanding of the entity and its environment and other evidence obtained during the audit; or

- performing other audit procedures to confirm the explanations received.

Where management are unable to offer any explanation, the auditor should carry out additional work to identify the cause of the inconsistency.

Analytical procedures

Not all explanations are capable of verification; nevertheless, the auditor may be able to decide on the reasonableness of those offered. For example, if a decrease in sales is attributed to a fall in demand, it may not be possible to verify this explanation directly nor quantify its effect (unless there are total market figures published and available in time for the audit). If the decrease is in line with the auditor's knowledge of the industry and prevailing market conditions, he may accept it as being reasonable. If the explanation cannot be verified, he must rely on other sources of evidence to satisfy himself in this area.

26 Audit sampling

26.1 Introduction

ISA (UK) 500 *Audit Evidence* requires the auditor to design and perform procedures to obtain sufficient appropriate audit evidence to be able to draw reasonable conclusions on which to base his opinion. It provides guidance on various means for selecting items for testing, of which sampling is one. ISA (UK) 500 was updated in July 2017.

The current ISA (UK) 530 *Audit Sampling* is effective for the audit of financial statements for periods ending on or after 15 December 2010. It was not revised by the FRC but was reissued as ISA (UK) 530 in June 2016. It covers:

- use of sampling;
- risk assessment;
- design of the sample;
- sample size;
- selecting the sample;
- performing audit procedures;
- deviations and misstatements; and
- evaluating results.

26.2 Use of sampling

The ISA recognises that the auditor does not normally examine all of the information available but reaches conclusions on, for example, account balances using audit sampling.

In the ISA, audit sampling is defined as 'the application of audit procedures to less than 100% of items within a population of audit relevance such that all sampling units have a chance of selection in order to provide the auditor with a reasonable basis on which to draw conclusions about the entire population'. It does not include procedures where individual items which have a particular significance are examined, e.g. all items over £10,000, as here the auditor is testing part of the population in its entirety and cannot use the results to draw conclusions about the rest of the population. Similarly, procedures such as walk-through tests are not sampling.

The auditor may use either tests of controls or substantive procedures in his work. When performing tests of controls, the auditor identifies a characteristic or attribute which indicates that a control has been implemented. This may be the signing of a purchase order or the completion of a credit check for new customers. The presence or absence of these attributes is then tested by the auditor. Audit sampling for tests of controls is generally appropriate when application of the control leaves audit evidence of performance, such as an approval stamp or the initials of an authorised person.

Substantive procedures can be broken down into substantive analytical procedures and tests of detail. Audit sampling will only relate to tests of detail.

26.3 Risk assessment

ISA (UK) 530 states that 'the auditor should use professional judgment to assess the risk of material misstatement … and design further audit procedures to ensure that this risk is reduced to an acceptably low level'.

A population will have a risk of material misstatement as assessed by the auditor at the planning stage. The level of risk of material misstatement will have a direct bearing on the sample size used. Where there is a high risk of material misstatement, the number of items tested from the population will be greater than in situations where the risk of material misstatement has been assessed as low. A higher sample size will result in lower sampling risk, increasing the auditor's confidence levels that the population does not contain a material misstatement. Other factors will also affect sample sizes (see **26.5**).

26.3.1 Sampling risk

Where sampling is used, the auditor must accept a risk that the sample is not representative of the population from which it is drawn and that he may draw the wrong conclusion from the test.

Sampling risk may result in:

- a population such as a file of reconciliations, which is acceptable, being rejected because the sample happens to pick a large proportion of the items in error. This normally results in additional, unnecessary audit work but should not affect the validity of the final audit conclusion; or

- a population, which contains a material error, being accepted as satisfactory because the sample happens not to select any of the items that contain errors. This risk is more serious because there is the possibility that an unqualified audit report is issued when the financial statements contain material misstatement (although the auditor should organise his other audit procedures so that it is, in fact, unlikely that such an error escapes detection).

Sampling risk does not only affect substantive procedures; tests of controls may result in:

- too high an assessment of control risk, because the error in the sample is greater than that in the population; or

- too low an assessment of control risk, because the error in the sample is less than the error in the population as a whole.

Sampling risk may be reduced by using a rational (possibly a statistical) basis for planning, selecting and testing the sample and for evaluating the results. This will ensure that the auditor has adequate assurance that the sample is representative of the population from which it is drawn.

26.3.2   Non-sampling risk

Non-sampling risk arises from factors that cause the auditor to reach an incorrect conclusion and is not related to the size of the sample. For example, the auditor may plan unsuitable audit procedures or misinterpret audit evidence and fail to recognise an error.

26.4   Design of the sample

26.4.1   Deciding whether to sample

When designing audit procedures, the auditor must decide whether to:

- select all items in a population (100% examination);

- select specific items;

- use audit sampling; or

- use a combination of specific items and sampling.

Selecting all items

This is most appropriate for tests of detail, for example where the population constitutes a small number of large value items or where CAATs are used to test or reperform all the transactions in the period.

Selecting specific items

The decision to select specific items from a population will be based on the auditor's knowledge of the client, the assessed risk of material misstatement and the characteristics of the population itself. Items selected may include:

- high value or key items (i.e. those which are themselves material, or have some other characteristic);

- all items over a certain amount;

- items to obtain information; and

- items to test control activities.

Audit sampling

Audit sampling may be applied to a class of transactions or account balances. Either non-statistical or statistical approaches may be used (see **26.10**).

26.4.2 Designing the sample

> When designing an audit sample, the auditor shall consider the purpose of the audit procedure and the characteristics of the population from which the sample will be drawn. ISA (UK) 530

Objectives

The auditor chooses the audit procedures that are most likely to achieve the stated audit objectives. Once the procedures have been decided, he designs the most appropriate form of sampling. This involves identifying conditions that are to be regarded as errors. For example, in a test of controls operating over purchases, non-compliance with the approval procedures may be assessed as an error. By contrast, the types of errors on a substantive test on sales invoices might be arithmetical inaccuracy and/or a failure to reflect them properly in the books of account.

Population

The auditor needs to ensure that he is extracting the sample from the appropriate population to test the specific audit objectives. This is more difficult when the audit objective is testing for understatement, such as the understatement of creditors, as the sample is chosen from a related population. The relevant population for such a test of understatement might be suppliers' statements, post-period payments or a list of all suppliers during the period, rather than unpaid invoices. In these cases, the auditor needs to take steps to ensure that the chosen population is complete, such as choosing suppliers' statements from a list taken from the purchase ledger.

The sampling unit is any of the individual items that make up the population and will vary according to the nature of the audit test. The auditor defines the sampling unit in order to obtain an efficient and effective sample to achieve his audit objective. For example, when testing the validity of debtors the sampling unit is the individual customer balances or invoices.

Stratification

By dividing a population into discrete sub-populations, sample sizes can be reduced without increasing sampling risk. Populations are often subdivided by monetary value, meaning greater audit effort can be directed to larger value items. However, the results of audit procedures performed on a stratified population can only be projected to items in the same stratum; other items will have to be tested separately.

Value-weighted selection

When sampling for tests of details, the auditor may define the sampling unit as the monetary unit that makes up the population, e.g. each £1 of the balance. The auditor will then test the balance containing the £1 sampling unit. This means that larger balances have more chance of being selected for testing than smaller ones.

26.5   Sample size

In determining the sample size, the auditor should consider whether sampling risk is reduced to an acceptably low level.

Sample size is affected by the level of sampling risk that the auditor is willing to accept. The lower the acceptable risk, the greater the sample size will need to be.

Examples of some factors affecting sample sizes, taken from the ISA, are shown in **Tables 1** and **2**.

TABLE 1: Some factors influencing sample size for substantive tests

Factor	Impact on sample size
Inherent risk[1]	The higher the assessment of inherent risk, the more audit evidence is required to support the auditor's conclusion.
Control risk[2]	The higher the assessment of control risk, the greater the reliance on audit evidence obtained from substantive procedures.

Factor	Impact on sample size
	A high control risk assessment may result in the decision not to perform tests of controls and place reliance entirely on substantive procedures.
Detection risk[3]	Sampling risk for substantive tests is one form of detection risk. The lower the sampling risk the auditor is willing to accept, the larger the sample size.
	Other substantive procedures may provide audit evidence regarding the same financial statement assertions and reduce detection risk. This may reduce the extent of the auditor's reliance on the results of the substantive procedure using audit sampling.
	The lower the reliance on the results of a substantive procedure using audit sampling, the higher the sampling risk the auditor is willing to accept, and, consequently, the smaller the sample size.
Tolerable error rate	The higher monetary value of the tolerable error rate, the smaller the sample size and vice versa.
Expected error rate	If errors are expected, a larger sample usually needs to be examined to confirm that the actual error rate is less than the tolerable error rate.
Population value	The less material the monetary value of the population to the financial statements, the smaller the sample size that may be required.
Numbers of items in population	Virtually no effect on sample size unless population is small.
Stratification	If it is appropriate to stratify the population, this may lead to a smaller sample size.

Notes

[1] Inherent risk is the susceptibility of an account balance or class of transactions to material misstatement, either individually or when aggregated with misstatements in other balances or classes, irrespective of related internal controls (see **Section 21**).

[2] Control risk is the risk that a misstatement could occur in an account balance or class of transactions. The misstatement could be material, either individually or when aggregated with misstatements in other balances or classes, and would not be prevented, or detected and corrected on a timely basis, by the accounting and internal control systems (see **Section 21**).

[3] Detection risk is the risk that the auditor's substantive procedures do not detect a misstatement that exists in an account balance or class of transactions, which could be material, either individually or when aggregated with misstatements in other balances or classes (see **Section 21**).

TABLE 2: Some factors influencing sample size for tests of controls

Factor	*Impact on sample size*
Sampling risk	The greater the reliance on the results of a test of controls using audit sampling, the lower the sampling risk the auditor is willing to accept and, consequently, the larger the sample size.
	The lower the assessment of control risk, the more likely the auditor is to place reliance on audit evidence from tests of controls.
Control risk	A high control risk assessment may result in a decision not to perform tests of controls.
Tolerable error rate	The higher the tolerable rate the lower the sample size and vice versa.
Expected error rate	If errors are expected, a larger sample usually needs to be examined to confirm that the actual error rate is less than the tolerable error rate.
	High expected error rates may result in a decision not to perform tests of controls.
Number of items in population	Virtually no effect on sample size unless population is small.

26.6   Selecting the sample

ISA (UK) 530 requires the auditor to select items for the sample with the expectation that all sampling units in the population have a chance of selection. In other words, all items in the population must have an opportunity of being selected although this need not be equal. For example, the auditor will often choose samples so as to give higher value items a greater chance of selection.

The three most common methods of selecting a sample are:

- random selection, where each item has an equal chance of selection, using random number tables or CAATs;

- systematic selection, using a constant interval between selections and a randomly selected starting point. Where this method is being used, it is important that the population is not structured in such a way that the sampling interval used corresponds to a particular pattern in the population; and

- haphazard selection, so long as there is no bias in the selection.

26.7   Performing audit procedures

The auditor performs the planned procedures on each item in the sample. If any item selected is not appropriate, a replacement item should be chosen. However, the auditor should consider whether the unsatisfactory item indicates an error. If procedures cannot be completed on a sample item, for example, the supporting documentation has been lost, alternative audit procedures should be considered for that item. If no alternative procedures are possible, the item should be considered to be an error.

26.8   Deviations and misstatements

ISA (UK) 530 requires the auditor to consider the sample results, the nature and cause of any deviations or misstatement identified, and their possible effect on the particular audit objective and other areas of the audit.

Before evaluating the results of a sample, the auditor needs to establish whether a matter detected is an error. There may be instances where such a matter does not meet the criteria for an error that were set in the planning of the test. For example, a substantive test of the validity of debtors may indicate that there has been a misposting between customer accounts. This does not lead to a misstatement of the total trade debtor balance; therefore in evaluating the sample it may be inappropriate to consider that this is an error. However, there may be implications for other areas of the audit, such as the recoverability of debtors.

The qualitative aspects of the error also need to be considered, particularly the nature and cause of the error, as they may have implications for other audit areas. It may be that all the errors fall within a particular time period or are at one location, in which case, it may be possible to identify the extent of the error in the rest of the population. For example, if the member of staff who inputs the sales invoices on to the system was away from work for a month and the replacement was entering the net amount of the invoice instead of the gross amount, an exercise could be undertaken to quantify the extent of the error by comparing the total of that month's gross and net sales.

26.8.1   Tolerable misstatement/deviation

Tolerable misstatement is the maximum error that is acceptable to the auditor, if he is to conclude that his audit objectives have been achieved. This is not necessarily the same as materiality, which relates to the financial statements as a whole rather than a particular balance or class of transactions, although it is the application of performance materiality in the case of substantive testing (see **Section 15**). The tolerable misstatement may be the same amount or an amount lower than performance materiality.

Where tests of controls are being performed, the tolerable rate of deviation will be the maximum rate of failure of an internal control that the auditor is prepared to accept in order to obtain reasonable assurance that the failure rate in the population as a whole is not unacceptably high.

26.8.2 Expected error

Before a test is performed, an error may already be expected. Here, a larger number of items may need to be tested to conclude that the actual error in the population is not greater than the planned tolerable error. This may be the case where previous years' audit tests have produced errors or the review of the internal controls indicates this.

26.8.3 Projecting errors

For tests of details, the auditor should project monetary errors found in the sample to the population, and should consider the effect of the projected error on the particular audit objective and on other areas of the audit.

When projecting errors found in the sample for tests of detail to the population from which it was drawn, the method used must be consistent with that used to select the sample. Projection commonly involves extrapolating the errors in the sample and estimating any further error not detected due to the imprecision of the methods used.

Anomalous errors, i.e. errors which arise from an isolated event that has not recurred other than on a specifically identifiable occasion, may be excluded when projecting errors to the population. This is because anomalous errors will not be representative of the population as a whole. However, their effect still needs to be considered in addition to the projection of non-anomalous errors.

To assess whether errors in the population might exceed the tolerable error, the projected population error plus anomalous errors (net of adjustments made by the entity) should be compared with the tolerable error, taking into account the results of other audit procedures relevant to that financial statement assertion.

Where projected errors plus anomalous errors approach or exceed the tolerable error, the auditor reassesses sampling risk and if he concludes that it is unacceptable (for example, he has insufficient confidence in the results of the sample), he should consider:

- extending his own audit procedures; or

- performing alternative procedures (which may involve reviewing a client's exercise to investigate errors).

This will enable him to conclude on the test and may result in identifying the need for an adjustment to the financial statements.

Projection of errors is not appropriate for tests of controls. On discovering errors in a test of controls, the auditor should consider whether the error is indicative of a general weakness in the control system.

26.9 Evaluating results

The auditor should assess the results of the sample tested to determine if the objectives of the test have been met.

For tests of controls, a high incidence of errors may lead the auditor to increase his assessment of the risk of material misstatement. For tests of detail, high error rates may indicate that a class of transactions or an account balance is materially misstated.

The auditor should use judgment where the projected error in a sample, plus any anomalous error which was not subject to projection, is close to his assessment of tolerable error. The auditor should be aware that sampling risk may mean that selection of a different sample may have provided an error which was greater than tolerable error. The auditor should consider the results of other audit procedures when assessing whether an adjustment to the financial statements is required.

If the auditor determines that test objectives have not been met, he may:

- request those charged with governance to investigate identified errors and the potential for further errors and to make any necessary adjustments; and/or

- modify the nature, timing and extent of further audit procedures. For example, in the case of tests of controls, the auditor might extend the sample size, test an alternative control or modify related substantive procedures; and/or

- consider the effect on the audit report.

26.10   Statistical and non-statistical sampling

Statistical sampling is an approach to sampling that involves random selection of the sample items and the use of probability theory to evaluate the sample results, including the measurement of sampling risk. Any other approach is described as being 'non-statistical'.

Both statistical and non-statistical approaches:

- examine less than the total population to enable the auditor to draw conclusions about the whole population;
- involve consideration of sampling risk;
- provide approximate, not exact, knowledge about the population;
- require performance of similar audit procedures; and
- require audit judgment.

Most audit testing is not performed on a rigorous statistical basis. Selection of items for testing on a genuinely random basis is often practically difficult and time consuming and the auditor may conclude that a judgmental approach to sample selection will provide the assurance required.

When using non-statistical methods, the auditor nevertheless needs to be satisfied that the selection is sufficiently representative of the population and of a sufficient size to enable him to draw reasonable conclusions regarding the population as a whole.

In both statistical and non-statistical approaches sample sizes will depend on factors such as population size, materiality and identified risk (see **26.5**).

27 Audit of accounting estimates

27.1 Introduction

ISA (UK) 540 (Revised June 2016) *Auditing Accounting Estimates, Including Fair Value Accounting Estimates, and Related Disclosures* is effective for the audit of financial statements for periods commencing on or after 17 June 2016.

Changes made in the 2016 revision of ISA (UK) 540 (Revised June 2016) related mostly to the application material and are covered by **Sections 10** and **21**. The only change in the main body of the ISA was the introduction of an Audit Directive requirement for the auditor to maintain professional scepticism. This is detailed in **27.7**.

ISA (UK) 540 (Revised June 2016) defines an accounting estimate as 'an approximation of a monetary amount in the absence of a precise means of measurement'. The term is used for an amount measured at fair value where there is an inherent lack of precision its measurement, as well as for other amounts that require estimation.

Commonly encountered estimates include:

- stock provisions;
- bad debt provisions;
- depreciation, amortisation or impairment;
- revenue recognition in complex arrangements or long-term contracts;
- deferred taxation;
- warranty provisions;
- provisions in respect of other liabilities;
- fair values of complex financial instruments;
- share based payments;
- valuation of certain assets or liabilities acquired in a business combination; and
- transactions involving exchange of assets without monetary consideration.

27.2 Obtaining an understanding

ISA (UK) 540 (Revised June 2016) requires that the auditor should obtain an understanding of the following in order to provide a basis for his identification and assessment of the risks associated with accounting estimates:

- requirements of the applicable financial reporting framework, including disclosures;

- how management identifies transactions, events and conditions that may give rise to the need for accounting estimates, and whether there has been any change in circumstances that would affect this; and

- how management makes the accounting estimates, and the data on which such estimates are based.

Consideration of how management makes accounting estimates includes consideration of:

- the method, and any models or specialist techniques used;

- relevant controls;

- use of an expert;

- assumptions underlying the estimates;

- changes from the prior year in methods used, and whether there should have been any changes;

- whether and how management has assessed the effect of estimation uncertainty.

The auditor is also required to review the outcome of prior period estimates (or any re-estimation for the purposes of the current period). Such a review is not intended to call into question the judgments made in prior periods but may provide the auditor with information relevant to his assessment of the risks of material misstatement in relation to similar estimates in the current period.

27.3 Risk relating to the use of accounting estimates

In assessing the risk of material misstatement associated with an accounting estimate, the auditor is required by ISA (UK) 540 (Revised June 2016) to assess the degree of estimation uncertainty, which is defined as the susceptibility of the estimate and related disclosure to an inherent lack of precision in its measurement. Factors affecting estimation uncertainty include:

- the extent to which the estimate relies on judgment;

- sensitivity of the estimate to changes in assumptions;

- use of recognised techniques or models to reduce estimation uncertainty, although the choice of technique or model may itself be affected by factors affecting estimation uncertainty;

- length of any forecast period;

- availability of reliable input data; and

- the extent to which inputs to the estimate are observable or unobservable.

Estimates may also be susceptible to management bias, whether intentional or unintentional; for example in selection of inputs, assumptions made, length of forecast period etc.

Where any accounting estimates are considered to have a high level of estimation uncertainty, the auditor should consider whether these give rise to significant risks.

27.4   Audit procedures

The ISA requires that the auditor should obtain sufficient audit evidence as to whether an accounting estimate is reasonable in the circumstances and when required, is appropriately disclosed. To this end, the auditor should adopt one, or a combination, of the following approaches in the audit of an accounting estimate:

(a) review and test the process used by management to develop the estimate, including consideration of whether the method used is appropriate and whether the assumptions used are reasonable;

(b) test the operating effectiveness of the controls over how management made the accounting estimate together with appropriate substantive procedures;

(c) develop his own estimate or range to compare to the estimate generated by management; or

(d) review subsequent events up to the date of his auditor's report.

Where the auditor determines a range rather than a point estimate, he should ensure that he narrows the range such that all outcomes within the range would be considered to be reasonable.

A review of subsequent events may remove the need for the auditor to obtain other evidence to support an accounting estimate. For example, if an estimate is made concerning an insurance claim for loss of profits after a fire and a provisional settlement is agreed during the course of the audit, this will provide evidence supporting the amount of the estimate and means that the auditor may reduce the attention he gives to the process by which management originally derived the estimate.

27.4.1 Significant risks

Where accounting estimates give rise to significant risks, the auditor should carry out further substantive procedures as appropriate and should also evaluate:

- whether the significant assumptions used by management are reasonable;

- whether management intend and are able to carry out any courses of action required by those assumptions; and

- how management have considered alternative assumptions and why they have been rejected.

The ISA also requires the auditor to obtain evidence concerning management's decision whether or not to recognise the estimate in the financial statements and if the measurement basis used for that estimate is in accordance with the requirements of the applicable financial reporting framework.

27.4.2 Testing management's methods

Testing management's methods and models for determining accounting estimates may be an effective audit tool when:

- the estimate is derived from a routine processing of data by the entity's accounting system;

- previous experience of similar estimates has shown that management's processes have been effective; and

- the accounting estimate is based on a large population of items of a similar nature, which individually are not significant.

Testing how management made the accounting estimate may involve:

- testing the reliability, accuracy, completeness and relevance of the data on which the estimate is based. This may be internal or external data supplied by experts;

- recalculating the estimate or assessing the validity of the model used (see **Table 1**);

- considering the process used to assess or review the calculated amount before approving it for use in the financial statements.

Where a model is used to determine the accounting estimate, the auditor may consider the procedures in **Table 1**.

TABLE 1: Audit procedures to assess the validity of models used to determine accounting estimates

The auditor may test whether:

- the model is validated prior to use, with periodic ongoing reviews. This should include evaluation of:

    - the theoretical soundness and mathematical integrity of the model;

    - the consistency and completeness of the model's inputs with market practices; and

    - the model's output as compared to actual transactions;

- appropriate change control policies and procedures exist to eliminate the risk of unauthorised changes being made;

- the model is periodically calibrated and tested for validity;

- necessary adjustments are made to the output of the model to reflect changing assumptions in the market place; and

- the model is adequately documented including its applications and limitations, key parameters, required inputs and results of any validation analysis performed.

In addition, if the financial reporting framework does not set out a fixed method for determining a particular accounting estimate, the auditor may consider:

- management's rationale for selecting the method used;

- whether management has applied any criteria set out in the financial reporting framework when selecting the chosen method;

- if the method is appropriate given the nature of the asset or liability being estimated; and

- if the method is appropriate in relation to the business, industry and environment in which the entity operates.

27.5   Evaluation of results

The ISA requires that the auditor should make a final assessment of the reasonableness of the accounting estimate based on the auditor's knowledge of the entity and its industry and whether it is consistent with other evidence obtained during the audit and subsequent events.

If the auditor believes management's estimate to be unreasonable and management refuses to revise its estimate, the difference between management's estimate and the auditor's estimate must be considered with all other misstatements in assessing whether the effect on the financial statements is material.

27.6 Disclosure

The auditor is required to obtain sufficient evidence as to whether disclosure of the accounting estimate in the financial statements is in accordance with the applicable financial reporting framework.

Where accounting estimates give rise to significant risks, the ISA also requires the auditor to evaluate the adequacy of the disclosure of the estimation uncertainty. In some situations, the auditor may consider it appropriate to encourage management to provide additional information regarding estimation uncertainty in the notes to the financial statements. Where the auditor believes that management's disclosure of estimation uncertainty in the financial statements is inadequate or misleading, this may have implications for the auditor's opinion.

27.7 Indicators of possible management bias

The auditor is required to review the decisions and judgments made by management in making their estimates and identify whether there are any indicators of possible management bias. Indicators of possible management bias do not themselves constitute misstatements, however, where identified the auditor should consider whether they affect his risk assessment and the implications for the rest of his audit. Examples of possible management bias include:

- changes in accounting estimate, or the method for making it, where management has made a subjective assessment that there has been a change in circumstances;

- use of an entity's own assumptions for fair value estimates when they are inconsistent with observable marketplace assumptions;

- selection of significant assumptions that yield a point estimate favourable for management objectives; and

- selection of a point estimate that may indicate a pattern of optimism or pessimism.

ISA (UK) 200 (Revised June 2016) *Overall Objectives of the Independent Auditor and the Conduct of an Audit in Accordance with International Standards on Auditing (UK)* requires the auditor to maintain professional scepticism throughout the audit. ISA (UK) 540 (Revised June 2016) now also contains a directive requirement for the auditor to apply professional scepticism, in particular when reviewing management estimates relating to fair values, the impairment of assets and provisions. Scepticism is an essential feature of any audit and the subject is discussed further in **23.9**.

27.8   Written representations

The auditor is required to obtain written representations from management, and where appropriate those charged with governance, whether they believe significant assumptions used in making their accounting estimates are reasonable.

An assumption used in making an accounting estimate is considered to be significant if a reasonable variation in the assumption would materially affect the measurement of the accounting estimate.

Depending on the nature, materiality and extent of estimation uncertainty, other representations about accounting estimates may cover:

- appropriateness of measurement processes including related assumptions and models, and consistency in application of measurement processes;
- confirmation that assumptions reflect management's intent and ability to carry out specific courses of action, where relevant to the accounting estimates and disclosures;
- confirmation that disclosures are complete and appropriate under the relevant accounting framework; and
- that no subsequent events require adjustment to the accounting estimates or disclosures in the financial statements.

27.9   Documentation

The auditor is required to include in his documentation:

- the basis for his conclusions about the reasonableness of the accounting estimates and their disclosure that give rise to significant risks; and
- indicators, if any, of possible management bias.

27.10   International developments

The IAASB is currently engaged in a project to update ISA 540. As part of the project, the IAASB is considering how to strengthen auditor scepticism in relation to accounting estimates and ensure that adequate consideration is given to the possibility of management bias, whether intentional or unintentional.

28 Auditing financial instruments

28.1 Introduction

Certain financial assets and financial liabilities may be presented or disclosed at fair value in the financial statements. The fair value used may arise from the initial recording of that asset or liability or from a subsequent change in its value. The use and determination of fair values is governed by the applicable financial reporting framework.

The measurement of fair value can be simple, for example, if assets are bought and sold in an active and open market, or more complex. Examples of fair values that can be difficult to determine include investment properties or complex financial derivatives. In these cases, an estimation of fair value may be achieved by using the work of an expert valuer or a valuation model.

28.2 Guidance

ISA (UK) 540 (Revised June 2016) *Auditing Accounting Estimates, Including Fair Value Accounting Estimates, and Related Disclosures* is effective for the audit of financial statements for periods commencing on or after 17 June 2016 and applies to estimates of fair values for financial instruments as well as other assets and liabilities.

Further guidance is contained in Practice Note 23 *Special Considerations in Auditing Financial Instruments* (PN 23). The current version of this was issued by the FRC in July 2013 and is based on International Auditing Practice Note (IAPN) 1000, *Special Considerations in Auditing Financial Instruments*, supplemented with further UK guidance.

The Practice Note is intended to assist auditors in understanding the nature of, and risks associated with, financial instruments, the different valuation techniques and types of controls that may be used by entities in relation to them, and identifies the important audit considerations.

APB Bulletin 2008/1 *Audit Issues when Financial Market Conditions are Difficult and Credit Facilities may be Restricted* provided additional guidance in the specific circumstances of the 'credit crunch' but contains guidance that may still be of relevance in similar circumstances.

28.3 Background information

Section 1 of PN 23 sets out background information about financial instruments including:

- The purpose and risks of using financial instruments

  As well as the normally expected risks such as credit risk, market risk, liquidity risk etc., this includes discussion of operational risk relating to the specific processing required for financial instruments and model risk, being the risk that imperfections and subjectivity of valuation models are not properly understood and accounted for or adjusted for.

- Controls relating to financial instruments

  An entity's controls over financial instruments are more likely to be effective where management and those charged with governance have:

    - established an appropriate control environment with active participation by those charged with governance in controlling use of financial instruments, clear rules, organisational structure, assignment of roles and responsibilities;

    - established a risk management process;

    - established information systems to provide those charged with governance with an understanding of the nature of activities involving financial instruments and the associated risks;

    - designed and documented a system of internal control to provide assurance that use of financial instruments is within the entity's risk management policies and in accordance with its 'risk appetite', ensure compliance with laws and regulations and monitor risk.

  An appendix to the Practice Note provides further background information and examples of controls that may exist in an entity dealing in a high volume of financial instrument transactions.

- Completeness, accuracy and existence

  The PN discusses issues that may arise in establishing completeness, accuracy and existence, especially in situations involving high volumes of trading and different counterparties such as clearing houses, banks and custodians.

- Valuation

  The PN considers issues in relation to the valuation process for financial instruments including determination of appropriate inputs, classification of inputs as level 1, 2 or 3, the use of models, third party pricing sources and external valuation experts.

- Presentation and disclosure in the financial statements

  The PN notes that most financial reporting frameworks require disclosures in the financial statements to enable users to make meaningful assessments of the entity's activities involving use of financial instruments. These will generally include:

  - quantitative disclosures regarding amounts recognised in the financial statements as assets, liabilities or transactions;

  - quantitative disclosures about significant judgments made e.g. sensitivity analysis;

  - qualitative disclosures about policies, procedures and controls; and

  - disclosures regarding exposure to risk and any changes to this, and policies and processes for managing risk.

28.4 Audit considerations

Section 2 of the Practice Note deals with audit considerations.

Certain factors may make auditing financial instruments particularly challenging. For example:

- it may be difficult for both management and the auditor to understand the nature of financial instruments and what they are used for, and the risks to which the entity is exposed;

- market sentiment and liquidity can change quickly, placing pressure on management to manage their exposures effectively;

- evidence supporting valuations may be difficult to obtain;

- individual payments associated with certain financial instruments may be significant, which may increase the risk of misappropriation of assets;

- the amounts recorded in the financial statements relating to financial instruments may not be significant, but there may be significant risks and exposures associated with these financial instruments;

- a few employees may exert significant influence on the entity's financial instrument transactions, in particular where their compensation arrangements are tied to revenue from financial instruments, and there may be possible undue reliance on these individuals by others within the entity.

These factors may cause risks and relevant facts to be obscured, which may affect the auditor's assessment of the risks of material misstatement, and latent risks can emerge rapidly, especially in adverse market conditions.

The PN emphasises the need for the auditor to maintain professional scepticism throughout the audit to reduce the risks of:

- overlooking unusual circumstances;

- over generalising when drawing conclusions from audit observations;

- using inappropriate assumptions in determining the nature, timing, and extent of the audit procedures and evaluating the results thereof; and

- not identifying management bias or over-optimism.

The PN also provides detailed guidance on planning, obtaining an understanding, risk assessment, substantive procedures and valuation matters as well as guidance on applying other aspects of ISAs (UK).

28.5   Using the work of an expert

Where valuation methods are complex or specialised, the auditor may require the assistance of an expert when assessing the entity's methods and procedures. Where an expert is used, the auditor should refer to ISA (UK) 620 (Revised June 2016) *Using the Work of an Auditor's Expert* (see **Section 31**).

Involvement of one or more experts or specialists may also be needed in gaining an understanding of an entity's use of financial instruments, including an understanding of the entity's control environment and in carrying out the auditor's risk assessment. This may be particularly appropriate where:

- financial instruments are complex;

- relatively simple financial instruments are combined to produce a more complex product; or

- the entity is engaged in trading of complex financial instruments.

29 The audit of retirement benefits

29.1 Introduction

Both UK and international accounting frameworks contain standards for accounting for retirement benefits and dealing with the related disclosures.

Where an entity contributes to a pension scheme designed to provide future retirement benefits for employees, the detailed accounting and disclosure will depend on the accounting framework applied, the nature of the scheme (defined contribution or defined benefit) and in some cases (e.g group or multi-employer schemes), the relationship between the scheme and the entity.

In the case of defined benefit schemes (other than those where the framework permits the entity to account for contributions as if the scheme was a defined contribution scheme), the accounting will involve a number of estimates and judgments. For example, determination of the entity's share of future pension liabilities involves calculations based on length of future service, inflation rates, life expectancy, etc. as well as a discount rate to establish present value of the liability. Calculations of asset values may also involve fair value estimates depending on the nature of the assets involved.

In determining amounts to be accounted for and disclosed in the financial statements, entities will usually involve one or more experts (management's experts) including an actuary. Other experts may be involved in asset valuations. Schemes may be managed by third party administrators and assets held by independent asset managers and/or custodians. Information relating to the scheme may therefore be obtained from a number of different sources.

29.2 Guidance for auditors

In November 2001, the APB issued Practice Note 22 *The Auditors' Consideration of FRS 17 Retirement Benefits – Defined Benefit Schemes* ('the Practice Note').

This was followed in February 2002 by the issue of Technical Release Audit 1/02 *Practical Points for Auditors in Connection with the Implementation of FRS 17 'Retirement Benefits' – Defined Benefit*

The audit of retirement benefits

Schemes ('the Technical Release') by the Audit and Assurance Faculty of the ICAEW.

Although the Practice Note and Technical Release referred specifically to FRS 17 which was the applicable accounting standard at that time, many of the principles continued to be relevant in the context of subsequent accounting standards and other frameworks.

However, the Practice Note and Technical Release were based also on Auditing Standards extant at that time, all of which have been subsequently revised or superseded. In recognition of this, the FRC withdrew Practice Note 22 in November 2017.

In auditing the accounting treatment and disclosures relating to pension arrangements in the financial statements of companies and other entities, the auditor should therefore be guided by the requirements of ISAs (UK) and the guidance set out elsewhere in this publication. Of particular relevance will be the sections dealing with estimates and fair values, reliance on others (management's experts), use of auditor's experts and service organisations.

At the time of writing, the ICAEW Technical Release was still available on the ICAEW website although it is likely to be of limited use.

30 Audits of group financial statements

30.1 Introduction

This section examines those situations where the auditor acts as auditor of a set of group financial statements and relies on audit work performed by other auditors on financial information of components of the group. The section does not cover reliance on internal audit functions or on experts, these are covered in **Section 31**.

30.2 Auditing standards and guidance

ISA (UK) 600 (Revised June 2016) *Special Considerations – Audits of Group Financial Statements (Including the Work of Component Auditors)* is effective for periods commencing on or after 17 June 2016.

Changes made in the 2016 revision to ISA (UK) 600 include Audit Directive requirements regarding responsibilities of the group engagement team. These include specific requirements for confirming the component auditor's independence and for the component auditor transferring relevant documentation to the group engagement team. Additionally, the group auditor must introduce procedures to enable him to comply with requests from regulators to obtain access to the working papers of component auditors. These issues are covered in **30.8** and **30.16.1**.

The ISA sets standards for auditors and provides guidance covering:

- responsibilities;
- acceptance and continuance as group engagement team;
- overall audit strategy and audit plan;
- understanding the group, its components and their environments;
- understanding the component auditor;
- materiality;
- responding to assessed risks;
- consolidation process;
- subsequent events;

- communication with the component auditor;

- evaluating the sufficiency and appropriateness of audit evidence obtained;

- communication with group management and those charged with governance of the group; and

- documentation.

In November 2013, the ICAEW issued *Auditing Groups: A Practical Guide*, replacing an earlier version issued in 2008. This guide draws on the experience of auditors who have acted as both group and component auditors to provide additional practical guidance on some of the more challenging aspects of group audits. Although it has not been updated for the latest ISA (UK) 600 (Revised June 2016), it remains useful guidance. Supplementary Material relating to the component auditor's report to the group engagement team was published in March 2014. Further details are set out in **30.17**.

30.3 Definitions

A 'component' of a group is an entity or business unit for which financial information that should be included in the group accounts is prepared. A component may be a separate legal entity such as a subsidiary, joint venture or associate or it may be a branch or division of an entity which prepares financial information separately from the remainder of the entity.

A 'significant component' is a component determined by the group engagement team to be of such significance to the group, by virtue either of its size or its circumstances, that it is likely to include significant risks of material misstatement of the group financial statements.

A 'component auditor' is the person or firm who provides an audit opinion on the financial information of a component, on which reliance is placed by the group engagement team. This may be another firm (which may or may not be a member of the group engagement team's network) or may be another office or audit team from the auditor's own firm.

The 'group engagement team' is the partners, including the group engagement partner, and staff who formulate the overall group audit strategy and plan, communicate with component auditors as necessary and perform the work on the consolidation necessary to form an overall audit opinion on the group financial statements.

30.4   Responsibilities

ISA (UK) 600 (Revised June 2016) sets out that although component auditors may perform work on the financial information of the components for the group audit, and as such are responsible for their overall findings, conclusions and opinions, it is the group engagement partner who is responsible for the direction, supervision and performance of the group audit and for the group audit opinion.

The ISA does not deal specifically with the situation where the group audit is carried out by two or more auditors acting as joint auditors.

30.5   Acceptance and continuance

ISA (UK) 600 (Revised June 2016) requires that, before deciding to act for a particular organisation, the group engagement partner should consider whether sufficient appropriate audit evidence can reasonably be expected to be obtained in relation to the consolidation process and the financial information of the components on which to base the group opinion.

In order to do this, the auditor should consider:

- the group structure including how the financial reporting system is organised;

- the industry and the regulatory, economic and political environments in which the significant components' business activities take place;

- the use of service organisations;

- a description of group-wide controls;

- the complexity of the consolidation process;

- whether any of the component auditors are from outside the group engagement team's firm or network;

- whether the group engagement team will have unrestricted access to the management and those charged with governance of both the group and the components as well as the component auditors; and

- whether the group engagement team will be able to perform necessary work on the financial information of the components.

This is intended to ensure that the group engagement team is sufficiently involved with the component auditors to the extent necessary to obtain sufficient appropriate audit evidence.

If the group engagement partner concludes that it will not be possible for the group engagement team to obtain sufficient appropriate audit evidence due to restrictions imposed by group management and that this may lead to a disclaimer of opinion on the group financial statements, the group engagement partner should either:

- not accept the engagement, or, in the case of a continuing engagement, withdraw from the engagement, where withdrawal is possible under applicable law or regulation; or

- where law or regulation prohibits an auditor from declining an engagement or where withdrawal from the engagement is not otherwise possible, having performed the audit of the group financial statements to the extent possible, he disclaims an opinion on the group financial statements.

30.6 Overall audit strategy and audit plan

ISA (UK) 600 (Revised June 2016) requires the group engagement team to formulate an overall audit strategy and audit plan for the group as a whole. This is to be reviewed by the group engagement partner.

In respect of any component considered to be a significant component, the plan should include an audit of the financial information relating to that component. In respect of components that are not significant components, the group engagement team should determine the nature and extent of work to be done in order to obtain sufficient appropriate evidence for group audit purposes. This may involve a full audit (for example where an audit is required for local statutory purposes anyway) or it may be limited in scope to relate only to those matters that are considered to be of greatest relevance to the group audit. For components that are individually and collectively not material, it may be possible for the group engagement team to obtain sufficient evidence by performing review procedures and making enquiries without involving a component auditor.

It is important, when planning a group audit, to ensure that the involvement of component auditors and the role of the group audit team in directing their work is established and communicated at an early stage.

30.7 Understanding the group, its components and their environments

The auditor is required to identify and assess the risks of material misstatement through obtaining an understanding of the entity and its environment. The ISA requires the group engagement team to perform procedures to update its understanding of the group, its components and their environments, and also to obtain an understanding of management's consolidation process. This understanding should be sufficient to confirm, or revise, the group engagement team's initial identification of significant components and to assess the risks of material misstatement to the group financial statements. Areas requiring an understanding include:

- group-wide controls, including internal audit functions;
- the consolidation process, including:
  - the instructions issued by group management to components;
  - matters relating to the applicable financial reporting framework;
  - the group's processes for ensuring complete, accurate and timely financial reporting by the components;
  - the process for recording consolidation adjustments,
  - the consolidation adjustments required by the applicable financial reporting framework; and
  - procedures for monitoring, controlling, reconciling and eliminating intra-group transactions and unrealised profits, and intra-group account balances.

ISA (UK) 240 (Revised June 2016) *The Auditor's Responsibilities Relating to Fraud in an Audit of Financial Statements* requires the key members of the engagement team to discuss the susceptibility of the entity's financial statements to material misstatement due to fraud. In a group audit, these discussions may include the component auditors. The group engagement partner determines who to include in these discussions based on a number of factors including his prior experience with the group.

From this work, the group engagement team should determine which components are likely to be significant and assess the risks of material misstatement in the group financial statements.

30.8   Understanding the component auditor

ISA (UK) 600 (Revised June 2016) requires the group engagement team to consider the professional competence of the component auditor in the context of the assignment including whether they understand, and will comply with, the ethical requirements that are relevant to the group audit, and in particular is independent[1]. The group engagement team also

---

[1] Component auditors in the UK should comply with the Revised Ethical Standard 2016. This standard is also the relevant standard for overseas component auditors who are members of the same network as the group auditor and whose work is used in the conduct of an audit of a public interest entity. In other cases, the relevant ethical requirements are contained in the IESBA Code.

considers whether they will be able to be involved with the work of the component auditor to the extent necessary and whether the component auditor operates in a regulatory environment which actively oversees auditors.

If a component auditor does not meet the relevant independence requirements or the group engagement team has serious concerns about the other matters noted in the previous paragraph, the group engagement team needs to obtain sufficient appropriate audit evidence relating to the financial information of the component without asking the component auditor to perform any work.

The component auditor is also asked to agree to transfer any relevant documentation to the group engagement team during the audit of the group financial statements. If this request is refused, the group engagement team will be unable to rely on the work of the component auditor.

There are various factors that affect the group engagement team's assessment of the component auditors, including:

- previous experience of their work;

- any affiliation of the other firm;

- membership of relevant professional bodies;

- the resources available to the component auditor to perform the necessary work; and

- discussions with the component auditors.

These factors are not mutually exclusive and the group engagement team considers them together when gaining his understanding of component auditors, as shown in the following example.

Example

The auditor of component A consistently applies quality control and monitoring policies and procedures and a methodology which are in common with the group engagement team's or he operates in the same jurisdiction as the group engagement team.

The auditor of component B does not have quality control and monitoring policies and procedures or a methodology which are the same as those of the group engagement team and/or he operates in a foreign jurisdiction.

The extent of the group engagement team's procedures to obtain an understanding of each component is likely to vary. The procedures for component A's auditor are likely to be less than those required to obtain an understanding of component B's auditor. The nature of the procedures performed in relation to each component is also likely to differ.

30.9   Materiality

ISA (UK) 600 (Revised June 2016) requires the group engagement team to determine:

- the materiality level for the group financial statements as a whole;

- any materiality level to be applied to particular classes of transactions, account balances or disclosures which are lower than the general materiality level;

- materiality for individual components; and

- the threshold above which misstatements cannot be regarded as clearly trivial to the group financial statements. This will normally be the level at which the component auditor will be requested to report any identified misstatements to the group engagement team.

Where a component is also subject to a local statutory audit requirement it is likely that the component auditor will want to use a materiality level lower than that which the group engagement team considers to be appropriate for group purposes. This is generally not a problem. Problems may arise, however, where the group engagement team specifies a materiality level lower than that which would normally be used by the component auditor. In this case the matter needs to be resolved by discussion with the component auditor.

30.10   Responding to assessed risks

Having assessed the risks of material misstatement of the financial statements (see **30.7**), the auditor is required to design and implement appropriate responses to address those risks. It is the role of the group engagement team to determine the type of work to be performed by the group engagement team, or the component auditors on its behalf. The group engagement team also needs to determine the nature, timing and extent of its involvement in the work of any component auditors. The type of audit procedures to be performed in relation to components and the level of involvement the group engagement team will have in the component auditor's work will depend on the:

- significance of the component;

- identified significant risks of material misstatement of the group financial statements;

- group engagement team's evaluation of the design of group-wide controls and determination of whether they have been implemented; and

- group engagement team's understanding of the component auditor.

Audits of group financial statements

Where individual components are not significant, either in terms of size or a significant risk of material misstatement, ISA (UK) 600 (Revised June 2016) requires only that analytical procedures at group level need be performed. The group engagement team may supplement this as required with additional procedures relating to the component, performed either by the group engagement team or the component auditor on their behalf.

The ISA also specifically requires that if the nature, timing and extent of the work to be performed on the consolidation process or the financial information of the components are based on an expectation that group-wide controls are operating effectively, or if substantive procedures alone cannot provide sufficient appropriate audit evidence at the assertion level, the group engagement team must themselves test, or request a component auditor to test, the operating effectiveness of those controls.

The diagram in **Table 1** shows how the significance of the component affects the group engagement team's determination of the type of work to be performed on the financial information of the component.

TABLE 1: Determining the type of work to be performed on components

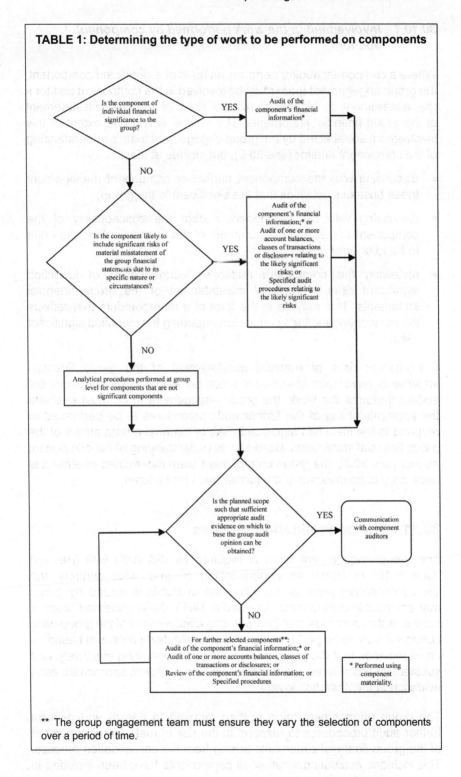

Is the component of individual financial significance to the group?

YES → Audit of the component's financial information*

NO ↓

Is the component likely to include significant risks of material misstatement of the group financial statements due to its specific nature or circumstances?

YES → Audit of the component's financial information;* or Audit of one or more account balances, classes of transactions or disclosures relating to the likely significant risks; or Specified audit procedures relating to the likely significant risks

NO ↓

Analytical procedures performed at group level for components that are not significant components

Is the planned scope such that sufficient appropriate audit evidence on which to base the group audit opinion can be obtained?

YES → Communication with component auditors

NO ↓

For further selected components**:
Audit of the component's financial information;* or
Audit of one or more accounts balances, classes of transactions or disclosures; or
Review of the component's financial information; or
Specified procedures

* Performed using component materiality.

** The group engagement team must ensure they vary the selection of components over a period of time.

30.10.1 Involvement in the work performed by component auditors

Where a component auditor performs an audit of a significant component, the group engagement team must be involved in the component auditor's risk assessment to identify significant risks of material misstatement of the group financial statements. The nature, timing and extent of this involvement are affected by the group engagement team's understanding of the component auditor (see **30.8**), but include at least:

- discussing with the component auditor or component management those business activities that are significant to the group;

- discussing with the component auditor the susceptibility of the component to material misstatement of the financial information due to fraud or error; and

- reviewing the component auditor's documentation of identified significant risks of material misstatement of the group financial statements. This may be in the form of a memorandum that reflects the component auditor's conclusion regarding the identified significant risks.

If significant risks of material misstatement of the group financial statements have been identified in a component on which a component auditor performs the work, the group engagement team must evaluate the appropriateness of the further audit procedures to be performed to respond to the identified significant risks of material misstatement of the group financial statements. Based on its understanding of the component auditor (see **30.8**), the group engagement team determines whether it is necessary to be involved in the further audit procedures.

30.11 The consolidation process

The group engagement team is required by ISA (UK) 600 (Revised June 2016) to obtain an understanding of group-wide controls and the consolidation process, including the instructions issued by group management to components. As noted in **30.10**, the engagement team or component auditor must test the operating effectiveness of the group-wide controls if work to be performed on the consolidation process is based on an expectation that the group-wide controls are operating effectively, or if substantive procedures alone cannot provide sufficient appropriate audit evidence at the assertion level.

The group engagement team is then required to design and perform further audit procedures to respond to the risk of material misstatement of the group financial statements arising from the consolidation process. This includes evaluating whether all components have been included in the group financial statements. The group engagement team's evaluation of the appropriateness, completeness and accuracy of the consolidation adjustments may include:

- evaluating whether significant adjustments appropriately reflect the events and transactions underlying them;
- determining whether significant adjustments have been correctly calculated, processed and authorised by group management and, where applicable, component management;
- determining whether significant adjustments are properly supported by documentation; and
- checking reconciliations and eliminations of intra-group transactions and balances.

The group engagement team should also evaluate whether any fraud risk factors or indicators of possible management bias exist.

Where the financial information of a component has not been prepared in accordance with the same accounting policies applied to the group financial statements, the group engagement team must evaluate whether the financial information of that component has been appropriately adjusted, for purposes of preparing and presenting the group financial statements.

The group engagement team determines whether the financial information on which the component auditor is reporting is the same information that is incorporated in the group financial statements.

If the group financial statements include a component with a financial reporting period-end that differs from that of the group, the group engagement team evaluates whether appropriate adjustments have been made to the component's financial statements in accordance with the applicable financial reporting framework.

30.12   Subsequent events

ISA (UK) 600 (Revised June 2016) requires either the group engagement team or the component auditors to perform procedures designed to identify any events that occur between the dates on which they reported on the financial information of the components and the date of the auditor's report on the group financial statements, where those events may require adjustment to, or disclosure in, the group financial statements.

Where component auditors perform work other than audits of the financial information of components, ISA (UK) 600 (Revised June 2016) requires the group engagement team to request the component auditors to notify the group engagement team if they become aware of subsequent events that may require an adjustment to or disclosure in the group financial statements.

30.13   Communication with the component auditor

The group engagement team should communicate with the component auditor on a timely basis, setting out the work to be performed, what use is to be made of that work and what form reports back to the group engagement team should take. The ISA states that the group audit team should:

- request that the component auditor confirms that he will cooperate with the group engagement team;

- set out the ethical requirements[2] that are relevant to the group audit;

- set out relevant materiality levels and reporting thresholds;

- identify risks of material misstatement to the group financial statements that are relevant to the component auditor; and

- provide a list of related parties prepared by group management, and any other related parties of which the group engagement team is aware.

The group engagement team should request that the component auditor communicates the following matters back to the group engagement team:

- whether he has complied with ethical requirements that are relevant to the group audit, including independence and professional competence;

- whether he has complied with the group engagement team's requirements;

- identification of the financial information of the component on which the component auditor is reporting;

- information on instances of non-compliance with laws and regulations that could give rise to a material misstatement of the group financial statements;

- a list of uncorrected misstatements of the financial information of the component (the list does not need to include those misstatements below the level of 'clearly trivial' communicated to the component auditor by the group engagement team);

---

[2] For UK entities, the relevant ethical requirements will be the FRC's Revised Ethical Standard 2016 and the ICAEW's Code of Ethics. Where component audits are carried out overseas, it may be appropriate to ask component auditors to confirm compliance with IESBA's Code of Ethics.

- indicators of possible management bias;

- any identified significant deficiencies in internal control at component level;

- other significant matters that the component auditor has, or expects to, communicate to those charged with governance;

- any other matters relevant to the group audit, including exceptions noted in the written representations from component management; and

- the component auditor's overall conclusion or opinion.

If effective two-way communication between the group and component auditors does not happen, there is a risk that the group engagement team may not obtain sufficient appropriate audit evidence on which to base the group's audit opinion.

In addition to two-way communication, cooperation between auditors is also needed.

For UK subsidiaries (of a UK group), the component auditors have a statutory duty to communicate such information and explanations as may be reasonably required by the group engagement team. Where there is no such obligation, the component auditors should obtain the permission of the component's management before giving such assistance.

Where the component auditors have been unable to conclude on a matter, or feel that there is something that should be brought to the attention of the group engagement team, they should do so bearing in mind their statutory obligation as noted in the previous paragraph.

There is no complementary obligation, but the group engagement team may inform component auditors of such matters if they consider it appropriate after due consultation with those charged with governance at the parent entity.

30.14 Evaluating the sufficiency and appropriateness of audit evidence

The group engagement team should consider the communication with the component auditor (see **30.13**) and discuss significant matters arising with the component auditor, component management or group management, as appropriate. They also consider whether it is necessary to review other relevant parts of the component auditor's audit documentation.

The Audit Directive specifically requires that for audits of group financial statements, the group engagement team shall:

(a) evaluate the audit work performed by the component auditor for the purpose of the group audit; and

(b) either:

   (i) review the audit work performed by the component auditor for the purpose of the group audit; or

   (ii) where the group engagement team is unable to secure agreement of the component auditor for the transfer of relevant audit documentation for the purposes of such a review, the group engagement team takes appropriate measures and informs the relevant competent authority[3]. Such measures shall, as appropriate, include carrying out additional audit work, either directly or by outsourcing such tasks, in the relevant component.

If the group engagement team concludes the work of the component auditor is insufficient, the group engagement team determines what additional procedures are necessary, and whether they are to be performed by the group engagement team or the component auditor.

ISA (UK) 200 (Revised June 2016) *Overall Objectives of the Independent Auditor and the Conduct of an Audit in Accordance with International Standards on Auditing (UK)* requires the auditor to obtain sufficient appropriate audit evidence to reduce audit risk to an acceptably low level and thereby enable him to draw reasonable conclusions on which to base his audit opinion.

As such, the group engagement team evaluates whether sufficient appropriate audit evidence has been obtained from the audit procedures performed on the consolidation process and the work performed by the group engagement team and the component auditors on the financial information of the components, on which to base the group audit opinion.

The group engagement partner evaluates the effect on the group audit opinion of any uncorrected misstatements and any instances where there has been an inability to obtain sufficient appropriate audit evidence.

30.15 Communication with those charged with governance of the group

The group engagement team needs to determine which identified deficiencies in internal control to communicate to those charged with governance and group management. In making this decision, the group engagement team will consider deficiencies in internal control:

---

[3] The competent authority is the FRC although for non-public interest audits certain regulatory tasks may be delegated to the auditor's Recognised Supervisory Body.

- identified by the group engagement team that affect the whole group;
- identified by the group engagement team that affect components; and
- identified by component auditors that affect components.

If fraud has been identified by the group engagement team or informed to the group engagement team by any of the component auditors, this should be reported to management of the group on a timely basis.

There may be situations where a component auditor is required to express an audit opinion on the financial statements of a component, and where the group engagement team is aware of a matter of significance to the component's financial statements, of which component management may be unaware. In this case, the group engagement team requests group management to inform component management of the matter. If group management refuse to communicate the matter to component management, the group engagement team discusses the matter with those charged with governance of the group. If the matter remains unresolved, the group engagement team, subject to legal and professional confidentiality considerations, consider whether to advise the component auditor not to issue the auditor's report on the financial statements of the component until the matter is resolved.

In addition to those items required by ISA (UK) 260 (Revised June 2016) *Communication with those Charged with Governance* and detailed in **Section 10**, ISA (UK) 600 (Revised June 2016) requires the group engagement team to communicate the following to those charged with governance of the group:

- an overview of the type of work to be performed on the financial information of the components;
- an overview of the nature of the group engagement team's planned involvement in the work to be performed by the component auditors of significant components;
- instances where the group engagement team's evaluation of the work of a component auditor gave rise to a concern about the quality of that auditor's work;
- any limitations on the group audit, for example, where the group engagement team's access to information may have been restricted; and
- fraud or suspected fraud involving group management, component management, employees who have significant roles in group-wide controls or others where the fraud resulted in a material misstatement of the group financial statements.

Audits of group financial statements

The revised ISA specifically notes that for group financial statements of public interest entities, the group engagement partner's firm bears the full responsibility for the additional report to the audit committee as required by ISA (UK) 260 (Revised June 2016) and covered in **10.7.2**.

30.15.1 Public interest entities

For public interest entities, there is certain information regarding the component audits that the group engagement team is also required to include in the additional report to the audit committee as detailed in **10.7.2**. This includes:

- where any of the auditor's activities have been carried out by another firm that is not a member of the same network, confirming that the group engagement team received a confirmation from the other firm (component auditor) regarding the component auditor's independence;

- reporting on any significant deficiencies in the parent undertaking's internal financial control system and/or in the accounting system and stating whether or not the deficiencies reported have been resolved by management;

- explaining the scope of consolidation and the exclusion criteria applied to non-consolidated entities, and whether those criteria are in accordance with the applicable financial reporting framework; and

- identifying any audit work performed by component auditors.

30.16   Documentation

ISA (UK) 600 (Revised June 2016) requires the group engagement team to include the following in their audit documentation:

- an analysis of components, indicating those that are significant, and the type of work performed on the financial information of the components;

- the nature, timing and extent of the work performed by the component auditor and of the group engagement team's involvement in the work performed by the component auditors on significant components, including, where applicable, the group engagement team's review of relevant parts of the component auditors' audit documentation and conclusions thereon; and

- written communications between the group engagement team and the component auditors about the group engagement team's requirements.

The group engagement team must retain sufficient and appropriate documentation to enable the competent authority to review the work of the auditor of the group financial statements.

In addition, the group audit team must make arrangements as described in **30.16.1** to enable them to comply with requests from regulators for access to working papers of component auditors, should the need arise. This does not, however, mean that the group team needs to obtain or retain a complete set of component auditor working papers.

30.16.1   External monitoring

ISQC (UK) 1 (Revised June 2016) states that where the audit firm is subject to a quality assurance review or an investigation concerning a group audit, the firm is responsible for complying with, and shall establish policies and procedures which require the group engagement team to comply with any request by the competent authority for:

(a) any relevant audit documentation retained by the team relating to the work of a component auditor; or

(b) to deliver any additional documentation of the work performed by any component auditor from a non-EEA member state.

In order to be able to comply with any such request, the firm must establish policies and procedures that require the group engagement team to either:

(a) obtain and keep copies of the documentation of the work carried out by the component auditor for the purpose of the group audit (including the component auditor's working papers relevant to the group audit);

(b) obtain the agreement of the component auditor that the group engagement team shall have unrestricted access to such documentation on request;

(c) retain documentation to show that the group engagement team has undertaken appropriate procedures to gain access to the audit documentation, together with evidence supporting the existence of any impediments to such access; or

(d) take any other appropriate action.

30.16.2   Examples

Table 2 provides some examples of documentation that may be sent to component auditors.

TABLE 2: Possible documentation to send to component auditors

This is not a definitive list and should be tailored to the circumstances of the individual group.

Referral instructions

Including:

- timetable for the work;

- auditing and ethical standards to be applied;

- request for confirmation of independence;

- details of component(s) to be audited together with required scope of work, arrangements for coordination of work at the planning stage and during the audit, including the group engagement team's involvement in their work;

- confirmation of arrangements for review of the component auditor's work, including access to working papers and translation of key documents where appropriate;

- request for confirmation that the component auditor (if not EEA based) will provide unrestricted access to audit working papers relevant to the group audit should these be requested by the competent authority for the purposes of a quality assurance review or regulatory investigation;

- details of the applicable financial reporting framework, auditing standards and any other statutory reporting responsibilities, including group accounting policies and applicable laws and regulations;

- details of any known related parties, and request for information about other related parties of which the component auditor may be aware;

- level of materiality to be applied for the purposes of the group audit (component materiality) and threshold for reporting misstatements to the group engagement team;

- details of specific risks and areas of focus for the group audit, including fraud risks and specific procedures required including work to be done on intra-group transactions and balances;

- request for component auditor's views on other areas of significant risk;

- details and timing of work to be done on subsequent events; and

- description of any group-wide controls including any testing by the group engagement team relevant to the work of other auditors.

Letter from other auditor acknowledging instructions

Including:

- the use that will be made of their work and that they will perform the work required;

- confirmation of independence and, for unrelated firms, of whether the quality control system complies with ISQC (UK) 1[4] and any relevant issues noted in recent monitoring reports;

- confirmation of understanding of the applicable financial reporting framework and auditing standards;

- confirmation of review arrangements and availability of working papers; and

- details of other known related parties, significant risks or other information relevant to the group audit.

Specimen reports to the group engagement team

Including:

- template for planning memorandum to describe proposed audit approach;

- template for clearance memos, summary memoranda and/or questionnaires to report findings including significant accounting, financial reporting and auditing matters including accounting estimates and related judgments, going concern matters;

- template for specimen management letter/report to those charged with governance of components including details of any significant deficiencies in internal control and/or for reporting such issues to the group engagement team;

- template for reporting uncorrected misstatements;

- template for reporting any actual fraud or information obtained that indicates a fraud may exist, including any suspected or alleged fraud affecting the component and any instances of non-compliance with laws and regulations that may have a material effect on the group financial statements;

- template for reporting audit component auditor's opinion on financial information of the component;

- subsequent events review sign-off; and

- confirmation of independence including details of fees for non-audit services.

30.17   ICAEW practical guidance

In November 2013, the Audit and Assurance Faculty of the ICAEW published *Auditing Groups: A Practical Guide*, to provide practical guidance on some of the more challenging aspects of group audits. The

---

[4] For component auditors based outside the UK, it may be appropriate to refer instead to ISQC 1 as issued by the IAASB.

guidance was based on the experience of auditors who have acted as both group and component auditors and replaces previous guidance documents on group audits issued by the ICAEW. It does not, however, address all the requirements of ISA (UK) 600 (Revised June 2016) and is not a substitute for the ISA in any way. Supplementary material dealing with the component auditor's report to the group engagement team was issued in March 2014.

30.18   International developments

In 2014, the IAASB set up a project with the aim of looking at issues relating to group audits, including feedback from inspection reports of regulators.

A Staff Practice Alert *Responsibilities of the Engagement Partner in Circumstances when the Engagement Partner Is Not Located Where the Majority of the Audit Work is Performed* was issued in March 2015. Whilst this provides useful reading, it is not a substitute for the ISA.

This paper aims to address concerns related to the performance of audits when the engagement partner is not located where the majority of the audit work is performed, for example, when an entity is structured such that the entity is legally registered in one jurisdiction and the majority of the general and financial management, business activities and transaction processing are undertaken in a different jurisdiction. In these circumstances, the group engagement partner and group engagement team may be located where the entity is legally registered, with the majority of the audit work being performed in the other jurisdiction(s). Because the engagement partner is not physically located where the audit work is being performed, meeting the objectives of the ISAs can pose different challenges than in situations when the engagement partner is located where the majority of the work is performed. In particular, concerns have been raised about how the engagement partner has taken responsibility for the direction, supervision, performance and review of the work, the adequacy of the audit documentation and whether, and how, the engagement partner has become satisfied that sufficient appropriate audit evidence has been obtained to enable the engagement partner to take responsibility for the auditor's report in these circumstances.

The Group Audits Task Force is now working on the broader aspects of group audits and a document entitled *Enhancing Audit Quality in the Public Interest* was issued for comment in December 2015. In summary, the issues considered, and possible responses relating specifically to group audits were:

(a)   scoping a group audit – to clarify how a group engagement team is expected to apply the requirements in the standards related to identifying and assessing risks of material misstatement, and responding to those risks;

(b) acceptance and continuance issues – considering the need for clarified requirements or enhanced guidance to drive more informed decisions. This includes proactive consideration of the situations where there may be restricted access to component financial information, to component management or component auditors when deciding to accept or continue the audit engagement, as well as addressing the related effect on planning and performing the group audit;

(c) using the work of component auditors – strengthening the engagement team's required understanding of the component auditors; enhancing and clarifying the requirements and guidance addressing direction, supervision and review of the work of the component auditors; emphasising the importance and relevance of the evaluation of the competence and capabilities of component auditors;

(d) involvement of the group engagement partner in the group audit – strengthening requirements and guidance around the involvement of the group engagement partner and engagement team in the group audit;

(e) two-way communication – more robust requirements or guidance for timely two-way communication between the engagement team and the component auditors;

(f) component materiality – clarifying the guidance relating to determining and applying component materiality;

(g) link with other ISAs – clarifying the interaction with other ISAs, e.g. with:

- ISQC 1 and ISA 220 on quality control considerations;

- ISA 315 on understanding the entity and its environment (including internal control) and the identification of risks of material misstatement;

- ISA 330 on responding to the identified risks of material misstatement; and

- ISA 230 on related documentation.

A project update was published by the Task Force in September 2017. This notes that the IAASB is committed to revising ISA 600 but has a number of priority projects on its current agenda and has finite resources and capacity. In addition, a number of revisions to ISA 600 are contingent upon the foundational revisions being made to other standards. As these projects progress, the Task Force will commence revising ISA 600 to reflect revisions in the other standards as well as on working on the other issues that need to be addressed.

31 Reliance on others

31.1 Introduction

This section examines situations where the auditor relies on others for part of the audit evidence. It examines reliance on:

- the internal audit function; and

- experts appointed by the auditor.

The section does not cover the audit of group financial statements and reliance on component auditors, these are covered in **Section 30**. Nor does it cover the situation where the auditor relies on work performed by an expert appointed by management ('management's expert'); this is covered in **Section 23**.

31.2 Internal audit function

31.2.1 Auditing Standards

The current version of ISA (UK) 610 (Revised June 2013) *Using the Work of Internal Auditors* was issued in June 2013 and is effective for the audit of financial statements for periods ending on or after 15 June 2014. It was not revised by the FRC but was reissued as ISA (UK) 610 in June 2016.

The ISA covers:

- determining whether, in which areas, and to what extent the work of the internal audit function can be used;

- using the work of the internal audit function; and

- documentation.

The ISA also covers determining whether, in which areas, and to what extent an internal auditor can be used to provide direct assistance and then further detail on using the internal auditor to provide the direct assistance. However, this is prohibited under ISAs (UK) as explained in **31.2.5**.

31.2.2   *Understanding the internal audit function*

Even where the entity has an internal audit function, the auditor is not required to use its work to modify the nature or timing, or reduce the extent of audit procedures to be performed directly by the external auditor. Use of the internal audit function remains a decision of the auditor in establishing his overall audit strategy.

However, where an internal audit function exists, in accordance with ISA (UK) 315 (Revised June 2016) *Identifying and Assessing the Risks of Material Misstatement through Understanding of the Entity and its Environment*, the auditor must make enquiries of appropriate individuals within the internal audit function as part of his risk assessment. In addition, regardless of whether he plans to use the work of internal audit, he must obtain an understanding of the nature of the function's responsibilities, its organisational status, and the activities performed, or to be performed. The auditor should document his enquiries and understanding of the internal audit function as part of his understanding of the entity and its environment, and his identification and assessment of risks of material misstatement (see **Chapter 21**).

The objectives and scope of an internal audit function, the nature of its responsibilities and its status within the entity, all vary widely from entity to entity. These matters depend on the size and structure of the entity and the requirements of management and those charged with governance. Depending on the responsibilities of the internal audit function, it may play an important role in the entity's monitoring of internal control over financial reporting. Equally, however, its responsibilities may be more focused on evaluating the efficiency and effectiveness of operations and if so, its work may not relate directly to the entity's financial reporting.

The auditor's enquiries of appropriate individuals within the internal audit function help him to obtain an understanding of the nature of the internal audit function's responsibilities. If he determines that the function's responsibilities are related to the entity's financial reporting, he may obtain further understanding of the activities performed, or to be performed, by the internal audit function and may then determine whether to use this work (see **31.2.3**).

Establishing communications with the appropriate individuals within an entity's internal audit function early in the engagement, and maintaining such communications throughout the engagement, can facilitate effective sharing of information. It creates an environment in which the auditor can be informed of significant matters that may come to the attention of the internal audit function when such matters may affect the work of the auditor.

31.2.3 Use of the work of the internal audit function

The internal audit function is defined by the ISA as 'a function of an entity that performs assurance and consulting activities designed to evaluate and improve the effectiveness of the entity's governance, risk management and internal control processes'. It requires that the external auditor considers the activities of this function and their effect, if any, on external audit procedures, although it does not relieve him of any of his responsibilities.

The activities of an internal audit function may include:

- assessment of the governance process in its accomplishment of objectives on ethics and values, performance management and accountability;

- identifying and evaluating significant exposures to risk and contributing to the improvement of risk management and internal control;

- performing procedures to assist the entity in the detection of fraud;

- reviewing controls, evaluating their operation and recommending improvements;

- examination of financial and operating information;

- review of the economy, efficiency and effectiveness of operations; and

- review of the compliance with laws, regulations and other external requirements and with management policies and directives.

Some of these activities will concern non-financial information and as such will not generally be of direct relevance to the external auditor. The level of precision that an internal auditor works to, may also be higher than that of the external auditor who is primarily concerned with material misstatement in the financial statements, but some of the methods used will be common.

Some entities will sub-contract the internal audit function to a third party but as this is still within the control of the entity, the external auditor may consider its impact on his own procedures.

Where the entity has an internal audit function and the external auditor expects to use the work of that function to modify the nature or timing, or reduce the extent, of audit procedures to be performed directly by the external auditor, the external auditor must:

(a) determine whether the work of the internal audit function can be used, and if so, in which areas and to what extent; and having made that determination:

(b) if using the work of the internal audit function, determine whether that work is adequate for purposes of the audit.

The external auditor should obtain a sufficient understanding of the activities of the internal audit function to identify and assess the risks of material misstatement of the financial statements and to design and perform further audit procedures.

Where an internal audit function is effective, the external auditor may be able to reduce the extent of his own testing. However, he will not be able to rely solely on the work of the internal audit function to the extent of performing no additional testing himself. Additionally, if the internal audit function is effective, this may be a consideration in the external auditor's assessment of the entity's control environment and risk assessment.

Evaluating the internal audit function

In order to determine whether, and to what extent the work of the internal audit function can be used, the external auditor needs to firstly evaluate the internal audit function.

The ISA sets out the criteria the auditor should use to make this evaluation. The external auditor should concentrate on the:

- extent to which the function's organisational status and relevant policies and procedures support the objectivity of the internal audit function;

- technical competence of the persons performing the work; and

- application of a systematic and disciplined approach to planning, performing, supervising, reviewing and documenting the work of the internal audit function.

The external auditor's evaluation of these criteria may indicate that the risks to the quality of the work of the function are too significant and that it is therefore not appropriate to use any of the work of the function as audit evidence.

In making this evaluation, it is important to consider the factors in aggregate since an individual factor may in itself not lead the auditor to the same conclusion as if that factor were considered in the light of others.

Determining the nature and extent of work of the internal audit function that can be used

Having determined that the work of the internal audit function can be used for purposes of the audit, the external auditor should consider whether the planned nature and scope of the internal audit function's work is relevant to his overall audit strategy and audit plan.

Examples of work of the internal audit function that may be used by the auditor include:

- testing of the operating effectiveness of controls;

- substantive procedures involving limited judgment;

- observations of inventory counts;

- tracing transactions through the information system relevant to financial reporting;

- testing of compliance with regulatory requirements; and

- in some circumstances, audits or reviews of the financial information of subsidiaries that are not significant components to the group.

Even where using the work of the internal audit function, the external auditor must still make all the significant judgments in the engagement and should therefore plan to perform more of the work himself in areas where:

- more judgment is involved, for example, in evaluating significant accounting estimates;

- he considers there to be a higher risk of material misstatement or where significant risks have been identified;

- the level of competence of the internal audit function is lower; and

- the organisational status and relevant policies and procedures of the function support their objectivity to a lesser degree.

Of course, in the latter two situations, the auditor would need to consider carefully whether any reliance on the internal audit function was appropriate.

The auditor also needs to evaluate whether, in aggregate, using the work of the internal audit function to the extent planned would still result in him being sufficiently involved in the audit, given his sole responsibility for the audit opinion. In addition, the external auditor needs to include in his communication with those charged with governance how he has planned to use the work of the internal audit function.

31.2.4   *Using the work of the internal audit function*

Where the external auditor plans to use the work of the internal audit function, he needs to:

- agree the timing, nature, extent of the work with the internal audit function as well as discussing materiality, sample methods, documentation and review and reporting procedures;

Reliance on others

- read the reports of the internal audit function that relate to the work the auditor plans to use to obtain an understanding of the nature and extent of the audit procedures performed by the internal audit function and the related findings;

- perform sufficient audit procedures on the internal audit function's work to determine its adequacy for purposes of the audit;

- reperform some of the internal audit function's work; and

- determine whether his initial evaluation of the internal audit function and the appropriateness of their work to the audit remains valid.

Coordination of the timing of the two auditors' work is best achieved by regular meetings throughout the year. This will normally ensure that the external auditor is made aware of any relevant matters as they come to light. The process also works in reverse, particularly at the end of the external audit when there may be matters in the report to management which are of concern to the internal audit function.

Table 1 gives examples of two scenarios and details the reliance that may be placed on the work of an internal audit function in each situation.

If the external auditor concludes that the internal audit function's work is not adequate for his purposes, he should consider what additional procedures of his own are necessary in order to have sufficient appropriate evidence to form an opinion.

TABLE 1: Evaluating the work of the internal audit function

Case A

An internal audit function is staffed by a number of qualified accountants. Reports go to the audit committee. Their programme of work consists of, among other things, systems checks and periodic audits of branch returns. The external auditor receives reports as and when produced.

Case B

Internal audits are carried out on a part-time basis by the controller of one subsidiary. Work is mainly of an ad hoc nature, looking at problem areas both in terms of control and efficiency and producing reports for the finance director.

Extent of reliance

Based upon the facts set out here, the possible extent of reliance in Case A would appear to be far greater than in Case B. The auditor may seek to rely on work performed on the internal control systems by the internal audit function together with some of the checks carried out during the audits of branch returns.

> In contrast, in Case B, the opportunities for reliance on the internal audit function would be greatly reduced. Some reliance may be possible in areas reported on which have relevance to the external audit. However, because of the status of the internal audit function and its method of operation, there would probably be less reliance and a greater level of procedures in the relevant area.

31.2.5   Direct assistance

Direct assistance is defined as the use of an internal auditor to perform audit procedures under the direction, supervision and review of the external auditor. Under the IAASB's ISA 610, direct assistance is permitted subject to certain restrictions.

However, the FRC has concluded that it is not appropriate to allow the use of direct assistance in audits under ISA (UK) 610 (Revised June 2013). This is because those individuals providing the direct assistance would not be independent of the audited entity under the Revised Ethical Standard 2016, which would seem to compromise the independence of the audit engagement team employed by the audit firm. Further, the risk to audit quality is heightened by the use of direct assistance since the individual providing direct assistance would not be familiar with the external auditor's processes, including those for quality control.

Therefore, the FRC has concluded that direct assistance should be prohibited for audits conducted in accordance with ISAs (UK) and that this should be extended in a group audit to any component auditor whose work is relied upon by the group auditor, including for overseas components. This does not represent a divergence from the IAASB's ISA 610, since the IAASB makes clear that its requirements in this area will not be applicable in jurisdictions where direct assistance is prohibited.

31.2.6   Documentation

When the auditor uses the work of the internal audit function, his documentation needs to include:

(1) an evaluation of:

    (a) whether the function's organisational status and relevant policies and procedures adequately support the objectivity of the internal auditor;

    (b) the level of competence of the function; and

    (c) whether the function applies a systematic and disciplined approach, including quality control;

(2) the nature and extent of the work used and the basis for that decision; and

(3) the audit procedures performed by the external auditor to evaluate the adequacy of the work used.

Where the auditor decides not to use the work of the internal audit function, he should nevertheless document his understanding of the internal audit function's responsibilities, its organisational status and the activities to be performed and the implications for his risk assessment.

31.3 Auditors' experts

31.3.1 Auditing standards

ISA (UK) 620 (Revised June 2016) *Using the Work of an Auditor's Expert* is effective for the audit of financial statements for periods commencing on or after 17 June 2016.

The ISA covers:

- determining the need for an auditor's expert;

- the nature, timing and extent of audit procedures;

- the competence, capabilities and objectivity of the expert;

- obtaining an understanding of the field of expertise of the expert;

- agreement with the expert;

- evaluating the adequacy of the expert's work; and

- reference to the expert in the audit report.

Changes made in the 2016 revision to ISA (UK) 620 include Audit Regulation requirements for public interest entities (see **31.3.5**) and Audit Directive requirements for statutory audits regarding documentation (see **31.3.10**).

Situations where the engagement team includes a member, or consults with an individual or organisation, with expertise in a specialised area of accounting and auditing are covered in **3.2**.

Where the auditor makes use of the work of a management's expert, i.e. an expert in a field other than accounting and auditing whose work has been used by the entity in preparing the financial statements, this is covered in **Section 23**.

31.3.2   Definition of an auditor's expert

An auditor's expert is an individual, or organisation, possessing expertise in a field other than accounting and auditing, whose work in that field is used by the auditor to assist him in obtaining sufficient appropriate audit evidence. The auditor's expert may be either an auditor's internal expert (who belongs to the auditor's firm or network) or an auditor's external expert. They are often members of another profession such as surveyors, actuaries or engineers.

The types of evidence that the auditor may obtain from experts will usually be a report, opinion or valuation, such as:

- valuation of an asset, for example property;

- determination of the quantity of an asset, for example minerals;

- determination of amounts using specialised techniques, for example actuarial valuation;

- measurement of work completed on contracts in progress; and

- legal opinions on interpretations of agreements.

Although the work of an expert may be used, the auditor retains sole responsibility for the audit opinion.

31.3.3   Determining the need for an auditor's expert

The auditor is required to determine whether it is necessary to use an auditor's expert to assist in obtaining appropriate audit evidence. The auditor may consider the following, when deciding whether or not to use an expert:

- whether those charged with governance have used an expert (management's expert) in preparing the financial statements;

- the nature and significance of the matter, including its complexity;

- the risks of material misstatement in the matter; and

- the expected nature of audit procedures planned to respond to identified risks.

31.3.4   The nature, timing and extent of audit procedures

The nature, timing and extent of audit procedures with respect to the expert will vary depending on the circumstances. In determining the nature, timing and extent of those procedures, however, the auditor considers the following matters:

- the nature of the matter to which the expert's work relates, i.e. whether it relates to an area involving subjective and complex judgments;

- the risks of material misstatement in the matter;

- the significance of the expert's work in the context of the audit;

- the auditor's knowledge of and experience with work performed previously by that expert; and

- whether the expert is subject to the auditor's firm's quality control policies and procedures.

31.3.5 *Competence, capabilities and objectivity of the expert*

When planning to use the work of an expert, the auditor should assess the competence, capabilities and objectivity of the expert. This assessment may use information from a number of sources, including:

- personal experience with previous work of that expert;

- discussions with the expert;

- discussions with others who are familiar with the work of that expert;

- knowledge of that expert's qualifications and membership of professional bodies; and

- the audit firm's quality control policies and procedures.

The objectivity of the expert will be impaired if he is either employed by the entity or related to it in some way (for example, they are a shareholder). The ISA states that where 'a proposed auditor's expert is an individual who has played a significant role in preparing the information that is being audited, that is, if the auditor's expert is a management's expert', there are no safeguards that can be applied to reduce the threats to objectivity to an acceptable level.

Where the expert is an employee of the auditor or his firm, the auditor will still need to assess aspects of the expert's work and results as if the expert was a third party, although he may not need to consider the expert's skills and competence for each assignment. The auditor, however, needs to have regard to the related ethical guidance when deciding if he can use employees of his firm as experts on an audit assignment. He must ensure that their objectivity and independence is not impaired, which would be the case where 'in house' experts have performed a valuation of an asset or liability of the client for inclusion in its balance sheet.

Public interest entities

For public interest entities, where the auditor has used the work of an auditor's external expert, he needs to obtain a confirmation from that external expert regarding his independence. In addition, ISA (UK) 260 (Revised June 2016) *Communication with those Charged with Governance* requires the auditor to communicate in the additional report to the audit committee when he has used the work of an external expert and to confirm that he has obtained confirmation from the external expert regarding his independence, see **10.7.2**.

31.3.6 Understanding the expert's field of expertise

Before using the work of an expert, the auditor needs to obtain a sufficient understanding of the field of expertise of the expert to enable him to:

(1) determine the nature, scope and objectivity of the expert's work for purposes of the audit; and

(2) evaluate the adequacy of that work.

This includes understanding whether the expert's field has areas of speciality that are relevant to the audit, whether any professional, legal or regulatory requirements apply, what assumptions and methods will be used by the expert and whether they are generally accepted within the field and appropriate for financial reporting purposes.

31.3.7 Agreement with the auditor's expert

The nature, scope and objectives of the auditor's expert's work may vary considerably depending on the circumstances. Therefore, these matters should be agreed before the expert commences his work and may be best clarified in writing.

The letter of instruction should contain details of:

- the nature, scope and objectives of the expert's work;

- the respective roles and responsibilities of the auditor and the expert;

- the nature, timing and extent of communication between the expert and the auditor and the form of any report to be provided; and

- the need for the expert to observe confidentiality requirements.

The letter of instruction may also contain details regarding access to, and retention of, each other's working papers and the expected method and frequency of communication between the auditor and the expert.

31.3.8 Evaluating the adequacy of the expert's work

The auditor should assess the appropriateness of the expert's report as audit evidence regarding the financial statement assertions being considered. This will involve assessment of:

- the relevance and reasonableness of the expert's findings and their consistency with other audit evidence;
- the assumptions and methods used and their relevance and reasonableness in the circumstances; and
- the source data used and its relevance, completeness and accuracy.

The auditor should ensure that the data used by the expert is sufficient, relevant and reliable and may consider reviewing or testing this data.

The expert's assumptions will not usually be challenged by the auditor as he does not have sufficient expertise, but he does need to understand the assumptions and consider whether they are reasonable given the auditor's knowledge of the business and the results of the other audit procedures.

Where the auditor determines that the work of the expert is not adequate for his purposes, he needs to agree with the expert on the nature and extent of further work to be performed by the expert or perform additional audit procedures himself.

31.3.9 Reference to the expert in the auditor's report

When the auditor is satisfied with the work of the expert, there is no need for him to refer to this in his report, unless specifically required by law or regulation. If the auditor needs to refer to the expert because such a reference is relevant to an understanding of a modification in the report, then the auditor has to make it clear in his report that the reference does not in any way reduce the auditor's responsibility for the opinion.

31.3.10 Documentation

The Audit Directive requires that for statutory audits of financial statements, when an auditor asks an auditor's expert for advice, the auditor must document the request made and the advice received.

Audit documentation will also normally include evidence supporting the auditor's assessment of the expert's competence, capabilities and objectivity and the auditor's evaluation of the adequacy of the expert's work. For public interest entities, this will include the required confirmation regarding the expert's independence (see **33.3.5**).

32 Management representations

32.1 Introduction

ISA (UK) 580 *Written Representations* was issued in October 2009 and is effective for the audit of financial statements for periods ending on or after 15 December 2010. It covers the need to gain written confirmation of management representations and includes:

- acknowledgement of management's responsibilities;
- representations as audit evidence; and
- the auditor's response where appropriate written representations cannot be obtained.

Although ISA (UK) 580 was not revised by the FRC when it revised a number of other ISAs in June 2016, it was reissued as ISA (UK) 580 in June 2016 with some minor changes to the application material.

Certain specific representations from management are required to be requested by the auditor. Other ISAs (UK) also require written representation to be obtained on specific matters as set out in **32.4**.

Additional guidance on written representations can be found in the ICAEW's technical release 04/02 AAF, *Management Representation Letters: Explanatory Note*, issued in November 2002 and updated in March 2018. The aim of the guidance is to remind auditors of the need to consider the reliability of written representations as audit evidence. The Explanatory Note is detailed in **32.10**.

32.2 Requirement to obtain written representations

Certain written representations are required by ISAs to be requested from management; in other cases, the auditor may seek written representations to confirm oral representations made by management during the course of the audit or in response to particular enquiries or in support of other audit evidence obtained by him.

References to 'management' in this context include references to those charged with governance as they have the primary responsibility for the financial statements. In the case of UK companies, written representations required by ISAs will need to be obtained from the directors but the auditor may also seek representations on specific matters from other members of senior management.

Written representations must be obtained in the form of a representation letter addressed to the auditor and signed by one or more persons with the appropriate authority. Usually, the letter is signed by one or more directors on behalf of the board. In this case, the letter may be discussed by the board before it approves the financial statements to ensure that all members are aware of the representations on which the auditor intends to rely in expressing his opinion on those financial statements.

Written representations should be obtained as near as practicable to the date of the auditor's report. Where there is a significant delay in signing the auditor's report after receipt of the representation letter, the auditor may need to obtain an updated letter or written confirmation that the representations made in the original letter remain valid.

The auditor may discuss the representations with those responsible for providing the written confirmation before they sign it to reduce the possibility of misunderstanding.

An example of a management representation letter in the case of a single entity is shown in **Table 1** at **32.9**. It should be tailored for the circumstances of each client.

32.3   Acknowledgement of directors' responsibilities

ISA (UK) 580 requires the auditor to request that those charged with governance provide a written representation that they have fulfilled their responsibility for the preparation of financial statements that give a true and fair view in accordance with the applicable financial reporting framework.

In addition, the auditor should request written representations from those charged with governance (and others as appropriate) that:

- they have provided the auditor with all relevant information and access agreed in the terms of the audit engagement; and

- all transactions have been recorded and are reflected in the financial statements.

This last representation may refer to a threshold amount agreed with the auditor or to state that all transactions that may have a material effect on the financial statements have been recorded.

The use of language to the effect that the representations are made to the best of management's knowledge and belief does not invalidate the representation as long as the auditor has found no evidence that the representations are incorrect.

In group situations, acknowledgement of the directors' responsibilities applies to the group financial statements as well as those of the parent undertaking.

32.4 Other written representations required by ISAs

Other ISAs also require that the auditor should obtain, in writing, from management or those charged with governance as appropriate:

ISA (UK) 240 (Revised June 2016), The Auditor's Responsibilities Relating to Fraud in an Audit of Financial Statements:

- representations regarding their responsibility for the design, implementation and maintenance of internal control; disclosure of management's assessment of the risk that the financial statements may be materially misstated as a result of fraud; disclosure of their knowledge of fraud or suspected fraud affecting the entity; and disclosure of their knowledge of any allegations of fraud, or suspected fraud, affecting the entity's financial statements communicated by employees or others (see **16.7**).

ISA (UK) 250 Section A (Revised December 2017) – Consideration of Laws and Regulations in an Audit of Financial Statements:

- representations regarding disclosure of all known instances of non-compliance or suspected non-compliance with laws and regulations where the consequences may affect the financial statements (see **17.5.1**).

ISA (UK) 450 (Revised June 2016), Evaluation of Misstatements Identified During the Audit:

- representations that they believe the effects of uncorrected misstatements are immaterial, individually and in aggregate, to the financial statements as a whole. A summary of uncorrected misstatements must be included in or attached to the written representation (see **15.9**).

ISA (UK) 501, Evidence – Specific Considerations for Selected Items:

- representations that all known actual or possible litigation and claims which may affect the preparation of the financial statements have been disclosed to the auditor and treated in the financial statements in accordance with the applicable financial reporting framework (see **23.6.2**).

ISA (UK) 540 (Revised June 2016), Auditing Accounting Estimates, including Fair Value Accounting Estimates, and Related Disclosures:

- representations that they believe significant assumptions used in making accounting estimates are reasonable. For this purpose, an assumption used in making an accounting estimate is considered significant if a reasonable variation in the assumption would materially affect the measurement of the estimate (see **27.8**).

ISA (UK) 550, Related Parties:

- representations that they have disclosed to the auditor the identity of the entity's related parties and all the related party relationships and transactions of which they are aware; and have appropriately accounted for and disclosed such relationships and transactions (see **20.8**).

ISA (UK) 560, Subsequent Events:

- representations that all events occurring subsequent to the date of the financial statements and for adjustment or disclosure have been adjusted or disclosed where required in accordance with the applicable financial reporting framework (see **33.3**).

ISA (UK) 570 (Revised June 2016), Going Concern:

- where events or conditions have been identified that may cast significant doubt on the entity's ability to continue as a going concern, representations regarding their plans for future action and the feasibility of these plans (see **11.9**).

ISA (UK) 710, Comparative Information – Corresponding Figures and Comparative Financial Statements:

- a specific representation regarding any restatement made to correct a material misstatement in prior period financial statements that affects the comparative information (see **19.4**).

32.5 Additional written representations

The application material in ISA (UK) 580 notes that the auditor may also consider it necessary to request representations on other matters including:

- whether the selection and application of accounting policies are appropriate;

- whether matters relevant under the financial reporting framework have been recognised, measured, presented or disclosed in accordance with that framework. These might include plans or intentions that may affect the carrying value or classification of assets and liabilities; contingent liabilities; title to or control over assets, liens or encumbrances on assets or assets pledged as collateral or aspects of laws, regulations or contractual arrangements that may affect the financial statements including non-compliance;

- a written representation from management that it has communicated to the auditor all deficiencies in internal control of which it is aware; and

- written representations about specific assertions in the financial statements; in particular, to support an understanding that the auditor has obtained from other audit evidence of management's judgment or intent in relation to, or the completeness of, a specific assertion.

32.6 Representations by management as audit evidence

ISA (UK) 580 asserts that, although written representations provide necessary audit evidence, they support other audit evidence obtained and do not on their own provide sufficient appropriate audit evidence about any of the matters with which they deal. Where no other evidence is available, it could lead to a qualification to the auditor's report because of a limitation of scope.

This also applies to cases where there is a genuine limitation of scope and the auditor does not expect any other evidence to be available. For example, where the auditor is appointed after the end of the reporting period and is unable to find any means of verifying material quantities of stock, management representations could never be considered sufficient evidence on their own to support quantities.

There will, however, be instances when no supporting evidence is available and cannot reasonably be expected to be available, and where written confirmation of the representation, when taken into consideration with other information of which the auditor is aware, will constitute sufficient evidence. For example, when auditing a deferred tax provision, the auditor may need to accept representations about management's intentions in regard to future capital spending. Similarly, the classification of financial instruments may depend on management's intentions regarding the use of the instrument. In such cases, the auditor should ensure that nothing conflicts with the representations and that they are consistent with other evidence obtained during the course of the audit regarding management's plans and intentions.

32.7 Reliability of representations

If the auditor has concerns about the integrity, competence or diligence of those from whom representations are sought, he needs to consider whether this affects the reliability of the written representations and their value as audit evidence.

Where there is an apparent contradiction between the representation and other audit evidence, the auditor should investigate the circumstances through discussions with management and other substantive procedures, and seek to resolve the difference.

Where the auditor concludes that representations are not reliable, he should consider the implications for the audit including the possible impact on the auditor's report. In particular, if the auditor concludes that the required representations regarding management's responsibilities (see **32.3**) are unreliable he should disclaim an opinion.

32.8 Refusal to provide written confirmation

Where management refuse to provide the auditor with written confirmation of representations, the auditor should re-evaluate the integrity of management and consider the implications for the reliability of other representations and audit evidence in general. He should also consider the implications for the auditor's report including whether this leads to a limitation of scope requiring either a qualified opinion or a disclaimer of opinion.

Where management refuse to provide the written representations requested in accordance with ISA (UK) 580 acknowledging management's responsibilities for the financial statements (see **32.3**), the auditor should disclaim an opinion.

32.9 Example representation letter

Table 1 provides an example of a representation letter.

TABLE 1: Example letter of representation

ABC & Co 1 High Street London

Dear Sirs

Financial Statements for the year ended 31 March 20 ...

We confirm that the following representations are made on the basis of enquiries of management and staff with relevant knowledge and experience (and where appropriate, of inspection of supporting documentation) sufficient to satisfy

---

ourselves that we can properly make each of the following representations to you in connection with your audit of the company's financial statements for the year ended 31 March 20 ...

We acknowledge as directors our responsibility under the *Companies Act* 2006 for preparing the financial statements which give a true and fair view and have been prepared in accordance with the relevant accounting framework and applicable law. All the accounting records have been made available to you for the purpose of your audit and all the transactions undertaken by the company have been properly reflected and recorded in the accounting records. All other records and related information, including minutes of all management and shareholder's meetings have been made available to you.

Uncorrected misstatements

We confirm that we believe that the effects of the uncorrected misstatements listed in the attached schedule are not material to the financial statements, either individually or in aggregate.

Significant assumptions

We confirm that the following significant assumptions used in making accounting estimates, including those measured at fair value, are reasonable.

[Details ...]

Accounting policies

We confirm that the selection and application of the accounting policies used in the preparation of the financial statements are appropriate.

Plans or intentions

We have no plans or intentions that may materially alter the carrying value and, where relevant, the fair value measurements or classification of assets and liabilities reflected in the financial statements.

Litigation and claims

Either

We have disclosed to you the following actual or possible litigation and claims, the effects of which should be considered when preparing the financial statements and these have been accounted for and disclosed in accordance with the applicable financial reporting framework.

[Details ...]

Or

We confirm that there are no actual or possible litigation and claims affecting the company.

Related parties

Either

We have disclosed to you the identity of all related parties and all the related party relationships and transactions of which we are aware. We have appropriately accounted for and disclosed such relationships and transactions in accordance with the requirements of the applicable accounting framework.

Or

We confirm that there have been no material transactions with related parties [other than transactions with group undertakings which are not required to be disclosed].

Subsequent events

Either

We have disclosed to you the following events occurring subsequent to the date of the financial statements for which the applicable financial reporting framework requires adjustment or disclosure:

[Details ...]

Or

There have been no events since the balance sheet date which necessitate revision of the figures included in the financial statements or inclusion of a note thereto. Should any material events occur, which may necessitate revision of the figures included in the financial statements or inclusion of a note thereto, we will advise you accordingly.

Going concern

Either

We confirm that we are satisfied that it is appropriate for the financial statements to have been drawn up on the going concern basis. In reaching this conclusion, we have taken into account all relevant matters of which we are aware, including the availability of working capital and have considered a future period of at least one year from the date on which the financial statements [were/will be] approved. [In particular, we have considered (give details of any matters relating to going concern on which specific representations are required, e.g. promises of support from other companies, negotiations with bankers or suppliers, etc.).]

Or

We confirm that we are satisfied that the use of the going concern assumption is inappropriate as the company will not continue in operational existence for the foreseeable future, and that, it is appropriate for the financial statements to have been drawn up on an alternative basis.

We have also considered the adequacy of the disclosures in the financial statements relating to going concern and are satisfied that sufficient disclosure has been made in order to give a true and fair view.

[Comparative information

We confirm that, in respect of the restatement to correct a material misstatement in prior period financial statements that affects the comparative information, [the adjustment relates to a change in accounting policy as we believe that the new accounting policy is more appropriate, and accordingly, to ensure the consistency of accounting treatment between periods, it is necessary to restate the current and corresponding periods on the basis of the new policy] [the adjustment relates to the correction of a fundamental error which has no bearing on the results of the current period, and accordingly, should be accounted for by restating prior periods].]

Internal control

We acknowledge our responsibility for the design, implementation and maintenance of internal control to prevent and detect fraud.

Either

We have disclosed to you the following deficiencies in internal control of which we are aware:

[Details …]

Or

There have been no deficiencies in internal control of which we are aware.

Fraud

We have disclosed to you the results of our assessment of the risk that the financial statements may be materially misstated as a result of fraud.

Either

We have disclosed to you our knowledge of fraud or suspected fraud affecting the company, and of any allegations of fraud or suspected fraud affecting the financial statements communicated to us by employees, former employees, analysts, regulators or others, involving management, employees who have significant roles in internal control, or others.

Or

We are not aware of any fraud or suspected fraud affecting the company and no allegations of fraud or suspected fraud affecting the financial statements have been communicated to us by employees, former employees, analysts, regulators or others.

Compliance with laws and regulations

Either

We have disclosed to you the following instances of non-compliance or suspected non-compliance with laws and regulations, whose effects should be considered when preparing the financial statements, together with the actual or contingent consequences which may arise therefrom:

[Details …]

Other than these matters, we are not aware of any actual or possible instances of non-compliance with laws or regulations whose effects should be considered when preparing financial statements of the company.

> *Or*
>
> We are not aware of any actual or possible instances of non-compliance with laws or regulations whose effects should be considered when preparing financial statements of the company.
>
> *Control*
>
> We confirm that the company is controlled by [...] and that the ultimate controlling party is [...].
>
> *Related parties*
>
> We confirm that we have disclosed to you the identity of all the company's related parties, related party relationships and transactions of which we are aware.
>
> *Liabilities, contingent liabilities or guarantees*
>
> There are no liabilities, contingent liabilities or guarantees to third parties other than those disclosed in the financial statements.
>
> *Title to assets*
>
> The company has satisfactory title to all assets and there are no liens or encumbrances on the assets except for those disclosed in the financial statements.
>
> *Contractual agreements*
>
> The company has complied with all aspects of contractual agreements that could have a material effect on the financial statements in the event of non-compliance.
>
> *[Additional matters*
>
> Any other matters relevant to the financial statements on which written representations are sought.]
>
> Yours faithfully,
>
> Signed on behalf of the board of directors
>
> .... Date ....

32.10   Technical release 04/02 AAF

In November 2002, the ICAEW issued an Explanatory Note on *Management Representation Letters* (Audit 04/02 following a High Court decision concerning the audit of Barings Futures (Singapore) Pte Ltd (BFS) by Deloitte & Touche (D&T). The guidance was updated and reissued in March 2018 as Technical release 04/02 *Management representation letters: Explanatory note.*

32.10.1   The case

Following an audit by D&T, BFS collapsed as a result of losses arising from unauthorised trading activity by one of its employees. D&T faced a claim for damages and attempted to defend themselves by stating that written representations provided to them by a director of the company were recklessly fraudulent. The auditor's claim ultimately failed as the judge was not satisfied that the director had signed representation letters knowing they were untrue or being indifferent as to whether or not they were true and knowing that he had no reasonable grounds for making the statements or being indifferent as to whether he had or not. The judge did, however, conclude that had a case for fraudulent misrepresentation been established he would have held the company vicariously liable for the director's actions and the auditor's claim would have succeeded.

32.10.2   Directors' ability to make representations

The guidance refers to the application material in ISA (UK) 580 which points out that whilst directors would be expected to have knowledge of the process followed by the entity in preparing and presenting the financial statements, directors may wish to make enquiries of others and may also wish to include qualifying language such as 'to the best of our knowledge and belief'. It also notes that the auditor may request the directors to include in the representations, confirmation that they have made enquiries of others where appropriate.

The illustrative letter in ISA (UK) 580 includes the caveat 'to the best of our knowledge and belief' and a reference to having made enquiries. However, for clarity and in order to avoid giving the impression that use of phrases such as 'to the best of our knowledge and belief' may enable directors not to make proper enquiries, the ICAEW guidance suggests alternative wording as follows:

> 'We confirm that the following representations are made on the basis of enquiries of management and staff with relevant knowledge and experience (and where appropriate, of inspection of supporting documentation) sufficient to satisfy ourselves that we can properly make each of the following representations to you.'

The guidance also recommends that the auditor should ask signatories of the representation letter what steps they took to obtain comfort that a particular assertion had substance or suggest that individual members of management themselves provide specialist representations to the board. In this case, it may be useful for the directors' letter of representation to attach and refer to this specialist representation.

Management representations

The auditor may also wish to remind directors and other client's staff that it is an offence under the *Companies Act* 2006, s. 501 to knowingly or recklessly make a misleading or false statement to the company's auditor. Similarly under the *Companies Act* 2006, s. 418, the directors are required to confirm in the directors' report that they have taken all the steps they should have to make themselves aware of any relevant audit information.

33 Subsequent events

33.1 Introduction

The current version of ISA (UK) 560 *Subsequent Events* was issued in October 2009 and is effective for the audit of financial statements for periods ending on or after 15 December 2010. It was not revised by the FRC but was reissued as ISA (UK) 560 in June 2016. The current version includes some revised application material largely dealing with the implications of facts that become known to the auditor after the financial statements have been issued. The ISA covers:

- events between the period end and the date of the audit report;

- matters of which the auditor becomes aware after the date of the audit report but before the financial statements are issued; and

- matters of which the auditor becomes aware after the financial statements have been issued.

ISA (UK) 560 does not deal with any matters relating to the auditor's responsibilities for other information obtained after the date of the auditor's report; these are covered in **Section 34**. However, it is worth noting that such other information may bring to light a matter which is within the scope of ISA (UK) 560.

33.2 Subsequent events

Subsequent events are events occurring between the balance sheet date and the date of the auditor's report, and the facts that become known to the auditor after the date of the auditor's report.

Events occurring after the year end either:

- provide additional evidence of conditions existing at the balance sheet date; or

- concern conditions which arose after the balance sheet date.

In forming his audit opinion, the auditor is required to consider the effects of events and transactions of which he becomes aware, and that occurred up to the date of his auditor's report. Such matters may directly affect the reported performance or financial position of the entity or may otherwise affect or require disclosure in the financial statements.

In addition, the auditor needs to respond appropriately to facts that become known to him after the date of the auditor's report, which had they been known at the time would have caused him to amend the auditor's report.

33.3 Events occurring before the date of the auditor's report

The auditor should perform audit procedures designed to obtain sufficient appropriate audit evidence that all events occurring between the date of the financial statements and the date of the auditor's report that require adjustment of, or disclosure in, the financial statements have been identified.

The nature and extent of procedures carried out by the auditor will depend on the circumstances and on the auditor's risk assessment. Procedures should be performed as near as practicable to the date of the audit report and must include:

- obtaining an understanding of procedures that management has established to identify subsequent events;

- making enquiries of management and, where appropriate, those charged with governance;

- reviewing minutes of meetings of members, directors, and audit and executive committees held since the period end and enquiring about any matters discussed at meetings for which minutes are not available; and

- reading the latest subsequent interim financial statements, if any.

The extent of these procedures will depend on the length of the period between the balance sheet date and the date of the audit report and the records available.

Other procedures may include review of, or testing of, accounting records, review of other information such as the latest available budgets and forecasts and enquiries into:

- the current status of litigation and claims, including further enquiries of legal counsel, if appropriate;

- the current status of items involving subjective judgment or which were accounted for on the basis of preliminary or inconclusive data;

- whether sales of assets are planned or have occurred;

- whether any assets have been appropriated by government or destroyed, for example, by fire or flood;

- whether other events have occurred that are relevant to the recoverability of assets

- whether new commitments, borrowings or guarantees have been entered into;

- whether events have occurred that are relevant to the measurement of estimates or provisions made in the financial statements;

- whether the issue of new shares or debentures or an agreement to merge or liquidate has been made or is planned;

- whether there have been developments regarding risk areas and contingencies;

- whether any unusual accounting adjustments have been made or are contemplated; and

- whether any events have occurred or are likely to occur which might bring into question the appropriateness of accounting policies used in the financial statements – for example, any that would bring the validity of the going concern basis of accounting into question.

One area which is the frequent subject of specific enquiries by the auditor is the appropriateness of the going concern basis of accounting and consideration of material uncertainties in relation thereto. This is considered in **Section 11**.

In all cases, the auditor should request a written representation from those charged with governance, in accordance with ISA (UK) 580 *Written Representations*, that all events occurring subsequent to the date of the financial statements and which require adjustment or disclosure have been adjusted or disclosed.

In a group audit situation, the auditor should make arrangements to ensure that an appropriate review of subsequent events at component level is carried out either by the group engagement team or by component auditors (if any) up to the date of the audit opinion on the group accounts, and that the results are reported back to the group engagement team for consideration (see **30.12**).

When the auditor becomes aware of an event which materially affects the financial statements, he should consider whether the events are properly accounted for and adequately disclosed in the financial statements.

33.4   Before the financial statements are issued

Once his report has been dated, the auditor has no responsibility to perform procedures to review subsequent events. However, if there is a delay between the issue of the auditor's report and the issue of the financial statements, the auditor may reasonably expect management to inform him of any events discovered which may affect the financial statements.

If, subsequent to the date of his auditor's report but before the financial statements are issued, the auditor becomes aware of facts that, had they been known prior to the date of the auditor's report, may have caused the auditor to amend his report, discuss the matter with management, and where appropriate, those charged with governance. He should also determine whether the financial statements need amendment.

33.4.1 Directors make the required amendments

Where the directors agree to make necessary amendments to the financial statements, there are a two possible scenarios:

(a) in the simplest case the financial statements are amended and re-approved by the directors, the auditor extends his subsequent review procedures to cover the period from the previous report date and issues a new report dated on or after the date of approval of the amended financial statements;

(b) the directors restrict the amendment of the financial statements to the effects of the subsequent event. In this case, the auditor may either reissue his audit report on a 'dual dated basis' or issue a new report with an appropriate emphasis of matter or other matter paragraph explaining that the auditor's procedures on the subsequent event were restricted to the amendment as described in the financial statements.

The version of ISA (UK) 560 issued in October 2009, introduced the concept of dual dating where events occur subsequent to the signing of the audit report which require amendment to an element of the financial statements. This concept is not permitted by some laws, regulations or financial reporting frameworks covered by the International ISA, but the UK specific guidance in the ISA (UK) does not restrict its use.

An example of a dual dated report would be:

[Date of auditor's report], except as to Note Y, which is as of [date of completion of audit procedures restricted to amendment described in Note Y].

33.4.2 Failure to amend financial statements

If the financial statements are not amended, the auditor should consider the implications for his report and issue a qualified report if the original report has not been issued to the entity. When the original report has been issued, the auditor should request management not to issue the financial statements until necessary amendments have been made; but if the financial statements are issued, the auditor will need to take appropriate action to prevent reliance on the audit report and may need to take legal advice.

33.5   Revising or withdrawing financial statements

In situations where the auditor becomes aware, after the financial statements have been issued, of facts that, had they been known at the time, would have led him to amend his report, he should discuss the matter with management, and where appropriate, those charged with governance. He should also determine whether the financial statements need amendment.

There is no formal procedure for the withdrawal of an auditor's report once issued but the auditor should consider and review the steps taken by the entity to ensure that anyone in receipt of the financial statements and auditor's report is informed of the situation.

Where financial statements have had a limited distribution, it may be possible to recall the issued copies and for those charged with governance to approve and issue amended financial statements on which the auditor has issued an updated and amended auditor's report, having extended his review of subsequent events to the date of his revised report. To avoid confusion, it may be appropriate for such financial statements and auditor's report to indicate that they replace the originally issued financial statements and report.

Where it is not possible to recall financial statements in this way, for example when company financial statements have been filed at Companies House, those charged with governance will need to consider how best to inform users in order to prevent reliance being placed on incorrect financial statements or an inappropriate auditor's report.

In the case of a company, the directors may follow the statutory procedure set out in *Companies Act* 2006 and regulations thereunder for the revision of defective accounts and reports, which include the provision of an auditor's report. These procedures are set out in **6.2**.

Auditors of UK companies may also wish to make use of powers under the Companies Act to address a general meeting of the company at which the members consider the financial statements.

In these situations, it may be appropriate for the entity or the auditor (or both) to seek legal advice.

34 The auditor's responsibilities in relation to other information

34.1 Introduction

Companies often issue, because of legal requirement, custom or investor demand, other information as part of the annual report containing the audited financial statements or otherwise accompanying the financial statements. This 'other information' may include both financial and non-financial information. Under ISAs (UK), the auditor has certain responsibilities in respect of this information.

In addition, in the UK the auditor has certain statutory responsibilities in respect of other information contained in, for example, the directors' report, strategic report, directors' remuneration report and other reports that may be required under applicable legislation. Further responsibilities are imposed by the Listing Rules of the Financial Conduct Authority (FCA) in respect of premium listed companies.

The principal reason for the auditor's consideration of other information is that there may be information therein that is materially inconsistent with the auditor's knowledge which, in turn, may indicate the existence of matters that should be reflected in the financial statements or would otherwise affect the auditor's opinion. Additionally, the other information may contain items that are materially incorrect or misleading and would inappropriately affect the economic decisions of users of the financial statements. Consideration of other information may also assist the auditor in complying with ethical requirements to avoid allowing himself to be associated with information that is false or misleading.

Annual reports may also include, or be accompanied by, other reports on which the auditor provides separate assurance, usually in the form of an assurance report separate from his report on the financial statements. Such additional assurance reports on, e.g. greenhouse gas emissions statements or corporate responsibility statements are becoming more popular with large companies but derive from separate assurance engagements outside the scope of a financial statements audit. See **Section 41** for further guidance on such reports.

34.2   Auditing standards

ISA (UK) 720 (Revised June 2016) *The Auditor's Responsibilities Relating to Other Information* is effective for periods commencing on or after 17 June 2016. Changes made in this latest revision:

- reflect revisions made to the international standard in 2015 by the IAASB;

- update the standard to reflect recent changes in UK company law;

- incorporate certain material, previously contained in ISA (UK) 700 relating to entities applying the UK Corporate Governance Code; and

- incorporate amendments deriving from the EU Audit Directive.

34.3   The auditor's consideration of other information

34.3.1   *Other information and statutory other information*

'Other information' is defined in ISA (UK) 720 (Revised June 2016) as the other financial and non-financial information, apart from the financial statements and the auditor's report on them, that is contained in an entity's 'annual report'. The 'annual report' in this context may be a single document or a combination of documents, the purpose of which is to provide stakeholders of the entity with information about the entity's operations, results and financial position. This is a widening of the definition compared with the previous version of the ISA and to some extent means that the determination of what constitutes other information may be a matter of judgment for the auditor.

The ISA also defines 'statutory other information' as being those documents or reports that are required to be produced and issued by the entity and on which the auditor is required to report in accordance with law or regulation. For UK companies, this will include the directors' report and strategic report, where required, and, if applicable, the separate governance statement for listed companies. For UK charities, this will also include the trustees' annual report as the auditor is required to report publicly on these reports in accordance with law or regulation. For all charities, the auditor is required to report on whether the information given in the trustees' annual report is inconsistent with the financial statements. For charitable companies, the auditor is required to give an opinion on such matters; whereas for non-company charities, the auditor reports by exception. This principle would apply in other sectors where law or regulation requires the auditor to report by exception on elements of the annual report.

'Other information' includes at least any statutory other information that is required for the entity. In addition, it includes information that is incorporated by cross reference in, or distributed to shareholders with, statutory other information. For example, if the entity decides to present a voluntary Operating and Financial Review (OFR) which includes some or all of the matters required for the business performance review section of the strategic report or the directors' report, then rather than duplicate the information, the entity may cross refer from the strategic report or the directors' report to the relevant information provided in the OFR. This information in the OFR would then be included in the definition of 'other information'.

The auditor's responsibilities relate to other information regardless of whether or not the information is obtained by the auditor prior to, or after, the date of his report. Whilst the ISA is based on the international standard which envisages situations in which the auditor may issue his report on the financial statements before all other information has been obtained, this is not permitted under ISAs (UK) and the ISA does note in this context that ISA (UK) 700 (Revised June 2016) *Forming an Opinion and Reporting on Financial Statements* requires that the auditor must obtain and examine all other information before he can sign or date his report.

34.3.2   *The auditor's responsibility*

ISA (UK) 720 (Revised June 2016) states that the objectives of the auditor, having read the other information, are to:

- consider whether there is a material inconsistency between the other information and the financial statements;

- consider whether there is a material inconsistency between the other information and his knowledge gained during the course of performing the audit;

- respond appropriately where he believes such inconsistencies exist or where he becomes aware that other information appears to be materially misstated;

- report in accordance with the ISA (UK); and

- form an opinion on whether the other information is consistent with the financial statements and the auditor's knowledge and report in accordance with applicable legal and regulatory requirements.

Except in respect of his responsibilities in respect of statutory other information, the auditor is not expressing assurance on the other information and is not required to obtain audit evidence beyond that which would be required to form an opinion on the financial statements.

34.3.3   Obtaining an understanding

As part of his obtaining an understanding of the entity and its environment (see **Section 21**), the auditor is also required to obtain an understanding of the legal and regulatory requirements applicable to the preparation of statutory other information by the entity, and how the entity is complying with those requirements.

34.3.4   Obtaining the other information

The auditor determines, through discussion with management, which documents are part of the annual report, when and how they will be issued and arranges to get copies of these, prior to the date of the audit report.

34.3.5   Reading and considering the other information

The auditor reads the other information and:

- considers whether there is a material inconsistency between the other information and the financial statements; and

- considers whether there is a material inconsistency between the other information and his knowledge obtained in the audit, in the context of audit evidence obtained and conclusions reached in the audit.

In order to consider whether there is a material inconsistency, the auditor selects specific amounts or items in the other information and compares them with the amounts in the financial statements to which they relate. For example, the auditor may compare a statement such as 'total research and development expense in 20X1 was £x' with the amounts shown in the financial statements.

The auditor is not expected to compare all amounts and items, and selecting the amounts to compare is a matter of professional judgment.

In considering whether there is a material inconsistency between the other information and the auditor's knowledge, the more experienced and the more familiar the auditor is with the key aspects of the audit, the more likely it is that his recollection of relevant matters will be sufficient. There may be instances, however, where he needs to refer to the audit documentation or to make enquiries of team members to determine whether an inconsistency exists. For example, if the other information describes important details of a lawsuit relevant to the audit, reference to the audit documentation will probably be necessary.

In reading and considering this other information, the auditor maintains professional scepticism and recognises that management may be overly optimistic as regards their future plans.

At the same time, he remains alert for any indications that other information that is not related to the financial statements or to the knowledge he has obtained in the course of the audit, appears to be materially misstated.

Statutory other information

In addition to the above, when reading the statutory other information, the auditor considers, based on the work undertaken in the course of the audit, whether the statutory other information appears to be materially misstated in the context of his understanding of the applicable legal and regulatory framework. The auditor performs such procedures as are necessary, in his professional judgment, to determine whether any material inconsistencies exist between the other information and the financial statements, or between the other information and the auditor's knowledge obtained in the audit; and whether the statutory other information appears to be materially misstated.

Procedures

The ISA makes it clear that the determination of the nature and extent of procedures to be applied when checking for consistency in other information is a matter of judgment for the auditor. It is clear, however, that some procedures are required and that a quick casual glance will not suffice.

34.4   Responding to inconsistencies and misstatements

ISA (UK) 720 (Revised June 2016) requires that if, as a result of his consideration of any 'other information', he identifies that a material inconsistency appears to exist (or becomes aware that the other information appears to be materially misstated), the auditor should discuss the matter with management and, if necessary, perform other procedures to conclude whether:

(a) a material misstatement of the other information exists;

(b) a material misstatement of the financial statements exists; or

(c) the auditor's understanding of the entity and its environment needs to be updated.

34.4.1   *Responding when a material misstatement of the other information exists*

In situation (a) in **34.4**, if the auditor concludes that a material misstatement of the other information exists, he asks management to correct the other information. If they agree to make the correction, he checks that this has been done. If management refuse to make the correction, the auditor communicates with those charged with governance to ask that the correction be made.

Prior to the date of the audit report

If the auditor concludes that a material misstatement exists in other information obtained prior to the date of his report, and the other information is not corrected after communicating with those charged with governance, he needs to take appropriate action. This includes:

(a) considering the implications for his audit report and communicating with those charged with governance about how the auditor plans to address the material misstatement in his report. This will normally involve including a statement that describes the misstatement in the Other information section of the auditor's report (see **34.6.1**). However, in rare circumstances, a disclaimer of opinion on the financial statement may be appropriate when a refusal to correct a misstatement of other information casts such doubt on the integrity of management or those charged with governance as to call into question the reliability of audit evidence in general; or

(b) withdrawing from the engagement, where withdrawal is possible under applicable law or regulation.

If the auditor considers that a material misstatement of the other information exists, and he cannot resolve the issues through discussion, he considers asking those charged with governance to consult with a third party, such as the entity's legal counsel.

Where the matter remains unresolved, the auditor may also use his right to be heard at the entity's general meeting.

After the date of the audit report

The situation in which the auditor concludes that a material misstatement exists in other information obtained after the date of his report is not applicable in the UK since the auditor is required by ISAs (UK) to obtain and review all other information prior to the issue of the audit report.

34.4.2 Responding when a material misstatement in the financial statements exists or the auditor's understanding needs to be updated

If, as a result of performing the procedures in **34.3.5**, the auditor concludes that a material misstatement in the financial statements exists or his understanding of the entity and its environment needs to be updated, the auditor responds appropriately. This may include:

- revising his risk assessment (see **Section 21**);

- evaluating the effect of misstatements on the audit and of uncorrected misstatements, if any, on the financial statements (see **Section 15**); and

- considering his responsibilities relating to subsequent events (see **Section 33**).

34.5 Timing

The auditor's reading of the 'other information' should be carried out in the final phase of the audit, once other evidence has been obtained. Such a review requires a person with 'appropriate levels of experience and skills'. As with other parts of the audit, the auditor considers materiality when performing this review. The review complements his other evidence and is not intended to be the only procedure that the auditor carries out in order to give his opinion.

The auditor should obtain the other information as soon as possible to allow time for any inconsistencies to be resolved.

34.6 Reporting

34.6.1 *All entities*

In the UK, the auditor is not permitted to sign, and hence date, his report earlier than the date on which all the other information has been approved by those charged with governance and the auditor has considered all necessary available evidence. As such, his report will always include a separate section headed 'Other Information', or other appropriate heading.

ISA 720 (UK) (Revised June 2016) now contains specific detailed reporting requirements related to other information. As a result, the 'Other Information' section of the report will need to include:

- a statement that management is responsible for the other information and an identification of the other information;

- a statement that the auditor's opinion on the financial statements does not cover the other information and that (except where explicitly stated otherwise) the auditor does not express any assurance thereon;

- a description of the auditor's responsibilities relating to reading, considering and reporting on other information; and

- a statement that the auditor has nothing to report or otherwise describes any uncorrected material misstatement of the other information.

(Note that inconsistencies do not get reported as they are supposed to be resolved and concluded on in accordance with **34.4**.)

34.6.2 Directors' report and strategic report

For companies required to prepare a strategic report and/or directors' report, the *Companies Act* 2006, s. 496 requires the auditor to state in his report:

(a) whether, in his opinion, based on the work undertaken in the course of the audit:
   (i) the information given in the strategic report (if any) and the directors' report for the financial year for which the accounts are prepared is consistent with those accounts; and
   (ii) any such strategic report and the directors' report have been prepared in accordance with applicable legal requirements;

(b) whether, in the light of the knowledge and understanding of the company and its environment obtained in the course of the audit, he has identified material misstatements in the strategic report (if any) and the directors' report; and

(c) if applicable, give an indication of the nature of each of the misstatements referred to in (b).

34.6.3 Separate corporate governance statement

Where a company prepares a separate corporate governance statement[1] in respect of a financial year, the *Companies Act* 2006, s. 497A requires that the auditor must, in his report:

(a) state whether, in his opinion, based on the work undertaken in the course of the audit, the information given in the statement in compliance with rules 7.2.5 and 7.2.6 in the Disclosure Rules and Transparency Rules sourcebook made by the Financial Conduct Authority (information about internal control and risk management systems in relation to financial reporting processes and about share capital structures):
   (i) is consistent with those accounts; and
   (ii) has been prepared in accordance with applicable legal requirements;

---

[1] Applies to listed companies only. However, a separate corporate governance statement is not required if the relevant information is included within the directors' report.

(b) state whether, in the light of the knowledge and understanding of the company and its environment obtained in the course of the audit, he has identified material misstatements in the information;

(c) if applicable, give an indication of the nature of each of the misstatements referred to in (b); and

(d) state whether, in his opinion, based on the work undertaken in the course of the audit, rules 7.2.2, 7.2.3 and 7.2.7 in the Disclosure Rules and Transparency Rules sourcebook made by the Financial Conduct Authority (information about the company's corporate governance code and practices and about its administrative, management and supervisory bodies and their committees) have been complied with, if applicable.

34.7   UK Corporate Governance Code reporting

For entities that are required, and those that choose voluntarily, to report on how they have applied the UK Corporate Governance Code or to explain why they have not, the auditor shall specifically address each of the following elements of the other information:

(a) the statement given by the directors that they consider the annual report and accounts taken as a whole is fair, balanced and understandable and provides the information necessary for shareholders to assess the entity's performance, business model and strategy, that is materially inconsistent with the auditor's knowledge obtained in the audit;

(b) the section describing the work of the audit committee that does not appropriately address matters communicated by the auditor to the audit committee;

(c) the explanation as to why the annual report does not include such a statement or section that is materially inconsistent with the auditor's knowledge obtained in the audit;

(d) the parts of the directors' statement required under the Listing Rules relating to the entity's compliance with the UK Corporate Governance Code containing provisions specified for review by the auditor in accordance with Listing Rule 9.8.10R(2) that do not properly disclose a departure from a relevant provision of the UK Corporate Governance Code; and

(e) the directors' statement relating to Going Concern required under the Listing Rules in accordance with Listing Rule 9.8.6R(3) that is materially inconsistent with the auditor's knowledge obtained in the audit.

In reporting on other information, the auditor shall describe the specific reporting responsibility relating to these matters and shall report on each of these matters.

34.7.1 Statement on the directors' assessment of the principal risks that would threaten the solvency or liquidity of the entity

For entities reporting on their application of the UK Corporate Governance Code, the auditor shall also give a statement as to whether he has anything material to add or draw attention to in respect of:

(a) the directors' confirmation in the annual report that they have carried out a robust assessment of the principal risks facing the entity, including those that would threaten its business model, future performance, solvency or liquidity;

(b) the disclosures in the annual report that describe those risks and explain how they are being managed or mitigated; and

(c) the directors' explanation in the annual report as to how they have assessed the prospects of the entity, over what period they have done so and why they consider that period to be appropriate, and their statement as to whether they have a reasonable expectation that the entity will be able to continue in operation and meet its liabilities as they fall due over the period of their assessment, including any related disclosures drawing attention to any necessary qualifications or assumptions.

In reporting on Other Information (under paragraph 22 of ISA (UK) 720 (Revised June 2016)), the description of the auditor's responsibilities in relation to the other information required by paragraph 22(d) shall also include the auditor's additional responsibilities under paragraph 18-2 of ISA (UK) 570 (Revised June 2016) *Going Concern* and the auditor's responsibility to report whether the auditor has anything material to add or draw attention to in relation to each of the above elements of the other information. In addition, where the auditor has identified anything material to add or draw attention to in respect of these elements of the other information, the auditor shall include in the auditor's report a statement that describes any other material information that the auditor considers it appropriate to add or draw attention to.

34.8 Modified audit reports

When the auditor's opinion on the financial statements is adverse or qualified, he should consider whether the matter giving rise to the modification of the opinion has any implications for his conclusions he is reporting in relation to other information.

34.9   Documentation

The auditor must ensure that he fully documents the procedures he performed on 'other information' and that he includes in his file the final version of the 'other information' on which he has performed this work.

34.10   Electronic publication

The Electronic Communication provisions of the *Companies Act* 2006 allow companies to meet, subject to certain conditions, their statutory reporting obligations to shareholders by distributing their annual financial statements and certain other reports electronically, or to post their financial statements on their website and advise shareholders of this. The implications for the auditor's work and report are set out in **4.27**.

35 Data analytics

35.1 Introduction

Data analytics is essentially the science of examining raw data with the purpose of drawing conclusions about that information. Data analytics is used in many industries to allow companies and organisations to make better business decisions and in the sciences to verify or disprove existing models or theories. It has been used in a basic form for many years by auditors using Computer Assisted Audit Techniques (CAATs), however developments in information technology have led to an increase in the speed and volume of data interrogated, such that data analytics can now be used for many more areas in the audit to improve the quality of the audit.

Companies are changing their business models in innovative ways in response to these developments. In addition, expectations on auditors are changing and stakeholders now expect the entity's auditor to make greater use of technology in the financial statement audit. Developments in technology, both within the financial reporting systems used to initiate, process, record and store data representing the information in the financial statements, and the tools and techniques available to analyse that data, are resulting in questions from stakeholders regarding how data analytics fits into the current risk based audit model. For larger and listed entities, it is now common place on tendering for an audit engagement, for the entity to inquire about the auditor's data analytics capabilities and in some cases, expecting the auditor to perform an audit that includes the increased use of technology, particularly data analytics.

35.2 Guidance

The ISAs neither prohibit nor require the use of data analytics. They do, however, acknowledge the use of technology by the auditor in executing the audit, through use of Computer Assisted Audit Techniques (CAATs). The reference to CAATs in the ISAs was created in a completely different technological era however, and CAATs have evolved significantly into what is now being referred to as data analytics.

As data analytics is still a relatively new area, there is not yet any guidance on how and when they should be used by auditors. There have been, however, a number of papers written on the subject over recent years and audit firms, standard setters and regulators have been giving considerable thought to the matter.

In August 2016, the IAASB's Data Analytics Working Group (DAWG) issued a 'Request for Input *Exploring the Growing Use of Technology in the Audit, with a Focus on Data Analytics*'. A feedback statement summarising the responses to this paper was published in January 2018.

In May 2016, the ICAEW issued *Data Analytics for External Auditors* as part of its series of publications on international auditing perspectives. This paper is discussed further in **35.3.2** and **35.3.3**.

In December 2016, the ICAEW then issued *Audit Insights: Data Analytics* (December 2016) – this is discussed further in **35.3.3**.

In January 2017, the FRC produced the latest in its series of Audit Quality Thematic Reviews, entitled Audit Quality Thematic Review: *The Use of Data Analytics in the Audit of Financial Statements*. This can be found online at Croner-i Tax and Accounting and is discussed in **35.3.4**.

35.3   Use of data analytics in external audits

The term 'data analytics' covers a wide range of activities including:

- the review of full data sets to find exceptions and then drilling down into the detail;

- the development of meaningful linkages between different data sets and other information; and

- predictive analytics, including complex modelling, which supports the optimisation of decision-making.

Data analytics also involves the use of algorithms, visualisation and modelling techniques. The skills needed at various points in this spectrum are correspondingly wide-ranging. They include the ability to manipulate data, mathematical and statistical skills and, just as importantly, the experience, judgment and flexibility to make the right linkages, interpret analyses and use them appropriately to support decisions. How this skill set is developed is an important area of current debate.

Larger firms are already investing heavily in data analytics but this is not exclusively the preserve of larger firms and third party accounting and auditing software providers will inevitably develop data analytics facilities to work alongside existing tools. Many smaller firms may also make use of data analytics in the context of Google Analytics and Excel. The market for free and low cost tools is being developed and a number of tools are emerging. The ICAEW's *Audit Insights* paper discusses some of these.

35.3.1 Audit quality

The IAASB's DAWG notes in its paper that the quality of a financial statement audit can be enhanced by the use of data analytics.

The use of technology and data analytics offers opportunities for the auditor to obtain a more effective and robust understanding of the entity and its environment, enhancing the quality of the auditor's risk assessment and response. Data analytics also enhances the auditor's ability to gather audit evidence from the analysis of larger populations, including enabling better risk-based selections from those populations for further testing by the auditor and allows the auditor to gain a broader and deeper insight of the entity and its environment, which provides the entity being audited with additional valuable information to inform its own risk assessment and business operations.

However, there are also limitations auditors need to be aware of in using data analytics. For example:

- Auditors need to have a clear understanding of the data they are analysing, particularly the relevance of the data to the audit. Analysis of data that is not relevant to the audit, is not well-controlled, is unreliable or the source of which (internal or external) is not well-understood could have negative consequences to audit quality. While the analysis of relevant and reliable data provides valuable insights to the auditor, it will not provide everything the auditor needs to know.

- Due to the need for the auditor to exercise professional judgments in relation to accounting and auditing, as well as issues related to data completeness and validity, being able to test 100% of a population does not imply that the auditor is able to provide something more than a reasonable assurance opinion or that the meaning of 'reasonable assurance' changes.

- In the financial statements of the majority of entities, there are significant amounts and disclosures that are accounting estimates (or that are based on accounting estimates) or that contain qualitative information. Professional judgment is necessary to assess the reasonableness of the entity's estimated value and disclosures of those items. While the data analytics technology of today is able to unlock valuable insights for the auditor to consider, its use in a financial statement audit will not replace the need for professional judgement and professional scepticism.

- The effective use of technology can support the auditor in obtaining sufficient and appropriate audit evidence. However, caution should be exercised regarding the auditor's and stakeholders' potential 'overconfidence' in technology, in which auditors lacking a clear understanding of the uses and limitations of technology falsely believe the results to be infallible (i.e. the output must be 100% accurate because a software program produced it).

As well as the speed and quantity of data that can be interrogated using data analytics, the presentation of the results is also evolving, making them more user-friendly. Tools now can filter, sort, slice and highlight data in a spreadsheet and then present it visually in variety of charts and dashboards.

35.3.2 Common data analytic routines

Data analytics can be used in a variety of ways and the ICAEW's *Data Analytics for External Auditors* paper gives the following examples of commonly performed data analytics routines.

- Comparing the last time an item was bought with the last time it was sold, for cost/NRV purposes.

- Inventory ageing and how many days inventory is in stock by item.

- Receivables and payables ageing and the reduction in overdue debt over time by customer.

- Analyses of revenue trends split by product or region.

- Analyses of gross margins and sales, highlighting items with negative margins.

- Matches of orders to cash and purchases to payments.

- 'Can do did do testing' of user codes to test whether segregation of duties is appropriate, and whether any inappropriate combinations of users have been involved in processing transactions.

- Detailed recalculations of depreciation on fixed assets by item, either using approximations (such as assuming sales and purchases are mid-month) or using the entire data set and exact dates.

- Analyses of capital expenditure v repairs and maintenance.

- Three-way matches between purchase/sales orders, goods received/ despatched documentation and invoices.

35.3.3 ICAEW papers

The ICAEW paper *Data Analytics for External Auditors* provides very useful reading for auditors considering how data analytics could be used in their work. It discusses what data analytics are, how they can contribute to audit quality, how useful they can be for the client as well as considering how differing sized firms may develop their use of data analytics and the issues around this.

Audit Insights: Data Analytics also provides useful reading for the auditor, although it also considers issues for the entity itself, such as culture, control and governance issues and how analytics can help to improve business performance.

35.3.4   Audit quality thematic review

During 2016, the FRC undertook a review of 19 audits which made use of data analytics for the year ending in 2015 and published their findings in January 2017 in Audit Quality Thematic Review: *The Use of Data Analytics in the Audit of Financial Statements*.

The report found that:

- the use of data analytics in the audit is not as prevalent as the market may expect. Audit firms and teams sometimes feel pressure to promote the use of data analytic techniques on audits to meet audit committee expectations, to achieve efficiencies and to win competitive tenders, however, this may result in the pace of development and usage of data analytics being overemphasised;

- thoughtful use of data analytic techniques can provide audit evidence that is more focused to the audit risks and provide useful insights to an entity's management and the audit committee;

- where firms focus efforts on supporting a small number of tools, use is more successful and uptake by audit teams increases, whereas where firms try to offer a wide variety of ADA tools, their use on audits is reduced;

- where audit teams are able to obtain entity data efficiently, they are more encouraged to use data analytic tools, improving their successful use on audits. This is helped where specialist dedicated support is available;

- audit teams need to have a clear understanding of the purpose of the technique within the audit methodology to ensure that they obtain sufficient and appropriate audit evidence;

- an experienced auditor should be able to understand the nature, timing and extent of the audit procedures performed, including where data analytic tools have been used; however, there were a number of instances where this evidencing was insufficient;

- audit regulators need to consider how they assess the integrity of data analytic tools used by audit teams and in particular whether they are functioning as intended;

- where tools are adopted globally, group teams can instruct that specific tools are used. Where entities use global systems, such tools can be used to execute testing centrally. This promotes efficiency and central oversight, but provides additional evidential challenges for component auditors.

It also highlighted that, although outside the scope of the report, the capture, storage and processing of entity data presents firms with challenges in relation to data confidentiality and security.

35.4 Future developments

It is expected that there will be many developments in data analytics in the short to medium term. Software developments are also expected to bring the use of data analytics more firmly within reach of the smaller practices.

Feedback from the IAASB's 'Request for input' paper will provide input to other IAASB projects and is likely to influence auditing standards in due course.

Key messages from the feedback include the following.

- ISAs should remain principles-based, but need to reflect the digital era in application guidance. Respondents overwhelmingly described a strong desire for practical guidance on the use of data analytics technology. Most respondents believe that the principles in the extant ISAs are still appropriate and accommodate the use of data analytics, and caution against prematurely rushing to change requirements in the standards.

- Applying professional scepticism when using data analytics remains paramount, as professional scepticism is integral to understanding the benefits and limitations of data analytics in view of its intended use in the audit.

36   The audit of small businesses

36.1   Introduction

In 2015, the Government confirmed its intention to increase the threshold for audit exemption in line with increases to small company size limits. As a result, an increasing number of small companies do not now require an annual audit.

In order to claim exemption from audit under the *Companies Act* 2006, s. 477, a company must qualify as a small company in relation to the financial year in question. A company qualifies as small in its first year if it satisfies two out of the following criteria: turnover, total assets, and employees.

In subsequent years, a small company will continue to qualify as small unless the criteria are not met for two successive years. The relevant criteria are shown in the table below:

	For periods beginning before 1 January 2016	For periods beginning on or after 1 January 2016
Turnover	Less than £6.5m	Less than £10.2m
Total assets	Less than £3.26m	Less than £5.1m
Employees (average monthly number)	Less than 50	Less than 50

The turnover and asset thresholds for small companies increased to £10.2m and £5.1m respectively for years commencing on or after 1 January 2016 as a result of the EU Accounting Directive. Small companies may apply the new limits shown for accounting purposes for periods commencing on or after 1 January 2015 but will not be able to use them to claim audit exemption for periods commencing before 1 January 2016 if they would not have otherwise been so entitled. This means that for periods commencing in 2015 there is a mismatch between the limits for accounting and auditing purposes. For periods beginning on or after 1 January 2016, however, the limits are lined up again.

Audit exemption is subject to the rights of members of the company to require an audit and is conditional on certain statements being made by the directors on the balance sheet. For years ended prior to 1 October 2012, companies also needed to satisfy both the turnover and asset criteria above. This is no longer the case.

Certain companies, such as public companies, banks and insurance companies will not qualify as small companies and will not be entitled to the exemption. Special rules also apply to companies that are members of a group. Dormant companies (including dormant public companies) may also be entitled to audit exemption under the *Companies Act* 2006, s. 480.

There are, however, many small businesses which still require an audit because they do not qualify for the exemptions and even some which fall within the exemptions but for which its shareholders or some third party, for example a lender, requests an audit. Whilst ISAs (UK) apply equally to the audit of smaller entities as to larger ones, the standards applicable do, in some cases, contain some considerations for smaller entities.

For more guidance on the accounting framework for small and micro-entities, refer to the book *Preparing Company Accounts: Small and Micros* published by Croner-i Ltd and available on CCH Online.

36.2 Guidance

Guidance to assist the auditors of small businesses in applying the documentation requirements contained within ISAs (UK) is contained in Practice Note 26, *Guidance on Smaller Entity Audit Documentation*. The current version of this was issued in December 2009 so does not specifically address documentation issues arising from subsequent amendments to the ISAs, including the revisions in 2016. It is detailed in **36.10**.

Further guidance on considerations specific to smaller entities is contained within the application material sections of many of the ISAs.

36.3 Characteristics of small businesses

The definition of a 'small business' cannot be a solely quantitative one, i.e. by reference to some measure of the size such as turnover. It also depends more upon qualitative characteristics.

Practice Note 26 notes that smaller, simpler entities are typically those where:

(a) ownership is concentrated in a small number of individuals (or one individual) who are actively involved in managing the business;

(b) the operations are uncomplicated with few sources of income and activities;

(c) business processes and accounting systems are simple; and

(d) internal controls are relatively few and may be informal.

A restriction on the number of managers that an entity has may mean that there is only limited management time to devote to such matters as formal internal control procedures. However, this lack of formality may not necessarily mean an increased risk of fraud or error. Indeed, supervisory controls exercised on a day-to-day basis by the owner-manager may also have a significant beneficial effect.

On the other hand, owner-managers may have the ability to override controls, and this may have an adverse effect on the control environment and lead to an increased risk of misstatement. The auditor must assess this based upon his knowledge of the attitude and motives of the owner-manager. In auditing small businesses, as with any other audit, the auditor should not assume that management is dishonest, but likewise should not assume unquestioned honesty.

Where a business has few sources of income and simple record-keeping procedures, this may make it easier to acquire, record and maintain knowledge of the business. Accounting populations may be very easily analysed and many analytical review tests may be simple to perform, with easily corroborated explanations for any variations found. Analytical review procedures may, as a result, significantly reduce the amounts of tests of detail to be performed.

By contrast, small businesses may have very informal accounting systems and completeness of records may therefore be a specific audit risk.

36.4 The relationship between small businesses and their auditors

Because they do not employ many people, small businesses often engage the auditor to provide additional services such as accounting, advising on accounting and computer systems, taxation and other matters such as the preparation of budgets and forecasts and assisting with obtaining finance.

This in-depth involvement with a small business will allow the auditor to keep his knowledge of the business up to date and help him to plan and conduct the audit as efficiently as possible.

Where assistance with the keeping of accounting records and the preparation of financial statements is given, the auditor is able to use the information gained as audit evidence, which may reduce the need for separate audit procedures.

Note, however, that provision of other services must always be limited by the knowledge that the client value of an audit derives from its objectivity. The auditor must always strive therefore to ensure that his relationship with small business does not prejudice his ability to form an objective opinion. To maintain this independence, he must ensure that he does not take over the role of management. This is a particular problem where management are not aware of the nature and extent of their own responsibilities in certain areas (for example, choice of accounting policies and preparation of financial statements), which they may otherwise regard as part of the audit.

The Revised Ethical Standard 2016 Section 6 – *Provisions available for small entities* provides useful guidance to the auditor in managing the potential self-review threat arising from performing non-audit services for small entities.

36.5   Responsibilities

36.5.1   *The auditor's responsibilities relating to fraud*

The fact that small businesses are often controlled by a single individual makes them more susceptible to the risk of fraud and error described in ISA (UK) 240 (Revised June 2016) *The Auditor's Responsibilities Relating to Fraud in an Audit of Financial Statements*. The auditor's knowledge of the owner-manager's general attitude to control issues and the way they exercise supervisory control will have a significant influence on his approach.

Examples of conditions or events typical of, but not exclusive to, small businesses, which may increase the likelihood of fraud or error or be indicative that it is occurring, include those set out in **Table 1**:

TABLE 1: Conditions which may indicate fraud or error

- the owner-manager has a specific motive to distort the financial statements, and has the ability to do so;
- there is confusion between personal and business transactions;
- the owner-manager's lifestyle is inconsistent with his remuneration;
- the owner-manager has not taken any holiday for a long period;
- there have been frequent changes in professional advisers;
- the audit start date is repeatedly delayed;

- there are demands to complete the audit in an unreasonably short period of time;

- accounting records are unavailable or have been lost;

- significant level of cash transactions with inadequate documentation;

- numerous unexplained aspects of audit evidence (e.g. differences with third-party confirmations, etc.);

- inappropriate use of accounting estimates;

- unusual transactions around the year end with a material effect on profit;

- unusual related party transactions; and

- excessive fees for agents or consultants.

36.5.2   Consideration of laws and regulations

The laws and regulations governing small companies tend to be largely identical to those of larger entities. A possible difference though, is the fact that small businesses tend to have less complicated activities, and thus are subject to a less complex regulatory environment. However, the auditor must assess each situation on its own merits.

36.5.3   Going concern

The same considerations apply to smaller entities as they do to larger ones; however, the forecasts and projections may be more informal and less detailed than those prepared by management of a larger entity. The auditor will need to consider whether the directors have given sufficient attention to going concern issues and the use of the going concern basis of accounting and matters affecting the entity's ability to continue as a going concern.

In many cases, management of smaller entities may not have prepared a detailed assessment of the entity's ability to continue as a going concern, but instead may rely on in-depth knowledge of the business and its future prospects. Nevertheless, the auditor needs to evaluate management's assessment and it may be appropriate to discuss the medium and long-term financing of the entity with management, provided their views can be corroborated. Continued financial support by owner-managers is often important to smaller entities' ability to continue as a going concern and the auditor may need to evaluate the owner-manager's ability to meet the obligations under the support arrangements.

Although smaller entities may be able to respond quickly to exploit opportunities, they may lack the reserves to sustain their operations in difficult times. The impact of the bank ceasing to support the entity, for example, or the loss of a principal supplier or customer may be greater than the impact on a larger entity.

Where the auditor assists an owner-manager with the assessment of going concern and the production of projections and budgets, he must ensure that the owner-manager is aware that he remains responsible for this information and the reasonableness of the assumptions on which the information is based.

36.5.4   *Agreeing the terms of the engagement*

One way of ensuring that owner-managers are aware of their responsibilities in areas such as going concern, as mentioned in **36.5.3**, and their responsibilities for financial statements, even when these have been prepared by the auditor, is to ensure that this is stated in the engagement letter.

36.5.5   *Subsequent events*

Because of the lack of reporting deadlines often associated with small companies, the length of time to be considered in a subsequent events review will often be greater.

In addition, accounting records and minutes may not have been written up since the year end and the auditor may need to rely on representations from the owner-managers. Here a representation letter, dated when the financial statements are approved and which ensures that the entire period since the year end has been covered, becomes increasingly important.

36.6   Planning, controlling and recording

36.6.1   *Planning an audit of financial statements*

The basic considerations relating to planning are identical to entities of all sizes; however, planning the audit of a small business need not be a complex or time consuming exercise. With a smaller team, coordination of, and communication between, team members should be easier.

Where accountancy work is being performed, the planning process must be properly co-ordinated in order to gain the most benefit from effort and cost. Planning should also be reconsidered as the accountancy work progresses.

Planning the audits of smaller businesses may also be easier in that much of the information may be obtained from:

- discussion with the owner-manager; and
- the knowledge of the audit engagement partner who is often involved in the provision of other services and will have some first-hand knowledge.

There will be cases where an audit is carried out entirely by the engagement partner, meaning that the issue of direction and supervision of engagement team members and review of their work does not arise. In such cases, the engagement partner, having personally conducted all aspects of the work, will be aware of all material issues. This can present other issues, however, for example, the ability to form an objective view on the appropriateness of the judgments made in the course of the audit can present practical problems when the same individual also performs the entire audit. If particularly complex or unusual issues are involved, and the audit is performed by a sole practitioner, it may be desirable to consult with other suitably-experienced auditors or the auditor's professional body.

36.6.2 *Identifying and assessing risks of material misstatement*

Often the provision of other services to small businesses enables the auditor to gain additional information about the client's accounting system, activities, management style, plans for the future, etc. However, this information may be obtained incidentally, and therefore, it is important to document such findings so that they can be taken into account when planning and conducting the audit. Irrespective of the circumstances, inquiry about identified risks and how they are addressed by management is still necessary for the audit.

The documentation must be of a level sufficient to:

- facilitate proper planning of the audit; and
- enable any change of responsibility within the audit firm (either partner or staff) to occur smoothly.

Many smaller entities will not have interim or monthly financial information that can be used for purposes of analytical procedures. In these circumstances, although the auditor may be able to perform limited analytical procedures for planning the audit or obtain some information through inquiry, he may need to plan to perform analytical procedures to identify and assess the risks of material misstatement when an early draft of the entity's financial statements is available.

36.6.3 *Materiality*

The levels of materiality used for the preparation of financial statements by the auditor and the audit work itself are likely to be different as management will want to ensure that their accounting records are as accurate as possible, which involves a greater degree of accuracy than would be necessary to give an unqualified audit opinion.

In the case of small businesses, draft financial statements may not be available on which to assess planning materiality. Therefore, it is important for any initial judgments to be revisited once the final figures are available.

To focus the auditor's attention on the more significant financial statement items, while determining the audit strategy, materiality is generally assessed by reference to some measure of the size of the business. One method is to use a percentage of a figure in the financial statements, such as:

- profit or loss before tax (adjusted, if appropriate, for the effect of any abnormal levels of items of expenditure such as directors' remuneration);

- turnover; or

- balance sheet total.

If an entity is at or near 'break-even' point, as may more often be the case with small businesses, assessing materiality as a percentage of pre-tax results alone may be inappropriate and lead to excessive audit work.

36.7   Accounting systems and internal control

36.7.1   *Identifying and assessing risks and the auditor's responses to them*

The information system and related business processes relevant to financial reporting in small entities is likely to be less sophisticated than in larger entities, but its role is just as significant. Small entities with active management involvement may not need extensive descriptions of accounting procedures, sophisticated accounting records, or written policies. Understanding the entity's information system relevant to financial reporting may therefore be easier in an audit of smaller entities, and may be more dependent on inquiry than on review of documentation. The need to obtain an understanding, however, remains important.

In applying ISAs to small entities, control risk is invariably assessed as high and therefore it is extremely unlikely that the audit of a small business will involve tests of controls. In many small businesses, there will be no formal system of internal control. This does not make such businesses 'unauditable' as it only raises the possibility of a risk of error. Such a risk may be offset by a number of factors and the absence of error may be established by reference to evidence obtained externally to the company.

In fact, a strong control environment will more often than not offset the potential problems that could result from lack of formal internal controls. Even where controls exist, they will not generally be ones that are easy to test. Thus, it is rarely cost-effective to plan to rely on them. In these circumstances, audit evidence may have to be obtained entirely through substantive procedures.

As small businesses tend to have few internal controls, the assessment of audit risk will often depend entirely on the assessment of inherent risk, as the risks identified here cannot be mitigated by a strong control environment. Therefore, it is important that the assessment of inherent risk is performed carefully and in possession of full knowledge of the client, its business and trading position.

In addition, the risks of small businesses are often mitigated by the auditor's providing of other services, such as accountancy, and this should also be taken into account.

The auditor needs to remember that although disclosures in financial statements of smaller entities may be less detailed or less complex, this does not relieve him of the responsibility to obtain an understanding of the entity and its environment, including internal control, as it relates to disclosures.

36.7.2 Service organisations

Smaller entities often make use of service organisations, for example, by using an external bookkeeping service which may do anything from the processing of certain transactions (for example, payment of payroll taxes) and maintenance of their accounting records to the preparation of their financial statements.

The use of such a service organisation for the preparation of its financial statements does not relieve management and, where appropriate, those charged with governance, of their responsibilities for the financial statements.

36.8 Evidence

36.8.1 Audit evidence and external confirmations

Although the ISAs recognise that audit evidence may be obtained from a number of sources (such as tests of controls and substantive procedures), where segregation of duties is limited and evidence of supervisory control is lacking, evidence may be obtained entirely from substantive procedures. This would often be the case for small businesses.

Assurance gained from accountancy procedures may lead to a reduction in the level of other audit procedures. This assurance may be gained through:

- examining prime documentation which supports a transaction or balance;
- calculating a balance for inclusion in the financial statements; or
- posting entries in the accounting records.

While the work may not be performed by those directly involved with the audit, it is important to ensure that the accountancy work is planned with the needs of the audit in mind.

While some verification work may be undertaken in connection with accountancy services provided to the entity, there will always be a need for some additional audit procedures in areas where this does not on its own provide sufficient assurance, for example, on the recovery of debtors, the valuation and ownership of stock, the carrying value of fixed assets and investments and the completeness of creditors. For convenience, this work may be carried out at the same time as the accountancy work.

In the case of small businesses, the completeness assertion may cause the auditor particular problems. The two main reasons for this are:

- the owner-manager occupies a dominant position and may be able to ensure that some transactions are not recorded; and
- the business may not have internal control procedures that provide documentary evidence that all transactions are recorded.

With small entities, as with other audits, the auditor should plan and conduct the audit with an 'attitude of professional scepticism', and should not accept representations from management as a substitute for other audit evidence that would be expected to be available. However, unless the audit reveals evidence to the contrary, the auditor is entitled to accept representations as truthful and records as genuine.

36.8.2 Analytical procedures

The use of analytical review procedures when planning the audit of a small business may be limited due to lack of reliable information such as interim or monthly financial reports. Therefore, analytical procedures at the planning stage may be more worthwhile once some of the accountancy work is completed. In some cases, a brief review of the general ledger or discussions with the owner-manager may prove sufficient.

When the activities of a business are uncomplicated and the number of variables to be considered is limited, analytical procedures may often be a very cost-effective way of obtaining audit assurance.

Such analytical review may also provide effective evidence regarding completeness, where expected results can be predicted with a reasonable degree of precision and confidence.

All auditors are required to perform a final analytical review to assess whether the financial statements are consistent with their knowledge of the business. However, due to the relative simplicity of small businesses many of the procedures performed are very similar to those used as substantive procedures. These may include:

- comparison to prior year;

- comparison to budget or forecast;

- review of trends in ratios;

- consideration of whether any changes in business are adequately reflected; and

- enquiry into unusual and unexplained features of the financial statements.

36.8.3 Audit sampling

The smaller populations normally encountered in small businesses may occasionally make it feasible to test:

- the whole population; or

- some part of the population – for example, all items above a given amount – applying analytical procedures to the balance of the population, if it is material.

Where the auditor decides to sample a population, the same underlying principles apply to a small business as to a larger one.

36.8.4 Written representations

An important issue in respect of audit evidence in relation to the completeness assertion is that of acceptance of management representations. In many smaller businesses, the accounting system is often controlled by one or two individuals and the auditor may have difficulty in obtaining sufficient reliable evidence to assure himself of the completeness of populations. This is particularly the case with cash businesses but may also apply to service industries or in businesses where stock is not purchased for specific customers. The auditor may also need to rely on representations when establishing that all expenditure is a valid charge on the business, given the confusion between the company and the owner in many small companies.

On their own, representations as to the completeness and accuracy of the accounting records cannot be sufficient. They may only be used if they are supported by or support the results of substantive tests of transactions and analytical review of costs and margins (or possibly one of them).

36.8.5   Initial audit engagements and comparative information

A small business which is a limited company may find itself in the position where its comparatives are taken from preceding period financial statements which were covered by the exemption from audit conferred on small companies.

The auditor will still need to obtain sufficient assurance about the opening balances and comparatives. Some information may be easily available (such as cash and debtors), but where he is unable to obtain the required evidence, he must consider qualifying his audit report. This issue is discussed in more detail in **Section 19** where a suitable report for use in this situation is set out.

36.8.6   Estimates and fair values

In smaller entities, the circumstances requiring an accounting estimate often are such that the owner-manager is capable of making the required point estimate himself. In some cases, however, an expert will be needed. Discussion with the owner-manager early in the audit process about the nature of any accounting estimates, the completeness of such estimates, and the adequacy of the estimating process may assist the owner-manager in determining the need to use an expert.

The process for making accounting estimates is likely to be less structured than in larger entities. However, just because the entity has no formal established process, it does not mean that management is not able to provide a basis upon which the auditor can test the accounting estimate.

36.8.7   Related parties

Small businesses are as likely as larger businesses to enter into related party transactions, and the disclosures are identical.

Control activities in smaller entities are likely to be less formal and smaller entities may have no documented processes for dealing with related party relationships and transactions. An owner-manager may mitigate some of the risks arising from related party transactions, or potentially increase those risks, through active involvement in all the main aspects of the transactions. For such entities, the auditor may obtain an understanding of the related party relationships and transactions, and any relevant controls that exist, through inquiry of management combined with other procedures, such as observation of management's oversight and review activities, and inspection of available relevant documentation.

Equally, auditors of small businesses are more likely to be closely involved in the preparation of the financial statements, and may have a relatively detailed knowledge of the businesses' transactions, enabling them to identify those that are disclosable.

36.9   Reporting

36.9.1   *The independent auditor's report on financial statements*

The auditor's reports, including the auditor's report on a small company are discussed in **Section 4** (see **4.25**).

36.9.2   *Communication with those charged with governance*

In the case of smaller entities, the auditor may communicate in a less structured manner with those charged with governance than in the case of listed or larger entities. This is acceptable provided communication is still relevant and appropriate.

Small businesses will often have simple, informal accounting systems and the scope for detailed internal control procedures based on segregation of duties will be limited. This is not necessarily a weakness, as the accounting system in place may be suitable for the size and complexity of the business and the degree of owner-manager involvement. The auditor must, therefore, ensure that recommendations to management are relevant and realistic to their business.

In addition, if management has not acted upon points made in previous management letters as the suggestions are not practical or cost-effective, the auditor is likely to gain little from repeating the same recommendations again. However, he should continue to check that the recommendations remain valid.

While the concepts underlying control activities in smaller entities are likely to be similar to those in larger entities, they are likely to operate in a less formal manner.

Smaller entities may also find that certain types of control activities are not necessary because of controls applied by management. For example, management's sole authority for granting credit to customers and approving significant purchases can provide effective control over important account balances and transactions, lessening or removing the need for more detailed control activities.

This higher level of management involvement needs to be balanced against the greater potential for management override of controls.

36.10 Practice Note 26 and documentation

36.10.1 Background

Practice Note 26, *Guidance on Smaller Entity Audit Documentation* is aimed at auditors of companies that are exempt from audit, but have chosen to have a voluntary audit. It provides guidance on the application of the documentation requirements set out in the ISAs (UK) for the audits of such entities.

Practice Note 26 provides examples of documentation where working papers have been prepared to meet the requirements of the ISAs, but without documenting the entirety of the auditor's understanding of the entity and matters related to it. The illustrative examples are not, however, mandatory.

It is also worth remembering that the auditor of a smaller entity may find it helpful and efficient to record various aspects of the audit together in a single document, with cross-references to supporting working papers as appropriate.

36.10.2 The purpose of audit documentation

ISA (UK) 230 (Revised June 2016) *Audit Documentation* requires auditors to prepare audit documentation that provides:

- a sufficient and appropriate record of the basis for the auditor's report; and

- evidence that the audit was performed in accordance with ISAs (UK) and applicable legal and regulatory requirements.

In addition, good documentation serves a number of purposes, including:

- assisting the audit team to plan and perform the audit;

- assisting members of the audit team to fulfil their review responsibilities;

- enabling the audit team to be accountable for its work;

- retaining a record of matters of continuing significance to future audits; and

- enabling an experienced auditor to conduct quality control reviews or external inspections as required.

These points remain relevant irrespective of the size of the entity. However, the audit documentation for the audit of a smaller entity will generally be less extensive than that for the audit of a larger entity.

36.10.3   *Special considerations for smaller entities*

A number of factors will influence the nature and extent of documentation required for a small company:

- the qualitative indicators of a simple entity:

    - ownership is concentrated in a small number of individuals who are actively involved in managing the business;

    - the operations are uncomplicated;

    - business processes and accounting systems are simple; and

    - internal controls are relatively few and may be informal;

- the characteristics of a smaller entity audit team and the way they carry out their work, including:

    - the provision of accounting and business related advice;

    - relatively small team size; and

    - the use of proprietary audit systems.

Concentration of ownership and management

For small entities, there are often few owners who are typically involved in the day to day running of the company, and this means that documentation of ownership is typically brief. Particular care should be taken, however, when documenting family and other close relationships which may impact the auditor's risk assessment in respect of related parties.

Uncomplicated operations

Typically, smaller entities have a limited range of products or services and a limited number of locations. This means that documentation of the auditor's understanding of their operations is likely to be simple and relatively brief. Such documentation may be in free-form narrative notes or by completing a structured form.

Simple accounting systems

For small companies, accounting systems are typically uncomplicated, with few, if any, personnel solely engaged in record keeping. There are likely to be no documented descriptions of accounting policies and procedures and limited opportunities for segregation of duties.

Small entities will typically use well known accounting systems, and previous knowledge of that system can help the auditor focus on areas of risk.

Limited and informal controls

For the audit of smaller entities, most of the audit evidence will typically come from substantive tests of detail. However, there is still a requirement for the auditor to document his understanding of the entity's system of internal control relevant to the audit.

Both size and economic considerations mean that internal controls are usually limited in such operations, but the direct control that management is able to exert will be an important feature of the control environment. Therefore, the extent and nature of management's involvement is likely to be a key aspect of the auditor's documentation, including whether the dominant position of management may be abused, leading to an override of controls.

Professional relationship between auditors and small entity clients

It is common for audit firms to provide non-audit services to smaller clients. The provision of such services can help the auditor gain further understanding of the entity and keep his knowledge up to date. The auditor must keep in mind, however, the need to maintain objectivity throughout his work.

The Practice Note lists the following considerations associated with providing non-audit services:

- to achieve completeness of audit documentation, information, gained as a result of the provision of other services, which is used as audit evidence needs to be incorporated or cross-referenced into the audit documentation;

- the auditor's assessment of his objectivity and independence is documented, including a description of the threats identified and the safeguards applied to eliminate or reduce the threats to an acceptable level; and

- the respective responsibilities of directors (or equivalent) and the auditor are documented in an engagement letter. This is particularly important where the audit firm is involved in the preparation of the financial statements.

Small audit team

Whatever the size of the audit team, even if it is an audit partner working alone, the documentation must be sufficient to enable an experienced auditor, having no previous connection with the audit, to understand the audit approach adopted, the audit evidence obtained, and the significant matters arising during the audit and the conclusions reached thereon.

If the audit team size increases, further documentation may be useful in enabling the team to obtain an appropriate understanding of the entity.

Use of proprietary audit system

Where the auditor of a small entity operates in a small practice, proprietary audit systems are likely to be used. Such systems are designed to deal with a wide variety of situations and must be tailored or adapted to meet each client's circumstances.

Sections of such systems relating to documenting the client, its operations and controls are usually checklists or blank spaces for narrative notes. Audit team members should be adequately trained before using such tools to ensure that they do not prepare excessive and, therefore, costly audit documentation.

36.10.4 Audit documentation requirements in the ISAs

The Practice Note lists the documentation requirements set out in each ISA on an ISA by ISA basis. The table is not reproduced here. The Practice Note, and hence the table, has not been updated since it was written in 2009. This means that the documentation requirements listed have not been updated for any amendments in recent revisions of ISAs (UK), including those in the June 2016 revisions.

36.11 International guidance

IFAC has also issued a *Guide to Using ISAs in the Audits of Small- and Medium-Sized Entities*. The guide is based on ISAs; however, it is still applicable to audits under ISAs (UK) and is useful reading for auditors of smaller entities. The guide can be found on the IFAC website (www.ifac.org).

37 Other operational issues

37.1 Introduction

This section covers various guidance issued by the ICAEW and FRC covering:

- the auditing implications of FRS 102;
- implications of IFRS transition;
- XBRL tagging of information in financial statements;
- paid cheques;
- auditing when financial market conditions are difficult; and
- the auditing implications of Brexit.

37.2 The auditing implications of FRS 102

FRS 102 *The Financial Reporting Standard applicable in the UK and Ireland* became effective for accounting periods beginning on or after 1 January 2015 and replaced almost all previous UK accounting standards, from which it differed in a number of significant respects. For periods commencing on or after 1 January 2016, FRS 102 was extended to apply to small entities through the inclusion of Section 1A, replacing the FRSSE. Adoption of the new standard and the differences between it and the previous standards gives rise to issues for both companies and their auditors.

The new UK GAAP standards and detailed guidance are available online from Croner-i Tax and Accounting as well as in various books published by Croner-i Ltd.

37.2.1 Guidance for auditors

In September 2014, the ICAEW published Technical Release TECH 13/14AAF *Issues for Auditors Arising from the Implementation of FRS 102, The Financial Reporting Standard applicable in the UK and Republic of Ireland*. This Technical Release was updated and reissued in November 2017.

FRS 102 is applicable to all entities which are neither required nor elect to apply EU-adopted IFRSs, FRS 101 *Reduced Disclosure Framework* or FRS 105 *The Financial Reporting Standard applicable to the Micro-entities Regime*. It is therefore applied by the majority of UK entities subject to audit.

There are significant implications for the auditors of the entities subject to this change and TECH 13/14AAF addresses the key issues of concern to those auditors. It covers the technical and process challenges arising for them and the risks that they will need to address, as well as ethical issues that may arise. Auditors should consider at an early stage both what they should expect their clients to be doing and also what they should be doing themselves. Auditors should take early action and advise their clients to start preparing for transition as early as possible, if they have not done so already.

There are a number of things the auditor should expect the entity to consider. To ensure the client entity is appropriately prepared for the transition, the auditor may wish to have an early discussion with the client about their plans, including considering the following areas:

- clarifying the responsibilities of management;

- establishing a timeline for transition;

- communicating changes with stakeholders;

- assessing the need for any additional resources or training;

- identifying the differences between the entity's current accounting policies and FRS 102;

- identifying any changes in financial data and additional information needed to meet the revised requirements;

- identifying any impact on wider business issues, such as considering bank covenant arrangements;

- planning the transition process; and

- implementing the changes.

37.2.2 Ethical considerations

Many entities are likely to benefit from the support of their auditors in the transition process, however, the auditor needs to ensure he considers ethical matters before providing assistance to clients. For example, clients may ask the auditor to provide accounting assistance in the preparation of financial statements under FRS 102, or ask for advice on the tax consequences that might arise as a result of FRS 102, or assistance with valuations under FRS 102. In all of these situations, the auditor must carefully document the nature of the service and consider all threats and safeguards before concluding whether he is able to assist the client.

In providing such advice, the auditor needs to guard against giving bookkeeping advice or making specific accounting entries that go beyond those permitted by the FRC's Revised Ethical Standard 2016, Section 5, i.e. beyond those considered to be of a technical, mechanical or informative nature (see **Section 2**). When considering the extent to which the auditor may provide advice to his clients on the transition to FRS 102, it should be clearly established that management retains full responsibility for all financial information, including the selection and application of appropriate accounting policies. Management cannot ask their auditor to make decisions about the preparation and presentation of financial statements under the new standard. Whilst the auditor can assist in identifying the choices that need to be made and discussing them with management, he cannot make any of these choices for management.

Similarly, the Revised Ethical Standard 2016 contains strict prohibitions on the provision of valuations by the auditor. On transition to FRS 102, many entities will be required to carry more items at a valuation than under their previous GAAP. Where the entity is not familiar with valuation techniques for such items, they may ask the auditor for assistance. However, in accordance with the Revised Ethical Standard 2016, the auditor is not permitted to provide a valuation for a listed entity where the valuation is material, nor for any other entity where the valuation involves a significant degree of subjective judgment and has a material effect on the financial statements, either separately or in aggregate with other valuations provided.

TECH 13/14AAF provides further details of ethical considerations and scenarios.

37.2.3 Potential problem areas

With the adoption of FRS 102, **Table 1** shows some of the areas which may present problems for the client and/or auditor:

TABLE 1: Potential problem areas with the adoption of FRS 102	
Audit team members and engagement partner	Do the audit team, and the engagement partner, themselves have the necessary skills and competence or do they themselves require additional training in FRS 102?
Ethical requirements	As noted in **37.2.2**, there may be an increased likelihood of threats arising from the provision of non-audit services.

TABLE 1: Potential problem areas with the adoption of FRS 102	
Fraud risk assessment	Changes to accounting systems may provide increased opportunity for aggressive earnings management and fraud.
Comparatives	The date of transition is the commencement of the comparative period. Comparatives will need to be restated under FRS 102 and an opening statement of balances at the date of transition also prepared. There may be some items in the financial statements for which management may find it difficult to obtain historical valuations and such information should be gathered as soon as possible.
Transitional adjustments	Transitional adjustments may be permitted and/or required in certain areas, for example, property valuation, recognition of forex forward contracts, deferred tax provisions. Such adjustments may reduce reserves to such a level that they affect dividends already paid out if not considered in good time.
Goodwill	FRS 102 has different requirements around the determination of a useful economic life for goodwill.
Fair values	FRS 102 may require assets to be revalued to fair value. This includes investment properties previously valued at market value. This may create problems in setting a fair value for the first time. The auditor will also need to ensure that exceptions granted by FRS 102 are not abused by client entities.
Pension schemes	Under FRS 102, for groups, the pension deficit will likely need to be recognised in at least one entity rather than just at a group level. This can impact on reserves and tax and the auditor should be aware of this when auditing component entities.

TECH 13/14AAF contains detailed guidance on the implementation of FRS 102, and also contains a very helpful table in Appendix 1 highlighting some of the specific issues likely to arise during the period of implementing FRS 102.

37.3 Implications of IFRS transition

Where an entity is required, or chooses, to adopt EU adopted IFRSs in its financial statements, similar issues arise as with transition to FRS 102 and auditors may wish to refer to TECH 13/14AAF.

In 2014, the ICAEW's Audit and Assurance Faculty issued Technical Release Audit 03/04 *Auditing Implications of IFRS Transition* providing specific guidance for auditors in this area. This technical release remains extant although auditors will need to bear in mind that IFRS and auditing and ethical standards have changed considerably since then.

TECH 13/13AAF notes that Audit 03/04 may also be relevant to entities applying FRS 101 *Reduced Disclosure Framework*.

37.4   XBRL tagging of information in financial statements

37.4.1   Background

In February 2010, the APB issued Bulletin 2010/1, *XBRL tagging of information in audited financial statements – Guidance for auditors*. This was in response to the joint statement by HMRC and Companies House made in September 2009, that the Company Tax Return, including the supporting statutory accounts and tax computations showing the derivation from those accounts of the entries in the Company Tax Return, must be delivered electronically using the Inline XBRL (iXBRL) format. This requirement has been mandatory since accounting periods ending on or after 31 March 2010 where the tax return is submitted to HMRC after 31 March 2011.

XBRL stands for Extensible Business Reporting Language and it is a computer-based language for the electronic communication of business data. It works by tagging individual items of information with machine-readable codes which are drawn from a library of codes referred to as a 'taxonomy'. The use of XBRL allows data to be more easily accessed, manipulated and reviewed. In line XBRL uses tags which can still be read by the human eye, for example, by hovering the computer mouse over the tagged item.

37.4.2   Auditor's involvement

Aspects of XBRL tagging can be automated, but there is likely to remain an element of judgment over which tag to map to which piece of data.

There is no requirement for an audit of the data or the XBRL tagging and the ISAs (UK) do not impose a general requirement on the auditor to check the tagging. In addition, because the XBRL tag is just a machine-readable rendering of the data in the financial statements it does not constitute 'other information' as defined in ISA (UK) 720 (Revised June 2016) *The Auditor's Responsibilities Relating to Other Information*, and the requirement to read the other information with the purpose of identifying material inconsistencies or material misstatement is not invoked (see **Section 34**).

There is a possibility that regulators may impose a requirement for companies to obtain assurance from their auditor on XBRL-tagged data in the future.

However, some companies may wish to engage an audit or accountancy firm to:

- perform the tagging exercise;
- perform an agreed upon procedures engagement to provide assurance about the tagging process;
- provide advice on the selection of individual tags;
- supply accounts preparation software that automates the tagging; or
- train management in XBRL tagging.

If such non-audit services are provided by the company's auditor, he must consider whether any possible threats to independence and objectivity arise. Particular care must be taken not to take decisions that are the responsibility of the management of the entity and suitable safeguards should be put in place.

Although there is currently no audit requirement in relation to XBRL tagging, firms should carefully consider how services provided either to set up a system for XBRL tagging or to tag data on behalf of a client may become a self-review threat if an audit requirement is introduced in future years. If XBRL becomes integrated into accounting systems, it may be difficult to separate tagging from accounting services. In such situations, the prohibition in the Revised Ethical Standard 2016 Section 5 that auditors of listed companies (or significant affiliates of listed companies) cannot provide accounting services to those clients will apply (see **2.6.7**).

37.4.3   *Technical Release AAF 04/10*

In June 2011, the Audit and Assurance Faculty of the ICAEW issued Technical Release AAF 04/10 *Guidance for performing agreed-upon procedures engagements that address XBRL-tagged data included within financial statements prepared in iXBRL format* to provide guidance for practitioners who are requested to perform agreed upon procedures engagements in relation to XBRL-tagged data.

In order for iXBRL to be useful, the data included must be accurate and reliable. Businesses may request practitioners to perform additional procedures to address the accuracy, existence, completeness or consistency of XBRL tagged information included within financial statements.

Terms of engagement

As a company's tax return to HMRC is a private submission, the majority of such agreed upon procedures engagements will not involve a third party and the terms of engagement should be agreed between practitioners and management. Where a company's auditor is requested to perform the procedures, he should ensure that he has satisfied himself that there are no threats to independence that arise in relation to the Revised Ethical Standard 2016 (see **Section 2**). Particular attention should be applied to the management threat and the self-review threat.

The entity's management is responsible for selecting the XBRL tags to be used and for applying them to the financial information. The practitioner will provide a factual report on his findings and will provide no assurance or opinion. The report should be addressed solely to those who have agreed to the procedures being performed.

An example engagement letter is given in the Technical Release.

Planning

Practitioners must obtain a general understanding of the tags or taxonomies relevant to the engagement and should be mindful that taxonomies are subject to periodic revision and may not remain relevant year on year. If the engagement requires expertise beyond that possessed by the practitioner, an expert may be used to assist with the engagement (see **Section 31**).

Procedures

The extent of procedures performed will be agreed between the practitioner and management. The level of testing required will be determined by:

- the length of the financial statements and the number of taggable items contained therein;

- the relevant taxonomies used;

- the method of preparation of the financial statements and the controls over their preparation; and

- management's expectations of the competence and experience of those who performed the tagging.

Possible procedures may include checking:

- the consistency of the human-readable element of the iXBRL financial statements with the source signed financial statements which were previously approved by the directors;

- whether the correct taxonomies have been applied;

- the accuracy, existence, completeness and consistency of XBRL-tagged data; and

- any company-specific extensions to the relevant taxonomies.

Further possible procedures are provided in an appendix to the Technical Release.

Reporting

The report should be factual in nature and not give an opinion. An example report is given the Technical Release.

37.5 Paid cheques

Changes in legislation and audit practices have made it less important for the auditor to review paid cheques returned to entities by their clearing bank.

37.5.1 Existing guidance

Guidance in this area was updated in February 2009 with the publication of the ICAEW's Audit and Assurance Faculty Technical Release AAF 1/09 *Paid Cheques*. The guidance encourages the auditor to:

- consider using alternative procedures;

- advise his clients to adopt more rigorous controls over cheque payments; and

- use cost-effective methods of examining paid cheques where they consider it to be necessary.

The statement does not provide detailed procedural guidance.

37.5.2 Audit evidence

Where adequate controls exist over purchasing and cheque payments, it may not be necessary to examine returned cheques. In cases where controls are weak, the auditor may want evidence that:

- there has been no fraudulent endorsement of cheques;

- cheques are properly recorded and controlled; and

- the cash book accurately reflects details of them.

With regard to purchase ledger items, other forms of evidence may be sufficient such as the reconciliation of supplier statements. Evidence on other items may be obtained from analytical review or examination of supporting evidence.

Additionally, the entity may use other forms of payment, such as electronic funds transfers, standing orders or direct debits.

37.5.3   Cheques Act 1992

Further controls against fraudulent endorsement comes from the *Cheques Act* 1992, which means that cheques crossed 'account payee' cannot be transferred by way of endorsement. Many banks now pre-print their cheques with this, which greatly reduces the risk and, in turn, the auditor's need to examine paid cheques.

37.5.4   Obtaining paid cheques

Where the auditor decides that he needs to review paid cheques, he should aim to choose the most cost-effective method of obtaining this evidence. Discussions with the client and their bank will normally be necessary as to the most appropriate method. Options include:

- returning all paid cheques to the client;
- providing the auditor with an agreed number of paid cheques directly, the selection being left to the bank;
- providing photocopies of paid cheques;
- extracting cheques before they are stored and forwarding them to the auditor directly; and
- providing specific paid cheques at the auditor's request.

Where paid cheques are to be sent to the auditor directly by the bank, authority will have to be provided by the client.

37.6   Auditing when financial market conditions are difficult

In January 2008, the APB issued Bulletin 2008/1 *Auditing issues when financial market conditions are difficult and credit facilities may be restricted* in response to developments in the financial markets commonly termed 'the credit crunch'.

As financial markets are characterised by difficult trading conditions made worse by a reduction in liquidity, entities with exposure to the financial markets through debt, equity, derivative and leveraged finance activities may experience a significant difficulty both trading in and valuing certain investments. This in turn will lead to an increased risk of material misstatement in the financial statements.

Even for those businesses outside the financial sector, the effect may be felt through:

- reduced liquidity making it expensive or impossible to replace finance arrangements that have expired, which may lead to going concern issues; and

- an increased difficulty in valuing investments where there has been a curtailment or cessation in market trading.

The Bulletin did not establish any new requirements, but pulled together guidance from the APB's other material into one place and provides useful guidance should such conditions be experienced again.

37.7 Auditing implications of Brexit

The UK's decision to leave the European Union has resulted, for some businesses, in a period of significant uncertainty which may lead to entities encountering difficulties trading and uncertainties about their futures. In turn, this may lead to an increased risk of material misstatement in financial statements.

Auditors will need to ensure they consider a variety of related issues, including:

- the volatility of foreign exchange rates and the potential impact on financial statements;

- the possible impact on any overseas trading that the entity may be involved in;

- the potential increase in supply prices and availability;

- the potential impact on asset valuations, and on valuation of pension deficits; and

- whether the going concern assessment and viability statement review remain appropriate.

Auditors will also wish to see appropriate disclosures relating to significant risks and ensure that statements made in the directors report or strategic report regarding risks or future prospects are consistent with the information in the financial statements and with their own knowledge gained during the course of the audit.

38 Change of auditor

38.1 Introduction

There are three main ways in which an auditor can cease to hold office under the *Companies Act* 2006 ('the Act'):

- removal (s. 510–513), where the auditor is removed by the company by ordinary resolution at a general meeting;

- resignation (s. 516–518), where the auditor sends a notice in writing to the company's registered office; or

- failure to reappoint an auditor (s. 514–515), which occurs when a company proposes a resolution (either written or at a general meeting), the effect of which is to appoint a person as auditor in place of the outgoing auditor whose term of office has expired, or is due to expire.

Under the Act, each of these methods of ceasing to hold office require certain statements to be made by the auditor and the company. These are set out in **38.2**.

For periods commencing on or after 1 October 2015, the *Deregulation Act* 2015, s. 18 and Sch. 5 amended the *Companies Act* 2006, s. 519–525 regarding statements to be made by the auditor when ceasing to hold appointment. These latest rules distinguish between 'public interest companies' (companies with any securities listed in the UK or equity securities officially listed in an EEA state) and other companies and provide exemptions where the auditor ceases to hold office because the company becomes audit exempt, enters into insolvency proceedings or, in the case of a subsidiary, the audit is taken over by the group auditor. The main purpose of the changes to the rules was to simplify procedures and remove some of the duplication of reporting that existed previously, especially in situations where the change in appointment resulted from a change in the company's circumstances rather than a change in the relationship between auditor and client.

It should be noted that whilst in many cases a 'public interest company' will also be a 'public interest entity' (PIE) as referred to by the ISAs, the two definitions are not the same.

For example, an entity can be a PIE without being a company under the Companies Act, whereas only companies under the Act can be 'public interest companies'. Another example is a company with debt (as opposed to equity) listed in the EEA which would not fall into the 'public interest company' definition, but would fall into the PIE definition.

Once an auditor has been replaced, the incoming auditor may wish to use information gathered by the outgoing auditor. Under the Act, and for periods commencing on or after 6 April 2008, the outgoing auditor is required to provide access to relevant information where the newly appointed auditor makes a written request for such access. Guidance on obtaining this access is given in the ICAEW's Technical Release AAF 01/08 *Access to Information by Successor Auditors*. This is discussed in **38.3**.

The ICAEW has also issued, in November 2016, two helpsheets to explain changes to the statutory procedures required when an auditor resigns, following the *Deregulation Act* 2015. These are entitled *Auditor responsibilities on resignation from a non-public interest company for financial years beginning on or after 1 October 2015* and *Non-public interest company responsibilities when the auditor ceases to act for financial years beginning on or after 1 October 2015*. The second of these shows the responsibilities of the company using a flowchart.

38.2   Procedures on cessation of office as auditor

38.2.1   The Companies Act 2006 requirements

The *Deregulation Act* 2015 made a number of changes to the provisions of the *Companies Act* 2006 dealing with auditor resignation and removal. The result is that new procedures apply where an auditor resigns in respect of a financial period commencing on or after 1 October 2015.

Slightly different procedures apply depending on whether or not:

- the company is a 'public interest company' (a company with any securities included in the Official List of the Financial Conduct Authority or equity securities officially listed in an EEA state);

- the auditor ceases to hold office at the end of his term of office;

- the reasons for the auditor ceasing to hold office are 'exempt' reasons; and

- there are matters which the auditor considers need to be brought to the attention of members or creditors.

38.2.2 All companies

The rules essentially require that:

- except in certain circumstances in the case of a non-public interest company, the outgoing auditor provides a statement of reasons for the change;
- where appropriate, the auditor will also provide a statement of matters that he considers should be brought to the attention of members and creditors;
- statements are filed by the auditor with the appropriate regulatory body (ICAEW or FRC);
- where the auditor ceases mid-term or where the reasons are not all exempt reasons the company is also required to file a statement with the appropriate audit authority;
- the company may apply to the court if it thinks that the auditor's statement is defamatory, otherwise it is obliged to send the auditor's statement to members (except in the case of non-public interest companies where there are no matters to be brought to the attention of members or creditors);
- for public interest companies and others where there are matters to be brought to the attention of members or creditors, statements are filed at Companies House.

38.2.3 Non-public interest companies

Auditor appointment ceases at end of term

Where, in the case of a private company, the auditor ceases to hold office at the end of a period for appointing auditors, or, in the case of a public company, at the end of an accounts meeting:

- the auditor notifies the company of ceasing to act; and
- no further actions are necessary.

This is the most straightforward situation, but unfortunately one which is least likely in practice as, in the case of private companies, it is not always easy to determine when the end of the period for appointing auditors is and in any case this may well not coincide with the timing of the company's decision to change auditor.

EXAMPLE

An auditor is appointed to perform the audit of a non-major private company for the year ended 30 April 2016. The period for appointing an auditor to perform the audit for the year ended 30 April 2017 ends on 27 February 2017 (i.e. filing deadline of 30 January 2017 plus 28 days) or, if earlier, 28 days after the April 2016 accounts are sent to members.

Note – the period for appointing auditors is a period of 28 days beginning with the end of the time allowed for sending out the annual report and accounts for the previous financial year or, if earlier, the date on which the annual report and accounts were actually sent out to members.

Auditor appointment ceases mid-term

The auditor has to consider first whether the reasons for his ceasing to hold office are all exempt reasons.

Exempt reasons are:

- the auditor is ceasing to carry out statutory audit work within the meaning of the *Companies Act* 2006, s. 1210;
- the company intends to take advantage of audit exemption under the *Companies Act* 2006;
- the company is a subsidiary of a UK company that prepares group accounts and the audit is to be carried out by the group auditor (provided that the group auditor is to take over the audit of all UK subsidiaries where an audit is required);
- the company is being wound up under the Insolvency Act or a petition for winding up has been presented and not withdrawn.

If all reasons are exempt reasons AND the auditor has no matters which he considers should be drawn to the attention of members or creditors, he simply needs to deposit a notice of resignation and no further actions are necessary.

If the reasons are not all exempt reasons, OR there are matters to be brought to the attention of members or creditors then the auditor is required to prepare and send to the company a statement of reasons for his ceasing to hold office (a 'section 519 statement').

38.2.4   *Section 519 statement*

Where a s. 519 statement is required, this must be sent to the company's registered office and state:

- the auditor's name and address;

- the auditor's registered number (as entered in the register of auditors);

- the company's name and registered number;

- the auditor's reasons for ceasing to hold office;

- details of any matters connected with his ceasing to hold office which the auditor considers need to be brought to the attention of members or creditors of the company – or if there are none, a statement to that effect.

The s. 519 statement must be sent as follows:

Reason for cessation of appointment	Timeframe for delivery of s. 519 statement to the company
Resignation	Must accompany the notice of resignation
Failure to seek reappointment	At least 14 days before the end of the time allowed for next appointing an auditor
Removal/not reappointed	Up to 14 days after ceasing to hold office

38.2.5   Notifications – non-public interest companies

Notification to ICAEW (auditor and company)

Where a s. 519 statement has been prepared, the auditor, at the same time, sends a copy to the appropriate audit authority which will be the Recognised Supervisory Body ('RSB') with which he is registered. In the case of auditors registered with the ICAEW, notifications should be sent to:

Change of Auditor Notifications
Quality Assurance Department
ICAEW
Metropolitan House
321 Avebury Boulevard
Milton Keynes
MK9 2FZ

or by e-mail to auditorchange@icaew.com.

Under the *Companies Act* 2006, s. 523, the company is also required to notify the audit authority. This can be done by preparing a statement that the auditor is ceasing to hold office, including what the company believes are the reasons for the auditor ceasing to hold office and containing the auditor's name and registered number and the company's name and registered number. Alternatively, the company can simply endorse a copy of the s. 519 statement and send that to the RSB. In either case, the notification should be sent within 28 days of the auditor ceasing to hold office.

Notification to members (by company)

Where circumstances are set out in the s. 519 statement, the company may apply to the court if it believes the auditor is using the statement to secure needless publicity for a defamatory matter. The application to the court must be made by the company within 14 days of receiving the statement.

In other cases, the company must send the statement, within 14 days of receipt, to members and any other person who is entitled to receive copies of the accounts under the *Companies Act* 2006, s. 423.

Notification to registrar (by auditor)

Where the s. 519 statement includes a statement to the effect that the auditor considers that none of the reasons for his ceasing to hold office and no matters (if any) connected with his ceasing to hold office need to be brought to the attention of members or creditors of the company, there is no need for either the auditor or the company to send a copy to the registrar.

Where the s. 519 statement does include such matters then the auditor should send a copy to the registrar. In this situation, he should wait 21 days after depositing the statement with the company and, provided he has not, in that time, received notice from the company of an application to the court, then he should send the statement to the registrar within a further seven days.

38.2.6 Public interest companies

In the case of a public interest company, the auditor must always prepare a s. 519 statement, as in **38.2.4**, regardless of the reasons for ceasing to hold office or circumstances connected with this. The auditor cannot, in this statement, say that there are no matters to bring to the attention of members or creditors as the statement in respect of a public interest entity will always be sent to the members and be filed at Companies House.

The auditor sends his s. 519 statement to the company and, at the same time, to the appropriate audit authority, which for a public interest company is the FRC:

Change of Auditor Notifications
Financial Reporting Council
8th Floor, 125 London Wall
London
EC2Y 5AS

or by e-mail to auditorchange@frc.org.uk.

Notification to members (by company)

As in **38.2.5**, the company may, within 14 days, apply to the court if it thinks that the auditor is using the statement to secure needless publicity for a defamatory matter. In all other cases, the company must, within 14 days send the statement to members and others entitled to receive the accounts of the company under the *Companies Act* 2006, s. 423.

Notification to registrar (by auditor)

In all cases, the auditor should send a copy of the section 519 statement to the registrar. In this situation, he should wait 21 days after depositing the statement with the company and, provided he has not, in that time, received notice from the company of an application to the court (as noted in the previous paragraph) then he should send the statement to the registrar within a further seven days.

Auditor appointment ceases at end of term

A public interest company will always be a public company and the auditor's term of office will cease at the conclusion of the accounts meeting (the general meeting of the company at which accounts are laid before members) unless he is re-appointed.

For most public interest companies, the timing of issue of the s. 519 statement is important as the company will generally want to send out the statement to members along with the notice of AGM. This will usually be at least 21 days in advance of the AGM date.

Auditor appointment ceases mid-term

Where the appointment ceases mid-term, the procedure is the same as for cessation at the end of term with one exception which is that if the auditor's reasons for ceasing to hold office are not all exempt reasons, then the company should also send a statement to the FRC. As with a non-public interest company, this can be done by the company sending its own statement of reasons or endorsing and forwarding the auditor's s. 519 statement.

38.2.7 Legal advice

In most situations, the reasons for the change in appointment are straightforward and uncontentious and there are no matters that the auditor considers need to be brought to the attention of members or creditors. However, auditors should be alert to the fact that where there are such matters, and in all cases for public interest entities, the s. 519 statement will be on public record and may be considered sensitive. Auditors may wish to ensure that all s. 519 statements are reviewed by someone with appropriate seniority in the firm before issue and in difficult cases seek legal advice.

TABLE 1: Auditor cessation – non-public interest company

Non-public interest company	Auditor notifies company of resignation or company notifies auditor of termination	Section 519 statement required				Company statement of reasons (s. 523)
		Auditor sends section 519 statement to company and audit authority (ICAEW)	Includes matters for attention of members/creditors OR statement that there are no such matters	Company sends to members or applies to court	Auditor waits 21 days then sends to registrar if no court application made	Company sends statement of reasons to audit authority (ICAEW)
Cessation at end of term – no action required						
Cessation mid term but all reasons are exempt reasons and no matters for attention of members/creditors	✓					
Other situations (non-exempt reasons and/or matters for attention of members/creditors)		✓	✓			✓ (but only if reasons are non-exempt)
If there are matters for attention of members or creditors				✓	✓	

TABLE 2: Auditor cessation – public interest company

Public interest company	Section 519 statement always required			Company statement of reasons (s. 523)
	Auditor sends section 519 statement to company and audit authority (FRC)	Company sends to members or applies to court.	Auditor waits 21 days then sends to registrar if no court application made	Company sends statement of reasons to audit authority (FRC)
In all cases	✓	✓	✓	
AND Where cessation is mid-term AND reasons are not all exempt reasons				✓

TABLE 3: Example section 519 statement for a non-public interest company

Statement under the *Companies Act* 2006, s. 519

To the Directors of [Company Name and Registered Number]

In accordance with s. 519 of the Act, we set out the following reason[s] for ceasing to hold office as auditor of the company:

- [SPECIFY REASONS ...]

These [are/are not] all considered to be exempt reasons as defined in s. 519A of the Act.

Either:

We consider that the following matter(s) connected with our ceasing to hold office as auditors need to be brought to the attention of members or creditors of the company:

- [GIVE DETAILS ...]

Or:

We consider that none of the reasons for us ceasing to hold office and no matters connected with our ceasing to hold office need to be brought to the attention of members or creditors of the company.

[Auditor name]
[Auditor registered number]
[Date]

TABLE 4: Example letter of resignation of auditors of a non-public interest company in circumstances where no section 519 statement required

The Directors

[Company]

[Address]

Dear Sirs

Cessation as auditors

If ceasing at end of term

As discussed, we confirm that we will cease to be auditors of the company when our term of office expires 28 days after the date you send the company's financial statements to members or the latest date on which they are due for filing at Companies House, if later.

We would like to take this opportunity to remind you of your obligation to appoint new auditors under s. 485 of the *Companies Act* 2006 ('the Act') unless you consider you will meet the conditions for exemption from audit under the Act.

OR

If ceasing mid term

We hereby resign as auditors of the company with effect from [date]. We consider that our reasons for ceasing to hold office are considered exempt reasons under *Companies Act* 2006, s. 519A(3) and we have no matters to bring to the attention of members or creditors.

Yours faithfully

Auditor

TABLE 5: Example letter of resignation of auditors of a non-public interest private company in non-exempt circumstances – s. 519 statement required

The Directors

[Company]

[Address]

Dear Sirs

Cessation as auditors

We hereby resign as auditors of the company with effect from [date]. We consider that our reasons for ceasing to hold office are not all considered exempt reasons under *Companies Act* 2006, s. 519A(3) and accordingly, we enclose the statement required under s. 519 of the Act setting out the reasons for our ceasing to hold office.

As required under the Companies Act, we have sent a copy of the statement to the ICAEW as the appropriate audit authority. You are also required to notify the ICAEW of the reasons for our ceasing to hold office. If you agree with our statement, you may do this simply by endorsing a copy of the statement indicating your agreement and sending it to:

Change of Auditor Notifications

Quality Assurance Department

ICAEW

Metropolitan House

321 Avebury Boulevard

Milton Keynes

MK9 2FZ

or by e-mail to auditorchange@icaew.com.

If you do not agree, you should write separately to ICAEW setting out what you consider the reasons to be. In either case, the Act provides that your notification should be sent within 28 days from the date on which we cease to hold office.

[*If the statement contains matters to be brought to the attention of members or creditors*

The statement also sets out matters we consider need to be brought to the attention of members or creditors of the company. You are required, within 14 days of receipt, either to send a copy of the statement to members of the company and all others entitled to receive copies of the company's annual report and accounts, or to apply to the Court for a direction. If you apply to the court, you should let us know. If we do not receive notification that you have applied to the Court, we will send a copy of the statement to the registrar of companies for filing.]

Yours faithfully

Auditor

TABLE 6: Example letter of resignation of auditors of a public interest company

The Directors

[Company]

[Address]

Dear Sirs

Cessation as auditors

Either

We hereby resign as auditors of the company with effect from [date] and enclose the statement required under *Companies Act* 2006, s. 519 setting out the reasons for our ceasing to hold office.

Or

Our term of office as auditor of the company expires at the conclusion of the next accounts meeting and we will not be seeking re-appointment. Accordingly, we enclose the statement required under *Companies Act* 2006, s. 519 setting out the reasons for our ceasing to hold office.

You are required, within 14 days of receipt, either to send a copy of the statement to members of the company and all others entitled to receive copies of the company's annual report and accounts, or to apply to the Court for a direction. If you apply to the court, you should let us know. If we do not receive notification that you have applied to the Court, we will send a copy of the statement to the registrar of companies for filing.

As required under the Companies Act, we have also sent a copy of the statement to the FRC as the appropriate audit authority. [You are also required to notify the FRC of the reasons for our ceasing to hold office. If you agree with our statement, you may do this simply by endorsing a copy of the statement indicating your agreement and sending it to:

Change of Auditor Notifications

Financial Reporting Council

8th Floor

125 London Wall

London

EC2Y 5AS

By e-mail to auditorchange@frc.org.uk.]

If you do not agree, you should write separately to the FRC setting out what you consider the reasons to be. In either case, the Act provides that your notification should be sent within 28 days from the date on which we cease to hold office.][1]

Yours faithfully

Auditor

[1] Omit this section if cessation is at end of term or if all reasons are exempt reasons.

38.3 Access to information by a successor auditor

38.3.1 *Requirements of the Act*

Prior to 2008, it was unusual for a predecessor auditor to share audit working papers with his successors, due mainly to liability concerns. However, the European Union's Statutory Audit Directive states that:

'where a statutory auditor or audit firm is replaced by another statutory auditor or audit firm, the former statutory auditor or audit firm shall provide the incoming statutory auditor or audit firm with access to all relevant information concerning the audited entity.'

As a result, the Recognised Supervisory Bodies were required under the *Companies Act* 2006 to introduce rules to give effect to this requirement which are now incorporated into Audit Regulation 3.09 as follows:

'When a Registered Auditor (the "predecessor") ceases to hold an audit appointment and another Registered Auditor (the "successor") is appointed the predecessor must, if required in writing by the successor, allow the successor access to all relevant information held by the predecessor in respect of its audit work … Any information obtained by the successor is for the purposes of its audit and must not be disclosed to a third party unless the successor is required to do so by a legal or professional obligation.'

The aim of the Audit Regulation is to maintain the effectiveness, including cost effectiveness, and efficiency of the audit process and to reduce the actual or perceived risk of changing auditor.

The Regulation is effective for the audits of financial periods commencing on or after 6 April 2008.

38.3.2   Technical Release AAF 01/08

The Audit and Assurance Faculty of the ICAEW issued Technical Release AAF 01/08, *Access to Information by Successor Auditors*. AAF 01/08 provides practical guidance on the application of Audit Regulation 3.09 and accompanying guidance.

Information requested

As well as the current year's audit working papers, information requested by a successor auditor may include permanent information on any standing or systems audit file as well as prior year audit papers if these are relevant. AAF 01/08 suggests that the successor auditor asks for the most recent audit working papers in the first instance and then, if his review suggests it is necessary, ask for older papers in another request.

As well as the papers relating to the standard audit, the following are set out in the 2006 Act as areas where a registered auditor may be required to perform specific functions, and therefore, for which access to working papers can be requested:

- a company applying to re-register as a public company (s. 92);

- a statement on summary financial statements issued by a quoted company (s. 428);

- abbreviated accounts (s. 449);

- when a private company makes a payment out of capital for the redemption or purchase of its own shares (s. 714);

- when a distribution is to be made by a company and the audit report was qualified (s. 837); and

- when initial accounts are prepared for a proposed distribution by a public company (s. 838).

There is no requirement for a successor auditor to make a request to see working papers from the predecessor auditor and he must, as part of his planning process, decide if such access is required and the areas to cover and amount of information to request.

There are specific references to reviewing a predecessor's audit work in ISA (UK) 510 (Revised June 2016) *Initial Audit Engagements – Opening Balances*, ISA (UK) 710 *Comparative Information – Corresponding Figures and Comparative Financial Statements* and ISA (UK) 300 (Revised June 2016) *Planning an Audit of Financial Statements*, and information is likely to be necessary in these areas. This includes, for public interest entities, the Audit Regulation imposing a requirement on a predecessor auditor to grant the incoming auditor access to the additional report to the audit committee from previous years.

An example request letter from successor to predecessor is set out in **Table 7**.

TABLE 7: Specimen letter from the successor requesting access

[Predecessor firm]

[Address]

For the attention of [Name of Senior Statutory Auditor]

Dear Sirs

Provision of information pursuant to Audit Regulation 3.09 relating to the audit of [audit client]

This firm was duly appointed statutory auditor (as defined by the *Companies Act* 2006, s. 1210 ('the Act')) on [date] to [company] ('the Company') [and its UK subsidiaries as listed in the schedule to this letter (together 'the Companies')].

Pursuant to para. 9(3) of Sch. 10 to the *Companies Act* 2006 and Audit Regulation 3.09, and in accordance with Technical Release AAF 01/08 issued by the Institute of Chartered Accountants in England and Wales, we request for the purposes of our audit work, access to the following information:

[*Set out information necessary at this stage, noting the guidance under Audit Regulation 3.09 that wherever possible a request framed simply as a request for 'all relevant information held by the predecessor and concerning the audited entity' or 'all relevant information held by the predecessor in relation to the office of auditor' should be avoided. The successor should strive to identify the information required, or the type of information required, as precisely as possible.*]

[*Where the request is for access to audit working papers and subsequent interim review working papers, insert where applicable:*

[The working papers in respect of your audit report on the financial statements of the [Company/Companies] relating to [insert period between the beginning of the last financial statements on which the predecessor reported and the date of cessation of the predecessor's appointment]].

[Where in your capacity as auditor you conducted a review of interim financial information subsequent to the audit report referred to above, this request

---

> includes a request for access to the working papers relating to that review also.]
>
> We may also request explanations from you in connection with our consideration of the above information, and on the same basis.
>
> [We/the Company will meet reasonable costs that you will incur in giving access/providing copies, provided that a maximum amount is agreed first.]
>
> We look forward to receiving your confirmation letter in response to this request, which should be addressed for the attention of [name of successor engagement partner].
>
> Yours faithfully
>
> [Successor]
>
> **[Schedule of UK subsidiaries to which this letter applies in addition to the Company**
>
> Company 2 Limited
>
> Company 3 Limited
>
> ...]

Audit files may contain information in a number of formats such as text, electronic file, sound or image and they may be kept in hard copy or electronic format, or a mixture of the two. Allowing another auditor access to information may mean that the successor auditor may gain access to the proprietary audit software of the outgoing auditor. If this is the case the successor cannot use the intellectual property or copyright of the software in any way. The predecessor auditor may prefer to make paper copies of working papers for the incoming auditor to review.

Care should also be taken where audit files also contain other documents relating to the client such as tax working papers. Papers to which the successor auditor has no right of access should be removed from the file before the successor auditor commences his review.

Where successors require access to tax papers, the Technical Release suggests that this would be best done directly from the client.

Relevant period

The period for which relevant information is normally requested would be in respect of any audit report relating to a period falling between the beginning of the last financial statement on which the predecessor reported and the date of cessation of the predecessor's audit appointment.

Example: An auditor resigns from an audit on 1 March 2010. The last accounting period for which he acted as auditor was the year ended 31 December 2009. The successor auditor can request access to relevant working papers for any reports prepared by the predecessor in the period 1 January 2009 to 1 March 2010.

The request for information can be made by the immediate successor only.

Liability

In order to ensure that there is no involvement of one auditor in liability for the other's work, an exchange of letters as set out in **Tables 7** and **8**, should be undertaken. These letters should also be copied to the audit client.

Copying

There is no obligation to allow a successor auditor to copy working papers, but it would be usual to allow extracts of the papers to be copied. The predecessor and successor should come to an agreement about what it is reasonable to copy prior to the meeting. Typically, this would include documents such as the breakdown of analyses of financial statements figures and documentation of the client's systems and processes.

The Technical Release suggests that predecessors check through any document that the successor asks to copy and to keep a log of documents that have been copied on the audit file.

Timing

A request for relevant information may be made by a successor once the successor has formally been appointed to the audit client and will typically be made soon after appointment when the incoming auditor commences his planning.

Access should be granted by the predecessor on a timely basis, with regard to:

- the point at which the predecessor's audit file will be complete as ISA (UK) 230 (Revised June 2016) *Audit Documentation* allows up to 60 days from the date of the audit report for the audit file to be completed; and

- the successor's reporting timetable.

The predecessor should also provide oral or written explanations in response to any further questions by the successor following the review of the working papers on a timely basis.

In providing such explanations, the predecessor should remember that:

- its obligation does not extend beyond relevant information;
- explanation should be given a factual or evidential reference point; and
- an internal written note or record of the request made and the explanation given should be put on file.

Location

The location where access is to be granted will be decided by the predecessor and will usually be his premises. The predecessor should be mindful of the confidentiality of other clients' information where access is granted at the predecessor's office.

Costs

Some recovery of the predecessor's costs of providing access may be reasonably recovered, but the legislation is silent on this point. Excessive charging may, however, be seen as a barrier to competition and choice, and it would not be reasonable to include an element of profit.

It may be reasonable to charge the successor auditor for the cost of:

- copying documents;
- paying someone to make the copies;
- retrieving documents from archive sources; and
- paying someone to attend to such retrieval and to provide documents for inspection by the successor.

Confidentiality

The predecessor is not breaching client confidentiality by allowing the successor access to its working papers. However, as a matter of courtesy a letter would be sent by the predecessor to the successor prior to granting access, in line with the example in **Table 8**.

TABLE 8: Specimen letter from predecessor responding to the successor's request for access

[Successor firm]

[Address]

Dear Sir

Provision of information pursuant to Audit Regulation 3.09 relating to the audit of [audit client]

We refer to your letter dated [date] following your appointment as statutory auditor of [company] ('the Company') [and its UK subsidiaries listed in the schedule to your letter (together 'the Companies')].

We confirm we will provide access to the information requested, namely:

[This should reflect the information set out in the successor's request letter. The successor should have identified the information required, or the type of information required, as precisely as possible.]

We understand that you may also request explanations from us in connection with your consideration of the above information, and on the same basis.

In accordance with the guidance under Audit Regulation 3.09 and Technical Release AAF 01/08 issued by the Institute of Chartered Accountants in England and Wales this letter sets out the basis on which the information and explanations (if any) are to be provided. Should you request or we provide any supplementary information to that set out above, such provision will be made on the same basis.

This access is provided to you:

(a)   solely in your capacity as duly appointed statutory auditor (as defined by the *Companies Act* 2006, s. 1210 ('the Act')) of the [Company/ Companies];

(b)   solely because we are required to give you access to information pursuant to para. 9(3) of Sch. 10 to the Act and Audit Regulation 3.09.

The provision of access does not and will not alter any responsibility that we may have accepted or assumed to the [Company/Companies] or the [Company's/respective Companies'] members as a body, in accordance with the statutory requirements for audit, for our audit work, for our audit report or for the opinions we have formed in the course of our work as auditor.

To the fullest extent permitted by law we do not accept or assume responsibility to you or to anyone else:

(a)   as a result of the access given;

(b)   for the information to which we provide access;

(c)   for any explanation given to you;

(d) in respect of any audit work you may undertake, any audit you may complete, and audit report you may issue, or any audit opinion you may give.

Where access is provided to audit [and interim review] working papers, those papers were not created or prepared for, and should not be treated as suitable for, any purpose other than the statutory audit that was the subject of our audit report [and respectively the interim review we carried out]. The statutory audit was planned and undertaken solely for the purpose of forming and giving the audit opinion required by the relevant statutory provision to the persons contemplated by that statutory provision. [The interim review was planned and undertaken solely for the purpose of meeting the requirements of the relevant standard.] The statutory audit [and the interim review] [was/were] not planned or undertaken, and the working papers were not prepared in contemplation of your appointment as statutory auditor or for the purpose of assisting you in carrying out your appointment as statutory auditor.

Neither you nor anyone else should rely on the information to which access is provided or any explanations given in relation to that information. The information cannot in any way serve as a substitute for the enquiries and procedures you should undertake and the judgments that you must make for any purpose in connection with the audit for which you are solely responsible as the auditor.

If notwithstanding this letter you rely on the information for any purpose and to any degree, you will do so entirely at your own risk.

[We will remove/have removed from the audit working papers all material in respect of which legal professional privilege is asserted.]

[Thank you for your confirmation that you/the Company will meet the reasonable costs that we will incur in giving access. [As already agreed] these will not exceed £x.]

In accordance with the guidance issued under Audit Regulation 3.09:

(a) you should refuse to accept an additional engagement, such as to act as an expert witness or to review the quality of our audit work, where the engagement would involve the use of the information obtained by you under the Regulation;

(b) you should not comment on the quality of our audit work unless required to do so by a legal or professional obligation; and

(c) the information should not be disclosed beyond persons who have a need to access the information where to do so is a necessary part of your audit work, nor should the information be disclosed to a third party including the [Company/Companies] (although this does not prevent you discussing the information with the [Company/Companies] where to do so is a necessary part of your audit work, or providing information to any third party if that is required of you by a legal or professional obligation).

In the event that access to information involves your having access to any intellectual property of ours or any material in which we have copyright, we do not grant permission to you to use or exploit that intellectual property or copyright and you must respect the same at all times.

When in this letter we refer to ourselves, we include [any person or organisation associated with this firm through membership of the international association of professional service firms to which this firm belongs,] our [and their] partners, directors, members, employees and agents. This letter is for the benefit of all those referred to in the previous sentence and each of them may rely on and enforce in their own right all of the terms of this letter.

Yours faithfully

[Predecessor]

cc The Company/Companies

Money laundering

In accordance with the Anti-Money Laundering Guidance for the Accountancy Sector issued by the CCAB (see **Section 18**), any request for information regarding suspicious activity should be declined. The risk of tipping off greatly restricts the ability to make disclosures of this type.

39 Review of interim financial information

39.1 Introduction

With some limited exceptions, a company whose shares or debt securities are listed on the London Stock Exchange must issue a half-yearly financial report covering the first six months of each financial year. This is sometimes referred to as an interim report. Rules governing the preparation of half-yearly reports are contained in the Disclosure and Transparency Rules (DTR) of the Financial Conduct Authority (FCA), which are derived from the EU's Transparency Directive (2004/109/EC).

The half-yearly financial report must include:

- a condensed set of financial statements;
- an interim management report; and
- responsibility statements.

If the company is required to prepare consolidated accounts, the condensed set of financial statements must be prepared in accordance with IAS 34 *Interim Financial Reporting*, as adopted by the European Union.

If the company is not required to prepare consolidated accounts, the condensed set of financial statements should be prepared in accordance with IAS 34 or FRS 104 *Interim Financial Reporting*, depending on the accounting framework used for the annual accounts.

Companies may choose to have the half-yearly report audited or reviewed by their auditor. If the half-yearly financial report has been audited or reviewed by the auditor pursuant to the APB's guidance (see **39.2**), the audit report or review report must be reproduced in full. If the half-yearly financial report has not been audited or reviewed by the auditor pursuant to the APB's guidance, the company must make a statement to this effect in its report.

AIM companies must also prepare half-yearly reports in accordance with the AIM Rules for Companies issued by the London Stock Exchange (AIM Rules).

The information contained in a half-yearly report for an AIM company must include at least a balance sheet, an income statement, a cash flow statement and must contain comparative figures for the corresponding period in the preceding financial year. Additionally, the half-yearly report must be presented and prepared in a form consistent with that which will be adopted in the company's annual accounts, having regard to the accounting standards applicable to such annual accounts. Half-yearly reports for AIM companies are not required to comply with IAS 34 or FRS 104, although companies may choose to do so.

Guidance notes contained in the AIM Rules state that where the half-yearly report of an AIM company has been audited, it must contain a statement to this effect. AIM Rules do not require publication of review reports.

In practice, whilst reviews of half-yearly reports are common, it is rare for such reports to be audited.

39.2 Guidance for the auditor

The APB issued standards on these engagements in International Standard on Review Engagements (UK and Ireland) 2410, *Review of interim financial information performed by the independent auditor of the entity*. As with the ISAs, the ISRE is the text of the international version, supplemented by UK and Ireland specific guidance. The ISRE is effective for the reviews of interim financial information for periods ending on or after 20 September 2007.

39.3 General principles

Although a review engagement is different in scope to a full audit, the auditor should comply with the ethical requirements relevant to the audit of the entity's annual financial statements and implement the same relevant quality control procedures such as leadership responsibilities, acceptance arrangements and monitoring. The same attitude of professional scepticism should be applied to an interim review as to a full annual audit.

39.4 Assurance provided

The interim financial information may be significantly less in scope than that included in the annual financial statements. The work performed does not provide a basis for expressing a true and fair opinion or that the interim financial information is free from material misstatement. The procedures are designed so that the auditor can give an opinion that the interim financial information has been prepared in accordance with the applicable financial reporting framework. The review will not generally include:

- inspection, observation or confirmation of accounting records;
- obtaining corroborative evidence in response to enquiries; or
- other typical audit tests such as tests of controls or verification of assets and liabilities.

Where the auditor has not audited the latest annual financial statements or has not reviewed the corresponding financial information in the preceding year, additional review procedures are likely to be necessary.

Additional guidance on cases where there are changes of auditor is given in **39.6**.

39.5   Engagement letters

An engagement letter for the review, or a separate section in the main audit engagement letter, confirms the auditor's acceptance of the appointment and helps to avoid misunderstandings about the level of assurance provided by the review. It also clarifies the extent of the auditor's responsibilities for the review.

An illustrative engagement letter is shown in **Table 1**.

TABLE 1: Example engagement letter for interim review report

Board of Directors XYZ PLC

Date

Dear Sirs

XYZ Plc Financial information for the six months ended 30 June 20 ...

We are providing this letter to confirm our understanding of the terms and objectives of our engagement to review the entity's interim balance sheet as at 30 June 20.. and the related statements of income, changes in equity and cash flows for the six-month period then ended.

As directors of XYZ plc, you are responsible under the *Companies Act* 2006 for keeping adequate accounting records. You are also responsible for presenting the half-yearly financial report in accordance with [International Accounting Standard 34, 'Interim Financial Reporting', as adopted by the European Union] [FRS 104 'Interim Financial Reporting'] and the requirements

---

of the Disclosure and Transparency Rules of the Financial Services Authority. *[The second sentence identifies the applicable financial reporting framework for the entity and should be amended as necessary.]*

For the purpose of our review, you will make available to us all of the company's accounting records and all other related information, including minutes of directors', shareholders' and audit committee meetings and of all relevant management meetings that we consider necessary.

Our review will be conducted in accordance with International Standard on Review Engagements (UK and Ireland) 2410, 'Review of Interim Financial Information Performed by the Independent Auditor of the Entity' issued by the Auditing Practices Board with the objective of providing us with a basis for reporting whether anything has come to our attention that causes us to believe that the interim financial information is not prepared, in all material respects, in accordance with the [indicate applicable financial reporting framework, including a reference to the jurisdiction or county of origin of the financial reporting framework when the financial reporting framework used is not International Financial Reporting Standards]. Such a review consists of making inquiries, primarily of persons responsible for financial and accounting matters, and applying analytical and other review procedures and does not, ordinarily, require corroboration of the information obtained. The scope of a review of interim financial information is substantially less than the scope of an audit conducted in accordance with International Standards on Auditing (UK) whose objective is the expression of an opinion regarding the financial statements and, accordingly we shall express no such opinion.

We expect to report on the interim financial information as follows:

[include text of sample report]

Responsibility for the interim financial information, including adequate disclosure, is that of management of the entity. This includes designing, implementing and maintaining internal control relevant to the preparation and presentation of interim financial information that is free from material misstatement, whether due to fraud or error; selecting and applying appropriate accounting policies; and making accounting estimates that are reasonable in the circumstances. As part of our review, we will request written representations from management concerning assertions made in connection with the review. We will also request that where any document containing interim financial information indicates that the interim financial information has been reviewed, our report will also be included in the document.

A review of interim financial information does not provide assurance that we will become aware of all significant matters that might be identified in an audit. Further, our engagement cannot be relied upon to disclose whether fraud or errors, or illegal acts exist. However, we will inform you of any material matters that come to our attention.

[Insert additional information regarding fee arrangements and billings, as appropriate.]

This letter will be effective for future years unless it is terminated, amended or superseded [*if applicable*].

Please sign and return the attached copy of this letter to indicate that it is in accordance with your understanding of the arrangements for our review of the financial statements.

39.6 Planning

As with any other engagement, the auditor should plan his review so that it is carried out effectively. The planning process, which should focus on areas of potential risk of material misstatement, will include:

- updating the auditor's knowledge of the business;

- consideration of the company's organisation, accounting and control systems and operating characteristics; and

- consideration of the nature of its assets, liabilities, revenues and expenses.

The auditor's understanding of the entity and its environment should be sufficient to allow him to identify potential material misstatement and consider the likelihood of it occurring and to select the review procedures required.

Where the auditor has previously been engaged to report on the most recent full financial statements, it will be sufficient for him to update his existing understanding of the business. Typical procedures implemented to do this are listed in **Table 2**.

TABLE 2: Example procedures to update the auditor's understanding of the entity and its environment

- reading the documentation, to the extent necessary, of the preceding year's audit and reviews of prior interim period(s) of the current year and corresponding interim period(s) of the prior year, to enable the auditor to identify matters that may affect the current period interim financial information;

- considering any significant risks, including the risk of management override of controls, that were identified in the audit of the prior year's financial statements;

- reading the most recent annual and comparable prior period interim financial information;

- considering materiality with reference to the applicable financial reporting framework as it relates to interim financial information to assist in determining the nature and extent of the procedures to be performed and evaluating the effect of misstatements;

- considering the nature of any corrected material misstatements and any identified uncorrected immaterial misstatements in the prior year's financial statements;

- considering significant financial accounting and reporting matters that may be of continuing significance, such as significant deficiencies in internal control;

- considering the results of any audit procedures performed with respect to the current year's financial statements;

- considering the results of any internal audit performed and the subsequent actions taken by management;

- reading management accounts and commentaries for the period;

- considering any findings from prior periods relating to the quality and reliability of management accounts;

- enquiring of management about the results of management's assessment of the risk that the interim financial information may be materially misstated as a result of fraud;

- enquiring of management about the effect of changes in the entity's business activities;

- enquiring of management about significant changes in internal control and the potential effect of any such changes on the preparation of interim financial information; and

- enquiring of management of the process by which the interim financial information has been prepared and the reliability of the underlying accounting records to which the interim financial information is agreed or reconciled.

Where the auditor has not previously been involved with the audit of the full year financial statements, he will have to perform more rigorous procedures, particularly in relation to:

- knowledge of the business;

- assessment of inherent risk;

- understanding the accounting systems; and

- verification of opening balances.

However, any work performed at the interim stage will reduce the year-end workload.

The planning exercise should determine the extent of the review work required, if any, for the different parts of the business, such as divisions, subsidiaries and associates or joint ventures. The following factors will influence this decision:

- the materiality of, and risk of misstatement in, the financial information associated with each part of the business;

- the extent to which management control is centralised within the group, and therefore the degree to which central management have a detailed understanding of operations and financial information in those parts of the business; and

- the strength of the control environment including the group accounting and reporting processes.

Where other auditors are involved, the principal auditor should ensure that the work of the other auditors is adequate for the purposes of the review.

39.7   Procedures and evidence

The auditor's evidence will be obtained primarily through enquiry and analytical review procedures. In the context of the review of interim financial information, analytical procedures are:

- comparison with comparable information for the prior period – both interim and full;

- evaluation of the information by consideration of plausible relationships between financial data and also between non-financial and financial data elements; and

- comparison of amounts and ratios with the auditor's expectations, based on his knowledge of the business.

The extent of the procedures necessary will be based on the auditor's assessment of the risk of material misstatement. In determining the procedures necessary, the auditor should consider:

- the financial position and trading conditions of the company;

- his knowledge of the business derived through previous audits;

- his knowledge of the company's accounting systems;

- the extent to which an item is affected by management judgment;

- management's own assessment of risks and the controls in place; and

- the materiality of transactions and account balances.

The ISRE suggests various procedures that the auditor may use as part of his review. These include:

- reviewing prior year matters which may have a material effect on the financial information;

- considering whether the financial information is prepared on a basis which is consistent with the previous period and with the stated accounting policies;

- reviewing significant consolidation adjustments for consistency with the previous period;

- reading the financial information and considering it in the light of matters which have come to his attention during the course of his review work, and reading the rest of the interim report to ensure there are no inconsistencies or misstatements;

- considering the disclosures;

- considering the going concern status of the entity and the disclosures of any significant uncertainties;

- obtaining management representations (see **39.12**); and

- ascertaining whether the financial information has been approved by the directors and the audit committee.

Where the auditor considers that there is a high risk of material misstatement, he should carry out additional procedures in order to be able to issue an unmodified review report.

In addition, the ISRE requires the auditor to obtain evidence that the interim financial information agrees or reconciles to the underlying accounting records. For consolidated group accounts, it is sufficient to agree the financial information of group components to the consolidation working papers.

The auditor may perform many of the review procedures before or simultaneously with the entity's preparation of the interim financial information. In addition, for convenience, some of the procedures required for the full period audit may also be performed at the interim stage, for example, reading minutes or procedures relating to unusual transactions in the period.

39.8 Documentation

The auditor should record in his working papers:

- details of the planning of the engagement;

- the nature, timing and extent of the procedures performed and his conclusions; and

- his reasoning and conclusions on all significant matters which require the exercise of judgment.

39.9 Subsequent events

To ensure that any relevant subsequent events are properly dealt with in the financial information, the auditor should make enquiries about events up to the date of the approval of the financial information.

39.10 Going concern

At the interim period end, directors should undertake a review of the going concern assessment they made at the previous full year end. In the light of the directors' review, the auditor should consider whether any significant factors identified at the previous audit have changed to such an extent as to affect the appropriateness of the going concern basis of accounting. Particular attention should be paid to the period since the sign off of the full financial statements.

Where the auditor does not have significant concerns, he should limit his enquiries to discussions with management about changes to cash flow and banking arrangements.

Where there are significant concerns, the ISRE notes that additional procedures will be necessary and the auditor should consider whether adequate disclosure has been made.

39.11 Comparative periods

Where comparative financial information is presented, the auditor should consider whether the accounting policies used for the comparative interim report are consistent with those used for the current period. Where this is not the case, appropriate adjustments and disclosures should be made. The auditor should also check that the comparatives used have been correctly extracted from the prior year's interim report.

Extra review procedures will be required where the auditor did not review the corresponding prior year interim financial information. The Listing Rules require comparatives to be given and readers will have expectations that these comparatives have been reviewed on the same basis as the prior period figures. If the auditor is unable to perform additional procedures on the comparatives, he should modify his report to indicate that the comparative figures have not been reviewed.

39.12 Management representations

As with the year end audit, the auditor may obtain from directors written representations to confirm matters arising throughout the review. The confirmation should include an acknowledgement of the limited scope of the review and of the directors' responsibilities for the interim report and the completeness of the financial records and minutes.

An example representation letter is included in the ISRE and this is shown in **Table 3**, which should be tailored to suit the circumstances of the review engagement.

TABLE 3: Illustrative management representation letter for review of interim financial information

[Entity Letterhead]

[To auditor]   [Date]

This representation letter is provided in connection with your review of the balance sheet of ABC Entity as of 31 March 20X1 and the related statements of income, changes in equity and cash flows for the three-month period then ended and a summary of the significant accounting policies and other explanatory notes for the purposes of expressing a conclusion whether anything has come to your attention that causes you to believe that the interim financial information does not give a true and fair view of (*or 'does not present fairly, in all material respects,'*) the financial position of ABC Entity as at 31 March 20X1, and of its financial performance and its cash flows in accordance with [IAS 34 as adopted by the European Union/FRS 104] and the Disclosure and transparency Rules of the Financial Conduct Authority.

We acknowledge our responsibility for the fair presentation of the interim financial information in accordance with [indicate applicable financial reporting framework].

We confirm, to the best of our knowledge and belief, the following representations:

- The interim financial information referred to above has been prepared and presented in accordance with [indicate applicable financial reporting framework].

- We have made available to you all books of account and supporting documentation, and all minutes of meetings of shareholders and the board of directors (namely those held on [insert applicable dates]).

- There are no material transactions that have not been properly recorded in the accounting records underlying the interim financial information.

- There has been no known actual or possible non-compliance with laws and regulations that could have a material effect on the interim financial information in the event of non-compliance.

- We acknowledge responsibility for the design and implementation of internal control to prevent and detect fraud and error.

- We have disclosed to you all significant facts relating to any known frauds or suspected frauds that may have affected the entity.

- We have disclosed to you the results of our assessment of the risk that the interim financial information may be materially misstated as the result of fraud.

- We believe the effects of uncorrected misstatements summarised in the accompanying schedule are immaterial, both individually and in the aggregate, to the interim financial information taken as a whole.

- We confirm the completeness of the information provided to you regarding the identification of related parties.

- The following have been properly recorded, and when appropriate, adequately disclosed in the interim financial information:

  - related party transactions, including sales, purchases, loans, transfers, leasing arrangements and guarantees, and amounts receivable from or payable to related parties;

  - guarantees, whether written or oral, under which the entity is contingently liable; and

  - agreements and options to buy back assets previously sold.

- The presentation and disclosure of the fair value measurements of assets and liabilities are in accordance with [indicate applicable financial reporting framework]. The assumptions used reflect our intent and ability to carry out specific courses of action on behalf of the entity, where relevant to the fair value measurements or disclosure.

- We have no plans or intentions that may materially affect the carrying value or classification of assets and liabilities reflected in the interim financial information.

- We have no plans to abandon lines of product or other plans or intentions that will result in any excess or obsolete inventory, and no inventory is stated at an amount in excess of realisable value.

- The entity has satisfactory title to all assets and there are no liens or encumbrances on the entity's assets.

- We have recorded or disclosed, as appropriate, all liabilities, both actual and contingent.

- [Add any additional representations related to new accounting standards that are being implemented for the first time and consider any additional representations required by a new International Standard on Auditing (UK) that are relevant to interim financial information.]

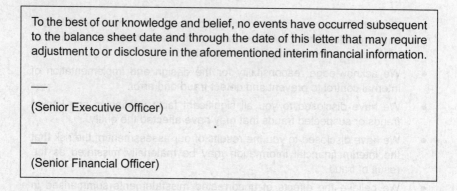

To the best of our knowledge and belief, no events have occurred subsequent to the balance sheet date and through the date of this letter that may require adjustment to or disclosure in the aforementioned interim financial information.

_____

(Senior Executive Officer)

_____

(Senior Financial Officer)

39.13   Other information

The other information in the interim report will often include:

- the management commentary;

- prospective information; and

- a chairman's statement.

The auditor should read any information to be published with the interim financial information and consider whether it is materially inconsistent with the interim financial information or his knowledge of the client and its circumstances. The auditor should only allow his review report to be included where he considers that the additional information is not in conflict with his report and that it is not misleading. Where there is an apparent misstatement or a material inconsistency between the other information and the financial information which cannot be resolved through discussion with the directors, the ISRE suggests that the auditor should consider taking legal advice and that he is likely to make reference to the matter in his review report.

39.14   Evaluating misstatements

The ISRE requires the auditor to assess misstatements individually and in aggregate to determine whether a material adjustment is required to the interim financial information. He is not required to aggregate any misstatements that are 'clearly trivial'.

39.15   Communication

The auditor should report matters which will necessitate a material adjustment to the interim financial information to the relevant level of management as soon as possible. If management does not respond adequately, the matter should be escalated to those charged with governance. If those charged with governance do not make the relevant changes to the interim financial information, the auditor considers:

- whether to modify his report;
- the possibility of withdrawing from the engagement; and
- the possibility of resigning from the full audit.

If matters come to the attention of the auditor which suggest that fraudulent activity has taken place, it should be reported to the appropriate level of management, unless management are involved in the fraud, and then the matter should be reported directly to those charged with governance.

39.16 Reporting

The auditor should issue a written report at the end of his work, and **Table 4** gives the example report taken from the ISRE.

TABLE 4: Unmodified review report

This example assumes that the reporting framework is IAS 34 as adopted by the European Union. References to IAS 34 should be changed if the framework applied is FRS 104.

Independent review report to XYZ plc

Introduction

We have been engaged by the company to review the condensed set of financial statements in the half-yearly financial report for the six months ended [date] which comprises [specify the primary financial statements and the related explanatory notes that have been reviewed].

We have read the other information contained in the half-yearly financial report and considered whether it contains any apparent misstatements or material inconsistencies with the information in the condensed set of financial statements.

Directors' responsibilities

The half-yearly report is the responsibility of, and has been approved by the directors. The directors are responsible for preparing the half-yearly financial report in accordance with the Disclosure and Transparency Rules of the United Kingdom's Financial Services Authority.

As disclosed in note X, the annual financial statements of the [group/company] are prepared in accordance with IFRSs as adopted by the European Union. The condensed set of financial statements included in this half-yearly financial

---

report has been prepared in accordance with International Accounting Standard 34, 'Interim Financial Reporting', as adopted by the European Union.

Our responsibility

Our responsibility is to express to the Company a conclusion on the condensed set of financial statements in the half-yearly financial report based on our review.

Scope of review

We conducted our review in accordance with International Standard on Reporting Engagements (UK and Ireland) 2410, 'Review of Interim Financial Information Performed by the Independent Auditor of the Entity' issued by the Auditing Practices Board for use in the United Kingdom. A review of interim financial information consists of making enquiries, primarily of persons responsible for financial and accounting matters, and applying analytical and other review procedures. A review is substantially less in scope than an audit conducted in accordance with International Standards on Auditing (UK) and consequently does not enable us to obtain assurance that we would become aware of all significant matters that might be identified in an audit. Accordingly, we do not express an audit opinion.

Conclusion

Based on our review, nothing has come to our attention that causes us to believe that the condensed set of financial statements in the half-yearly financial report for the six months ended … is not prepared, in all material respects, in accordance with International Accounting Standard 34 as adopted by the European Union and the Disclosure and Transparency Rules of the United Kingdom's Financial Services Authority.

Auditor

Address

Date

39.16.1 Modification of the review report

The auditor's review report will be modified if he considers that there is or has been:

- a departure from the applicable financial reporting framework;
- a limitation on scope; or
- going concern or significant uncertainties.

Departure from applicable financial reporting framework

Where the auditor concludes that the interim financial information has not been prepared in accordance with the applicable financial reporting framework and a material adjustment is required, he should issue a qualified or adverse opinion, depending on the severity of the departure.

Limitation on scope

Where the auditor cannot finish his review because of a limitation on scope, he should write to the appropriate level of management or those charged with governance to set out the reasons why. He should also consider the implications for his report.

The auditor should not accept an engagement to review the interim financial information if he is aware that a limitation on scope would be imposed by management. If the limitation is imposed after the auditor has accepted the engagement, and management refuse all requests to remove the limitation, he would ordinarily issue a disclaimer of opinion and ensure that his report outlines the reasons for issuing such a report.

Going concern or significant uncertainties

If there are going concern issues, and these are adequately disclosed in the interim financial information, the auditor does not qualify his report, but instead should add an emphasis of matter paragraph to highlight the material uncertainty relating to going concern. An example of such a report is given in **Table 5**.

If there is not adequate disclosure of any going concern issue in the interim financial information, the auditor will issue a qualified or adverse conclusion.

Emphasis of matter paragraphs should also be used for other significant uncertainties which are disclosed in the interim financial information. An example is given in **Table 6**.

TABLE 5: Extract from review report with emphasis of matter relating to going concern

Review work performed

...

Emphasis of matter – going concern

In arriving at our review conclusion, we have considered the adequacy of disclosures made in the condensed set of financial statements concerning the company's ability to continue as a going concern. The company incurred a loss of £x during the period to 30 June 20 ... and at that date its liabilities

---

exceeded its assets by £y. These conditions, along with the other matters explained in note x to the financial information, indicate the existence of a material uncertainty that may cast significant doubt about the company's ability to continue as a going concern. The financial information does not include the adjustments that would result if the company was unable to continue as a going concern.

Review conclusion

On the basis of our review, we are not aware of any material modifications that should be made to the condensed set of financial statements as presented for the six months ended 30 June 20.. .

TABLE 6: Extract from review report with significant uncertainty

Review work performed

...

Emphasis of matter – possible outcome of litigation

In arriving at our review conclusion, we have considered the adequacy of disclosures made in the note ... concerning the possible outcome of litigation against B Limited, a subsidiary undertaking of the company, for an alleged breach of environmental regulations. The future settlement of this litigation could result in additional liabilities and the closure of B's business, whose net assets included in the summarised balance sheet total £y and whose profit before tax for the year is £z. Details of the circumstances relating to this significant uncertainty are described in note x.

Review conclusion

On the basis of our review we are not aware of any material modifications that should be made to the condensed set of financial statements as presented for the six months ended 30 June 20.. .

39.16.2 *Prior period modifications*

Where the prior period review report was modified or the audit report on the most recent financial statements was qualified and the matter has not been resolved, the review report should refer to the earlier modification or qualification and discuss the current status of the matter.

39.16.3 *Date of review report*

The date the auditor signs his report should not be earlier than the date on which the directors approve the financial information.

39.17   Complete set of interim financial information

The Listing Rules of the UK Stock Exchange requires condensed half yearly financial reports to be prepared. However, on some occasions where the company is not listed on the UK Stock Exchange, the interim financial information may comprise a complete set of general purpose financial statements prepared in accordance with a financial reporting framework designed to achieve fair presentation. The appendices to the ISRE provide example engagement letter paragraphs, representation letter paragraphs, review reports and modified review reports for such circumstances.

39.18   Requests to discontinue an interim review engagement

As a review of the interim statement is not mandatory, directors may request the auditor to discontinue his review engagement if it becomes clear that a modified review report will be given.

If this is the case, the auditor must inform the audit committee of this in writing. If, in the auditor's opinion, the company does not take appropriate action to address his concerns about the interim financial information, the auditor may request the directors discuss the issue with the company's brokers. The directors and brokers should then consider whether the matter should be reported to the Stock Exchange.

In such a case, the auditor should also consider whether as a result he should resign as the company's auditor. The ISRE suggests that he may consider taking legal advice in these circumstances. If the auditor decides to resign, the details of the issue should be included, after taking appropriate legal advice, in his statement to shareholders (see **Section 38**).

40 Reports for special purposes and to third parties

40.1 Introduction

Managing their own risk is important to auditors, and one major area of concern is reliance by parties other than those with whom the auditor has contractual relations. For example, where loans and other facilities are made available to businesses, the extent to which the auditor is responsible to the lender is often ambiguous. This becomes more difficult and potentially more dangerous where the auditor has an obligation to report to other third parties, for example, regulatory authorities. Managing the terms under which third parties can, or more importantly cannot, place reliance on reports is an area in which increasing guidance has been produced. This section provides an overview of this guidance and covers a number of areas where it is likely to happen. It covers:

- an overview of applicable guidance (**40.2** and **40.3**);
- auditor's duties to lenders (**40.4**);
- covenants in loan agreements (**40.5**);
- engagements to report on covenant compliance (**40.6**);
- reports on internal controls of service organisations (**40.7**);
- reports to other third parties (**40.8**); and
- discussion of examples of claims by third parties (**40.9**).

Section 41 covers the following related areas:

- reviews of historical financial statements (**41.2**);
- assurance on non-financial information (**41.5**);
- reports on special purpose financial statements (**41.4**); and
- agreed upon procedures engagements (**41.3**).

Reporting to regulators of regulated entities is covered in **Section 49**. Reporting on grant claims is covered in **Section 48**. Compilation engagements are covered in **Section 8**.

40.2   Development of guidance

In November 2000, the Consultative Committee of Accountancy Bodies (CCAB) issued a Statement which contains guidance aimed at helping all parties involved in financing arrangements. This addresses issues such as the appropriate form of report, firms' duties of care and reporting in connection with covenants in loan agreements and other facilities.

The Statement was reissued by the Audit and Assurance Faculty of the ICAEW as Technical Release 4/00 *Firms' Reports and Duties to Lenders in Connection with Loans and Other Facilities to Clients and Related Covenants*.

The guidance also deals with reports on client's compliance with loan covenants, including the scope of work to be performed and the format of the report to be given.

Since 2001, a number of further publications have been issued addressing various aspects of liability to third parties. The main additional guidance is contained in:

- ICAEW Technical Release TECH 10/12AAF: *Reporting to Third Parties* (see **40.8**);

- ICAEW Technical Release Audit 2/01: *Requests for References on Clients' Financial Status and their Ability to Service Loans* (see **40.8**);

- ICAEW Technical Release AAF 01/06: *Assurance Reports on Internal Controls of Service Organisations Made Available to Third Parties* (see **40.7**); and

- ICAEW TECH 09/13 AAF: *Assurance Review Engagements on Historical Financial Statements* (see **Section 41**).

In addition, ICAEW Technical Release AAF 02/07 *A Framework for Assurance Reports on Third Party Operations* is intended to provide high-level yet practical guidance for practitioners who provide assurance services on operations or arrangements agreed between two or more organisations (third party operations). TECH 04/13AAF, *Assurance Reporting on Relevant Trustees* is a supplement to AAF 02/07. Although not specifically detailed in this section, the reader should be aware of the existence of these pieces of guidance.

Further guidance has been issued by the ICAEW to develop the guidance in TECH 10/12AAF for specific circumstances:

- TECH 09/16AAF (previously TECH 07/12AAF): *Revised Arrangements for ATOL Reporting Accountants Reporting to the Civil Aviation Authority*[1];

- AAF 01/11: *Reporting to the Audit Bureau of Circulations Limited (ABC)*;

- AAF 01/07: *Independent Accountants Report on Packaging Waste*; and

- AAF 04/06: *Assurance Engagements: Management of Risk and Liability*, see **40.3**.

A study of the legal cases involving claims by third parties against auditors was completed by the Audit and Assurance Faculty in 2005, in conjunction with the law firm Simmons & Simmons. The review, *Audit liability: Claims by third parties*, summarises the key matters arising from the relevant cases and is considered in **40.9**.

40.3 General guidance

AAF 04/06, *Assurance Engagements: Management of Risk and Liability* provides principles for reporting accountants to consider in relation to managing their risk and liability when agreeing to undertake assurance engagements and providing assurance reports to third parties. It does not seek to provide detailed advice on the planning and conduct of the work involved in such engagements or how to manage risk and liability in particular circumstances. Such detail will be provided in other technical releases which will cross-refer to this over arching guidance.

Additional general guidance on these issues is also given in TECH 09/15BL (previously TECH 02/11), *Managing the Professional Liability of Accountants*.

40.3.1 Accepting an engagement

Reporting accountants should have appropriate engagement acceptance procedures to assess the risks associated with taking on a particular engagement. Reporting accountants should consider the:

---

[1] From 1 April 2016, auditors carrying out ATOL reporting work must be individually licensed under the ATOL Reporting Accountants Scheme administered by the CAA and professional accountancy bodies including the ICAEW. Details of the scheme can be found on the ICAEW's website or in CAA's revised Guidance Note 10 which includes details of the licensing process, reporting requirements for ATOL holders and their ATOL Reporting Accountants and the purpose for which the ATOL holders' reports are used by the CAA and the ATT.

- purpose for which the work is being sought;
- party or parties seeking to benefit from the work, whether they are directly party to the engagement or not yet identified;
- use that will be made of the work; and
- professional competence of the engagement team.

40.3.2 *Managing professional liability*

AAF 04/06 outlines the following arrangements into which reporting accountants may enter:

- a tri-partite or multi-partite engagement contract with the client and the third parties, accepting that they owe a duty of care not only to the client but also to those third parties. Provisions to limit liability may be appropriate;
- an engagement with the client, with the option for third parties to join the duty of care if they accept the relevant terms of the engagement letter. Again, liability may be limited;
- an engagement with the client alone, but allowing access to the audit report for third parties as long as they:
  - acknowledge in writing that the reporting accountant owes them no duty of care; and
  - agree in writing that no claims will be brought against the reporting accountant in relation to the assurance report; and
- an engagement with the client alone, disclaiming any liability or duty to others by notice in the assurance report. This may be in conjunction with the client indemnifying the reporting accountant if a third party makes a claim against the reporting accountant, although such indemnities may not be commercially attractive or reliable if the client is not financially stable.

Alternatively, if the risks are too high or reporting accountants are unable to reach acceptable terms with the client or third parties, reporting accountants may decline to accept the engagement.

40.3.3 *Agreeing the terms of the engagement*

Reporting accountants must manage their relationship with the client and any third party, and clarify that any assurance engagements are separate from statutory audit engagements. Depending on the type of contractual arrangement agreed upon (see **40.3.2**), reporting accountants will need to agree specific terms with all parties to the engagement and record them in writing in the engagement letter. The engagement letter should include details of the purpose of the report to be issued, its agreed use and any accompanying disclosure restrictions setting out the extent to which, the context in which, and the basis on which the report may be made available by the client to the third parties.

It is often useful to include a draft pro forma report as an appendix to the engagement letter.

40.4   Duties to lenders

The position of the auditor in relation to the provider of loans and other facilities can be ambiguous. Technical Release 4/00 *Firms' Reports and Duties to Lenders in Connection with Loans and Other Facilities to Clients and Related Covenants* provides guidance in relation to various aspects of the relationship of auditors with providers of finance to their clients.

40.4.1   Case law

The guidance issued in Technical Release 4/00 is based on case law. In his judgment in the case of *Caparo Industries plc v Dickman* (1990) 2 WLR 353, Lord Bridge stated that a duty of care to a third party will exist if the person who owes the duty of care is aware:

- of the transaction to be undertaken by the third party;
- that the advice given will be passed to the third party, either directly or indirectly; and
- that it is likely that the third party will rely on that information in deciding whether to enter into the transaction.

Since this judgment, banks and other lenders have sought to document a direct and sufficient relationship between themselves and their customer's auditor so as to be able to rely on statutory audit reports.

40.4.2   Duties of care for the statutory audit report

An auditor's duty of care in respect of his audit report would not normally be expected to extend beyond that owed to his client. However, the general trend of authorities since *Caparo* makes it clear that, unless there is an effective disclaimer, an auditor may owe a duty of care to a lender or other third party. The test is whether the auditor, in making the statements in his audit report, assumed a responsibility to a lender who may subsequently be given a copy of those statements. The important issue is not whether the auditor in question intended to assume the responsibility towards the third party, but rather whether a reasonable auditor would have assumed the responsibility in those circumstances.

Therefore, the auditor must be aware that he may inadvertently accept responsibility unless steps are taken to limit his exposure. The auditor may assume responsibility without his knowledge by the client having discussions with the lender, or the lender being passed a set of the most recent audited financial statements, if it is deemed that a reasonable auditor would assume such responsibility.

The use of a *'Bannerman'* paragraph in the auditor's report to clarify the auditor's responsibilities is discussed in **4.28**.

Lenders will often seek to establish a relationship with the auditor. In this regard, certain banks have included a clause in the conditions attached to a loan, which requires the auditor of the borrower to provide written acknowledgement to the bank that the bank may rely on the audited financial statements of the borrower in connection with the facilities offered. Where the auditor is aware, or is in receipt, of a request to provide acknowledgement, he should not let it go unanswered.

In addition, banks may write directly to auditors stating that they do intend to rely on audited financial statements in connection with a proposed transaction. In this situation, a duty of care will be created unless the auditor vigorously denies it. A firm should normally disclaim all responsibility in this situation in writing. Where the auditor has included a *'Bannerman'* style paragraph in his auditor's report on the financial statements, it may also be appropriate to refer to this in any separate disclaimer issued to lenders or others. See **4.28** for further details of *Bannerman* paragraphs.

40.4.3   Draft accounts

The courts have held that reliance on draft audited accounts was not actionable, since a reasonable auditor would not intend such reliance to occur. However, there may be circumstances in which a duty of care may arise and care must be taken, therefore, when circulating draft audited accounts. The status of the accounts must be clearly stated and the giving of assurances or representations about the reliability of the accounts (or whether the final position is likely to differ greatly from that shown in the draft) should be avoided.

40.4.4   Disclaimer of responsibility

Disclaimers of responsibility can only be relied upon if they pass the reasonableness test set out in the *Unfair Contract Terms Act* 1977, s. 2. If the disclaimer is not reasonable, it will be void.

Disclaimers can be worded to pass the reasonableness test and are therefore an effective way of limiting an auditor's liability to lenders and other third parties who seek to claim reliance on a report. They may also be useful in avoiding any doubt that a firm does not have a duty of care to a lender or third party to whom a report is shown or a reference to a report is made.

However, it is important to note that a disclaimer of responsibility does not exempt an auditor or an accountant issuing a review report from carrying out his work in accordance with auditing standards or other applicable standards.

40.4.5   The Contracts (Rights of Third Parties) Act 1999

The *Contracts (Rights of Third Parties) Act* 1999 came into force on 11 November 1999 and applies to all contracts entered into after 10 May 2000. Under the Act, a third party to a contract has the right to enforce a term of that contract if it confers a benefit or right to the third party. This equates to a partial abolition of the concept of 'privity of contract', which has been a central feature of the English law of contract for more than 100 years. Therefore, if a reference is made to the provision of a set of financial statements to a lender, or to a lender requiring the financial statements for a specific purpose, within a contract between an auditor and his client, a benefit may have been conferred upon the lender.

Audit engagement letters should state clearly that they do not confer any rights on any third party and that, for the avoidance of doubt, any rights conferred on third parties pursuant to the *Contracts (Rights of Third Parties) Act* 1999 shall be excluded.

The Act does not apply to Scotland, which has long recognised the concept of *ius quaesitum tertio*, a right vested in and secured to a third party in and by a contract between two parties. Accordingly, a third party has the right to enforce a contract between two parties if the intention to confer a benefit on that third party can be gathered from the terms of the document.

40.4.6   Separate engagements to provide specific assurances to lenders

If a firm decides that it is able to provide specific assurances to a lender, it should be the subject of a separate engagement between the firm, the client and the lender. There should be a separate engagement letter in place for this work, normally the subject of separate financial arrangements.

A firm should also consider whether entering into such an agreement with both client and lender could present it with a conflict of interest. Reference should be made to the ethical guidance of the Institute which governs the firm.

40.5 Covenants in agreement for loans and other facilities

Agreements for certain financing arrangements often contain a number of covenants with which the borrower is expected to comply. Typically, the directors of the borrower are required to prepare a periodic statement or report, a 'Statement of Covenant Compliance', to confirm continuing compliance with the covenant terms agreed when arranging the finance.

Imposed covenants will be either financial or non-financial. Non-financial covenants tend to be more common and take the form of commitments by the borrower as to its future actions. Financial covenants may also need to be maintained by the borrower. These will often be financial statement ratios, the intention of which is to provide the lender with some assurance as to the continuing financial condition of the business.

40.5.1 Common financial and non-financial covenants

A list of common financial and non-financial covenants is given in **Table 1**. In specialised industries, lenders may require the maintenance of industry key performance indicators (KPIs), which are derived from management information outside the financial statements, such as room occupancy rates for hotels or pollution levels for heavy industry.

TABLE 1: Common covenants for borrowings

Financial

- cash flow to total debt service;
- dividend cover;
- minimum share capital and reserves;
- PBIT-based interest cover;
- gearing;
- cash flow-based interest cover;
- net current assets/borrowings;
- proportion of debtors below certain days outstanding;
- current ratio;
- quick asset ratio;
- EBITDA;
- gross profit margin;
- rent roll ratios.

Non-financial

- first charge over specified assets;

- audited annual accounts within a specified period;

- cross default clauses;

- monthly management accounts within a specified period;

- restrictions on changes to ownership;

- restrictions on additional borrowings (from other sources);

- maintenance of adequate fire, theft and other insurances;

- restrictions in mergers/acquisitions;

- restrictions on asset disposals;

- no capital expenditure beyond certain limits without approval;

- compliance with environmental laws and regulations;

- compliance with other laws and regulations;

- no redemption of preference shares while loans outstanding;

- charges over key-man insurance;

- key-man critical illness policy;

- limits on directors' remuneration.

40.5.2   The lender's requirement for evidence of covenant compliance

The lender will require from the directors of the borrower, a written confirmation that they have complied with all covenants for the period under review. This confirmation should set out the computation of the relevant financial covenants for the applicable accounting date. Simple calculations of gearing and interest cover are often self-evident and can easily be reperformed by the lender to ensure compliance. However, where information for covenants is not readily available to the lender, or it is not contained in the borrower's financial statements, the lender may require a report from the borrower's auditors.

The auditor is not compelled to accept such an engagement, as he cannot be bound to comply with the terms of an agreement to which he is not party. Therefore, if the auditor becomes aware that a client is negotiating a loan or other facility, it is good practice to enquire whether the draft loan agreement seeks to place any reporting obligations on him.

Where a requirement to report is found, the auditor should write to the lender to clarify the basis of preparation. This is particularly important if the lender approaches the auditor directly, rather than through the borrower. An example letter for this purpose is set out in **Table 2**.

TABLE 2: Example letter to lender setting out basis on which reports under a loan agreement will be provided

[Lender plc]

Dear Sirs

XYZ plc – [Loan Agreement Reference]

XYZ plc has provided us with a copy of [and you have written to us in connection with], the Loan Agreement referred to above, Clause X of which contemplates that reports will periodically be provided to you by the auditors of XYZ plc in connections with XYZ plc's compliance with certain covenants.

As auditors of XYZ plc, we confirm that, provided that XYZ plc authorises us to do so and you sign an engagement letter with us substantially in the attached form, we will report to you on the following matters:

- whether the financial information contained in the Statement of Covenant Compliance prepared by the directors of XYZ plc has been accurately extracted from the sources identified therein and, where applicable, agrees with the underlying accounting records;

- whether the calculations shown in the Statement, made in accordance with Clause X of the loan agreement, are arithmetically accurate; and

- where the elements and composition of the financial information contained in the Statement are the subject of objective accounting definition in the Loan Agreement, or have subsequently been agreed by Lender plc and XYZ plc, whether the financial information is presented in compliance with the relevant definitions and agreement.

As regards our audit work on XYZ plc's financial statements for future periods, our work will be carried out in accordance with our statutory and professional obligations and will not be planned or conducted in contemplation of your requirements or any matters which might be set out in the Loan Agreement. In particular, the scope of our audit work will be set and judgments made by reference to our assessment of materiality in the context of the audited accounts taken as a whole, rather than in the context of your needs. For this reason, our work will not necessarily address or reflect matters in which you may be primarily interested as lenders. Therefore, we cannot accept any responsibility to you in relation to our audit opinions and disclaim all liability to you in connection therewith.

Yours faithfully

cc. XYZ plc

Enc. Form of engagement letter [see **Table 3**]

40.5.3   The firm's duty of care

Auditors accepting an engagement to report on compliance with covenants acknowledge a duty of care to the lender. Firms will use their established risk management techniques to control this duty. One key method of achieving this is to issue an engagement letter which limits the use of the report to the intended addressee of the report, includes a disclaimer of responsibility to all other parties and specifies liability limits.

In addition, an engagement letter normally includes an exclusion of liability to the lender in respect of their normal audit or review report. This ensures that no responsibility to lenders is assumed for these reports.

Firms must consider whether the engagement is between themselves and the lender, or if it is a separate engagement between themselves and their client. In either case, a separate engagement letter is sent. An example wording is set out in **Table 3**.

The example wording also includes clauses excluding liability in respect of any loss or damage caused by, or arising from, fraudulent acts, misrepresentation or concealment on the part of the client entity, its directors, employees or agents, and excluding all liability to third parties.

TABLE 3: Example engagement letter

[Lender plc]

[Other addressees as provided for in the second paragraph of the letter]

Dear Sirs

XYZ plc – [Loan Agreement reference]

Under the terms of Clause [X] of the agreement dated [date] between XYZ plc and Lender plc ('the Loan Agreement'), the Directors of XYZ plc are required to procure that their auditors report to you in connection with the Directors' Statement of Covenant Compliance ('the Statement'), prepared in accordance with Clause [X] of the Loan Agreement. At the request of the Directors of XYZ plc, we are writing to set out our understanding of the work you wish us to perform and the terms and conditions upon which we are prepared to provide such a report for your use. A copy of this letter is being sent to the Directors of XYZ plc to confirm their authorisation and understanding of the basis on which we will report to you.

[This engagement letter is addressed to Lender plc, as lead manager/arranger of the facility/syndication agreement, and to each of the other lenders participating in the facility/syndication agreement whose names, as set out in Attachment 1, have been notified to us by Lender plc as having validly authorised it to accept this engagement letter on their behalf. By signing and accepting the terms of this engagement letter, Lender plc confirms that it will ensure that it receives prima facie authority from each other lender identified in

---

Attachment 1, as participating in the facility/syndication agreement authorising it to enter into this engagement letter on the relevant lender's behalf.]

Respective responsibilities of directors and auditors

The Directors of XYZ plc are responsible for ensuring that XYZ plc complies with all of the terms and conditions of the Loan Agreement including each of the Covenants set out in Clauses [X] to [X] thereof. Under Clause [X] thereof, the Directors are responsible for preparing their Statement of Covenant Compliance. Our responsibility is to prepare a report to you on the computation of those financial covenants which pertain to accounting matters as identified below.

We are auditors of XYZ plc and have audited the annual accounts of XYZ plc ('the audited accounts') and reported to its members in accordance with our responsibilities under the Companies Act on [date]. Our audit of the accounts of XYZ plc was not intended to address compliance with financial covenants or other matters in which the addressees of this letter may be primarily interested. In particular, the scope of our audit work was set and our judgments made by reference to our assessment of materiality in the context of the audited accounts taken as a whole, rather than in the context of the report contemplated in this letter. Accordingly, we do not acknowledge any responsibility, and deny any liability, to the addressees of this letter in relation to the audited accounts.

Basis of report

Our work will be conducted in accordance with the framework for reporting in connection with loan covenants set out in guidance issued by the Consultative Committee of Accountancy Bodies and published as Audit Technical Release 4/00 by the Institute of Chartered Accountants in England and Wales [*or alternative CCAB member*]. We will read the Statement prepared by the Directors. Our work will be based on obtaining an understanding of the compilation of the Statement and by enquiry of management, reference to the Loan Agreement, comparison of the financial information in the Statement to the sources from which it was obtained and re-computation of the calculations in the Statement. [The specific procedures that we have agreed to conduct are set out in the Appendix to this letter.] Other than as set out herein, we will not carry out any work by way of audit, review or verification of the financial information nor of the management accounts, accounting records or other sources from which that information is to be extracted for the purpose of providing you with our report.

Use of report

Our report will be provided solely for your use in connection with the Loan Agreement and should not be made available to any other party without our written consent. The report is confidential to you and will be provided only for the purpose of your assessment of XYZ plc's compliance with the terms of Clause [X] of the Loan Agreement. We accept no liability to any other party who is shown or gains access to our report.

Obligations and liabilities

We undertake that we will exercise reasonable professional skill and care in the performance of our work as set out in this letter in accordance with applicable professional standards. This engagement is undertaken subject to certain terms excluding liability where information is or has been misrepresented to us, or withheld or concealed from us, and providing for our aggregate liability to the addressees of this letter and XYZ plc to be limited to a maximum aggregate amount of £[X] and subject to that cap, to the part of any loss suffered which is proportional to our responsibility.

It is agreed that the allocation between addressees of the limit of liability specified above will be entirely a matter for the addressees, who shall be under no obligation to inform us of it, provided always that if (for whatever reason) no such allocation is agreed, no addressee shall dispute the validity, enforceability or operation of the limit of liability on the ground that no such allocation was agreed.

Our detailed Terms of Business are set out in the attachment to this letter which shall apply as if set out in full herein.

Acknowledgement and acceptance

We will be grateful if, having considered the provisions of this letter together with the attachments and having concluded that they are reasonable in the context of all the factors relating to our proposed engagement, you will indicate your agreement to these arrangements by signing and returning to us the enclosed copy of this letter.

Yours faithfully

The terms and conditions contained in this letter and the attached Terms of Business are agreed and accepted on behalf of Lender plc by:

.... (authorised person)

Authorised and accepted on behalf of XYZ plc by:

.... (authorised person)

40.5.4   The firm's consideration of acceptance of the engagement

Before accepting the engagement, the auditor must ensure that the respective responsibilities of the borrower and the auditor are clearly defined. It is the responsibility of the directors of the borrower to prepare the financial information and the Statement of Covenant Compliance, and the auditor's responsibility is to report on that information to the extent that it relates to financial and accounting matters.

The Statement of Covenant Compliance will normally set out the calculations of financial ratios, etc. as provided for under the loan agreement. The loan agreement will usually require the borrower to comply with the covenants at all times during the period being reported upon, but the auditor's report will only refer to compliance at specific dates. A firm would not normally accept an engagement which requires confirmation of compliance with covenants over an extended period of time, or for which confirmation that the borrower will comply with covenants in the future based on prospective information is required.

Firms should also consider carefully the implications of accepting an engagement to report on a Statement of Covenant Compliance based on financial covenants whose terms are imprecise.

40.6 Engagements to report on covenant compliance

40.6.1 Scope of work performed

The scope of work will vary from engagement to engagement and should be agreed with both the client and the lender. Typical procedures will include:

- reading the relevant clauses of the loan agreement and gaining an understanding of the operation of the covenants;

- reading the directors' Statement of Covenant Compliance;

- agreeing the financial information in the Statement to the sources from which it has been extracted;

- re-computing the calculations and ratios set out in the Statement in order to ascertain their arithmetical accuracy; and

- obtaining a representation from the client as to the completeness of disclosure in the Statement.

Firms will not undertake procedures to confirm the reliability of the financial information in the Statement nor of the sources from which the data has been extracted. In addition, they will not report on non-financial information in the Statement, such as directors' judgments on future business trends.

An example representation letter is provided in **Table 4**.

TABLE 4: Example representation letter

[Auditor's name and address]

Dear Sirs

[Loan Agreement Reference]

In connection with your proposed report in accordance with the arrangements set out in your letter of [date], we are writing to confirm to the best of our knowledge and belief the following representations we have made to you

---

and on which you need to rely in providing your report on the Statement of Covenant Compliance ('the Statement') to Lender plc.

We are responsible for preparing the Statement, accurately reflecting the matters contained therein at the relevant dates.

The Statement is complete and accurate and reflects all matters of significance relating to Lender plc's assessment of XYZ plc's compliance with the Covenants set out therein as at the relevant dates and all significant matters relevant to that assessment have been brought to your attention.

Throughout the period since [date], the Company has at all times been in compliance with the terms of the Loan Agreement or, if not, all such instances of non-compliance have been notified to Lender plc in accordance with the terms of the Loan Agreement. Copies of such notifications have been made available to you.

[No events have occurred subsequent to [date of last audited financial statements] that would have required adjustment to, or disclosure in, the audited financial statements had their approval by the Board been deferred until the date of this letter.]

Yours faithfully

.... (signature of authorised person on behalf of XYZ plc)

40.6.2 The report

The report should be prepared in accordance with the engagement letter. The report will:

- identify the addressees who can rely on it;
- contain a statement concerning the scope of the report and the respective responsibilities of the directors and the auditor;
- refer to the Statement of Covenant Compliance;
- set out the basis for the report;
- provide a description of the procedures undertaken (either in the body of the report or in an appendix);
- report on the arithmetical accuracy of the extraction and calculation of the financial information within the Statement; and
- where the elements and composition of the financial information in the Statement are the subject of objective accounting definition in the loan agreement, or have been subsequently agreed by the parties, report whether the financial information is presented in compliance with the relevant definitions and agreement.

An illustrative form of report is given in **Table 5**.

TABLE 5: Example report

[Lender plc]

[Other addressees as provided for in the engagement letter]

Dear Sirs

XYZ plc – [Loan Agreement reference]

We refer to the above-mentioned agreement ('the Loan Agreement'). Under the terms of Clause [X] thereof, XYZ plc is required to comply with specified financial covenants and to supply the addressees of this letter with information in connection therewith reported upon by its auditors.

The directors of XYZ plc have prepared a Statement of Covenant Compliance ('the Statement'), a copy of which is appended to this letter.

This report letter is provided pursuant to, and must be read in conjunction with, our engagement letter dated [date] and is subject to the terms and limitations set out therein.

Basis of report

Our work was conducted in accordance with the framework for reporting in connection with loan covenants set out in guidance issued by the Consultative Committee of Accountancy Bodies [and published as Audit Technical Release 4/00 by the Institute of Chartered Accountants in England and Wales, *or alternative CCAB member*]. We have read the attached Statement prepared by the Directors. Our work was based on obtaining an understanding of the compilation of the Statement by enquiry of management, reference to the Loan Agreement, comparison of the financial information in the Statement to the sources from which it was obtained and recomputation of the calculations in the Statement. [The specific procedures we performed are set out in the Appendix to this letter.] For the purpose of providing you with this letter, other than as set out herein, we have not carried out any work by way of audit, review or verification of the financial information nor of the management accounts, accounting records or other sources from which that information has been extracted.

Report

Based solely on the procedures described above, we confirm that:

- the financial information contained in the accompanying Statement has been accurately extracted from the sources identified therein and, where applicable, agrees with the underlying accounting records;

- the calculations shown in the Statement made in accordance with Clause [X] of the Loan Agreement are arithmetically accurate; and

- the financial information in the Statement is presented in compliance with the relevant accounting definitions as to its elements and composition set out in Clause [X] of the Loan Agreement [and as agreed between Lender plc and XYZ plc and confirmed to us in a letter dated [date]].

Our report as set out herein is confidential to the addressees of this letter and should not be made available to any other party without our written consent. It is provided solely for the purpose of your assessment of XYZ plc's compliance with the terms of [Clause [X] of] the Loan Agreement. We accept no liability to any other party who is shown or gains access to this letter.

Yours faithfully

cc. XYZ plc

40.7   Reports on internal controls of service organisations

40.7.1   Background

Many entities use service organisations to perform various tasks for them. These services may vary from performing a certain task, such as preparing the payroll, to replacing entire business units. Many of the functions undertaken by service organisations affect an entity's financial statements and so the auditor may seek information about the control procedures put in place by the service organisation.

Reporting accountants may be asked by service organisations to provide a report on their internal controls which they can supply to their customers and the customers' auditor.

In June 2006, the Audit and Assurance Faculty of the ICAEW issued AAF 01/06 *Assurance Reports on Internal Controls of Service Organisations Made Available to Third Parties* specifically in relation to financial service activities, including:

- custody;
- investment management;
- pension administration;
- property management;
- fund accounting; and
- transfer agency.

The guidance may be applied to other areas, such as payroll processing, but further considerations may be required.

AAF 01/06 replaced guidance previously issued as FRAG 21/94 and Audit 4/97. AAF 01/06 was most recently updated in July 2016 and currently includes an Appendix 8 to reflect the issue by the IAASB of ISAE 3402, *Assurance Reports on Controls at a Third Party Service*

Organisation, as well as a Stewardship supplement, covering assurance reporting on principles of the UK Stewardship Code for institutional investors.

Guidance on using reports on service organisations when conducting the audit of an entity is covered in **Section 22**.

40.7.2 Responsibilities of the service organisation

The directors of the service organisation are required to identify control objectives and the control procedures which they consider appropriate to ensure that these control objectives are met. Their key responsibilities are:

- accepting responsibility for internal control;

- evaluating the effectiveness of the service organisation's control procedures using suitable criteria;

- supporting their evaluation with sufficient evidence, including documentation; and

- providing a written report of the effectiveness of those control procedures for the relevant period.

The appendices to AAF 01/06 include a list of detailed control objectives for the financial services activities listed in **40.7.1**. The list is not exhaustive and the directors of the service organisation are responsible for considering whether the objectives are sufficient for their organisation. The directors are required to make a statement in their report that they have referred to the examples in the appendices.

Service organisations are also responsible for:

- providing the reporting accountants with access to appropriate service organisation resources, such as service organisation personnel, systems documentation, contracts and minutes of management or audit committee meetings;

- disclosing to the reporting accountants any significant changes in control procedures that have occurred since the service organisation's last examination or within the last 12 months if the service organisation has not previously engaged reporting accountants to issue an assurance report;

- disclosing to the reporting accountants and the affected customers any illegal acts, fraud, or uncorrected errors attributable to the service organisation's management or employees that may affect its customers and the entity's whistle-blowing arrangements;

- disclosing to the reporting accountants any relevant design deficiencies in control procedures of which it is aware, including those for which the directors believe the cost of corrective action may exceed the benefits;

- disclosing to the reporting accountants all significant instances of which it is aware when control procedures have not operated with sufficient effectiveness to achieve the specified control objectives; and

- providing the reporting accountants with a letter of representation.

40.7.3 *Accepting the engagement*

As with other reports where third parties may be seeking to place reliance on their report, reporting accountants may:

- accept that they owe a duty of care to the third parties and enter into a tri-partite or multi-partite engagement contract with the client and the third parties. Provisions to limit liability may be appropriate. A multi-partite engagement contract may be difficult where the service organisation has numerous customers;

- engage with the service organisation with the ability for its customers to be afforded the same duty of care agreed between the reporting accountant and the service organisation if they subsequently accept the relevant terms of the engagement letter, including any limitations on liability;

- proceed with an engagement with the client alone, but allowing access to the report for third parties as long as they:

  - acknowledge in writing that the reporting accountant owes them no duty of care; and

  - agree in writing that no claims will be brought against the reporting accountant in relation to the assurance report;

- engage with the client alone, disclaiming any liability or duty to others by notice in the assurance report. This may be in conjunction with the client indemnifying the reporting accountant if a third party makes a claim against the reporting accountant; or

- decline to accept the engagement.

Reporting accountants will always disclaim liability to the auditor of the service organisation's customers, as the auditor will have responsibility for his own audit report.

Example extract terms of engagement are shown in **Table 6**.

Reporting accountants may become aware of third parties other than the service organisation's customers who may request sight of the report. In such cases, accountants may decline the request, or access may be agreed if the third party acknowledges in writing that they owe the accountant no duty of care.

TABLE 6: Extracts of example engagement letter paragraphs for assurance reports on internal controls of service organisations

Responsibilities of directors

The Board of Directors ('the Directors') of [entity name] in relation to which the reporting accountant's assurance report is to be provided ('the Organisation') are and shall be responsible for the design, implementation and operation of control procedures that provide adequate level of control over customer's assets and related transactions. The Directors' responsibilities are and shall include:

- acceptance of responsibility for internal controls;

- evaluation of the effectiveness of the service organisation's control procedures using suitable criteria;

- supporting their evaluation with sufficient evidence including documentation; and

- providing a written report ('Directors' Report') of the effectiveness of the service organisation's internal controls for the relevant financial period.

In drafting this report, the Directors have regard to, as a minimum, the criteria specified within the Technical Release AAF 01/06 issued by the Institute of Chartered Accountants in England & Wales ('the Institute') but they may add to these to the extent that this is considered appropriate in order to meet customers' expectations.

Responsibilities of reporting accountants

It is our responsibility to form an independent conclusion, based on the work carried out in relation to the control procedures of the Organisation's [ ] function carried out at the specified business units of the Organisation [located at [ ]] as described in the Directors' Report and report this to the Directors.

Scope of the reporting accountants' work

We conduct our work in accordance with the procedures set out in AAF 01/06, issued by the Institute. Our work will include enquiries of management, together with tests of certain specific control procedures which will be set out in an appendix to our report.

In reaching our conclusion, the criteria against which the control procedures are to be evaluated are the internal control objectives developed for service organisations as set out within the AAF 01/06 issued by the Institute.

Any work already performed in connection with this engagement before the date of this letter will also be governed by the terms and conditions of this letter.

We may seek written representations from the Directors in relation to matters on which independent corroboration is not available. We shall seek

---

confirmation from the Directors that any significant matters of which we should be aware have been brought to our attention.

Inherent limitations

The Directors acknowledge that control procedures designed to address specified control objectives are subject to inherent limitations and, accordingly, errors or irregularities may occur and not be detected. Such procedures cannot guarantee protection against fraudulent collusion especially on the part of those holding positions of authority or trust. Furthermore, the opinion set out in our report will be based on historical information and the projection of any information or conclusion in our report to any future periods will be inappropriate.

Use of our report

Our report will, subject to the permitted disclosures set out in this letter, be made solely for the use of the Directors of the Organisation, and solely for the purpose of reporting on the internal controls of the Organisation, in accordance with these terms of our engagement.

Our work will be undertaken so that we might report to the Directors those matters that we have agreed to state to them in our report and for no other purpose.

Our report will be issued on the basis that it must not be recited or referred to or disclosed, in whole or in part, in any other document or to any other party, without the express prior written permission of the reporting accountants. We permit the disclosure of our report, in full only, to customers [of the Organisation using the Organisation's [financial services] ('customers')] [(as defined in appendix [ ] to this letter),] and to the auditors of such customers, to enable customers and their auditors to verify that a report by reporting accountants has been commissioned by the Directors of the Organisation and issued in connection with the internal controls of the Organisation without assuming or accepting any responsibility or liability to them on our part.

To the fullest extent permitted by law, we do not and will not accept or assume responsibility to anyone other than the Directors as a body and the Organisation for our work, for our report or for the opinions we will have formed.

Liability provisions

We will perform the engagement with reasonable skill and care and acknowledge that we will be liable to the Directors as a body and Organisation for losses, damages, costs or expenses ('losses') suffered by the Directors as a body and the Organisation as a result of our breach of contract, negligence, fraud or other deliberate breach of duty. Our liability shall be subject to the following provisions:

- we will not be so liable if such losses are due to the provision of false, misleading or incomplete information or documentation or due to the acts or omissions of any person other than us, except where, on the basis of the enquiries normally undertaken by us within the scope set out in these terms of engagement, it would have been reasonable for us to discover such defects;

- we accept liability without limit for the consequences of our own fraud or other deliberate breach of duty and for any other liability which it is not permitted by law to limit or exclude;

- subject to the previous provisions of this Liability paragraph, our total aggregate liability, whether in contract, tort (including negligence) or otherwise, to the Directors as a body and the Organisation, arising from or in connection with the work which is the subject of these terms (including any addition or variation to the work), shall not exceed the amount of [to be discussed and negotiated].

To the fullest extent permitted by law, the Organisation agrees to indemnify and hold harmless [name of reporting accountants] and its partners and staff against all actions, proceedings and claims brought or threatened against [name of reporting accountants] or against any of its partners and staff by any persons other than the Directors as a body and the Organisation, and all loss, damage and expense (including legal expenses) relating thereto, where any such action, proceeding or claim in any way relates to or concerns or is connected with any of [name of reporting accountant]'s work under this engagement letter.

The Directors as a body and the Organisation agree that they will not bring any claims or proceedings against any of our individual partners, members, directors or employees. This clause is intended to benefit such partners, members, directors and employees who may enforce this clause pursuant to the *Contracts (Right of Third Parties) Act* 1999 ('the Act'). Notwithstanding any benefits or rights conferred by this agreement on such partners, members, directors or employees by virtue of the Act, we and the Directors as a body may together agree in writing to vary or rescind the agreement set out in this letter without the consent of any such partners, members, directors or employees. Other than as expressly provided in this paragraph, the provision of the Act are excluded.

Any claims, whether in contract, negligence or otherwise, must be formally commenced within [years] after the party bringing the claim become aware (or ought reasonably to have become aware) of the facts which give rise to the action and in any event no later than [years] after any alleged breach of contract, negligence or other cause of action. This expressly overrides any statutory provision which would otherwise apply.

This engagement is separate from, and unrelated to, our audit work on the financial statements of the Organisation for the purposes of the *Companies Act* 2006 (or its successor) or other legislation and nothing herein creates obligations or liabilities regarding our statutory audit work, which would not otherwise exist.

[*Appendix*]

List of customers to whom the assurance report may be made available.]

40.7.4 Reporting accountant's procedures

Reporting accountants will read the directors' description of the control procedures and undertake procedures to determine whether that description is a fair presentation. Procedures may include:

- discussing aspects of the control framework and relevant control procedures with management and other personnel;

- determining who the customers are and how the services provided by the service organisation are likely to affect the customers;

- reviewing standard terms of contracts with the customers to gain an understanding of the service organisation's contractual obligations;

- observing the procedures performed by the service organisation's personnel;

- reviewing the service organisation's policy and procedure manual and other systems documentation; and

- performing walkthrough tests on selected transactions and control procedures.

Reporting accountants should consider whether the control procedures are suitably designed. Their assessment may include:

- considering the linkage between the control procedure and the associated control objectives;

- considering the ability of the control procedures to prevent or detect errors; and

- performing further procedures such as enquiries of personnel, inspection of documentation and observation of control procedures to determine whether they are adequately designed and operated as prescribed.

Where reporting accountants become aware that the control objectives are incomplete or inappropriate, they discuss their findings with the directors and request that the directors amend their report accordingly. If the directors refuse to make suitable amendments, reporting accountants will highlight this fact in their report.

40.7.5 Reporting

The engagement performed by the reporting accountant is a reasonable assurance engagement, that is sufficient evidence is obtained to allow them to express a positive conclusion on the directors' report.

The report concludes on the fairness of the description and the design and operating effectiveness of control procedures over a specified period. An example report is given in **Table 7**.

TABLE 7: Example report on internal controls of service organisations

To the directors of [name of entity]

Use of report

This report is made solely for the use of the directors, as a body, of [name of entity], and solely for the purpose of reporting on the internal controls of [name of entity], in accordance with the terms of our engagement letter dated [date] [and attached as appendix [ ]].

Our work has been undertaken so that we might report to the directors those matters that we have agreed to state to them in this report and for no other purpose. Our report must not be recited or referred to in whole or in part in any other document nor made available, copied or recited to any other party, in any circumstances, without our express prior written permission.

We permit the disclosure of this report, in full only, by the directors at their discretion to customers [of [name of entity] using [name of entity]'s [financial services] ('customers'),] and to the auditors of such customers, to enable customers and their auditors to verify that a report by reporting accountants has been commissioned by the directors of [name of entity] and issued in connection with the internal controls of [name of entity], and without assuming or accepting any responsibility or liability to customers or their auditors on our part.

To the fullest extent permitted by law, we do not accept or assume responsibility to anyone other than the directors as a body and [name of entity] for our work, for this report or for the conclusions we have formed.

Subject matter

This report covers solely the internal controls of [name of entity] as described in your report as at [date]. Internal controls are processes designed to provide reasonable assurance regarding the level of control over customers' assets and related transactions achieved by [name of entity] in the provision of [outsourced activities] by [name of entity].

Respective responsibilities

The directors' responsibilities and assertions are set out on page [ ] of your report. Our responsibility is to form an independent conclusion, based on the work carried out in relation to the control procedures of [name of entity]'s [ ] function carried out at the specified business units of [name of entity] [located at [ ]] as described in your report and report this to you as the directors of [name of entity].

Criteria and scope

We conducted our engagement in accordance with International Standard on Assurance Engagement (ISAE) 3000 and the Institute of Chartered Accountants in England & Wales Technical Release AAF 01/06. The criteria against which the control procedures were evaluated are the internal control objectives developed for service organisations as set out within the Technical Release AAF 01/06 and identified by the directors as relevant control objective relating to the level of control over customers' assets and related transactions in the provision of [outsourced activities]. Our work was based upon obtaining an understanding of the control procedures as described on page [ ] to [ ] in the report by the directors, and evaluating the directors' assertions as described on page [ ] to [ ] in the same report to obtain reasonable assurance so as to form our conclusion. Our work also included tests of specific control procedures, to obtain evidence about their effectiveness in meeting the related control objectives. The nature, timing and extent of the tests we applied are detailed on pages [ ] to [ ].

Our tests are related to [name of entity] as a whole rather than performed to meet the needs of any or any particular customer.

Inherent limitations

Control procedures designed to address specific control objectives are subject to inherent limitations and, accordingly, errors or irregularities may occur and not be detected. Such control procedures cannot guarantee protection against (among other things) fraudulent collusion especially on the part of those holding positions of authority or trust. Furthermore, our conclusion is based on historical information and the projection of any information or conclusions in this report to any future periods would be inappropriate.

Conclusion

In our opinion, in all material respects:

* the accompanying report by the directors describes fairly the control procedures that relate to the control objectives referred to above which were in place as at [date];

* the control procedures described on pages [ ] to [ ] were suitably designed such that there is reasonable, but not absolute assurance that the specified control objective would have been achieved if the described control procedures were complied with satisfactorily [and customers applied the control procedures contemplated]; and

* the control procedures that were tested, as set out in the attachment to this report, were operating with sufficient effectiveness for us to obtain reasonable, but not absolute, assurance that the related control objectives were achieved in the period [x] to [y].

Name of firm

Chartered Accountants

Location

Date

40.8 Reports to other third parties

40.8.1 Introduction

The Audit and Assurance Faculty increased the scope of the original guidance on reporting to lenders to other third parties by publishing two further Technical Releases: Audit 1/01, *Reporting to Third Parties* and 2/01 *Requests for References on Clients' Financial Status and their Ability to Service Loans*.

Audit 1/01 was revised in 2012 and released as TECH 10/12AAF.

The aim of TECH 10/12AAF is to establish the same type of approach as set out in Audit 4/00 for all special reporting engagements. Firms should be on their guard to avoid circumstances that may result in a duty of care for the statutory audit report becoming established with a third party without sufficient disclaimers being put in place.

The guidance in Audit 2/01 is only appropriate where there is no need to perform any work, research or investigation to produce the reference. If further work is required, then a formal engagement should be agreed under TECH 10/12AAF.

40.8.2 TECH 10/12AAF: Reporting to third parties

Accountants have no obligation to sign reports requested by third parties such as trade bodies, regulators or other third parties, but may wish to do so in order to assist their clients. Accountants should endeavour to become familiar with third parties' demands for customised reports as early as possible in the relationship with their client so that appropriate engagement terms can be negotiated.

Technical Release TECH 10/12AAF aims to help accountants to manage their risk in relation to providing such reports. However, it does not cover corporate finance engagements, reports made under UK company legislation, (covered by APB Bulletin 2008/9), or reports relating to public sector entities or requests for references, which are covered by Audit 2/01.

The Technical Release sets out, under a number of headings, the process accountants should follow in response to requests from third parties. The process is illustrated by the flowchart in **Table 8**.

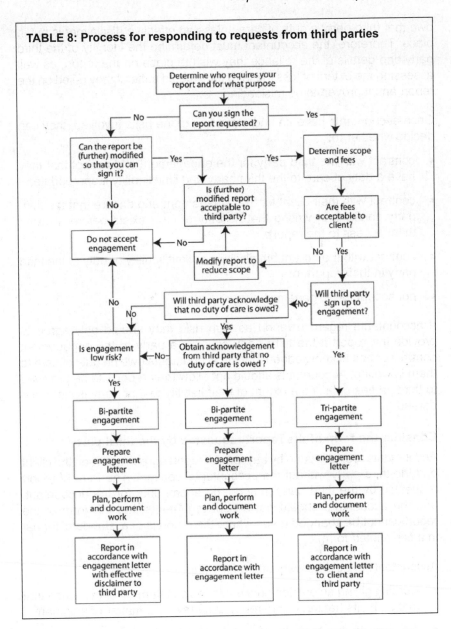

TABLE 8: Process for responding to requests from third parties

Determine who will rely on the accountants' work and for what purpose

When accountants become aware that a report has been requested, and will be relied upon, by a third party there is a risk that the accountant will owe that third party a duty of care unless an effective disclaimer is put in place. Therefore, the accountant must determine the identity of the third party and details of the reliance they wish to place on the report, as well assessing the extent of loss the third party could suffer if they relied on the report and it proved to be misleading.

Once accountants have an understanding of the risks involved, they can decide whether to:

- contract with the third party for the engagement and accept that they have a duty of care to the third party and limit liability if appropriate;

- contract with their client for the engagement and ensure that the third party confirms in writing that no duty of care exists before allowing them access to the report;

- contract with their client but disclaim or limit liability or duty to the third party in their report; or

- not accept the engagement.

If accountants regard a report as high risk, they should only agree to provide the report if the third party either is a party to the engagement contract or has acknowledged that the accountants owe no duty of care to them in writing. Accountants should not allow their reports to be provided to third parties unless the extent of their liability to that party is clear and agreed.

Consider the form of the report requested by the third party

Accountants are not bound by any form of report agreed between the client and the third party without the accountants' consent. The form of report requested by the third party may not be appropriate for the accountant, and the accountant should not accept arguments that the form of the report cannot be changed (even where the report is of a 'standard' format in a pre-printed form).

Accountants should be wary of the following:

- wording giving an opinion on a matter as a statement of fact when that matter, by its nature, is inherently uncertain or a matter of judgment;

- the use of the term 'true and fair' when financial information is not prepared under an acceptable financial reporting framework (e.g. Financial Reporting Standards or International Financial Reporting Standards);

- 'fair and reasonable' opinions, which are usually associated with investment banks making recommendations to shareholders in respect of transactions;

- wording that might suggest that the third party is able to rely on the statutory audit of the client;

- opinions that are open-ended or otherwise cannot be supported by the work carried out by the accountants;

- opinions which accountants do not have the necessary competence to provide such as actuarial opinions or property valuations;

- opinions on matters beyond the accountants' knowledge and experience, particularly in relation to the detailed and specific operational circumstances of the client;

- wording that is open to interpretation;

- reports on internal controls where there are inadequate criteria for a sound control system;

- reports without addressees;

- reports on financial information which is not explicitly approved by the client;

- modifications or qualifications in covering letters only; and

- opinions which would impair the accountants' independence.

Accountants must only sign reports if they have performed sufficient work to support the statements they are asked to make. In some circumstances, such as reports on future solvency or performance of the client, statements cannot be supported by any amount of work, and accountants should refuse to sign such reports. Instead an agreed upon procedures form of report may be given.

Agree the work to be performed and the form of the report to be given

In agreeing the work to be performed and form of report, accountants must make clear to clients and third parties that these engagements are separate from the statutory audit engagement and will be subject to separate terms and a separate fee. The terms for the report to third parties may include a limitation of liability.

The accountant must agree the form of report that is appropriate and the timescale in which it is to be delivered. The timescale must be realistic in relation to the amount of work the accountant will need to perform to provide the required opinion.

No UK auditing standards cover the forms of report which may be given, though some guidance is available in international standards. International standards break the types of report down into four types:

- *reasonable assurance*, where a conclusion is expressed in positive terms;

- *limited assurance*, requiring performance of limited procedures and possibly involving the provision of negative assurance in the style of 'nothing has come to our attention ...';

- *agreed upon procedures,* which involves performing certain defined procedures on factual information and reporting findings without any form of opinion on the implications of the work done; and

- *compilation engagements*, which involve preparing financial information on behalf of clients.

Where reports are to be given to third parties an agreed upon procedures report is usually most suited to the requirements of the client and the third party. Accountants must consider the level of risk of giving the type of report requested by the third party (even after appropriate liability limits are set) and consider whether the engagement should be accepted.

Agree appropriate terms of agreement

The accountant should agree terms of engagement in writing with both the client and third party. If the third party refuses to sign an engagement letter, the accountant should either refuse to provide a report, or do so only subject to a disclaimer of liability to the third party. Disclaimers must be reasonable to be effective. An example disclaimer notice is given in **Table 9**.

TABLE 9: Example disclaimer notices

Where the third party does not sign the engagement letter:

Our report is prepared solely for the confidential use of [client's name] and solely for the purpose of [details]. It may not be relied upon by [client's name] for any other purpose whatsoever. Our report must not be recited or referred to in whole or in part in any other document. Our report must not be made available, copied or recited to any other party [without our express permission]. [Accountant's name] neither owes nor accepts any duty to any other party and shall not be liable for any loss, damage or expense of whatsoever nature which is caused by their reliance on our report.

Where the third party signs the engagement letter:

Our report is prepared solely for the confidential use of [client's name] and [name of third party], and solely for the purpose of [details]. It may not be relied upon by [client's name] or [name of third party] for any other purpose whatsoever. Our report must not be recited or referred to in whole or in part in any other document. Our report must not be made available, copied or recited to any other party [without our express written permission]. [Accountant's name] neither owes nor accepts any duty to any other party and shall not be liable for any loss, damage or expense of whatsoever nature which is caused by their reliance on our report.

Example engagement letter extracts for an agreed upon procedures engagement are set out in **Table 10**.

TABLE 10: Example extracts from an engagement letter for an agreed upon procedures engagement

Services to be provided

We will complete the specified limited scope procedures set out below:

(Describe the nature, timing and extent of the procedures to be performed, including specific reference, where applicable, to the identity of the documents and records to be read, individuals to be contacted and parties from whom confirmations will be obtained.)

The above procedures will be performed solely for your purposes. You are responsible for determining whether the scope of our work specified above is sufficient for your purposes.

Upon completion of the procedures we will provide you with a report of our findings in the form of that attached to this letter, solely for your information. Our report is not to be used for any other purpose or disclosed to any other third party without our consent. [We consent to the report being released to [third party name] provided that [third party name] acknowledges in writing that we owe no duty of care to [third party name] and we will not be liable to [third party name] for any reliance it chooses to place on the report.]

We have agreed that, under this engagement, we will not perform any verification procedures other than those which are specified in the scope section above. [If we were to perform additional procedures or if we were to perform an audit or any more limited review, other matters might come to our attention that would be reported to you.] Our report will not extend to any financial statements of the Company taken as a whole.

Audit work

Our audit work on the financial statements of the Company is carried out in accordance with our statutory obligations and is subject to a separate engagement letter. Our audit report is intended for the sole benefit of the Company's shareholders as a body, to whom it is addressed, to enable them to exercise their rights in general meeting. Our audits of the Company's financial statements are not planned or conducted to address or reflect matters in which anyone other than such shareholders as a body may be interested.

We do not, and will not, by virtue of this report or otherwise, assume any responsibility whether in contract, negligence or otherwise in relation to our audits of the Company's financial statements; we and our employees shall have no liability whether in contract, negligence or otherwise to [third party name if addressee to this letter, or to] any [other] third parties in relation to our audits of the Company's financial statements.

Timetable

We will be able to commence our limited scope procedures on [date] and we expect our work to be completed by [date]. Our work will depend upon

---

receiving without undue delay full cooperation from all relevant officials of the Company and their disclosure to us of all [the accounting records of the Company and all other] records and related information (including certain representations) we may need for the purpose of our work.

Staffing

[X] will be the partner in charge of the engagement. [Y] will act as manager.

Scope of our work

The scope of our work and the procedures we shall carry out in preparing our report, together with the limitations inherent therein, are outlined above. If the scope and procedures do not meet your requirements, please tell us so that we can discuss a different scope or additional or alternative procedures. [You should understand that there is no guarantee that these procedures will result in the identification of all matters which may be of interest to you.]

Our work will be based primarily on internal management information and will be carried out on the assumption that information provided to us by the management of the Company is reliable and, in all material respects, accurate and complete. We will not subject the information contained in our reports and letters to checking or verification procedures except to the extent expressly stated. This is normal practice when carrying out such limited scope procedures, but contrasts significantly with, for example, an audit. Even audit work provides no guarantee that fraud will be detected. You will therefore understand that the Services are not designed to and are not likely to reveal fraud or misrepresentation by the management of the Company. Accordingly, we cannot accept responsibility for detecting fraud (whether by management or by external parties) or misrepresentation by the management of the Company.

Any engagement letter should include the following:

- an unambiguous description of the scope of work and form of report to be given;

- a description of the client's obligations and responsibilities;

- a statement that the engagement is separate from the statutory audit and that no duty of care will arise in relation to the statutory audit;

- if agreed, an appropriate liability cap;

- details of the addressee for the report, together with details of restrictions on who is entitled to see and rely on the report; and

- a copy of the report that will be provided.

Example wording for a liability cap is set out in **Table 11**.

TABLE 11: Example liability cap

The aggregate liability, whether to [client's name] or [third party name] or any other party, of whatever nature, whether in contract, tort or otherwise, of [Accountant's name] for any losses whatsoever and howsoever caused arising from or in any way connected with this engagement [and this transaction] shall not exceed [amount] (including interest).

Perform the work

The work for a third party report is separate to that for the statutory audit, and the audit team should put together a separate working paper file for this engagement.

Report

The report should reflect the terms set out in the engagement letter, and should not include undefined terms such as 'review' without specifying what the terms mean.

Accountants should not modify the wording of their reports at the client's or third party's request unless the modification is appropriate and they have the opportunity to perform any additional work that is required to support the change in wording. If a different form of report is required to that set out in the engagement letter, the accountants should either reissue their terms of engagement or refuse to report, giving their reasons in writing.

Illustrative contents of a report of factual findings for an agreed upon procedures engagement are set out in **Table 12**.

TABLE 12: Illustrative contents of a report of factual findings for an agreed upon procedures engagement

These include:

- addressee;
- identification of the applicable engagement letter and specific information to which the agreed upon procedures have been applied;
- a statement that the procedures performed were those agreed with the client (and third party, if applicable);
- identification of the purpose for which the agreed upon procedures were performed;
- a listing of the specific procedures performed;

- a description of the accountants' factual findings, including sufficient details of errors and exceptions found;

- a statement that the procedures performed do not constitute either an audit or a review;

- a statement that had the accountants performed additional procedures, an audit or a review, other matters might have come to light that would have been reported;

- a statement that the report is restricted to those parties that have agreed to the procedures performed;

- a statement that the report relates only to the matters specified and that it does not extend to the entity's financial statements taken as a whole; and

- the date of the report.

40.8.3   *Requests for references on clients' financial status*

Accountants may be asked to provide references to banks, building societies and a range of other bodies about their clients' financial position, ability to pay debts as they fall due or service a loan. This is particularly relevant for individuals or small businesses that may not have audited accounts. Audit 2/01 *Requests for References on Clients' Financial Status and their Ability to Service Loans* provides guidance on how reporting accountants can manage their risks effectively when asked to perform such procedures.

The guidance is only appropriate where the accountant does not have to perform any additional work, research or investigation to give the reference. Where extra procedures have to be performed the guidance in TECH 10/12AAF should be followed.

The main issues

Third parties would like accountants to confirm that their client will have sufficient future income to service a loan or other commitment. However, no amount of enquiry can provide accountants with the assurance required to give such a confirmation.

Reporting on the present solvency of a client is only possible if the accountant is engaged to report on accounts, computations and projections as at a stated date. It is likely that the costs involved in producing such a report will be prohibitive to any third party.

References covered by Audit 2/01 require no extra work, and therefore incur no fee. This avoids the possibility of an implied contract. The fact that no extra work has been performed is stated in the reference.

Accountants may legitimately refuse to give a reference if they think the risks of doing so are too high, e.g. if the amounts involved are judged to be too large.

Unincorporated entities

Lenders who are entering into agreements with individuals and other unincorporated small borrowers, will not have audited reports to consider when making their lending decision. Accountants can, however, supply information that might be useful to a lender. This will include:

- the length of time the accountant has acted for the client;

- the net income or profits declared to HMRC; and

- a statement that the accountant has no reason to suppose that the client would have entered into a commitment which they would not expect to fulfil.

The third item of these bullet points is a matter of judgment and will be based on the accountants' past experience of the client and the client's attitude to commercial obligations. Where accountants have insufficient knowledge of their client (for example, they have only just started to act) or there is any doubt about the judgment, they can decline to comment.

If the accountants' knowledge of the client is out of date, this will also be noted in the report.

Reporting

Accountants should report in a manner suitable for the particular circumstances. Third parties may provide a standard form of report, but accountants should amend the wording if necessary to reflect any limitations to the information requested.

Accountants should ensure that all technical terms are sufficiently defined, and should refer the third party to information provided directly by the client if this is more appropriate.

An example report is given in **Table 13**.

TABLE 13: Example of an accountants' reference in connection with a lending application made by an individual or other small borrower

Without responsibility

[Name of lender]

[Address]

Dear Sirs

REFERENCE IN CONNECTION WITH THE LENDING APPLICATION MADE BY [name of client and application reference, as appropriate]

Our above named client has approached us for a reference in connection with the proposed loan by you of [amount] [repayable by monthly instalments of amount over number years].

We have acted in connection with our client's [personal/business/corporate tax] affairs since [date]. However, it should be noted that our knowledge of our client's affairs may not be fully up to date. In addition, we have not carried out any specific work with regard to this statement.

Our client's net income [insert definition] declared by our client to HMRC as at [date] amounted to [amount]. (To be adapted for borrowers who are not individuals.)

(Income/profits for previous years and identification of those agreed with HMRC may be added.)

Whilst we have no reason to believe that our client would enter into a commitment such as that proposed which our client did not expect to be able to fulfil, we can make no assessment of our client's continuing income or future outgoings.

Whilst the information provided above is believed to be true, it is provided without acceptance by [Accountant's name] of any responsibility whatsoever, and any use you wish to make of the information is, therefore, entirely at your own risk.

Yours faithfully

Signed ....

Dated ....

40.9   Audit liability: Claims by third parties

In June 2005, the Audit and Assurance Faculty of the ICAEW, in conjunction with the law firm Simmons & Simmons, published a review of the legal cases involving claims by third parties against auditors. It sets out the key matters arising from the cases of which auditors in practice should take note.

All the cases have in common an institution seeking assurance or reassurance from a company's auditor as to that company's financial strengths at a particular point in time, whether by reference to its audited accounts or by means of some other independent confirmation from the auditor that the company is financially sound.

As stated in **40.4**, the case law surrounding the auditor's duty of care was set out in the *Caparo v Dickman* judgment. That case set out that there would only be sufficient grounds to establish a duty of care to a third party where:

- the work produced was required for a purpose made known to the auditor; and

- the auditor knew, or should have known, that its work would be communicated to the non-client party for that purpose; and

- the auditor, knew or should have known, that its work would be likely to be relied upon by that third party for that purpose, without independent enquiry.

The main categories of cases where the application of these principles has been considered in the paper are:

- potential investors;

- creditors and lenders;

- regulators and trade bodies; and

- affiliates/associates of the audit client.

40.9.1 *Potential investors*

A duty of care to potential investors may occur other than in written form. In *ADT v Binder Hamlyn*, ADT, the potential investor, argued that a duty of care had been created when the audit partner made a comment in a meeting that the firm stood by its earlier unmodified audit opinion. ADT stated that they made further investment in Britannia Securities Group plc as a result of this affirmation and therefore sought damages from Binder Hamlyn when that investment lost money. By orally restating the true and fair opinion to the potential investor, the audit partner had assumed a duty of care to ADT which did not exist from the earlier audit report itself, as this had been prepared only with the shareholders of Britannia in mind.

An important element of the *Caparo* decision is whether the third party would have had another way of obtaining the assurance it sought from the auditor. In *Barker v Grant Thornton*, where potential investors sued the auditor, no duty of care was found to exist as it was reasoned that it would have been practical for the investor to have instructed investigating accountants to obtain the necessary assurance for them rather than rely on the statutory audit report. In addition, Grant Thornton had already specifically disclaimed responsibility to the investor.

In *Yorkshire Enterprises Ltd v Robson Rhodes*, however, as the auditor was aware that he was completing the audit promptly because the financial statements were to be passed on to venture capitalists, it was not judged reasonable to require the investors to instruct their own investigating accountants. In addition, Robson Rhodes had not specifically disclaimed responsibility to Yorkshire Enterprises.

Two other cases set out in the study, *Electra Private Equity Partners v KPMG* and *Man Nutzfahrzeuge Aktiengesellschaft v Ernst & Young* demonstrate that the auditor may have a duty of care to a third party arising not from what he said or did when auditing the financial statements, but merely on the basis of what he was told during the audit, for example, that the audited financial statements were to be relied upon as the basis of a proposed sale.

40.9.2 Creditors and lenders

The same principles apply to those that lend money rather than invest in a company. In the case of *Royal Bank of Scotland v Bannerman Johnstone Maclay*, it was sufficient that the auditor should have been aware that a lender would rely on audited financial statements to create a duty of care. This case is discussed in **Section 4**.

40.9.3 Regulators and trade bodies

In a similar manner, in *Andrew v Kounnis Freeman*, the auditor ought to have known that the audited financial statements which they forwarded to the Civil Aviation Authority (CAA) would be relied upon by the CAA in determining whether to renew a company's ATOL licence, and by sending the audited financial statements, they assumed a duty of care.

In another case, audited financial statements were forwarded by the client to ABTA and IATA. In addition, they were sent to the provider of bond facilities to the travel agent. A travel agent is required to hold such bonds in order to be a member of ABTA and IATA. A duty of care was found to exist between the auditor and the bond provider, despite the auditor not knowing who would be providing the bond facilities. In this situation, it was sufficient that the auditor, with experience of clients in the travel business, should be aware that a bond provider would be required and that this provider would need sight of the audited financial statements.

40.9.4 Affiliates or associates of the audit client

As well as separate third parties pursuing claims against auditors, there are situations where a claim is made by entities affiliated or associated with the audit client. In *Barings plc (in administration) v Coopers & Lybrand*, Barings sought damages from the auditor of one of its own indirect subsidiaries. It was judged that Coopers & Lybrand knew that their audit report on the subsidiary would be required to allow directors of the parent company to prepare group financial statements which showed a true and fair view. In addition, the auditor of the subsidiary had liaised directly with the auditor of the parent company, reporting to them any matters of significance so that they could inform the parent company management. Both these matters created a duty of care between the subsidiary auditor and the parent company, independent of the duty of care the subsidiary auditor had to his own client.

41 Other engagements

41.1 Introduction

Increases in audit exemption limits in recent years have led to an increasing number of companies being entitled to take advantage of audit exemption. The thresholds for audit exemption are set out in **36.1**. Whilst many such companies still choose, or are required for other reasons, to have their financial statements audited, this has created an expanding market for services that add credibility to financial statements, without being a full audit. In summary, the options available are:

- A limited assurance review engagement in which the accountant carries out procedures and enquiries that are limited in scope and do not constitute a full audit, in order to provide a basis for his conclusion. International Standard for Review Engagements (ISRE) 2400 (Revised) *Engagements to Review Historical Financial Statements* issued by the IAASB and effective for periods ending on or after 31 December 2013 sets standards and provides guidance on the conduct of such a review. In the UK, ISRE 2400 (Revised) is supplemented by ICAEW technical release TECH 09/13 AAF *Assurance Review Engagements on Historical Financial Statements* (see **41.2**).

- Agreed-upon procedures, which result in a report of purely factual findings relating to procedures carried out. The user is left to draw his own conclusions, but will have increased confidence as these conclusions will be based on facts that have been checked by an independent accountant. More information can be found in the International Standard for Related Services (ISRS) 4400 *Agreed-upon Procedures regarding Financial Information*, and in the ICAEW technical release TECH10/12 AAF *Reporting to Third Parties* (see **40.8** and **41.3**).

- A compilation engagement, where the accountant is engaged to prepare the financial statements from an entity's accounting records but without carrying out any verification of those records. Guidance can be found in technical releases TECH 07/16AAF (incorporated entities) and TECH 08/16AAF (unincorporated entities) (see **Section 8**). IFAC has also issued further guidance on these engagements, in its *Guide to Compilation Engagements* published in September 2015. Although based on the International Standard on Related Services 4410 (Revised) *Compilation Engagements*, it provides useful guidance applicable to the UK.

The differences between these various types of engagement are illustrated in **Table 1**.

TABLE 1: Rules of engagement

Type of engagement	Assurance engagement		Agreed upon procedures engagement	Compilation engagement
	Reasonable assurance	**Limited assurance ('review')**		
Example	Audit in accordance with ISAs (UK)	Review in accordance with ISRE 2400 (Revised)/ TECH 09/13 AAF		
Type of conclusion	Positive opinion, e.g. 'true and fair'	Negative opinion, e.g. 'nothing has come to our attention'	Factual report of results of procedures, no conclusion given	Confirm facts of compilation only, no conclusion given

For entities not required to prepare general purpose financial statements, accountants may also be asked to provide assurance on financial statements, or elements of financial statements prepared for a specific purpose or on non-financial information. New ISAs (UK) 800 and 805 were issued in October 2016 and set out standards and guidance for use in such situations. These new standards are based on the IAASB's ISAs 800 and 805 (Revised).

Engagements to report on special purpose financial statements under ISA (UK) 800 (Revised), *Special Considerations – Audits of Financial Statements Prepared in Accordance with Special Purpose Frameworks* and ISA (UK) 805 (Revised), *Special Considerations – Audits of Single Financial Statements and Specific Elements, Accounts or Items of a Financial Statement* are covered in **41.4**;

Engagements to provide assurance on non-financial information, using guidance in ISAE 3000 (Revised) *Assurance Engagements Other than Audits or Reviews of Historical Financial Information* are covered in **41.5**.

41.2   Review engagements

41.2.1   Guidance

Guidance on the performance of review engagements is given in TECH 09/13 AAF *Assurance Review Engagements on Historical Financial Statements* which is based on the IAASB's International Standard on Review Engagements (ISRE) 2400 (Revised) *Engagements to Review Historical Financial Statements*, issued in September 2012.

In an assurance engagement, the accountant expresses a conclusion on the financial statements. In those review engagements covered by TECH 09/13 AAF, the accountant gives a negative form of conclusion on the unaudited financial statements. This is known as a limited assurance engagement, as opposed to a reasonable assurance engagement where positive assurance is given, usually in terms of a true and fair view.

ISRE 2400 (Revised) applies when a practitioner who is not the auditor of an entity undertakes an engagement to review financial statements. The principles contained therein may also be applied to reviews of other historical information. ISRE 2400 (Revised) helps practitioners performing review engagements to follow a globally accepted benchmark for undertaking such engagements, and aims to promote clarity for users about the nature of a review.

TECH 09/13 AAF issued by the ICAEW aims to provide guidance to assist with compliance with ISRE 2400 (Revised) and includes example letters and reports to support these engagements.

41.2.2   Features of a review engagement

The IAASB believes that an engagement performed under the revised standard should:

- enhance users' degree of confidence in the entity's financial statements, by reporting on them in a manner commensurate with the limited assurance obtained by the practitioner;

- be able to be performed on a cost-effective basis; and

- be clearly distinguishable from an audit of financial statements.

The ISRE sets out guidance in the following areas:

- conduct of a review engagement in accordance with the ISRE;

- ethical requirements;

- professional scepticism and judgment;

- engagement level quality control;

Other engagements

- acceptance and continuance of review engagements;
- communication with management and those charged with governance;
- performing the engagement;
- subsequent events;
- written representations;
- evaluating evidence;
- forming a conclusion on the financial statements;
- reporting; and
- documentation.

41.2.3 Accepting the engagement

The terms of the engagement should be agreed in writing. Example engagement letter wording is given in **Table 2**. The assurance report may be received by people not party to the engagement and the accountant should assess the risks of litigation arising from third parties prior to accepting the engagement. The engagement letter should be suitably worded to ensure that no liability is assumed to any third party.

TABLE 2: Example extracts from an engagement letter for a limited assurance review engagement for an audit exempt company

Your responsibilities as directors

As directors of the company, you are responsible for preparing financial statements which give a true and fair view and which have been prepared in accordance with the *Companies Act* 2006 (the Act). As directors, you must not approve the financial statements unless you are satisfied that they give a true and fair view of the assets, liabilities, financial position and profit or loss of the company.

In preparing the financial statements, you are required to:

- select suitable accounting policies and then apply them consistently;
- make judgments and estimates that are reasonable and prudent; and
- prepare the financial statements on the going concern basis unless it is inappropriate to presume that the company will continue in business.

You are responsible for keeping adequate accounting records that set out with reasonable accuracy at any time the company's financial position, and for ensuring that the financial statements comply with United Kingdom Generally Accepted Accounting Practice (UK GAAP) and with the *Companies Act* 2006 and give a true and fair view.

You are also responsible for such internal control as you determine is necessary to enable the preparation of financial statements that are free from material misstatement whether due to fraud or error.

You are also responsible for safeguarding the assets of the company and hence for taking reasonable steps to prevent and detect fraud and other irregularities.

You are responsible for ensuring that the company complies with laws and regulations that apply to its activities, and for preventing non-compliance and detecting any that occurs.

You have undertaken to make available to us, as and when required, all the company's accounting records and related financial information, including minutes of management and shareholders' and directors' meetings, that we need to do our work.

Our responsibilities when carrying out a review

Our review will be conducted with the objective of expressing our conclusion on the financial statements. Our conclusion, if unmodified, will be in the form:

'Based on our review, nothing has come to our attention that causes us to believe that the financial statements have not been prepared:

- so as to give a true and fair view of the state of the company's affairs as at [date], and of its profit [loss] for the year then ended;
- in accordance with United Kingdom Generally Accepted Accounting Practice; and
- in accordance with the requirements of the *Companies Act* 2006.'

We will conduct our review in accordance with International Standard on Review Engagements (ISRE) 2400 (Revised) *Engagements to Review Historical Financial Statements* and ICAEW Technical Release TECH 09/13AAF *Assurance Review Engagements on Historical Financial Statements*. ISRE 2400 (Revised) requires us to conclude whether anything has come to our attention that causes us to believe that the financial statements, taken as a whole, are not prepared in all material respects in accordance with the applicable financial reporting framework. ISRE 2400 (Revised) also requires us to comply with relevant ethical requirements.

A review of financial statements in accordance with ISRE 2400 (Revised) is a limited assurance engagement. We will perform procedures, primarily consisting of making enquiries of management and others within the entity, as appropriate, applying analytical procedures, and evaluating the evidence obtained. We will also perform additional procedures if we become aware of matters that cause us to believe the financial statements as a whole may be materially misstated. These procedures are performed to enable us to express our conclusion on the financial statements in accordance with ISRE 2400 (Revised). The procedures selected will depend on what we consider necessary applying our professional judgment, based on our understanding of the company and its environment, and our understanding of UK GAAP and its application in the context of your company.

A review is not an audit of the financial statements, therefore:

(a) there is a commensurate higher risk than there would be in an audit, that any material misstatements that exist in the financial statements reviewed may not be revealed by the review, even though the review is properly performed in accordance with ISRE 2400 (Revised);

(b) in expressing our conclusion from the review of the financial statements, our report on the financial statements will expressly disclaim any audit opinion on the financial statements.

Our report will be made solely to the company's directors, as a body, in accordance with the terms of this engagement letter. Our work will be undertaken so that we might state to the directors those matters that we have agreed to state to them in a review report and for no other purpose. To the fullest extent permitted by law, we will not accept or assume responsibility to anyone other than the Company and the Company's directors as a body for our work, for our report or the conclusions we form.

We have discussed with you the extent of our liability to you in respect of the professional services described within this engagement letter (the professional services). Having considered both your circumstances and our own, we have reached a mutual agreement that £ … represents a fair maximum limit to our liability.

In reaching this agreement, it is also agreed that:

(a) in the event of any claim for loss or damage arising from the professional services, you have agreed that the sum of £ … represents the maximum total liability to you in respect of the firm, [its] [principals] [directors] [members] [and staff]. This maximum total liability applies to any and all claims made on any basis and therefore includes any claims in respect of breaches of contract, tort (including negligence) or otherwise in respect of the professional services and shall also include interest;

(b) we confirm that the limit in respect of our total aggregate liability will not apply to any acts, omissions or representations that are in any way criminal, dishonest or fraudulent on the part of the firm, [its] [principals] [directors] [members] [or employees]; and

(c) you have agreed that you will not bring any claim of a kind that is included within the subject of the limit against any of our [principals] [directors] [members] [or employees] on a personal basis.

As part of their risk management process, accountants should consider whether there are third parties who may seek to rely on their report. Depending on circumstances, and similar to the general guidance for managing professional liability set out in **40.3.2**, accountants may:

- accept that they owe a duty of care to the third parties and enter into a tri-partite or multi-partite engagement contract with the client and the third parties. Provisions to limit liability may be appropriate;

- proceed with an engagement with the client alone, but allowing access to the report for third parties as long as they:

  - acknowledge in writing that the reporting accountant owes them no duty of care; and

  - agree in writing that no claims will be brought against the reporting accountant in relation to the assurance report;

- engage with the client alone, disclaiming any liability or duty to others by notice in the assurance report. This may be in conjunction with the client indemnifying the reporting accountant if a third party makes a claim against the reporting accountant; or

- decline to accept the engagement.

41.2.4   Reliance by third parties

During the performance of the engagement, or after the report has been issued, the accountant may become aware of third parties, such as banks or lenders, who may request sight of the report. In such cases, the accountant may decline the request, or access may be agreed if the third party acknowledges in writing that they owe the accountant no duty of care.

When the accountant becomes aware that a third party has obtained a copy of his report, he should consider writing to the third party informing them that he did not undertake the work for the use of third parties and that he does not accept any responsibility to them and that all liability is denied.

It is likely that most assurance review reports will relate to general purpose financial statements, including statutory financial statements for audit exempt companies. These may become widely available, for example, they may be filed at Companies House although there is no obligation on the company to do so. This will make it impossible to restrict who has access to them, and it may therefore not be possible for the accountant to limit liability purely by means of a contract. An assurance review report appended to general financial statements may, however, include a paragraph disclaiming liabilities to third parties. The illustrative report in **Table 3** includes a paragraph to this effect, which is equivalent to the 'Bannerman' paragraph used in audit reports, and relies on the same legal precedent (see **4.28**).

41.2.5   Performing the engagement

Further guidance on performing the engagement is given in the ISRE. In particular, the accountant should be aware that he is still subject to the *Money Laundering Regulations* 2007 and the requirements of the

Other engagements

Proceeds of Crime Act 2002. In addition, although the depth of work carried out on going concern will be less than that for an audit, the accountant will still need to consider the disclosures in this area in accordance with the applicable accounting framework and the FRC guidance for directors.

An emphasis of matter paragraph is required when the accountant considers a matter to be of such importance that it is fundamental to users' understanding of the financial statements. This will include situations where there is material uncertainty related to events or conditions that may cast significant doubt on the entity's ability to continue as a going concern.

41.2.6 Written representations

Written representations are still required from management and example wording is given in TECH 09/13.

41.2.7 Reporting

The accountant's report helps addressees derive comfort from the involvement of an independent accountant. It also assists in clarifying the scope of the engagement and ensuring that readers are aware that a full audit has not taken place. **Table 3** includes an example report to directors.

TABLE 3: Example accountant's report to directors

Independent Chartered Accountant's review report to the directors of [entity name]

To the Board of Directors of [entity name] ('the Company')

We have reviewed the financial statements of XYZ Limited for the year ended [date], which comprise the [Profit and Loss Account, the Balance Sheet, the Cash Flow Statement, the Statement of Total Recognised Gains and Losses,] and notes to the financial statements including a summary of significant accounting policies. The financial reporting framework that has been applied in their preparation is applicable law and United Kingdom Accounting Standards, including FRS 102: The Financial Reporting Standard applicable in the UK and Republic of Ireland (United Kingdom Generally Accepted Accounting Practice).

Directors' Responsibility for the Financial Statements

As explained more fully in the Directors' Responsibilities Statement [set out on pages ...], the directors are responsible for the preparation of the financial statements and for being satisfied that they give a true and fair view.

Accountants' Responsibility

Our responsibility is to express a conclusion based on our review of the financial statements. We conducted our review in accordance with International

---

Standard on Review Engagements (ISRE) 2400 (Revised), *Engagements to Review Historical Financial Statements* and ICAEW Technical Release TECH 09/13AAF *Assurance Review Engagements on Historical Financial Statements*. ISRE 2400 (Revised) also requires us to comply with the ICAEW Code of Ethics.

Scope of the Assurance Review

A review of financial statements in accordance with ISRE 2400 (Revised) is a limited assurance engagement. We have performed additional procedures to those required under a compilation engagement. These primarily consist of making enquiries of management and others within the entity, as appropriate, applying analytical procedures and evaluating the evidence obtained. The procedures performed in a review are substantially less than those performed in an audit conducted in accordance with International Standards on Auditing (UK). Accordingly, we do not express an audit opinion on these financial statements.

Conclusion

Based on our review, nothing has come to our attention that causes us to believe that the financial statements have not been prepared:

- so as to give a true and fair view of the state of the company's affairs as at [date], and of its profit [loss] for the year then ended;

- in accordance with United Kingdom Generally Accepted Accounting Practice; and

- in accordance with the requirements of the *Companies Act* 2006.

Use of our report

This report is made solely to the Company's directors, as a body, in accordance with the terms of our engagement letter dated [date]. Our review has been undertaken so that we may state to the company's directors those matters we have agreed with them in our engagement letter and for no other purpose. To the fullest extent permitted by law, we do not accept or assume responsibility to anyone other than the Company and the Company's directors as a body for our work, for this report or the conclusions we have formed.

[Accountant's signature – name of individual or firm]

[Firm name] Chartered Accountants [Address]

[Date]

41.3   Agreed upon procedures

Guidance in the area of agreed upon procedures reports to third parties is provided by International Standard on Related Services (ISRS) 4400, *Engagements to Perform Agreed-Upon Procedures Regarding Financial Information*. ISRS 4400 sets out the general principles and standards to be applied by the accountant when an engagement to perform agreed-upon procedures is undertaken.

In an agreed-upon procedures engagement, the accountant will carry out procedures of an audit nature on which he and the entity, together with any relevant third parties, have agreed, and report on his findings.

As the accountant simply provides a report of the factual findings of agreed-upon procedures, no assurance is expressed. Instead, users of the report assess for themselves the procedures and findings reported by the accountant and draw their own conclusions from the results of the work performed. Under ISRS 4400, the accountant's report is restricted to those parties that have agreed to the procedures to be performed since others, unaware of the reasons for the procedures, may misinterpret the results.

ISRS 4400 contains detailed guidance on:

- defining the terms of the engagement;
- planning;
- documentation;
- procedures and evidence; and
- reporting.

Further matters to consider and example engagement letters and reports in respect of an agreed upon procedures engagement are discussed in **40.8**.

41.4 Auditor's reports on special purpose financial statements

Guidance covering reports by the auditor on special purpose financial statements is given in ISA (UK) 800 (Revised), *Special Considerations – Audits of Financial Statements Prepared in Accordance with Special Purpose Frameworks* and ISA (UK) 805 Revised, *Special Considerations – Audits of Single Financial Statements and Specific Elements, Accounts or Items of a Financial Statement.*

ISA (UK) 800 (Revised) and ISA (UK) 805 (Revised) were issued in October 2016 and are effective for audits of financial statements for periods commencing on or after 1 January 2017.

These ISAs (UK) are based on the IAASB's ISA 800 (Revised) and ISA 805 (Revised) published in January 2016. Prior to the issue of the ISAs (UK) in October 2016, there had been no direct UK equivalents of these ISAs and, where appropriate, UK auditors had referred to the international standards.

These standards are not appropriate for engagements to report on statutory accounts of UK companies which are required to be general purposes financial statements, even where an audit is not required.

41.4.1 Special purpose frameworks

ISA (UK) 800 (Revised) is applicable where an audit opinion (i.e. reasonable rather than limited assurance) is given on a complete set of financial statements but the financial statements have been prepared in accordance with a special purpose framework rather than a generally accepted one. A special purpose framework is one designed to meet the financial information needs of specific users and will usually be based on a generally accepted framework but deviate from it in one or more material respects because the information required by the framework is either inappropriate or irrelevant for the special purpose for which the financial statements are prepared. Examples of such frameworks include:

- a tax basis of accounting for a set of financial statements accompanying an entity's tax return;

- cash receipts and payments basis of accounting for cash flow information that an entity may be requested to prepare for creditors;

- the financial reporting provisions established by a regulator to meet the requirements of that regulator; and

- the financial reporting provisions of a contract, such as a bond indenture, loan agreement, or a project grant.

ISA (UK) 800 (Revised) deals with special considerations in the application of ISAs to an audit of financial statements prepared in accordance with a special purpose framework and in particular sets standards and provides guidance on accepting the engagement, planning and performing procedures and forming an opinion and reporting.

Accepting the engagement

In an audit of special purpose financial statements, ISA (UK) 800 (Revised) requires the auditor to obtain an understanding of the purpose for which the financial statements are prepared; the intended users; and the steps taken by management to determine that the applicable financial reporting framework is acceptable in the circumstances.

Planning and performing the audit

ISA (UK) 200 (Revised June 2016) *Overall Objectives of the Independent Auditor and the Conduct of an Audit in Accordance with International Standards on Auditing (UK)* requires the auditor to comply with all relevant ethical requirements and all ISAs (UK) relevant to the audit. It also requires the auditor to comply with each requirement of an ISA (UK) unless, in the circumstances of the audit, the entire ISA (UK) is not relevant or the requirement is not relevant because it is conditional and the condition does not exist. In planning and performing an audit of special purpose financial statements, the auditor needs to determine whether application of the ISAs (UK) requires special consideration in the circumstances of the engagement.

For example, in ISA (UK) 320 (Revised June 2016) *Materiality in Planning and Performing an Audit*, judgments about matters that are material to users of the financial statements are based on a consideration of the common financial information needs of users as a group. In the case of an audit of special purpose financial statements, however, those judgments are based on a consideration of the financial information needs of the intended users.

In the case of special purpose financial statements, such as those prepared in accordance with the requirements of a contract, management may agree with the intended users on a threshold below which misstatements identified during the audit will not be corrected or otherwise adjusted. The existence of such a threshold does not relieve the auditor from the requirement to determine materiality in accordance with ISA (UK) 320 (Revised June 2016) for purposes of planning and performing the audit of the special purpose financial statements.

ISA (UK) 315 (Revised June 2016) *Identifying and Assessing the Risks of Material Misstatement through Understanding of the Entity and its Environment* requires the auditor to obtain an understanding of the entity's selection and application of accounting policies. ISA (UK) 800 (Revised) specifically notes that in the case of financial statements prepared in accordance with the provisions of a contract, the auditor shall obtain an understanding of any significant interpretations of the contract that management made in the preparation of those financial statements. An interpretation is significant when adoption of another reasonable interpretation would have produced a material difference in the information presented in the financial statements.

Forming an opinion and reporting

In forming an opinion and reporting on special purpose financial statements, the auditor still applies the requirements of ISA (UK) 700 (Revised June 2016) *Forming an Opinion and Reporting on Financial Statements*, as well as reporting requirements contained in other ISAs (UK) as appropriate. This includes evaluating whether the financial statements adequately refer to or describe the applicable financial reporting framework. In the case of financial statements prepared in accordance with the provisions of a contract, the auditor evaluates whether the financial statements adequately describe any significant interpretations of the contract on which the financial statements are based.

As well as following the requirements of ISA (UK) 700 (Revised June 2016) regarding the form and content of the auditor's report, in the case of an auditor's report on special purpose financial statements:

- the auditor's report shall also describe the purpose for which the financial statements are prepared and, if necessary, the intended users, or refer to a note in the special purpose financial statements that contains that information; and

- if management has a choice of financial reporting frameworks in the preparation of such financial statements, the explanation of management's responsibility for the financial statements shall also make reference to its responsibility for determining that the applicable financial reporting framework is acceptable in the circumstances.

The auditor specifically describes the financial reporting framework as a special purpose framework in the auditor's report. He also specifically states that the audit has been carried out in accordance with ISAs (UK), including ISA (UK) 800 and/or ISA (UK) 805.

An example audit report is given in **Table 4**:

TABLE 4: Example of an audit report in accordance with ISA (UK) 800 (Revised)[1]

Independent Auditor's Report to [Appropriate Addressee]

Opinion

We have audited the financial statements of ABC Company, which comprise the balance sheet as at December 31, 20X1, and the income statement, statement of changes in equity and cash flow statement for the year then ended, and a summary of significant accounting policies and other explanatory information.

In our opinion, the accompanying financial statements of ABC Company for the year ended December 31, 20X1 are prepared, in all material respects, in accordance with the financial reporting provisions of Section Z of the contract dated January 1, 20X1 between ABC Company and DEF Company ('the contract').

Basis for Opinion

We conducted our audit in accordance with International Standards on Auditing (UK). Our responsibilities under those standards are further described in the *Auditor's Responsibilities for the Audit of the Financial Statements* section of our report. We are independent of the Company in accordance with the ethical requirements that are relevant to our audit of the financial statements in [jurisdiction], and we have fulfilled our other ethical responsibilities in accordance with these requirements. We believe that the audit evidence we

---

have obtained is sufficient and appropriate to provide a basis for our audit opinion.

Emphasis of Matter – Basis of Accounting and Restriction on Distribution and Use

We draw attention to Note X to the financial statements, which describes the basis of accounting. The financial statements are prepared to assist ABC Company in complying with the financial reporting provisions of the contract referred to above. As a result, the financial statements may not be suitable for another purpose. Our report is intended solely for ABC Company and DEF Company and should not be distributed to or used by parties other than ABC Company or DEF Company. Our opinion is not modified in respect of this matter.

Management's Responsibility for the Financial Statements

Management is responsible for the preparation of these financial statements in accordance with the financial reporting provisions of Section Z of the contract, and for such internal control as management determines is necessary to enable the preparation of financial statements that are free from material misstatement, whether due to fraud or error.

In preparing the financial statements, management is responsible for assessing the Company's ability to continue as a going concern, disclosing, as applicable, matters relating to going concern and using the going concern basis of accounting unless management either intends to liquidate the Company or to cease operations, or has no realistic alternative but to do so.

Those charged with governance are responsible for overseeing the Company's financial reporting process.

Auditor's Responsibility for the Audit of the Financial Statements

Our objectives are to obtain reasonable assurance about whether the financial statements as a whole are free from material misstatement, whether due to fraud or error, and to issue an auditor's report that includes our opinion. Reasonable assurance is a high level of assurance, but is not a guarantee that an audit conducted in accordance with ISAs will always detect a material misstatement when it exists. Misstatements can arise from fraud or error and are considered material if, individually or in the aggregate, they could reasonably be expected to influence the economic decisions of users taken on the basis of these financial statements.

As part of an audit in accordance with ISAs, we exercise professional judgment and maintain professional scepticism throughout the audit. We also:

- identify and assess the risks of material misstatement of the financial statements, whether due to fraud or error, design and perform audit procedures responsive to those risks, and obtain audit evidence that is sufficient and appropriate to provide a basis for our opinion. The risk of not detecting a material misstatement resulting from fraud is higher than for one resulting from error, as fraud may involve collusion, forgery, intentional omissions, misrepresentations, or the override of internal control.

- obtain an understanding of internal control relevant to the audit in order to design audit procedures that are appropriate in the circumstances, but not for the purpose of expressing an opinion on the effectiveness of the Company's internal control.

- evaluate the appropriateness of accounting policies used and the reasonableness of accounting estimates and related disclosures made by management.

- conclude on the appropriateness of management's use of the going concern basis of accounting and, based on the audit evidence obtained, whether a material uncertainty exists related to events or conditions that may cast significant doubt on the Company's ability to continue as a going concern. If we conclude that a material uncertainty exists, we are required to draw attention in our auditor's report to the related disclosures in the financial statements or, if such disclosures are inadequate, to modify our opinion. Our conclusions are based on the audit evidence obtained up to the date of our auditor's report. However, future events or conditions may cause the Company to cease to continue as a going concern.

We communicate with those charged with governance regarding, among other matters, the planned scope and timing of the audit and significant audit findings, including any significant deficiencies in internal control that we identify during our audit.

[Auditor's signature]

[Auditor's address]

[Date of the auditor's report]

[1] This example is based on the IAASB's version of ISA 800 and does not include any UK specific amendments.

41.4.2 Reports on a single financial statement or a specific element

ISA (UK) 805 (Revised) deals with special considerations in the application of ISAs to an audit of a single financial statement or of a specific element, account or item of a financial statement. The single financial statement or the specific element, account or item of a financial statement may be prepared in accordance with a general or special purpose framework. If prepared in accordance with a special purpose framework, ISA (UK) 800 (Revised) also applies to the audit.

Accepting the engagement

As with an audit in accordance with ISA (UK) 800 (Revised) as detailed in **41.4.1**, ISA (UK) 200 (Revised June 2016) requires the auditor to comply with all ISAs (UK) relevant to the audit.

Other engagements

In the case of an audit of a single financial statement or of a specific element of a financial statement, this requirement applies irrespective of whether the auditor is also engaged to audit the entity's complete set of financial statements. The auditor needs to determine whether it is indeed practicable to audit a single financial statement or of a specific element of those financial statements in accordance with ISAs (UK).

When the auditor is not also engaged to audit the entity's complete set of financial statements, he may not have the same understanding of the entity and its environment, including its internal control, as an auditor who also audits the entity's complete set of financial statements. The auditor also does not have the audit evidence about the general quality of the accounting records or other accounting information that would be acquired in an audit of the entity's complete set of financial statements. Accordingly, he may need further evidence to corroborate audit evidence acquired from the accounting records.

If the auditor concludes that an audit of a single financial statement or of a specific element of a financial statement in accordance with ISAs (UK) may not be practicable, he discusses with management whether another type of engagement might be more practicable.

The auditor is also required to determine the acceptability of the financial reporting framework applied. In the case of an audit of a single financial statements or specific element, ISA (UK) 805 (Revised) requires this to include whether application of the financial reporting framework will result in a presentation that provides adequate disclosures to enable the intended users to understand the information conveyed, and the effect of material transactions and events on the information conveyed in the financial statement or the specific element.

The agreed terms of the audit engagement must also include the expected form of any reports to be issued by the auditor, including whether the expected form of opinion is appropriate in the circumstances.

Planning and performing the audit

Although the audit must be conducted in accordance with all ISAs (UK), in planning and performing the audit of a single financial statement or of a specific element of a financial statement, the auditor shall adapt ISAs (UK) relevant to the audit as necessary in the circumstances of the engagement. The relevance of each ISA (UK) requires careful consideration. For example, even when only a specific element of a financial statement is subject to audit, ISAs (UK) 240, 550 or 570 may still be relevant as the item may be misstated as a result of fraud, the effect of related party transactions or the application of the going concern basis of accounting.

Forming an opinion and reporting

In forming an opinion and reporting on a single financial statement or on a specific element of a financial statement, the auditor still applies the requirements of ISA (UK) 700 (Revised June 2016), and where applicable the requirements of ISA (UK) 800 (Revised).

Where the auditor undertakes an engagement to report on a single financial statement or on a specific element of a financial statement in conjunction with an engagement to audit the entity's complete set of financial statements, the auditor expresses a separate opinion for each engagement. The single element may however be published together with the entity's audited complete set of financial statements, provided the single element is sufficiently differentiated from the complete set of financial statements, and subject to the following exceptions. The auditor should not issue his opinion until he is satisfied with this differentiation.

If the auditor's report on the entity's complete set of financial statements includes a modified opinion, an Emphasis of Matter paragraph or an Other Matter paragraph, a Material Uncertainty Related to Going Concern section, communication of key audit matters, or a statement that describes an uncorrected material misstatement of the other information then the auditor needs to consider the implications, if any, that these matters have for the audit of the single financial statement or of the specific element of a financial statement and for his report thereon.

If the auditor issues an adverse opinion or disclaims an opinion on the complete set of financial statements, then he is not permitted to include an unmodified opinion on a single element of those financial statements in the same audit report, since it would contradict the opinion on the complete set of financial statements. If the auditor considers that an unmodified opinion on a specific element of the financial statements is appropriate, then he can only express that opinion if it is published separately to the audit report containing the adverse or disclaimed opinion, and provided the single element is not a major proportion of the complete set of financial statements.

The auditor is not permitted, however, to express an unmodified opinion on a single financial statement of a complete set of financial statements if the auditor has expressed an adverse opinion or disclaimed an opinion on the complete set of financial statements as a whole. This applies even if the auditor's report on the single financial statement is not published together with his report containing the adverse opinion or disclaimer of opinion, since a single financial statement is deemed to constitute a major portion of those financial statements.

41.5 Assurance on non-financial information

41.5.1 Non-financial information

There are a number of areas where entities currently report on non-financial information, and these include:

- statements and information contained in the annual report, such as the enhanced business review, corporate governance statements and information on risk management policies, internal controls or wider operating data;

- corporate responsibility reporting on environmental, economic and social performance;

- reports to Regulators on matters such as risk exposures, pricing policies or compliance with regulatory requirements; and

- reporting on public interest concerns, for example, quality of service provision, carbon emissions or the conduct of public competitions.

Demand for credible information in these areas is growing, and therefore, there has been an increasing requirement for practitioners to provide assurance reports.

41.5.2 Current practices and guidance

The current version of the International Standard on Assurance Engagements (ISAE) 3000 (Revised) *Assurance Engagements Other than Audits or Reviews of Historical Financial Information*, published by the IAASB, was issued in December 2013 and is effective for assurance reports dated on or after 15 December 2015. It covers all aspects of assurance engagements including:

- engagement acceptance;

- agreeing the terms of engagement;

- planning and performing the engagement;

- using the work of experts;

- obtaining evidence;

- considering subsequent events;

- documentation; and

- preparing the external assurance report.

Reference may be made to this standard where an assurance engagement is being conducted which is not an audit, or a review of historical financial information.

This standard is increasingly being used in the UK by accountants who are engaged to provide assurance on non-financial information produced by entities such as greenhouse gas emissions statements or sustainability reports. Such statements may form part of a company's annual report to members or may be a separate report(s) published on a website or prepared specifically for use by third parties.

Corporate responsibility

Corporate responsibility reports provide non-financial information on the social, economic and environmental performance of an organisation. There is no generally accepted framework or standard for preparing a corporate responsibility report, however, the sustainability reporting guidelines issued by the Global Reporting Initiative (GRI) are the best-known global voluntary code for sustainability reporting.

Regulatory reporting

Many regulatory bodies require information from the entities that they regulate in order to perform their duties, but the nature and volume of the information required varies significantly from Regulator to Regulator. Practitioners should ensure that they are fully conversant with the requirements of the relevant Regulator prior to accepting an engagement to provide assurance on such information.

Where Regulators request reports on non-financial information, the form of report made by the regulated entity and the nature of external assurance requirements will be set out by the Regulator.

Other reports

Other areas where practitioners may be asked to report on non-financial information include:

- the application of quality assurance standards in relation to information security or customer service; and

- the administration of public competitions and telephone voting.

There is no external framework of guidance to assist practitioners with this type of engagement, but ISAE 3000 (Revised) should be helpful, and ISO 9000 may also provide some useful guidance on quality assurance.

41.5.3   *Considerations for practitioners*

By providing external assurance reports, practitioners are enhancing the credibility of non-financial information by:

- following rigorous ethical standards covering independence;

- following a defined framework and standards which cover the whole assurance engagement; and

Other engagements

- having the relevant skills and experience in carrying out assurance engagements, following professional standards, complying with CPD and training requirements and having internal quality control procedures in place.

When accepting such an engagement, practitioners should:

- consider the motivations and purpose behind the request to ensure that they are able to meet this need;

- understand the needs of the users of the non-financial information;

- be clear about what the information is that they are reporting on and why it is needed;

- have agreed criteria by which they can measure the information; and

- clearly communicate these considerations in their report to help to avoid any expectation gap.

Skills

Practitioners' auditing experience may be valuable when carrying out assurance engagements on non-financial information. They are used to applying professional judgment and are familiar with assessing materiality, understanding the business and obtaining sufficient appropriate evidence.

Specialists can be consulted or a multi-disciplinary team can be used where practitioners have less experience in assessing qualitative, rather than quantitative, information or have a lack of in-depth technical knowledge, such as in engineering or surveying.

Subjective information

Compared to financial information, established measurement conventions do not exist for non-financial information. In such situations, it may not be possible to establish consistent measurement criteria that are acceptable to all interested parties, and practitioners must consider whether the criteria used are relevant to the needs of the intended users of the information.

A reference to the measurement criteria used should be made in the external assurance report so that the basis of the practitioners' conclusion is clear.

Information from third parties

Reported non-financial information may include data sourced from third parties, such as retail statistics, average market prices, etc. In line with the requirements of ISA (UK) 402, *Audit Considerations Relating to Entities Using Service Organisations* (see **Section 22**), practitioners should consider whether the bodies producing this information have suitable controls and procedures in place to ensure that the information produced is accurate. This assurance may be in the form of an external assurance report on their operations (see **40.7**). If any such evidence is lacking, practitioners may exclude the associated data from the scope of their assurance report.

Evidence

Practitioners need to be aware that non-financial information is often qualitative, and therefore, it is often difficult to determine criteria against which to measure the information. Evidence may also be harder to obtain as there is likely to be less documentation to support disclosure and third-party verification is likely to be less readily available. In addition, determining materiality can be difficult in areas which are less quantitative in nature.

Control environment

Internal controls related to non-financial business activities and operations are not always well monitored or documented and may not be as robust as those related to financial reporting. Therefore, at the planning stage of the engagement, practitioners consider how they will obtain evidence that the information is robust enough to express an opinion on.

42 Corporate governance

42.1 Background

42.1.1 Corporate governance framework

Corporate governance has been developed over many years since the early 1990s and over that time a number of committees and reports (for example, the Cadbury Report, the Greenbury Report and the Combined Code) have been developed, resulting in today's governance framework.

For listed companies, the principal relevant document is the *UK Corporate Governance Code*, referred to as 'the Code', issued by the FRC. This is supported by a number of FRC documents aimed at assisting boards and audit committees with the application of the Code. These include:

- *Guidance on Board Effectiveness*, published in 2011;

- *Guidance on Audit Committees*, updated in 2016 and considered in **42.8**;

- *Guidance on Risk Management, Internal Control and Related Financial and Business Reporting*, published in 2014 and consolidating and updating earlier guidance; and

- an *Audit Quality Practice Aid* for audit committees, issued in March 2015 and covered in **Section 3**.

The latest edition of the Code was issued in April 2016 and applies to accounting periods beginning on or after 17 June 2016.

The Code is not mandatory but is intended to be applied on a 'comply or explain' basis under which entities applying the Code will make a statement of compliance in which they identify those provisions of the Code with which they have not complied and provide an explanation for their non-compliance.

The Code contains broad principles and more specific provisions. All companies with a Premium Listing of equity shares in the UK are required under the Listing Rules to report in their annual report and accounts on how they have applied the main principles of the Code, and either to confirm that they have complied throughout the reporting period with all relevant provisions of the Code or, where they have not, to provide an explanation. The relevant section of the Listing Rules can be found at www.fshandbook.info/FS/html/handbook/LR/9/8. Auditors of such companies are required to review this statement of compliance, but only insofar as it relates to certain specified provisions of the Code.

These requirements do not apply to companies with a standard listing only, nor to AIM listed companies. However, revised AIM Rules issued in March 2018 now require AIM companies to provide on their website details of a recognised corporate governance code that the board of directors of the AIM company has decided to apply (see **42.10**).

42.1.2 Directors' remuneration

Directors' remuneration remains a key issue for corporate governance and one of the main principles of the Code is that a company's remuneration policy should be designed to promote the long-term success of the company.

Under the *Companies Act* 2006, quoted companies are required to prepare a separate Directors' Remuneration Report. Some, but not all of the information in the Directors' Remuneration Report is required to be examined and reported on by the auditor.

The detailed requirements relating to the Directors' Remuneration Report are set out in the *Large and Medium-Sized Companies and Groups (Accounts and Reports) Regulations* 2008 (SI 2008/410), Sch. 8. A new Sch. 8 was substituted for financial years ending on or after 30 September 2013 by the *Large and Medium-sized Companies and Groups (Accounts and Reports) (Amendment) Regulations* 2013 (SI 2013/1981).

The requirement to prepare a Directors' Remuneration Report applies not only to premium listed companies but to any 'quoted' company which is defined as a company incorporated under the *Companies Act* 2006:

- whose equity share capital has been included in the official list; or
- is officially listed in an European Economic Area (EEA) state; or
- is admitted to dealing on either the New York Stock Exchange or the exchange known as Nasdaq.

The definition includes companies with standard listed equity shares but does not include companies traded on the Alternative Investment Market (AIM) or entities with standard listed debt or non-equity shares only.

42.1.3 Disclosure and transparency rules

With effect for financial years beginning on or after 29 June 2008, certain disclosures relating to corporate governance, and auditors' responsibilities in relation thereto, came into effect as a result of the European Union directives. The requirements were incorporated into the Disclosure Rules and Transparency Rules (now part of the Financial Conduct Authority (FCA) Handbook) and the *Companies Act* 2006. These included a requirement for listed companies to produce a Corporate Governance Statement and to include in it a description of the main features of their internal control and risk management systems in relation to the financial reporting process. Details of requirements relating to the Corporate Governance Statement are set out in **42.7.1**.

42.2 Guidance

42.2.1 FRC – companies and investors

In addition to the UK Corporate Governance Code, the FRC publishes a series of guidance notes intended to assist companies address specific aspects of governance and accountability. Currently, these cover:

- board effectiveness;

- the role of audit committees; and

- risk management, internal control and assessing and reporting on whether the business is a going concern.

The FRC also publishes the UK Stewardship Code which sets standards for investors for monitoring and engaging with companies. The Stewardship Code sets out a number of areas of good practice to which the FRC believes institutional investors should aspire and also operates on a 'comply or explain' basis. The FCA requires UK authorised asset managers to report on whether or not they apply the Code.

The FRC publication *UK Approach to Corporate Governance* explains the code-based approach, and how it fits into the UK's regulatory regime.

42.2.2 FRC – auditors

In September 2006, the APB issued Bulletin 2006/5, *The combined code on corporate governance: requirements of auditors under the Listing Rules of the Financial Services Authority and the Irish Stock Exchange* to update guidance for auditors when reviewing a company's statement made in relation to the Combined Code (now the UK Corporate Governance Code).

Additionally, in December 2009, the APB issued Bulletin 2009/4 *Developments in corporate governance affecting the responsibilities of auditors of UK companies*. This new bulletin:

- updated and superseded guidance in paragraphs 68 to 72 of Bulletin 2006/5 relating to the requirement for the auditor to review the directors' statement on going concern (see **42.6.4**);

- provided guidance in relation to the corporate governance statements required by the Disclosure Rules and Transparency Rules of the Financial Conduct Authority (see **42.7.1**); and

- provided guidance for reporting on standard listed companies (see **42.7.2**).

The FRC now seeks to maintain standards and guidance for auditors in parallel with its guidance for companies and recent developments in the UK Corporate Governance Code have been accompanied, where applicable, by changes to ISAs (UK).

The 2016 version of ISA (UK) 720 (Revised June 2016) *The Auditor's Responsibilities Relating to Other Information* contains a number of requirements and associated guidance applicable only to those entities that are required, or choose voluntarily to report on how they have applied the Code. This version of ISA (UK) 720 (Revised June 2016) is applicable for periods commencing on or after 17 June 2016. For earlier periods, these requirements were covered in ISA (UK) 700 *The Independent Auditor's Report on Financial Statements.*

The FRC's Bulletin: *Compendium of illustrative auditor's reports on United Kingdom private sector financial statements for periods commencing on or after 17 June 2016* was issued in October 2016, and contains examples of how these requirements might be applied in an auditor's report.

The implications for the auditor's report of compliance with the Code and the Listing Rules are considered in **Section 4**.

ISA (UK) 260 (Revised June 2016) *Communication with those Charged with Governance* contains specific requirements applicable to auditors of entities that report on application of the Code and sets out the matters that should be communicated by the auditor to the audit committee in connection with the responsibilities of those charged with governance under the Code.

ISA (UK) 570 (Revised June 2016) *Going Concern* contains specific requirements relating to the auditor's responsibility in relation to statements and disclosures made by the directors in the annual report in relation to risk, going concern and longer term viability.

42.3   Terms of engagement

Bulletin 2006/5 recommended that for premium listed companies, in order to clarify the auditor's responsibilities:

- the engagement letter explains the scope of the auditor's review of the directors' statement of compliance with the Code; and

- the auditor discusses the findings of his review with those charged with governance, prior to the publication of his report.

The Bulletin contains an example of suitable paragraphs to include in an engagement letter with respect to the company's compliance with the Listing Rule (LR) 9.8.10R.

The example terms of engagement also include paragraphs relating to the auditor's responsibilities in relation to the Directors' Remuneration Report, where applicable.

42.4   Auditor's responsibilities for the 'comply or explain' statement

The Listing Rules require listed companies to include a two-part statement in their annual report relating to the Code:

- *Part one*: explaining how the company has applied the main principles of the UK Corporate Governance Code, in a manner that would enable shareholders to evaluate how the principles have been applied;

- *Part two*: either:

  - *Comply* – include 'a statement as to whether it has complied throughout the accounting period with all relevant provisions set out in the UK Corporate Governance Code'; or

  - *Explain* – include 'a statement as to whether it has not complied throughout the accounting period with all relevant provisions set out in the UK Corporate Governance Code' and if so, set out:

    (i)   those provisions, it has not complied with;

    (ii)   in the case of provisions whose requirements are of a continuing nature, the period within which, if any, it did not comply with some or all of those provisions; and

    (iii)   the company's reasons for any non-compliance.

Auditors have no responsibility to assess and comment upon a company's decision to depart from the provisions of the Code. The auditor is, however, required by LR 9.8.10R(2), to review the parts of the statement that relate to certain of the objectively verifiable Code provisions as set out in **Table 1**.

In February 2012, the FRC published a paper titled *What Constitutes an Explanation under 'Comply or Explain'?* which was based on discussion meetings between senior investors and companies and identified a number of features of a meaningful explanation. These included, for example, providing a clear rationale for the action taken and describing any mitigating actions and ensuring that explanations – and corporate governance reporting generally – are specific to the company's position, not generic or off-the-shelf.

42.5   Provisions of the UK Corporate Governance Code

The Listing Rules require that the auditor reviews the company's statement, see **42.4**, insofar as it relates to the company's compliance with certain specified provisions of the Code. The relevant provisions are set out in **Table 1**. If the auditor has any matters to report in respect of this review, he should include them in his report.

TABLE 1: Provisions of the UK Corporate Governance Code which the auditor is required to review

C.1.1

The directors should explain in the annual report their responsibility for preparing the annual report and accounts, and state that they consider the annual report and accounts, taken as a whole, is fair, balanced and understandable and provides the information necessary for shareholders to assess the company's performance, business model and strategy. There should be a statement by the auditor about their reporting responsibilities.

C.2.1

The directors should confirm in the annual report that they have carried out a robust assessment of the principal risks facing the company, including those that would threaten its business model, future performance, solvency or liquidity. The directors should describe those risks and explain how they are being managed or mitigated.

C.2.3

The board should monitor the company's risk management and internal control systems and, at least annually, carry out a review of their effectiveness, and report on that review in the annual report. The monitoring and review should cover all material controls, including financial, operational and compliance controls.

C.3.1

The board should establish an audit committee of at least three, or in the case of smaller companies two, independent non-executive directors. In smaller companies, the company chairman may be a member of, but not chair, the committee in addition to the independent non-executive directors, provided he or she was considered independent on appointment as chairman. The

---

board should satisfy itself that at least one member of the audit committee has recent and relevant financial experience. The audit committee as a whole shall have competence relevant to the sector in which the company operates.

C.3.2

The main role and responsibilities of the audit committee should be set out in written terms of reference and should include:

- to monitor the integrity of the financial statements of the company, and any formal announcements relating to the company's financial performance, reviewing significant financial reporting judgments contained in them;

- to review the company's internal financial control and, unless expressly addressed by a separate board risk committee composed of independent directors, or by the board itself, to review the company's internal control and risk management systems;

- to monitor and review the effectiveness of the company's internal audit function;

- to make recommendations to the board, for it to put to the shareholders for their approval in general meeting, in relation to the appointment, reappointment and removal of the external auditor and to approve the remuneration and terms of engagement of the external auditor;

- to review and monitor the external auditor's independence and objectivity and the effectiveness of the audit process, taking into consideration relevant UK professional and regulatory requirements;

- to develop and implement policy on the engagement of the external auditor to supply non-audit services, taking into account relevant ethical guidance regarding the provision of non-audit services by the external audit firm; and to report to the board, identifying any matters in respect of which it considers that action or improvement is needed and making recommendations as to the steps to be taken; and

- to report to the board on how it has discharged its responsibilities.

C.3.3

The terms of reference of the audit committee, including its role and the authority delegated to it by the board, should be made available.

C.3.4

Where requested by the board, the audit committee should provide advice on whether the annual report and accounts, taken as a whole, is fair, balanced and understandable and provides the information necessary for shareholders to assess the company's position and performance, business model and strategy.

C.3.5

The audit committee should review arrangements by which staff of the company may, in confidence, raise concerns about possible improprieties in matters of financial reporting or other matters. The audit committee's objective should be to ensure that arrangements are in place for the proportionate and independent investigation of such matters and for appropriate follow-up action.

C.3.6

The audit committee should monitor and review the effectiveness of the internal audit activities. Where there is no internal audit function, the audit committee should consider annually whether there is a need for an internal audit function and make a recommendation to the board, and the reasons for the absence of such a function should be explained in the relevant section of the annual report.

C.3.7

The audit committee should have primary responsibility for making a recommendation on the appointment, reappointment and removal of the external auditors. If the board does not accept the audit committee's recommendation, it should include in the annual report, and in any papers recommending appointment or reappointment, a statement from the audit committee explaining the recommendation and should set out reasons why the board has taken a different position.

C.3.8

A separate section of the annual report should describe the work of the committee in discharging its responsibilities. The report should include:

- the significant issues that the committee considered in relation to the financial statements, and how these issues were addressed;

- an explanation of how it has assessed the effectiveness of the external audit process and the approach taken to the appointment or reappointment of the external auditor, and information on the length of tenure of the current audit firm and when a tender was last conducted and advance notice of retendering plans; and

- if the external auditor provides non-audit services, an explanation of how the auditor's objectivity and independence are safeguarded.

The Listing Rules also require that the auditor reviews the going concern statement and longer term viability statement made by the directors in compliance with the Code (Listing Rule 9.8.10R).

42.6 Procedures

42.6.1 Statement of compliance

Bulletin 2006/5 sets out a number of general procedures relating to the auditor's review of the statement of compliance, and specific procedures relating to each Code provision that is to be reviewed. However, both the Code and corporate reporting practices have evolved since the Bulletin was issued, as have the auditor's responsibilities in relation to other information under ISA (UK) 720. Guidance in the Bulletin is therefore incomplete and may not reflect current practice.

42.6.2 Specific procedures – the verifiable code provisions

Responsibilities of directors and the auditor (Code provision C.1.1)

Directors' responsibilities

The auditor should ensure that the directors' responsibility for preparing the accounts is explained in the annual report. This is usually contained within the directors' report or in separate statement of responsibilities.

Auditor's responsibilities

The auditor has responsibilities to audit, review or read different parts of the annual report. These should be clarified by inclusion of a statement of auditor's responsibilities in the audit report or as a separate statement and by inclusion of a paragraph in the engagement letter. In practice, the standard form of audit report used by the FRC in its published examples deals adequately with the auditor's responsibilities and a separate statement is rare.

Directors' assessment of risks (Code provision C.2.1)

Not covered by the Bulletin.

Monitoring of risk management and internal control (Code provision C.2.3)

Directors' responsibilities

Under the FRC's guidance on internal control issued in October 2005, boards were recommended to 'confirm that necessary actions have been or are being taken to remedy any significant failings or weaknesses identified from [their review of the effectiveness of the system of internal control]' in their statement on internal control. In addition, FCA Rule DTR 7.2.5 R requires companies to describe the main features of the internal control and risk management systems in relation to the financial reporting process.

Auditor's responsibilities with respect to the directors' narrative statement

The annual report will contain a narrative statement about how the company has applied Code principle C.2.1. This should, as a minimum, disclose that there is an ongoing process for identifying, evaluating and managing the significant risks faced by the company that is regularly reviewed by the Board. This statement is likely to vary significantly from company to company.

The auditor has no responsibility to review this narrative statement, but is expected to read it in line with the requirements of ISA (UK) 720 (Revised June 2016).

However, in relation to the additional recommendation that the Board should confirm that actions have been or are being taken to remedy significant weaknesses, Bulletin 2006/5 recommends that the auditor:

- review the documentation prepared to support the Board's statement in relation to any significant failings or weaknesses and consider whether or not this documentation provides sound support for the Board's statement;

- discuss actions already taken or about to be taken with directors; and

- consider the statement made in relation to his knowledge of the company obtained during the audit of the financial statements. This would include whether the directors have considered any significant deficiencies in internal control reported to those charged with governance in accordance with ISA (UK) 260 (Revised June 2016) (see **Section 10**).

The auditor is not required, however, to assess the Board's decision as to what constitutes a 'significant' failing or weakness or whether the actions taken or planned will actually remedy the failure identified.

Auditor's review of compliance

The auditor is, as part of his review, required to assess whether the summary of the process given by the board is supported by documentation and reflects the actual process that took place. The auditor's procedures will include:

- discussing the process used with the directors and comparing the understanding this provides with the statement made in the annual report;

- reviewing the documentation connected with the process and considering whether it supports the statement; and

- considering whether the statement is reasonable given the knowledge gained about the company during the audit of the financial statements.

The auditor should also consider whether the directors' statement covers the year under review and the period to the date of approval of the annual report and accounts.

As his knowledge of the client is narrower than the directors', the auditor is not expected to assess whether all risks and controls have been addressed or that risks are satisfactorily addressed by internal controls. However, if the auditor discovers a significant deficiency in internal control as part of his audit work, he should report it to those charged with governance as soon as possible so that it can be considered as part of the statement on internal control.

Significant problems in the annual report

The FRC's internal control guidance recommended that the internal control aspects of any 'significant problems' disclosed in the annual report and accounts are discussed in the Board's statement. Unfortunately, the term 'significant problem' is not defined, and in practice this is likely to be highly subjective and include both financial and non-financial items.

Auditors have a responsibility to:

- discuss the steps the directors have taken to identify 'significant problems' disclosed in the annual report and accounts; and

- assess whether the narrative disclosure of the process applied to deal with any internal control aspects of these problems is an appropriate reflection of the actual process undertaken.

If the auditor is aware of a significant problem in the annual report and accounts which has not been considered in the statement, this should be brought to the attention of the directors. If the matter cannot be resolved, the auditor should consider whether there is an impact on his report.

Groups of companies

The review of effectiveness of internal control should be from a group perspective and where material joint ventures and associated companies have been excluded, this fact should be disclosed. Using his knowledge of the client, the auditor should assess whether any material joint ventures or associated companies have been excluded.

Non-executive Directors (Code provision C.3.1)

Bulletin 2006/5 recommends that the auditor should:

- check the number of members of the audit committee complies with the Code requirements (at least three members, or two for smaller companies);

- obtain an understanding of the process used by the Board to determine:

- if the audit committee are all independent non-executive directors; and

- that at least one member of the audit committee has recent and relevant financial experience; and

- review evidence, such as minutes and other documentation, to support the above.

The auditor is not responsible for determining whether the directors are independent or whether a particular audit committee member has the relevant financial experience. However, if he has doubts over either of these areas, they should be communicated to the audit committee and board.

Audit Committee (Code provision C.3.2)

The Bulletin recommends that the auditor should obtain a copy of the terms of reference of the audit committee and review whether the roles and responsibilities described therein reflect the recommendations of Code provision C3.2.

The auditor is not responsible for considering whether the audit committee has fulfilled its roles and responsibilities.

Audit Committee Terms of Reference (Code provision C.3.3)

The auditor should review whether the terms of reference for the audit committee are posted on the company's website or otherwise made readily available.

Audit Committee Advice on Annual Report (Code provision C.3.4)

The Bulletin does not provide guidance for the auditor in respect of this Code provision.

Raising Staff Concerns (Code provision C.3.5)

The auditor should review:

- supporting documentation to determine whether there is evidence that the audit committee has reviewed the arrangements and discuss the review with staff as necessary; and

- documentation supporting the company's arrangements for 'proportionate and independent' investigations.

The auditor is not responsible for considering whether the arrangements do allow 'proportionate and independent' investigations or whether follow-up action is appropriate, but rather should review the process undertaken to assure the audit committee that this is the case.

Internal Audit (Code provision C.3.6)

The Bulletin states that the auditor should perform the following procedures:

- hold discussions with the audit committee chairman and review supporting documentation to establish that the effectiveness of any internal audit function has been monitored and reviewed;

- where no internal audit function exists, review whether:

  - the audit committee has considered the need for an internal audit function;

  - there is documentation that this recommendation has been made to the Board; and

  - the reasons for not having an internal audit function are included in the relevant section of the annual report.

The auditor is not responsible for considering whether the internal audit function is effective or whether the reasons disclosed in the annual report for not having an internal audit function are reasonable.

Appointment, Reappointment and Removal of the External Auditor (Code provision C.3.7)

The auditor should:

- review the terms of reference of the audit committee, or other documentation, to ensure that the audit committee has primary responsibility for making a recommendation on the appointment, reappointment and removal of the auditor;

- review documentation of the audit committee's recommendation to the board;

- where the board has not accepted the audit committee's recommendation, review the annual report and any papers recommending appointment or reappointment of the auditor, to ensure inclusion of:

  - a statement from the audit committee explaining its recommendation; and

  - a statement from the board setting out reasons why they have taken a different position from that recommended by the audit committee.

Non-audit services (Code provision C.3.8)

The auditor should review whether a description of the work performed by the audit committee is included in a separate section of the annual report, and is not materially inconsistent with the information that the auditor has obtained in the course of his audit work.

The auditor should review whether the annual report includes a statement explaining how the objectivity and independence of the auditor is safeguarded where non-audit services are also provided. He should consider this statement and:

- notify the audit committee and board if the audit committee has not fulfilled its responsibilities to review and monitor the independence and objectivity of the external auditor and to develop and implement policy on the engagement of the external auditor to supply non-audit services; and

- consider the requirements of ISA (UK) 720 (Revised June 2016) in relation to other information issued with audited financial statements if they believe the explanation is misleading. This will involve attempting to resolve differences with the board, and considering the implications for his report if they are not able to do so.

42.6.3 *Non-compliance with the code*

Where the auditor discovers a non-compliance with a Code provision that is within the scope of his review, he should ascertain whether adequate disclosure has been made in the directors' statement of compliance. He need not perform any additional procedures in this respect, and as long as the non-compliance has been adequately disclosed, he need not refer to it in his audit report.

If the non-compliance is not adequately disclosed, the auditor should report this in the 'Matters on which we are required to report by exception' section of his report. This does not affect the opinion on the financial statements.

42.6.4 *Going concern*

The Listing Rules (LR 9.8.6R (3)) require the directors of all UK companies with a premium listing to include in the annual report a statement on:

(a) the appropriateness of adopting the going concern basis of accounting (containing the information set out in provision C.1.3 of the *UK Corporate Governance Code*); and

(b) their assessment of the prospects of the company (containing the information set out in provision C.2.2 of the *UK Corporate Governance Code*);

prepared in accordance with the *Guidance on Risk Management, Internal Control and Related Financial and Business Reporting* published by the Financial Reporting Council in September 2014.

Auditor's procedures

The Listing Rules require a UK company with a premium listing to ensure that the auditor reviews the going concern and longer term viability statements prior to publication of the annual financial report (LR 9.8.10R).

The guidance in the Bulletin is out of date in this respect as it has been overtaken by changes to the Code requirement, changes to ISA (UK) 570 (Revised June 2016) and changes to the auditor's reporting responsibilities as set out in ISA (UK) 700 (Revised June 2016) and ISA (UK) 720 (Revised June 2016).

ISAs (UK) now explicitly require the auditor to make a statement as to whether he has anything material to add or to draw attention to in relation to:

(a) the directors' confirmation in the annual report that they have carried out a robust assessment of the principal risks facing the entity, including those that would threaten its business model, future performance, solvency or liquidity;

(b) the disclosures in the annual report that describe those risks and explain how they are being managed or mitigated;

(c) the directors' statement in the financial statements about whether they considered it appropriate to adopt the going concern basis of accounting in preparing them, and their identification of any material uncertainties to the entity's ability to continue to do so over a period of at least 12 months from the date of approval of the financial statements; and

(d) the director's explanation in the annual report as to how they have assessed the prospects of the entity, over what period they have done so and why they consider that period to be appropriate, and their statement as to whether they have a reasonable expectation that the entity will be able to continue in operation and meet its liabilities as they fall due over the period of their assessment, including any related disclosures drawing attention to any necessary qualifications or assumptions.

This statement should be made by the auditor:

- having regard to the work performed by him in accordance with ISA (UK) 570 (Revised June 2016); and

- having read and considered the directors' statements and disclosures in the annual report in the light of the knowledge he has acquired during the audit, including that acquired in the evaluation of management's assessment of the entity's ability to continue as a going concern.

Matters that the auditor considers should include:

- whether the auditor is aware of information that would indicate that the annual report and accounts taken as a whole are not fair, balanced and understandable in relation to the principal risks facing the entity including those that would threaten its business model, future performance, solvency or liquidity; and

- matters relating to the robustness of the directors' assessment of the principal risks facing the entity and its outcome, including the related disclosures in the annual report and accounts, that the auditor communicated to the audit committee and that are not appropriately addressed in the section of the annual report that describes the work of the audit committee.

42.7 Other disclosures and reporting requirements

42.7.1 Disclosures under the 'Disclosure Rules and Transparency Rules'

European Directive 2006/46 requires that listed companies include a Corporate Governance Statement in the annual report. This includes all issuers with a Premium or Standard listing. In the UK, this has been implemented through:

- section 7.2 of the *Disclosure Rules and Transparency Rules* (DTR) of the FCA; and

- various amendments to the *Companies Act* 2006.

The disclosure requirements set out in the DTR may be fulfilled by including the Corporate Governance Statement:

- as a separate section of the directors' report; or

- in a separate report, which is either:

  - published together with the annual report; or

  - available on the company's website with its location cross-referenced in the director's report.

Wherever the disclosure is made, the auditor is responsible for forming an opinion on whether the information in the Statement is consistent with the financial statements and contains the information it is supposed to contain.

Where the required disclosures are made in the directors' report, the auditor is not required to make specific reference to them in his report as this is covered by his review of consistency of the directors' report and compliance with relevant legislation.

When there is no Corporate Governance Statement in the directors' report, CA 2006, s. 498A requires the auditor to ascertain whether or not such a statement has been prepared. If no statement has been prepared, this must be stated in the auditor's report.

If the disclosure is made in a separate Corporate Governance Statement, the auditor is required by CA 2006, s. 497A to review the Statement and report certain matters in his audit report on the annual financial statements. Section 497A was amended by the *Companies, Partnerships and Groups (Accounts and Reports) Regulations* 2015 (SI 2015/980).

The auditor is required to state:

- whether, in his opinion, based on the work undertaken in the course of the audit, the information given in the statement in compliance with rules 7.2.5 and 7.2.6 in the Disclosure Rules and Transparency Rules sourcebook made by the Financial Conduct Authority (information about internal control and risk management systems in relation to financial reporting processes and about capital structures) is consistent with the financial statements;

- whether the separate corporate governance statement has been prepared in accordance with applicable legal requirements. The auditor shall also state whether, in the light of the knowledge and understanding of the company and its environment obtained in the course of the audit, he has identified any material misstatements in the statement and, if applicable, give an indication of the nature of each of the misstatements; and

- whether in his opinion, based on the work undertaken in the course of the audit, rules 7.2.2, 7.2.3 and 7.2.7 in the Disclosure Rules and Transparency Rules sourcebook made by the Financial Conduct Authority (information about the company's corporate governance code and practices and about its administrative, management and supervisory bodies and committees) have been complied with, if applicable.

An example extract from an auditor's report where a listed company has produced a separate corporate governance statement is given in **Table 2**.

TABLE 2: Extract from an example auditor's report where the Corporate Governance Statement is a separate report rather than being included in the directors' report

- *Company is a listed company required to comply with Disclosure and Transparency Rules*

- *Company is a quoted company preparing a directors' remuneration report*

- *Report is for a period commencing on or after 1 January 2016 or an earlier application of the Companies, Partnerships and Groups (Accounts and Reports) Regulations 2015*

Opinion on other matters prescribed by the Companies Act 2006

In our opinion, the part of the Directors' Remuneration Report to be audited has been properly prepared in accordance with the *Companies Act* 2006.

In our opinion, based on the work undertaken in the course of the audit:

- the information given in the Strategic Report and the Directors' Report for the financial year for which the financial statements are prepared is consistent with the financial statements and those reports have been prepared in accordance with applicable legal requirements;

- the information about internal control and risk management systems in relation to financial reporting processes and about share capital structures given in compliance with rules 7.2.5 and 7.2.6 in the Disclosure Rules and Transparency Rules sourcebook made by the Financial Conduct Authority (the FCA Rules) is consistent with the financial statements and has been prepared in accordance with applicable legal requirements; and

- information about the company's corporate governance code and practices and about its administrative, management and supervisory bodies and their committees complies with rules 7.2.2, 7.2.3 and 7.2.7 of the FCA Rules.

Matters on which we are required to report by exception

In the light of the knowledge and understanding of the company and its environment obtained in the course of the audit, we have not identified any material misstatements in:

- the strategic report or the directors' report; or

- the information about internal control and risk management systems in relation to financial reporting processes and about share capital structures, given in compliance with rules 7.2.5 and 7.2.6 of the FCA Rules.

We have nothing to report in respect of the following matters in relation to which the *Companies Act* 2006 requires us to report to you if, in our opinion:

- adequate accounting records have not been kept, or returns adequate for our audit have not been received from branches not visited by us; or

- the financial statements and the part of the Directors' Remuneration Report to be audited are not in agreement with the accounting records and returns; or

- certain disclosures of directors' remuneration specified by law are not made; or

- we have not received all the information and explanations we require for our audit; or

- a Corporate Governance Statement has not been prepared by the company.

42.7.2   Standard listed companies

Companies with only a standard listing of securities are not required to make the going concern statement required by Listing Rule 9.8.6R(3) or the corporate governance statement required by Listing Rule 9.8.6R(6). The section of the auditor's report dealing with matters set out by the Listing Rules to be reported on by exception does not therefore apply to such companies. However, should such companies choose voluntarily report on how they have applied the UK Corporate Governance Code or to explain why they have not, the auditor will be required under ISA (UK) 720 to report on statements made in the annual report in compliance with the Code, as, described in **42.6.4**.

Standard listed companies are required to comply with the DTR requirements. Elements of the auditor's report referring to these requirements will be applicable in such cases.

42.8   Audit committees and the external auditor

42.8.1   Role and responsibilities of the audit committee

The roles and responsibilities of audit committees have been clarified and reinforced over recent years and there are now a number of publications available to audit committees to assist with their role.

The principal source of guidance is the FRC's *Guidance on Audit Committees* which was last revised in 2016. Key aspects of the guidance insofar as it relates to relationships with the external auditor are discussed in **42.8.2**.

In February 2012, the FRC published jointly with the Institute of Chartered Accountants of Scotland and the Institute of Chartered Accountants in Australia *Walk the Line: Discussions and insights with leading audit committee members*, a report summarising discussions with the audit committee chairs of leading companies in the UK, Australian and other markets. The report covers issues such as the role and composition of the audit committee and its relationship and communications with the board, management and the external auditor.

In November 2014, the Quoted Companies Alliance published an *Audit Committee Guide for Small and Mid-Size Quoted Companies* to assist audit committee members to be effective in their roles, meeting the expectations of investors and complying with best regulatory best practice for small and mid-size quoted companies. It covers the operational aspects of the committee; the roles and responsibilities of those on the committee and those that work with the committee; the internal focus of the committee on risk management and internal control; the external focus of the committee on the corporate reporting cycle; and the audit committee report in the annual reports and accounts.

Earlier guidance which is now a bit dated but may nevertheless contain some useful information includes:

- *The Power of Three: Understanding the roles and relationships of internal and external auditors and audit committees* published in 2003;

- the ICAEW series of seven booklets published in 2003 and 2004 covering:

   - *Working with your auditor;*

   - *Company reporting and audit requirements;*

   - *Reviewing auditor independence;*

   - *Evaluating your auditor;*

   - *Monitoring the integrity of financial statements;*

   - *The internal audit function; and*

   - *Whistleblowing arrangements.*

42.8.2 FRC guidance on audit committees

In respect of the external audit process, the guidance states that the audit committee is the body responsible for overseeing the company's relations with the external auditor. It recommends the following:

Appointment and tendering

- The audit committee should have primary responsibility for making a recommendation on the appointment, reappointment and removal of the external auditor. This includes negotiating the fee and scope of the audit and influencing the selection of the engagement partner.

- Where it recommends considering the selection of a possible new auditor, the committee should be responsible for and oversee the selection process.

- The audit committee should annually assess, and report to the board on, the qualification, expertise and resources, and independence of the external auditors and the effectiveness of the audit process and make a recommendation regarding reappointment of the auditor. This assessment will involve the audit committee obtaining a report on the auditor's own internal quality control procedure and their annual transparency report.

- If the external auditor resigns, the audit committee should investigate the issues giving rise to such resignation and consider whether any action is required.

- The audit committee should evaluate risks to audit quality and the effectiveness of the financial reporting process.

Terms and remuneration

- The audit committee should approve the terms of engagement and the remuneration to be paid to the external auditor in respect of audit services provided.

- The committee should review and agree the engagement letter issued by the external auditor at the start of each audit and should satisfy itself as to the adequacy of the scope of the external audit proposed by the auditor.

- The committee should satisfy itself that the fee payable in respect of the audit is appropriate and that an effective, high quality, audit can be conducted for such a fee.

Annual audit cycle

- At the start of each annual audit cycle, the audit committee should ensure that appropriate plans are in place for the audit. The committee should consider whether the auditor's overall work plan, including planned levels of materiality, and proposed resources available is consistent with the proposed scope of the audit, having regard also to the seniority, expertise and experience of the audit team.

- The audit committee should review, with the external auditors, the findings of their work and should:

  - discuss with the auditor any major issues, both resolved and unresolved, that arose during the audit;

  - ask the auditor to explain how they addressed the risks to audit quality identified earlier;

  - weigh the evidence they have received in relation to each of the areas of significant judgment and review key accounting and audit judgments;

  - ask the auditor for their perception of their interactions with senior management and other members of the finance team; and

  - review errors identified during the audit obtaining explanations as to why certain errors might remain unadjusted.

- The audit committee should review and monitor management's responsiveness to the auditor's findings and recommendations. It should also review audit representation letters before signature and give particular consideration to matters where representation has been requested that relate to non-standard issues. It should consider whether the information provided is complete and appropriate based on its own knowledge.

- The audit committee should assess the effectiveness of the audit process. This includes consideration of mind-set, culture, skills, knowledge and judgment including the robustness of the auditor in dealing with key judgments and their assessment of internal control;

- The audit committee should:

  - ask the auditor to explain the risks to audit quality that they identified and how they have been addressed;

  - discuss with the auditor the key audit firm and network level controls the auditor relied on to address the identified risks to audit quality and enquire about the findings from internal and external inspections of their audit and their audit firm;

  - review whether the auditor has met the agreed audit plan and understand the reasons for any changes to the audit plan, including changes in perceived audit risks and the work undertaken by the external auditors to address those risks;

  - obtain feedback about the conduct of the audit from key people involved; and

  - review and monitor the content of the external auditor's management letter and other communications with the audit committee, in order to assess whether it is based on a good understanding of the company's business and establish whether recommendations have been acted upon and, if not, the reasons why they have not been acted upon.

Independence, including the provision of non-audit services

The audit committee should:

- assess the independence and objectivity of the external auditor annually, including consideration of all relationships between the company and the audit firm, including throughout the group and with the audit firm's network firms, and any safeguards established by the external auditor;

- develop and recommend to the board the company's policy in relation to the provision of non-audit services by the auditor, and keep the policy under review;

- be responsible for approving non-audit services, ensuring that the provision of such services does not impair the external auditor's independence or objectivity. They should make an assessment considering threats to independence and objectivity and any safeguards in place; the nature of the non-audit services; whether the skills and experience of the audit firm make it the most suitable supplier of the non-audit service; the fees incurred for non-audit services, both for individual services and in aggregate, relative to the audit fee; and the criteria which govern the compensation of the individuals performing the audit;

- set and apply a formal policy specifying the types of non-audit service (if any) for which the use of the external auditor is pre-approved (but this should only apply to matters that are clearly trivial);

- set a policy for how it will assess whether non-audit services have a direct or material effect on the audited financial statements, how it will assess and explain the estimation of the effect on the financial statements and how it will consider the external auditors' independence;

- develop and monitor the application of the company's policy for the employment of former employees of the external auditor, taking into account the Revised Ethical Standard 2016 for auditors and paying particular attention to the policy regarding former employees of the audit firm who were part of the audit team and moved directly to the company; and

- monitor the external audit firm's compliance with the Revised Ethical Standard 2016, the level of fees that the company pays in proportion to the overall fee income of the firm, or relevant part of it, and other related regulatory requirements;

- seek information from the audit firm annually about policies and processes for maintaining independence and monitoring compliance with relevant requirements, including those regarding the rotation of audit partners and staff;

- where the audit committee decides that it is necessary to allow the audit engagement partner to stay in the position for up to two years beyond the normal rotation period of five years, in order to safeguard the quality of the audit without compromising the independence and objectivity of the external auditor, they should disclose this fact and the reasons for it to the shareholders as early as practicable.

42.8.3 Communication between the auditor and the audit committee

ISA (UK) 260 (Revised June 2016) includes a number of matters which are included in an additional report to the audit committee; this is covered in **Section 10**. It requires that, in the case of companies reporting compliance with the Code, the auditor shall communicate to the audit committee the information that the auditor believes will be relevant to the board (in the context of fulfilling its responsibilities under Code provisions C.1.1, C.1.3, C.2.1, C.2.2 and C.2.3) and the audit committee (in the context of fulfilling its responsibilities under Code provision C.3.4); and to the audit committee (in the context of fulfilling its responsibilities under Code provision C.3.2).

This information includes the auditor's views:

(a) on business risks relevant to financial reporting, the application of materiality and the consequent implications for the overall audit strategy, the audit plan and the evaluation of misstatements;

(b) on significant accounting policies (both individually and in aggregate);

(c) on management's valuations of the entity's material assets and liabilities and the related disclosures;

(d) without expressing an opinion on the effectiveness of the entity's system of internal control as a whole, and based solely on the audit procedures performed in the audit of the financial statements, about:

(i)   the effectiveness of the entity's system of internal control relevant to risks that may affect financial reporting; and

(ii) other risks arising from the entity's business model and the effectiveness of related internal controls;

(e) about the robustness of the directors' assessment of the principal risks facing the entity, including those that would threaten its business model, future performance, solvency or liquidity and its outcome, including the related disclosures in the annual report confirming that they have carried out such an assessment and describing those risks and explaining how they are being managed or mitigated (in accordance with Code provision C.2.1);

(f) about the directors' explanation in the annual report as to how they have assessed the prospects of the entity, over what period they have done so and why they consider that period to be appropriate (in accordance with Code provision C.2.2), and their statements:

(i)   in the financial statements, as to whether they considered it appropriate to adopt the going concern basis of accounting in preparing them, including any related disclosures identifying any material uncertainties to the entity's ability to continue to do so over a period of at least 12 months from the date of approval of the financial statements (in accordance with Code provision C.1.3); and

(ii) in the annual report as to whether they have a reasonable expectation that the entity will be able to continue in operation and meet its liabilities as they fall due over the period of their assessment, including any related disclosures drawing attention to any necessary qualifications or assumptions (in accordance with Code provision C.2.2); and

(g) on any other matters identified in the course of the audit that the auditor believes will be relevant to the board or the audit committee in the context of fulfilling their responsibilities referred to above.

42.9   Monitoring

Since 2011, the FRC has published reports on the impact and implementation of the UK Corporate Governance Code and its Stewardship Code for institutional investors. The latest report is *Developments in Corporate Governance and Stewardship 2016* which is available from the FRC's website.

42.10   Other Codes

42.10.1   *Investment companies*

Many investment companies refer to the AIC Code of Corporate Governance. Published by the Association of Investment Companies (AIC), the AIC Code of Corporate Governance sets out a framework of best practice in respect of the governance of investment companies. It has been endorsed by the Financial Reporting Council as an alternative means for AIC members to meet their obligations in relation to the UK Corporate Governance Code.

42.10.2   *Smaller quoted companies*

In April 2018, the Quoted Companies Alliance (QCA) issued an updated version of its Corporate Governance Code. Its Corporate Governance Code (2018) is intended to be a practical, outcome-oriented approach to corporate governance that is tailored for small and mid-size companies.

This new and updated version of the Code includes ten corporate governance principles that companies should follow, and step-by-step guidance on how to effectively apply these principles.

The revision of the QCA Code may be especially relevant in that the AIM Rules (March 2018) of the London Stock Exchange now require that from September 2018, an AIM company must publish details of a recognised corporate governance code that the board of directors of the AIM company has decided to apply; how the AIM company complies with that code; and where it departs from its chosen corporate governance code, an explanation of the reasons for doing so. This information should be reviewed annually and the website should include the date on which this information was last reviewed.

42.11 Future plans

In December 2017, the FRC published proposals for a revised UK Corporate Governance Code which focuses on the importance of long-term success and sustainability, addresses issues of public trust in business and aims to ensure the attractiveness of the UK capital market to global investors.

This was the result of a wide-ranging review, building on the FRC's Culture report published in 2016, responding to the recommendations made in the Government's response to the Green Paper *Consultation on Corporate Governance Reform* (published in August 2017) and taking into account issues raised by the House of Commons' Business, Energy and Industrial Strategy Committee's Report on Corporate Governance, published in April 2017.

The revised Code sets out good practice so that the boards of companies can:

- establish a company's purpose, strategy and values and satisfy themselves that these and their culture are aligned;

- undertake effective engagement with wider stakeholders, to improve trust and achieve mutual benefit, and to have regard to wider society;

- gather views of the workforce;

- ensure appointments to boards and succession plans are based on merit and objective criteria to avoid group think, and promote diversity of gender, social and ethnic backgrounds, cognitive and personal strengths;

- be more specific about actions when they encounter significant shareholder opposition on any resolution, including those on executive pay policies and awards; and

- give remuneration committees broader responsibility and discretion for overseeing how remuneration and workforce policies align with strategic objectives.

Following consultation, the FRC will consider the responses and aims to publish a final version of the Code by summer 2018, to apply to accounting periods beginning on or after 1 January 2019.

43 Charities

43.1 Legal background

There are a number of different regulators with responsibility for charities throughout the UK. The Charity Commission regulates charities in England and Wales, the Office of the Scottish Charity Regulator ('the OSCR') regulates charities registered in Scotland and also, to some extent, English or Welsh charities operating in Scotland. Northern Ireland also has its own Charity Commission, the CCNI. This section mainly addresses the regime governing English and Welsh charities.

The main laws that relate to a charity's financial statements and audit are:

All charitable companies	*Companies Act* 2006
Registered charities in England and Wales	*Charities Act* 2011
All charities registered in Scotland with the Office of the Scottish Charity Regulator (OSCR)	*Charities and Trustee Investment (Scotland) Act* 2005
Non-company charities in Northern Ireland	*Charities Act (Northern Ireland)* 2008 and the *Charities Act (Northern Ireland)* 1964 (to the extent this has not been superseded by the *Charities Act (Northern Ireland)* 2008)

By virtue of an order under the *Charities Act* 2011, s. 144 and 147, the audit regimes of companies and non-company charities are identical if the company elects for exemption from audit under the Companies Act. (The option to elect for audit exemption is only available to charitable companies who meet two of the following three criteria: income is under £10.2m, gross assets are under £5.1m and the average number of employees is 50 or fewer.) Larger company audits continue to be performed under the Companies Act regime. Charitable companies (if they elect for exemption from the Companies Act audit requirement) are subject to the same independent examination and audit regime, depending upon their gross income and gross assets, as non-company charities.

By virtue of the *Charities Act* 2011, charitable parent companies of small groups are required to prepare accounts and be audited under both the *Companies Act* 2006 and the *Charities Act* 2011. As a result, the audit requirement and trustees' responsibilities need to reflect the legal requirements of both pieces of legislation.

Charities that are subject to alternative legislative requirements to the Charities Act (such as the Companies Act for larger charities that are limited companies), or alternative SORPs to the Charities' SORP (for example, Registered Providers of Social Housing) should follow the accounting and auditing requirements in the alternative legislation or SORP. For charities which are limited companies, the Department for Business, Innovation and Skills considers the FRS 102 Charities SORP ('the FRS 102 SORP') to be indicative of the accounting practices necessary for charities to produce financial statements which show a true and fair view. This section deals mainly with charities applying the FRS 102 SORP or subject to the *Charities Act* 2011 accounting and auditing requirement. While academies prepare their accounts in accordance with the FRS 102 SORP, there are additional requirements for auditors as set by the Department for Education. Auditors of academies should refer to the DfE website for details of these requirements.

In charitable companies, the directors are also the charity trustees and the term 'trustees' has been used throughout to refer to both.

Furthermore, charities established in Scotland register separately as Scottish charities and charities registered in Northern Ireland are required to register separately as Northern Irish charities.

Dual registered charities preparing accruals accounts (i.e. registered with the Charity Commission and with the OSCR and/or with the Charity Commission for Northern Ireland) need to comply with the FRS 102 SORP, but the audit requirement, annual report, and trustees' responsibilities need to reflect the legal requirements of all countries in which they are registered.

The FRSSE SORP for small charities was withdrawn for accounting periods beginning on or after 1 January 2016.

The legislation, SORP and further accounting guidance can be found online from Croner-i Tax and Accounting and in the Croner-i Ltd publication *Preparing Charity Accounts*. In addition, Croner-i Tax and Accounting has produced a separate industry guide *Charities: Industry Tax, Accounting and Auditing Guide* which covers the material in this section in greater detail.

43.1.1 General

The *Charities (Accounts and Reports) Regulations* 2008 continue to set out the requirements for preparation of accounts in respect of English and Welsh charities. Guidance has been issued by the Charity Commission on their application in conjunction with the FRS 102 SORP. Whilst all charities must prepare accounts, the impact of these regulations depends on the threshold requirements as set out in the 2011 Act and on whether the charity is registered or not. These requirements can be summarised as follows:

- registered charities with gross income and total expenditure of £25,000 or less, and charities which are not registered, are not required to submit annual reports or accounts to the Charity Commission, unless requested to do so. All registered charities must prepare an annual report, even if they are not requested to submit it to the Charity Commission;

- non-company charities with gross income of £250,000 or less may prepare a receipts and payments account and a statement of assets and liabilities; and

- all charitable companies and non-company charities that exceed this £250,000 threshold must prepare accounts on an accruals basis to give a true and fair view. Certain additional disclosure requirements are placed on charities whose gross income exceeds the audit exemption threshold.

The audit or examination requirements for charitable companies and non-company charities are as follows:

- gross income does not exceed £25,000 – no statutory requirement for either an audit or an independent examination;

- gross income does not exceed £250,000 – an election may be made for the accounts to be independently examined;

- gross income does not exceed £1m in the year and gross assets do not exceed £3.26m – an election may be made for the accounts to be independently examined but the examiner must be a member of a specified body (note – for charities registered with OSCR, the income limit is £500,000); and

- gross income exceeds £1m in the year (£500,000 for charities registered with OSCR), or gross income exceeds £250,000 and gross assets exceed £3.26m – a statutory audit is required.

An audit can only be undertaken by a registered auditor, unless the Charity Commission gives a dispensation.

As noted in **43.1**, where the charity is a company and has not elected for exemption from the Companies Act audit requirement then the audit is conducted under the Companies Act.

43.1.2   Independent examination

An independent examination for a charity below the thresholds discussed in **43.1.1**, does not have to be carried out by a professionally qualified individual but should be by a person suitable to the circumstances of the charity. The examiner must be 'an independent person who is reasonably believed by the trustees to have the requisite ability and practical experience to carry out a competent examination of the accounts'.

The independent examiner's report to the charity's trustees is intended to provide a moderate level of assurance (negative assurance) and should:

- specify that it is a report in respect of an examination carried out under the Charities Act and in accordance with any directions given by the Commissioners which are applicable;

- state whether or not any matter has come to the examiner's attention which gives him reasonable cause to believe that in any material respect:

  - accounting records have not been kept in accordance with the Act;

  - the accounts do not accord with the records; or

  - the accounts do not comply with the regulations;

- state whether or not any matter has come to his attention which should be drawn to the attention of the trustees;

- disclose any material expenditure or action which appears not to be in accordance with the trusts of the charity; and

- disclose any information or explanation provided or any information in the accounts which is materially inconsistent with the trustees' report.

The duties of an examiner are set out in CC32 issued by the Charity Commission, which is available from the Commission's website. The most recent version was issued in September 2017.

43.1.3   Whistle-blowing duties for auditors and examiners

The *Charities Act* 2011 imposes the same duties on auditors and independent examiners of all charities, whether or not they are limited companies.[1] Under this whistle-blowing requirement, they have to report in writing, under s. 156 (Duty of auditors, etc. to report matters to the Commission) of the 2011 Act, any matters which may be of material

---

[1] 'Exempt' charities are excluded from the CCEW's supervision and monitoring, and consequently, the auditor is not required to report matters of material significance to CCEW. Instead, the auditor of an exempt charity reports such matters to the charity's principal regulator. There is, however, no disapplication of the reporting duty for exempt company charities.

significance to the Charity Commission's function as a regulator, which came to light as a result of their work.

The Charity Commission issued revised guidance on whistleblowing during 2017. Major changes relate to extending the list of matters that are considered reportable to include:

- reporting a modified auditor's or independent examiner's report or opinion;

- where the auditor or independent examiner has identified evidence that conflicts of interest have not been managed by the trustees, or that related party transactions have not been disclosed in the financial statements as required by the SORP.

The revised guidance has removed the duty for auditors to report to the Charity Commission those matters reported to the charity's trustees on ceasing to hold office or resigning from office.

Further details are given in **43.9**.

43.2 Audit guidance

The major source of guidance for auditors is Practice Note 11 (Revised) *The Audit of Charities in the United Kingdom*, issued by the FRC. Practice Note 11 was revised in November 2017 and applied for audits of periods commencing on or after 17 June 2016.

The Practice Note provides a useful summary of the legislative and regulatory framework including an appendix setting out in detail the accounting and audit requirements applicable to charities in the UK. It also provides guidance on the application of ISAs (UK) in the specific context of a charity and contains a separate section on reporting matters of material significance to charity regulators.

Further guidance is issued regularly by the Charity Commission and also HMRC. Reference should be made to these sources as appropriate.

43.3 Agreeing the terms of audit engagements

Under UK law, the trustees are responsible for preparing the financial statements, and engagement terms will normally be agreed with the trustees, although in some cases engagement letters may need to be sent to a different appointing authority.

Where the charity's constitution, organisation or funding arrangements require reports from the auditor in addition to the auditor's report on the statutory financial statements, it is the responsibility of the trustees to determine what is required and to instruct the auditor accordingly. It is not practicable for the auditor to check the documentation for all funds received by a charity to determine the need for additional reporting. Non-audit work undertaken on behalf of the charity or its trustees should be the subject of a separate engagement letter(s).

43.4 Quality control for an audit of financial statements

The auditor must comply with the FRC's Ethical Standard (Revised 2016). Particular issues relating to charities include:

- self interest – the auditor needs to be aware of other interests in the charity which may affect the conduct or outcome of the audit. The auditor therefore ensures that none of the audit team is in any way dependent upon the charity or provide significant support to the charity;

- self review – auditors will often be asked to provide additional help and advice, often on a pro-bono basis. The provision of this service is regarded in the same way as other non-audit services in assessing whether there is a threat to objectivity;

- other relationships, e.g. if the audit firm has made significant donations or provided other support for the charity, this could be considered to be an other relationship impacting the independence as described in the Ethical Standard; and

- persons in the audit firm acting as trustees.

As well as ensuring that the engagement team has an appropriate level of knowledge of the charity sector, the engagement partner also satisfies himself that the members of the engagement team have sufficient knowledge, commensurate with their roles in the engagement, of:

- the type of charity being audited;

- key risks affecting the charity;

- the Charities SORP;

- the governing document of the charity;

- the legal responsibilities and duties of charity trustees;

- the regulatory framework within which charities operate; and

- the guidance issued by charity regulators regarding matters that should be reported to them by auditors.

The auditor also considers if an engagement quality control review is required based on the nature of the engagement, including the extent to which it involves a matter of public interest. What is a matter of public interest is difficult to define: factors that may apply to a charity include:

- the size of the charity;

- its national or local profile; and

- its source of funds, including the extent to which the charity receives public funds.

43.5   The auditor's responsibilities relating to fraud

In applying ISA (UK) 240 (Revised June 2016) *The Auditor's Responsibilities Relating to Fraud in an Audit of Financial Statements* to charities, the auditor must be aware that the trustees are responsible for the prevention or detection of fraud in relation to the charity. However, the planning process of the audit must include an assessment of the possibility of fraud being committed by any of the people involved in the operation of the charity as well as by third parties. Certain features of charities may increase the risk of fraud, namely:

- the limited involvement of trustees in key decision making or monitoring transactions, and limited engagement with charity staff;

- widespread branches or operations, such as those established in response to emergency appeals in countries where there is no effective system of law and order;

- reliance on management and staff with limited management or supervision and a lack of segregation and rotation of duties;

- transactions often undertaken in cash;

- unpredictable patterns of giving by members of the public, both in terms of timing and point of donation;

- informal banking or cash transfer methods used in areas remote from conventional banking systems;

- inconsistent regulation across international borders; and

- international transfer of funds.

Auditors are required by ISA (UK) 240 (Revised June 2016) to consider whether one or more fraud risk factors are present and to investigate whether unusual or unexpected relationships may indicate risks of material misstatement due to fraud.

The auditor should also consider the extent of the trustees' day-to-day involvement in the charity, trustees' and senior management's access to resource and their ability, collectively or individually to override controls.

The charity's records may also be incomplete as a result of fraud – one common type of fraud being diversion of donations or non-routine income.

Whilst charities are not-for-profit entities, there may still be risk of fraudulent financial reporting relating to income recognition although this may be rebutted, for example, in some public sector bodies receiving grant-in-aid income.

43.6 Consideration of laws and regulations

Because there are laws and regulations specifically made to cover charities and their activities, including laws which affect charities which undertake fundraising, auditors must have an understanding of applicable law and regulation. Auditors must be aware of the risk of money laundering given the relatively large sums of cash which many charities receive.

43.6.1 Laws and regulations relating directly to the preparation of financial statements

Auditors here must be aware of, in particular, the *Charities (Accounts and Reports Regulations)* 2008, the *Charities Accounts (Scotland) Regulations* 2006, the *Companies Act* 2006 and the Charities SORP. In addition, charities may also be subject to other laws and regulations such as those which relate to housing associations.

Auditors should also check whether the charity's governing document contains any special disclosure or reporting requirements. The Practice Note states that in order to give a true and fair view, due regard needs to be given to disclosure of any significant non-compliance with the governing documents. These, for example, may take the form of Articles of Association, a trust deed, a constitution or a will. Auditors should obtain an understanding of the governing documents and ensure that the audit covers the charity's compliance with the governing documents.

43.6.2 Laws and regulations where non-compliance may have a material effect on the financial statements

Determination of laws and regulations where instances of non-compliance may have a material effect on the financial statements requires consideration of its governing documents, the activities it undertakes and laws specifically applicable to those entities as well as the requirements of charity law. To assist in identifying instances of non-compliance, the auditor should inspect recent correspondence between the charity and relevant charity regulators.

Failure to comply with tax laws and regulations may have a material direct effect on the determination of amounts disclosed in the financial statements. It may also have an indirect material effect that would require disclosure, for example, the failure to maintain tax exempt status would be a matter that would probably require disclosure and may ultimately impact on the charity's ability to continue its operations.

Other laws and regulations that may be relevant include:

- Charities Act requirements relating to fundraising, property and borrowing transaction;
- laws on raising funds through lotteries;
- laws relating to house to house or street collections;
- Trustee Act;
- Children Act requirements;
- Registered Homes Act;
- Environmental Protection Act; and
- food safety and hygiene regulations.

Auditors should be aware that identified or suspected instances of non-compliance with laws or regulations may be indicative of money laundering and should be reported to the auditor's MLRO in accordance with anti-money laundering and terrorist financing procedures (see **Section 18**). Auditors should also be careful to avoid 'tipping off' in such situations.

43.7   The auditor's right and duty to report to regulators

The auditor of a charity has, in certain circumstances, a statutory right to report matters to the charity's regulator. The auditor also has a statutory duty to report to certain matters to the regulator.

Charities legislation in England and Wales, Scotland and Northern Ireland impose a duty on the auditor to report certain matters to the relevant regulator. The legislation also establishes a right to report to the regulator a matter which does not appear to fall within the duty to report but which the auditor has reason to believe is likely to be relevant to the regulator in the exercise of its functions. Both the right and duty to report apply to company and non-company charities.

Matters which give rise to a duty to make an immediate report to the regulator are those which:

(a) relate to the activities of the charity or any connected institution or body; and

(b) the auditor has reasonable cause to believe is, or is likely to be, of material significance for the exercise, in relation to the charity, of the relevant regulator's functions.

Where a charity is registered in multiple jurisdictions and there is any doubt as to which regulator the auditor should report, he should report to all relevant regulators.

In determining what is a 'matter of material significance', auditors should refer to Practice Note 11 and to the guidance *Matters of material significance reportable to UK charity regulators: A guide for auditors and independent examiners,* issued jointly by charity regulators. This guidance was updated in April 2017, to take effect from 1 May 2017 and provides detailed guidance on the legislative requirement, matters to be reported and the form of report required.

The guidance includes a list of nine topics which are always considered to be of material significance and hence reportable. In summary, these are:

(1) Dishonesty and Fraud – matters suggesting dishonesty or fraud involving a significant loss of, or a material risk to, charitable funds or assets.

(2) Internal Controls and Governance – failure(s) of internal controls or charity governance that resulted in, or could give rise to, a material loss or misappropriation of charitable funds, or which leads to significant charitable funds being put at major risk.

(3) Money Laundering and Criminal Activity – knowledge or suspicion that the charity or charitable funds including the charity's bank account(s) have been used for money laundering or such funds are the proceeds of serious organised crime or that the charity is a conduit for criminal activity.

(4) Support of Terrorism – matters leading to the knowledge or suspicion that the charity, its trustees, employees or assets, have been involved in or used to support terrorism or proscribed organisations in the UK or outside of the UK.

(5) Risk to charity's beneficiaries – evidence suggesting that in the way the charity carries out its work relating to the care and welfare of beneficiaries, the charity's beneficiaries have been or were put at significant risk of abuse or mistreatment.

(6) Breaches of law or the charity's trusts – single or recurring breach(es) of either a legislative requirement or of the charity's trusts leading to material charitable funds being misapplied.

(7) Breach of an order or direction made by a charity regulator – evidence suggesting a deliberate or significant breach of an order or direction made by a charity regulator under statutory powers.

(8) Modified audit opinion or qualified independent examiner's report – on making a modified audit opinion, emphasis of matter, material uncertainty related to going concern, or issuing of a qualified independent examiner's report, the auditor or examiner must notify the regulator with supporting reasons including notification of the action taken, if any, by the trustees subsequent to the report.

(9) Conflicts of interest and related party transactions – evidence that significant conflicts of interest have not been managed appropriately by the trustees and/or related party transactions have not been fully disclosed.

The auditor does not need to perform additional work as a result of the statutory duty although he will need to make members of the audit team aware of reportable matters which are likely to be encountered.

ISA (UK) 250 Section B (Revised June 2016) – *The Auditor's Statutory Right and Duty to Report to Regulators of Public Interest Entities and Regulators of Other Entities in the Financial Sector* does not apply to charities unless they are also regulated entities as defined in that standard.

43.8 Communication with those charged with governance

For the purposes of ISA (UK) 260 (Revised June 2016) *Communication with those Charged with Governance,* those charged with governance will normally be the trustees of the charity. In some situations, the auditor may agree with the charity that a subcommittee of the board, such as an audit committee, may fulfil this role.

43.9 Communicating deficiencies in internal control

Charity regulators issue general guidance for trustees in implementing appropriate financial controls. Such guidance may be of assistance to the auditor in determining whether significant weaknesses exist in internal control. Significant weaknesses should be communicated to those charged with governance and may call into question the integrity of those charged with governance or management of the charity. Such weaknesses may represent a matter of material significance to the regulator.

43.10 Planning an audit of financial statements

Particular issues the auditor considers at the planning stage include:

- the applicable reporting framework including:

  - the legislative requirements, e.g. the *Companies Act* 2006 or, in England and Wales the *Charities Act* 2011 or, in Scotland the *Charities and Trustee Investment (Scotland) Act* 2005;

  - the relevant Charities SORP (or sector specific SORP where one applies);

  - the governing document for the charity, which may also include specific reporting requirements. Auditors should also be aware of the changes introduced to the *Charities Act* 2011 by the *Charities and Social Investment Act* 2016;

- governance arrangements, including planning with the trustees the form and timing of communications;

- operating structures, branches and overseas operations including:

  - the extent to which the charity's activities (either of a fundraising or a charitable nature) are undertaken through branches or overseas activities and the impact this has on the auditor's required knowledge of the business (for laws and regulations applicable to the charity's overseas operations), the auditor's risk assessment and sources of audit evidence; and

  - the structure and management of any related or connected entities, in particular the degree to which the entities are managed and controlled by the trustees and management of the charity;

- the charity's activities in the context of its stated objects and powers, including any limitations within the charity's governing document, or terms and restrictions placed on material gifts or donations received;

- the likely impact on the financial statements of the charity of the activities of any related or connected entities (for example, a separate limited company set up to undertake commercial activities for the charity);

- the statutory duty to report matters to the charity regulators including whether members of the audit team have sufficient understanding (in the context of their role) to enable them to identify situations which may give reasonable cause to believe that a matter should be reported to the regulator; and

- whether other auditors' reports are required – for example, special reports to funders of the charity, grant donors or EU agencies.

43.11   Identifying and assessing risks of material misstatement

The auditor will need knowledge of the special features of charity audits, and in carrying out a risk assessment, he will need to be aware of the following:

- the existence of special regulations governing the conduct of charities;

- sources of income which may include grants from public authorities or funds held on trust. Breaches of the conditions relating to the use of such income can have serious implications to the charity;

- tax relief dependent upon a charity complying with the governing document submitted to HMRC;

- activities of the charity which bring it within the scope of other regulations, as well as those relating to charities;

- the level of involvement in the administration of the charity which can be expected of trustees; and

- the way in which the charity is managed on a day-to-day basis.

43.11.1   Control environment

ISA (UK) 315 (Revised June 2016) requires the auditor to obtain an understanding of the accounting and internal control systems sufficient to plan the audit and develop an effective audit approach. There is a wide variation between different charities in terms of size, activity and organisation so that there can be no standard approach to internal control and risk. Even large national charities with sophisticated control systems may have local branches that are run by voluntary staff on an informal basis.

Maintenance of an effective system of internal control is as important for charities as it is for other entities. Trustees have responsibility for ensuring that an adequate system of internal control is maintained to ensure proper administration of the charity and that assets are properly safeguarded.

The auditor of certain charities may be subject to specific reporting requirements in respect of internal controls (e.g. friendly societies, registered social landlords and charitable non-departmental public bodies). Where this is the case, the auditor should plan his work bearing in mind the duty to report if a satisfactory system of internal control is not maintained.

The auditor should also assess the charity's governance structure and overall control environment. This includes assessment of the skills of trustees and management, the extent of their involvement in the activities of the charity and the policies and procedures established by them.

Charities

Larger charities are required by the SORP to include in the annual report a summary of the risk and uncertainties faced by the charity, together with any plans for managing those risks. The auditor should consider the trustees' risk management process in order to gain an understanding of the principal risks identified by the trustees and consider the implications for the audit.

43.11.2   Accounting policies

The auditor must review accounting policies and ensure these are in line with the applicable accounting framework including the Charities SORP. Policies that may require particularly careful consideration include those for the recognition of:

- legacies receivable;
- grants receivable as voluntary income;
- grants receivable or payable on performance related conditions;
- liabilities resulting from constructive obligations;
- gifts in kind and donated services; and
- heritage assets.

For group audits, the auditor should consider the consistency of policies applied in the preparation of financial information of components of the group.

43.11.3   Risk of misstatement

Appendix 1 to the Practice Note includes a list of conditions and events that may indicate risks of material misstatement in the financial statements. These include:

General

- evidence of failure to act in accordance with those objects and powers in the charity's governing documents;
- extent and nature of non-primary purpose trading activities;
- difficulties of the charity in establishing ownership and timing of voluntary income where funds are raised by non-controlled bodies;
- overseas operations.

Classes of transactions, account balances and disclosures

- allocation of costs between different expenditure categories in the Statement of Financial Activities (SoFA);

- restricted funds which require special considerations as to use and accounting, including clawback of restricted grants or contracts;
- grants payable or receivable;
- contracts with performance related conditions;
- legacies;
- heritage assets;
- events or transactions that involve significant measurement and recognition uncertainty, including accounting estimates, and related disclosures. In particular:
  - pension schemes;
  - investments;
  - properties which are partly used for investment purposes;
  - fair value of assets and liabilities acquired where acquisition accounting is applied;
  - recognition of second hand goods received and other donations in kind or donated services;
  - other arrangements which are offered or received on extended terms of more than 12 months discounted to their present value;
  - taxation matters including income from gift aid and the gift aid small donations scheme, the identification of tainted donations and the recognition of irrecoverable VAT;
  - commitments and liabilities, including constructive obligations;
  - departures from the Charities SORP.

43.12 Materiality in planning and performing an audit

The general principles underlying the consideration of materiality apply to audits of charities in a similar way to other entities. Judgments about materiality are affected by the information needs of users and in general this will be the trustees although auditors should consider whether there are other users who are relevant in the particular circumstances of the charity.

As charities are generally not profit driven, benchmarks used for the determination of materiality are usually based on gross income or expenditure.

Having determined an overall financial statement materiality level, the auditor may apply lower materiality levels to specific classes of transactions, balance or disclosures where appropriate or where there is a particular interest in such items. Transactions with trustees may be regarded as being material by their nature, regardless of size.

Many charities receive funds subject to specific trusts, which must be accounted for separately in accordance with the relevant Charities SORP. There is no presumption that the auditor will set a different monetary materiality level for such funds.

43.13   The auditor's responses to assessed risks

ISA (UK) 330 (Revised June 2016) *The Auditor's Responses to Assessed Risks* requires the auditor to design and implement responses to the identified risks of material misstatement in the financial statements. Practice Note 11 provides guidance in relation to a number of risks commonly encountered in the charity sector including:

- completeness of income;

- overseas operations;

- restricted funds;

- heritage assets; and

- grants payable.

43.13.1   *Completeness of income*

Typically, income from charities comes from a number of different sources, such as grants and public donations, and its amount and timing is often difficult to predict. Trustees cannot be expected to have responsibility for funds until they are, or should be, within the control of the charity, but as soon as this happens, trustees should implement procedures to ensure appropriate recording and safeguarding of the funds.

The Practice Note suggests that the auditor should consider:

- tax effective giving – for most tax effective schemes there are required procedures and detailed rules to prevent abuse;

- completeness of income – often difficult to substantiate, especially where cash is involved. The auditor may wish to consider the effectiveness of controls in this area;

- recognition of income from third party fundraisers – the auditor should consider the agreement between the charity and the fundraiser and other documents supporting the transfer of funds to the charity;

- income from branches, associates or subsidiaries – the auditor should review arrangements to determine the point at which it is appropriate to recognise funds;

- legacy income – at what point is it appropriate to recognise this, and how much. Subsequent events may provide evidence of the existence, completeness and amount. Review of legal documentation may assist in understanding terms attached to legacies and there are agencies who can provide charities with notification when probate is granted;

- grants or contractual income – review of legal documentation and correspondence may assist in determining the appropriate accounting treatment. The auditor may wish to obtain direct confirmation form the provider;

- non-cash donations – the auditor needs to consider how to obtain assurance over completeness.

43.13.2   Overseas operations

Overseas operations may be conducted through a variety of organisational structures. The financial statements nevertheless need to reflect the results of all the charity's operations.

The Practice Note suggests the following procedures:

- consideration of control procedures put in place by the charity, and how adherence to procedures is monitored;

- obtaining evidence from field officers' reports as to work undertaken;

- comparison of accounting returns of expenditure with field reports and plans for consistency and reasonableness;

- analytical review of accounting returns received from overseas branches or local agents;

- consideration of any inspection or internal control visit reports undertaken by any internal audit function;

- consideration of audit work undertaken by local auditors, and consideration of any audit reports carried out on behalf of international donors, for example, government departments; and

- evidence from the audit work of another audit firm.

Where material assets are held or material funds are applied by overseas operations, the Practice Note suggests that the auditor may seek observational evidence by way of site visit.

Where a charity makes a grant to an autonomous overseas charity, the auditor ensures:

- receipt of the funding; and

- that the charity has exercised reasonable diligence in ensuring that the funds are used for charitable purposes in order that adverse tax consequences are not suffered.

In some cases, it may be appropriate to arrange for an overseas component auditor to carry out audit work on the financial information of a component, especially where the operations form a significant part of the charities activities. In this case, the requirements of ISA (UK) 600 (Revised June 2016) *Special Considerations – Audits of Group Financial Statements (Including the Work of Component Auditors)* apply.

43.13.3 Restricted funds

Restricted funds which are subject to specific rules about their application may give rise to a significant risk of material misstatement. The auditor should consider:

- the terms or conditions attached to the restricted funds;

- any funds in deficit;

- any income funds held in illiquid assets, preventing application of the fund; and

- capital being expended without authority.

The Practice Note suggests the following audit procedures:

- consideration of internal control procedures put in place by the charity to identify restricted funds;

- consideration of the methods used in cost allocation;

- comparison of expenditure with the terms of the restricted funds;

- consideration of the future funding to recover negative balances;

- consideration of the validity of the transfer between funds;

- consideration of the ability of the fund to meets its obligations in view of its underlying assets; and

- consideration of whether the capital of an endowed fund has been expended without express authority.

43.13.4 Heritage assets

Factors to consider include:

- sufficiency of information available to value heritage assets, including availability of experts and valuations of comparable assets;

- completeness of heritage assets – the auditor may consider the controls adopted by the entity and perform searches to identify significant or high profile movements;
- existence/rights and obligations – the auditor considers what documentary or other evidence may be available to support ownership.

43.13.5 Grants payable

Where charities make grants to third parties, auditors may consider factors such as:

- internal controls and processes including oversight by those charged with governance;
- diversion of grants to inappropriate recipients – the auditor may choose to obtain confirmation of receipt from recipients.

43.14 Audit considerations relating to an entity using a service organisation

The requirements for the auditor to review and consider arrangements between charities and their service organisations are no different from those applying in any audit situation.

The use of service organisations by charities is not uncommon and includes services provided to the charity such as:

- maintenance of accounting records and payroll services;
- fundraising; and
- custodianship of assets, and investment management services.

43.15 Initial audit engagements – opening balances

Because of the possibility that charities will qualify by reason of size for an audit where previously they were exempt, cases will arise where charities will not have had opening balances audited and the receipts and payments basis of accounting may have been used.

Where there has been a change in the basis of accounting, procedures may include checking bank statements, reviewing receipts and payments after the year end and physically checking any tangible fixed assets. For analytical review procedures, the auditor is likely to need to adjust the prior year management information prepared on a receipts and payments basis to enable a proper comparison.

If prior year financial statements were audited by a predecessor auditor, the auditor should take into account the professional competence and independence of the predecessor, including whether the predecessor auditor had other relevant charity experience, in determining whether a review of the predecessor's working papers provides sufficient appropriate audit evidence in relation to opening balances.

43.16 Auditing accounting estimates, including fair value accounting estimates, and related disclosures

On occasion, evidence obtained from post balance sheet review and observation may be insufficiently conclusive. Where such estimates are likely to be material, the auditor reviews the process by which the estimate was arrived at and considers the basis of the calculation in terms of its reasonableness, justifiability and consistency. In so doing, the auditor will draw heavily on its knowledge of the charity in testing the consistency of principles adopted. Estimates of this nature may include:

- the quantification of future charitable commitments and constructive liabilities;
- valuations of gifts in kind, particularly property;
- valuation of assets received for onwards distribution;
- valuation of fixed asset investments where no market price exists;
- valuation of heritage assets;
- valuation of intangible income derived from donated services or use of facilities;
- estimates of ongoing service potential of fixed assets, in the absence of a cash flow, in an impairment review;
- impairment of programme-related investments made in furtherance of a charity's objectives, rather than for financial return; and
- recoverability of loans made to beneficiaries in the furtherance of a charity's objects.

43.17 Related parties

It is a fundamental principle of trust law that a trustee should not benefit directly or indirectly from his or her trust. Neither charity trustees nor persons or businesses connected with them should obtain benefit from the charity unless expressly permitted by the charities governing document or an appropriate authority. There are also disclosure requirements in the relevant Charities SORP and in the regulations.

The auditor needs to understand the controls management have put in place to authorise and approve significant transactions.

43.18 Subsequent events

The determination after the balance sheet date of the amount of a gift aid payment to a parent charity by a subsidiary undertaking, if the subsidiary had a present legal obligation at the balance sheet date, is an adjusting post balance sheet event. However, reference should also be made to the ICAEW Technical Release 16/14BL *Guidance on donations by a company to its parent charity.*

43.19 Going concern

This can be a difficult area in the audit of charities as many charities have an apparent financial weakness which is often compounded by the uncertainty of future income. Their ability to raise revenue will often be outside their direct control, and be dependent on such matters as the voting of grants and spending of the public.

It may also be difficult for a charity to cut back on a project or grant funding in the event of a liquidity problem, and although it may have an apparently large bank balance, it may be unable to meet general liabilities because the balance in question belongs to a restricted fund.

The Charities SORP requires that where there are material uncertainties related to events or conditions that may cast significant doubt on the charity's ability to continue as a going concern, these should be disclosed in the financial statements. Where there are no such material uncertainties, the financial statements should state this.

Charity specific indicators of potential going concern issues include:

- inability of the charity to finance its operations from its own resources or unrestricted funds;
- decision by the trustees to curtail or cease activities;
- transfer to, or take-over by, another entity of the charity's activities;
- loss of essential resources or key staff;
- existence of tax liabilities which cannot be met from existing resources;
- deficits on unrestricted funds;
- loss of clients, for example, where a public authority ends a practice or contract to refer (and pay for) clients to the charity;
- loss of operating licence;

- significant changes in strategy of major funders and significant decline in donations by the public;
- investigation by a charity regulator;
- loans made to subsidiaries which cannot be repaid;
- claw-back of grant received and gift aid refunds; and
- failure to meet reserves policy targets.

The going concern concept does not apply to the preparation of financial statements on a receipts and payments basis (allowed for small non limited company charities in England and Wales which are within the income thresholds defined by legislation). In these circumstances, the auditor should consider whether there are matters that affect the charities' ability to continue in operational existence for the foreseeable future. The auditor should not issue his report unless he is satisfied with explanations received from trustees concerning future funding arrangements. If he is not satisfied, he may find it appropriate to include an explanatory paragraph in his report. He will not qualify his report on the proper presentation of the receipts and payments account.

43.20   Written representations

A representation letter in respect of the financial statements of the charity is normally signed by the trustees who are responsible for the contents and presentation of the financial statements.

Where day-to-day management of the charity is delegated to senior management by trustees and representations are taken from those staff, the auditor should ensure that the staff involved have the necessary authority and all such representations are considered and approved by the trustees.

In addition to representation required by ISAs (UK), the auditor of a charity also considers obtaining confirmation that:

- all income has been recorded;
- the restricted funds have been properly applied;
- constructive obligations for grants have been recognised;
- all correspondence with regulators has been made available to the auditor including any serious incident reports (for charities registered in England and Wales) and any notifiable events reports (for charities registered in Scotland); and
- the trustees consider there to be appropriate controls in place to ensure overseas payments are applied for charitable purposes.

43.21 Audits of group financial statements

Where other auditors are used because they act for local branches, subsidiaries or other units, the group auditor must assess the degree of reliance he intends to place on the other auditors' work. Where the charity is a limited company, there is a statutory obligation on the component auditors of any subsidiary undertaking that is a company to communicate such information and explanations as may be reasonably required by the group auditor. Where the charity is unincorporated, the auditor has rights under s. 15 of the 2011 Act of access to books, documents and records which relate to the charity. This extends beyond those actually in the ownership of the charity.

Where charitable groups have components overseas, there may be added complications for the group auditor to ensure the results of the components are appropriately consolidated into the group financial statements. The group auditor:

- obtains an understanding of the component business;
- obtains an understanding of the accounting framework and policies under which the component accounts will be prepared;
- considers the need to review the charity's conversion of the component financial statements into UK GAAP format;
- considers the need for the component auditors to perform work on UK GAAP specific areas. Depending on the local accounting framework, this may require details of the accounting requirements under the Charities SORP to be explained to the component auditors.

Section 30 provides further guidance on group audit situations, including consideration of overseas components.

43.22 The auditor's report on financial statements

The 2008 Regulations determine that audit reports should be addressed to the trustees unless the auditor has been appointed by the Charity Commission. Companies and Friendly Societies statutes require audit reports to be addressed to the members. Scottish law requires company audit reports to be addressed to trustees and members.

The trustees' responsibilities may vary depending upon the constitution and size of the particular charity. The Companies Act and the Co-operative and Community Benefit Societies Act establish duties under law. Where a charity is not subject to other regulation, appendix four of the Practice Note recommends the form of words to be used in the statement of trustees' responsibilities within the financial statements.

The Charities SORP has been developed and issued under the code of practice established by the Financial Reporting Council for the production and issue of SORPs. They are authoritative guidance on the application of accounting standards to charities.

As the 2011 Act requires trustees to state whether financial statements have been prepared in accordance with SORP, this provision, taken with the general status of the SORPs, implies a strong presumption that the financial statements will need to follow the relevant SORP in order to give a true and fair view.

In addition, UK GAAP and the SORP indicate that it is necessary for a reporting entity to prepare consolidated financial statements in certain circumstances.

In October 2016, the FRC issued Bulletin: *Compendium of illustrative auditor's reports on United Kingdom private sector financial statements for periods commencing on or after 17 June 2016*. This bulletin is based on the new reporting requirements in revised ISAs (UK) and replaces the guidance and examples previously contained in Bulletin 2010/2: *Compendium of Illustrative Auditor's Reports on United Kingdom Private Sector Financial Statements for periods ended on or after 15 December 2010 (Revised)*.

However, the 2016 bulletin does not specifically provide examples of suitable audit reports specifically tailored in respect of charity audits. As a result, the auditor will need to take care in combining the charitable law requirements with the ISA (UK) 700 (Revised June 2016) and other reporting requirements set out in the October 2016 bulletin.

The Audit and Assurance Faculty of the ICAEW has issued a helpsheet, *Preparing an audit report for a charity,* illustrating how audit reports for charities may be constructed.

43.23   Other information

The Charities SORP requires trustees of larger charities which are subject to audit under charity law (see **43.1.1**)[2] to include in their report a description of the principal risks and uncertainties facing the charity, together with a summary of their plans and strategies for managing those risks. Smaller charities are not required to give this information, but it is considered good practice to make a statement about risk assessment

---

[2] For those charities operating in jurisdictions where there is no charity law audit requirement, the reference to larger charities is construed as applying to those charities with a gross income exceeding £500,000 (UK) or €500,000 (Republic of Ireland) in the reporting period.

and management. The Charity Commission is also encouraging larger charities to give expanded details on their risk management processes. Whilst the auditor is not expected to verify any risk management statement made by trustees, he should consider the disclosures made in relation to his knowledge of the charity's circumstances and systems.

The auditor of a charitable company audited under the *Companies Act* 2006 must report whether, in his opinion, the information in the trustees' report (directors' report) and strategic review (where applicable) is consistent with the financial statements and whether the reports have been prepared in accordance with applicable legal requirements.

The auditor of a non-company charity, or a small company choosing to be audited under the *Charities Act* 2011 rather than the *Companies Act* 2006, only needs to report under the Act where, in his opinion, the trustees' report is not consistent with the financial statements.

New requirements of ISA (UK) 720 (Revised June 2016) also apply to charities (see **Section 34**).

43.24   Summarised financial statements

The Practice Note makes reference to summarised financial statements but does not specifically cover such engagements.

Where a charity produces summarised financial statements, there is no requirement for a report by the auditor. However, should the charity wish such a report to be produced the auditor may do so. In this case, the auditor will need to decide whether to continue to refer to Bulletin 2008/3 or to refer to other guidance such as the IAASB's ISA 810 *Engagements to Report on Summary Financial Statements.* A revised version of ISA 810 was issued in March 2016.

44 Pension schemes

44.1 Introduction

Pension schemes operate in a complex legal environment and specific guidance to auditors of schemes is provided in Practice Note 15 (Revised) *The audit of occupational pension schemes in the United Kingdom,* most recently revised in November 2017 ('PN 15').

This section is intended to guide auditors of pension schemes to the key items addressed in PN 15 and to provide details of where other relevant information can be obtained.

In June 2016, the FRC issued a new suite of ISAs (UK), effective for the audit of financial statements for periods commencing on or after 17 June 2016, as set out in **1.6.4**. The November 2017 version of the Practice Note reflects the requirements of the revised ISAs (UK) as well as changes in the regulatory environment and the relevant financial reporting framework since it was last updated in 2011.

The Practice Note contains guidance on the application of auditing standards to the statutory audit of trust based occupational pension schemes established under the Pensions Acts in the United Kingdom. The guidance is also applicable to audits undertaken solely under the terms of a scheme's trust deed or other agreement requiring an auditor to provide a similar report, including requests from trustees where the scheme is otherwise exempt from audit or for financial statements prepared other than at the normal scheme year-end. Similar considerations apply to the audits of Common Investment Funds (CIFs) which are usually set up under trust and require an audit under their trust deed. PN 15 may also be of assistance to auditors of public sector pension schemes, although these schemes are subject to different financial reporting frameworks and different legislation.

The Practice Note sets out the special considerations relating to the audit of occupational pension schemes which arise from the individual ISAs (UK). It also provides useful background information on the legislative framework and useful example letters and reports.

44.2   Legal background

ISA (UK) 250 Section A (Revised December 2017) – *Consideration of Laws and Regulations in an Audit of Financial Statements* ('ISA (UK) 250A') sets out the auditor's responsibility to consider laws and regulations.

The legislative framework for pension schemes is dominated by the *Pension Schemes Act* 1993 ('PSA 1993'), the *Pensions Act* 1995 ('PA 1995'), the *Pensions Act* 2004 ('PA 2004') and regulations that accompany them. The subsequent *Pensions Act* 2007 ('PA 2007'), *Pensions Act* 2008 ('PA 2008'), *Pensions Act* 2011 ('PA 2011'), *Pensions Act* 2014 ('PA 2014') *Pensions Schemes Act* 2015 ('PSA 2015') and *Pensions Act* 2017 ('PA 2017') are also relevant for background knowledge but with less direct impact on pension scheme auditors.

PSA 1993 is consolidating legislation addressing the contracting out of the additional element of the state scheme (which ceased on 5 April 2016) and the protection of members through the disclosure of information to them and by placing restrictions on employer-related investment.

PA 2007 is primarily concerned with the provision of state pensions including the change in state pension age, increasing from 65 to 68 over the period 2019–46.

PA 2008 introduced the requirement on employers to auto-enrol all eligible employees into qualifying workplace pension schemes.

PA 2011 puts into law changes to the state pension age timetable established under PA 2007 and, together with associated Regulations, implements the automatic enrolment and related provisions first set out in PA 2008.

PA 2014 introduced the single-tier state pension from 6 April 2016, with consequent withdrawal of contracting out of NICs.

PSA 2015 introduces collective benefit schemes and details the 'pension flexibilities' which allow greater access to pension benefits to those aged 55 and above.

PA 2017 dealt with a new regulatory regime for master trusts. Key points are:

- the Act introduces an authorisation regime for master trusts which provide DC benefits (whether alone or in conjunction with other benefits);

- master trusts will have to demonstrate to TPR that they meet certain key criteria on establishment (or, for existing master trusts, when the relevant provisions are brought into force);

- TPR has been given new supervisory powers to authorise and de-authorise master trusts according to strict criteria, ensuring that master trusts continue to meet the required standards throughout their existence; and

- the Act introduces specific trustee requirements on wind up or closure of master trusts.

The Act also makes provision for regulations to be laid to introduce further measures on administration charges (the cap on early exit charges and the ban on member-borne commission charges).

PA 1995 and PA 2004 are both reforming legislation and primarily enabling Acts with detailed requirements set out in Regulations made under them. The principal Regulations that pension scheme auditors need to be aware of are:

- the *Occupational Pension Schemes (Disclosure of Information) Regulations* 1996 ('the Disclosure Regulations');

- the *Occupational Pension Schemes (Scheme Administration) Regulations* 1996 ('the Administration Regulations');

- the *Occupational Pension Schemes (Requirement to obtain Audited Accounts and a Statement from the Auditor) Regulations* 1996 ('the Audited Accounts Regulations'); and

- the *Occupational Pension Schemes (Investment) Regulations* 2005 ('the Investment Regulations').

In addition to specific pensions legislation, many schemes are constituted as trusts and are also subject to the requirements of trust law.

The Pension Acts and the Regulations referred to above have been amended frequently since they were first issued, and care should be taken to refer to the latest amended versions.

PA 1995, PA 2004 and the Regulations set out the basis on which auditors are appointed, auditors' responsibilities and the form and content of pension scheme financial statements and annual reports. They also set out responsibilities for trustees such as obtaining the annual report and financial statements and the establishment and operation of internal controls.

PA 2004 also introduced the Pensions Regulator ('the Regulator'). The Regulator replaced the Occupational Pensions Regulatory Authority ('OPRA') from April 2005.

The Regulator, which is sometimes abbreviated to 'TPR' or 'tPR', has a range of powers, which include issuing:

- codes of practice, as explained further below, and other regulatory guidance;

- improvement notices: the ability to prevent those responsible for a scheme contravening pensions legislation;

- third party notices: the ability to take action against a third party who is preventing a person from complying with the law;

- contribution notices: to order contributions from parties attempting to avoid employer debt to a defined benefit scheme; and

- financial support directions: to secure financial support from a party associated with the principal employer if the employer is either a service organisation or insufficiently funded.

Codes of Practice are primarily directed at trustees. They are not statements of law, but are an indication of what is considered to be best practice. Any departure from them should, therefore, be justifiable and not be in breach of any underlying legal requirements. All professionals involved with pension schemes should be aware of the Codes of Practice and should refer regularly to the Pension Regulator's website (www. thepensionsregulator.gov.uk), which also provides guidance related to each code of practice. There have been 14 Codes of Practice issued to date. Those which are particularly relevant to the responsibilities and work of a pension scheme auditor are:

01 Reporting breaches of the law

03 Funding defined benefits

05 Reporting late payment of contributions to occupational pension schemes

07 Trustee knowledge and understanding

09 Internal controls

13 Governance and administration of occupational defined contribution trust-based schemes*

14 Governance and administration of public service pension schemes

* Code 13 has been significantly updated and a revised code came into effect in July 2016.

The Codes of Practice referred to above are explained in more detail in the relevant parts of this section.

The Pensions Regulator also issues guidance to help understand what the law requires with regard to regulating pension provision.

In explaining the legal environment in which pension schemes operate, Code of Practice 01 refers to 'enactments or rule of law', which are broadly defined to include the *Theft Act* 1968, the *Trustee Act* 2000 and other trust law and common law. Auditors of pension schemes must, therefore, maintain an understanding of many legal requirements. In addition, there must also be familiarity with the scheme's own rules and regulations which are set out in its trust deed and rules.

44.3   Accounting guidance

The accounting guidance for pension schemes is contained in the Statement of Recommended Practice *Financial Reports of Pension Schemes* ('the SORP'). The SORP is issued by the Pensions Research Accountants Group ('PRAG') who also issue other guidance for the accounting and governance of pension schemes. Auditors of pension schemes should refer to the PRAG website (www.prag.org.uk) for details of the latest guidance.

The current version of the SORP was issued in November 2014 and applies to accounting periods commencing on or after 1 January 2015. It implements the requirements of FRS 102 for pension scheme accounts. Compared to the previous version, the 2014 SORP requires significantly more disclosures in the financial statements relating to investments, and particularly about the risks attached to investments, with both qualitative and quantitative disclosures. This poses an additional challenge for auditors in gathering sufficient, appropriate, reliable evidence.

In March 2016, the Financial Reporting Council published a change to FRS 102 allowing financial institutions and retirement benefit plans to use the investment fair value hierarchy required by International Financial Reporting Standards rather than that previously required by FRS 102 and incorporated in the 2014 SORP. This change applies for periods commencing 1 January 2017 onwards but may be early adopted and thus effectively applied retrospectively. The guidance and further details can be found online at Croner-i Tax and Accounting.

Auditors are required by the *Audited Accounts Regulations* to report whether the financial statements contain the information specified in reg. 3A of those Regulations. This sets out certain disclosures that need to be made and in particular whether the financial statements have been prepared in accordance with the 'relevant financial reporting framework applicable to occupational pension schemes' (generally understood to include the SORP) and if not, an indication of material departures.

PN 15 explains that it is normally necessary to follow the guidance in the SORP in order for pension scheme accounts to show a true and fair view. Auditors must, therefore, be familiar with the requirements of the SORP and be prepared to refer to any material non-compliance with it in the audit opinion.

It should be noted that pension scheme financial statements do not include the scheme's liabilities to pay pensions and other benefits that fall due after the end of the scheme year. A statement of net assets is required instead of a balance sheet.

44.4 Schemes exempt from audit

A number of categories of scheme are exempt under the Administration Regulations from the requirement to appoint an auditor. The principal exemptions relate to:

- occupational pension schemes with fewer than two members;

- certain public sector schemes;

- occupational money purchase small schemes (prior to *Finance Act* 2004, these were known as Small Self Administered Schemes or 'SSASs') meeting specified criteria in respect of unanimous decision making and membership of the trustee board;

- schemes not registered under *Finance Act* 2004; and

- unfunded occupational schemes.

Any of the above schemes may be audited on a 'voluntary basis', for example, where the trustees request an audit to be performed or where the scheme rules require an audit.

In addition, money-purchase schemes which invest only in one or more insurance policies which specifically allocate benefits to individual members ('ear-marked schemes') are also exempt from the requirement to prepare audited accounts, but are still required to obtain an auditor's statement about contributions.

44.5 Appointment and resignation

To be effective, the appointment of a scheme auditor must be made in accordance with the Administration Regulations. The trustees or managers of the scheme must forward a notice of appointment to the auditor which specifies the effective date of appointment, to whom the auditor is to report, and from whom the auditor will take instructions. For the appointment to be effective, PA 1995 requires the auditor to acknowledge receipt of the notice of appointment within one month of receipt. It also requires the auditor to state that he will notify the trustees immediately if he becomes aware of the existence of any conflict of interest.

On resignation, the Administration Regulations require the auditor to provide a written notice of resignation to the trustees. This must contain either a statement specifying any circumstances connected with the resignation which, in his opinion, significantly affect the interests of the members or prospective members of, or beneficiaries under, the scheme or a declaration that there are no such circumstances.

PN 15 provides examples of notice of appointment, acknowledgement of notice of appointment and resignation letters.

The scheme auditor does not have a right of access to information held by third parties and it is necessary for the auditor to request such information through the trustees when required for the audit. It is generally appropriate therefore to include in the engagement letter a paragraph relating to access to third parties to whom the trustees delegate functions, and to their records relating to the scheme. Such parties may include:

- scheme administrator;

- investment manager(s);

- custodian(s);

- sponsoring employer(s) and sponsoring employer's auditor; and

- scheme actuary.

44.6   Considerations of fraud

Although PN 15 comments that the potential for fraud exists in all schemes. Even if the auditor considers that the nature of pension schemes (not profit-making and not trading) reduces the risk of fraudulent financial reporting, the risk of misappropriation of assets remains and professional scepticism remains key. PN 15 explains that, even if activities are delegated, the trustees retain responsibility for the prevention and detection of fraud.

Examples of the type of fraud that may occur in a pension scheme are:

- misappropriation of assets;

- deliberate non-payment of employee and/or employer contributions to the scheme;

- use of assets of the scheme either directly or as collateral for borrowing by either the employer or an associate of the employer;

- misapplication of the assets of a scheme to meet the obligations and expenses of either another scheme or of the sponsoring employer;

- dealing in scheme assets by the investment manager without the required mandate or authorisation;

- lending of scheme assets by the custodian without authorisation;

- exchange of assets without sufficient valuable consideration (for example, selling assets such as property at below market value);

- assets of the scheme used for the personal preferment of the trustees or used for the personal preferment of an individual scheme member;

- benefit claims by members or their beneficiaries to which they are not entitled (for example, failure to notify a scheme of the death of a member or other beneficiary); and

- creation of fictitious scheme records by the administrator (for example, dummy beneficiary records).

There are circumstances that increase the risk of fraud and the auditor needs to be aware of these when planning the audit. These include:

- failure by the trustees to establish and operate adequate internal control mechanisms;

- trustees or scheme management displaying a significant disregard for the various regulatory authorities;

- trustees or scheme management having little or no involvement in the day-to-day administration of the scheme;

- trustees or scheme management having ready access to the scheme's assets and an ability to override any internal controls;

- trustees or scheme management failing to put in place arrangements to monitor activities undertaken by third parties, including the employer;

- trustees or scheme management displaying a lack of candour in dealings with members, the actuary or the auditor on significant matters affecting scheme assets;

- the sponsoring employer operating in an industry with increasing business failures, or itself having financial difficulties;

- significant levels, or unusual types, of related-party transactions (including employer-related investments) involving unaudited entities or entities audited by other firms; and

- opaque investment arrangements where the flow of information to the trustees is restricted and therefore it is more difficult to control and monitor the investment.

To properly assess the above circumstances, scheme auditors should be communicating with the trustees and those responsible for the management of the scheme, which may include the sponsoring employer, its directors or staff and third parties to whom the trustees have delegated the conduct of scheme activities. Scheme auditors should also conduct analytical procedures and hold a fraud brain-storming discussion. As with all entities, an appropriate response to identified fraud risks should be determined and management representation sought on fraud.

In accordance with ISA (UK) 240 (Revised June 2016), the auditor should consider the risk of fraud in relation to revenue recognition. As there is usually little scope or incentive for revenue to be fraudulently misstated, the auditor may conclude that the presumed risk of fraud is not relevant to the engagement. The auditor should nevertheless record his reasoning for such a conclusion having regard to the types of fraud that may occur in pension schemes and any risk indicators that may exist.

44.7   Use of service organisations

Many pension schemes delegate activities, most commonly administration and investment management, to third parties. Of particular relevance to pension scheme auditors is, therefore, ISA (UK) 402 *Audit Considerations relating to entities using a service organisation*. The responsibility for the operation of the scheme does, however, remain with the trustees when they have outsourced activities and they are responsible for ensuring that scheme has appropriate procedures and controls. Any weaknesses or gaps in the controls operated by trustees may lead to additional audit risk. In such circumstances, the auditor will need to design audit procedures to address that risk.

It is necessary for scheme auditors to gain an understanding of how the scheme's use of a service organisation affects the scheme's internal control. The following should, therefore, be documented and understood:

- the nature and significance of services provided;

- the nature and materiality of transactions processed or accounts processes affected;

- the nature of the relationship including contractual terms;

- interaction of the control systems of the scheme and the service organisation;

- the scheme's controls relevant to the service organisation and how risks are identified and controlled;

- the trustees' assessment procedures covering the capability of the service organisation; and

- information available to the trustees in respect of the service organisation's operations including general and IT controls.

The service organisation may provide information to the trustees by producing an 'internal control report' in accordance with *AAF 01/06 Assurance reports on internal controls of service organisations made available to third parties* ('AAF 01/06') (see **Section 40**).

The essential content of an internal control report under AAF 01/06 is for the service organisation to explain how control procedures achieve control objectives. Control objectives are set by the management of the service organisation, but AAF 01/06 provides mandatory objectives for pension scheme administrators, custodians and investment managers. An internal control report produced under AAF 01/06 will also contain a report from a Reporting Accountant providing information on the description and the design and operating effectiveness of control procedures.

Service organisations with an international clientele may alternatively produce an internal control report in accordance with the International Auditing and Assurance Standards Board standard ISAE 3402 *Assurance reports on controls at a service organisation* which has similar objectives to AAF 01/06.

Trustees should seek to obtain such reports from service providers and incorporate an assessment of them into their control procedures.

Having gained an understanding of the service organisation's controls, it may be concluded that these controls do not impact on the overall assessment of the audit risk in respect of the scheme. This could, for example, be because either the activities are not significant to the audit of the scheme or because the trustees have appropriate controls in place over their use of the service organisation.

If, however, the activities of the service organisation do result in audit risk, appropriate audit procedures will need to be designed. The nature of the procedures will be specific to each scheme and are dependent upon the service and the risks that have been assessed. Access to the service organisation will not always be necessary as the trustees may either hold sufficient documentation, or the service organisation provides periodic reports which contain adequate information. The internal control reports provided to trustees may also provide useful information to the scheme auditor.

44.8 Communication with trustees

Scheme auditors must ensure that there is interaction with those charged with governance at various stages of the audit. For pension schemes, those charged with governance will normally be the trustees, or the directors of the corporate trustee. As well as being a requirement of ISA (UK) 260 (Revised June 2016) *Communication with those Charged with Governance*, it is fundamental to the planning of the audit and compliance with ISA (UK) 315 (Revised June 2016).

Auditors will communicate with the trustees on a range of matters including:

- the responsibilities of the auditor;
- independence;
- scope of the audit, the audit plan and any additional procedures;
- timetable;
- fees;
- access to third parties and information;
- fraud;
- procedures, controls and internal audit;
- changes to the scheme;
- issues arising from a review of the minutes;
- significant findings from the audit;
- unadjusted errors other than those that are clearly trivial; and
- communication with the Regulator.

As part of their assessment and communication of matters concerning their independence, scheme auditors should also consider services provided to the sponsoring employer of the scheme. Regulatory guidance issued by the Regulator in 2008 highlights trustees' responsibilities to assess and manage conflicts of interest, including advisor conflicts.

At the end of the audit process, the auditor will also communicate with trustees. ISA (UK) 265 *Communicating Deficiencies in Internal Control to those Charged with Governance and Management* requires the auditor to report deficiencies to the extent that the auditor considers that they warrant the trustees' attention. In making that assessment, the auditor should have regard to factors such as:

- the significance and nature of the risk(s) to the scheme that are not being addressed as a result of the deficiency;
- the possible impact on scheme assets;
- the possible impact on member benefits;
- the extent to which the operation of controls is formal and documented or otherwise;
- whether alternative preventative controls are operating; and
- whether other parties such as third-party administrators compensate for the deficiencies.

Trustees should be notified of all breaches of duties relevant to the administration of the scheme discovered in the course of the audit work. These duties include those imposed by any enactment or rule of law on the trustees or managers, the employer, any professional adviser or any prescribed person acting in connection with the scheme. The notification to the trustees should be made, regardless of whether the matter gave rise to a statutory duty to report to the Regulator. If there are no matters that need to be notified, the trustees should be advised in writing accordingly.

44.9   Going concern

In April 2018, the Pensions Research Accountancy Group (PRAG) published guidance *Pension Scheme Accounts and Going Concern* to assist trustees and auditors in dealing with going concern matters in the preparation and audit of financial statements of pension schemes.

As with any other entity, in assessing whether the going concern assumption is appropriate or whether material uncertainties exist, trustees should assess a period of at least 12 months from the date of approval of the accounts, based on information available at the time of approval of the accounts.

In making their assessment, trustees should consider information available to them in the ordinary course of running the scheme. Possible considerations for trustees could include the following:

(1)   Has a decision been made to wind up the scheme (by employer or trustee)?

(2)   Has a formal decision been made to buy out a scheme's liabilities?

(3)   Have any trigger events occurred that cause a wind up under the trust deed and rules?

(4)   Are there concerns over the employer covenant?

   (a)   Are the results of an employer covenant review poor?

   (b)   Is the employer experiencing financial difficulties which give concerns about its ability to pay future contributions? Financial difficulties could be indicated where banking facilities are being renegotiated, there are profitability issues, loss of key customers and/or cash flow issues. For listed companies, there may be profit warnings. There also may be disclosures around going concern issues in the employer accounts.

   (c)   Are there any events notifiable to the Pensions Regulator?

   (d)   Has the employer experienced an insolvency event?

(5) Scheme funding

  (a) For defined benefit schemes, is the actuarial valuation complete and a recovery plan in place?

  (b) Are contributions payments up-to-date or are there any significant late contributions or a history of significant late contributions?

(6) Are there contingent assets in place?

(7) Does another group company provide financial support?

(8) Is the scheme in the PPF assessment period?

(9) Has the Pensions Regulator issued a freezing order?

(10) Has the Pensions Regulator ordered the scheme to be wound up?

This is not an exhaustive list and there may be others specific to the scheme circumstances. In addition, some of these considerations may not be relevant to all schemes. If any of the above situations apply, trustees should consider the implication for the use of the going concern basis and consider whether any material uncertainties in relation to going concern exist.

Suggested good practice is for trustees to document their assessment as a short paper and/or a formal minute.

Trustees' responsibilities in respect of going concern should be included in the Statement of Trustee Responsibilities accompanying the financial statements.

Auditors may wish to seek specific representations in this area via the representation letter.

44.10   Other information

The auditor, in considering his audit opinion should also consider other information contained in the annual report, as required by ISA (UK) 720 (Revised June 2016) *The Auditor's Responsibilities Relating to Other Information* (see **Section 34**). The auditor reads the other information contained in the annual report in the light of the knowledge acquired during the audit with a view to identifying whether there are any apparent misstatements therein or matters which are inconsistent with the financial statements or the auditor's knowledge gained in the course of performing the audit. The auditor is not expected specifically to verify any of the other information. It is important to ensure that the trustees are aware of their own responsibilities in respect of the other information and those of the auditor, and the extent of those responsibilities may be specifically outlined in the engagement letter.

The 'other information' which may accompany the financial statements of a pension scheme and examples of matters that the auditor may consider include:

- Trustees' report – membership reconciliation: are the changes in membership numbers consistent with the financial information?

- Trustees' report – pension increases: is the rate of increase reflected in the benefit payments?

- Actuary's certificate as to the adequacy of contributions: are the recommended rates of contribution the same as those received by the scheme?

- Report on actuarial liabilities – are the net assets consistent with net assets in the financial statements?

- Trustees' report/Investment report: is the asset total and investment income/return consistent with the amounts shown in the financial statements?

- Chair's Statement regarding governance (re schemes with defined contributions assets): are the assertions made consistent with the auditor's knowledge of the scheme?

- Report on actuarial liabilities: is the net assets data consistent with the financial statements?

If, on reading the other information, the auditor identifies a material misstatement in the other information and it is not corrected after communicating with the trustees, the auditor should take appropriate action including:

- modifying the opinion in the auditor's report (following the requirements of ISA (UK) 706 (Revised June 2016) *Emphasis of Matter paragraphs and Other Matter Paragraphs in the independent auditor's report*); or

- withdrawing from the engagement.

44.11   Reporting

The form and content of auditor's reports on the financial statements of pension schemes follow the requirements established by ISA (UK) 700 (Revised June 2016) *Forming an opinion and reporting on financial statements*, and the particular detailed requirements of the Audited Accounts Regulations. Those regulations require the trustees of a scheme to obtain audited financial statements and so it is to the trustees that the auditor's report is addressed, although other parties may be added if required by the trust deed or other applicable rules.

A statement of trustees' responsibilities, usually included within the trustees' report, assists in meeting the requirement to distinguish between the auditor's responsibilities and the responsibilities of those charged with governance (in the case of a pension scheme, its trustees). The exact responsibilities of the trustees may vary according to the constitution of the particular pension scheme. An example trustee responsibility statement is set out in an appendix to PN 15.

Unlike company law, pension scheme law does not impose on the trustees a direct responsibility for the preparation of the financial statements. The trustees' responsibility statement should, however, make it clear that it is the trustees (not the auditor) who are primarily responsible for the preparation and content of the financial statements.

The Audited Accounts Regulations set out the requirements of the auditor to report on whether, in their opinion, the financial statements:

- show a true and fair view of the financial transactions of the scheme during the year, and of the amount and disposition at its year-end of its assets and liabilities, other than the liabilities to pay pensions and benefits after the end of the year; and

- contain the information specified in the *Occupational Pension Schemes (Requirement to Obtain Audited Accounts and a Statement from the Auditor) Regulations* 1996, reg. 3 and 3A, made under the *Pensions Act* 1995.

An example of an unmodified audit report on the statutory financial statements of a pension scheme is set out in **Table 1**. Note that this example does not include the auditor's separate statement on contributions which is often given as a separate report (see **44.12**).

TABLE 1: Unqualified audit opinion

INDEPENDENT AUDITOR'S REPORT TO THE TRUSTEES OF XYZ PENSION SCHEME

Opinion

We have audited the financial statements of [XYZ Pension Scheme] ('the scheme') for the year ended [*date*] which comprise the fund account, the statement of net assets and notes to the financial statements, including a summary of significant accounting policies. The financial reporting framework that has been applied in their preparation is applicable law and United Kingdom Accounting Standards, including Financial Reporting Standard 102 *The Financial Reporting Standard applicable in the UK and Republic of Ireland* (United Kingdom Generally Accepted Accounting Practice).

In our opinion, the financial statements:

- show a true and fair view of the financial transactions of the scheme during the year ended [...], and of the amount and disposition at that date of its assets and liabilities, other than the liabilities to pay pensions and benefits after the end of the year;

- have been properly prepared in accordance with United Kingdom Generally Accepted Accounting Practice; and

- contain the information specified in regulations 3 and 3A of the *Occupational Pension Schemes (Requirement to obtain Audited Accounts and a Statement from the Auditor) Regulations* 1996, made under the *Pensions Act* 1995.

Basis for opinion

We conducted our audit in accordance with International Standards on Auditing (UK) (ISAs (UK)) and applicable law. Our responsibilities under those standards are further described in the Auditor's responsibilities for the audit of the financial statements section of our report. We are independent of the scheme in accordance with the ethical requirements that are relevant to our audit of the financial statements in the UK, including the FRC's Ethical Standard, and we have fulfilled our other ethical responsibilities in accordance with these requirements. We believe that the audit evidence we have obtained is sufficient and appropriate to provide a basis for our opinion.

Conclusions relating to going concern

We have nothing to report in respect of the following matters in relation to which the ISAs (UK) require us to report to you where:

- the trustees' use of the going concern basis of accounting in the preparation of the financial statements is not appropriate; or

- the trustees have not disclosed in the financial statements any identified material uncertainties that may cast significant doubt about the scheme's ability to continue to adopt the going concern basis of accounting for a period of at least 12 months from the date when the financial statements are authorised for issue.

Other information

The other information comprises the information included in the [*annual report*], other than the financial statements and our auditor's report thereon. The trustees are responsible for the other information. Our opinion on the financial statements does not cover the other information and, except to the extent otherwise explicitly stated in our report, we do not express any form of assurance conclusion thereon.

In connection with our audit of the financial statements, our responsibility is to read the other information [, including (*specify titles of other information*)] and, in doing so, consider whether the other information is materially inconsistent with the financial statements or our knowledge obtained in the audit or otherwise appears to be materially misstated. If we identify such material inconsistencies or apparent material misstatements, we are required to determine whether there is a material misstatement in the financial statements or a material misstatement of the other information. If, based on the work we have performed, we conclude that there is a material misstatement of this other information, we are required to report that fact.

We have nothing to report in this regard.

Responsibilities of trustees

As explained more fully in the statement of trustees' responsibilities [set out on page ...], the trustees are responsible for the preparation of the financial statements and for being satisfied that they show a true and fair view, and for such internal control as the trustees determine is necessary to enable the preparation of financial statements that are free from material misstatement, whether due to fraud or error.

In preparing the financial statements, the trustees are responsible for assessing the scheme's ability to continue as a going concern, disclosing, as applicable, matters related to going concern and using the going concern basis of accounting unless the trustees intend to wind up the scheme, or have no realistic alternative but to do so.

Auditor's responsibilities for the audit of the financial statements

Our objectives are to obtain reasonable assurance about whether the financial statements as a whole are free from material misstatement, whether due to fraud or error, and to issue an auditor's report that includes our opinion. Reasonable assurance is a high level of assurance, but is not a guarantee that an audit conducted in accordance with ISAs (UK) will always detect a material misstatement when it exists.

Misstatements can arise from fraud or error and are considered material if, individually or in the aggregate, they could reasonably be expected to influence the economic decisions of users taken on the basis of these financial statements.

A further description of our responsibilities for the audit of the financial statements is located on the Financial Reporting Council's website at www.frc.org.uk/auditorsresponsibilities. This description forms part of our auditor's report.

Use of our report

This report is made solely to the scheme's trustees, as a body, in accordance with the *Pensions Act* 1995. Our audit work has been undertaken so that we might state to the scheme's trustees those matters we are required to state to them in an auditor's report and for no other purpose. To the fullest extent permitted by law, we do not accept or assume responsibility to anyone other than the trustees, as a body, for our audit work, for this report, or for the opinions we have formed.

44.11.1 Key audit matters

ISA (UK) 701 *Communicating Key Audit Matters in the Independent Auditor's Report* does not apply automatically to audits of pension schemes, but the auditor may nevertheless decide to communicate key audit matters in his report. Where he does so the sections of the report dealing with key audit matters, an overview of the scope of the audit and application of materiality should be included in accordance with ISA (UK) 701 (see **Section 4**).

44.12 Contributions

Scheme auditors are required by the Audited Accounts Regulations to make a statement about contributions. This is separate to the opinion that is given on the financial statements. The statement is whether contributions have, in all material respects, been paid at least in accordance with the payment schedule or the schedule of contributions.

The requirement for an auditor's statement about contributions applies to most schemes that are required to appoint an auditor, irrespective of the size or nature of the scheme. However, with effect from 6 April 2016, an amendment to the Audited Accounts Regulations has removed the requirement for any scheme which, on the first day of the scheme year, had at least 20 participating employers.

Auditors need to understand the basis under which contributions are paid to the scheme by the employer. Money purchase schemes are required to have a payment schedule under PA 1995, s. 87 and defined benefit schemes are required to have a schedule of contributions under PA 2004, s. 227 ('the schedule(s)').

Pension scheme auditors need to be familiar with the form and content of the schedule relevant to the scheme. Since 2005, contributions to defined benefit schemes come under the 'scheme specific funding' regime, which replaced the previous minimum funding requirements.

The schedule of contributions must be prepared in accordance with the *Occupational Pension Schemes (Scheme Funding) Regulations* 2005 and is required to show separately any deficit funding and 'other' contributions due from the employer. It must also be signed by the trustees and the employer.

Auditors need to ascertain when a schedule becomes effective. PN 15 provides guidance on the issues that need to be considered, but it is important to be aware that a schedule of contributions cannot be effective until it is certified by the actuary and that it cannot be backdated.

The Regulator's Code of Practice 03 *Funding defined benefits* and Code of Practice 05 *Reporting late payment of contributions to occupational pension schemes* provide guidance for trustees on the monitoring of contributions and the reporting responsibilities in the event of late or incorrect payments being made.

In order to make his statement about contributions, the auditor must obtain the schedule and undertake procedures to obtain sufficient appropriate evidence to conclude whether or not contributions payable have, in all material respects, been paid at least for the amounts and within the timeframe set out in the schedule.

The auditor needs to consider a range of issues, including:

- changes in rates of contributions payable and the extent to which these have been included in the schedule;
- changes in the definition of salary on which the contributions are based;
- whether the schedule is sufficiently clear;
- whether the schedule complies with legal requirements and guidance issued by the Regulator;
- whether there have been any member complaints about incorrect contributions;
- the scheme's systems for recording and monitoring contributions; and
- any reports to the Regulator of late or inaccurate contributions.

As the statement about contributions is separate to the audit opinion, PN 15 indicates that it should be a separate report. PN 15 notes that it is important for readers of the auditor's statement about contributions to understand which contributions are covered by it and which are not. To assist in this, it is recommended that a summary of contributions paid during the scheme year under the schedule is produced by the trustees and included with the annual report ('the summary'). It is also helpful to include a reconciliation of contributions under the schedule to the total of contributions reported in the financial statements.

As the schedule refers to both the quantum and the timing of the payment of contributions, materiality must be considered in terms of both value and time. It is normal to apply materiality to values and the pension scheme auditor should consider this in the same manner as for any other transaction stream. The application of materiality to timing is more complex.

The application of materiality is a matter of judgment for individual pension scheme auditors and the only guidance provided by PN 15 is that there should be regard to the nature and frequency of any breaches and the cumulative, as well as the individual, impact of the breaches.

In considering the application of materiality to timing, there are, however, some salient factors which may be considered:

- the statement about contributions is on an aggregate basis and so materiality should not be applied based on the perception of a single member's contribution;

- late contributions are usually more significant in a money purchase arrangement; and

- the manner of the monitoring of contributions, the identification of any late contributions and the timeliness of such identification should be considered.

Example wording of the auditor's statement about contributions and guidance on the wording of qualified statements about contributions is given in the following tables. **Table 2** provides an example of an unmodified statement and **Table 3** gives a qualified statement.

TABLE 2: Example of an Unmodified Auditor's Statement about Contributions

INDEPENDENT AUDITOR'S STATEMENT ABOUT CONTRIBUTIONS TO THE TRUSTEES OF XYZ PENSION SCHEME

We have examined the summary of contributions to the [name of scheme] for the scheme year ended [...] [to which this statement is attached/which is set out in the Trustees' Report on page [x].

Respective responsibilities of Trustees and the auditor

As explained more fully in the Statement of Trustees' Responsibilities [set out on page ...], the scheme's Trustees are responsible for ensuring that there is prepared, maintained and from time to time revised a [schedule of contributions/payment schedule] showing the rates and due dates of certain contributions payable towards the scheme by or on behalf of the employer and the active members of the scheme. The Trustees are also responsible for keeping records in respect of contributions received in respect of active members of the scheme and for monitoring whether contributions are made to the scheme by the employer in accordance with the [schedule of contributions/ payment schedule].

It is our responsibility to provide a Statement about Contributions paid under the [schedule of contributions/payment schedule] and to report our opinion to you.

Scope of work on Statement about Contributions

Our examination involves obtaining evidence sufficient to give reasonable assurance that contributions reported in the [attached] summary of contributions have in all material respects been paid at least in accordance

---

with the [schedule of contributions/payment schedule]. This includes an examination, on a test basis, of evidence relevant to the amounts of contributions payable to the scheme and the timing of those payments under the [schedule of contributions/payment schedule].

Statement about Contributions payable under the [schedule of contributions]/[payment schedule]

In our opinion, contributions for the scheme year ended [...] as reported in the summary of contributions and payable under the [schedule of contributions]/ [payment schedule] have in all material respects been paid at least in accordance with the [schedule of contributions certified by the scheme actuary on [date]/payment schedule dated [...]].

Statutory Auditor

Address

Date

TABLE 3: Extract from a Modified Auditor's Statement about Contributions

Basis for qualified statement about contributions

As explained on page [...], [give brief details of the departure from the schedule including an indication of the frequency of late payments, and quantification of the amounts involved – e.g. 'during the year, three months' contributions amounting in total to £X were paid [specify timing of payment] later than the due date set out in the schedule of contributions'].

Qualified statement about contributions payable under the [schedule of contributions]/[payment schedule]

In our opinion, except for the effects of the departure from the schedule of contributions set out above, contributions for the scheme year ended [...] as reported in the summary of contributions and payable under the [schedule of contributions]/[payment schedule] have in all material respects been paid at least in accordance with the [schedule of contributions certified by the scheme actuary on [date ...]/payment schedule dated [...]].

In the event that the auditor's statement about contributions is qualified, trustees should have already considered the need to report to the Regulator because of their responsibility to monitor the receipt of contributions. In such circumstances, the auditor will need to consider the following.

- If a report has been made by the trustees, did it contain all relevant information that the Regulator would expect?

- If the trustees were aware of the issue giving rise to the qualification, have they documented why a report was not made to the Regulator and is the conclusion reasonable?

- If the trustees were not aware of the issue, are their monitoring procedures insufficient and are there wider implications?

Depending upon the results of the above, it may be necessary for a report to be made to the Regulator by either the trustees or the auditor. Further guidance on the necessity of a report to the Regulator is provided in the Regulator's Code of Practice 05 *Reporting late payment of contributions to occupational pension schemes*. A qualified statement about contributions does not automatically result in a report to the Regulator. A report by the trustees to the Regulator on the timing of contributions is, however, more likely to result in a qualified statement about contributions, but the pension scheme auditor should give the matter proper consideration.

44.13   Schemes in the process of winding up

Schemes in winding up are not exempt from the requirement to produce an annual report and audited financial statements until the wind up is complete. The Administration Regulations do not require the appointment of an auditor if the membership is less than two, so potentially, the statutory requirement for an audit can cease before the wind up is finalised. However, trust law and best practice indicate that financial statements should still be prepared. In these circumstances, the audit becomes non-statutory and the auditor needs to consider whether the existing engagement terms remain appropriate.

A schedule of contributions is no longer required once the wind up of a defined benefit pension scheme commences and the auditor should only express an opinion in his statement about contributions on compliance with the schedule of contributions up to the date the wind up commences. In relation to subsequent periods, the statement concerns compliance with the scheme rules and, where appropriate, the recommendations of the actuary.

For a money purchase scheme, the payment schedule is still required during the wind up period. Trustees should revise the payment schedule to reflect the basis on which contributions are payable from the start of winding up, which is normally nil. The auditor expresses an opinion on the payment schedule in force up to the commencement of winding up and thereafter on the revised schedule if one has been produced.

Once winding up is formally concluded the auditor's appointment automatically lapses without the need for formal resignation. Evidence of winding up should be obtained, but, if no such evidence is available, the auditor should consider formal resignation. Where no audit work has been performed for several months, it may be appropriate for the auditor to include in the statement on resignation that he is not able to know of any circumstances which might affect members' interests.

44.14 Other reporting situations

There are situations when audited financial statements are required for periods other than the usual agreed accounting reference date. These will normally coincide with the requirement for an actuarial valuation in circumstances such as:

- the present recovery plan being significantly inadequate;

- a claim against an employer under PA 1995, s. 75 due to an employer ceasing to participate in a multi-employer scheme;

- following a bulk transfer into or out of a scheme and/or a significant change in membership; or

- for the purpose of the Pension Protection Fund following the entry of the scheme into the assessment period.

The financial statements in all of these situations should be prepared in accordance with the Audited Accounts Regulations. A trustee report is not usually required, although a statement of trustee responsibilities should be included, and the notes to the financial statements should specify the purpose for which the financial statements have been prepared. The auditor will report on the financial statements in the usual manner, again specifying the purpose for which they have been prepared. There is not usually a requirement to give a separate statement about contributions. In each of these situations, it is likely that the auditor will need to issue a revised engagement letter to recognise the altered scope and purpose of the engagement compared with a normal annual audit.

44.15 Whistle-blowing responsibilities

The *Pensions Act* 2004, s. 70 imposes on the auditor (and virtually everyone associated with the running of a scheme) a duty to report to the Regulator any breaches of the law that are likely to be of material significance to the Regulator. PN 15 provides comprehensive information on the auditor's considerations leading to such a report and the manner in which this should be undertaken.

The Regulator's Code of Practice 01 explains the 'whistle-blowing' requirements and this, together with further guidance issued by the Regulator, should be understood by the scheme auditor. The duty to report to the Regulator arises where the trustees or others associated with the scheme have failed to comply with their legal duties. The Regulator has, however, indicated that it expects most reporting to be by trustees and, if a report has already been made, the auditor should only report if there is additional information to be provided. Note that the auditor is only required to report matters that are of 'material significance to the Regulator', not all breaches of regulations or law. The auditor is not required to undertake any additional work other than to fulfil his responsibilities.

44.16   Non-statutory audits

Many schemes that are not required under the Regulations to obtain audited financial statements nevertheless choose to do so, either because it is a requirement or at the request of trustees or members.

44.16.1   Appointment and removal

A non-statutory auditor falls within the definition of the term 'professional adviser' used in the Occupational Pension Schemes (Scheme Administration) Regulations, so the provisions relating to the appointment and removal of the scheme auditor (as discussed in **44.5**) apply also to the appointment of a non-statutory auditor.

44.16.2   Engagement letter

Some tailoring of the engagement letter will be required to remove references to statutory obligations and responsibilities and to reflect the particular circumstances of the engagement and /or requirements of the trust deed.

Where the auditor is asked to provide a 'true and fair' opinion then the financial statements will still need to be prepared in accordance with relevant UK Accounting Standards and the SORP.

Similarly, the auditor's work will be governed by the requirements of ISAs (UK) and will not differ in any significant respect from an audit carried out for statutory purposes.

Whether or not the auditor is required to issue a statement regarding contributions will depend on the requirements of the scheme and the trust deed. References to responsibilities of the trustees and the auditor in this regard will need to be tailored appropriately to the circumstances, without reference to statutory requirements that are not applicable.

44.16.3   Reporting to the Pensions Regulator (TPR)

As a 'professional adviser' to the scheme, a non-statutory auditor of an occupational pension scheme, like the statutory auditor, is subject to the duty to report to TPR under the *Pensions Act* 2004, s. 70.

44.16.4   Auditor's statement about contributions

It is unlikely that a non-statutory auditor will be required to report about contributions by reference to a Payment Schedule. However, the trust deed may impose a requirement to report whether contributions have been paid in accordance with the trust deed and rules, or something similar. In these situations the auditor should tailor his work appropriately, and report accordingly.

44.16.5   Termination of appointment

The termination of the appointment of a non-statutory auditor is subject to the same legal requirements as the termination of a statutory appointment.

44.16.6   Trustees' responsibilities statement

The first part of the example statement shown in the appendix to PN 15 will typically need to be amended to read as follows:

'The non-statutory financial statements are the responsibility of the trustees. The trust deed and rules of the scheme require the trustees to prepare audited financial statements for each scheme year which:

- show a true and fair view of the financial transactions of the scheme during the scheme year and of the amount and disposition at the end of that year of the assets and liabilities, other than liabilities to pay pensions and benefits after the end of the scheme year, and

- contain the information specified in the Statement of Recommended Practice "Financial Reports of Pension Schemes (Revised November 2014)" and the Trust Deed.'

Reference to a statutory obligation to maintain a payment schedule or a schedule of contributions will be omitted.

44.16.7   Auditor's report

The auditor's report in respect of a non-statutory audit has the same structure as a statutory audit report (see **Table 1**) but some of the wording needs to be tailored for the particular circumstances. In particular:

- it may be appropriate to refer to the financial statements as 'the non-statutory financial statements' for clarity;

- in the opinion paragraph the last bullet, which refers to compliance with the regulations, should be replaced with 'have been prepared in accordance with the requirements of the Trust Deed'.

45 Solicitors' Accounts Rules

45.1 Background

The rules dealing with solicitors' accounts are contained in the SRA Accounts Rules 2011 ('the Rules'). The Solicitors Regulation Authority (SRA) is the independent regulatory body for solicitors in England and Wales.

The Rules, together with the SRA Authorisation Rules 2011 and the SRA Indemnity Rules 2012 can be found in the SRA Handbook, version 19 of which was issued on 1 November 2017. Further details and guidance can be found in the Croner-i publications *Solicitors and Other Client Money Programmes* and the *Solicitor's Industry Accounting and Auditing Guide*, available online at Croner-i Tax and Accounting.

45.1.1 Summary of recent changes

All practising solicitors who, at any time during an accounting period, held or received client money, or operated a client's own account as signatory, must obtain an accountant's report for that accounting period within six months of the end of the accounting period. If the report has been qualified, the solicitor is responsible for delivering it to the SRA within six months of the end of the accounting period.

There have been a number of changes to the reporting regime over the past few years. In November 2014, the Rules were changed to require submission of accountants' reports to the SRA only where they contained qualifications. For periods ending on or after 1 November 2015, a new format of report was introduced with changes to the Rules to require qualification of the report only in respect of material breaches and/or significant weaknesses in the firm's systems and controls for compliance with the Accounts Rules; and to remove Rule 39 which covered defined procedures to be undertaken by the reporting accountant.

The SRA issued its own guidance related to the changes *Guidance on completing the new annual accountant's report (AR1 form)*. The ICAEW has also issued a Technical Release, TECH 16/15AAF *Solicitors Regulation Authority (SRA) Accounts Rules: interim guidance for reporting accountants following changes to the accountant's report requirements*.

This section deals with the reporting regime as at 30 April 2018. However, following a recent consultation, the SRA is planning further changes to the regime although it is not yet clear when new rules will come into effect. An overview of the consultation and possible future changes is covered in the future developments section (**45.6**).

45.1.2 Compliance with the rules

Ten high level Principles overlay the Rules. These are mandatory and underpin all aspects of regulation, including the Rules.

A firm's first point of reference when considering compliance with the Rules must always be the principles set out in **Table 1**.

TABLE 1: High level principles

- uphold the rule of law and the proper administration of justice;

- act with integrity;

- not allow your independence to be compromised;

- act in the best interests of each client;

- provide a proper standard of service to your clients;

- behave in a way that maintains the trust the public places in you and in the provision of legal services;

- comply with your legal and regulatory obligations and deal with your regulators and ombudsman in an open, timely and cooperative manner;

- run your business or carry out your role in the business effectively and in accordance with proper governance and sound financial and risk management principles;

- run your business or carry out your role in the business in a way that encourages equality of opportunity and respect for diversity; and

- protect client money and assets.

The Rules apply to 'you' (as defined in Rule 2) and include ABSs (licensed bodies), and their managers and employees, as well as if you are a solicitor, a registered European lawyer (REL), a registered foreign lawyer (RFL), a recognised body or a licensed body. There are additional categories and detailed definitions contained in Rule 4. The Rules apply to all those who carry on or work in a firm and to the firm itself. In relation to multi-disciplinary practices (MDPs), the Rules apply only in respect of those activities for which the practice is regulated by the SRA.

Solicitors who practise outside England and Wales are governed by Part 7 of the Rules. These are similar to the rules governing those who practice in England and Wales, but are less detailed and less onerous in their requirements.

All practising solicitors (subject to the exemptions below) who handle clients' money are required to obtain a report confirming their compliance with the Rules within six months of the solicitor's firm's year end. This must be given by an authorised reporting accountant. Firms are not required to submit a report if:

- all of the client money held or received during an accounting period is money held or received from the Legal Aid Agency or in the circumstances set out in rule 19.3; or

- in the accounting period, the statement or passbook balance of client money you have held or received does not exceed:

  (i)   an average of £10,000; and

  (ii) a maximum of £250,000,

  or the equivalent in foreign currency.

The report is only required to be submitted to the SRA if it contains qualifications. The responsibility for delivery is that of the firm and not the reporting accountant. A clean accountant's report must be retained by the law firm and also the reporting accountant for a period of six years, for inspection on request by the SRA.

45.1.3   Objective

The purpose of the Rules is to keep client money safe. More specifically, as stated in Rule 1, 'you' must:

- keep other people's money separate from money belonging to you or your firm, safely in a bank or building society account identifiable as a client account; ensure that each client's money is used for that client's matters only;

- ensure that money held as trustee of a trust is used for the purposes of that trust only;

- establish and maintain proper accounting systems, proper internal controls over those systems, and proper accounting records to ensure compliance with the rules and accurately show the position with regard to the money held for each client or trust;

- account for interest on other people's money in accordance with the rules;

- cooperate with the SRA in checking compliance; and

- obtain annual accountant's reports as required by the rules.

All the principals in a practice must ensure compliance with the rules both by themselves and by everyone employed in the practice. This duty also extends to the directors of a recognised body or a licensed body which is a company, or to the members of a recognised body which is an LLP. The Rules also extend this duty to the Compliance Officer for Finance and Administration (COFA) of a firm (whether the COFA is a manager or non-manager). Under r. 8.5(e) of the SRA Authorisation Rules 2011, the COFA must keep a record of any failure to comply with the Rules for production to the SRA on request, and also report any breaches to the SRA.

Breaches of the Rules must be rectified promptly upon discovery, including the replacement of money improperly withheld or withdrawn from a client account. The duty to remedy breaches rests not only on the person causing or discovering the breach but also on all the principals. This duty extends to replacing missing client money from principals' own resources, even if the money has been misappropriated by an employee or another principal and whether or not a claim is made on the solicitors' indemnity or the Compensation Fund.

The basic principle is that any money received from a client by a solicitor must be paid into a client account unless it is received in respect of a bill rendered to the client for time costs or disbursements that have already been paid by the solicitor. Money may only be withdrawn from a client account in accordance with the client's instructions, or to settle a solicitor's fee after a fee invoice has been given to the client. The money earmarked for costs in the office account becomes office money and must be transferred out of the client account within 14 days of the fee invoice being raised. There are more specific and prescriptive rules/definitions regarding the receipt and transfer of costs in r. 17.

The books of account maintained by the solicitor must show the current balance on each client's ledger and balances must be reconciled with the cash books and the bank statements every five weeks. The records must be kept for a period of six years and any bank statements must be kept as issued and printed by the bank. Further details are contained in r. 29.

45.2 Engagement letter

There is a formal requirement for engagement letters to be issued to and agreed with solicitors by the reporting accountant and both parties must keep these for six years after termination of the retainer. Rule 35 details a number of terms which need to be incorporated into the engagement letter. An example of suitable paragraphs for inclusion in the engagement letter is shown in **Table 2**.

TABLE 2: Paragraphs to include in an engagement letter concerning whistle-blowing and other matters

In accordance with r. 35 of the SRA Accounts Rules 2011, we are instructed as follows:

(a) I/this firm/this company/this limited liability partnership recognises that, if during the course of preparing an accountant's report:

(i) we discover evidence of fraud or theft in relation to money:

(A) held by a solicitor (or registered European lawyer, or registered foreign lawyer, or recognised body, or licensed body, or employee of a solicitor or registered European lawyer, or manager or employee of a recognised body or licensed body) for a client or any other person (including money held on trust); or

(B) held in an account of a client, or an account of another person, which is operated by a solicitor (or registered European lawyer, registered foreign lawyer, recognised body, licensed body, employee of a solicitor or registered European lawyer, or manager or employee of a recognised body); or

(ii) we obtain information which we have reasonable cause to believe is likely to be of material significance in determining whether a solicitor (or registered European lawyer, or registered foreign lawyer, or recognised body, or licensed body, or employee of a solicitor or registered European lawyer, or manager or employee of a recognised body) is a fit and proper person:

(A) to hold money for clients or other persons (including money held on trust); or

(B) to operate an account of a client or an account of another person,

(iii) we discover a failure by the firm to submit a qualified accountant's report to the Solicitors Regulation Authority, as required by these rules,

we must immediately give a report of the matter to the Solicitors Regulation Authority if required to do so under the *Solicitors Act* 1974, s. 34(9) or the *Legal Services Act 2007 (Designation as a Licensing Authority) (No. 2) Order* 2011, art. 3(1) as appropriate;

(b) we may, and are encouraged to, make that report without prior reference to you;

(c) we are to report directly to the Solicitors Regulation Authority should our appointment be terminated following the issue of, or indication of intention to issue, a qualified accountant's report, or following the raising of concerns prior to the preparation of an accountant's report;

(d)   we are to deliver to you our report which you should retain for at least six years from the date of its signature and to produce the copy to the Solicitors Regulation Authority on request;

(e)   you are to retain these terms of engagement for at least six years after the termination of the retainer and to produce them to the Solicitors Regulation Authority on request; and

(f)   following any direct report made to the Solicitors Regulation Authority under (a) or (c) above, we are to provide to the Solicitors Regulation Authority on request any further relevant information in our possession or in the possession of our firm.

To the extent necessary to enable us to comply with (a) to (f) above, you waive your right of confidentiality. This waiver extends to any report made, document produced or information disclosed to the Solicitors Regulation Authority in good faith pursuant to these instructions, even though it may subsequently transpire that we were mistaken in our belief that there was cause for concern.

45.2.1   'Whistle-blowing'

In addition to the accountant's obligations under money laundering regulations (see **Section 18**), the reporting accountant has a mandatory whistle-blowing duty if he discovers evidence of fraud or theft in relation to money:

- held by a solicitor (or registered European lawyer, registered foreign lawyer, recognised body, or licensed body, or employee of a solicitor or registered European lawyer, or manager or employee of a recognised body or licensed body) for a client or any other person (including money held on trust); or

- held in an account of a client, or an account of another person, which is operated by a solicitor (or registered European lawyer, registered foreign lawyer, recognised body, or licensed body, employee of a solicitor or registered European lawyer, or manager or employee of a recognised body or licensed body).

The mandatory whistle-blowing duty also applies if he obtains information which gives reasonable cause to believe it is likely to be of material significance in determining whether a solicitor is a fit and proper person to hold money for clients or other persons (including money held on trust), or to operate an account of a client or an account of another person.

The reporting accountant is encouraged to report directly to the SRA, without reference to the solicitors.

Matters which may indicate a requirement on the reporting accountant to report to the SRA include:

- false accounting, theft or misappropriation by any solicitor in the firm;

- evidence of theft or misappropriation by any employee, fee-earner, consultant or third party not reported to the police authorities;

- evidence leading to concerns about honesty or integrity of any solicitor;

- evidence of attempted tax evasion (either direct or indirect taxes);

- failure to properly control client money;

- failure to keep proper accounting records under the Accounts Rules which is so significant that the reporting accountant is unable to express an opinion in his report;

- failure to take professional advice without due consideration;

- evidence of indifference or recklessness in connection with client money or operation of a client's own account as signatory; or

- any other matters or indications of fraud or theft in connection with client money or operation of a client's own account as signatory.

Please note that the above indicators were taken from the Solicitor's Accounts Rules 1998 and not the SRA Accounts Rules 2011, but they are still considered to be good indicators of when a whistle-blowing obligation might arise.

45.2.2   Termination of appointment

The reporting accountant is also required to communicate with the SRA on the termination of his appointment where this has arisen from the issue of, or an indication of the intention to issue, a qualified accountant's report or following the raising of concerns prior to the preparation of an accountant's report.

45.2.3   Independence

Reporting accountants must document any possible connections with the solicitors that may influence their independence.

Typical factors that should be considered include whether the reporting accountant, his principals, directors, members or employees of the accountancy practice:

- are related to the solicitor;

- normally maintain the solicitor's client accounts;

- place substantial reliance on the solicitor for referral of clients;

- are clients or former clients of the solicitor; and

- whether there are any other circumstances which may affect the reporting accountant's independence.

45.3 Procedures

The reporting accountant should:

- determine for himself what is the correct type and level of work to be performed for each particular law firm – based on their professional assessment of risk, the size of the law firm and the range of services provided; and

- qualify the report only in respect of 'material breaches of the Accounts Rules and/or significant weaknesses in the firm's systems and controls for compliance with the Accounts Rules'.

Rule 43A states:

'43A.1 The accountant should exercise his or her professional judgement in determining the work required for the firm they are instructed to obtain the report on in order to assess risks to client money arising from compliance with these rules. This should cover the work that the accountant considers is appropriate to enable completion of the report required by the SRA at the date the report is commissioned.'

The most notable impact of Rule 43A is that it now falls to the reporting accountant, to decide on the actual work and to report based explicitly on risk assessment and judgment.

The latest accountant's report (AR1) together with guidance notes prepared by the SRA can be located at www.sra.org.uk/AR1.

Accountants should closely consider both the contents of the form and the guidance notes and examples of what are considered likely to be qualifications contained therein.

The SRA has emphasised that the examples in its guidance are intended to be helpful but are not definitive nor prescriptive, and the reporting accountant is expected to exercise professional judgment in completing the AR1 accountant's report form, whether qualified or not.

In practice, reporting accountants will need to focus on the systems and controls and documenting their methodology to support both the type of work they are undertaking and the volume in the context of the risk profile of their client.

Under Rule 43A, sufficient time should be spent at the planning stage in tailoring any work programmes used to match the specific law firm involved. This will be important to ensure that the work is directed in the most appropriate areas for the law firm concerned and its specific risk profile. It will also be important in terms of being able to justify to the SRA the sufficiency of the work undertaken.

Holding a planning meeting with the COLP (Compliance Officer for Legal Practice), COFA (Compliance Officer for Finance and Administration) and/or the firm's finance team is perhaps a useful source of information at the planning stage to identify and discuss risks with the client.

Under Rule 43A, there is there is an expectation that the reporting accountant will consider the control systems and procedures that a law firm has in place. This involves some consideration and work being directed to:

- documenting the control systems (both IT and non-IT controls);

- assessing their adequacy/effectiveness for their intended purpose; and

- testing the application of the control systems.

The SRA has confirmed that there is no intention to drive the work of the reporting accountant towards a controls-based approach. The SRA expects the reporting accountant to undertake a risk based approach towards planning the work and expects substantive testing to form a significant element of the reporting accountants work.

The SRA requires reporting accountants to assess compliance with the provisions of certain elements of the Accounts Rules. Work programmes will need to be modified to take these into account. These are specified in the accountant's report. These provisions are:

- Rule 1 The overarching objective and underlying principles;

- Rule 7 Duty to remedy breaches;

- Rule 13 Client accounts;

- Rule 14 Uses of a client account;

- Rule 17 Receipt and transfer of costs;

- Rule 18 Receipt of mixed payments;

- Rule 20 Withdrawals from a client account;

- Rule 21 Method of and authority for withdrawal from a client account;

- Rule 27 Restrictions on transfers between clients;

- Rule 29 Accounting records for client accounts.

If the circumstances outlined in Rule(s) 8, 9, 10, 15, 16 and 19 are applicable, the accountant is required to assess compliance accordingly.

It will be the responsibility of the reporting accountant to assess the nature and amount of work they should perform given the risk profile of the client. Areas considered low risk may therefore involve less work compared to high risk areas. This will vary firm by firm and should be documented in the planning sections of the file.

The ICAEW Technical Release provides some useful guidance on possible reduced areas of work and also where more work might need to be focused. Examples of areas where historically few breaches have arisen, and hence which could be deemed low risk might include:

- checking transactions from the bank statements to transaction records or nominal ledger;
- detailed testing of bills of costs to transaction records;
- paid cheque testing;
- detailed transactional testing work at reconciliation dates; and
- reliance on bank audit letters at the two selected dates.

Conversely, work may need to be focused in the following areas:

- review of monthly client funds three way reconciliations across the year;
- greater focus on the office account and office account reconciliations as a source of breaches;
- review of client funds reconciliation to look for shortfalls/differences compared to the bank balances and how these are managed and dealt with (as opposed to the current regime of examining two specific dates in detail);
- reviewing instances of suspense accounts being used and compliance of their use with the SRA Accounts Rules; and
- testing treatment of old residual balances – specifically for sweeping up, acting as banker and charging of inappropriate expenses.

45.3.1 The role of the reporting accountant

In the vast majority of cases, despite the changes made in the last few years, reporting accountants will find the same sort of issues they have found in the past. There is also no reason to suggest that reporting accountants will identify different types of risks to client money or serious breaches.

The key difference is that there is now guidance from the SRA, referred to above, to help reporting accountants conclude on which of the breaches/ weaknesses they identify are material/significant and reportable to the SRA on the AR1 accountant's report form, and which are reportable only to the law firm by way of management letter or discussions with the COFA and/or COLP. As noted in **45.1.1**, the ICAEW technical release TECH 16/15 AAF is also a useful point of reference. This includes an appendix covering examples of material breaches and significant weaknesses in systems/controls. A further appendix discusses some of the most common, and in some cases potentially more serious, breaches of the Rules, with examples of potential conclusions on the qualification of an accountant's report.

A fundamental challenge remains for reporting accountants, in that their perceived risk and exposure to the SRA will be deemed to be reduced if they qualify the accountant's report. On the other hand, the reporting accountant may also come under pressure from law firms not to qualify the accountant's report and may not come to the same conclusion about whether a breach/weakness is considered material/significant or not.

In a situation where there was an adverse client fund issue with a law firm where no qualification had been issued in the accountant's report by the reporting accountant, the ICAEW have provided guidance which states that if the reporting accountant can demonstrate:

- a reasonable understanding of the systems, procedures, transactions and control systems that the law firm has in place and were operative in the relevant period;
- that they have planned and undertaken an appropriate level of work in completing the accountant's report; and
- that they have formed reasonable and well-supported conclusions based upon the information received and matters of concern identified,

the SRA would not take the view that the work they have performed nor conclusions reached were inadequate in the event that the law firm or the SRA subsequently identifies a risk to or actual loss of client funds in the law firm concerned.

45.4 Common breaches

The reporting accountant should ensure that he is aware of the following areas as part of his knowledge of the business, as they are the common areas in which solicitors breach the Rules. The ICAEW technical release provides other useful examples.

45.4.1 Debit balances

No client account may go into debit in the solicitor's ledger. Each client should be treated in isolation and it is not permissible to net off debits and credits on the client ledger. This would indicate a shortage of funds that should be disclosed.

The SRA does not allow debit balances to be offset against credit balances when stating the liabilities to clients as shown by the ledgers on the accountant's report form.

45.4.2 Client confidentiality

Solicitors may refuse to allow the accountant access to certain documents (privileged documents) on the grounds of client confidentiality (or privilege) and where this is the case the accountant should qualify the report, setting out the circumstances.

45.4.3 'Without delay'

'Without delay' is defined in the Rules as meaning, in normal circumstances, the day of receipt or the next working day. This means that solicitors must have procedures to ensure that cheque receipts are banked 'without delay'. Any cheques that are not banked within this time period will constitute a breach of the Rules.

45.4.4 Receipt and transfer of costs – the '14 day rule'

Rule 17.2 states that a bill of costs or other written notification of costs must be sent to the client if payment of the solicitors' fees is required from money held in a client account. Once Rule 17.2 is complied with (i.e. the bill or notification has been sent), the money earmarked for costs becomes office money and must be transferred out of the client account within 14 days.

Guidance note (vii) to r. 17 gives an example of when costs are 'properly' due under r. 17.2 and should be transferred out of the client account. Guidance note (viii) explains what is meant by 'earmarking' in r. 17.3, and deals with the issue where the firm wants to obtain clients' prior approval of its costs.

45.4.5 Reconciliations

Rule 29.12 states that a three-way reconciliation between the client cash account, statement/passbook and the client ledger account of the liabilities to clients must be undertaken at least once every five weeks.

45.4.6 Prompt return of client money and residual balances

Rule 14.3 states that client money must be returned to the client (or other person on whose behalf the money is held) promptly, as soon as there is no longer any proper reason to retain those funds. Rule 14.4 goes on to state that the client must be informed in writing of the amount of any client money retained at the end of a matter (or the substantial conclusion of a matter), and the reason for that retention. This also needs to be done in writing at least once every 12 months thereafter, again covering off the amount of client money still held and the reason for the retention.

The reporting accountant should be aware of the above and, if considered a particular risk at planning, should design procedures beyond just sample examination of files/matters. As well as discussing the firm's systems and controls to deal with this requirement, the reporting accountant might consider checking exception reports of residual client balances. It is likely the firm's system will be able to generate reports showing residual balances or client balances where no time has been charged for a certain period of time.

45.4.7   *Providing bank facilities*

Rule 14.5 states that banking facilities should not be provided through a client account. Payments into, and transfers or withdrawals from, a client account must be in respect of instructions relating to an underlying transaction or to a service forming part of normal regulated activities provided to clients. During testing, the reporting accountant should be alert to transactions not involving normal legal activities, such as payment of school fees on a conveyancing matter or banking of cheques on behalf of a client. It is likely that any such instances identified by the reporting accountant will lead to a qualification as firms are strictly prohibited from providing banking facilities.

45.5   Reporting

The accountant's report has to be prepared by an accountant who is a member of one of the Institutes listed in Rule 34.1(a) who is also a registered auditor, and strict rules for its compilation are set out in Part 6 of the Rules.

Although it is called an accountant's report, many of the procedures involved are of an auditing nature, with a high degree of judgment in both the type of work to be undertaken and the classification of any breaches identified as material or not. The work is, however, still restricted to an examination of both client and office ledgers and the related bank accounts, and does not involve the audit of a profit and loss account and balance sheet of the practice. No accounts have to be filed with the SRA.

The reporting accountant is not required to check that the solicitor's practice holds professional indemnity insurance for the period covered by the report.

The reporting accountant is not required to complete a checklist covering the results of test checks, as prescribed by Rule 43. Along with Rule 39 this rule was removed in November 2015.

The accountant's report requires details of:

- firm details – the names used by the firm or in-house practice from the offices covered by this report. This must include the registered name of a recognised body/licensed body which is an LLP or company, and the name under which a partnership or sole practitioner is recognised;

- the period covered by the report;

- firm COFA;

- any qualification; and

- matters of significance.

There is a box in section 2 of the accountant's report form to include details of material breaches of the Accounts Rules and or significant weaknesses in the firm's systems and controls identified by the reporting accountant. The details given should be sufficient to enable the SRA to understand the nature of the breach and will have a section for client comments on the breaches.

45.6 Future developments

On 1 June 2016, the SRA issued for consultation a document entitled '*Looking to the Future: Accounts Rules review*' in which the SRA looked more widely at the existing Accounts Rules and made proposals for broader change. The formal consultation closed on 21 September 2016 and the SRA published its decisions and consultation response documents in July 2017 with the key changes being:

- new SRA principles that clearly and concisely state the high ethical standards expected of those regulated by the SRA;

- two new Codes of Conduct: The code for individuals sets out the professional standards and behaviours expected of solicitors in practice. The code for firms provides clarity on what their responsibilities are as regulated businesses;

- solicitors offering services outside SRA regulated firms: Solicitors will be able to offer non-reserved legal services outside of firms overseen by the SRA or another approved legal services regulator; and

- revised and streamlined Account Rules: New rules are intended to strip out unnecessary bureaucracy and focus on keeping clients' money safe.

The overriding aim was to create shorter, clearer principles and codes, as well as much simpler Accounts Rules.

Although the changes have been agreed, a new handbook will not be implemented before autumn 2018 and the SRA has not yet confirmed when the new Accounts Rules will be effective from. It will be consulting on phase 2 of 'Looking to the Future', which includes the rest of the rules and the SRA's approach to enforcement, later in 2018. The SRA has confirmed that all Handbook changes will be implemented together.

46 Investment businesses

46.1 PN 21 withdrawn

In November 2017, the FRC announced that it had withdrawn, with immediate effect, Practice Note 21 *The Audit of Investment Businesses in the United Kingdom*.

Much of the Practice Note, which was issued in 2007, had been superseded by the issue of the FRC's Client Asset Assurance Standard in 2015, and the remaining material was considered to be dated. The PN had not been updated to reflect revisions to ISAs (UK) in 2016. As a result, it was no longer considered appropriate to support high quality work.

Client asset reporting is covered in **Section 9**.

47   Registered Providers of Social Housing

The term 'Registered Providers of Social Housing' (or 'Registered Provider') was introduced by the *Housing and Regeneration Act* 2008. The previous term, 'Registered Social Landlord' (RSL) was introduced by the *Housing Act* 1996. Registered Providers can now come from the profit-making sector as well as the traditional non-profit making sector. They can include housing associations, local housing companies, registered housing charitable trusts and housing care and support agencies. Local authorities managing social housing were within the regulatory framework for the first time from 1 April 2010. From 1 April 2010, a broader range of providers, such as profit-making organisations, were able to become Registered Providers. The entry of new forms of provider was intended to create greater competition and encourage innovation and the delivery of greater value for money by existing providers.

The *Housing and Regeneration Act* 2008 brought about a fundamental change to the way that housing and regeneration are regulated and funded, including the formation of the Homes and Communities Agency (HCA), the national housing and regeneration agency in England. Similar agencies exist for Wales, Scotland and Northern Ireland, with similar statutory objects to those applicable in England.

The *Housing and Regeneration Act* 2008 states that the regulation function can only be exercised by the Homes and Communities Agency acting through an independent Regulation Committee. The Regulation Committee, as a statutory committee of the HCA, is responsible for the regulation of social housing.

Changes made to the *Homes and Planning Act* 2016 had an impact on social housing regulation. These came into effect from 6 April 2017. Among the changes, there is no longer the need for non-profit providers to seek the regulator's consent for restructures, disposals of social housing and changes to governing documents and providers need only notify the regulator for certain types of restructures.

On 11 January 2018, the HCA's non-regulation arm adopted a new trading name 'Homes England'. One of the statutory committees of the HCA is the Regulation Committee, which is responsible for the regulation of social housing. The HCA's regulation directorate, now refers to itself as the Regulator of Social Housing (RSH). Until legislation is enacted, Homes England and RSH continue to be constituted as one body – the HCA – but operate with two separate identities.

Homes England provides investment for new affordable housing and for improvements to existing social housing, as well as for regenerating land. Its remit is the 'delivery of sufficient new homes, where they are most needed, to deliver a sustained improvement in affordability'.

RSH is the regulator for social housing providers in England. The overall objective of RSH is to promote a viable, efficient and well-governed social housing sector that can deliver homes to meet a range of needs.

RSH also sets consumer standards and can intervene in cases of serious detriment that have caused, or are likely to cause, harm. Homes England and RSH operate throughout England, including a regulatory role in London. However, responsibility for housing and regeneration activity in London lies with the Greater London Authority.

The objectives of the Regulator are set out in the *Housing and Regeneration Act* 2008. RSH regulates private registered providers of social housing to promote a viable, efficient and well-governed social housing sector able to deliver homes that meet a range of needs.

Regulatory standards are set out in the *Regulatory Framework Requirements* which can be found at www.gov.uk/government/collections/regulatory-framework-requirements.

These are important documents for auditors of Registered Providers of Social Housing to be familiar with, covering:

- regulatory requirements – what registered providers need to comply with;
- codes of practice – to amplify any economic standard to assist registered providers in understanding how compliance might be achieved;
- regulatory guidance – provides further explanatory information on the regulatory requirements and includes how the regulator will carry out its role of regulating the requirements.

The regulatory requirements include:

- economic standards:
    - governance and financial viability (accompanied by a Code of Practice);
    - value for money;
    - rent;

- consumer standards:
  - tenant involvement and empowerment;
  - home;
  - tenancy;
  - neighbourhood and community;
- registration requirements;
- de-registration requirements;
- information submission requirements;
- the accounting direction for private registered providers of social housing from April 2015;
- disposal proceeds fund requirements;
- requirement to obtain regulator's consent to disposals;
- requirement to obtain regulator's consent to changes to constitutions.

Each standard sets out the high-level outcome that landlords should achieve, followed by a series of 'specific requirements' related to that outcome.

There is also regulatory guidance as follows:

- regulating the standards;
- rent standard guidance (part of) and associated guidance documents;
- registration guidance and application form guidance notes;
- de-registration guidance;
- NROSH+ guidance documents;
- guidance on intervention, enforcement and use of powers;
- guidance for constitutional consents, restructuring and dissolution;
- disposal proceeds fund guidance;
- disposing of Land, and application form guidance notes;
- procedural guidance notes for constitutional changes.

The approach of the HCA continues to be one of 'co-regulation' which means an expectation of robust self-regulation by the boards and councillors of registered providers who govern the delivery of housing services, incorporating effective tenant involvement.

Of particular note are requirements in relation to:

- records of assets and liabilities – particularly those liabilities that may have recourse to social housing assets;

- risk flows in group structures;

- stress testing of business plans against identified risks and combinations of risks across a range of scenarios;

- certification of compliance with the Governance and Financial Viability Standard within the annual report; and

- a Code of Practice designed to amplify the requirements in the Governance and Financial Viability Standard.

The above is not a comprehensive list of requirements and so auditors should obtain a copy of relevant regulatory documents from the HCA's website.

47.1 Existing audit guidance

47.1.1 Practice Note 14

In January 2014, the Financial Reporting Council issued Practice Note 14 *The Audit of Housing Associations in the United Kingdom*. This provides guidance for auditors on the audit of housing associations in the light of the landscape in which the social housing sector now operates.

The latest Practice Note contains the following four principal sections:

- background information about the social housing sector to provide context for the other three sections below;

- a description of the four devolved regulatory regimes, focusing on the interface between the regulator and the auditor and the regulators' viability assessments. Four appendices summarise the regulatory background relating to each regulator;

- a description of generic business risks that could adversely affect a housing association from achieving its objectives or successfully executing strategies. These are also risks which may give rise to a risk of material misstatement in a housing association's financial statements; and

- a discussion of audit risks, primarily arising from the above generic business risks, which the auditor is likely to need to pay particular attention to. This section is written in the context of special considerations relating to the audit of housing associations which arise from those ISAs (UK) which are listed in the contents of the Practice Note. The Practice Note does not provide any material where there are no special considerations arising from an ISA.

In June 2016, the FRC issued a suite of revised ISAs (UK) (see **1.6.4**). At the time of writing, however, Practice Note 14 had not been updated and still referred to the previous version of ISAs. References to ISAs within this section have, however, been updated to the most recent version where applicable.

47.2 Background

47.2.1 *The nature of Registered Providers*

Most existing Registered Providers are not-for-profit housing associations, managed under the oversight of a board, independently from local and central government. They provide social housing accommodation (usually made available at less than market rents and allocated to applicants in greatest housing need) and other related services. Councils managing social housing are also registered providers as are profit-making organisations where they are managing social housing.

Registered Providers operate under a variety of legal frameworks, including co-operative and community benefit societies, limited companies and charitable trusts. They are required, under legislation, to have an annual independent audit, although the specific auditing requirements will vary depending on the legal status. For example, some may be eligible to apply exemptions applicable to small companies, charities and co-operative and community benefit societies. For community benefit societies, for example, the *Co-operative and Community Benefit Societies Act* 2014 sets out criteria to disapply the requirements for appointment of auditors depending on certain financial thresholds and other factors. Advantage of these exemptions is only possible if permitted under the Rules under which they are incorporated.

Auditors of Registered Providers must be registered auditors, i.e. eligible under the Companies Act and registered with a supervisory body recognised under companies legislation.

Registered Providers undertake new building, refurbishment of existing property, acquisition of existing satisfactory properties or regeneration activities, with the aim of providing affordable, low cost rented accommodation. Some provide more specialised housing, including care and support, student accommodation and key worker accommodation. Under certain conditions such housing may be sold to tenants (e.g. right to buy, right to acquire and shared ownership). Increasingly, larger Registered Providers are involved in commercial development for outright sale and the private rented sector.

Auditors must understand the statutory framework of their social housing clients as this will affect audit reporting requirements. This does differ slightly between England, Wales, Scotland and Northern Ireland. The majority of Registered Providers in the United Kingdom are registered with the HCA under the *Housing and Regeneration Act* 2008 and the term given to that body is the 'Regulator'. Under certain pieces of legislation, the Regulator has the power to determine the accounting requirements of Registered Providers which will be important for the auditor to understand.

The constitution of Registered Providers or the legal rules under which they are incorporated usually prohibit them from distributing any surpluses or assets to shareholding members, even if they are non-charitable. Non-profit making organisations that are registered providers are required to have within their objects:

- the provision of social housing;
- not-for-profit status; and
- non-distribution of assets to members.

Where a Registered Provider is charitable, it is classed as an 'exempt charity'. They are subject to the Charities Act but their principal regulator is the HCA rather than the Charity Commission. Principal regulators must promote exempt charities' compliance with charity law.

Co-operative and Community Benefit Societies Act 2014

The majority of Registered Providers are co-operative and community benefit societies and most reference is made to a consolidating piece of legislation, the *Co-operative and Community Benefit Societies Act* 2014. The *Co-operative and Community Benefit Societies Act* 2014 came into force on 1 August 2014. It consolidated previous Acts and subsequent legislation to modernise and simplify it.

As co-operative and community benefit societies, they fall under the administrative jurisdiction of the mutual societies division of the Financial Conduct Authority (FCA). This means that their constitution comprises 'Rules' which must be registered with the FCA. They will be governed by a board which is appointed by the members. The *Co-operative and Community Benefit Societies Act* 2014 contains some basic requirements for the accounts and audit. It requires proper financial records to be kept and that all financial statements agree with those records, that there is a satisfactory system of internal control over transactions and that the financial statements show a true and fair view of the social housing provider's financial position.

Companies Act 2006

Registered Providers that are limited companies are incorporated under the Companies Act and are generally companies limited by guarantee without share capital. They will therefore need to comply with the *Companies Act* 2006 and the accounting directions issued by the relevant regulator, e.g. the HCA.

47.2.2 *Responsibilities of the board*

Although day-to-day management of the Registered Provider may be delegated to subcommittees or staff, the board retains full responsibility for seeing that those functions are properly carried out.

The regulatory framework for social housing in England from 1 April 2015 is made up of:

- regulatory requirements, namely the standards that a registered provider must comply with;

- codes of practice, which expand and provide guidance on any economic standard; and

- regulatory guidance, which includes detail as to how the regulator will perform their role in regulating the standards.

The Governance and Financial Viability Standard sets out the responsibilities of the board of a provider. The board is responsible for ensuring that there are effective governance arrangements that deliver their aims, objectives and intended outcomes for tenants and potential tenants in an effective, transparent and accountable manner. Governance arrangements shall ensure registered providers:

(a) adhere to all relevant law;

(b) comply with their governing documents and all regulatory requirements;

(c) are accountable to tenants, the regulator and relevant stakeholders;

(d) safeguard taxpayers' interests and the reputation of the sector;

(e) have an effective risk management and internal controls assurance framework; and

(f) protect social housing assets.

Useful guidance is available through various representative bodies, such as the National Housing Federation (NHF) in England (www.housing.org. uk). The mission of the NHF is to support and promote the work that housing associations do and campaign for better housing and neighbourhoods. Examples of guidance for those charged with governance include:

- *code of governance – Promoting board excellence for housing associations (2015 edition);*

- *board members' resource pack;* and

- *leadership and control: a governance manual for board members.*

The NHF produces many other publications for housing associations covering:

- finance;

- assurance;

- development and regeneration;

- housing management;

- care and support;

- legislation;

- asset management and maintenance; and

- equality and diversity.

47.2.3   Responsibilities of audit committees

There is no requirement by the regulator to establish an audit committee as part of the governance arrangements in a housing association, however in following the NHF Code of Governance, which advises that boards may establish committees where the board determines that they will provide expertise that will enable them to provide good governance, many associations do have an audit committee in place.

There is no specific sector guidance for the operation of such a committee. In April 2016, the FRC issued *Guidance on Audit Committees*, which, whilst aimed at the boards of listed entities in their compliance with the UK Corporate Governance Code, provides useful best practice for committees operating in the housing sector.

A copy of the guidance can be obtained from https://frc.org.uk/Our-Work/Publications/Corporate-Governance/Guidance-on-Audit-Committees-(2).pdf and this is further considered in section **42.8**.

47.2.4   Financial reporting requirements

Generally, each Registered Provider is required to prepare financial statements which give a true and fair view and hence should comply with applicable law and generally accepted accounting standards.

The financial statements of Registered Providers are prepared in accordance with the requirements of applicable law and regulations. The precise nature of the requirements is determined by two factors:

- how the Registered Provider is constituted (for example, as a co-operative and community benefit society or non-profit making company); and

- whether the Registered Provider is registered with a relevant regulatory body.

The *Housing and Regeneration Act* 2008 sets out the requirements for accounts and audit in s. 127–143.

The *Accounting Direction for Private Registered Providers of Social Housing from 2015*, issued in September 2015, sets out the disclosure requirements that must be followed by English registered providers of social housing when preparing their annual accounts.

The 2015 accounting direction is essential reading for auditors.

UK GAAP

FRS 102 *The Financial Reporting Standard applicable in the UK and Republic of Ireland* is applicable to registered providers of social housing. FRS 102 introduced some significant changes to accounting requirements having a particular impact in the social housing sector.

A revised Housing SORP, reflecting requirements of FRS 102, was published in September 2014 and is applicable for financial years beginning on or after 1 January 2015. *Housing SORP 2014 Statement of Recommended Practice for social housing providers* is available from the National Housing Federation (www.housing.org.uk) and is essential reading for auditors of registered providers of social housing.

Formats for statutory accounts are prescribed by the social housing regulator in the *Accounting Direction for Private Registered Providers of Social Housing from 2015*, which takes into consideration the requirements of FRS 102 and the Housing SORP 2014.

47.2.5 *Responsibilities of the auditor*

Although Registered Providers may be subject to different legislation, the statutory duties of auditors are similar to those of ordinary companies. The auditor is required to express an opinion as to whether the financial statements give a true and fair view and have been properly prepared in accordance with the appropriate statutory requirements.

Depending on the legislation under which the Registered Provider is incorporated there are a number of matters upon which the auditor must report by exception. These include (but are not limited to):

- the information given in the Report of the Board for the financial year for which the financial statements are prepared is not consistent with the financial statements;

- where proper books of account have not been kept;

- where a satisfactory system of control over transactions has not been maintained; and

- if the financial statements are not in agreement with the books and records of the Registered Provider.

There are often other reports which are requested of auditors, for example, reporting on loan agreements with lenders may include the need for the auditor to report on compliance with financial covenants.

47.2.6   Features of social housing audits

Risk profile

There are housing federations which represent the best interests of Registered Providers in the United Kingdom. Auditors should be aware of guidance issued by these federations, for example, codes of governance and finance updates.

The various UK regulators of registered providers of social housing also publish regular sector risk profiles. These focus on the financial risks that may cause a provider to fail to comply with economic standards, in particular, the viability element of the Governance and Financial Viability standard in England. The key message running through these sector risk profiles relates to the role and responsibility of boards to ensure effective governance and risk management is at the heart of their business. They highlight the importance of boards and executives in the co-regulatory environment. The same regulators often publish quarterly survey reports on the state of the social housing sector. These cover financial indicators for the sector as a whole covering areas such as income, rent arrears, void levels, asset sale values, borrowing headroom and capacity, development completions and exposure to standalone derivatives.

These sector risk profiles and quarterly surveys are essential reading for auditors to obtain an understanding of the wider operating environment in which registered providers operate.

Substantial debt financing

It is common for Registered Providers to have significant amounts of borrowing. It is important for Registered Providers to assess their medium-term financial forecasts to ensure that the going concern basis remains appropriate. Such debt financing often brings with it loan covenant compliance requirements which are often reported on by the statutory auditor.

The Auditing Practices Board (APB) Bulletin 2008/1, *Audit Issues when Financial Market Conditions are Difficult and Credit Facilities may be Restricted* and the update in APB Bulletin 2008/10, are particularly relevant to Registered Providers (see **Section 37**). Both focus on the possible risks of misstatement to the financial statements arising from:

- the possibility of the reduced availability of finance; and

- difficulties with valuing some assets for balance sheet purposes, especially those that are required to be measured at 'fair value'.

Housebuilding activities

Many Registered Providers now have an element of housebuilding activity, either as shared ownership or properties developed for outright sale. These face significant exposure to the housing market, with forecast sales receipts – particularly those from market sales – contributing significantly to access to liquidity. The ability to successfully mitigate sales risk is key in ensuring the long-term viability of a provider.

A number of Registered Providers have had their viability rating downgraded due to what is perceived to be an undue reliance on profits from housebuilding activities.

Complex direct tax, indirect tax and employee tax rules

Registered Providers are heavily involved in property transactions and this brings with it complex corporation tax, stamp duty land tax and VAT requirements. As many Registered Providers are charitable housing associations, they need to be aware of their primary purpose when considering property development contracts involving mixed tenure (e.g. developments where a scheme may include an element of commercial units and units for outright sale). Other examples of complexities include:

- group structures and most often the inability to be considered a group for tax purposes, i.e. group relief;

- conflicts between social housing accounting requirements under accounting standards, and the social housing SORP and the tax treatment, e.g. first tranche shared ownership sales;

813

- transfer pricing, loan relationships and qualifying charitable donations (often referred to as Gift Aid) which can add complexity;

- partial exemption treatment for VAT purposes;

- the use of development company subsidiaries outside the VAT group to maximise the recovery of VAT on professional fees;

- tax risks associated with joint ventures and the use of special purpose vehicles for acquiring land or undertaking property construction;

- potential difficulties for stock transfer associations in claiming input VAT on certain property refurbishment costs;

- the effect of employee tax for employees transferring from local authorities and tax deduction requirements on payments made to overseas landlords, e.g. under temporary leasing arrangements;

- construction industry scheme administration; and

- self-employed tax rules when using consultants, especially in busy property development departments.

Auditors should be aware of joint guidance issued in May 2009 by HMRC, the Charity Commission and the Homes and Communities Agency titled *Affordable Home Ownership – Charitable Status and Tax.* This guidance was issued because Registered Providers increasingly venture into commercial activities which may not always fit with their 'primary purpose' or charitable status. The guidance sets out the authorities' understanding of what may or may not qualify as being covered by the charitable tax exemptions and considers the question of whether particular individual families would be suitable beneficiaries. Registered Providers with home ownership activities such as shared ownership will be affected by this as will those developing residential property for outright sale. The guidance can be found on the Charity Commission's website at www.charity-commission.gov.uk and HMRC's website at www.hmrc.gov.uk.

ICAEW Technical Release TECH 16/14BL (Revised) considers donation of profits to charitable entities by subsidiary trading companies and the tax implications, including the application of Gift Aid rules. This could affect registered providers of social housing. The Technical Release addresses situations where the donated amounts exceed distributable profits of the trading subsidiary and the practical remediation steps open to group entities in respect of past payments. More information can be found on the ICAEW website at www.icaew.com/-/media/corporate/files/technical/technical-releases/legal-and-regulatory/tech16-14bl-guidance-for-donations-by-a-company-to-its-parent-charity.ashx.

Supported housing

Registered Providers involved in supported housing and providing care services have access to various sources of funding, e.g. in England, 'Supporting People'. A large amount of this funding is available through contracts with local authorities. These contracts can be complex and the available funding may not always be sufficient to deliver the service or they can be only for short periods of time making it challenging to assess the long-term viability of this business stream.

Housing properties

Where housing properties are carried at a valuation, the SORP mandates Existing Use Value – Social Housing as the basis to use. A professional valuation is often obtained and, as set out in ISA (UK) 620 (Revised June 2016) *Using the Work of an Auditor's Expert*, the auditor must consider the proper inclusion of the valuation in the accounts, the information on which the valuer has relied and the reasons for any changes in the valuation from the previous period.

Capitalisation of works to existing properties

The principles within accounting standards are followed and further guidance is given in the Housing SORP 2014.

The SORP mandates the use of component accounting for housing properties. Registered Providers are expected to allocate the cost of a property over the major components (typically roof, structure, kitchens, bathrooms, etc.) and depreciate each component over its useful economic life.

Where any major works represent a replacement component, the existing component is disposed of and the cost of the replacement component capitalised.

For other major works, the SORP recommends that those which result in an increase in the net rental income stream should be capitalised as improvements. This may arise from works carried out to existing properties, through a combination of increased rents, reduction in future maintenance costs or a significant extension to the life of the property. It is often difficult to demonstrate that any enhancement of the economic benefits of tangible fixed assets is in excess of the previously assessed standard of performance anticipated when the assets were first acquired, constructed, last replaced or revalued and should be capitalised.

Impairment

Accounting standards relevant to impairment are important considerations in social housing audits. Impairments can be triggered under many circumstances for a Registered Provider. The SORP gives examples of events that would be classed as a trigger event. If a trigger event occurs, then a detailed review should be performed.

47.2.7 The auditor's relationship with the Regulators

The *Housing and Regeneration Act* 2008 sets out the general requirements in respect of accounts and audit. Section 127 of this Act sets out the powers of the Regulator to issue accounts directions for Registered Providers. Section 143 concerns the disclosure of information by the auditor to the relevant authority.

This section applies to information that a person has received while acting as auditor or as a reporting accountant of a Registered Provider. Such persons may disclose the information to the regulator for a purpose connected with the regulator's functions:

- despite any duty of confidentiality; and

- whether or not the regulator requests the information.

The reference to disclosing information includes expressing an opinion on it.

Where a Registered Provider is regulated by the Financial Conduct Authority (FCA), then there is an obligation on the auditor to report to the FCA information which comes to the auditor's attention during the course of the audit that may be of material significance to the FCA. Further information is given in section **47.6.2** and **Section 9**.

47.3 Audit engagement letters

Audit engagement letters are covered by ISA (UK) 210 (Revised June 2016) *Agreeing the Terms of Audit Engagements*.

An example of an audit engagement letter for a Community Benefit Society is shown in **Table 1**. References to the legislation and other aspects of the letter would need to be amended for other types of entity.

Separate engagement letters should be prepared for engagements in relation to Registered Providers, which may arise:

- under statute – such as additional returns to be reviewed;

- from recommendations issued to Registered Providers within the various codes and other recommendations from the relevant regulatory body or relevant housing federation; or

- by agreement with the Registered Provider – for example loan covenant reporting.

The recommendations made to Registered Providers by their regulatory bodies are not themselves binding on auditors, but Registered Providers and their auditor may agree to increase the scope of the auditor's work to ensure that the Registered Provider complies with best practice. This would be a separate engagement from the statutory audit.

The terms of any additional engagements should be prepared in accordance with relevant guidance. The framework for reporting in connection with loan covenants is set out in guidance issued by the Consultative Committee of Accountancy Bodies and published as Audit Technical Release 04/00 by the ICAEW and agreed upon procedures work is typically performed under the provisions of International Standard on Related Services (ISRS) 4400 *Engagements to Perform Agreed upon Procedures Regarding Financial Information*. These are further considered in **Sections 40** and **41**.

Statutory requirements may also result in additional returns which a Registered Provider may request its auditor to review or sign, such as service charge summaries under the *Landlord and Tenant Act* 1985.

TABLE 1: Extract from an example engagement letter for a Registered Provider which is a Community Benefit Society

To the Board of [name of Registered Provider]

The purpose of this letter is to set out the basis on which we are to act as auditors of the association and the respective areas of responsibility of the Board, comprising those charged with governance of the association, and of ourselves.

Financial statements, accounting records and internal controls

As members of the Board of the association, you are responsible for maintaining adequate accounting records and an appropriate system of internal control for the association. You are also responsible for preparing the annual report and the financial statements which give a true and fair view and have been prepared in accordance with applicable accounting standards; the *Co-operative and Community Benefit Societies Act* 2014 and, where the society is the parent of a group, the *Co-operative and Community Benefit Societies (Group Accounts) Regulations* 1969; the *Housing and Regeneration Act* 2008; and the most recent applicable Accounting Determinations and/or Accounting Direction as periodically issued.

In preparing the financial statements, you are required to:

- select suitable accounting policies and then apply them consistently;

- make judgments and estimates that are reasonable and prudent; and

- prepare the financial statements on the going concern basis unless it is inappropriate to presume that the association will continue in business.

You are responsible for keeping adequate accounting records that:

- show and explain the association's transactions;

- disclose with reasonable accuracy at any time the association's financial position; and

- enable you to ensure that the financial statements comply with the *Co-operative and Community Benefit Societies Act* 2014 and, where the society is the parent of a group, the *Co-operative and Community Benefit Societies (Group Accounts) Regulations* 1969; the *Housing and Regeneration Act* 2008; and the most recent applicable Accounting Direction as periodically issued.

You are also responsible for safeguarding the assets of the association and hence for taking reasonable steps to prevent and detect fraud and other irregularities.

As the board, you have a duty to prepare a board report for each financial year. You should have regard to the relevant Statements of Recommended Practice and Accounting Direction.

The *Co-operative and Community Benefit Societies Act* 2014 requires that as Board members you must prepare financial statements that give a true and fair view of the assets, liabilities, financial position and surplus or deficit of the association and the group.

It is usual for a statement of your responsibilities to be included in the board report or elsewhere in the annual report. We will refer to this statement in our report.

You are responsible for filing the financial statements with the registrar and with other regulators within the requisite time limits. Failure to do so can result in action being taken against yourself and the association.

You are responsible for ensuring that the association complies with laws and regulations that apply to its activities, and for preventing non-compliance and detecting any that occurs.

You are required by law to make available to us, as and when required, all the association's accounting records and related financial information, including minutes of management and board meetings, that we need to do our work. We are entitled to require from the officers of the association such information and explanations we think necessary for the performance of our audit. We are also entitled to attend all general meetings of the association and to receive all notices of, and other communications relating to such meetings.

Disclosure of information to auditors

You agree that the members of the board, having made enquiries of fellow members of the board and the association's auditors, will state in the board report that:

- so far as they are aware, there is no relevant audit information of which the association's auditors are unaware; and

- they have taken all reasonable steps they ought to have taken as board members in order to make themselves aware of any relevant audit information and to establish that the association's auditors are aware of that information.

Electronic publication

We recognise that you may wish to publish your financial statements and our audit report on your website or distribute them by means such as e-mail. If you choose to do so, it is your responsibility to ensure that such publication properly presents the financial information and any auditors' report.

You agree to advise us of any intended electronic publication before it occurs, and we reserve the right to withhold consent to the electronic publication of our audit report if we assess the audited financial statements or our report to be published in an inappropriate manner.

The members of the board are responsible for the controls over, and security of, the website used for this purpose, and examination of these controls is beyond the scope of our audit of the financial statements. You are also responsible for establishing and controlling the process for electronically distributing Annual Reports and other financial information to members.

If you choose to publish our audit report electronically, the following wording must also be published:

'*Financial statements are published on the association's website in accordance with legislation in the United Kingdom governing the preparation and dissemination of financial statements, which may vary from legislation in other jurisdictions. The maintenance and integrity of the association's website is the responsibility of the members of the board. The responsibility of the members of the board also extends to the ongoing integrity of the financial statements contained therein.*'

Access to audit working papers

Our working papers and other internal documentation created for the purpose of carrying out our duties as auditors belong solely to Example Firm LLP and will not be provided to you. We may however be required to give access to our audit working papers for regulatory purposes or because of other statutory obligations.

Where consolidated financial statements are produced, the Financial Reporting Council's staff may request access to audit working papers produced in relation to other affiliated or subsidiary parts of your group. This includes those entities located overseas, whether or not Example Firm LLP has acted as auditor. Where relevant, you agree to take all steps considered reasonable and necessary to ensure that your overseas affiliated and subsidiary entities comply with such requests.

Our responsibilities as auditors

Audit under the Co-operative and Community Benefit Societies Act 2014

The responsibility for safeguarding the assets of the association and for the prevention and detection of fraud, error and non-compliance with law or regulations rests with yourselves. However, we shall endeavour to plan our audit so that we have a reasonable expectation of detecting material misstatements in the financial statements or accounting records (including those resulting from fraud, error or non-compliance with law or regulations), but our examination should not be relied upon to disclose all such material misstatements or frauds, errors or instances of non-compliance as may exist.

Under the *Insolvency Act* 1986, you have a statutory duty of care to the creditors of the association. You must ensure that the association does not continue to trade if there is no reasonable prospect of avoiding insolvent liquidation. If during our audit, any factors come to our attention that indicate such a possibility we shall of course inform you. However, this will not relieve you of your statutory and other duties as members of the board.

The law requires us to report to the members of the association whether, in our opinion:

- the financial statements give a true and fair view of the state of the association's affairs and of its surplus or deficit for the year;

- the financial statements have been properly prepared in accordance with the relevant financial reporting framework; and

- the financial statements have been properly prepared in accordance with the *Co-operative and Community Benefit Societies Act* 2014 and, where the society is the parent of a group, the *Co-operative and Community Benefit Societies (Group Accounts) Regulations* 1969; the *Housing and Regeneration Act* 2008; and the most recent applicable Accounting Direction as periodically issued.

The law also requires us to consider whether:

- adequate accounting records have been kept by the association;

- the association has maintained a satisfactory system of control over its transactions;

- the association's individual accounts are in agreement with the accounting records and returns; and

- we have obtained all the information and explanations which we think are necessary for the purposes of our audit.

We will plan and perform our audit work to anticipate issuing an audit report in accordance with ISAs (UK). Should we conclude it to be necessary, our opinion on the financial statements will be modified in accordance with ISAs (UK) 705 and 706 as appropriate.

We are required to read the other information issued with audited financial statements and to consider whether it is consistent with the financial statements. This other information would include, where applicable, a chairman's statement, operating and financial review, financial highlights, corporate governance statement, the board's statement on internal control, etc. If we become aware of any apparent misstatements or material inconsistencies with the financial statements, we draw these to your attention. We will include in our report a description of our responsibilities in relation to the other information together with a statement that we have nothing to report in this regard or details of any uncorrected material misstatements of the other information we believe to exist.

We also have a professional responsibility to refer in our report to instances of material non-compliance with applicable accounting standards. We do not need to refer in our report to those areas where, in our opinion, the non-compliance is necessary for the financial statements to show a true and fair view and is adequately disclosed.

Scope of audit

Our audit will be conducted in accordance with International Standards on Auditing (UK) and will have particular regard to the FRC's Practice Note applicable to registered providers of social housing. It will include such tests of transactions and of the existence, ownership and valuation of assets and liabilities as we consider necessary. We shall obtain an understanding of the accounting and internal control systems in order to assess their adequacy as a basis for the preparation of the financial statements and to establish whether adequate accounting records have been maintained by the association. We shall expect to obtain such appropriate evidence as we consider sufficient to enable us to draw reasonable conclusions therefrom.

The nature and extent of our procedures will vary according to our assessment of the association's accounting system and, where we wish to place reliance on it, the internal control system, and may cover any aspect of the business's operations that we consider appropriate.

Because of the test nature and other inherent limitations of an audit, together with the inherent limitations of any accounting and internal control system, there is an unavoidable risk that even some material misstatements may remain undiscovered.

Our audit is not designed to identify all significant weaknesses in the association's systems but, if such weaknesses come to our notice during the course of our audit which we think should be brought to your attention, we shall report them to you.

We shall request sight of all documents or statements which are due to be issued with the financial statements.

Representations by management/board members

From time to time, we may have to rely on oral representations by management, which are uncorroborated by other audit evidence. Where they relate to matters which are material to the financial statements, we will request that you provide written confirmation of them. In particular, where misstatements in the financial statements that we bring to your attention are not adjusted, we are required to obtain your reasons in writing.

Use of reports

As noted above, our report will be made solely to the association's members, as a body, in accordance with the *Co-operative and Community Benefit Societies Act* 2014, s. 87 and the *Housing and Regeneration Act* 2008. Our audit work will be undertaken so that we might state to the association's members those matters we are required to state to them in an auditors' report and for no other purpose. In those circumstances, and to the fullest extent permitted by law, we will not accept or assume responsibility to anyone other than the association and the association's members as a body, for our audit work, for the audit report, or for the opinions we form.

We shall not be treated as having notice, for the purposes of our audit responsibilities, of information provided to members of our firm other than those engaged on the audit (for example, information provided in connection with accounting, taxation and other services).

Once we have issued our report, we have no further direct responsibility in relation to the financial statements for that financial year. However, where a general meeting is held at which the financial statements are laid, we expect that you will inform us of any material event occurring between the date of our report and the date of that meeting.

Communication with those charged with governance

We will communicate certain information to you, including:

- any matters relevant to the firm's independence and the integrity and objectivity of the audit engagement partner and audit staff;

- an outline of the nature and scope of the work that we propose to undertake;

- our views about the qualitative aspects of the association's accounting practices and financial reporting;

- uncorrected misstatements other than those that are clearly trivial; and

- material weaknesses in internal control identified during the audit.

Such communication may be oral or in writing. However, we will report in writing any findings from the audit that we consider to be significant or to confirm that there are no matters that we wish to report in writing. Any such report may not be disclosed to third parties without our prior written consent. Such consent will be granted only on the basis that such reports are not prepared with the interests of anyone other than the association in mind and that we accept no duty or responsibility to any other party as concerns the reports.

Communication

In carrying out the engagement, it may be necessary for us to communicate with auditors of divisions and subsidiary, associated or joint undertakings and to arrange for them to perform such work as we consider necessary. As part of this process, we may request you to communicate with directors or management of divisions and subsidiary, associated or joint undertakings in order to explain and expedite the necessary procedures.

If the association operates any pension or post-retirement benefit schemes, it may be necessary for us to communicate with the association's actuary in connection with accounting entries and disclosures in the financial statements relating to such schemes. You hereby give us permission to communicate directly with the actuary in order to establish the basis and reliability of the figures and information in the financial statements on which we are required to report.

47.4 Quality control

ISA (UK) 220 (Revised June 2016) *Quality Control for an Audit of Financial Statements* requires the engagement partner to be satisfied that the engagement team collectively has the appropriate capabilities, competence and time to perform the audit engagement in accordance with professional standards and regulatory and legal requirements, and to enable an auditor's report that is appropriate in the circumstances to be issued. For a registered provider of social housing, this should include:

- the scope and nature of the activities of the Registered Provider;

- the most significant parts of the relevant regulator's guidance; and

- the relevant general principles of the social housing SORP.

47.5 Responsibilities relating to fraud

ISA (UK) 240 (Revised June 2016) *The Auditor's Responsibilities Relating to Fraud in an Audit of Financial Statements* is of relevance to social housing due to the nature of the sector's assets and activities. Registered Providers have been encouraged by their respective regulatory bodies to establish adequate internal controls and to report frauds over a certain limit to their regulator. All frauds should be recorded in a fraud register.

As part of his risk assessment, the auditor should review any disclosures to the regulator and enquire whether the regulatory body has responded.

Various external issues could influence a Registered Provider's objectives and strategies. The auditor should be aware of the increase in consolidation within the sector, the increased focus on efficiency and cost control, and the desire to become or remain a HCA development partner. Registered Providers often also have significant borrowings with covenants attached (generally interest cover and gearing covenants). This may create pressures on the entity that, in turn, may motivate management to take action to improve the reported business performance, boost reserves for gearing purposes or to misstate the financial statements.

Where the auditor suspects that there may be any matters which he believes should be included in the fraud register, he should document his findings and, subject to any requirement to report them directly to a third party, raise them with senior management or a board member as soon as possible. He should also consider reporting the matter to the board and audit committee once he is aware of all the circumstances. When considering the appropriate person to discuss these matters with the auditor should bear in mind the management structure of the Registered Provider.

There is no requirement for the auditor to report suspected instances of fraud to a regulatory body unless he considers it a matter of public interest or, in the case of an unincorporated, non-exempt charity, he believes it would be a matter of material significance in the exercise of the Charity Commission's functions. **Section 47.2.7** sets out the implications of reporting matters to the regulator.

47.6   Laws and regulations

47.6.1   ISA (UK) 250 Section A (Revised December 2017) – Consideration of Laws and Regulations in an Audit of Financial Statements

The law relating to a specific Registered Provider depends on:

- whether the Registered Provider is constituted as a registered charity, a society registered under the *Co-operative and Community Benefit Societies Act* 2014 or as a non-profit making company; and

- which regulatory body has granted registration to the Registered Provider.

Although, as noted above, the regulations imply that the financial statements of a Registered Provider should be prepared in accordance with the social housing SORP, consideration must also be given to any specific requirements of its governing document.

The auditor should perform further audit procedures to help identify instances of non-compliance with those laws and regulations where non-compliance should be considered when preparing financial statements, specifically:

(a) inquiring of management as to whether the entity is in compliance with such laws and regulations;

(b) inspecting correspondence with the relevant licensing or regulatory authorities, e.g. the HCA; and

(c) enquiring of those charged with governance as to whether they are on notice of any such possible instances of non-compliance with law or regulations.

In the UK and Ireland, the auditor's procedures should be designed to help identify possible or actual instances of non-compliance with those laws and regulations which provide a legal framework within which the Registered Provider conducts its business and which are central to its ability to conduct its business and hence to its financial statements.

Laws and regulations which are likely to be central to a Registered Provider are those where a breach would have any of the following consequences:

- intervention by the regulatory body to direct the affairs of the Registered Provider – for example, non-compliance with the various laws relating to fraud and corruption under which the regulatory body possesses various powers of intervention;

- loss of necessary licences to continue a major element of the Registered Provider's work – primarily laws and regulations applicable to building and planning regulations or contaminated land, or health and safety regulations in relation to homes in multiple occupation; or

- financial effects resulting in liabilities which are likely to exceed the available resources of the Registered Provider – for example, expenditure or activities outside grant conditions imposed by the regulatory body which may lead to disallowance and repayment of grant.

Auditors of Registered Providers other than unincorporated charities have no statutory duty to report suspected or actual instances of non-compliance with the law or regulations to an appropriate authority, unless they believe it should be reported in the public interest.

Given the significant cash flows involved in the purchase and development of land, all Registered Providers should be aware of the risk of money laundering (see **Section 18**).

Instances of non-compliance with laws or regulations identified by the auditor should be reported to the appropriate level of management. However, if management are involved in the breach, the auditor may consider it appropriate to communicate with the Board.

The Governance and Financial Viability Standard requires all boards to assess their compliance with the standard at least once a year. Part of the requirement of the standard is that boards have in place a governance structure to ensure that they adhere to all relevant law and regulations.

Their compliance with the Governance and Financial Viability Standard should be certified in the financial statements. Therefore, auditors should be able to obtain from management appropriate documentation to support the statement made in the financial statements that can form the basis of audit testing in this area.

47.6.2 ISA (UK) 250 Section B (Revised June 2016)

Where a Registered Provider of social housing is regulated by the Financial Conduct Authority (FCA), it falls within the scope of ISA (UK) 250 Section B (Revised June 2016) – *The Auditor's Statutory Right and Duty to Report to Regulators of Public Interest Entities and Regulators of Other Entities in the Financial Sector.*

The FCA took over regulation of consumer credit from the Office of Fair Trading (OFT) in April 2014. Registered Providers may not carry out consumer credit activities unless authorised to do so.

Since 21 March 2016, changes to the Mortgage Credit Directive mean that the rules changed to bring second charge mortgage lending (such as HomeBuy) into the wider mortgage regime rather than the consumer credit regime. Where the lender is a Registered Provider these loans will be treated differently.

Those loans entered into on or after 1 April 2014 are exempt but loans that were entered into before 1 April 2014, and which were regulated credit agreements when they were entered into or became regulated credit agreements before that date, are to remain regulated under the *Consumer Credit Act* 1974 and did not move into the mortgage regime from 21 March 2016.

This change means that housing associations need the relevant consumer credit permission to continue holding such loans ('exercising, or having the right to exercise, the lender's rights and duties under a regulated credit agreement').

The status of any firm can be checked, together with the permissions they hold, by searching the Financial Services Register.

Activities that meet the definition of regulated activities in a Registered Provider are wide and varied. This is a specialist area where legal advice is often sought by the Registered Provider when determining whether they plan to carry out regulated activities.

Not-for-profit bodies may be able to apply for the limited permission regime for the full range of their consumer credit regulated, which may reduce the requirements that a regulated firm is required to comply with.

Registered Providers should be alert to the requirement to provide special reports to the FCA on a routine basis, if required, as set out in the FCA Handbook.

Section B of ISA 250 deals with the auditor's duty to report directly to a regulator information which comes to the auditor's attention in the course of work undertaken in his capacity as auditor of the regulated entity which might be of material significance to the regulator. This can relate to work undertaken in providing an audit opinion or other reports specified by the regulator or legislation.

Auditors are not required to actively perform additional procedures to identify such matters, however, they must remain alert to the possibility of such matters when performing audit work.

Auditors of Registered Providers should consider any additional terms to be added to standard terms of engagement to describe both auditor and board responsibilities in respect of the FCA regulation, alongside the internal policies of the audit firm in undertaking such work, for example, review of this area by an auditor specialising in Financial Services.

Further guidance on ISA (UK) 250 Section B (Revised June 2016) is in **Section 9**.

47.7   Communication with those charged with governance

ISA (UK) 260 (Revised June 2016) *Communication with those Charged with Governance* needs to be understood due to the governance structures within social housing providers. As responsibilities in Registered Providers are delegated by the Board to the management team, the auditor needs to consider to whom it would be most appropriate to address his reports. Whilst the management team may play a central role in the management of the Registered Provider, their powers come from the Board, and therefore, it is to the Audit Committee that the auditor will normally address his management letters.

The ISA sets out examples of areas to consider when communicating to those charged with governance:

- expected modifications to the auditor's report;
- unadjusted misstatements;
- significant deficiencies in the accounting and internal control systems;
- views about the qualitative aspects of the Registered Provider's accounting practices and financial reporting;
- matters specifically required by other ISAs to be communicated to those charged with governance, such as fraud and error; and
- any other relevant matters relating to the audit.

There is a requirement to provide a copy of the auditor's management letter, along with the management response, to the Regulator, within six months of the financial year end. It is recognised that the management letter addresses only those matters which have come to the attention of the auditor in the course of his audit.

47.8 Identifying and assessing risks of material misstatement

Under ISA (UK) 315 (Revised June 2016) *Identifying and Assessing Risks of Material Misstatement through Understanding the Entity and its Environment*, the auditor identifies and assesses the risks of material misstatement, whether due to fraud or error, at the financial statement and assertion levels, through understanding the entity and its environment, including the entity's internal control, thereby providing a basis for designing and implementing responses to the assessed risks of material misstatement. In practice, there is no significant difference in the activities performed for a Registered Provider than for other entities. Some particular matters that should be considered though include:

- the Constitution of Registered Providers, regulation and financial reporting requirements;

- obtaining an understanding of the nature of the entity including the overall structure, regulated and unregulated activities, finances, guarantees and governance of the Registered Provider;

- understanding of internal control relevant to the audit including the statutory requirement to report if the Registered Provider has not maintained a satisfactory system of control; the expectation or in some cases, requirement, that the management letter will be passed on to the regulatory body.

Auditors of Registered Providers also need to consider the risks surrounding significant and complex transactions and other factors such as:

- property development work including:
  - incorrect allocation of costs to schemes;
  - cost overruns due to poor budgeting or unauthorised expenditure leading to costs in excess of the original project appraisal;
  - fraud risks arising from procurement frauds, such as payment for services not supplied; or
  - collusion;
- lack of experience of the Registered Provider's staff in carrying out non-core activities;

- the complexity of the transactions, e.g. legal structures, guarantees, tax, accounting and complex funding arrangements;

- involvement of, and reliance on, third parties;

- viability concerns arising from cost overruns, reductions in government support, over reliance on property sales, etc.; and

- issues relating to the vires of the Registered Provider, if applicable.

47.9   Materiality

With regard to ISA (UK) 320 (Revised June 2016) *Materiality in Planning and Performing an Audit*, consideration of materiality for Registered Providers does not differ fundamentally from that for other entities. Auditors should set a materiality level for the financial statements as a whole, this will be based on a benchmark appropriate for the entity, for example, gross assets or turnover and a percentage is applied to this benchmark. The calculation of materiality is based on the professional judgment of the auditor.

In some cases, it may be appropriate to calculate and apply a specific materiality. This could apply to matters such as the remuneration of the board, or to items used in the calculation of loan covenants, such as interest expense or items contributing to operating surplus.

47.10   Responses to assessed risks

In accordance with ISA (UK) 330 (Revised July 2017) *The Auditor's Responses to Assessed Risks*, the auditor designs audit tests to address the risks that have been assessed in relation to the financial statements. Those audit tests can take the form of tests of controls or substantive tests. Many social housing activities involve a large number of small value, high volume transactions, e.g. rental income, and these streams lend themselves to tests of controls that are designed to test the operating effectiveness of relevant controls in place at the Registered Provider. Where the auditor is satisfied, through evaluation and testing, that there are appropriate and effective controls, including, for example, the effective reconciliation of housing management and finance systems, he can use the results of this control testing as a source of audit evidence about the completeness and accuracy of recorded transactions.

Irrespective of whether tests of controls have been performed, the auditor should perform substantive testing on the balances within the financial statements. The nature and extent of substantive procedures will depend on the risk of material misstatement for any assertion and whether tests of controls have been performed satisfactorily.

47.11   Using a service organisation

Under ISA (UK) 402 *Audit Considerations Relating to an Entity Using a Service Organisation*, where a Registered Provider makes use of a service organisation it does not alter the ultimate responsibility of the board or the audit committee to meet their legal responsibilities, neither does it diminish the auditor's responsibilities when reporting on financial statements.

Examples of activities undertaken by a service organisation may include:

- processing of the payroll;

- other financial functions which involve establishing the carrying value of items in financial statements, for example, calculation of pension liabilities and financial instruments;

- management of assets, including outsourcing of repairs, maintenance and development work;

- management of agency schemes;

- internal audit; and

- undertaking or making arrangements for transactions as agents of the user entity, e.g. property management contracts.

47.12   Audit evidence

In order for the auditor to obtain reliable audit evidence under ISA (UK) 500 *Audit Evidence*, the information upon which the audit procedures are based needs to be relevant and reliable. When an auditor is using information produced by the entity, they need to determine that the information is both accurate and complete.

For example, in auditing rental income, the auditor considers the accuracy and completeness of the information derived from the housing management system. Obtaining this assurance on the information produced by the housing management system may be performed concurrently with the actual audit procedure applied to the information when obtaining such audit evidence is an integral part of the audit procedure itself, for example, by agreeing a sample of rent amounts to the underlying tenant agreement.

In other situations, the auditor may have obtained audit evidence of the accuracy and completeness of such information by testing controls over the production and maintenance of the information and of the general controls over the IT applications that are used to produce the information (referred to as 'ITGCs'). The areas of ITGCs that are commonly tested can include:

- Logical access controls;

- System development controls;

- Program change management; and

- System and data backup and recovery controls.

Given the large number of housing properties owned and managed by Registered Providers, physical inspection is unlikely to be an appropriate means of testing existence. The auditor views or obtains confirmation of documents of title from solicitors or the Land Registry. However, such tests do not establish that the valuation of properties is appropriate.

47.13   External confirmations

With regard to ISA (UK) 505 *External Confirmations*, situations in which external confirmations may be used by Registered Provider auditors may include:

- bank balances and other information from bankers;

- loan balances and terms and conditions;

- balances with local authorities, agencies and other partners;

- property title deeds held by lawyers.

Confirmations are unlikely to be appropriate as a means of checking balances with tenants and leaseholders given the volume and size of individual balances.

47.14   Analytical procedures

When applying ISA (UK) 520 *Analytical Procedures*, certain elements of the income and expenditure of Registered Providers, and in particular interest payable and rental income, are predictable. This facilitates comparisons with budgets, with other organisations in the sector and proof in total tests.

In addition, as Registered Providers are required to submit a number of returns to their Regulator, many publish a comprehensive range of information and data, which may assist the auditor by indicating trends and current ratios.

Examples of items to consider and features of data are detailed in **Table 2**.

TABLE 2: Analytical procedures

Rental income:

- the relationship between the number of housing units available for occupation, the incidence of empty units and rents receivable;

- movements, and any unexpected or unusual relationships, between current and prior year budgets for rent received or service charges;

- movements, and unexpected or unusual relationships, between current year, prior year and budget for voids and bad debts as a percentage of rents;

- rents and service charges for each month.

Other income and administrative expenses:

- amounts are usually related to comparable information for prior periods;

- amounts are usually directly comparable to other Registered Providers of similar size and nature;

- some amounts are closely related to non-financial information such as the number of units, the number of employees and the size of office buildings.

Interest payable

Amounts are compared with average loan balances and the rates that are payable on the loans.

47.15 Auditing accounting estimates

In applying ISA (UK) 540 (Revised June 2016) *Auditing Accounting Estimates, Including Fair Value Accounting Estimates, and Related Disclosures*, the main areas where estimates are likely to be involved in the audit of Registered Providers are:

- depreciation of housing properties and amortisation of social housing grant, and especially the estimated useful economic life;

- the determination of pension liabilities;

- the determination of fair value of non-basic financial instruments;

- the level of bad and doubtful debt provisions against tenant arrears; and

- impairment provisions, particularly when an alternative measure of service potential has been used where assets are held for social purposes.

Where a business combination has been effected between Registered Providers, the combination is typically in substance the 'gift' of the business and assets of one Registered Provider to another with nil consideration. Under FRS 102, the identifiable assets and liabilities of the Registered Provider 'gifted' should be included in the acquirer's balance sheet at their fair value at the date of acquisition. This most likely will apply to housing properties and financial instruments. The auditor ensures that the valuation method and amount adopted is appropriately supported and properly reflected in the financial statements.

In principle, the fair value of social housing properties is the Existing Use Value Social Housing (EUV-SH) of these properties. The fair value of other property assets and liabilities can be assessed in accordance with the requirements of FRS 102. The auditor considers whether the information provided is consistent with the financial records subject to audit.

47.16   Related parties

Under ISA (UK) 550 *Related Parties*, the principles and procedures apply to the audit of Registered Providers as for other entities. In addition, those Registered Providers that are companies need to comply with relevant sections of the Companies Acts.

Subject to certain exemptions, members of the board and those associated with them, and those associated with key management personnel, are not allowed to benefit financially from their connection with the Registered Provider. If there is any evidence of the existence of such related party transactions, then both ISA (UK) 550 and ISA (UK) 250 Section A (Revised June 2016) apply.

The auditor considers in particular whether appropriate disclosure, as required by accounting standards, is made in the financial statements of transactions between the Registered Provider, board members and other key management personnel.

The provisions of accounting standards in the context of related parties and the Registered Provider's management, are applied to all members of 'key management' not just members of the board. Key management may be taken to include those persons having authority and responsibility for planning, directing and controlling the activities of the Registered Provider, directly or indirectly, including any director (whether executive or otherwise) or officer of that Registered Provider.

The 2015 accounting direction sets out specific, additional, disclosure requirements in relation to the transactions between a Registered Provider and non-registered entities within the Registered Provider group. This disclosure includes details of the basis of apportionment, for example, headcount, that has been used for costs between group entities, the amounts involved and the names of the entities involved.

47.17 Subsequent events

Under ISA (UK) 560 *Subsequent Events*, the requirements for the auditor to consider subsequent events do not differ for Registered Providers compared to other entities. Auditors should be aware, however, that in most Registered Providers, the non-executive board plays a crucial role in approving the financial statements. This may be a significant time after the formal audit clearance meeting has taken place and procedures should be performed up to the date of approval of the financial statements.

47.18 Going concern

Under ISA (UK) 570 (Revised June 2016) *Going Concern*, auditors should obtain sufficient audit evidence and conclude on, management's use of the going concern basis for the preparation of financial statements. This takes the same form as for other entities. The board has primary responsibility to make an assessment as to whether the going concern assumption is appropriate for the preparation of the financial statements.

As Registered Providers have a relatively long business cycle, the board may need to consider a longer period than normal. This is likely to involve an assessment of the extent to which there may be adverse variations or uncertainties, and because of this, it may be appropriate for the auditor to obtain representations from the board on these. Where there are uncertainties, confirmation of particular sources of funds or revenues of the Registered Provider may need to be obtained by the auditor in the same way as confirmation of facilities may be required for a company.

Factors which may indicate a potential going concern problem are listed in **Table 3**.

TABLE 3: Factors indicating potential going concern problems

- transfers of the entire housing stock, or a significant proportion of it;

- potential action from the regulatory body and the implications thereof, for example, a downgraded viability rating can affect the availability of, or rate at which, funding can be obtained;

- for a transferee Registered Provider, transfers of housing stock where the acquisition cost or carrying value is not covered by the long-term projected net rental income;

- onerous contract terms;

- inability to service interest payments;

- a significant amount of variable interest rate borrowings at a time when interest rates are rising or are predicted to rise;

- a significant short-term repair liability that the Registered Provider will have difficulty in meeting from its own resources;

- loan repayments or refinancing which cannot be met from the Registered Provider's own resources;

- housing property development commitments which cannot be met;

- breach of loan covenants; and

- significant loans to subsidiaries involved in activities such as shared ownership or developments for sale.

47.19   Written representations

In accordance with ISA (UK) 580 *Written Representations*, the auditor may include in his representation letters confirmation that all minutes and correspondence with the regulatory bodies have been made available to him.

47.20   Using the work of internal auditors

ISA (UK) 610 (Revised June 2013) *Using the Work of Internal Auditors* applies to auditors making use of any internal audit function in place at the Registered Provider. Larger Registered Providers are required to determine what is an appropriate internal audit function.

The extent to which an external auditor can use the work of an internal auditor will depend on an assessment of the objectivity of the internal audit function, the level of competence of the internal audit function and whether the internal audit function applies a systematic and disciplined approach.

If an external auditor plans to use the work of an internal auditor, they should perform audit procedures on the work of the internal auditor to determine its adequacy for external audit purposes.

47.21　Using the work of an auditor's expert

ISA (UK) 620 (Revised June 2016) may be particularly relevant where there are defined benefit pension liabilities on the balance sheet or non-basic financial instruments, such as derivatives.

In respect of defined benefit pension schemes, information is often supplied by the client actuary about the surpluses or deficits to be included on the balance sheet. An auditor may engage his own expert to assist in providing sufficient, appropriate audit evidence in this specialised area.

In a situation involving complex financial instruments, the housing association may have employed its own expert (management's expert) to assist in the provision of valuations or other relevant information. The auditor may however consider it appropriate to appoint his own expert to assist in the audit of those valuations and information.

Normal auditing considerations apply and these are dealt with in **Section 31**.

47.22　The auditor's report on financial statements

An example unqualified report in accordance with ISA (UK) 700 (Revised June 2016) *Forming an Opinion and Reporting on Financial Statements* is shown in **Table 4**. An example statement of board members' responsibilities is given in **Table 5**. These examples deal with a single entity that is a Community Benefit Society but is not a charity. Different reporting requirements apply to Registered Providers that are companies and/or charities.

TABLE 4: Audit report for single entity registered provider of social housing that is a community benefit society

Independent auditor's report to the members of Example Housing Association

Opinion

We have audited the financial statements of [name of entity] (the 'association') for the year ended [*date*] which comprise [*specify the titles of the primary statements*] and notes to the financial statements, including a summary of significant accounting policies. The financial reporting framework that has been applied in their preparation is applicable law and United Kingdom Accounting Standards, including Financial Reporting Standard 102 *The Financial Reporting Standard applicable in the UK and Republic of Ireland* (United Kingdom Generally Accepted Accounting Practice).

In our opinion, the financial statements:

● give a true and fair view of the state of the association's affairs as at [....] and of the its surplus [deficit] for the year then ended;

- have been properly prepared in accordance with United Kingdom Generally Accepted Accounting Practice; and

- have been prepared in accordance with the requirements of the *Co-operative and Community Benefit Societies Act* 2014, the *Housing and Regeneration Act* 2008 and the *Accounting Direction for Private Registered Providers of Social Housing* 2015.

Basis for opinion

We conducted our audit in accordance with International Standards on Auditing (UK) (ISAs (UK)) and applicable law. Our responsibilities under those standards are further described in the Auditor's responsibilities for the audit of the financial statements section of our report. We are independent of the association in accordance with the ethical requirements that are relevant to our audit of the financial statements in the UK, including the FRC's Ethical Standard, and we have fulfilled our other ethical responsibilities in accordance with these requirements. We believe that the audit evidence we have obtained is sufficient and appropriate to provide a basis for our opinion.

Conclusions relating to going concern

We have nothing to report in respect of the following matters in relation to which the ISAs (UK) require us to report to you where:

- the board's use of the going concern basis of accounting in the preparation of the financial statements is not appropriate; or

- the board has not disclosed in the financial statements any identified material uncertainties that may cast significant doubt about the association's ability to continue to adopt the going concern basis of accounting for a period of at least 12 months from the date when the financial statements are authorised for issue.

Other information

The other information comprises the information included in the [*annual report*], other than the financial statements and our auditor's report thereon. The board is responsible for the other information. Our opinion on the financial statements does not cover the other information and, except to the extent otherwise explicitly stated in our report, we do not express any form of assurance conclusion thereon.

In connection with our audit of the financial statements, our responsibility is to read the other information [, including (*specify titles of other information*)] and, in doing so, consider whether the other information is materially inconsistent with the financial statements or our knowledge obtained in the audit or otherwise appears to be materially misstated. If we identify such material inconsistencies or apparent material misstatements, we are required to determine whether there is a material misstatement in the financial statements or a material misstatement of the other information. If, based on the work we have performed, we conclude that there is a material misstatement of this other information, we are required to report that fact.

We have nothing to report in this regard.

Matters on which we are required to report by exception

We have nothing to report in respect of the following matters where we are required to report to you if, in our opinion:

- adequate accounting records have not been kept by the association;

- a satisfactory system of control has not been maintained over transactions; or

- the association's financial statements are not in agreement with the accounting records and returns; or

- we have not received all the information and explanations we require for our audit.

Responsibilities of the board

As explained more fully in the board's responsibilities statement [set out on page ...], the board is responsible for the preparation of the financial statements and for being satisfied that they give a true and fair view, and for such internal control as the board determines is necessary to enable the preparation of financial statements that are free from material misstatement, whether due to fraud or error.

In preparing the financial statements, the board is responsible for assessing the association's ability to continue as a going concern, disclosing, as applicable, matters related to going concern and using the going concern basis of accounting unless the board either intends to liquidate the association or to cease operations, or has no realistic alternative but to do so.

Auditor's responsibilities for the audit of the financial statements

This report is made solely to the association's members, as a body, in accordance with the *Housing and Regeneration Act* 2008 and the *Co-operative and Community Benefit Societies Act* 2014, s. 87. Our audit work has been undertaken so that we might state to the association's members those matters we are required to state to them in an auditor's report and for no other purpose. To the fullest extent permitted by law, we do not accept or assume responsibility to anyone other than the association and the association's members as a body, for our audit work, for this report, or for the opinions we have formed.[1]

Our objectives are to obtain reasonable assurance about whether the financial statements as a whole are free from material misstatement, whether due to fraud or error, and to issue an auditor's report that includes our opinion. Reasonable assurance is a high level of assurance, but is not a guarantee that an audit conducted in accordance with ISAs (UK) will always detect a material misstatement when it exists.

Misstatements can arise from fraud or error and are considered material if, individually or in the aggregate, they could reasonably be expected to influence the economic decisions of users taken on the basis of these financial statements.

A further description of our responsibilities for the audit of the financial statements is located on the Financial Reporting Council's website at www.frc.org.uk/auditorsresponsibilities. This description forms part of our auditor's report.

Use of our report

This report is made solely to the association's members, as a body, in accordance with the *Housing and Regeneration Act* 2008 and the *Co-operative and Community Benefit Societies Act* 2014, s. 87. Our audit work has been undertaken so that we might state to the association's members those matters we are required to state to them in an auditor's report and for no other purpose. To the fullest extent permitted by law, we do not accept or assume responsibility to anyone other than the association and the association's members as a body, for our audit work, for this report, or for the opinions we have formed.[1]

XYZ LLP, statutory auditor

Town,

United Kingdom

Date

[1] This Bannerman paragraph is optional and the use of such a paragraph is further discussed in **4.28**.

TABLE 5: Example responsibility statement for Registered Provider board

The board members are responsible for preparing the report of the board and the financial statements in accordance with applicable law and regulations.

Community and Co-operative Benefit Society law and social housing legislation require the board members to prepare financial statements for each financial year in accordance with United Kingdom Generally Accepted Accounting Practice (United Kingdom Accounting Standards and applicable law). The board must not approve the financial statements unless they are satisfied that they give a true and fair view of the state of affairs of the Association and of the surplus or deficit of the association for that period.

In preparing these financial statements, the board members are required to:

- select suitable accounting policies and then apply them consistently;

- make judgments and accounting estimates that are reasonable and prudent;

- state whether applicable UK Accounting Standards and Statement of Recommended Practice have been followed, subject to any material departures disclosed and explained in the financial statements; and

- prepare the financial statements on the going concern basis unless it is inappropriate to presume that the Association will continue in business.

> The board members are responsible for keeping adequate accounting records that are sufficient to show and explain the association's transactions and disclose with reasonable accuracy at any time the financial position of the association and enable them to ensure that the financial statements comply with the *Co-operative and Community Benefit Societies Act* 2014, the *Co-operative and Community Benefit Societies (Group Accounts) Regulations* 1969, the *Housing and Regeneration Act* 2008 and the *Accounting Direction for Private Registered Providers of Social Housing* 2015. They are also responsible for safeguarding the assets of the association and hence for taking reasonable steps for the prevention and detection of fraud and other irregularities.
>
> The board is responsible for ensuring that the report of the board is prepared in accordance with the *Accounting Direction for Private Registered Providers of Social Housing* 2015 and the applicable Statement of Recommended Practice.
>
> Financial statements are published on the association's website in accordance with legislation in the United Kingdom governing the preparation and dissemination of financial statements, which may vary from legislation in other jurisdictions. The maintenance and integrity of the association's website is the responsibility of the board members. The board members' responsibility also extends to the ongoing integrity of the financial statements contained therein.

ISA (UK) 700 (Revised June 2016) also requires auditor's reports to contain any further matters required by statute or other requirements applicable to the particular engagement. For Registered Providers, these matters may be set out in a number of areas, depending on the legal form and jurisdiction of the Registered Provider:

- the *Housing and Regeneration Act* 2008, together with any Statutory Instrument or Accounting Direction or Order issued under the Act;

- the *Co-operative and Community Benefit Societies Act* 2014;

- the *Companies Act* 2006;

- the *Charities Act* 2011;

- the trust deed.

Of particular note is the requirement for Registered Providers to maintain adequate books and records and satisfactory systems of internal control which vary depending on the legislation under which they are formed. Auditors are required to report if this is not the case, and consideration should also be given to a qualification on the grounds of limitation of scope.

47.22.1 UK Corporate Governance Code and enhanced audit reporting

Registered Providers of Social Housing are required to disclose in their financial statements the code of governance that has been adopted (*Accounting Direction for Private Registered Providers of Social Housing 2015*). Most choose to adopt the NHF's *Code of governance: promoting board excellence for housing associations* in which case there are no additional audit reporting requirements. However, some choose to voluntarily adopt the UK Corporate Governance Code (see **Section 42**) and report in their annual report on how they have applied the Code. This triggers the need for additional reporting by the auditor on key audit matters under ISA (UK) 701 *Communicating Key Audit Matters in the Auditor's Report*, and on other information under ISA (UK) 720 (Revised June 2016) *The Auditor's Responsibilities in Relation to Other Information* and ISA (UK) 570 (Revised 2016).

Those that 'cherry pick' some aspects of the UK Corporate Governance Code but do not include a statement explaining how they have applied the Code are unlikely to require enhanced audit reporting.

ISA (UK) 701 does not apply automatically to audits of Registered Providers unless they choose to report on their application of the UK Corporate Governance Code or have securities listed on a public market. The auditor may nevertheless decide to communicate key audit matters in his report. Where he does so the sections of the report dealing with key audit matters, an overview of the scope of the audit and application of materiality should be included in the report in accordance with ISA (UK) 701 (see **Section 4**).

47.23 Other information

As in any other audit of financial statements, ISA (UK) 720 (Revised June 2016) requires the auditor to read all other information contained in the annual report.

Examples of other information that may be included are:

- statements by the patron, president, chair or chief executive;
- an operating and financial review;
- a statement concerning arrangements for corporate governance;
- a narrative report on assessment of value for money as required by the 2015 Accounting Direction;

- the board's statement on risks and internal control;
- a treasurer's report;
- financial summaries; and
- projections of future expenditure based on planned activity.

The auditor considers whether there is a material inconsistency between the other information and the financial statements or the knowledge he has obtained in the course of the audit. He also remains alert for any indication that other information not related to the financial statements or the auditor's knowledge may be materially misstated.

In accordance with ISA (UK) 720, the auditor's report will contain a section headed 'Other information' which will describe the auditor's responsibilities in relation to the other information and contain details of any matters to be reported, or a statement that there are no such matters.

For Registered Providers that are incorporated under the *Companies Act* 2006, auditors are required to include an opinion on whether the information given in the strategic report (where required) and the directors' report for the financial year for which the financial statements are prepared is consistent with the financial statements; the strategic report and directors' report have been prepared in accordance with applicable legal requirements; and, based on their knowledge and understanding of the entity and its environment obtained during the course of the audit, that they have identified no material misstatements in the strategic report or the directors' report.

47.24 Miscellaneous reports

There are many returns where auditors are asked to report which will vary from one Registered Provider to another. Due to the variety, it is impracticable to list them in this guidance. Auditors should refer to guidance contained in Technical Release TECH 10/12AAF *Reporting to Third Parties* (see **40.8**) which can be adapted to such returns and also to Technical Release Audit 03/03 *Public Sector Special Reporting Engagements – Grant Claims* (see **Section 48**).

47.25 Service charge audits

The *Housing and Regeneration Act* 2008 contains the requirements for the provision of information to leaseholders and in respect of monies held for service charges in designated accounts.

ICAEW Technical Release TECH 03/11, *Residential Service Charge Accounts – Guidance on Accounting and Reporting in Relation to Service Charge Accounts for Residential Properties on which Variable Service Charges are Paid in Accordance with a Lease or Tenancy Agreement*.

The introduction to Tech 03/11 includes a section covering the scope of the guidance which states:

'Whatever the nature of the landlord entity (e.g. the landlord can be an individual, a partnership, a company or a community benefit society), if that person is entitled under the terms of a lease to levy variable service charges on residential property, it is subject to the provisions of the *Landlord and Tenant Acts* (LTAs) 1985 and 1987 in relation to accounting for service charges. Therefore, this guidance is relevant to lessee-owned companies such as RMCs [residents' management company], as well as to large for profit companies and registered providers of social housing.'

The guidance covers the preparation of service charge accounts for issue to the tenants/leaseholders of residential properties and considerations for independent accountants' reports on service charge accounts. It sets out the alternative types of examination that may be undertaken by the independent accountant depending upon the terms of the lease. The type of engagement, which should be agreed between the accountant and the housing association, will depend on the terms of the lease and should be proportionate to the size and nature of the property/scheme.

Section 3 of Tech 03/11 includes reporting guidance on service charge statements covering:

- audit;
- engagement to deliver a report of factual findings; and
- reporting under the *Landlord and Tenant Act* 1985, s. 21.

The appendices to the Technical Release provide further guidance on:

- comparison of audit to an engagement to report on factual findings;
- procedures for undertaking an audit of service charge accounts;
- work programme for making a factual report on service charge accounts;
- paragraphs for engagement letters;
- example paragraphs for a representation letter from landlord/managing agent to the reporting accountant; and
- example reports on service charge accounts covering:
  - audit report in accordance with ISA 800;
  - accountant's report of factual findings to the landlord.

48 Public sector audits

48.1 Introduction

In recent years, the accountability of central government departments and other public bodies has become a topic of increasing public interest. There has been continuing debate concerning their audit arrangements with increasingly more audits being carried out by private sector auditors.

In accordance with the FRC's Policy on Developing Statements of Recommended Practice, the Public Audit Forum, comprising the four UK National Audit Agencies has been recognised by the FRC for the purpose of issuing the Statement of Recommended Practice: Practice Note 10 *Audit of financial statements of public sector bodies in the United Kingdom*. This SORP (referred to hereafter as Practice Note 10 or 'PN10') was issued in November 2016 and replaced the previous Practice Note 10, *Audit of financial statements of public sector bodies in the United Kingdom* which was issued in October 2010.

As well as providing guidance on the application of each ISA (UK) and ISQC (UK) 1 to public sector audits in the UK, the Practice Note also considers the role of the public sector auditor. The Practice Note is based on auditing standards, legislation and regulations which were in effect at 1 September 2016, thus including the revisions issued for periods commencing on or after 17 June 2016. Part 1 of the Practice Note is concerned with the ISAs (UK), Part 2 relates to the audit of regularity, considered in **48.25**.

Additional guidance is given to public sector auditors in Technical Release AAF01/10 *Framework Document for Accountants' Reports on Grant Claims* (see **48.26**), issued in 2010.

48.2 The role of the public sector auditor

External auditors in the public sector give an independent opinion on the financial statements and may review and, where appropriate, report on aspects of the arrangements set in place by the audited body to ensure the proper conduct of its financial affairs and to manage its performance and use of resources. As such, external audit is an essential element in the process of accountability and makes an important contribution to the stewardship of public money and the corporate governance of public services.

Public sector auditors act and report in accordance with the mandates that govern their activities and provide the authority for the auditor to carry out and to report the results of the audit work. These mandates are embodied in legislation and, in some circumstances, set out in Codes of Audit Practice which may be established in accordance with legislation and issued by the national audit agencies. The mandates of public sector auditors vary in accordance with the requirements laid down in the legislation relevant to each jurisdiction within the public sector and within each geographical area.

Although the detail varies, these mandates establish broadly similar responsibilities for each jurisdiction in relation to:

- the financial statements;

- compliance with legislative and other authorities (sometimes referred to as 'regularity'); and

- economy, efficiency and effectiveness (sometimes referred to as 'performance audit', 'value for money' or 'use of resources').

In carrying out their audit responsibilities, auditors of public sector bodies are required to comply with ISAs (UK) and Practice Note 10 as well as any more specific guidance contained in Codes of Practice or other relevant guidance issued by the appropriate national audit agency.

Public sector auditors may also be required to review and report on other information prepared by public bodies. Such other information may include aspects of corporate governance or arrangements to secure economy, efficiency and effectiveness in the use of resources. Practice Note 10 does not provide guidance to the auditor on conducting these assignments, unless it is directly related to reporting on the audit of financial statements or regularity. The standards governing other reporting assignments in the public sector are a matter for the national audit agencies and certain regulators to determine. These may be included in a separate Code of Audit Practice.

48.3   Quality control

ISQC (UK) 1 (Revised June 2016) *Quality Control for Firms that Perform Audits and Reviews of Financial Statements, and Other Assurance and Related Services Engagements* is relevant in its entirety to the audit of financial statements of public sector entities. Practice Note 10 provides additional guidance in relation to withdrawing from an engagement and threats to auditor independence, as well as quality control considerations for 'contracted out' engagements and engagements on an 'appointment by' basis.

In the public sector, under statute the auditor may not be able to withdraw from an engagement. In most cases, there is a duty to publicly report matters that would have otherwise caused withdrawal from the engagement.

If a national audit agency is appointed by statute, there is no option to withdraw from an engagement where threats to independence have been identified and other steps should be taken to reduce these threats. Where an audit firm has been appointed as an agent of a national audit agency, that agency will assess the firm's independence when it is appointed. The firm must comply with the requirements of ISQC (UK) 1 (Revised June 2016) on independence when carrying out their work.

Auditors in the public sector may need to meet relevant ethical and propriety requirements in addition to the Revised Ethical Standard 2016, such as restrictions on political activities or requirements established by regulators. They may also have additional statutory obligations relating to confidentiality, for example the *Official Secrets Act* 1989 also covers some public sector activities.

48.4 Overall objectives of the auditor and the conduct of an audit

The general principles of auditing are the same in both private and public entities, but auditors of public entities often have wider duties and further responsibilities laid down in legislation, directives and codes of practice.

48.5 Agreeing the terms of audit engagements

With some exceptions, the statutory framework allows national audit agencies to mandate a substantial part of the scope and objectives of the audit. In other cases, an appointment letter or Code of Audit Practice issued by a national audit agency may determine the nature and scope of the audit engagement. For this reason, formal engagement letters for statutory engagements may not always be necessary. However, for audits of local bodies in England, for example where appointments have been made directly by the audited bodies under the *Local Audit and Accountability Act* 2014 or for the audit of Foundation Trusts, a letter of engagement is required.

Nevertheless, it remains important that management and the auditor formally recognise their respective responsibilities. It may also be necessary, where legislation does not provide sufficient detail on the scope of the audit, to ensure that it is appropriately understood by those charged with governance. A letter of understanding may therefore be necessary.

The auditor may find it appropriate to conclude letters of understanding with the audited entity to confirm the auditor's understanding of the roles of the parties with an interest in the engagement, the requirements of the audit, the responsibilities of each party, how the responsibilities will be met, and the expectations that each party can have of the other.

Where the auditor has not been appointed under statute, an engagement letter is required to set out the responsibilities of the auditor and the audited body. The auditor agrees the terms of engagement with the addressee of the auditor's report.

Where financial statements are laid before Parliament, either by statute or command, the auditor also considers whether HM Treasury agreement of these terms may be required.

48.6   Quality control

ISA (UK) 220 (Revised June 2016) *Quality Control for an Audit of Financial Statements* requires an engagement quality control review of the audit of listed entities and public interest entities. In the public sector, audit teams should consider whether such a review is necessary for each client. Reviews are likely to be appropriate for larger, more complex entities or those with a high profile.

48.7   The auditor's responsibilities relating to fraud

The public sector auditor's responsibilities relating to fraud may be a result of law, regulation or other authority applicable to public sector entities or separately covered by the auditor's mandate. Consequently, the public sector auditor's responsibilities may not be limited to consideration of risks of material misstatement of the financial statements, but may also include a broader responsibility to consider risks of fraud.

A public sector auditor needs to consider misstatements that may arise from fraudulent financial reporting where the audited body may manipulate its results to meet externally set targets, for example, the achievement of a statutory break-even duty by a health body or where financial results impact on achievement of objectives and/or wider performance reporting.

ISA (UK) 240 (Revised June 2016) *The Auditor's Responsibilities Relating to Fraud in an Audit of Financial Statements* states that the auditor ordinarily presumes that there are risks of fraud in revenue recognition, as material misstatements due to fraudulent financial reporting often result from a misstatement of revenue. The auditor may rebut this presumption, for example if revenue is considered immaterial or where there is a single type of simple revenue transaction. However, the auditor may need to consider whether there is a risk of material misstatements due to fraud related to revenue recognition where the audited body is required to meet externally set targets. For example, within central government departments, income may be an immaterial transaction stream but could be manipulated in order to ensure that net expenditure is within the resource limits.

In the public sector, auditors focus their consideration of the risk of fraud and error on expenditure. As most public bodies are net spending bodies, then the risk of material misstatement due to fraud related to expenditure may be greater than the risk of material misstatements due to fraud related to revenue recognition.

As well as misstatements resulting from the misappropriation of assets and misstatements resulting from fraudulent financial reporting, auditors in the public sector also consider the risk of external fraud. The risk of external fraud may be particularly high where there is an increased risk of fraudulent activity by individuals or groups outside the immediate control of the entity, for example fraudulent benefit or prescription claims.

In the public sector, requirements for reporting fraud, whether or not discovered through the audit process, may be subject to specific provisions of the audit mandate or related law, regulation or other authority. Where the public sector auditor considers that there is a duty to report instances of suspected or actual fraud to a third party, he determines the proper authority to whom he is initially expected to report.

48.8   Consideration of laws and regulations

ISA (UK) 250 Section A (Revised December 2017) – *Consideration of Laws and Regulations in an Audit of Financial Statements* is concerned with laws and regulations that, if not complied with, may materially affect the financial statements. These fall into two categories, those which set out the form or contents of the financial statements and those which set the provisions under which an entity is allowed to conduct its business. The auditor is required to obtain a general understanding of both categories of laws and regulations. Where the auditor is required to report on compliance with certain provisions of laws or regulations, for example, the regularity assertion for public entities, then as well as being familiar with the law itself, he must test the entity's compliance with its provisions.

Auditors of local government and health entities have separate statutory responsibilities when matters come to their attention that indicate that unlawful expenditure has been or will be incurred or that a financial loss or deficiency will arise. This is irrespective of the potential for material impact on the financial statements. In addition, the auditor must report on the elements of the local government or health entities' corporate governance arrangements that relate to the legality of transactions which might have a financial consequence.

48.8.1 Consideration of legislation on corruption

Public sector auditors need to consider to whom the auditor may report suspected or actual acts of corruption, irrespective of whether, in his opinion, the consequences of the corruption could have a material effect on the financial statements. Normally, he would bring the matter to the attention of those charged with governance and it is then their responsibility to report the matter to the proper authorities. If those charged with governance do not report the matter to the relevant third party, the auditor would need to take additional steps as set out in the ISA.

48.8.2 Reporting non-compliance

In some situations, the public sector auditor may be obliged to report on instances of non-compliance to the legislature or other governing body or to report them in the auditor's report.

48.9 Communication with those charged with governance

In the context of a public sector audit, those charged with governance may include the Accounting/Accountable Officer (or equivalent) and other individuals responsible for decision-making, for example a board, scrutiny committee, Council, governing body or another group.

In addition to the requirements of ISA (UK) 260 (Revised June 2016) *Communication with those Charged with Governance*, the Practice Note stresses the importance of reports to management as a means of reporting non-compliance with:

- regularity;
- propriety; and
- other official guidance to Accounting Officers.

Where matters relating to other duties and responsibilities are reported to management in the same letter as matters arising from the audit of the financial statements, the auditor must be sure that the letter still meets the requirements of ISA (UK) 260 (Revised June 2016).

Special arrangements may have developed for reporting to those charged with governance by auditors of some entities sponsored by government departments. In such cases the Accounting/Accountable Officer of the sponsor department must obtain assurance that the financial and other management controls applied by the sponsored entity are adequate to ensure regularity and propriety. Reports from the auditor of the lower tier entity may assist the Accounting/Accountable Officer in obtaining such assurance.

Public sector bodies may be required to make public communications, such as an annual audit letter, between the auditor and those charged with governance. Even where this is not the case, reports to management may come into the possession of third parties and the auditor may wish to include a caveat in any such report to make it clear that the report was not intended for third party use and that it should not be relied on for any purpose other than that for which it was prepared.

Public sector auditors may have additional responsibilities to communicate deficiencies in internal control that the auditor has identified during the audit, in ways, at a level of detail and to parties not envisaged in ISA (UK) 265 *Communicating Deficiencies in Internal Control to those Charged with Governance and Management*. For example, significant deficiencies may have to be communicated to the legislature or other governing body. Law, regulation or other authority may also mandate that public sector auditors report deficiencies in internal control, irrespective of the significance of the potential effects of those deficiencies. Further, legislation may require public sector auditors to report on broader internal control-related matters than the deficiencies in internal control required to be communicated by the ISA (UK), for example, controls related to compliance with legislative authorities, regulations, or provisions of contracts or grant agreements.

48.10   Identifying, assessing and responding to risks

Under ISA (UK) 315 (Revised June 2016) *Identifying and Assessing Risks of Material Misstatement through Understanding the Entity and its Environment* and ISA (UK) 330 (Revised July 2017) *The Auditor's Responses to Assessed Risks*, the auditor is required to obtain an understanding of the relevant financial reporting framework and regulatory factors and their impact on the audit. These include the financial reporting framework and other regulations set out in:

- the specific legislation that has established the audited entity and determines its activities;
- accounts directions;

- Managing Public Money and the Government Financial Reporting Manual (now based on IFRS);

- other HM Treasury guidance on the application of accounting standards, the *Companies Act* and the disclosure of information;

- manuals for accounts of NHS entities; and

- relevant SORPs.

An additional consideration for public sector auditors is the additional assertion of regularity. When assessing risk for reporting on the regularity assertion, the auditor should consider the following specific factors:

- the complexity of the regulations;

- the introduction of major new legislation or changes in existing regulations;

- services and programmes administered under European Union authorities, where the framework of authorities may be complex;

- services and programmes delivered through third parties; and

- payments and receipts made on the basis of claims or declarations.

ISA (UK) 315 (Revised June 2016) requires the auditor to obtain an understanding of an entity's business objectives and strategies and assess any resulting business risks. Public sector entities may have a number of additional business risks as a result of their closely regulated regimes, public reporting process and typically high number of transactions processed. These additional factors may arise where:

- major new legislation or expenditure programmes have been introduced;

- there is the possibility of manipulation by management to achieve performance or other targets;

- an entity is likely to be wound up, reorganised, merged, sold or privatised;

- there is political pressure on an entity to complete transactions quickly; or

- the final form of account does not reflect the underlying management and accounting processes.

In addition, as set out in ISA (UK) 240 (Revised June 2016), there will be a significant risk relating to management override of controls and a presumed risk of fraud in revenue recognition, as is the case in audits of private sector entities.

48.11   Materiality in planning and performing an audit

When assessing the qualitative aspects of materiality, the auditor should consider the interest of the body to whom the audit report is addressed. When considering materiality, the auditor should consider any higher body into whose financial statements the results of the audited entity is being consolidated, to be the addressee of the audit report. The auditor should also be aware of any special considerations applying to the reporting of certain classes of misstatement when assessing the materiality of uncorrected misstatements.

In an audit of a public sector entity, gross expenditure or gross assets/liabilities may be more appropriate than profit or revenue as benchmarks for setting materiality.

Where public sector auditors have a responsibility to report on matters that do not affect the opinion on the financial statements, they may adopt an appropriate level of materiality for these items which differs from the materiality level applied to the audit of the financial statements.

The concept of materiality applies to the audit of regularity as to any other assertions in the financial statements. Where required to report on regularity, auditors need only to obtain sufficient evidence to give an opinion on whether expenditure and income has been applied for the intended purposes 'in all material respects'. As with other financial statements assertions, the assessment of materiality will include both qualitative and quantitative judgments. Materiality for the purposes of regularity reporting may be set at a level lower than that which is applied to the financial statements as a whole.

48.12   Using a service organisation

The requirement for public sector auditors to give an opinion on the regularity of transactions may require inspection of records maintained by service organisations beyond that in other audits. ISA (UK) 402 *Audit Considerations Relating to an Entity using a Service Organisation* does not automatically secure access rights to this information, and so it is important that the contract terms between the public sector entity and its service provider allow sufficient access by the entity's auditor.

48.13   Evaluation of misstatements

In the case of an audit of a public sector entity, the evaluation as to whether a misstatement is material may also be affected by the auditor's responsibilities established by law, regulation or other authority to report specific matters.

Furthermore, issues such as public interest, accountability, probity and ensuring effective legislative oversight, in particular, may affect the assessment of whether an item is material by virtue of its nature. This is particularly so for items that relate to compliance with law, regulation or other authority.

48.14 Opening balances

ISA (UK) 510 (Revised June 2016) *Initial Audit Engagements – Opening Balances* is concerned with the opening balances for initial engagements. In the public sector, this can occur when the financial statements for the prior period were audited by another auditor, but is also relevant for 'machinery of government changes' that transfer functions from one part of the public sector to another as a going concern.

The Practice Note sets out guidance which is given in **Table 1**.

TABLE 1: Additional guidance on the audit of opening balances

Nature of opening balances	*Additional guidance*
Opening balance amounts are clearly identifiable from the preceding period's audited financial statements for the transferring entity.	The auditor adopts the requirements of paragraphs 6 and 7 of ISA (UK) 510 (Revised June 2016).
Opening balance amounts are not identifiable from the preceding period's audited financial statements for another entity, but have been derived from balances contained in those statements.	If relevant, the auditor discusses with the auditor of the predecessor organisation whether information is available that would provide substantive evidence for the opening balances. In the absence of such evidence, the auditor carries out substantive testing of opening balances to confirm they have been brought forward appropriately in accordance with the terms of the transfer, at an appropriate valuation in line with the accounting policies of the receiving body.
Opening balances have been calculated as part of a separate disaggregation/merger exercise, subject to a separate specific review and report by an auditor.	The auditor considers the scope and outcomes of that separate review, and considers whether the conclusions can be relied on in accordance with ISA (UK) 500 *Audit Evidence*.

Nature of opening balances	Additional guidance
	Where the work from the separate specific review cannot be used, the auditor considers carrying out substantive testing of opening balances in line with the box above.
Opening balances have been calculated as part of a separate disaggregation/merger exercise, but not subject to separate specific review and report.	The auditor considers carrying out substantive testing of opening balances. Completeness of assets and liabilities, together with appropriate valuation can be risks in a disaggregation exercise, and engagement with the audited body is made at an early stage.

Where, after performing the procedures in **Table 1**, the auditor is unable to obtain sufficient appropriate audit evidence concerning the opening balances of the entity, he considers the implications for his audit report.

In the public sector, the predecessor auditor is expected by the national audit agencies to adopt a co-operative approach in the interests of efficiency and reducing the audit burden. This may include enabling the incoming auditor to perform a review of the prior year audit documentation or have access to particular reports or papers that may be required rather than the transfer of all the relevant papers or data.

48.15 Accounting estimates

In the public sector, factors outside of the scope of the financial reporting framework can have a significant influence on management's estimates. For example, central government departments must adhere to HM Treasury budgetary controls, so estimates in the financial statements can be influenced by the impact they have on departmental expenditure limits or the administration budget. In the health sector, statutory limits or targets can similarly influence management decisions.

Auditors need to understand these influences, some of which come from elsewhere within a departmental or sector group, when considering the appropriateness of accounting estimates and the assumptions applied by management.

In addition, some public sector entities are reliant on accounting estimates provided by other entities within the public sector. The auditor needs to understand how these estimates have been derived, and may need to communicate with the auditors of the entities compiling the accounting estimates on which the public sector body relies.

48.16 Related parties

The public sector auditor's responsibilities regarding related party relationships and transactions may be affected by the audit mandate, or by obligations on public sector entities arising from law, regulation or other authority. Consequently, the public sector auditor's responsibilities may not be limited to addressing the risks of material misstatement associated with related party relationships and transactions, but may also include a broader responsibility to address the risks of non-compliance with law, regulation and other authority governing public sector bodies that lay down specific requirements in the conduct of business with related parties. Further, the public sector auditor may need to have regard to public sector financial reporting requirements for related party relationships and transactions that may differ from those in the private sector.

48.17 Subsequent events

For central government entities, the auditor must also consider matters arising from relevant parliamentary procedures as part of his subsequent events review. The auditor should consult relevant legislation to determine the dates the financial statements are deemed to be 'issued' and 'laid before members', as this varies for each central government entity.

For auditors of local government and health entities, the auditor may be required to give both an audit opinion on the financial statements and to:

- discharge certain other statutory responsibilities and duties; and

- issue a certificate ('audit completion certificate') confirming that the audit and all related responsibilities and duties have been completed in accordance with the legislation.

The issue of the audit completion certificate marks the end of the auditor's duties.

There may be a significant delay between the auditor completing the work on the financial statements and him being in a position to issue the audit completion certificate. The auditor should consider whether these additional statutory duties are likely to give rise to matters which would have a material effect on the financial statements, and if so, the opinion on the financial statements should not be given until the additional statutory duties have been completed.

48.18 Going concern

The Practice Note gives guidance on the following areas:

- the auditor's other responsibilities relating to going concern;

- circumstances affecting going concern;

- consideration of the foreseeable future;

- the auditor's responsibilities in considering going concern;

- entities that prepare their financial statements on a cash basis; and

- the auditor's responsibilities for reviewing and reporting on an entity's arrangements for securing value for money.

48.18.1 The auditor's other responsibilities relating to going concern

Due to the introduction of the revised auditing standards in June 2016, the guidance in this area of the Practice Note has been amended to reflect the change in the auditor's reporting responsibilities in respect of going concern. In particular, auditors should be aware of reporting by exception on the robustness of management's assessment and adequacy of disclosures in respect of the principal risks facing the entity, as well as reporting on material uncertainty in respect of going concern in a separate section of the auditor's report. Auditors should refer to the relevant version of the standard for audit requirements and further application guidance.

48.18.2 Circumstances affecting going concern

It is unlikely that a central government entity will cease to operate as a result of insolvency or inability to finance operations, unless they operate in a trading capacity at arm's length from the Government.

Cessation is most likely to result from a decision by the Government and may involve transferring the operations to another entity. In such cases, the individual circumstances should be considered when assessing whether the going concern basis is appropriate.

48.18.3 Consideration of the foreseeable future

Government policy is inherently subject to political uncertainty, but political decisions are no more uncertain than the risks faced by private entities. Therefore, the provisions in ISA (UK) 570 (Revised June 2016) *Going Concern* relating to 'foreseeable future' can be applied by the auditor of public sector entities.

48.18.4 The auditor's responsibilities in considering going concern

Public sector auditors should consider two factors:

- the risk associated with changes in policy direction (for example, where there is a change in Government); and

- the operational, or business, risk (for example, the entity has insufficient working capital).

Auditors need to obtain evidence concerning the Government's intentions in the particular area of policy that the entity operates in. This would include whether:

- they intend to review policy, for example, a manifesto commitment;

- a review has been announced;

- an efficiency review has concluded that rationalisation is necessary; or

- there is a known intention to privatise its activities.

Trading operations may also be subject to risks arising from changes in policy direction as well as operational and business risks.

48.18.5 *Entities that prepare their financial statements on a cash basis*

Where central government entities prepare financial statements on a cash basis, ISA (UK) 570 (Revised June 2016) does not apply to the audit as the going concern basis is not used in the preparation of the statements. However, the auditor still considers whether there are any matters affecting the audited entity's ability to continue as a going concern. Where the auditor identifies such matters, the auditor considers the need to report separately to Parliament on those matters or, where there is material uncertainty over the use of the going concern basis, the auditor draws attention to the going concern disclosures under the heading 'Material Uncertainty Related to Going Concern' in the auditor's report. The auditor does not, however, modify the audit opinion on the proper presentation of the financial statements.

48.18.6 *Auditors' responsibilities for reviewing and reporting on an entity's arrangements for securing value for money*

Auditing frameworks may require public sector auditors to review and report on the entity's arrangements for securing value for money and in such cases it may be appropriate for auditors to consider how the entity ensures that it is able to maintain the sustainability of its services and finances. But, where auditors identify concerns about an entity's general financial health, or its arrangements for maintaining the sustainability of its services and finances, this does not necessarily cast doubt upon the entity's ability to continue to prepare its financial statements on a going concern basis.

48.19   Written representations

Each type of public sector entity has a person or group of people with responsibility for the preparation and signing of the financial statements. The auditor should review relevant regulations to determine to whom this responsibility falls. The responsible person signs letters of representation, including specific representations on the regularity assertion.

48.20   Audits of group financial statements

Where the auditor is acting as group auditor and is relying on the work of one or more component auditors, the considerations set out in ISA (UK) 600 (Revised June 2016) *Special Considerations – Audits of Group Financial Statements (Including the Work of Component Auditors)* will apply.

48.21   Using the work of internal auditors

The requirements of ISA (UK) 610 (Revised June 2016) *Using the Work of Internal Auditors* are as relevant to the audit of public sector entities as to private companies. The internal audit function is normally a mandatory element of a public sector entity's internal control framework, and auditors may have a responsibility to provide negative assurance on a Statement of Internal Control. An assessment of the internal control function is required even if it is not possible to rely on its work in relation to the financial statements.

48.22   Using the work of an auditor's expert

In the public sector, there may be circumstances (in addition to those described in ISA (UK) 620 (Revised June 2016) *Using the Work of an Auditor's Expert*, where the auditor is required to use the work of an auditor's expert. For example, for the audit of specialist or complex accounting estimates, the auditor may need to appoint an expert to obtain understanding of the estimation process. Another example is when one auditor appoints an expert to provide assurance to a number of auditors, for example in respect of professional valuation of properties or a pension scheme.

48.23   Forming an opinion and reporting on financial statements

When reporting on central government financial statements, the requirements of the auditor reporting ISAs (UK) should be followed, bearing in mind any specific reporting requirements of the engagement, such as to whom the audit report is addressed.

The Practice Note gives additional guidance on responsibility statements which should draw attention to the responsibilities of the Accounting Officers or other financial officer with responsibility for the financial statements, separately from those of any other officers. **Table 2** sets out the expected disclosures in a public sector entity's Statement of Responsibilities.

TABLE 2: Expected disclosures in a public sector entity's Statement of Responsibilities

Responsibility for:

- proper accounting records that disclose with reasonable accuracy at any time the financial position of the entity and enable the entity to ensure that financial statements are prepared to comply with statutory requirements;

- safeguarding the assets of the entity and for taking reasonable steps for the prevention and detection of fraud and other irregularities;

- preparation of financial statements for each financial year that give a true and fair view of/present fairly the state of affairs of the entity and its performance for that period;

- in preparing financial statements:

  - selecting suitable accounting policies and then applying them consistently;

  - making judgments and estimates that are reasonable and prudent;

  - stating whether applicable accounting standards have been followed, subject to any material departures disclosed and explained in the financial statements; and

  - preparing the financial statements on the going concern basis, unless it is inappropriate to presume that the entity will continue in business;

- the regularity of the public finances for which the Accounting/Accountable Officer is answerable, where a regularity opinion is given.

The wording of the audit opinion depends on the particular auditing framework. The opinion paragraph should clearly indicate the financial reporting framework used to prepare the financial statements and the statute which requires the financial statements to be audited. These vary from body to body.

Where the auditor is reporting on regularity, a separate and explicit opinion is given on the regularity of transactions in the entity's financial statements. In addition, the auditor may provide separate reports, other than through his audit opinions, on issues of regularity. Where the auditor gives a qualified opinion on regularity, this does not in itself lead to a qualification of the truth and fairness, fair presentation or proper presentation part of the opinion.

48.24 The auditor's responsibilities relating to other information in documents containing audited financial statements

Most public sector entities are required to include a foreword in the same document as the financial statements. The foreword usually contains the information which would be included in the directors' report in a set of Companies Act financial statements, and the auditor's opinion does not extend to the contents of the foreword.

Other information required will vary depending on the type of public sector entity.

48.25 Regularity

For central government bodies in England, the external auditor has to report on whether transactions included in the financial statements conform with the legislation that authorises them. The Comptroller and Auditor General then satisfies himself that expenditure and income have been applied in accordance with Parliament's wishes and reports to Parliament accordingly. Similar requirements exist in Wales, Scotland and Northern Ireland.

A similar requirement also exists in England and Wales in relation to health authorities and other specified National Health Service entities which are consolidated respectively into the financial statements of the Department of Health and the National Assembly for Wales. In Northern Ireland, this requirement exists for health and social service boards.

In other health entities and in local government, there is no requirement for the external auditor to report on regularity, but he should be alert to questions of legality and review the procedures in place to ensure the legality of transactions that might have a significant financial consequence. Any transactions or events of questionable legality coming to light as a result of this review should be reported to the appropriate authorities.

The auditor's responsibilities in relation to regularity are discharged at the same time as the audit of the financial statements and are covered in a separate part of the audit report.

Guidance on regularity for the auditor is set out in Part 2 of the Practice Note. In particular, the section covers:

- understanding the concept of regularity;
- how regularity relates to other concepts including propriety and compliance with laws and regulations;
- the audit of regularity – an overview;
- understanding the entity and its environment;
- understanding the entity's internal controls;
- materiality for the audit of regularity;
- assessing the risk of material irregularity;
- planning and performing audit procedures;
- areas requiring special consideration;
- written representations;
- using the work of others;
- evaluating irregularities;
- the risk of fraud in the audit of regularity;
- regularity opinion on financial statements; and
- other reporting on regularity.

48.26 Grant claims

Many organisations, both in the public and private sectors, receive grant in aid or other grants from government departments or other funding bodies, often requiring the recipient to obtain a report from their accountant or auditor regarding their eligibility for and/or use of the grant.

In 2003, the ICAEW issued Technical Release Audit 03/03 *Public Sector Special Reporting Engagement – Grant Claims* to provide guidance in situations where a grant paying body has awarded a grant for a special purpose and requires that a special accountant's report be produced. Audit 03/03 does not apply in situations where a grant paying body has awarded grant in aid or grants and requires a regularity opinion on the use of these funds.

The Technical Release, which was agreed with the Treasury, builds on the principles outlined in Audit 1/01 *Reporting to Third Parties* (see **Section 40**), and applied from September 2003 for grant arrangements entered into before 2010.

In March 2010, the ICAEW issued Technical Release AAF 01/10 *Framework Document for Accountants' Reports on Grant Claims*. This document sets out a new framework for reporting accountants, to be applied for new schemes developed from 1 April 2010. The framework is intended to be helpful to those involved in providing special reports on grants and returns and also to the grant paying bodies that receive and rely on such reports. The new framework was not intended to be applied to existing schemes whose terms and conditions were already in place, although the Technical Release notes that there is nothing to stop grant paying bodies considering the good practice principles in the framework for such schemes.

49 Regulated entities

49.1 Introduction

Regulated entities (see **Table 1**) are often required to submit a large volume of financial information to their regulated body as part of the regulatory process and the exact requirements can vary significantly between industries. Regulators use this information in a number of ways, for example, in ensuring that costs and pricing are transparent, and the regulatory body often requires an independent accountant's report on elements of this information.

Guidance to assist accountants when reporting on regulatory information can be found in TECH 02/16AAF *Reporting to Regulators on Regulatory Accounts* issued by the ICAEW. This technical release is an update to the one issued in October 2003, Audit 5/03 *Reporting to Regulators of Regulated Entities*.

The guidance in the technical release is based on TECH 10/12AAF *Reporting to Third Parties* (see **Section 40**), and was developed after discussion and consultation with a number of regulators. It does not apply to reporting to other regulatory bodies such as the Financial Conduct Authority (see **Section 9**).

TABLE 1: Regulatory bodies

The Government appointed regulatory bodies that oversee the activities of regulated entities for the purpose of TECH 02/16AAF are:

- Ofgem (Office of Gas and Electricity Markets);

- Ofwat (The Water Services Regulation Authority);

- CAA (Civil Aviation Authority);

- ORR (Office of Rail and Road);

- URegNI (Utility Regulator, Northern Ireland);

- Ofcom (Office of Communications).

49.2   Duty of care and engagement contracts

As noted in **Section 40**, when an accountant knows that a third party obtains and relies on his report, the accountant will owe that third party a duty of care unless an effective disclaimer is in place.

Regulatory returns and regulatory accounts are required by an individual regulator, who will specify what information they will contain and who uses that information as part of its overall role. The accountant will only accept a duty of care to the regulator if either a tri-partite or bi-partite engagement contract with a written notice is in place. If the regulator will not enter into a suitable engagement contract, the accountant will not accept a duty of care to the regulator and will make it clear in his report. However, the report will be addressed to the company and the regulator in order to meet the requirements of the regulatory licence.

The accountant will exclude a duty of care to any other third party by including a suitable disclaimer in his report. A third party may only rely on the report once they have become party to the engagement contract.

49.2.1   Tri-partite engagement contracts

A tri-partite engagement contract is a written engagement contract between the accountant, the regulated entity and the regulator. The contract will contain appropriate terms clarifying and limiting the scope and extent of the accountant's responsibilities and liability.

An example tri-partite engagement contract can be found in TECH 02/ 16AAF *Reporting to Regulators on Regulatory Accounts*.

49.2.2   Bi-partite engagement contracts

A bi-partite engagement contract is a written engagement contract between the accountant and the regulated entity only. In order for the accountant to owe a duty of care to the regulator when a bi-partite engagement contract exists, there must be provision in that contract for the accountant to accept a responsibility to the regulator separately in a written notice. The contract will cap any financial liability to the regulator and regulated entity in aggregate to that which would have been paid to the regulated entity if no separate agreement had been made with the regulator.

A copy of the bi-partite engagement contract between the accountant and the regulated entity will be attached to the written notice. An example of both the bi-partite engagement contract and the written notice can be found in TECH 02/16AAF *Reporting to Regulators on Regulatory Accounts*.

49.3 Reporting

The regulated entity is usually required, under the terms of its regulatory licence, to provide certain information to the regulator and to obtain an accountant's report supporting some or all of that information. Each regulator will stipulate in its regulatory licence the information to be included in reports it receives but any financial information will not usually be in the form of complete financial statements or provide a 'true and fair view'.

However, ISA (UK) 700 (Revised June 2016) *Forming an Opinion and Reporting on Financial Statements* (see **Section 4**) deals with reports on accounts prepared under both 'true and fair' and 'compliance' frameworks and hence can be applied also to reports by independent accounts on regulatory accounts. An example report is given in TECH 02/16AAF *Reporting to Regulators on Regulatory Accounts* although this example has not been updated to reflect the new format and content of the report required under ISA (UK) 700 (Revised June 2016). The report should be further modified as appropriate for the particular circumstances of the engagement.

The accountant should make clear in his report the regulatory information on which he is providing assurance, and that on which he is not. Where the regulatory information is part of a wider report or return, the material covered by the accountant's report should be clearly identified.

49.4 Materiality

Increasingly regulators are requiring entities to include a number of different analyses of their business segments or operations and for accountants to report on them. In order to do this, the accountant must use his professional judgment to assess materiality in the context of the regulatory accounts as a whole and in line with the principles outlined in ISA (UK) 320 (Revised June 2016) *Materiality in Planning and Performing an Audit* (see **Section 15**). His opinion should be on the regulatory accounts as a whole, not on the individual analyses.

If the regulator requires specific items to be reported on in detail, this should form the basis of a separate, 'agreed upon procedures' engagement, which is reported on separately to the opinion on the accounts. Guidance on agreed upon procedures engagements is given in **41.3**.

49.5 Working with independent experts

Accountants may need to rely on the work of independent experts when reporting on regulatory accounts and other regulatory information, such as technical or engineering experts to determine whether the cost of projects should be capitalised or expensed.

Where this is the case, the accountant would follow the guidance in ISA (UK) 620 (Revised June 2016) *Using the Work of an Auditor's Expert* (see **31.3**), and would not refer to the expert's work in his audit report. If an 'agreed upon procedures' engagement is undertaken and no opinion is given in the accountant's report, reference to the expert's work is likely. Consent should be obtained from the experts prior to issuing any report which refers to them or includes extracts of their work.

Appendix 1

Existing guidance at 30 April 2018

Table A sets out the Ethical Standard and other FRC pronouncements. Table B lists the ISAs (UK). Table C sets out other Standards, Practice Notes and Bulletins. Except as noted these are all issued by the FRC, or its predecessors, and are extant as at 30 April 2018.

'Date issued' is the date on which the standard was issued, or, where applicable, the date on which it was last updated. Where a standard is listed twice the latest version contains requirements that may not be fully effective as at 30 April 2018.

Table D lists ICAEW Technical Releases extant on 30 April 2018.

TABLE A

FRC pronouncement	Date Issued
Scope and authority of audit and assurance pronouncements	June 2016
Glossary of terms (auditing and ethics) 2018	January 2018
Revised Ethical Standard 2016	June 2016
ISQC (UK) 1 (Revised June 2016) Quality control for firms that perform audits and reviews of historical financial statements, and other assurance and related services engagements	July 2017

TABLE B

ISAs (UK)	
200 (Revised June 2016) Overall objectives of the independent auditor and the conduct of an audit in accordance with international standards on auditing (UK)	June 2016
210 (Revised June 2016) Agreeing the terms of audit engagements	July 2017
220 (Revised June 2016) Quality control for an audit of financial statements	July 2017
230 (Revised June 2016) Audit documentation	June 2016
240 (Revised June 2016) The auditor's responsibilities relating to fraud in an audit of financial statements	July 2017

250 Section A (Revised June 2016) – Consideration of laws and regulations in an audit of financial statements	June 2016
250 Section A (Revised December 2017) – Consideration of laws and regulations in an audit of financial statements *(effective for audits of periods commencing on or after 15 December 2017)*	December 2017
250 Section B (Revised June 2016) – The auditor's statutory right and duty to report to regulators of public interest entities and regulators of other entities in the financial sector	June 2016
260 (Revised June 2016) Communication with those charged with governance	July 2017
265 Communicating deficiencies in internal control to those charged with governance and management	June 2016
300 (Revised June 2016) Planning an audit of financial statements	June 2016
315 (Revised June 2016) Identifying and assessing the risks of material misstatement through understanding of the entity and its environment	June 2016
320 (Revised June 2016) Materiality in planning and performing an audit	June 2016
330 (Revised June 2016) The auditor's responses to assessed risks	June 2016
330 (Revised July 2017) The auditor's responses to assessed risks *(effective for audits of periods commencing on or after 15 December 2017)*	July 2017
402 Audit considerations relating to an entity using a service organisation	June 2016
450 (Revised June 2016) Evaluation of misstatements identified during the audit	July 2017
500 Audit evidence	July 2017
501 Audit evidence – specific considerations for selected items	June 2016
505 External confirmations	July 2017
510 (Revised June 2016) Initial audit engagements – opening balances	June 2016
520 Analytical procedures	June 2016
530 Audit sampling	June 2016
540 (Revised June 2016) Auditing accounting estimates, including fair value accounting estimates, and related disclosures	June 2016
550 Related parties	June 2016
560 Subsequent events	June 2016
570 (Revised June 2016) Going concern	June 2016

580 Written representations	June 2016
600 (Revised June 2016) Special considerations – audits of group financial statements (including the work of component auditors)	June 2016
610 (Revised June 2013) Using the work of internal auditors	June 2016
620 (Revised June 2016) Using the work of an auditor's expert	June 2016
700 (Revised June 2016) Forming an opinion and reporting on financial statements	June 2016
701 Communicating key audit matters in the independent auditor's report	June 2016
705 (Revised June 2016) Modifications to the opinion in the independent auditor's report	June 2016
706 (Revised June 2016) Emphasis of matter paragraphs and other matter paragraphs in the independent auditor's report	June 2016
710 Comparative information – corresponding figures and comparative financial statements	June 2016
720 (Revised June 2016) The auditor's responsibilities relating to other information	June 2016
800 (Revised) Special considerations – audits of financial statements prepared in accordance with special purpose frameworks	October 2016
805 (Revised) Special considerations – audits of single financial statements and specific elements, accounts or items of a financial statement	October 2016

TABLE C

Other FRC standards

Standard: Providing assurance on client assets to the Financial Conduct Authority	November 2015
ISRE (UK and Ireland) 2410: Review of interim financial information performed by the independent auditor of the entity	July 2007

Practice Notes

SORP: PN10 Audit of financial statements of public sector bodies in the United Kingdom (now issued by the Public Audit Forum)	December 2016
PN11 (Revised) The audit of charities in the United Kingdom	November 2017
PN14 The audit of housing associations in the United Kingdom	January 2014
PN15 (Revised) The audit of occupational pension schemes in the United Kingdom	November 2017

PN19 (Revised) The audit of banks and building societies in the United Kingdom — March 2011

PN20 (Revised) The audit of insurers in the United Kingdom — January 2017

PN23 Special considerations in auditing financial instruments — July 2013

PN26 (Revised) Guidance on smaller entity audit documentation (Revised) — December 2009

Bulletins

Bulletin 2006/5 The Combined Code on Corporate Governance: Requirements of auditors under the Listing Rules of the Financial Services Authority and the Irish Stock Exchange — September 2006

Bulletin 2008/1 Audit issues when financial market conditions are difficult and credit facilities may be restricted — January 2008

Bulletin 2008/5 Auditor's reports on revised accounts and reports in the United Kingdom — April 2008

Bulletin 2008/9 Miscellaneous Reports by Auditors Required by the United Kingdom Companies Act 2006 — October 2008

Bulletin 2008/10 Going Concern Issues During the Current Economic Conditions — December 2008

Bulletin 2009/4 Developments in Corporate Governance Affecting the Responsibilities of Auditors of UK Companies — December 2009

Bulletin 2010/1 XBRL Tagging of Information in Audited Financial Statements – Guidance for Auditors — February 2010

Bulletin 2: Guidance for Reporting Accountants of Stakeholder Pension Schemes in the United Kingdom — February 2013

Bulletin: Compendium of illustrative auditor's reports on United Kingdom private sector financial statements for periods commencing on or after 17 June 2016 — October 2016

Bulletin: The auditor's association with preliminary announcements made in accordance with UK Listing Rules — December 2017

FRC staff guidance notes

SGN 01/2016 Provision of non-audit services to non-EU subsidiaries

SGN 02/2016 Playing any part in management or decision making

SGN 03/2016 Period of engagement

SGN 04/2016 Power of attorney

SGN 05/2016 Prohibited tax services

SGN 01/2017 Services Linked to Financing, Capital Structure and Allocation and Investment Strategy of the Audited Entity

SGN 02/2017 Explaining to what extent the audit was considered capable of detecting irregularities

SGN 03/2017 Materiality and Other Information

SGN 01/2018   The Auditor's Provision of Restructuring Services to Public interest Entity Participants in Bank Lending or Bond Funded Syndicates

TABLE D

ICAEW Technical Releases

The following list is not a complete list of ICAEW Technical Releases but provides details of those that are of particular relevance to auditors.

AAF 02/95: The ascertainment and confirmation of contingent liabilities arising from pending legal matters

AAF 02/99: Receipt of information in confidence by auditors

AUDIT 04/00: Firm's reports and duties to lenders in connection with loans and other facilities to clients and related covenants

AUDIT 02/01: Requests for references on clients' financial status and their ability to service loans

AUDIT 01/02: Practical points for auditors in connection with the implementation of FRS 17 'Retirement Benefits' – defined benefit schemes

AUDIT 02/02: New arrangements for reporting to the ABTA

AUDIT 04/02: Management representation letters: Explanatory note

AUDIT 01/03: The audit report and auditor's duty of care to third parties (Revised May 2018)

AUDIT 03/03: Public sector special reporting engagements – grant claims

AUDIT 04/03: Access to working papers by investigating accountants

AUDIT 03/04: Auditing implications of IFRS transition

AUDIT 02/05: Guidance on the implications of the *Freedom of Information Act* 2000

AAF 01/06 Assurance reports on internal controls of service organisations made available to third parties (Revised 2012)

AAF 02/06 Identifying and managing certain risks arising from the inclusion of reports from auditors and accountants in prospectuses (and certain other investment circulars)

AAF 04/06 Assurance engagements: management of risk and liability

AAF 01/07 Independent accountants report on packaging waste

AAF 02/07 A framework for assurance reports on third party operations

AAF 01/08 Access to information by successor auditors

AAF 01/09 Paid cheques

AAF 01/10 Framework document for accountants' reports on grant claims

AAF 04/10 Guidance for performing agreed-upon procedures engagements that address XBRL-tagged data included within financial statements prepared in an iXBRL format

AAF 01/11 Reporting to the Audit Bureau of Circulations Limited (ABC)

TECH 03/11 Residential service charge accounts

TECH 08/12AAF Regularity reporting for Academies 2011–12: Guidance

TECH 10/12AAF Reporting to third parties (superseded AUDIT 01/01)

TECH 04/13AAF Assurance reporting on relevant trustees

TECH 09/13 AAF Assurance review engagements on historical financial statements (supersedes AAF 03/06)

TECH 07/14 AAF Assurance reporting on master trusts (master trust supplement to AAF 02/07)

TECH 10/14 AAF Receipt of information in confidence by auditors (superseded AUDIT 02/99)

TECH 13/14 AAF Issues for auditors arising from the implementation of FRS 102 *The Financial Reporting Standard applicable in the UK and Republic of Ireland*

TECH 16/14 BL (Revised) Guidance on donations by a company to its parent charity

TECH 16/15 AAF Solicitors Regulation Authority (SRA) Accounts Rules: interim guidance for reporting accountants following changes to the accountant's report requirements

TECH 09/15 BL Managing the professional liability of accountants

TECH 02/16 AAF Reporting to regulators on regulatory accounts (supersedes AUDIT 05/03)

AAF 07/16 Chartered accountants' reports on the compilation of financial information of incorporated entities Revised March 2016 – updates AAF 02/10

AAF 08/16 Chartered accountants' reports on the compilation of historical financial information of unincorporated entities Revised March 2016 – updates AAF 03/10

TECH 09/16 AAF Revised arrangements for ATOL reporting accountants reporting to the Civil Aviation Authority (supersedes TECH 07/12AAF)

TECH 12/16 AAF Assurance reporting on Master Trusts (supplement to AAF 02/07)

Appendix 2

Specific ISA requirements relating to statutory audits of public interest entities

The requirements listed below are those that apply specifically to public interest entities, PIEs[1]. These are in addition to requirements applicable to audits of listed companies (for example in ISQC (UK) 1 and ISAs (UK) 220, 260, 700, 701 and 720) and entities that are required to or choose voluntarily to state how they have complied with the UK Corporate Governance Code (for example in ISAs (UK) 260, 570, 700, 701 and 720). Such entities may also be PIEs. Where additional guidance is given in the application material of ISAs rather than in the requirements, this is not included here.

ISA	Paragraph Reference	Summary of requirement	Chapter reference
ISQC1	27R-2	Additional requirements before accepting or continuing an engagement	3.2.6
ISQC1	36R-1	Additional requirements about the EQCR	3.2.8
ISQC1	39R-1	Additional requirements about the need for an EQCR and who is qualified to perform it	3.2.8
ISQC1	43-R1	Resolving disagreements between the audit partner and EQCR	3.2.8
220	21R-1	Areas of consideration for an EQCR	3.3.6
220	21R-2	Discussion of the results of the EQCR	3.3.6
220	25R-1	Documentation of the EQCR	3.3.8
220	25R-2	Documentation of the EQCR	3.3.8
240	41R-1	Suspicions about fraud or irregularities	16.8.1
240	43R-1	Informing the authorities when the entity does not investigate suspicions of fraud or irregularities	16.8.1

---

[1] See glossary for definition.

Appendix 2

ISA	Paragraph Reference	Summary of requirement	Chapter reference
250A (Revised June 2016)	22R-1	Suspicions about fraud or irregularities	17.8.4
250A (Revised June 2016)	28R-1	Informing the authorities when the entity does not investigate suspicions	17.8.4
250A (Revised December 2017)	23R-1	Suspicions about fraud or irregularities	17.8.4
250A (Revised December 2017)	29R-1	Informing the authorities when the entity does not investigate suspicions	17.8.4
250B	13R-1	Reporting to regulators	9.7
260	11R-1	Report to the equivalent of the audit committee where none exists	10.2
260	16R-2	Additional report to the audit committee	10.7.2
260	17R-1	Confirmation and discussion of independence	10.6.5
260	20R-1	Requirements regarding the additional report to the audit committee	10.4.2
260	21R-1	Timing of additional report to audit committee	10.7.2
260	23D-1	Retention of documents relating to the additional report to the audit committee	10.4.2
330	19R-1	Requirement to assess the valuation methods used	21.4.2
510	8R-1	Obtaining an understanding of the predecessor auditor's methodology	19.3.3
600	49D-1	Responsibility for additional report to audit committee	30.15
620	9R-1	Confirmation of the external expert's independence	31.3.5
700	30-1	Reporting on key audit matters for those entities that apply the Code	4.11
700	45R-1	Requirements regarding the audit report	4.18
701	All	Requirements relating to key audit matters	4.11

Appendix 3

Glossary

Annual report (for the purposes of ISA (UK) 720 *The auditor's responsibilities relating to other information*)	A document, or combination of documents, prepared typically on an annual basis by management or those charged with governance in accordance with law, regulation or custom, the purpose of which is to provide owners (or similar stakeholders) with information on the entity's operations and the entity's financial results and financial position as set out in the financial statements. An annual report contains or accompanies the financial statements and the auditor's report thereon and usually includes information about the entity's developments, its future outlook and risks and uncertainties, a statement by the entity's governing body, and reports covering governance matters. In the UK, an annual report includes at least: (a) the statutory other information; and (b) any other documents that are incorporated by cross-reference in, or distributed to shareholders with, statutory other information either voluntarily or pursuant to law or regulation or the requirements of a stock exchange listing.
FCA	Financial Conduct Authority
Key audit matters	Those matters that, in the auditor's professional judgment, were of most significance in the audit of the financial statements of the current period. Key audit matters are selected from matters communicated with those charged with governance.
Key audit partner	The key audit partner is defined in UK legislation as: (a) The statutory auditor designated by an audit firm for a particular audit engagement as being primarily responsible for carrying out the statutory audit on behalf of the audit firm; or (b) In the case of a group audit, the statutory auditor designated by an audit firm as being primarily responsible for carrying out the statutory audit at the level of the group and the statutory auditor designated at the level of material subsidiaries; or (c) The statutory auditor who signs the audit report.

Listed entity	A listed entity is one whose shares, stock or debt are quoted or listed on a recognised stock exchange, or are marketed under the regulations of a recognised stock exchange or other equivalent body. In the UK this includes those listed on the London Stock Exchange (including those admitted to trading on the Alternative Investments Market), ISDX Markets. It does not include entities whose quoted or listed shares, stock or debt are in substance not freely transferable or cannot be traded freely by the public or the entity.
Public interest entity (PIE)	Public interest entities are those whose transferable securities are admitted to trading on a regulated market, credit institutions and insurance undertakings. This includes companies listed on the main market of the London Stock Exchange but not those listed on AIM.

The FRC's *Scope and Authority of Audit and Assurance Pronouncements* makes clear that requirements in the Ethical and Auditing Standards applicable to public interest entities apply only to such entities as are governed by the law of an EU member state.

Statutory other information	For statutory audits of financial statements, those documents or reports that are required to be prepared and issued by the entity (including any reports or documents that are incorporated by cross reference) in relation to which the auditor is required to report publicly in accordance with law or regulation.

In the UK, the statutory other information includes, where required to be prepared:

(a) the directors' report;

(b) the strategic report;

(c) the separate corporate governance statement, where applicable.

INDEX

abbreviated accounts
auditor's report   6.4.2
guidance   6.4.3
preparation of   6.1

ACCA (Association of Chartered Certified Accountants)
as RSB   2.1
audit regulations   2.1.2

Access to Information by Successor Auditors (Technical Release 01/08)   38.1, 38.3.2

Access to Working Papers by Investigating Accountants (Technical Release Audit 04/03)   12.1, 12.9

accountants
determining who will rely on work of   40.8.2
engagement letters, example   8.3.1
from same firm as auditors   12.9.4
IFAC Code of Ethics   2.5
procedures   8.3.3, 8.4.6
professional ethics   8.2.1
reports – *see* accountants' compilation reports

accountants' compilation reports
aim   8.3.6
audit exemption   8.5
engagement letters   8.5.3
example   8.3.6
exemptions   8.1
guidance   8.2
incorporated entities – *see* incorporated entities, accountants' compilation reports
requirements when a company becomes exempt   8.5.2
resignation procedures   8.5.4
Solicitors' Accounts Rules   45.5–6
unincorporated entities – *see* unincorporated entities, accountants' compilation reports

accounting and auditing   1.2

accounting estimates
audit procedures   27.4
significant risks   27.4.1
testing management's methods   27.4.2
charities   43.16
documentation   27.9
evaluation of results   27.5
fraud risk   16.4.5
generally   27.1
indicators of   27.7
international developments   27.10
ISA (UK) 540 (Revised) (Auditing accounting estimates, including fair value accounting estimates, and related disclosures)   27.1
obtaining an understanding   27.2
possible management bias, indicators of   27.7

accounting estimates – *contd*
public sector audits   48.15
Registered Providers of Social Housing   47.15
risk assessment of   27.3
written representations   27.8

accounting policies – *see also* FRS 18 (Accounting Policies)
charities   43.11.2
significant, omission of in reports to management   10.6.4

accounting risks – *see also* risk assessment

accounting systems and internal control
custody assets and collateral   9.5.1
risk identification and assessment, auditor's responses   36.7.1
service organisations   36.7.2
simple, smaller entities   36.10.3

accounts
abbreviated – *see* abbreviated accounts
charities   43.1.1

actuaries – *see also* experts, use of
competence and objectivity   31.3.5

ad hoc reports, to FCA
auditing standards   9.6.1
auditor's right to report directly to regulators   9.6.5
communication by FSA   9.6.7
compliance with management requirements   9.6.3
cumulative minor breaches   9.6.4
fit and proper person requirement   9.6.3
form of report   9.6.6
going concern, doubt as to entity's status as   9.6.3
guidance   9.6.1, 9.6.3
identification of matters requiring report   9.6.4
material significance considerations   9.6.3
other auditors, use of   9.6.4
planning   9.6.4
procedures   9.6.4
public interest entities   9.7
relationship with other reporting responsibilities   9.6.8
reporting   9.6.5
right and duty to report   9.6.2
risk of loss   9.6.3
statutory provisions   9.6
supervision and control   9.6.4

'adverse' opinion – *see also* opinions, audit
client asset engagements   9.5.17
modified auditor's reports   5.4
modified opinion   5.5.3

Affordable Home Ownership – Charitable Status and Tax   47.2.6

American Institute of Certified Public Accountants (AICPA) – *see* AICPA (American Institute of Certified Public Accountants)

analytical procedures – *see also* **ISA (UK) 520 (Analytical procedures)**
audit evidence, evaluating   16.5
audit procedures   23.2.5
definition   25.2
end of audit   25.6
evidence   36.8.2
generally   25.1
investigating
unusual items   16.4.3
variances   25.7
practical problems   25.3
Registered Providers of Social Housing   47.14
risk assessment   21.3.2, 25.4
substantive procedure   25.5
acceptable differences   25.5.4
data reliability   25.5.2
precision of expected results   25.5.3
suitability of analytical procedures   25.5.1
substantive procedures as   21.4.2

announcements, preliminary – *see* **preliminary announcements**

annual report
auditor discovers non-compliance with the Code   42.6.3
significant problems   42.6.2

anti-money laundering measures – *see* **money laundering prevention**

Anti-Money Laundering Regulations 2017
effectivity   18.2

APB (Auditing Practices Board)
adoption of clarified ISAs   1.6.3
bulletins – *see* bulletins (APB)
ethical standards for auditors   2.1.1
Practice Notes issued by   1.7.1
predecessor body   1.5.3
Professional Scepticism project 23.9.1

APMs (alternative performance measures)
preliminary announcements   6.3.5

appointment and reappointment of auditors – *see also* **resignations**
acceptance of   2.8.1
corporate governance, auditor procedures in relation to   42.6.2

appointment and resignation
pension schemes   44.5

approval of financial information
incorporated entities   8.3.5
unincorporated entities   8.4.8

ARC (Audit Registration Committee)
guidance on technical standards   2.8

assertions
audit
account balances and related disclosures at period end   21.3.6
classes of transactions and events for the period under audit   21.3.6
other disclosures   21.3.6
presentation and disclosure   21.3.6
audit evidence, using to gather   23.2.4
definition   23.2.4
fraud, at assertion level   16.4.5
risks related to   21.3.6, 21.4.2

assets
client – *see* client assets
non-cash, transfer to public company by one of its members   7.6.1
responsible for   14.4
tangible, inspection of   23.2.5

Association of Chartered Certified Accountants (ACCA)
as RSB   2.1
audit regulations   2.1.2

Association of Investment Companies (AIC)   42.10.1

Assurance Engagements: Management of Risk and Liability (ICAEW AAF 04/06)   40.3, 40.3.2

Assurance Engagements other than Audits or Review of Historical Financial Information (ISAE) 3000 (Revised)   41.5.2

Assurance on Non-Financial Information: Existing Practices and Issues (ICAEW)   40.2
considerations for practitioners   41.5.3
practices and guidance   41.5.2
report on   41.5.1

Assurance reports on internal controls of service organisations made available to third parties (AAF 01/06)   40.2, 40.7.1, 40.7.2

Assurance review engagements on historical financial statements (Technical Release 09/13 AAF)   41.1, 41.2.1

Attendance at stocktaking (Practice Note 25) – *see also* **ISA (UK) 501 (Audit evidence – specific considerations for selected items)**
audit evidence   23.5.2
auditor unable to attend physical count   23.5.6
evaluation of management's instructions and procedures   23.5.4
guidance   23.5.1
inventory held by third parties   23.5.7
observation, inspection and test counts   23.5.5
planning   23.5.3

audit clients
partners joining   2.7.4
partners/audit firm employees not to accept governance role with   2.6.4

audit committees
communication with external auditors   42.8.3
guidance booklets, ICAEW   42.2.1
independence of auditors   42.8.1
responsibilities of audit committee   42.8.1
corporate governance, auditor procedures in
relation to   42.6.2
interim review engagement, notification of
requests to discontinue   39.18
Registered Providers of Social
Housing   47.2.3
responsibilites of   42.8.1
Revised Ethical Standard 2016   2.6
role of
designing communication to
complement   42.8.2
understanding   42.8.1

audit considerations
bank confirmations   24.2

audit engagement partners, rotation   2.6.5

audit evidence – *see* **evidence, audit**

audit exemption
charities   43.1
ineligible companies   8.5.1
requirements when a company becomes
exempt   8.5.2
resignation procedures   8.5.4

audit findings
reports to management   10.6.4

audit firm culture
audit quality   3.4.2

audit firms
control of   2.3

**Audit of Charities (Practice Note 11) 43.2 –
see also charities**
audit guidance   43.2
audit procedures   43.13
charities   43.7
going concern issues   43.19
governance, communication with those
charged with   43.8
summarised financial statements   43.24
terms of engagement   43.3

**Audit of Financial Statements of Public Sector
Bodies in the United Kingdom (Practice Note
10)   48.1**

**Audit of Housing Associations in the United
Kingdom (Practice Note 14)   47.1.1**
laws and regulations   47.6.1
responsibilities of the board   47.2.2

**Audit of Insurers in the United Kingdom
(Practice Note 20) (Revised)   9.6.1**

**Audit of Investment Businesses in the United
Kingdom (Practice Note 21) (Revised)**
auditing standards and guidance   9.2
generally   46.1

**Audit of Occupational Pension Schemes in
the United Kingdom (Practice Note 15)   44.1**
fraud considerations   44.6

**Audit of Registered Social Landlords in the
United Kingdom (Practice Note 14) 47.1.1**
responsibilities of the board   47.2.2

Audit of Related Parties in Practice (ICAEW)
five-point action plan   20.12.2
issue of   20.12.1

audit opinions – *see* **opinions, audit**
report on other legal and regulatory
requirements   4.13

audit procedures – *see* **procedures, audit**

audit process
audit quality   3.4.2

Audit Quality Framework (FRC)
audit firm culture   3.4.2
audit process   3.4.2
background   3.4.1
factors outside auditor's control   3.4.3
promoting audit quality   3.4.2
quality control   3.1
reliability of audit reporting   3.4.2
skills of partners and staff   3.4.2

audit regulation and ethics – *see* **regulation
and ethics, audit**

**Audit report and auditor's duty of care to third
parties (Technical Release Audit 01/03)   4.2.1**
introductory paragraph   4.8

audit reports – *see* **reports, audit**
objective   4.3
other planning and scoping matters   4.11.6

audit risk
assessment of – *see* risk assessment
setting materiality   15.4

audit sampling – *see* **sampling, audit**
evidence   36.8.3

auditing
and accounting   1.2

**Auditing Complex Financial Instruments -
Interim Guidance (Practice Note 23) (Revised)
– *see also* complex financial instruments**
audit evidence, evaluating   28.9.7
audit procedures   28.9.6
background   28.9.1
considerations in difficult market
conditions   28.9.9
general considerations   28.9.2
generally   28.2, 28.9.1
reliance on controls   28.9.5
responsibilities   28.9.3
understanding the entity   28.9.4
valuation guidance   28.9.2

**Auditing Issues when Financial Market
Conditions are Difficult and Credit Facilities
may be Restricted (APB Bulletin 2008/1)**
fair value auditing   28.2

Auditing Issues when Financial Market Conditions are Difficult and Credit Facilities may be Restricted (APB Bulletin 2008/1) – *contd*
    going concern   11.2
    Registered Providers of Social
        Housing   47.2.6
    risk assessment   37.6

auditing standards – *see also* **International Standards of Auditing (UK) (ISAs); individual ISAs**
    audit reports   4.2
    Auditing Practices Board – *see* APB (Auditing
        Practices Board)
    authoritative bodies   1.3
    bulletins – *see* bulletins (APB)
    conventions   1.9
    EU Audit Directive and Regulation – *see* EU
        Audit Directive and Regulation
    auditors' experts   31.3.1
    going concern   11.2
    IAASB – *see* IAASB (International Auditing
        and Assurance Standards Board)
    ICAEW – *see* ICAEW (Institute of Chartered
        Accountants in England and Wales)
    IFAC – *see* IFAC (International Federation of
        Accountants)
    internal audit   31.2.1
    International Standards on Auditing (UK)
        (ISAs)   1.6.1
    laws and regulations   17.1
    limitations of   1.2
    on Consultative Advisory Group (CAG)   1.4.2
    on Public Interest Oversight Board
        (PIOB)   1.4.2
    other auditors, reliance on   31.3.1
    other guidance   1.8
    other information   36.2
    Practice Notes – *see* Practice Notes
    related parties   20.2
    reports to FCA   9.2
    risk assessment   21.1
    summary financial statements   6.5
    transition period, clarified ISAs   1.6.1

auditor responsibilities
    audit reports   4.9
    'comply or explain' statement   42.4
    corporate governance   42.6.2
    error   16.4
    fraud   16.4
    ISA (UK) 600 (Revised June 2016)   4.16
    Kingston Cotton Mill Company case   16.4
    laws and regulations   17.4
    opening balances and comparatives   19.2
    other information   34.1
    professional scepticism   16.4.1
    public sector audits
        entity's arrangements for securing value for
            money   48.18.6
        going concern issues   48.18.4
    Registered Providers of Social
        Housing   47.2.5
    reporting by exception
        other entities   4.14
        small companies   4.14

auditor responsibilities – *contd*
    reporting by exception – *contd*
        UK companies   4.14
    review – *see* review, audit
    statement of   42.4
    UK Corporate Governance Code   42.4
        provisions   42.5
        reporting   34.7

auditors
    appointment
        acceptance of   2.8.1
        CASS auditors   9.5–9.5.1
        corporate governance, auditor procedures
            in relation to   42.6.2
    cessation of office procedure   38.2
        all companies   38.2.2
        Companies Act 2006 requirements   38.2.1
        legal advice   38.2.7
        non-public interest companies   38.2.3
        notifications – non-public interest
            companies   38.2.5
        public interest companies   38.2.6
        Section 519 statements   38.2.4
    changes in – *see* changes of auditors
    compliance with UK Corporate Governance
        Code   42.1.1
    auditor disclaims an opinion, other
        considerations   5.5.7
    component auditors
        communication with   30.3
        definition   30.3
    continuing, opening balances   19.1
    ethical standards   2.1.1, 2.6
    FRC guidance on audit committees   42.8.2
    incoming – *see* incoming auditors
        comparatives   19.5
        public interest entities   19.3.2
    independence of – *see* independence
    non-audit services, provision   2.6.7
    pension schemes – *see* pension schemes
    public interest entities   9.7
    Regulators, relationship with   47.2.7
    reliance on other – *see* other auditors, reliance
        on
    resignations
        audit exemption, increase in   8.5.4
        laws and regulations   17.9
    responsibilities of – *see* auditor responsibilities
    scepticism – *see* professional scepticism
    small businesses, relationship with   36.4

Auditors' Association with Preliminary Announcements Made in Accordance with Requirements of the UK and Irish Listing Rules (APB Bulletin 2008/2)   6.1, 6.3.2–6.3.3
    alternative performance measures   6.3.5
    superseded by Bulletin 2008/2   6.3.9

Auditors' consideration of FRS 17 (Practice Note 22)
    guidance   29.2

auditors' experts
    auditing standards   31.3.1
    considerations in using experts   31.3.3
    nature, timing and extent of audit
        procedures   31.3.4

auditor's report
public interest entities   4.18

Auditor's Reports on Revised Accounts and Reports in the United Kingdom (APB Bulletin 2008/5)   6.1, 6.2.2

authoritative bodies
outline of main bodies   1.3
role   1.1

authority
bank confirmations   24.4

balance sheet – *see also* post-balance sheet events
complex financial instruments   28.9.6
qualified, re-registration of companies   7.4.2

bank confirmations
audit considerations   24.2
authority   24.4
guidance   24.1
online confirmation   24.5
request letters   24.3

Bank Reports for Audit Purposes (Practice Note 16)   24.1

Bannerman case (audit reports)
Bannerman statements included in reports   4.2.1
generally   4.28
re-registration of companies   7.4.2
Technical Release Audit 1/03   4.2.1

BBA (British Bankers' Association) – *see also* bank confirmations
online confirmations   24.5

borrowing facilities
and going concern, assessment of   11.7.2

Brexit
auditing implications   37.7

British Bankers' Association – *see* BBA (British Bankers' Association), bank confirmations

Bulletins (APB)
Auditing Issues when Financial Market Conditions are Difficult and Credit Facilities may be Restricted (No 2008/1) – *see* Auditing Issues when Financial Market Conditions are Difficult and Credit Facilities may be Restricted (APB Bulletin 2008/1)
Auditors' association with preliminary announcements made in accordance with the requirements of the UK and Irish listing rules (No 2008/2)   6.1, 6.3.2–6.3.3
Auditor's reports on revised accounts and reports, in the United Kingdom (No 2008/5)   6.1, 6.2.2
Auditor's Statement on the Summary Financial Statement in the United Kingdom (No 2008/3)
summary financial statements   6.5

Bulletins (APB) – *contd*
Combined Code on Corporate Governance: Requirements of Auditors Under the Listing Rules of the Financial Services Authority and the Irish Stock Exchange (No 2006/5)   42.2.2, 42.6
Companies (Revision of Defective Accounts and Reports) Regulations 2008 (No 2008/4)   6.1
Compendium of illustrative auditor's reports on United Kingdom private sector financial statements for periods ending on or after 15 December 2010 (revised) (APB Bulletin 2010/2)
charities   43.2
going concern   11.2
Developments in Corporate Governance Affecting the Responsibilities of Auditors of UK Companies (No 2009/4)   42.2.2
Directors' Remuneration Report Regulations 2002 (No 2002/2) – *see* Directors' Remuneration Report Regulations 2002 (APB Bulletin 2002/2)
Going Concern Issues During the Current Economic Conditions (No 2008/10) – *see* Going Concern Issues During the Current Economic Conditions (APB Bulletin 2008/10)
Miscellaneous Reports by Auditors required by United Kingdom Companies Act 2006 (No 2008/9)   7.1
Providing assurance on client assets to the Financial Conduct Authority (No 2011/2)   9.2, 9.5.5
Special Auditor's Report on Abbreviated Accounts in the United Kingdom (No 2008/4)   6.1
The senior statutory auditor under the United Kingdom Companies Act 2006 (No 2008/6)   4.2.1
XBRL Tagging of Information in Audited Financial Statements – Guidance for Auditors (No 2010/1)   37.4.1

business refinancing, no acquisition
access to working papers   12.9.3

business relationships
Ethical Standard Section 2   2.6.4

CAATs (computer-assisted audit techniques)
data analytics   35.1
generally   23.2.5

capabilities
of experts   31.3.5

capitalisation of works
social housing audits   47.2.6

CASS auditors
assessment of engagement risk   9.5.8
auditing standards   9.2
experience   9.5.6
expert knowledge   9.5.16
generally   9.5–9.5.1
guidance   9.2
trust funds   9.5.9

CASS auditors – *contd*
  trust funds – *contd*
    custody assets 9.5.11
    expert assistance 9.5.16
    reconciliations 9.5.10

CASS (Client Assets Sourcebook) rule –
see also **client assets**
  compliance with 9.5.7
  generally 9.5.4–9.5.5
  objective 9.5.8
  trusts 9.5.9
    expert knowledge 9.5.16
    internal audits 9.5.15

CCAB (Consultative Committee of Accountancy Bodies) **1.5.2**
  anti-money laundering guidance, accountancy
    sector 18.3
  guidance to third parties 40.2

cessation of office as auditors, procedures
  all companies, rules 38.2.2
  Companies Act 2006 requirements 38.2.1
  legal advice 38.2.7
  non-public interest companies
    appointment ceases at end of term 38.2.3
    appointment ceases mid-term 38.2.3
  notifications, non-public interest companies
    ICAEW 38.2.5
    members 38.2.5
    registrar 38.2.5
  public interest companies 38.2.6
  Section 519 statement 38.2.4

changes in terms
  engagement letters 14.4.3

changes of auditors – *see also* **auditors**
  access to information by successors
    Companies Act 2006 38.3.1
    Technical Release 01/08 38.1, 38.3.2
  procedures on cessation of office, Companies
    Act 2006 requirements 38.2.1
  working papers 12.9.5

charities – *see also* **Audit of Charities (Practice Note 11)**
  accounts preparation 43.1.1
  audit
    exemptions 43.1
    guidance 43.2
    requirements 43.1.1
  communicating deficiencies 43.9
  FRS 102 43.1
  generally 43.1.1
  independent examination 43.1.2
  legislation 43.1
  material significance considerations 43.7
  planning, financial statements audit 43.10
  problems for auditors 43.2
  quality control, financial statements
    audit 43.4
  Registered Providers of Social
    Housing 47.2.6
  regulators 43.1
  risk of misstatement 43.11.3
  summarised financial statements 43.24

charities – *see also* **Audit of Charities (Practice Note 11)** – *contd*
  terms of audit engagements, agreement 43.3
  whistle-blowing duties 43.1.3

Charities (Accounts and Reports) Regulations 2008 **43.1.1**
  laws and regulations, consideration of
    financial statements preparation 43.6.1
    non-compliance may have a material effect
      on the financial statements 43.6.2

Charities Act 2011
  generally 43.1
  whistle-blowing duties 43.1.3

Charity Commission
  audit reports 43.22
  responsibilities 43.1
  whistle-blowing requirement 43.1.3

Chartered Accountants' Reports on the Compilation of Financial Statements of Incorporated Entities (Technical Release Audit 07/16) **8.2, 8.3.1, 8.3.6, 41.1**

Chartered Accountants' Reports on the Compilation of Historical Financial Statements of Unincorporated Entities (Technical Release Audit 08/16) **8.2, 8.4.1, 8.4.3, 41.1**

Cheques Act 1992
  paid cheques 37.5.3

claims
  enquiries 23.6
  grant – *see* grant claims
  meeting of 2.10

clarity project (IAASB) **1.6.2**

Client Asset Assurance Standard
  assurance procedures 9.5.7
  CASS rules
    client money (CASS 5, 7 and 11) 9.5.5
    client money distributions (CASS 5.6 and
      7A) 9.5.5
    collateral (CASS 3) 9.5.5
    custody assets (CASS 6) 9.5.5
    mandates (CASS 8) 9.5.5
  internal audit function 9.5.15
  scope 9.5.5

client asset reports
  adverse opinion 9.5.17
  examples 9.5.17
  generally 9.5.1
  types of
    limited assurance report 9.5.2
    reasonable assurance report 9.5.2

Client Asset Rules
  breaches 9.5.1, 9.5.7
  standards 1.7.3

client assets
  accepting engagement 9.5.6
  assurance standard – *see* Client Asset
    Assurance Standard
  background 9.5.1

client assets – *contd*
CASS auditor report 9.5.1
CASS rules 9.5.4, 9.5.13
client money 9.5.5, 9.5.12
client money distributions 9.5.5
collateral 9.5.5
custody assets 9.5.5, 9.5.11
mandates 9.5.5, 9.5.14
permission to hold 9.5.3
Providing Assurance on Client Assets to the
FSA (APB Bulletin 2011/2) 9.5.5
reports – *see* client asset reports
risk of loss 9.6.3
safeguarding 9.5.1

client investments – *see* **custody assets
(CASS Rule 6)**

client money – *see also* **Solicitors' Account
Rules**
CASS rules 9.5.5, 9.5.12

**client money distributions (CASS Rules 5.6
and 7A) 9.5.5**

clients, audit
responsibilities, accountants' report 8.4.4

collateral (CASS Rule 3) 9.5.5

Combined Code on Corporate Governance –
see also **corporate governance**

**Combined Code on Corporate Governance:
Requirements of Auditors Under the Listing
Rules of the Financial Services Authority
and the Irish Stock Exchange (APB Bulletin
2006/5)**
guidance in 42.2.2
procedures 42.6

**communicating deficiencies in internal
control**
deficiencies in 9.10.4
identifying and reporting deficiencies 10.10.1
reporting of
other deficiencies 10.10.4
significant deficiencies 10.10.3
significant deficiencies 10.10.2

**communicating with management and
those charged with governance** – *see also*
**communicating deficiencies in internal
control**
addressees 10.4.3
adequacy of communications 10.5
aims 10.3
auditor's responsibilities 10.6.2
determination 10.2
documentation 10.4.2
establishing expectations 10.4.1
form of communication 10.4.2
form of reports 10.4.4
fraud 16.8
generally 10.1
groups 10.8
planned scope and timing 10.6.3
public interest entities 16.8
significant findings from audit 10.6.4

**communicating with management and
those charged with governance** – *see also*
**communicating deficiencies in internal
control** – *contd*
third parties 10.9

communication with audit committees
companies applying UK Corporate
Governance Code 10.7.1

communications from auditors – *see also*
**interim reports, review of; communicating
with management and those charged with
governance**
interim financial information 39.15

**Companies (Audit, Investigations and
Community Enterprise) Act 2004**
RSBs 2.1

Companies Act 2006
approval of financial statements 8.3.5
audit documentation 12.1
audit opinions
directors' report 4.13
separate corporate governance
statement 4.13
strategic report 4.13
cessation of office as auditors,
procedures 38.2.1
changes of auditors 38.1
Directors' Remuneration Report
provisions 4.26.2
quoted companies 4.26.1
distributions
legal background 7.2.1
electronic publication
other information 34.10
overview 4.27.1
engagement letters
changes in terms 14.4.3
liability limitation 14.5.1
governance, responsibilities of those charged
with 16.3
laws and regulations 17.5.1
micro-entities 4.25.3
new small companies regime 6.5, 4.25.2
non-cash assets, transfer to a public company
by a member 7.6.1
other information
auditor's consideration of 34.3.1
procedures on cessation of office
requirements 38.2.1
Section 519 38.2.4
related parties
reporting 20.11
reporting, other information
directors' report and strategic
report 34.6.2
requirements
cessation of office as auditors,
procedures 38.2.1
revised financial statements and reports 6.3
separate corporate governance
statement 34.6.3
shares
allotment of, otherwise than for cash 7.5.1
small businesses, audit of 36.1

Companies Act 2006 – *contd*
summary financial statements   6.5

Companies Act 2006 (Commencement No. 5, Transitional Provisions and Savings) Order 2007
statutory audit reports   7.1

Companies, Partnerships and Groups (Accounts and Reports) Regulations 2015
new small companies regime   6.5, 4.25.2
reporting, other information
directors' report and strategic
report   34.6.2
separate corporate governance
statement   34.6.3

Companies (Revision of Defective Accounts and Reports) (Amendment) Regulations 2013   6.2.2

Companies (Summary Financial Statement) Regulations 2008   6.5

comparative periods
interim reports   39.11

comparatives – *see also* **opening balances**
incoming auditors   19.5
prior period financial statements issued by a
predecessor auditor   19.4.2
prior period financial statements not
audited   19.4.3
qualified reports   19.4.1

Compendium of Illustrative Auditor's Reports on UK Private Sector Financial Statements (APB Bulletin 2010/2)   4.2.1

competence
ICAEW Code of Ethics   2.7.2
maintaining   2.9
of experts   31.3.5

complaints
quality control   3.2.11

completeness
audit procedures   28.9.6
of income (charities)   43.13

complex financial instruments – *see also* **fair value**
audit evidence
evaluating   28.9.7
management representations   28.9.8
controls, reliance on   28.9.5
difficult financial market conditions   28.9.9
general considerations
examples   28.9.2
materiality   28.9.6
risk assessment   28.9.2
understanding entity   28.9.4
valuation   28.9.2

compliance – *see also* **laws and regulations**
auditors' review of   42.6.2
covenants in agreement for lending facilities –
see covenants in agreement for lending
facilities

compliance – *see also* **laws and regulations** – *contd*
investment businesses, reports to FSA   9.6.3
laws and regulations
affecting operations of the entity   17.5.2
other procedures and written
representations   17.5.3
with direct effect on financial
statements   17.5.1
non-compliance   17.7
UK Corporate Governance Code   42.1.1

'Comply or Explain' statement
auditor responsibilities   42.4

component auditors – *see also* **auditors**
communication with   30.3
definitions   30.3
examples of documentation   30.16.2
involvement in the work   30.10.1

Comptroller and Auditor General (C&AG)
public sector audits   48.25

computer-assisted audit techniques (CAATs) – *see* **CAATS (computer-assisted audit techniques)**

confidentiality
access to information by successors   38.3.2
cyber security, e-commerce   35.1
FSMA 2000   9.6.7
ICAEW Code of Ethics   2.5.2, 2.7.2
overriding of duty by anti-money laundering
legislation   16.9
Solicitors' Accounts Rules   45.4.2

confirmation
audit evidence   23.2.5

conflict resolution
ICAEW Code of Ethics   2.7.4

consultation
engagement performance   3.2.8, 3.3.6

Consultative Committee of Accountancy Bodies (CCAB) – *see* **CCAB (Consultative Committee of Accountancy Bodies)**

continuing auditors
opening balances   19.3.1

continuing professional education (CPE)   2.9

Contracts (Rights of Third Parties) Act 1999
duties to lenders   40.4.5

control environment
charities   43.11.1
cyber security   35.1
internal controls   21.3.5

control tests
extent of   21.4.2
risk assessment   21.4.2
sampling   26.2

controlled trust money
definition   45.1.2

Co-operative and Community Benefit Societies and Credit Unions Act 2010 **47.2**

copying
access to information by successors 38.3.2

corporate governance – *see also* **governance, persons charged with; UK Corporate Governance Code**
APB Bulletins
2006/5 42.2.2, 42.6
'Comply or Explain' statement, auditors'
responsibilities for 42.4
directors' remuneration 42.1.2
disclosures 42.1.3, 42.7.1
guidance 42.2
procedures
generally 42.6.1
going concern 42.6.4
non-compliance with Code 42.6.3
specific – nine verifiable Code
provisions 42.6.2
statement of auditors' responsibilities 42.4
terms of engagement 42.3
transparency rules 42.1.3

costs
access to information by successors 38.3.2
audit sampling 26.10

covenants in agreement for lending facilities
compliance
common financial and non-financial
covenants 40.5.1
engagements to report on 40.6.1, 40.6.2
lender's requirement for evidence
of 40.5.2
engagements to report on compliance with
report 40.6.2
scope of work performed 40.6.1
firm's consideration of acceptance of
engagement 40.5.4
firm's duty of care 40.5.3
Statement of Covenant Compliance
duty of care 40.5.3
firm's consideration of acceptance of
engagement 40.5.4

CPE (continuing professional education) **2.9**

credit crunch – *see* **difficult financial market conditions**

credit unions
small entity client 2.7.2

custody assets (CASS Rule 6) **9.5.5, 9.5.11**

customer due diligence (CDD) **18.7**

data analytics
computer-assisted audit techniques
(CAATs) 35.2
future developments 35.4
overview 35.1
use in external audits 35.3
audit quality 35.3.1
common data analytic routines 35.3.2
ICAEW papers 35.3.3
thematic review 35.3.4

data reliability
analytical procedures 25.5.2

debit balances
Solicitors' Accounts Rules 45.4.1

debt financing
social housing audits 47.2.6

Deregulation Act 2015
changes of auditor 38.1

derivative financial instruments **28.9.2**

Developments in Corporate Governance Affecting the Responsibilities of Auditors of UK Companies (APB Bulletin 2009/4) **42.2.2**

differences of opinion
engagement performance 3.2.7, 3.3.6

difficult financial market conditions – *see also* **Auditing Issues when Financial Market Conditions are difficult and Credit Facilities may be restricted (APB Bulletin 2008/1)**
auditor's report 37.6
complex financial instruments 28.9.9
fair values 28.9.7
going concern 37.6

direct tax
social housing audits 47.2.6

direction, supervision and review
planning 13.9

directors
narrative statement 42.6.2
non-executive 42.6.2
preliminary announcements, approval 6.3.7
remuneration of – *see* directors' remuneration
responsibilities – *see* directors' responsibilities

directors amendments to financial statements
subsequent events 33.4.1

directors' remuneration **42.1.2**
Remuneration Report – *see* Directors'
Remuneration Report

Directors' Remuneration Report
auditable part 4.26.3
overview 4.26.1
provisions 4.26.2
regulations – *see* Directors' Remuneration
Report Regulations 2002 (APB Bulletin
2002/2)
reporting 4.26.4

Directors' Remuneration Report Regulations 2002 (APB Bulletin 2002/2) – *see also* **directors' remuneration; Directors' Remuneration Report**

directors' reports
difficult financial market conditions 37.6
other information
reporting 34.6.2

directors' responsibilities
accountants' compilation reports 8.3.2

directors' responsibilities – *contd*
contents   14.4
corporate governance, auditor procedures in
    relation to   42.6.2
financial statements   4.15, 4.24
management representations   32.3

disclaimers of opinion
auditor's responsibilities, description of   5.5.6
modified auditors' reports   5.4, 5.5.4
other considerations   5.5.7

Disclosure Rules and Transparency Rules
disclosures   42.7.1

disclosures
accounting estimates   27.6
audit plan   13.5.1
audit procedures   28.9.6
control, related parties   20.7
corporate governance   42.7.1
fair value   28.7
misstatements   15.6.3

distributions
annual accounts   7.2.2
initial accounts   7.2.4
interim accounts   7.2.3
legal background   7.2.1

documentation
accounting estimates   27.9
assembly of final audit file   12.4
audit, changes to   12.5
audit directive   12.1
audit, purpose of   36.10.2
auditors not experts in authentication of   16.4
other information   34.9
engagement   3.2.8
experts, use of   31.3.10
form and content   12.3
    characteristics of items tested   12.3.2
    departures from ISAs (UK)   12.3.4
    factors affecting working papers   12.3.1
    identification of preparer and
        reviewer   12.3.5
    judgment areas   12.3.3
    specific requirements   12.3.6
fraud and error   16.10
generally   12.1
ICAEW   12.1
identification of preparer and reviewer   12.3.5
inspection of   23.2.5
interim reports   39.8
investigating accountants from same firm as
    auditors   12.9.4
materiality   15.7
other auditors, reliance on   38.3.9
public interest entities   3.3.8
purpose of   12.2
quality control system   3.2.11, 3.3.8
related parties   20.10
risk assessment   21.3.8, 21.4.5
specific requirements   12.3.6

**documentation of quality control
system   3.2.11, 3.3.8**

draft accounts
duties to lenders   40.4.3

**DTI Review (Review of Regulatory Regime of
the Accountancy Profession)   2.1**

due care
ICAEW Code of Ethics   2.7.2

duties of care
and engagement contracts
    bi-partite   49.2.2
    tri-partite   49.2.1
covenants in agreement for lending
    facilities   40.5.3
in statutory audit reports   40.4.2
lenders – *see* lenders, duties to

EBITDA (earnings figure)
preliminary announcements   6.3.5

economic dependence
ES-PASE (Ethical Standard – Provisions
    Available for Small Entities)   2.7.3

electronic commerce – *see* **e-commerce**

electronic publication
auditors and directors' responsibilities   4.27.2
other information   34.10
overview   4.27.1

employee tax rules
social housing audits   47.2.6

employment relationships
Ethical Standard Section 2   2.6.4

encryption-based security
e-commerce   35.1

engagement letters – *see also* **ISA (UK) 210
(Revised June 2016) (Updated July 2017)
(Agreeing the terms of audit engagements);
terms of engagement**
audit exemption   8.5, 8.5.3
changes in terms   14.4.3
contents   14.4
    changes in terms   14.4.3
    generally   14.3
    groups of companies   14.4.2
    recurring audits   14.4.1
disengagement   14.4.4
generally   14.1
interim reports   39.5
liability limitation
    agreements   14.5.3
    background   14.5.1
    FRC guidance   14.5.2
    other services   14.5.4
preconditions for an audit   14.3
purpose of   14.2
recurring audits   14.4.1
responsibilities as auditor   14.4
responsibilities as directors   14.4
scope of audit   14.4
Solicitors' Accounts Rules   45.2

engagement letters – see also ISA (UK) 210 (Revised June 2016) (Updated July 2017) (Agreeing the terms of audit engagements); terms of engagement – *contd*
  Solicitors' Accounts Rules – *contd*
    generally   45.2
    place of examination   45.2.3
    termination of appointment   45.2.2
    whistle-blowing   45.2.1
  true and fair view   14.4

engagement performance
  consultation   3.2.7
  differences of opinion   3.2.7
  engagement quality control review   3.2.7
  quality control   3.2.7, 3.3.6

engagement quality control review
  eligibility of reviewers   3.2.7
  engagement performance   3.2.7, 3.3.6
  nature, timing and extent of review   3.2.7
  public interest entities   3.2.7, 3.3.6, 3.3.8
  review documentation   3.2.7

engagement team discussion
  fraud   16.4.2
  risk assessment procedures   21.3.3

engagements
  accepting   40.3.1
    firm's consideration of   40.5.4
    responsibilities as directors   41.2.3
    responsibilities in carrying out a review   41.2.3
    service organisations, reports on internal controls   40.7.3
  auditor unable to continue   16.6
  quality control   3.2.7, 3.3.6
  specific assurances to lenders, providing   40.4.6
  terms of – *see* terms of engagement
  to report on covenant compliance report   40.6.2
    scope of work performed   40.6.1

Engagements to Perform Agreed-Upon Procedures Regarding Financial Information (ISRS 4400)   41.1, 41.3

enquiries about litigation and claims – *see also* **ISA (UK) 501 (Audit evidence – specific considerations for selected items)**
  audit procedures   23.6.1
  written representations   23.6.2

enquiry
  audit evidence   23.2.5
  negative, example   23.6.1
  positive, example   23.6.1

entities that report on application of the Code
  communication with   10.7.1
  ISA (UK) 701 requirement   4.5.1
  other information   4.17

error – *see also* **fraud**
  audit sampling – *see* sampling, audit
  auditors' responsibilities   16.4
  definition   16.2.2

error – see also fraud – *contd*
  governance, responsibilities of those charged with   16.3
  related parties   20.3
  risk assessment   16.4.3

ESs – *see* **ethical standards**

estimates – *see* **accounting estimates**

ethical issues
  quality control   3.2.4, 3.3.3

ethical policies and procedures
  Ethical Standard Section 1 (Integrity, Objectivity and Independence)   2.6.3

Ethical Standards for Auditors (FRC)
  and audit reports   4.6
  compliance with   1.6.6
  ISQC 1   3.2.1
  issue of   2.1
  publication of   2.1

ethics partners
  responsibilities   2.6.2

EU Audit Directive and Regulation
  changes to IAASB's standards   1.6.5
  changes to ISAs   1.6.4
  Ethical and Auditing Standards revision   1.6.4
  public interest entities
    definition   1.6.4
    statutory audit requirements   1.6.4
  UK Corporate Governance Code changes   1.6.4
  UK law amendments   1.6.4

evidence, audit – *see also* **ISA (UK) 500 (Updated July 2017) (Audit Evidence); ISA (UK) 501 (Audit evidence – specific considerations for selected Items)**
  and fraud   16.5
  assertions, using to gather   23.2.4
  attendance at stocktaking   23.5.2
  charities   43.10
  complex financial instruments   28.9.7
  concept of   23.2.1
  consistency of   23.2.2
  dealing with inconsistent or potentially unreliable evidence   23.2.7
  e-commerce – *see* e-commerce, evidence
  interim reports   39.7
  management representations as   28.9.8, 32.6
    directors' ability to make representations   32.10.2
  management's expert – *see* management's expert
  obtaining   19.3, 19.4
  paid cheques   37.5.2
  Registered Providers of Social Housing   47.12
  reliability of   23.2.2
  retirement benefits – *see* retirement benefits (FRS 17), audit evidence
  risk assessment   21.4.4
  selection and sampling of items for testing   23.2.6
  sources of   23.2.3

evidence, audit – see also ISA (UK) 500
(Updated July 2017) (Audit Evidence);
ISA (UK) 501 (Audit evidence – specific
considerations for selected Items) – *contd*
  sufficient appropriate   23.2.2
  written representation, reliability   32.7

examples of documentation
  letter from other auditor acknowledging
    instructions   30.16.2
  referral instructions   30.16.2
  specimen reports to the group engagement
    team   30.16.2

experts, use of
  actuaries – *see* actuaries
  agreement with the auditor   31.3.7
  auditor's expert, definition   31.3.2
  auditors not experts in authentication of
    documentation   16.4
  competence and objectivity   31.3.5
  documentation   31.3.10
  evaluating adequacy of work   31.3.8
  fair value   28.5, 28.9.3
  management's experts   23.3.1
  nature, scope and objectives of work   31.3.7
  nature, timing and extent of audit
    procedures   23.3.1
  reference to the expert in auditor's
    report   31.3.9
  Registered Providers of Social
    Housing   47.21
  regulated entities   49.5
  understanding of field of expertise   31.3.6

Extensible Business Reporting Language
(XBRL)
  and tagging of information   37.4.1–37.4.3

external confirmations
  debtors' confirmations   23.8.2
  Registered Providers of Social
    Housing   47.13
  use of   23.8.1

fair value – *see also* ISA (UK) 545 (Auditing
Fair Value Measurements and Disclosures);
Auditing Complex Financial Instruments
(Practice Note 23) (Revised)
  accounting estimates, ISAs   27.1
  audit considerations   28.4
  background information   28.3
  charities   43.16
  complex financial instruments – *see* complex
    financial instruments
  disclosures   28.7
  expert, use of   28.5, 28.9.3
  governance, communication with those
    charged with   28.8
  guidance on   28.2
  measurement of   28.1

family/personal relationships
  Ethical Standard Section 2 (Financial,
    Business, Employment and Personal
    Relationships)   2.6.4

FCA (Financial Conduct Authority)
  debt management firms   9.5.13
  Listing Rules – *see* Listing Rules
  Office of Fair Trading (OFT)   47.6.2
  Registered Providers of Social
    Housing   47.2.1, 47.6.2

fees
  Ethical Standard Section 4 (Fees,
    Remuneration and Evaluation Policies,
    Litigation, Gifts and Hospitality)   2.6.6

financial position
  risk of loss   9.6.3

financial relationships
  Ethical Standard Section 2 (Financial,
    Business, Employment and Personal
    Relationships)   2.6.4

financial reporting
  Registered Providers of Social
    Housing   47.2.4

Financial Reporting and Auditing Group
statements – *see* FRAGS (Financial Reporting
and Auditing Group Statements)

Financial Reporting Council – *see* FRC
(Financial Reporting Council)

Financial Reporting Standard for Smaller
Entities – *see* FRSSE (Financial Reporting
Standard for Smaller Entities)

Financial Reports of Pension Schemes
(SORP)   44.3

Financial Services and Markets
Act 2000   9.6.7

financial statements – *see also* historical
financial information; ISA (UK) 700 (Auditors'
report on financial statements); SAS 600
(Auditor's Report on Financial Statements)
  approval of   8.3.5
  charities   43.4, 43.21, 43.23
  code of ethics   8.3.4
  conclusions relating to going concern   4.10
  failure to amend, subsequent events   33.4
  interim, complete set   39.17
  laws with direct effect on   17.5.1
  material misstatement, causes of   5.3.1
  misleading, incorporated entities   8.3.4
  misstatements in – *see* misstatements
  preliminary announcements – *see* preliminary
    announcements
  revised – *see* revised financial statements and
    reports
  revising or withdrawing   33.5
  summary – *see* summary financial statements
  XBRL tagging in
    auditor's involvement   37.4.2
    background   37.4.1
    guidance   37.4.3

Firm's Reports and Duties to Lenders in connection with Loans and Other Facilities to Clients and Related Covenants (Technical Release 4/00) 40.2
lenders, duties to 40.4–4.1

fit and proper person requirement
audit regulation and ethics 2.4
investment businesses, reports to FSA 9.6.3

flotations
access to working papers 12.9.3

fraud – see also error; ISA (UK) 240 (Revised June 2016) (Updated July 2017) (Auditor's responsibilities relating to fraud in an audit of financial statements)
at assertion level 16.4.5
audit evidence, evaluating 16.5
auditor's responsibilities
  charities 43.5
  engagement team discussion 16.4.2
  professional scepticism 16.4
  risk assessment 16.4.3
auditor unable to continue engagement 16.6
charities
  auditor's responsibilities 43.5
communication with authorities 16.9
  public interest entities 16.9.1
definition 16.2.1
detection of as auditor's principal duty 39.1
documentation 16.10
error distinguished 16.2.2
financial statements 16.2.1
governance, responsibilities of those charged with 16.3
management representations 16.7
material misstatement 16.2.1
  audit evidence, evaluating 16.5
  responses to fraud risk 16.4.5
  revenue recognition 16.4.4
pension schemes 44.6
petty cash 16.5
public interest entities 16.8, 16.9
public sector audits 48.7
Registered Providers of Social Housing 47.5
related parties 20.3
reports to management 16.8
risk of
  governance, assessing those charged with 16.4.3
  identification and assessment 16.4.4
  journal entries 16.4.5
  management and others within entity, assessing 16.4.3
  other information 16.4.3
  responses to 16.4.5
  revenue recognition 16.4.4
  risk assessment 16.4.3
  risk factors 16.4.3
  unusual or unexpected relationships 16.4.3

FRC (Financial Reporting Council)
An Update for Directors of Listing Companies 11.20.2
as authoritative body 1.3
audit firm monitoring 2.14

FRC (Financial Reporting Council) – *contd*
audit quality, framework 3.1
Audit Quality Review (AQR) 2.13
bulletins 1.7.2
client asset reporting standard 1.7.3
Codes and Standards Committee 1.5.1
Conduct Committee 1.5.1
  responsibilities 2.12
Enforcement Division 2.12
engagement letters
  liability limitation 14.5.2, 14.5.3, 14.5.4
ethical issue 3.2.4
ethical standards 2.1.1
Going Concern and Liquidity Risk: Guidance for Directors of UK Companies 2009 11.2, 42.6.4, 42.7.1
on audit committee 42.8.2
POBA 2.12
Practice Notes 1.7.1
predecessor body 1.5.3
Promoting Audit Quality – *see* Promoting Audit Quality (FRC)
pronouncements
  Recognised Supervisory Body (RSB) 1.5.2
  Scope and Authority of Audit and Assurance Pronouncements 1.5.2
role and structure 1.5.1
standards for reporting accountants 1.7.5
Statements of Recommended Practice (SORPs) 1.7.4
UK Corporate Governance Code
  companies and investors 42.2.1
UK Stewardship Code 42.2.1

friendly societies
small entity client 2.7.1

FRS 8 (Related parties)
Registered Providers of Social Housing 47.16

FRS 12 (Provisions, Contingent Liabilities and Contingent Assets)
management responsibility 17.3

FRS 102 43.1
auditing implications
  ethical considerations 37.2.2
  framework 1.10
  guidance for accounting 44.3
  guidance for auditors 37.2.1
  implications of IFRS transition 37.3
  potential problem areas 37.2.3
small companies 4.25.1

FRS 104 (Interim Financial Reporting)
review 39.1

FRS 105 (Financial Reporting Standard applicable to the Micro-entities Regime)
auditing implications
  guidance for auditors 37.2.1

FRSSE (Financial Reporting Standard for Smaller Entities)
evidence 36.8.6
framework 1.10
guidance for auditors 37.2.1
reporting 36.9.1

891

FSMA (Financial Services and Markets Act) 2000
ad hoc reports, to FSA   9.6
communication by FSA   9.6.7

FSMA 2000 (Communications by Auditors) Regulations 2001
ad hoc reports   9.6

FSMA 2000 (Financial Services and Markets Act) 2000
material significance considerations   9.6.3

gifts
Ethical Standard Section 4 (Fees, Remuneration and Evaluation Policies, Litigation, Gifts and Hospitality)   2.6.6

Going Concern Issues During the Current Economic Conditions (APB Bulletin 2008/10)   11.2
detailed considerations   11.20.3
finance, availability of   11.20.4
general principles   11.20.2
need for guidance   11.20.1

going concern – *see also* ISA (UK) 570 (Revised June 2016) (Going concern)
additional procedures when events or conditions are identified   11.9
adequacy of disclosures   11.11
events or conditions identified, no material uncertainty exists   11.11.2
events or conditions identified with material uncertainty exists   11.11.1
auditing standards   11.2
auditor conclusions
entities applying the UK Corporate Governance Code   11.10.1, 11.12.7
example report extracts   11.16
auditor responsibilities   11.5
adequacy of disclosures   11.11
evaluating entity's assessment of going concern   11.7
events after period considered by those charged with governance   11.8
auditor's report, implications   11.12
conclusions   11.12.1
small and micro-entities   11.12.6
bank confirmations   24.6
basis of accounting
appropriate and material uncertainty exists   11.12.4
appropriate and no material uncertainty identified   11.12.3
inappropriate   11.12.2
other considerations   11.12.5
borrowing facilities   11.7.2
charities   43.19
circumstances affecting, public sector audits   48.18.2
communication with those charged with governance   11.14
public interest entities   11.14.1
corporate governance, auditor procedures in relation to   42.6.4
delay in approval of financial statements   11.15

going concern – *see also* ISA (UK) 570 (Revised June 2016) (Going concern) – *contd*
difficult financial market conditions   37.6
doubt as to entity's status as   9.6.3
entities that prepare their financial statements on a cash basis   48.18.5
entity unwilling to make or extend assessment   11.13
entity's responsibilities   11.4
evaluating entity's assessment of   11.7
example report extracts   11.16
general requirement   11.3
generally   11.1
groups   11.18
interim reports   39.10, 39.16.1
key audit matters   11.12.8
other information   11.12.9
possible audit procedures   11.7.1
preliminary announcements   11.19
public sector audits
auditor's other responsibilities   48.18.1
auditor's responsibilities   48.18.4
circumstances affecting going concern   48.18.2
consideration of foreseeable future   48.18.3
Registered Providers of Social Housing   47.18
regulated entities   11.17
risk assessment procedures and related activities   11.6

governance, persons charged with – *see also* corporate governance; ISA (UK) 260 (Revised June 2016) (Updated July 2017) (Communication with those charged with governance); SAS 610 (Communication of Audit Matters to those Charged with Governance)
accounting records   22.2.2
communication with
audit committees   10.7.1
charities   43.8–43.9
effectiveness of communications   10.5
fair value   28.8
form of communication   10.5
fraud and error   16.8
matters to be communicated   10.6.1–10.6.5
minimum contents of communications   2.6.3
non-audit services, significant facts   2.6.7
planning   13.10
public interest entities   11.14.1, 16.8, 17.8.4
public sector audits   48.9
Registered Providers of Social Housing   47.7
related parties   20.9
reporting to   17.8.1
risk assessment   21.3.7
definition   10.2
definition of
responsibility in relation to   16.3
risk assessment   16.4.3
engagement partner's name   4.19
fraud and error   16.1

governance, persons charged with – see also corporate governance; ISA (UK) 260 (Revised June 2016) (Updated July 2017) (Communication with those charged with governance); SAS 610 (Communication of Audit Matters to those Charged with Governance) – *contd*
  going concern
    determining whether entity is 11.4
    events following relevant period 11.8
  reporting to 17.8.1
  representations from 20.8

grants payable
  charities 43.13

groups of companies
  engagement letters 14.4.2
  going concern 11.18
  internal controls, review of
    effectiveness 42.6.2
  small and medium-sized – *see* small and
    medium-sized groups, exemptions for

Guidance on Smaller Entity Audit Documentation (Practice Note 26) 36.2
  audit documentation requirements 36.10.4
  background 36.10.1
  characteristics of small businesses 36.3
  issue of 36.2
  purpose of audit documentation 36.10.2
  responsibilities 36.5
  special considerations for smaller
    entities 36.10.3

Guide to Professional Ethics
  replacement by Code of Ethics
    (ICAEW) 2.5.1

heritage assets
  charities 43.13

historical financial information
  investment circular reporting – *see* SIR 2000
    (Investment Reporting Standards
    applicable to public reporting
    engagements on historical financial
    information)
  ISQC – *see* ISQC (UK) 1 (Revised June 2016)
    (Quality control for firms that perform
    audits and reviews of historical financial
    information)

Homes and Communities Agency (HCA) 46

hospitality
  Ethical Standard Section 4 (Fees,
    Remuneration and Evaluation Policies,
    Litigation, Gifts and Hospitality) 2.6.6

host contracts
  as complex financial instruments 28.9.2

housing
  – *see* Registered Providers of Social Housing

Housing and Regeneration Act 2008
  Registered Providers of Social
    Housing 47.2.7

human resources
  quality control 3.2.6

IAASB (International Auditing and Assurance Standards Board) 1.4
  A Framework for Audit Quality: Key Elements
    that Create an Environment for Audit
    Quality 3.1, 3.7
  as authoritative body 1.3
  auditor scepticism paper 23.9
  background 1.4.1
  clarity project 1.6.2
  development of International Standards on
    Auditing (UK) 1.6
  IAPN 1000, Special Considerations in Auditing
    Financial Instruments 28.2
  and IFAC 1.3, 1.4.1
  ISA 810 (Revised) Engagements to Report on
    Summary Financial Statements 6.5
  ISAs issued by 1.4.1
  ISAE 3402 40.7.1
  ISRE 2400 41.1
  other changes to ISAs 1.6.5
  pronouncements 1.4.3
  reporting standards 1.6.5
  structure and processes 1.4.2

IAPN 1000, Special Considerations in Auditing Financial Instruments 28.2

IAS 34 (Interim Financial Reporting)
  review 39.1

IAS 37 (Provisions, Contingent Liabilities and Contingent Assets)
  management responsibility 17.3

ICAEW (Institute of Chartered Accountants in England and Wales)
  Assurance Engagements: Management of
    Risk and Liability (AAF 04/06) 40.2,
    40.3, 40.3.2
  Assurance on Non-Financial Information:
    Existing Practices and Issues 40.2
  Assurance reports on internal controls of
    service organisations made available to
    third parties (AAF 01/06) 40.2, 40.7.1,
    40.7.2
  authoritative body 1.3
  Bannerman case
    engagement letters 4.28.4
    further developments 4.28.5
    guidance 4.28.2
    overview 4.28.1
    recommended wording and position in
      report 4.28.3
  Business Law Committee, on
    confidentiality 2.5.5
  Business Law Committee, on conflicts of
    interest 2.5.5
  Code of Ethics
    assurance engagement 2.5.1
    background 2.5.1
    conflict resolution 2.5.4
    conflicts of interest and
      confidentiality 2.5.5
    control of confidentiality and
      independence 2.5.6

ICAEW (Institute of Chartered Accountants in England and Wales) – *contd*
Code of Ethics – *contd*
fundamental principles 2.5.2
independence requirements 2.5.1
International Ethics Standards Board of Accountants' (IESBA) 2.5.1
receipt of information in confidence by auditors 2.5.7
threats and safeguards 2.5.3
guidance booklets 42.8.1
accountants 7.2
audit committees 42.2.1
Identifying and managing certain risks arising from the inclusion of reports from auditors and accountants in prospectuses (AAF 02/06) 4.2.1
Management Representation Letters (Audit 04/02) 32.1, 32.10
QAD 2.13
RSB 2.1
Technical Releases – *see* Technical Releases (ICAEW)

ICAI (Institute of Chartered Accountants of Ireland) 2.1

ICAS (Institute of Chartered Accountants of Scotland) 2.1

Identifying and managing certain risks arising from the inclusion of reports from auditors and accountants in prospectuses (ICAEW AAF 02/06) 4.2.1

IFAC (International Federation of Accountants)
Code of Ethics for Professional Accountants 2.6, 2.16
Guide to Using ISAs in the Audits of Small- and Medium-Sized Entities 36.11

incoming auditors
comparatives 19.5

incorporated entities, accountants' reports – *see also* **unincorporated entities**
aims 8.3.6
approving financial statements 8.3.5
directors' responsibilities 8.3.2
example 8.3.6
misleading financial statements 8.3.4
procedures 8.3.3
terms of engagement 8.3.1

independence
auditors 2.6
cyber security, e-commerce 35.1
definition 2.6.3
EC Recommendation 2.6
reports to management 10.6.5

indirect tax
social housing audits 47.2.6

Industrial and Provident Societies Act 1965
small entity clients 2.7.1

information systems
internal controls 21.3.5

information systems environment, audits – *see also* **CAATS**

initial audit engagement
opening balances
public sector audits 48.14
planning 13.7

insolvency
safeguarding of client assets 9.5.4, 9.5.8

inspections
audit procedures 23.2.5

Institute of Chartered Accountants in England and Wales – *see* **ICAEW (Institute of Chartered Accountants in England and Wales)**

Institute of Chartered Accountants of Ireland – *see* **ICAI (Institute of Chartered Accountants of Ireland)**

Institute of Chartered Secretaries and Administrators (ICSA) – *see* **ICSA (Institute of Chartered Secretaries and Administrators)**

insurance intermediaries, CASS audits 9.5.12

integrity
definition 2.6.3
ICAEW Code of Ethics 2.5.2
listed companies 10.6.5
reports to management 10.6.5

interim financial information
complete set 39.17

interim reports, review of
assurance provided 39.4
communication 39.15
comparative periods 39.11
date of review report 39.16.3
departure from applicable financial reporting framework 39.16.1
documentation 39.8
engagement letters 39.5
evidence 39.7
general principles 39.3
going concern 39.10, 39.16.1
guidance for auditors 39.2
half-yearly financial report requirements 39.1
limitation of audit scope 39.16.1
Listing Rules requirements 39.1
management representations 39.12
modification of review report 39.16.1
other information 39.13
planning 39.6
procedures 39.7
reporting
date of review report 39.16
modification of review report 39.16.1
prior period modifications 39.16.2
requirement for 39.16
review engagement, requests to discontinue 39.18
significant uncertainties 39.16.1

interim reports, review of – *contd*
  subsequent events   39.9

internal audit
  auditing standards   31.2.1
  client assets   9.5.15
  corporate governance, auditor procedures in
    relation to   42.6.2
  direct assistance   31.2.5
  documentation   31.2.6
  effect on external audit procedures   31.2.3
  evaluating of   31.2.3
  evaluating specific work   31.2.4
  nature and extent of work, determining
    the   31.2.3
  public sector audits   48.21
  Registered Providers of Social
    Housing   47.20
  understanding functions of   31.2.2
  using the work of   31.2.4

internal audit function
  definition   31.2.3

internal control – *see also* **communicating
deficiencies in internal control; risk
assessments**
  activities   21.3.5
  components   21.3.5
  control activities   21.3.5
  control environment   21.3.5
  corporate governance, auditor procedures in
    relation to   42.6.2
  failure to conduct review of   42.6.2
  information system   21.3.5
  limitations of   21.3.5
  management override of controls   16.4.5
  manual and automated elements   21.3.5
  monitoring of controls   21.3.5
  risk assessment process   21.3.5
  service organisations – *see* service
    organisations, internal controls reports
  understanding entity   28.9.4

**International Auditing and Assurance
Standards Board** – *see* **IAASB (International
Auditing and Assurance Standards Board)**

international developments
  A Framework for Audit Quality: Key Elements
    that Create an Environment for Audit
    Quality (IAASB)   3.5
  Enhancing Audit Quality in the Public
    Interest   30.18
  Group Audits Task Force   30.18
  group audits, documentation   30.18
  IESBA code of ethics   2.16

**International Ethics Standards Board for
Accountants' Code of Ethics for Professional
Accountants (IESBA Code)**
  compliance with the Code   2.6.1
  international developments   2.16
  ISQC (UK) 1 (Revised June 2016), ethical
    requirements   3.2.4, 3.3.3

**International Federation of Accountants
(IFAC)** – *see* **IFAC (International Federation of
Accountants)**

International Financial Reporting Standards –
see **IFRSS (International Financial Reporting
Standards)**
  example auditor's report for a premium listed
    company   4.23

**International Standard on Assurance
Engagements** – *see* **ISAE (International
Standard on Assurance Engagements)**

**International Standards on Auditing (UK)
(ISAs)** – *see also* **specific ISAs**
  adoption of clarified   1.6.3
  APB, issued by   1.3
  application of   1.6.6
  authoritative bodies   1.3
  clarity project – *see* clarity project (IAASB)
  existing and clarified standards
    going concern issues   11.2
    nature of auditing standards   1.6.1
  issue   1.6.1
  review of   1.6.1

International Standard on Quality Control –
see **ISQC (UK) 1 (Revised June 2016) (Quality
Control for Firms that Perform Audits and
Reviews of Historical Financial Information)**

investigations
  unusual items   16.4.3
  variances   25.7

investment businesses
  audits – *see* Audit of Investment Businesses in
    the United Kingdom (Practice Note 21)
    (Revised)
  client assets – *see* client assets
  reports to FSA – *see* investment businesses,
    reports to FCA

investment businesses, reports to FCA –
see also **ISA (UK) 250B (Revised June 2016)
(Section B, Auditor's statutory right and
duty to report to regulators of public interest
entities and regulators); reports, audit**
  ad hoc reports – *see* ad hoc reports to FCA
  auditing standards   9.2
  client assets – *see* client assets
  guidance   9.2
  legal background   9.1
    entities in the financial sector   9.1.2
    overview   9.1.1
    public interest entities   9.1.3
  auditor's responsibilities   9.4
  types of report   9.3

Irish Stock Exchanges
  interim financial information   39.7

**ISA (UK) 200 (Revised June 2016) (Objective
and General Principles Governing an Audit of
Financial Statements)**
  accounting estimates
    management bias, indicators   27.7
  as grandfather standard   1.6.6

ISA (UK) 200 (Revised June 2016) (Objective and General Principles Governing an Audit of Financial Statements) – *contd*
sceptical mindset   23.9.2

ISA (UK) 200 (Revised June 2016) (Overall Objectives of the Independent Auditor and the Conduct of an Audit in Accordance with International Standards on Auditing)
audit evidence   30.14
risk assessment
generally   21.1

ISA (UK) 210 (Revised June 2016) (Updated July 2017) (Agreeing the terms of audit engagements)
access to audit working papers   47.3
audit engagement letters   47.3
communication   47.3
disclosure of information to auditors   47.3
electronic publication   47.3
engagement letter   12.6
imposed limitation of scope   5.3.3
issue of   14.1
Landlord and Tenant Act 1985   47.3
preconditions for an audit   14.3
preliminary engagement activities   13.3
purpose of engagement letters   14.2
Registered Providers of Social Housing   47.3
small companies and micro-entities   14.6

ISA (UK) 220 (Revised June 2016) (Updated July 2017) (Quality control for an audit of financial statements) – *see also* **misstatements; quality control**
and fair value   28.9.3
documentation, specific requirements   12.3.6
engagement quality control review   3.2.7
ethical requirements   3.3.3
general requirement   3.3.1
initial audit engagement   13.7
ISQC (UK) 1 (Revised)   3.3.1
issue   3.1
leadership responsibilities for quality   3.3.2
other documentation requirements   12.6
planning an initial engagement   19.2
preliminary engagement activities   13.3
public sector audits   48.6
purpose of engagement letters   14.2
Registered Providers of Social Housing   47.4

ISA (UK) 230 (Revised June 2016) (Audit documentation) – *see also* **documentation**
assembly of final audit file   12.4
changes to audit documentation   12.5
form and content of documentation
characteristics of items tested   12.3.2
factors affecting working papers   12.3.1
judgment areas   12.3.3
generally   12.1
other documentation requirements   12.6
purpose of documentation   12.2, 36.10.2

ISA (UK) 230 (Revised June 2016) (Documentation) – *see also* **working papers**
other documentation requirements   12.6

ISA (UK) 240 (Revised June 2016) (Updated July 2017) (Auditor's responsibilities relating to fraud in an audit of financial statements) – *see also* **fraud; fraud risk**
and small businesses   36.5.1
audit of related parties in practice
five-point action plan   20.12.2
auditor responsibilities   16.1, 16.4
engagement team discussion   16.4.2, 21.3.3
risk assessment   16.4.3, 21.1
auditor unable to continue engagement   16.6
charities
fraud   43.5
issue of   16.2
management representations   16.7
matters to be communicated   10.6.1
other documentation requirements   12.6
other written representations   32.4
Registered Providers of Social Housing   47.5
related party transactions   20.3
responses to fraud risk   16.4.5
revenue recognition   16.4.4
risk assessment
generally   21.1
procedures   21.3.2, 21.3.6
significant risks   21.3.6
skeptical mindset   23.9.2
understanding the group, its components and their environments   30.7

ISA (UK) 250A (Revised December 2017) (Section A, Consideration of laws and regulations in an audit of financial statements) – *see also* **laws and regulations   17.1**
matters to be communicated   10.6.1
money laundering   18.3
non-compliance   17.7
other documentation requirements   12.6
pension schemes   44.2
public sector audits   48.8
Registered Providers of Social Housing   47.6.1
written representations   32.4

ISA (UK) 250B (Revised June 2016) (Section B, Auditor's statutory right and duty to report to regulators of public interest entities and regulators)
ad hoc reports
auditing standards   9.6.1
cumulative minor breaches   9.6.4
form of   9.6.6
guidance   9.6.1
material significance
considerations   9.6.3
procedures   9.6.4
public interest entities   9.7
reporting   9.6.5
right and duty to report   9.6.2
supervision and control   9.6.4
auditing standards and guidance   9.2
charities   43.1.3, 43.7
guidance   8.3, 17.1
public interest entities   9.7
Registered Providers of Social Housing   47.6.1–47.6.2

ISA (UK) 250B (Revised June 2016) (Section B, Auditor's statutory right and duty to report to regulators of public interest entities and regulators) – *contd*
    third parties, reporting to 17.8.3

ISA (UK) 260 (Revised June 2016) (Updated July 2017) (Communication with those charged with governance) – *see also* **governance, persons charged with; communicating with management and those charged with governance**
    addresses 10.4.3
    aims of reports to management 10.3
    audit committees 10.7.1
    communication between external auditor and audit committee 42.8.3
    determination 10.2
    directors' narrative statement, auditors' responsibilities with respect to 42.6.2
    effectiveness of communications 10.5
    form of communication and documentation 10.4.2
    form of reports 10.4.4
    issue of 10.1
    listed companies 10.6.5
    misstatements, communication of 15.8
    other documentation requirements 12.6
    pension schemes 44.8
    planning information 10.6.3
    public interest entities 10.6.5, 10.7.2, 10.10.3, 19.3.2, 30.15, 30.15.1, 31.3.5
    public sector audits 48.9
    Registered Providers of Social Housing 47.7
    significant findings from audit 10.6.4

ISA (UK) 265 (Communicating deficiencies in internal control to those charged with governance and management)
    background
        identifying and reporting deficiencies 10.1, 10.10.1
    pension schemes 44.8
    public sector audits 48.9

ISA (UK) 300 (Revised June 2016) (Planning an audit of financial statements) – *see also* **planning; risk assessment**
    audit plan 13.5
    documentation 13.6
    guidance applying to initial audits 19.1
    other documentation requirements 12.6
    planning an initial engagement 19.2

ISA (UK) 315 (Revised June 2016) (Identifying and assessing the risks of material misstatement through understanding the entity and its environment)
    analytical procedures 25.1, 25.4
    and fair value 28.9.4
    and internal controls 21.3.5
    and ISA 250 9.6.4
    assertions, using to gather evidence 23.2.4
    assessment of risk 20.5.5
    audit plan 13.5
    control environment 21.3.5
    documentation 16.10, 21.3.8
    engagement team discussion 16.4.2, 21.3.3

ISA (UK) 315 (Revised June 2016) (Identifying and assessing the risks of material misstatement through understanding the entity and its environment) – *contd*
    enquiries 20.5.1
    financial performance, measurement and review 21.3.4
    governance, communicating with those charged with 21.3.7
    key audit matters 4.11.1
    management override of controls, responses to 16.4.5
    material misstatement, assessing risks of 21.3.6
    monitoring of controls 21.3.5
    nature of entity 21.3.4
    objectives, strategies and related business risks 21.3.4
    other documentation requirements 12.6
    pension schemes
        communication with trustees 44.8
        public sector audits 48.10
    Registered Providers of Social Housing 47.8
    requirements 21.3.1
    risk assessment
        generally 21.1
        requirements 21.3.1
    team discussion 20.5.3
    understanding audit function 31.2.2
    understanding entity, its environment and internal controls 21.3.4

ISA (UK) 320 (Revised June 2016) (Materiality in planning and performing an audit) – *see also* **materiality**
    charities
        misstatements, uncorrected 15.6.2, 15.6.3
    other documentation requirements 12.6
    Registered Providers of Social Housing 47.9
    regulated entities 49.4
    revision to assessments 15.5

ISA (UK) 330 (Revised July 2017) (Auditor's responses to assessed risks) – *see also* **risk assessment**
    analytical procedures 25.1, 25.5
    assertion level, responses at 21.4.2
    audit evidence, evaluating 16.5
    audit plan 13.5
    bank confirmations 24.1
    charities
        completeness of income 43.13.1
        grants payable 43.13.5
        heritage assets 43.13.4
        overseas operations 43.13.2
        restricted funds 43.13.3
    other documentation requirements 12.6
    overall responses 21.4.1
    planning 13.5
    public sector audits 48.10
    Registered Providers of Social Housing 47.10
    risk assessment
        generally 21.1
    significant risks 21.3.6
    substantive procedure 25.5
        suitability of analytical procedures 25.5.1

ISA (UK) 402 (Audit considerations relating to an entity using a service organisation) – *see also* **service organisations**
and fair value 28.9.4
background information 28.3
fraud, non-compliance and uncorrected misstatements 22.5
pension schemes 44.7
public sector audits 48.12
Registered Providers of Social Housing 47.11
subservice organisations 22.4

ISA (UK) 450 (Revised June 2016) (Updated July 2017) (Evaluation of misstatements identified during the audit)
documentation 15.7
materiality 15.1
matters to be communicated 10.6.1
other documentation requirements 12.6
planning information 10.6.3
written representations 32.4

ISA (UK) 500 (Updated July 2017) (Audit evidence) – *see also* **evidence, audit**
audit procedures 23.2.5
clarified, guidance in 23.1
concept of audit evidence 23.2.1
Registered Providers of Social Housing 47.12
sampling, audit 26.1

ISA (UK) 501 (Audit evidence – specific considerations for selected items) – *see also* **evidence, audit**
audit procedures 23.6.1
claims, enquiries about 23.6
clarified 23.1
litigation enquiries 23.6
segment information 23.7
specific considerations 23.4
stocktaking, attendance at 23.5.1, 23.5.2
written representations 32.4

ISA (UK) 505 (Updated July 2017) (External confirmations)
audit procedures 23.2.5
bank confirmations 24.1
clarified, guidance in 23.1
matters to be communicated 10.6.1
Registered Providers of Social Housing 47.13
use of external confirmations 23.8.1

ISA (UK) 510 (Revised June 2016) (Initial audit engagements – opening balances)
and documentation of departures from ISAs (UK) 12.3.4
guidance in 19.1
matters to be communicated 10.6.1
predecessor auditor's report 19.3.1
public interest entities 19.3.2
public sector audits 48.14
to carry out 19.3.2
version of 19.1

ISA (UK) 520 (Analytical procedures) – *see also* **analytical procedures**
analytical procedures end of audit 25.6

ISA (UK) 520 (Analytical procedures) – see also analytical procedures – *contd*
clarified 25.1
investigation of variances 25.7
Registered Providers of Social Housing 47.14

ISA (UK) 530 (Audit sampling) – *see also* **sampling, audit**
designing the sample 26.4.2
deviations and misstatements 26.8
guidance 26.1
issue 26.1
risk assessment 26.3
misstatements, material 26.4.1
sampling risk 26.3.1
sample size 26.5
selecting sample 26.6
substantive procedures, extent of 21.4.2
use of sampling 26.2

ISA (UK) 540 (Revised June 2016) (Auditing accounting estimates, including fair value accounting estimates and related disclosures) – *see also* **accounting estimates; disclosures; fair value**
accounting estimates, ISA concerning 27.1
and Practice Note 23 28.2
audit procedures 27.4
clarified
disclosures 27.6
guidance in 27.1
risk assessment 27.3
evaluation of results 27.5
fair value 28.2
management bias, indicators 27.7
obtaining an understanding 27.2
other documentation requirements 12.6
Registered Providers of Social Housing 47.15
written representations 32.4

ISA (UK) 550 (Related parties) – *see also* **related parties**
arm's length transactions 20.6.1
auditing standards 20.2
charities
control disclosures 20.7
documentation 20.10
generally 20.1
governance, representations from those charged with 20.8
matters to be communicated 10.6.1
other documentation requirements 12.6
Registered Providers of Social Housing 47.16
remaining alert 20.5.4
significant risks 21.3.6
small businesses 36.8.6
team discussion 20.5.3
written representations 32.4

ISA (UK) 560 (Subsequent events) – *see also* **subsequent events**
dual dating 33.4.1
issue of 33.1
matters to be communicated 10.6.1
other matter 5.8

ISA (UK) 560 (Subsequent events) – see also subsequent events – *contd*
  Registered Providers of Social
    Housing 47.17
  written representations 32.4

ISA (UK) 570 (Revised June 2016) (Going concern) – *see also* going concern; Going Concern Issues During the Current Economic Conditions (APB Bulletin 2008/10)
  auditing standards 11.2
  auditor's procedures
    going concern 42.6.4
  auditors' responsibilities 34.7.1
  current version of 11.2
  detailed considerations 11.20.3
  evaluating entity's assessment of going
    concern 11.7
  general principles 11.20.2
  general requirement 11.3
  group financial statements 11.18
  matters to be communicated 10.6.1
  public sector audits
    auditor's other responsibilities 48.18.1
    entities that prepare their financial
      statements on a cash basis 48.18.5
  Registered Providers of Social
    Housing 47.18
  written representations 32.4

ISA (UK) 580 (Written representations) – *see also* management representations
  additional written representations 32.5
  audit evidence, representations as 32.6
  directors' responsibility,
    acknowledgement 32.3
  issue of 32.1
  management representations as audit
    evidence 32.6
  public sector audits 48.19
  refusal to provide written confirmation 32.8
  Registered Providers of Social
    Housing 47.19
  requirement to obtain written
    representations 32.2
  subsequent events 33.3

ISA (UK) 600 (Revised) (Special considerations – audits of group financial statements)
  acceptance and continuance 30.5
  auditing standards and guidance 30.2
  clarified materiality 15.1
  communication with component
    auditor 30.13
  communication with those charged with
    governance of group 30.15
  consolidation process 30.11
  documentation 30.16
  evaluating sufficiency and appropriateness of
    audit evidence 30.14
  ICAEW practical guidance 30.17
  materiality 30.9
  matters to be communicated 10.6.1
  other documentation requirements 12.6
  overall audit strategy and audit plan 30.6
  overview 30.1
  public sector audits 48.20

ISA (UK) 600 (Revised) (Special considerations – audits of group financial statements) – *contd*
  responding to assessed risks 30.10
  responsibilities 4.16, 30.4
  subsequent events 30.12
  understanding the component auditor 30.8
  understanding the group, its components and
    their environment 30.7

ISA (UK) 610 (Revised June 2016) (Using the work of internal auditors) – *see also* internal auditors
  covers to 31.2.1
  internal audit
    direct assistance 31.2.5
  issue of clarified 31.2.1
  other documentation requirements 12.6
  public sector audits 48.21
  Registered Providers of Social
    Housing 47.20

ISA (UK) 620 (Revised June 2016) (Using the work of an auditor's expert) – *see also* experts, use of
  and non-compliance 17.7
  auditing standards 31.3.1
  fair value 28.5
  housing properties 47.2.6
  management's experts 23.3.1
  other documentation requirements 12.6
  public sector audits 48.22
  Registered Providers of Social
    Housing 47.21
  regulated entities 49.5

ISA (UK) 700 (Revised June 2016) (The independent auditor's report on financial statements) – *see also* financial statements; reports, audit
  adoption by APB 1.6.3
  and other guidance 4.2.1
  auditor's procedures
    going concern 42.6.4
  auditor's responsibilities, description of 5.5.6
  Bulletin 2010/2 (Revised) Compendium of
    Illustrative Auditor's Reports on United
    Kingdom Private Sector Financial
    Statements 4.2.1
  charities 43.22
  contents of report 4.5
  date 4.22
  emphasis of matter 5.7
  engagement partner's name 4.19
  forming an opinion 4.4
  going concern 11.2
  material uncertainty in relation to going
    concern 4.10
  matters to be communicated 10.6.1
  modified auditor's reports 5.1
  other information 4.12
  other matters 5.2
  Registered Providers of Social
    Housing 47.22
  regulated entities 49.3
  standards and guidance 4.2
  unmodified auditor's reports examples

ISA (UK) 700 (Revised June 2016) (The independent auditor's report on financial statements) – see also financial statements; reports, audit – *contd*
    unmodified auditor's reports examples – *contd*
        example auditor's report for a premium
           listed company using IFRSs 4.23
        example simple auditor's report 4.23

ISA (UK) 700 (Revised June 2016) Forming an opinion and reporting on financial statements
    auditor's consideration of other
        information 34.3.1
    guidance 6.2.2
    placement 5.9
    reporting 44.11

ISA (UK) 701 (Communicating key audit matters in the independent auditor's report)
    auditor disclaims an opinion, other
        considerations 5.5.7
    contents 14.4
    key audit matters 4.11.1, 44.11.1
    matters to be communicated 10.6.1
    other matter 5.8
    planning information 10.6.3
    prior period financial statements not
        audited 19.4.3
    Smaller Entities and FRS 105 4.25.1

ISA (UK) 705 (Revised June 2016) (Modifications to the opinion in the independent auditor's report) – *see also* opinions, audit; qualified reports
    imposed limitation of scope 5.3.3
    interaction between key audit matters and
        going concern matters 4.11.4
    key audit matters 4.11.2
    matters to be communicated 10.6.1
    modified auditor's reports 5.1
    reporting 20.11, 22.6

ISA (UK) 706 (Revised June 2016) (Emphasis of matter) 5.7
    matters to be communicated 10.6.1
    modified auditor's reports 5.1, 5.5, 5.9
    other matter 5.8

ISA (UK) 710 (Comparative information – corresponding figures and comparative financial statements) – *see also* comparatives
    evidence, obtaining 19.4
    matters to be communicated 10.6.1
    other documentation requirements 12.6
    other matter 5.5, 5.8
    qualified reports 19.4.1
    version of 19.1
    written representations 32.4

ISA (UK) 720 (Revised June 2016) (The auditor's responsibilities relating to other information) – *see also* other information
    audit procedures 42.6.2
    auditing standards 34.2
    auditor's consideration of
        auditor's responsibility 34.3.2
        other information, definition 34.3.1
    contents 14.4

ISA (UK) 720 (Revised June 2016) (The auditor's responsibilities relating to other information) – see also other information – *contd*
    directors' assessment 34.7.1
    directors' narrative statement, auditors'
        responsibilities with respect to 42.6.2
    disclosures 42.7.1
    electronic publication of auditors'
        reports 4.27.1
    going concern
        auditor's procedures 42.6.4
    matters to be communicated 10.6.1
    other documentation requirements 12.6
    other matter 5.8
    pension schemes 44.10
    Registered Providers of Social
        Housing 47.23
    responding to inconsistencies and
        misstatements 34.4
    Revised June 2016
        auditor disclaims an opinion, other
           considerations 5.5.7
        Auditor's responsibilities relating to other
           information 4.12, 6.3.3–6.3.4
        procedures 6.3.4
        reporting 34.6.1
        terms of engagement 6.3.3
        Section A (The auditor's responsibilities
           relating to other information in
           documents containing audited financial
           statements)
        other matter 5.5
        Registered Providers of Social
           Housing 47.22.1
        XBRL tagging in financial
           statements 37.4.2

ISA (UK) 800 (Special Considerations – Audits of Financial Statements Prepared in Accordance with Special Purpose Framework)
    special purpose financial statements
        audits of 41.4.1

ISA (UK) 805 (Special Considerations – Audits of Single Financial Statements and Specific Elements, Accounts or Items of a Financial Statement)
    special purpose financial statements
        audits of 41.4, 41.4.2
        reports on 41.4, 41.4.2

ISAE (International Standards on Assurance Engagements)
    service organisations 40.7.1

ISQC (UK) 1 (Revised June 2016)
    accepting engagement 9.5.6
    and ISA (UK) 220 (Revised) 3.3.1
    assembly of final audit file 12.4
    basic requirement 3.2.1
    client acceptance and continuance 3.3.4
        public interest entities 3.2.5
    complaints 3.2.10
    complex financial instruments 28.9.3
    confidentiality, custody, ownership of working
        papers 12.7

ISQC (UK) 1 (Revised June 2016) – *contd*
documentation of quality control
system   3.2.11, 3.3.8
documentation, specific requirements   12.3.6
elements of quality control system   3.2.2
engagement documentation   3.2.8
engagement performance   3.2.7, 3.5
ethical requirements   3.2.4, 3.3.3
external monitoring   30.16.1
human resources   3.2.6
issue of   3.1
leadership   3.2.3
leadership responsibilities for quality   3.3.2
matters to be communicated   10.6.1
monitoring   3.2.9, 3.3.7, 3.5
other documentation requirements   12.6
retetion of working papers   12.8
team assignment   3.3.5

ISRE (UK and Ireland) 2410 (Review of interim financial information)   39.2

ISRE 2400 (Revised) (Engagements to Review Historical Financial Statements)   41.2.1

ISRS 4400 (Engagements to Perform Agreed-Upon Procedures Regarding Financial Information)   41.1, 41.3, 47.3

ius quaesitum tertio concept
duties to lenders   40.4.5

journal entries
fraud risk, responses to   16.4.5

key audit matters
audit documentation   4.11.8
auditor's decision   4.11.1
circumstances in which a key audit matter is
not communicated   4.11.3
communication with those charged with
governance   4.11.7
introductory language   4.11.2
no matters to report   4.11.5

key audit partners
rotation of   2.6.5

Large and Medium-sized Companies and Groups (Accounts and Reports) (Amendment) Regulations 2013
Directors' Remuneration Report
auditable part   4.26.3

Large and Medium-Sized Companies and Groups (Accounts and Reports) Regulations 2008
Directors' Remuneration Report
auditable part   4.26.3
quoted companies   4.26.1
reporting   4.26.4
laws and regulations   17.5.1

laws and regulations – *see also* **ISA (UK) 250A (Revised December 2017) (Section A, Consideration of laws and regulations in an audit of financial statements)**
auditor responsibilities   17.4
compliance, consideration of
laws affecting operations of entity   17.5.2

laws and regulations – *see also* **ISA (UK) 250A (Revised December 2017) (Section A, Consideration of laws and regulations in an audit of financial statements)** – *contd*
compliance, consideration of – *contd*
laws governing small businesses   36.5.2
other procedures and written
representations   17.5.3
legal and regulatory framework   17.2
management responsibility   17.3
money laundering prevention   17.6
non-compliance   17.7
public sector audits   48.8
Registered Providers of Social Housing   47.6
reporting
in auditor's report   17.8.2
public interest entities   17.8.4
to third parties   17.8.3
to those charged with governance   17.8.1
resignations   17.9

leadership
quality control   3.2.3

leadership responsibilities for quality
quality control   3.3.2

lenders, duties to
case law   40.4.1
Contracts (Rights of Third Parties)
Act 1999   40.4.5
disclaimer of responsibility   40.4.4
draft accounts   40.4.3
specific assurances, separate engagements to
provide   40.4.6
statutory audit reports   40.4.2

liabilities
access to information by successors   38.3.2

liability limitation
agreements   14.5.3
background   14.5.1
FRC guidance   14.5.2
other services   14.5.4

limitation of audit scope
interim reports   39.16.1
modified auditors' reports   5.3.3

Listing Rules – *see also* **FCA (Financial Conduct Authority)**
Combined Code, statements of compliance
with   42.1.1
interim reports   39.1, 39.7
modified auditors' reports   6.3.8
preliminary announcements   6.4
and going concern   11.19
UK Corporate Governance Code reporting
other information   4.17, 34.7

litigation
enquiries   23.6
Ethical Standard Section 4 (Fees,
Remuneration and Evaluation Policies,
Litigation, Gifts and Hospitality)   2.6.6

loans and guarantees
Ethical Standard Section 2 (Financial,
Business, Employment and Personal
Relationships) 2.6.4

Local Audit and Accountability Act 2014 48.5

**management – *see also* governance, persons
charged with; management representations**
audit procedures 27.7
controls, override of 16.4.5
reports to – *see* communicating with
management and those charged with
governance
responsibility, laws and regulations 17.3
smaller entities 2.7.1, 36.10.3

**Management Representation Letters (Audit
04/02) 32.10**

**management representations – *see also*
ISA (UK) 240 (Revised June 2016) (Updated
July 2017) (Auditor's responsibilities relating
to fraud in an audit of financial statements);
ISA (UK) 580 (Written representations)**
as audit evidence 32.6
complex financial instruments 28.9.8
reliability of written representations 32.7
charities 43.20
directors' ability to make
representations 32.10.2
directors' responsibility,
acknowledgement 32.3
Explanatory Note (ICAEW) 32.1
fraud 16.7
High Court decision (Barings Futures
(Singapore) Pte Ltd) 32.10
details of case 32.10.1
interim reports 39.12
public sector audits 48.19
refusal to provide written confirmation 32.8
Registered Providers of Social
Housing 47.19
representation letter, example 32.9
requirement to obtain written
representations 32.2

management's experts
evaluating appropriateness of expert's
work 23.3.4
evaluating expert's competence, capabilities
and objectivity 23.3.2
obtaining an understanding of the expert's
work 23.3.3
using the work of 23.3.1

**Managing the professional liability of
accountants 14.1**

mandates (CASS Rule 8) 9.5.5, 9.5.14

**market conditions, difficult – *see* difficult
financial market conditions**

**material misstatement – *see also*
misstatements**
definitions 15.2
fair value 28.9.4
fraud – *see* fraud

**material misstatement – *see also*
misstatements – *contd***
planning 39.6
public sector audits 48.10
Registered Providers of Social Housing 47.9
risk assessment 21.2, 21.3.6

**materiality – *see also* ISA (UK) 320 (Revised
June 2016) (Materiality in planning and
performing an audit)**
benchmarks 15.4
charities 43.7, 43.12
complex financial instruments 28.9.6
concept of 15.3
definitions 15.2
documentation 15.7
FRC Audit Quality Thematic Review 15.10
future developments 15.11
consequential amendments 15.11.2
ICAEW views 15.11.1
misstatements – *see* misstatements
overall financial statement materiality 15.4.1
performance 15.4.2
public sector audits 48.11
Registered Providers of Social Housing 47.9
regulated entities 49.4
related parties 20.4
revision to assessments 15.5
small business 36.6.3
written representations 15.9, 32.4

misleading financial statements
incorporated entities 8.3.4
unincorporated entities 8.4.7

**misstatements – *see also* ISA (UK) 315
(Revised June 2016) (Identifying and
assessing the risk of material misstatement
through understanding the entity and its
environment); materiality**
'clearly trivial' 15.6.1
communication of 15.8
disclosures 15.6.3
evaluation of 39.14
material – *see* material misstatements
misstatements, communication of 15.8
qualitative 15.3
tolerable 26.8.1
unadjusted 10.6.4
uncorrected
at completion phase 15.6.2
during audit 15.6.1

MLRO (Money Laundering Reporting Officer)
reporting suspicious activity 18.8

modified audit reports
other information 34.8

**modified auditors' reports going
concern 11.2**

**modified auditor's reports – *see also* qualified
reports**
adverse opinions 5.4
applicable situations 5.2
auditing standards 5.1
communication with regulators and
others 5.11

modified auditor's reports – see also qualified reports – *contd*
  disclaimers of opinion   5.4
  emphasis of matter   5.7
    placement   5.9
  examples   5.6
    modifications to opinions   5.6.1
  financial statements
    material misstatement, causes of   5.3.1
  form and content
    adverse opinion   5.5.3
    auditor disclaims an opinion, other
      considerations   5.5.7
    auditor's responsibilities, description
      of   5.5.6
    basis for modification paragraph   5.5.5
    disclaimer of   5.5.4
    ICAEW guidance   5.5.9
    opinion paragraph   5.5.1
    other implications of modified
      opinions   5.5.8
    qualified opinion   5.5.2
  governance, communication with those
    charged with   5.10
  inability to obtain sufficient audit
    evidence   5.3.2
  ISA (UK) 705 (Modifications to the opinion
    in the independent auditor's report)   5.1
  ISA (UK) 706 (Emphasis of matter)   5.1
  limitation of audit scope   5.3.2, 5.3.3
  modifications, emphasis of matter   5.2, 5.4,
    5.8
  modified opinion, types of
    'adverse' opinion   5.4, 5.4.1, 5.5.3
    'disclaimer' of opinion   5.4, 5.4.1, 5.5.4
    basis for modification paragraph   5.5.5
    qualified opinion   5.4, 5.5.2
  multiple uncertainties   5.4
  other matter   5.8
    placement   5.9
  preliminary announcements   6.3.8
  prior period modifications   39.16.2
  qualified opinion   5.4
  review report   39.16.1

**Money Laundering – Guidance for Auditors
in the United Kingdom (Practice Note 12)
(Revised)   18.3**

money laundering prevention
  access to information by successors   38.3.2
  Anti-Money Laundering
    Regulations 2017   18.2
  auditor's report on financial statements   18.9
  customer due diligence (CDD)   18.7
    enhanced CDD   18.7.2
    simplified CDD   18.7.1
  definition of 'money laundering'   18.4
  laws and regulations   17.6
  MLRO
    NCA, reporting to   18.8
    reporting suspicious activity   18.8
    roles and responsibilities   18.5.1
  Money Laundering Regulations 2003   17.6
  policies and procedures
    client due diligence   18.5.2

money laundering prevention – *contd*
  policies and procedures – *contd*
    compliance management
      communication   18.5.2
    internal control   18.5.2
    ongoing monitoring   18.5.2
    record keeping   18.5.2
    reporting procedures   18.5.2
    risk based approach, risk assessment and
      management   18.5.2
  Politically Exposed Person   18.7.3
  privileged circumstances   18.8.3
  reporting to regulators
    National Crime Agency (NCA)   18.8.2
  resignation and communication with successor
    auditors   18.10
  risk based approach   18.6
  statutory provisions, updated   18.1, 18.2
  tipping off – *see* tipping off, money laundering
  training
    anti-money laundering supervisory
      authority   18.5.3
    customer (or client) due diligence
      (CDD)   18.5.3
    reporting   18.5.3
    scope of audit   18.5.3

monitoring
  external monitoring of group audits   3.2.9
  internal controls   21.3.5
  quality control   3.2.9, 3.3.7

multiple uncertainties
  disclaimer of opinion   5.4

National Crime Agency (NCA)
  Money Laundering Reporting Officer (MLRO)
    reporting suspicious activity   18.8

National Housing Federation (NFS)   47.2.2

nature, timing and extent of review
  engagement quality control review   3.2.7

**net assets statement (pension
schemes)   44.3**

new small companies regime
  auditor's report   6.4.2
  guidance   6.4.3
  legal background   6.4.1

non-audit services
  corporate governance, auditor procedures in
    relation to   42.6.2
  provision to audited entities   2.6.7

**non-cash, transfer to public company by one
of its members**
  guidance   7.6.2
  legal background   7.6.1

non-compliance – *see also* **laws and
regulations**
  laws and regulations   17.7
    consequences   17.3
    with direct effect on financial
      statements   17.5.1
    with Combined Code   42.6.2

non-statutory audits
appointment and removal   44.16.1
auditor's report   44.16.7
auditor's statement about
    contributions   44.16.4
engagement letter   44.16.2
reporting to The Pensions Regulator   44.16.3
termination of appointment   44.16.5
trustees' responsibilities   44.16.6

objectivity
definition   2.6.3
ICAEW Code of Ethics   2.5.2
of experts   31.3.5
risks or threats to   2.6.3, 2.6.7

observation
audit evidence   23.2.5

occupational pension schemes, money purchase
exemption from audit   44.4

Official Secrets Act 1989   48.3

online confirmation
bank confirmations   24.5

opening balances – *see also* **comparatives**
charities   43.15
evidence, obtaining   19.3
modifications to the predecessor auditor's
    report   19.3.1
public interest entities   19.3.2
public sector audits   48.10
to carry out   19.3.2

operational issues
paid cheques – *see* paid cheques
service organisations – *see* service
    organisations
stock – *see* stocktaking

opinions, audit – *see also* **modified auditor's reports**
adverse – *see* adverse opinion
basis for modification   5.5.5
disclaimers   5.5.4
qualified   5.4, 5.5.2

other auditors, reliance on
auditing standards   31.2.1, 31.3.1
charities   43.21
direct assistance   31.2.5
documentation   31.2.6
experts, use of   31.3.1
    agreement with the auditor's expert   31.3.7
    competence, capabilities and
        objectivity   31.3.5
    considering nature, timing and extent of
        audit procedure   31.3.4
    auditor's expert, definition   31.3.2
    evaluating adequacy of expert's
        work   31.3.8
    need for an auditor's expert   31.3.3, 48.22
    public interest entities   31.3.5
    reference to the expert in auditor's
        report   31.3.9
    understanding of field of expertise   31.3.6

other auditors, reliance on – *contd*
investment businesses, reports to FSA   9.6.4
public sector audits   48.21

other engagements
audit exemption   41.1

other information – *see also* **ISA (UK) 720 (Revised June 2016) (The auditor's responsibilities relating to other information)**
auditor's consideration of
    auditor's responsibility   34.3.2
    obtaining an understanding   34.3.3
    Operating and Financial Review
        (OFR)   34.3.1
    obtaining information   34.3.4, 34.4.4
    other information, definition   34.3.1
    procedures   34.3.7
    reading and considering   34.3.5
    statutory other information   34.3.6
auditor's responsibilities
    auditing standards   34.2
    generally   34.1
charities   43.23
documentation   34.9
electronic publication   34.10
modified audit reports   34.8
pension schemes   44.10
reporting   34.6
    all entities   34.6.1
    directors' report and strategic
        report   34.6.2
    separate corporate governance
        statement   34.6.3
responding to inconsistencies and
    misstatements
    after the date of audit report   34.4.1
    auditor's understanding needs to be
        updated   34.4.2
    when material misstatement of other
        information exists   34.4.1
    prior to the date of audit report   34.4.1
    when material misstatement in financial
        statements exists   34.4.2
timing   34.5
UK Corporate Governance Code
    reporting   4.17, 34.7

overseas operations
charities   43.13

paid cheques
audit evidence   37.5.2
Cheques Act 1992   37.5.3
existing guidance   37.5.1
obtaining   37.5.4

Paid Cheques (AAF 1/09)   37.5.1

partners – *see also* **ethics partners; key audit partners**
'cooling off' period where accepting
    management role   2.7.4
Ethical Standard Section 2 (Financial,
    Business, Employment and Personal
    Relationships)   2.6.4
ethics partners, responsibilities   2.6.3
joining audit client   2.7.4

partners – see also ethics partners; key audit partners – *contd*
    key audit partners, rotation 2.6.5
    new, financial interests of 2.6.4
    rotation periods 2.6.5

ES-PASE (Ethical Standard – Provisions Available for Small Entities) 2.6, 2.7.1

Pensions Act 1995 44.2

Pensions Act 2004 44.2, 44.15

Pensions Act 2007 44.2

Pensions Act 2008 44.2

Pensions Act 2011 44.2

Pensions Act 2014 44.2

Pensions Act 2017 44.2

Pension Schemes Act 1993 44.2

Pension Schemes Act 2015 (PSA) 44.2

pension schemes – see also retirement benefits (FRS 17), audit evidence
    accounting guidance 44.3
    appointment and resignation 44.5
    auditor's statement, contributions 44.12
    auto-enrolment of employees 44.2
    communication with trustees 44.8
    contributions 44.12
    enactments or rule of law 44.2
    financial interests held by 2.6.4
    Financial Reports of Pension Schemes (SORP) 44.3
    financial statements outside or normal accounting reference date 44.14
    fraud, consideration of 44.6
    going concern 44.9
    guidance for auditors 44.1
    legal background 44.2
    net assets statements 44.3
    other information 44.10
    Regulations 44.2
    reporting situations 44.14
    schemes exempt from audit 44.4
    use of service organisations 44.7
    whistle-blowing responsibilities 44.15
    winding up, schemes in process of 44.13

Pensions Research Accountants Group (PRAG) 44.3, 44.9

performance materiality 15.4.2

planning – see also ISA (UK) 300 (Planning an audit of financial statements)
    accountants' reports, unincorporated entities 8.4.5
    audit committees and external auditors, communication between 42.8.3
    audit plan 13.5
        disclosures 13.5.1
    changes to planning decisions during course of audit 13.8
    direction, supervision and review 13.9
    documentation 13.6

planning – see also ISA (UK) 300 (Planning an audit of financial statements) – *contd*
    FRS 17 (Retirement Benefits) 26.4.1–26.4.2
    governance, communication with those charged with 13.10
    guidance applying to initial audits 19.1
    initial audit engagement 13.7
    interim reports 39.6
    investment businesses 9.6.4
    materiality and audit risk 15.4
    objectives of 13.2
    overall audit strategy
        significant factors and preliminary activities 13.4
        reporting objectives, timing of audit and communications required 13.4
        scope of audit engagement 13.4
    preliminary engagement activities 13.3

POBA (Professional Oversight Board for Accountancy)
    generally 2.12
    responsibilities 2.12

Politically Exposed Person (PEP) 18.7.3

Power of Three (ICAEW Audit and Assurance Faculty) 42.2.1

Practical Points for Auditors in Connection with the Implementation of FRS 17 (No 1/02) 29.2

Practice Notes
    ad hoc reports 9.6.1
    Attendance at stocktaking (PN 25) 23.5.1
    Audit of Charities (PN 11) – see Audit of Charities (Practice Note 11)
    Audit of Investment Businesses in the United Kingdom (PN 21) – see Audit of Investment Businesses in the United Kingdom (Practice Note 21) (Revised)
    Audit of Occupational Pension Schemes in the United Kingdom (PN 15) 44.6
    Audit of Small Business (PN 13) 36.8.2
    Auditing Complex Financial Instruments (PN 23) – see Auditing Complex Financial Instruments (Practice Note 23) (Revised)
    Auditors' consideration of FRS 17 (PN 22) – see Auditor's consideration of FRS 17 (Practice Note 22)
    Bank Reports for Audit Purposes (PN16) 24.1
    Guidance on Smaller Entity Audit Documentation (PN 26) – see Guidance on Smaller Entity Audit Documentation (Practice Note 26)
    Money Laundering – Guidance for Auditors in the United Kingdom (PN 12) (Revised) 18.3

preconditions for audits
    engagement letters 14.3

preliminary announcements
    alternative performance measures 6.3.5
    background 6.3.1
    directors' approval 6.3.7
    going concern 11.19

preliminary announcements – *contd*
guidance   6.3.2
management commentary   6.3.6
modified auditors' reports   6.3.8
not agreed   6.3.10
procedures   6.3.4
reporting   6.3.9
terms of engagement   6.3.3

presumptive doubt   23.9.2

prior period modifications
review reports   39.16.2

prior year information
risk assessment procedures   21.3.2

privileged circumstances
money laundering prevention   18.8.3

procedures, audit
accounting estimates   27.4
testing management's methods   27.4.2
analytical procedures   23.2.5
and materiality   15.4
audit evidence   23.2.5
auditor responsibilities   17.4
completeness   28.9.6
compliance, review of   42.6.2
confirmation   23.2.5
considering nature, timing and extent
of   31.3.4
corporate governance   42.6.2
disclosures   28.9.6
enquiry   23.2.5
existence, rights and obligations   28.9.6
group engagement team   30.3
external monitoring   30.16.1
inspection of records or documents   23.2.5
interim reports   39.7
observation   23.2.5
preliminary announcements   6.3.4
purpose of   23.2.5
recalculation   23.2.5
Registered Providers of Social
Housing   47.10
reperformance   23.2.5
revised financial statements and
reports   6.2.4
role of   45.3
reporting accountant   45.3.1
sampling   26.4.1, 26.7
Solicitors' Accounts Rules   45.3
substantive – *see* substantive procedures
summary financial statements   6.5
tangible assets, inspection of   23.2.5
valuation   28.9.6

Proceeds of Crime Act 2002
fraud   16.9
money laundering prevention   17.6

professional behaviour
ICAEW Code of Ethics   2.5.2, 17.4
background   2.5.1

professional competence and due care
ICAEW Code of Ethics   2.5.2

professional indemnity insurance (PII)
claims   2.10

professional liability
managing   40.3.2

**Professional Oversight Board for
Accountancy** – *see* POBA (Professional
Oversight Board for Accountancy)

professional scepticism
APB project   23.9.1
danger of audit methodologies   23.9.5
difficulties surrounding   23.9.5
fraud   16.4
IAASB paper   23.9.1
importance   23.9.4
improvement of
conditions   23.9.6
presumptive doubt   23.9.2
role of
audit committees   23.9.6
management   23.9.6
sceptical mindset   23.9.2
throughout all stages of audit   23.9.3

Promoting Audit Quality (FRC)
audit firm culture   3.4.2
audit process   3.4.2
background   3.4.1
factors outside auditor's control   3.4.3
reliability of audit reporting   3.4.2
skills of partners and staff   3.4.2

**Provisions available for small entities –
Section 6   2.7**
and non-audit services   2.7.2
audit report wording   2.7.5
background   2.7.1
economic dependence   2.7.3
example disclosures where exemptions
used   2.7.5
partners joining audit client   2.7.4
relationship between small businesses and
auditors   36.4
small entity client, defined   2.7.1

public interest entities
auditor's report   4.18
ISA (UK) 700   4.5.2

Public Interest Oversight Board (PIOB)   1.4.2

public sector audits
agreeing terms of engagement   48.5
audit conduct   48.4
auditor objectives   48.4
auditor responsibilities   48.18.4
documents containing audited financial
statements   48.24
going concern   48.18.1
Comptroller and Auditor General (C&AG)
regularity   48.25
corruption   48.8.1
evaluation of misstatements   48.13
forming an opinion and reporting on financial
statements   48.23
generally   48.1
going concern

public sector audits – *contd*
  going concern – *contd*
    auditor's other responsibilities 48.18.1
    auditor's responsibilities 48.18.4
    circumstances affecting 48.18.2
    consideration of foreseeable
      future 48.18.3
  grant claims 48.26
  International Standards of Auditing (UK) (ISAs)
    ISA (UK) 220 48.6
    ISA (UK) 250A 48.8
    ISA (UK) 260 48.9
    ISA (UK) 315 48.10
    ISA (UK) 402 48.12
    ISA (UK) 510 48.14
    ISA (UK) 610 48.21
  ISQC (UK) 1 (Revised June 2016) 12.1, 48.3
  reporting non-compliance 48.8.2
  role of auditor 48.2

public sector bodies **48.1**

Public Sector Special Reporting Engagements – Grant Claims (Technical Release Audit 03/03) **48.26**

qualified opinion
  modified auditors' reports 5.4
  modified opinion 5.5.2

qualified reports – *see also* **modified auditors' reports**
  client assets 9.5.7
  comparatives 19.4.1

Quality Assurance Directorate (QAD) **2.13**

quality control – *see also* **documentation; ISA (UK) 220 (Revised June 2016) (Updated July 2017) (Quality control for an audit of financial statements); working papers**
  Audit Quality Framework 3.1
  charities 43.4
  documentation of system 3.2.11, 3.3.8
  engagement performance 3.2.7, 3.3.6
  engagement quality control review
    engagement performance 3.2.7, 3.3.6
  IAASB consultation paper 3.5
  monitoring 3.2.9, 3.3.7
  Promoting Audit Quality – *see* Promoting Audit
    Quality (FRC)
  public sector audits 48.3, 48.6
  Registered Providers of Social Housing 47.4
  technical standards 2.8.2

quoted companies
  affected by the rules
    admitted to dealing at New York Stock
      Exchange or Nasdaq 4.26.2
    listed in an European Economic Area
      (EEA) 4.26.2
    definition 4.26.2

Quoted Companies Alliance (QCA) **42.10.2**

reasonableness test
  disclaimer of responsibility 40.4.4

recalculation
  audit evidence 23.2.5

reconciliations, CASS audits 9.5.10

recurring audits
  engagement letters 14.4.1

Registered Providers of Social Housing – *see also* **housing**
  accounting standards 47.2.6
  audit committees, responsibilities 47.2.3
  audit engagement letters 47.3
  audit enhancement 47.22.1
  auditors
    relationship with Regulators 47.2.7
    responsibilities 47.2.5
  financial reporting requirements 47.2.4
  generally 47
  guidance
    commercial activities 47.2.6
  Housing and Regeneration Act 2008 47.2.4, 47.2.7
  miscellaneous reports 47.24
  National Housing Federation 47.2.2
  nature of 47.2.1
  Practice Note 14 47.1.1
  regulatory framework 47
  responsibilities of the board 47.2.2
  service charge audits 47.25
  social housing audits, features 47.2.6
  standards 47
  Statement of Recommended Practice 47.2.4
  UK Corporate Governance Code 47.22.1

regulated entities
  duty of care and engagement contracts
    bi-partite engagement contracts 49.2.2
    tri-partite engagement contracts 49.2.1
  going concern 11.7
  materiality 49.4
  reporting 49.3
  working with independent experts 49.5

regulation and ethics, audit
  audit, definition 2.1
  audit firms, control of 2.3
  claims, meeting of 2.10
  competence, maintaining 2.9
  control of audit firms 2.3
  ethical standards – *see* ES-PASE (Ethical
    Standard – Provisions Available for
    Small Entities)
  fit and proper person requirement 2.4
  generally 2.1
  Professional Oversight Board for Accountancy
    – *see* POBA (Professional Oversight
    Board for Accountancy)
  qualifications, recognition 2.2
  quality control 2.13
  reports 2.15
  RSB regulations 2.1
  RSBs 2.1
  rules 2.11
  technical standards – *see* technical standards

related parties – *see also* **Audit of Related Parties in Practice (ICAEW Exposure Draft); ISA (UK) 550 (Related parties)**
  charities 43.17
  control disclosures 20.7

related parties – see also Audit of Related
Parties in Practice (ICAEW Exposure Draft);
ISA (UK) 550 (Related parties) – *contd*
   documentation   20.10
   enquiries   20.5.1
   general requirement   20.3
   generally   20.1
   governance, those charged with
      communication with   20.9
      representations from   20.8
   materiality   20.4
   public sector audits   48.16
   Registered Providers of Social
      Housing   47.16
   reporting   20.11
   response to risk   20.6
   risk assessment   20.5
   small business   36.8.7

related party transactions
   arm's length transactions   20.5.2
   assessment of risk   20.5.5
   remaining alert   20.5.4
   response to risk   20.6
   understanding of controls   20.5.2

reliance on others – *see* internal audit; other
auditors, reliance on

remuneration and evaluation policies
   Ethical Standard Section 4 (Fees,
      Remuneration and Evaluation Policies,
      Litigation, Gifts and Hospitality)   2.6.6

reperformance
   audit evidence   23.2.5

reporting requirements
   corporate governance   42.7.1

Reporting to Regulators of Regulated Entities
(Technical Release Audit 5/03)   49.1

Reporting to regulators on regulatory
accounts (TECH 02/16 AAF)
   Bi-partite   49.2.2
   regulated entities   49.1
   Tri-partite   49.2.1

Reporting to Third Parties (TECH 10/12 AAF)
   generally   40.2, 40.8.1
   other engagements   41.1
   regulated entities   49.1

reports, audit – *see also* accountants'
reports; ISA (UK) 700 (Revised June 2016)
(Auditor's report on financial statement);
Directors' Remuneration Report; Directors'
Remuneration Report Regulations 2002 (APB
Bulletin 2002/2)
   addressees   4.7
   annual report, significant problems   2.3.1,
      3.11.2, 42.6.2
   audit opinions – *see* opinions, audit
   audit regulation and ethics   2.15
   auditor's location   4.21
   auditor's opinions   4.8
   Bannerman case – *see* Bannerman case
      (audit reports)

reports, audit – see also accountants'
reports; ISA (UK) 700 (Revised June 2016)
(Auditor's report on financial statement);
Directors' Remuneration Report; Directors'
Remuneration Report Regulations 2002 (APB
Bulletin 2002/2) – *contd*
   basis for opinion   4.9
   charities   43.22
   conclusions relating to going concern   4.10
   contents   4.5
   date   4.22
   distributions – *see* distributions
   electronic publication – *see* electronic
      publication
   forming an opinion   4.4
   guidance   4.2
   interim – *see* interim reports
   introduction of   4.1
   investment businesses – *see* investment
      businesses, reports to FSA
   material uncertainty in relation to going
      concern   4.10
   reporting to   17.8.2
   to management – *see* communicating with
      management and those charged with
      governance
   modified – *see* modified auditors' reports
   money laundering prevention   18.9
   pension schemes   44.11
   preliminary announcements   6.3.9
   qualified – *see* qualified reports
   Registered Providers of Social
      Housing   47.22
   regulation, small businesses   2.7.5
   signature
      audit regulations   4.20.1
      date   4.22
      joint auditors   4.20.4
      senior statutory auditor   4.2.1, 4.20.2
      signing of auditors' report   4.2.1, 4.20.3
   small businesses
      regulation   2.7.5
   standards
      APB Bulletins – *see* bulletins (APB)
      Statements of Auditing Standards (SAS) –
         see under specific SAS
   subsequent events   33.3
   summary financial statements   6.5
   title   4.6
   wording
      ES-PASE (Ethical Standard – Provisions
         Available for Small Entities)   2.7.5
   XBRL tagged data   37.4.3

representation letters – *see also* management
representations
   Audit 04/02   32.1, 32.10

Republic of Ireland, use of UK ISAs in   4.2

request letters
   bank confirmations   24.3

Requests for References on Clients' Financial
Status and their Ability to Service Loans
(Audit 2/01)   40.8.1
   reports to other third parties   40.2, 40.8.3

re-registration of companies
guidance 7.4.2
legal background 7.4.1

response to risk
arm's length transactions 20.6.1

restricted funds
charities 43.13

retirement benefits
audit evidence – *see* retirement benefits, audit
evidence
guidance for auditors 29.2
overview 29.1

retirement benefits, audit evidence
actuaries – *see* actuaries

revenue recognition
fraud risk 16.4.4

review, audit
interim reports 39.13

review engagements
acceptance of engagement 41.2.3
accepting engagement 41.2.3
features 41.2.2
guidance 41.2.1
limited assurance engagement 41.2.1
performing the engagement 41.2.5
reliance by third parties 41.2.4
reporting 41.2.7
responsibilites as directors 41.2.3
responsibilites in carrying out a review 41.2.3
written representations 41.2.6

**Review of Regulatory Regime of the
Accountancy Profession (DTI)** 2.1, 2.6

Revised Ethical Standard 2016
contents
Part A 2.6.2
Part B 2.6.2
Ethical Standard Section 1 (Integrity,
Objectivity and Independence) 2.6.3,
10.6.5
Ethical Standard Section 2 (Financial,
Business, Employment and Personal
Relationships) 2.6.4
partners joining audit client 2.7.4
Ethical Standard Section 3 (Long Association
with Audit Engagement) 2.6.5
Ethical Standard Section 4 (Fees,
Remuneration and Evaluation Policies,
Litigation, Gifts and Hospitality) 2.6.6
Ethical Standard Section 5 (Non-audit
Services Provided to Audited
Entities) 2.6.7
Ethical Standard Section 6 (Provisions
Available for Small Entities) 2.7
scope
compliance with IESBA Code 2.6.1
European Directive and Regulation 2.6.1
small businesses – *see* ES-PASE (Ethical
Standard – Provisions Available for
Small Entities)

revised financial statements and reports
guidance 6.2.2
legal background 6.2.1
procedures 6.2.4
types of revision 6.2.3

risk assessment – *see also* **ISA (UK) 315
(Revised June 2016) (Identifying and
assessing the risks of material misstatements
through understanding the entity and
its environment); ISA (UK) 330 (Revised
July 2017) (Auditor's responses to assessed
risks)**
accounting estimates 27.3
analytical procedures 21.3.2, 25.4
assertions, risks related to 21.3.6
charities 43.11.1, 43.13
complex financial instruments 28.9.2
enquiries 20.5.1
extent of procedures 21.4.2
fraud and error 16.4.3
internal controls 21.3.5
materiality 15.4, 21.3.6
misstatements 21.3.6
nature of procedures 21.4.2
overview 21.2
pervasive risks 21.3.6
prior periods' assessments/work, relying
on 21.4.2
procedure 20.5
process 21.3.5
public sector audits 48.10
Registered Providers of Social
Housing 47.10
relying on prior periods' work 21.4.2
responses to assessed risks
at assertion level 21.4.2
audit evidence, evaluating 21.4.4
documentation 21.4.5
material misstatement 22.3
overall 21.4.1
presentation of financial statements 21.4.3
Registered Providers of Social
Housing 47.10
risks unable to be mitigated by substantive
procedures alone 21.3.6
sampling risk 26.3.1
non-sampling risk 26.3.2
significant risks 21.3.6
substantive procedures 21.4.2
tests of control
extent of 21.4.2
timing of procedures 21.4.2
unusual or unexpected relationships 16.4.3

risk management
auditor procedures 42.6.2

RSBs (Recognised Supervisory Bodies)
control of audit firms 2.3
CPE 2.9
fit and proper person requirement 2.4
regulations 2.1

sampling, audit – *see also* **ISA (UK) 530 (Audit
sampling)**
audit procedures 26.7
cost-benefit analysis 26.10

sampling, audit – see also ISA (UK) 530 (Audit sampling) – *contd*
deciding whether to sample   26.4.1
definitions   26.2
designing the sample   26.4.2
deviations and misstatements
  anomalous errors   26.8.3
  expected error   26.8.2
  projecting error   26.8.3
  tolerable   26.8.1
evaluation of results   26.9
objectives   26.4.2
population   26.4.2
sample size   26.5, 26.10
selecting sample   26.6
selection of items   23.2.6, 26.4.1
statistical and non-statistical   26.10
stratification   26.4.2
use of   26.2
value-weighted selection   26.4.2

SAR 98 (Solicitors' Accounts Rules) – *see* **Solicitors' Account Rules 2011**

SAS 600 (Auditor's Report on Financial Statements) – *see also* **reports, audit**

SAS 610 (Communication of Audit Matters to those Charged with Governance) – *see also* **governance, persons charged with**
scepticism – *see* professional scepticism

Scope and Authority of Audit and Assurance Pronouncements   1.5.2

segment information – *see also* **ISA (UK) 501 (Audit evidence – specific considerations for selected items)**
evidence, audit   23.7

selection of items for testing
evidence, audit   23.2.6

Senior Statutory Auditor
audit reports signed by   4.2.1

Senior Statutory Auditor under the United Kingdom Companies Act 2006 (APB Bulletin 2008/6)   4.2.1

Serious Organised Crime and Police Act 2005   18.2

service charge audits
Registered Providers of Social
  Housing   47.25

service organisations
AAF 01/06   22.1, 22.2.1
accounting records   22.2.2
accounting systems and internal
  control   36.7.2
charities   43.14
definition   22.1
fraud   22.5
internal controls reports
  accepting engagement   40.7.3
  background   40.7.1
  reporting   40.7.5
  reporting accountant's procedures   40.7.4

service organisations – *contd*
internal controls reports – *contd*
  responsibilities of service
    organisation   40.7.2
ISA (UK) 402   22.1
ISAE 3402   22.1, 22.2.1, 40.7.1
misstatements, uncorrected   22.5
non-compliance with laws and
  regulations   22.5
pension schemes   44.7
public sector audits   48.12
Registered Providers of Social Housing   47.11
reporting   22.6
responding to the assessed risks of material
  misstatement   22.3
responsibilities   40.7.2
risk assessment   22.3
subservice organisations   22.4
understanding the services provided by a
  service organisation, including internal
  control
  accounting records   22.2.2
  using type 1 or type 2 report   22.2.1

shares
allotment of, otherwise than for cash
  guidance   7.5.2
  legal background   7.5.1
purchase and redemption of own
  guidance   7.3.2
  legal background   7.3.1

signature of audit reports
audit regulations   4.20.1
date   4.22
joint auditors   4.20.4
Senior Statutory Auditor   4.2.1, 4.20.2
signing of   4.2.1, 4.20.3

significant uncertainties
modified reports   4.2, 39.16.1

skills and competence
audit quality, promoting   3.4.2

Small Audit Firms
economic dependence   2.7.3

small businesses – *see also* **Guidance on Smaller Entity Audit Documentation (Practice Note 26)**
accounting systems and internal control   36.7
  risks identification and assessment,
    auditor's responses   36.7.1
  service organisations   36.7.2
audit documentation requirements   36.10.4
audit of   36.1
audit system   36.10.3
audit team   36.10.3
auditors, relationship with   36.4
auditor's report   6.4.2
characteristics   36.3
concentration of ownership and
  management   36.10.3
'cooling off' period for partners accepting
  management role   2.7.4
definitions   2.7.1, 36.3
estimates and fair values   36.8.6

small businesses – see also Guidance on Smaller Entity Audit Documentation (Practice Note 26) – *contd*
  ethical standard – *see* ES-PASE (Ethical Standard – Provisions Available for Small Entities)
  evidence 36.8
    analytical procedures 36.8.2
    audit evidence and external confirmations 36.8.1
    audit sampling 36.8.3
    estimates and fair values 36.8.6
    initial audit engagements and comparative information 36.8.5
    related parties 36.8.7
    written representations 36.8.4
  Financial Reporting Standard for Smaller Entities – *see* FRSSE (Financial Reporting Standard for Smaller Entities)
  guidance 36.2
  laws and regulations
    consideration of 36.5.2
  legal background 6.4.1
  limited and informal controls 36.10.3
  planning, controlling and recording 36.6
    financial statements, audit 36.6.1
    materiality 36.6.3
    material misstatement, risk identification and assessment 36.6.2
  Practice Note
  professional relationship with auditors 36.10.3
  related parties 38.6.7
  reporting 36.9
    governance, communication with those charged with 36.9.2
    independent auditor's report on financial statements 36.9.1
  responsibilities 36.5
    engagement letter 36.5.4
    going concern 36.5.3
    relating to fraud 36.5.1
    subsequent events 36.5.5
  uncomplicated operations 36.10.3

Small Companies (Micro-Entities' Accounts) Regulations 2013
  micro-entities 4.25.3

Small Companies and Groups (Accounts and Directors' Report) Regulations 2008
  micro-entities 4.25.3
  new small companies regime 6.5, 4.25.2

small companies and micro-entities
  engagement letters 14.6

social housing
  features of audits 47.2.6
  Registered Providers – *see* Registered Providers of Social Housing

Solicitors' Accounts Rules 2011
  accountant's report changes 45.1.1
  breaches 45.4
    debit balances 45.4.1
    client confidentiality 45.4.2

Solicitors' Accounts Rules 2011 – *contd*
  breaches – *contd*
    prompt return of client money, residual balances 45.4.6
    providing bank facilities 45.4.7
    receipt and transfer of costs 45.4.4
    reconciliations 45.4.5
    'without delay' 45.4.3
  compliance 45.1.2
  engagement letters
    place of examination 45.2.3
    termination of appointment 45.2.2
    whistle-blowing 45.2.1
  future developments 45.6
  generally 45.1
  high-level principles 45.1.2
  objective 45.1.3
  procedures 45.3
    reporting accountant, role of 45.3.1
  reporting 45.5
  Rule 39 removal of 45.1.1

Solicitors' Regulation Authority (SRA) **45.1**
  future developments 45.6

Special Auditor's Report on Abbreviated Accounts in the United Kingdom (APB Bulletin 2008/4) **6.1**

special purpose financial statements
  audits of 41.4
  reports on 41.4
    a single financial statement or a specific element 41.4.2

staff concerns
  raising 42.6.2

state pension age, changes to **44.2**

Statement on the Directors' Assessment of the Principal Risks that Would Threaten the Solvency or Liquidity of the Entity
  UK Corporate Governance Code reporting other information 34.7

Statements of Recommended Practice – *see* SORPS (Statements of Recommended Practice)

statutory audit reports
  distributions
    annual accounts 7.2.2
    legal background 7.2.1
  duties of care 40.4.2
  guidance 7.1
  non-cash assets, transfer to a public company by one of its members 7.6.1
  re-registration of companies
    guidance 7.4.2
    legal background 7.4.1
  shares – *see* shares

subsequent events – *see also* ISA (UK) 560 (Subsequent events); post-balance sheet events
  before date of auditor's report 33.3
  before issue of financial statements 33.4
  charities 43.18

**subsequent events – see also ISA (UK) 560
(Subsequent events); post-balance sheet
events** – *contd*
definition 33.2
failure to amend financial statements 33.4.2
interim reports 39.9
public sector audits 48.17
Registered Providers of Social
Housing 47.17
revising or withdrawing financial
statements 33.5

substantive procedures
analytical procedures as – *see* analytical
procedures, substantive procedures
complex financial instruments 28.9.6
extent of 21.4.2
public interest entities 21.4.2
risks unable to be mitigated alone by 21.3.6
sampling 26.2

summary financial statements 6.5
charities 43.24

supervision and control
investment businesses, ad hoc reports to
FSA 9.6.4

supported housing – *see* social housing

syndicated financings
access to working papers 12.9.3

taxation issues
Company Tax Return, and XBRL
tagging 37.4.1
e-commerce 49.5.3
social housing audits 47.2.6

Taxes Acts
laws and regulations 17.5.1

taxonomy
tagging of information 37.4.1

Technical Release (ICAEW)
Access to Information by Successor Auditors
(No 01/08) 38.3.2
Audit report and auditor's duty of care to third
parties (No 01/03) – *see* Audit report
and auditor's duty of care to third parties
(Technical Release Audit 01/03)
Chartered Accountants' Reports on the
Compilation of Historical Financial
Statements of Incorporated Entities (No
02/10) 8.2
Chartered Accountants' Reports on the
Compilation of Historical Financial
Statements of Unincorporated Entities
(No 03/10) 8.2, 8.4.1, 8.4.3
Firm's Reports and Duties to Lenders in
connection with Loans and Other
Facilities to Clients and Related
Covenants (No 4/00) 40.2
Guidance on XBRL tagging (No
04/10) 37.4.3
Residential service charge accounts –
guidance on accounting and reporting
in relation to service charge accounts

Technical Release (ICAEW) – *contd*
for residential properties on which
variable service charges are paid in
accordance with a lease or tenancy
agreement 47.2.7
third parties 40.2

technical standards
acceptance of appointment and
reappointment 2.8.1
quality control 2.8.2

term of office
procedure on cessation of office 38.2.1

termination of appointment
Solicitors' Accounts Rules 45.2.2

**terms of engagement – *see also* engagement
letters; engagements**
accountants' compilation reports
incorporated entities 8.3.1
unincorporated entities 8.4.3
agreeing 40.3.3
reports to third parties 40.8.2
charities 43.3
corporate governance 42.3
general guidance
agreeing terms of engagement 40.3.3,
48.5
managing professional liability 40.3.2
preliminary announcements 6.3.3
Registered Providers of Social Housing 47.3
XBRL tagged data 37.4.3

tests of controls see control tests

third parties
claims by
affiliates or associates of audit
client 40.9.4
case law 40.9.1–40.9.2
creditors and lenders 40.9.2
potential investors 40.9.1
regulators and trade bodies 40.9.3
Contracts (Rights of Third Parties)
Act 1999 40.4.5
duties to lenders – *see* lenders, duties to
guidance 40.2
reporting to 17.8.3
reports to
agreeing work to be performed 40.8.2
duties of care – *see* covenants in
agreement for lending facilities; duties
of care
form requested by 40.8.2
performance of work 40.8.2
reports to management 10.9

time limits
other information 34.5
partner rotations 2.6.5

'tipping off', money laundering 18.8.1, 18.9
auditors' right to report directly to
regulators 9.6.5
reporting in auditor's report 17.8.2

transactions, business rationale
fraud risk   16.4.5

true and fair view
governance, responsibilities of those charged
with   4.15, 16.3

trustees of pensions schemes
communication with   44.8
statement of responsibilities   44.10

trusts, CASS rules   9.5.9, 9.5.12

UK Code on Corporate Governance – *see also*
corporate governance
auditor's statement   9.13.3
engagement letters   14.2
future plans   42.11
generally   42.1.1
listed companies   42.7.2
monitoring   42.9
non-compliance with   42.6.2
other codes
investment companies   42.10.1
smaller quoted companies   42.10.2
provisions which auditors must review   42.1.1

UK Corporate Governance Code reporting
auditor responsibilities   34.7
directors' assessment   34.7.1
entities reporting on application   4.17
other information   34.7
other planning and scoping matters   4.11.6

UK GAAP
directors' responsibility statements   4.24
example simple auditor's report   4.23
Smaller Entities and FRS 105   4.25.1

Unfair Contract Terms Act 1977
contract terms   14.5
disclaimer of responsibility   40.4.4

**unincorporated entities (accountants'
reports)   8.4.9**
accounting basis   8.4.2
approval of financial information   8.4.8
client's responsibilities   8.4.4
guidance, scope   8.4.1

**unincorporated entities (accountants'
reports) –** *contd*
misleading financial information   8.4.7
planning   8.4.5
procedures   8.4.6
requests for references on financial
status   40.8.3
terms of engagement   8.4.3

unusual items
investigations   16.4.3

valuation
audit procedures   28.9.6

variances
investigation, analytical procedures   25.7

vendor due diligence
access to working papers   12.9.3

whistle-blowing
charities   43.1.3
pension schemes   44.15
Solicitors' Accounts Rules   45.2.1

winding up
pension schemes   44.13

working papers – *see also* **documentation;
reports, audit**
access to
change of auditor   12.9.5
further explanations   12.9.2
for other parties   12.9.3
ownership and access   12.9.1
confidentiality, custody and ownership
of   12.7
definition   12.2
form and content   12.3
factors affecting   12.3.1
judgment areas   12.3.3
requirements for   12.3; 12.6
retention   12.8

**XBRL Tagging of Information in Audited
Financial Statements – Guidance for Auditors
(APB Bulletin 2010/1)   37.4.1–37.4.3**